831 - 462 - 2755
CAROL

JOE
604 - 327 - 8992

Adventure Guide

Mexico's Pacific Coast

Adventure Guide

Mexico's Pacific Coast

Vivien Lougheed

HUNTER

HUNTER PUBLISHING, INC,
130 Campus Drive, Edison, NJ 08818
732-225-1900; 800-255-0343; fax 732-417-1744
www.hunterpublishing.com

Ulysses Travel Publications
4176 Saint-Denis, Montréal, Québec
Canada H2W 2M5
514-843-9882, ext. 2232; fax 514-843-9448

Windsor Books
The Boundary, Wheatley Road, Garsington
Oxford, OX44 9EJ England
01865-361122; fax 01865-361133

ISBN 1-58843-395-1

© 2005 Hunter Publishing, Inc.

Printed in the United States

This guide focuses on recreational activities. As all such activities contain elements of risk, the publisher, author, affiliated individuals and
companies disclaim responsibility for any injury, harm, or illness that
may occur to anyone through, or by use of, the information in this book.
Every effort was made to insure the accuracy of information in this book,
but the publisher and author do not assume, and hereby disclaim, liability for any loss or damage caused by errors, omissions, misleading information or potential travel problems caused by this guide, even if such
errors or omissions result from negligence, accident or any other cause.

Cover photo: Colorful door, © Viesti Associates, Inc
Back cover image and interior color images provided compliments of the
Mexico Tourist Board
Black and white images by Vivien Lougheed
Index by: Nancy Wolff

Maps by Kim André, © 2005 Hunter Publishing, Inc.

www.hunterpublishing.com

Hunter's full range of guides to all corners of the globe is featured on our website. You'll find guidebooks to suit every type of traveler, no matter what their budget, lifestyle, or idea of fun.

Adventure Guides – There are now over 40 titles in this series, covering destinations from Costa Rica and the Yucatán to Tampa Bay & Florida's West Coast, Canada's Atlantic Provinces and the Alaska Highway. Complete with information on what to do, as well as where to stay and eat, *Adventure Guides* are tailor-made for the active traveler, with all the practical travel information you need, as well as details of the best places for hiking, biking, canoeing, horseback riding, trekking, skiing, watersports, and all other kinds of fun.

Alive Guides – This ever-popular line of books takes a unique look at the best each destination offers: fine dining, jazz clubs, first-class hotels and resorts. In-margin icons direct the reader at a glance. Top-sellers include *St. Martin & St. Barts*, *The US Virgin Islands* and *Aruba, Bonaire & Curaçao*.

Our *Romantic Weekends* guidebooks provide escapes for couples of all ages and lifestyles. Unlike most"romantic" travel books, ours cover more than charming hotels and delightful restaurants, with a host of activities that you and your partner will remember forever.

One-of-a-kind travel books available from Hunter include *Best Dives of the Caribbean; Golf Resorts; Cruising Alaska* and many more.

Full descriptions are given for each book at www.hunterpublishing.com, along with reviewers' comments and a cover image. You can also view pages and the table of contents. Books may be purchased on-line via our secure transaction facility.

DEDICATION

This book is for Panama Pat Corcoran,
who got me my first review that helped
push me along this path.

Contents

APPENDIX

■ Maps

Introduction

The lure of isolated beaches rimmed with palm trees brought John Huston to Puerto Vallarta in the 1960s to film *Night of the Iguana*. His cast included Elizabeth Taylor and Richard Burton. While working, the two fell in love. Richard bought Elizabeth a house similar to his own that was perched on the side of a hill overlooking Bandera Bay. The houses were across the road from each other.

The couple then built a walkway between the two places so they could visit each other more discreetly. Elizabeth left Eddie Fisher, her husband at the time, and married Burton. Their story became one of the great love stories of that century.

This romance resulted in thousands of people swarming to the shores of Mexico's west coast in search of sun, sand, palm trees and love. Some even came looking for iguanas. The Mexicans soon realized the potential of tourism and, with the help of international companies, built a first-class infrastructure of hotels, shops and restaurants around the bay.

However, not all visitors wanted what had been built, so they moved up and down the coast to little villages where they could ride horses or donkeys, snorkel among the tropical fish, trek in the jungle looking for exotic birds and animals, watch cliff divers perform or just lay where it was quiet and sip on tequila.

In the jungles along the shore, Mexicans built viewing stations connected by cables where tourists could swing like monkeys while looking for exotic birds and strange amphibians. The usual adjustments took place. Some Mexicans and tourists didn't like the environmental effects caused by chasing around in motorboats looking for big fish, building hotels on the beach, and bungee jumping off bridges. Ecologically-sensitive practices were followed so that wildlife was protected. Garbage was picked up and pollution-control devices were put on vehicles. They left some of the jungle in its wild state and planted flowers in their gardens. More people came.

Today, the west coast of Mexico is as popular as ever. This is because it offers every possible recreational activity, suitable for almost any skill level and budget. The area has both economical and lush accommodations. The food is safe to eat and the bottled water, found in every hotel hallway, grocery store and café is safe to drink. The crime rate is low in tourist areas and the locals are friendly, though the usual pressures of tourism often show. But the best draw of all is that the price for a comparable vacation in any other tropical paradise is about twice what it is here.

The best time to visit the Pacific coast of Mexico is between November and May, when humidity and temperatures are down. This is when most North American and European countries are cold. It is also when the whales move south looking for warmer waters and when the migratory birds are passing by on their way to winter nesting grounds.

But Mexico also has lots to offer during the summer. The Sierra Madres butt up against the ocean, offering relief from the heat just a few hours away by car or public bus. At higher elevations, muscle-powered sports like hiking or cycling are possible any time of year. Museums in the state capitals offer endless intellectual stimulation and the live entertainment often found in towns and city plazas is enthralling. There are ruins to visit and architecture to admire, history to relive and exotic foods to taste.

Regardless of when you come or where you go along Mexico's west coast, you can enjoy any style of vacation, and your trip will be one that you will remember for a long time.

History

Anywhere I go I want to know who was there before me. I want to know their stories.

■ Paleo-Indians

The main pattern of Paleo-Indian settlement in the Americas (20,000-7,000 BC approx) is generally agreed upon, though dates and details keep changing and infighting among anthropologists and archeologists is intense. By about 20,000 BC, the last ice age was into a long decline. The ice pack that covered most of Canada and Northeastern United States receded, creating a corridor from Beringia (connecting Asia and North America) down into ice-free southern Alberta. From there the rest of the Americas was wide open, but the migrants kept moving south down the mountain chains. They stuck to the highlands because these areas supported the large herbivores that they ate: mammoth, mastodon, caribou, bison, horse, giant armadillo, giant sloth, guanaco (ancestor of the llama), llama and vicuña.

The dating of sites in the Americas shows the progression, first north to south, then east and west. These dates also show how long the process took. Sites like Monte Verde in southern Chile have been reliably dated to about 12,000-10,000 BC. Estimates are that in Mesoamerica, the occupied parts of pre-Columbian Mexico and Central America, the highlands may have been populated as early as 18,000 BC.

Archeologists also learn from the sites how the Paleo-Indians lived. In Monte Verde, wood and skin huts contained brazier pits. Mastodon and other large herbivore bones were found, along with the remains of seeds, nuts, berries and roots. Tools included stone hand axes, choppers and scrapers; some of these tools may have had wooden handles. The weapons were wooden lances and stones chosen or shaped so that they could be hurled from slings.

Once the Americas were occupied from top to bottom, population pressure and global warming resulted in movement into the lowlands, along the coastlines (which at that time were farther out to sea), and onto the Caribbean islands. Increasing temperatures changed the highlands in particular, leaving them less habitable. In Mesoamerica the grasslands turned to deserts, and the large herbivores disappeared, leaving smaller game like rabbit and deer.

Along the Gulf of Mexico and the Caribbean, grasslands turned into forests. Since Mesoamerica was, and still is, rich in edible plants – like mesquite, cactus and agave – people ate more grains, fruits and vegetables and less meat, though ducks and dogs were being domesticated as a meat supply. By 11,000 BC, people were eating wild corn, onions, amaranth, avocado, acorns, piñon nuts, chili peppers, maguey and prickly pear. By 8,000 BC, the Paleo-Indian period of Mesoamerica was coming to an end. Chasing game was giving way to clearing land, cultivating domestic plants, and raising domestic animals.

By 7,000 BC, the nomadic hunters were growing crops, especially squash, avocado and chili pepper. By 5,000 BC, maize – a small, wheatlike ancestor of corn – was being grown in the Tehuacan Valley of Southern Mexico. By 3,000 BC, pit house settlements were popular. A pit house was a tent-like wood, wattle and daubed-mud structure erected over a hole dug into the ground. By 2,300 BC, pottery replaced stone jars and bowls, village life was the norm, and population growth was exploding. One of the sites, found in 1947 at Tepexpan, confirmed many of these facts for archeologists.

As civilization grew, four classical groups formed in Mexico. They were the **Teotihuacans**, who lived in and around Mexico City; the **Zapotecs**, who lived in the Oaxaca and Tehuantepec areas; and the **Olmecs** and **Totonacs**, who lived in the Vera Cruz part of the country. The Maya lived mostly in Southern Mexico, Belize and Guatemala and as far south as Honduras and Nicaragua.

The Olmecs and Totonacs were most powerful around 1700 BC and had developed a unique artistic style in the carving of huge stone heads. In contrast to these stone heads, they also carved intricate jade figurines. However, their greatest contribution was the development of hieroglyphic writing and of the calendar that had dots for days and dashes representing months. The Olmecs disappeared around 600 BC. Archeologists have not decided what ultimately happened to the Olmecs. The present evidence shows that they could have disappeared because of starvation, invasion and assimilation, or genocide.

The Teotihuacans were so impressive to the **Aztecs**, who came later, that the Aztecs named the city as the "place of the gods." The Teotihuacans had good town planning with all activities taking place in the main plaza that was marked by an impressive pyramid. From the plaza, a complex road system splayed out into the countyside, where the urban population worked the fields. Their trade was so extensive that evidence of their presence was found as far south as Guatemala.

While Teotihuacans grew, the Zapotecs to the south also gained power. Their city of Monte Alban grew to about 20,000 people, almost as big as the powerful Maya center of Tikal in Guatemala. The people of Monte Alban continued to flourish until about 700 AD, when they fell into decline. They are mainly known for their black pottery.

The **Maya** became the next prominent civilization, followed by the **Toltecs** who, like the Maya, disappeared due to drought around 1100 AD.

The Aztecs were a warring group who, by forming alliances with lesser groups, soon took control of central Mexico. Their empire eventually included over five million people. They had a hierarchy that was headed by a king and queen, followed by nobility and then the military. Those in commerce, farming and art belonged to the lower classes. The Aztec's religious ceremonies were complex and included human sacrifice to appease the gods.

AZTEC LORE

The Aztecs believed that the sun and earth had died and been reborn four times. They also believed that the fifth cycle of birth and death would result in the final death.

All in all, Mexican civilizations developed organized religions, written language, monumental architecture, sophisticated art forms and an understanding of mathematics and astronomy. They also had an accurate calendar. But their main focus was, as with modern people, on war and trade. This resulted in the Toltecs from the north interbreeding with the Maya and, by 1200 AD, the Aztecs intermingling with southern tribes.

The most famous leader of this group was Montezuma, who is credited with uniting most of the tribes of Mexico as far south as Oaxaca. He was also the leader who had to deal with the Spanish.

■ The Spanish

In 1511 a boat loaded with Spaniards traveling from South America to the Caribbean was marooned on the coast of the Yucatán. Among the shipwrecked survivors was **Jeronimo de Alguilar** who, rather than returning to South America, chose to live among the Maya and learn their language.

Six years later, **Diego Velasquez** decided that Mexico should be explored and exploited so he sent **Francisco Fernández de Cordoba** to start the process. Cordoba did some exploration and was soon followed by **Hernan Cortez**. After two years of exploration under the command of Cortez, thousands of Aztec people and all the Aztec chiefs had been executed, and thousands had succumbed to smallpox, typhoid and dysentery. Others who resisted Spanish intrusions were killed. The land was open for grabs. Cortez became the Marquis of Oaxaca, with 25,000 square miles/65,000 square km of land and 100,000 Indians to control.

By 1528 the first court with executive powers was established in Mexico and **Antonio de Mendoza** became the first viceroy of New Spain. Mendoza was succeeded in 1535 by **Luis de Velasco**, who ruled until 1564. This was the beginning of 300 years of Spanish dominance in Mexico, during which time the Indians became impoverished slaves and the Spanish became ruling landowners. The Spanish wanted a feudal system like they had at home – only in Mexico the Indians would be the serfs.

Under Spanish leadership agricultural practices were extended, mining was modernized and new crops (such as citrus fruits, wheat, sugarcane and olives) were introduced. Also, chickens, horses, mules and donkeys were brought into the country. The Spanish secured the caste system and placed themselves at the top of the heap. They ensured expansion by bringing in Catholicism and allowing the missionaries to go into the hinterland to secure more souls.

■ Independence

Exploitation of the masses caused discontent mostly among the miners in Mexico. Miners, who had the sympathy of most peasants, were drawn by an inspiring speech by **Miguel Hidalgo**, a Creole, in Guanajuato on September 16, 1810. They started the War of Independence that resulted in Hidalgo and his machete-wielding army meeting the Spanish royalists near Mexico City. Intimidated by the enemy, Hidalgo retreated to Guadalajara and then to the north. He and some of his men were captured, executed and had their heads hung on a granary wall as a warning to other would-be rebels. Today, September 16th is celebrated as Independence Day and Hidalgo is considered the hero, although true independence didn't come for a long time.

After Hidelgo's death, his loyal follower, **José Maria Morelos**, another Creole, became the leader of the areas now known as Guerrero and Oaxaca. His main goal was to establish independence for Mexico by forming a constitution and improving the economy. In November of 1813, and before he could accomplish what he wanted, Morelos was executed. Two years later, civil war broke out with the royalists fighting the Indians and Creoles. It lasted a total of five years. Although peace of sorts followed, the Spanish government continued to rule without a constitution.

In Spain, liberal revolts influenced the Creoles (Mexican-born Spaniards) of Mexico to change sides and join forces with the Indians in the hope of bringing true independence to the country. On September 27, 1821, **Agustine de Iturbide** entered Mexico City. He declared Mexico a nation with independent rule and himself Emperor. His promise to the peasants was independence, Catholicism and equality. Although Mexico was now independent of Spanish rule, the people had no experience at governing themselves. Iturbide lost power within a year.

The country continued to be surreptitiously ruled by a clergy that was backed by a wealthy Spanish-ruled church. By 1824 a constitution was adopted as the Creoles managed to gain equality with the Spanish. The Indians, on the other hand, along with the mestizos (people with a mixture of Spanish and Indian or Negro blood), were still considered inferior. Power struggles were fierce between the clergy and the ruling Creoles who controlled the military. The government, on average, changed hands yearly.

Antonio Lopez Santa Anna, a Creole who became the governor of Veracruz under Iturbide, rebelled and became the elected president of Mexico. The following year, he decided that Mexico was not ready for democracy and became a dictator. Santa Ana was elected to power six times in all and when others became president, he ruled almost as strongly from position of vice president.

In 1836, Santa Anna led forces to Texas in order to keep the Americans at bay and the land in Mexican control. However, during an afternoon sleep when he failed to post guards, the Americans attacked and won. The battle resulted in Santa Anna becoming prisoner. He quickly signed a treaty giving Texas to the US.

It wasn't long before Santa Anna's errors, oppression, high taxes and personal extravagance irritated the people. This resulted in the middle class professionals taking power. Their leader was **Benito Juarez** who, in 1854, drove Santa Anna out of office and into exile.

Juarez brought economic reforms, had the military and religious courts abolished in regard to civil matters, and outlawed corporate ownership of land. The last law caused discontent with the Indians when it was used against them in their communal land holdings. However, in 1857, Juarez also drafted a new constitution that gave more freedoms to the people and declared Mexico a democratic republic.

It took three years of war for the government to implement the idealism it had written into the constitution and secularize the state. But during that struggle they nationalized church property.

The French still regarded Napoleon's conquest of Spain as a claim on Mexico. By 1862 the French marched toward Mexico City with the intention of pushing Juarez out of power and installing a conservative king. With the help of the right-wing groups in Mexico, this happened, but it took two years.

Although he retreated into the hills, Juarez continued to have a strong following. The French were beaten at the village of Puebla on May 5th (a day still celebrated in Mexico), but the following year, the French regrouped and successfully took the city. They put the Hapsburg prince, **Maximilian** into power. Within five years, Juarez and his followers overthrew Maximilian's government and had the flamboyant emperor executed. Juarez then brought in more social reforms, one of which was compulsory education for everyone.

Nationalism strengthened and the constitution was amended in the hope of improving life for ordinary people. In 1876, **Porfirio Diaz** took over administration and ruled for 35 years. Any opposition to him was instantly snuffed, but the economy flourished. Railways were built and telegraph lines were hung, banks were established and industry grew. Economic growth benefitted the ruling class and foreign investors, but the Indians and mestizos continued to live under difficult conditions. When inflation became a problem, the lower classes starved. This became fodder for another revolution.

■ The Mexican Revolution

 By the early 1900s conditions in Mexico for the peasants were unbearable. They rebelled, demanding, food, water, land and schools for their children.

The first rebellion, started in 1908, was called the **Madero Revolution** and was led by Francisco I. Madero, who came from a wealthy Mexican family. He tried to beat Diaz in the 1910 election but failed, so he decided to use force. In November of that year he overthrew the government and sent Diaz into exile. The following year Madero was elected by public vote, but he held power for only 15 months before he was murdered by one of his turncoat military leaders.

The death of Madero and the reign by his successor **Victoriano Huerta** caused the different factions to again take sides. Those wanting a constitutional government joined forces. The leaders of this group were **Francisco (Pancho) Villa, Alvaro Obregón, Venustiano Carranza** and **Emiliano Zapata**. In 1914, with the help of the Americans and then-president Woodrow Wilson, they brought down Huerta. The four split up the responsibilities of ruling the country, with Obregón taking Mexico City, Carranza ruling Veracruz, Pancho Villa ruling in the north and Zapata in the south.

Internal scuffles soon – including a few with the United States – but it also resulted in a new constitution, one that offered free elementary schooling for everyone, labor laws that were in favor of the worker and land reforms stating that the subsoil belonged to the nation. However, passing a law and enforcing it are two different matters. Unrest continued until about 1920, when Alvaro Obregón took power and tried to appease the people with actual change. Opposition and corruption prevailed until Obregón was assassinated in 1928.

By the mid-1930s a new form of campaigning took place. A man by the name of **Lazaro Cardenas** approached the people directly, gaining their support. As the new ruler, Cardenas started a period of prosperity. Land was redistributed, education became prevalent for everyone and labor conditions improved. Cardenas also expropriated foreign petroleum enterprises, thus allowing the profits from that industry to benefit the country.

The 1940s sent the government to the right and, with the help of the United States, they strengthened the peso, constructed the Pan American Highway and modernized industry.

After the war and until the early 1960s, the government saw a period of expansion – hydroelectric dams were built, the Pan Am highway was completed, and a modern university was constructed in Mexico City. Social services were expanded and women won the right to vote.

Even after all these changes, the country remained an agrarian nation struggling toward industrialization and a piece in the global economy. Inflation and debt resulted in more poverty for the working class.

The 60s saw discontent, and many people were killed in demonstrations or riots that opposed the practices of the rich. In 1982, **Miguel de la Madrid** came to power. At that time, the world oil crises caused huge financial troubles in Mexico and, as a result, the country was unable to pay back foreign debt. Inflation was rampant and the peso dropped so much it became one of the world's most devalued currency.

The 1988 elections resulted in Harvard-educated **Carlos Salinas de Gorari** winning, but only after numerous recounts. It was the worst showing that the Institutional Revolutionary Party (PRI) had ever gotten. But Salinas was dedicated to improving life for the poor, for women and for the indigenous groups. His biggest claim to fame was that he signed the North American Free Trade Agreement (NAFTA) with Canada and the US. It came into effect on January 1, 1994. On the same day, the Zapatistas in the Chiapas rebelled and captured a number of small towns. While the government tried to settle the problems in the north, **Luis Donaldo Colosio**, the man many thought would be the successor to Salinas, was gunned down in Mexico City. **Ernesto Zedillo** became the next PRI ruler of the country. The next 10 years resulted in economic problems with the peso dropping and being artificially propped up, and the struggles with the Zapatistas in the Chiapas causing massacres of police, military and peasants. There was a killing of 45 indigenous people in Chiapas that was linked to PRI officials, and then a second event where anti-government speeches in Ayutla, Guerrero resulted in torture of those who supported the Indians. These atrocities are still being studied by human rights groups in the hope of getting restitution for people who were mistreated.

The biggest news of all for Mexican politics was the coming of leader **Vincente Fox**, former president of Coca-Cola Mexico and National Action Party (PAN) governor of Guanajuato State. He put an end to the PRI's 71 years of rule.

The signing of NAFTA was done with the hope that prosperity would finally arrive. While traveling through the western coast of Mexico, you might believe that this may, in fact, have happened. The inflation rate has dropped below 15% and investment dollars are again returning. But best of all, Mexico has repaid all the money it received to help in the bailout of the economic slump.

POLITICAL PARTIES

The three main parties active today are the **National Action Party** (PAN) headed by Vincente Fox, the **Institutional Revolutionary Party** (PRI) that is headed by Francisco Labastida, and the **Party of the Democratic Revolution** (PRD), headed by Cuauhtemoc Cardenas.

Government

The **United Mexican States** is the official name of the country commonly known as Mexico. The capital of the country is **Mexico City**. Mexico is a federal republic with 31 administrative divisions called states.

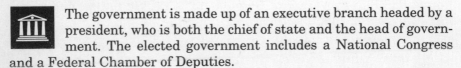

MEXICAN STATES

The following is a list of all Mexican states. Those marked with an asterisk (*) are covered, either partially or in whole, in this book.

Aguascalientes, Baja California, Baja California Sur, Campeche, Chiapas, **Chihuahua***, Coahuila, **Colima***, Distrito Federal, **Durango***, **Guerrero***, Guanajuato, Hidalgo, **Jalisco***, Mexico, **Michoacan***, Morelos, **Nayarit***, Nuevo Leon, **Oaxaca***, Puebla, Quntana Roo, **Sinaloa***, San Luis Potosi, **Sonora***, Tabasco, Tamaulipas, Tlaxcala, Veracruz, Yucatán, Zacatecas.

■ Officials

The government is made up of an executive branch headed by a president, who is both the chief of state and the head of government. The elected government includes a National Congress and a Federal Chamber of Deputies.

In 2000, the people of the country elected the flamboyant **Vincente Fox** to be their leader for the next six years. He won by almost 43% of the vote.

The **Cabinet** is appointed by the president after an election, but the assigning of an attorney general requires the consent of the Senate. The **National Congress** is made up of 128 seats, with 96 of those being elected by the people in each district. The 32 non-elected seats are given to members of the elected parties and are proportionally split up according to the number of votes won in the election. This provides for fairer representation. Each member serves a six-year term.

The **Federal Chamber of Deputies** consists of 500 seats, 300 of which are elected by popular vote. The other 200 seats are given to members of the elected parties and, as in Congress, are proportionally split according to the number of votes each party has won in the election. The deputies serve a three-year term.

Mexico officially won independence from Spain on September 16, 1810 and celebrates that day as a national holiday. The present constitution, drawn up on February 5, 1917, is a mixture of constitutional theory and civil law. It ensures voting rights to all citizens over the age of 18 and makes education compulsory for everyone between the ages of six and 15. Also, education is to be free of religious doctrine.

The **Supreme Court of Justice** is appointed by the president, but must have the approval of the Senate. There are 21 judges who function as the full court or tribunal. Circuit judges and district judges are appointed by the Supreme Court and they must all have law degrees awarded from recognized law schools.

■ Military Service

Men and women can enter the military at the age of 18 and the forces consist of an army, navy and air force. There are presently almost 200,000 active persons in the military working under an annual expenditure of $4 billion. There are also 300,000 on reserve. It is compulsory for men at the age of 18 to enlist and those 16 years of age may volunteer to receive training as technicians. Women may volunteer at the age of 18. Conscientious objectors are not exempt from service. Which sector of the military one serves is a game of chance. Those who draw a white ball from the bag go into the army or air force, while those who get a blue ball must enter the navy. Mexico offers those in the service an opportunity for secondary education or special training in fields such as social work.

■ The Police Force

The Mexican police force is notorious for its corruption. Getting into trouble is usually dealt with by paying a bribe. Because of the low pay, police officers are often people with low education, and many are interested only in expanding their criminal connections. These facts were researched and reported in the *World Policy Journal*, Volume 17, No. 3 in the fall of 2000. The story was also published in *Nexos*, a monthly magazine based in Mexico City, in April and August of 1998. Andrew Reding, a director of the Americas Project at the World Policy Institute, translated the article. For a complete report, go to www.worldpolicy.org/globalrights/ mexico/2000-fall-wpj-mexpolice.html.

But there is a good side to the Mexican police force. The **tourist police** found in areas popular with visitors don't seem too corrupt. It appears to me that they have managed to clean up most of the crime in those regions of the country. While walking around I never felt threatened or that I was being watched by potential robbers.

However, I still wouldn't take a chance of walking on the beach alone after dark. I also highly recommend that you don't wander around drunk in a public place, that you stay away from the drug trade (of which there is plenty) and that you avoid things like nude bathing except on beaches designated as such. These things are not tolerated and will get you a jail sentence.

Those driving may be stopped and asked for a small contribution, called a *mordida*. Whether you are guilty or not, I suggest you ask for the ticket, or *boleto*. The best that can happen is that the officer will walk away and let you go. The worst that can happen is you will pay a fine for the infraction you have committed. If you pay a traffic ticket within 24 hours, the cost is half.

Economy

Mexico is a free market economy with industry, public services and agriculture owned mostly by the private sector. Tourism is a big draw for the Mexican government and it works hard to attract investors to build the infrastructure tourists require. When visiting the resorts, you will find high-quality rooms, service, food, entertainment and security.

A devaluation of the peso in 1994 threw Mexico into economic disaster that caused a recession. Concerns included wages, underemployment, unequal income distribution and few advancement opportunities for the Indians. At time of writing, the exchange rate was 9.6 pesos to US $1.

The signing of NAFTA, the **North American Free Trade Agreement**, was done in the hope of improving the economy. According to *The New York Times*, November 19, 2003, the agreement has tripled trade with the US and Canada, but the wages of workers in the manufacturing industry, in agriculture and in the service industry has decreased. The inequality of wages between the middle class and the peasant class has increased, and immigration to the US has continued to rise. The World Bank reports that Mexico has benefited from the agreement. The main problem seems to be that small farmers, who were no longer subsidized for growing staple crops, left the farms for the factories, but there weren't enough jobs to go around. The farms were bought out by big producers who, in turn, sold the crops at higher prices.

Mexico is now looking to negotiate a new bilateral trade deal that would include the rest of Latin America and improve Mexico's situation.

At present, Mexico has free trade agreements with the US, Canada, Guatemala, Honduras, El Salvador and Europe. Over 90% of the country's trading power is under these agreements. In 2002 this increased Mexico's purchasing power to $900 billion, which resulted in a growth rate of 1%.

Foreign investment had risen to over $25 billion in 2001 and recent reports show that this flow has remained fairly constant, although investments in Latin America in general are down about 20%. In 1998 the government lifted foreign ownership restrictions on banks and the third-largest bank, Serfin, was sold to Santander Central Hispano of Spain. Bancomer, another large bank, was sold to BBVA, also of Spain. It is believed that foreign management will help stabilize the peso.

The **GDP** in 2002 was $637.2 billion, or $6,030 per person. Of this, 4% came from agriculture, 26.6% from industry, 8.9% from manufacturing, and 69.4% from services. This results in 40% of the population living below the poverty line. Although only 3% of the population is unemployed, there is a huge underemployed group. But it's not all bad. The inflation rate dropped from 52% in 1995 to 6.4% in 2002, the lowest rate in 30 years. Exports have reached a sum of $171.3 billion, but this has fallen recently due to a decline in the demand for goods by the United States. Mexico's imports are worth $184.6 billion. Due to economic slowdown worldwide, both the exports and imports have recently declined.

▪ The Maquiladoras

An unpredicted result of the free trade agreements and foreign investment was the emergence of the Maquiladora. Maquiladoras are towns along the Mexican/American border where there are no tariffs on exports. Mexico has few ecological restraints in these areas, so cheap construction and operation costs are also a big draw. Additionally, the companies can hire cheap labor. The results are cheap goods going back into the rest of North America with no tariffs attached. The backlash of this is that the people of United States and Canada have lost millions of jobs and, in turn, millions of dollars in tax revenue.

People & Culture

■ Cultural Groups

After the Spanish came, it took just two generations to depopulate Mexico of its indigenous peoples. This happened through disease, war and intermarriage. The population is now predominantly *mestizo*, people with a mixture of Spanish and Indian or Negro blood. Today, this group makes up about 60% of the total population. Pure indigenous people are 30% of the population, and whites are about 9%.

There is an unspoken class system that puts the pure European white person at the top. These are the **Creoles**, those born in the country but originating from unmixed European stock. The first Creoles to populate Mexico were the children of the Spanish settlers. Later, they came as refugees from the Spanish Civil War.

Beneath the Creoles on the class scale are the *mestizos* and beneath them are the pure **Amerindians**.

There are also a number of **Asians** in the country, who arrived after they were refused entry into the United States in the late 19th and early 20th centuries. This group shares equal status with the Amerindians.

The total population is presently over 100 million, a figure that has doubled in the last 30 years. However, recently the rate has slowed due to the migration of workers to the United States and Canada.

Sixty-two percent of the population is between the ages of 15 and 64. Those under 15 make up about 34% of the population. Life expectancy for females is 75 years of age, seven years longer than males.

The Nahuatl (Aztec language) speaking people number about two million and are concentrated in the States of Guerrero and Oaxaca. The numbers of Maya language speakers are low. The Maya are concentrated in the state of Chiapas and in the Yucatán Peninsula.

■ Traditional Arts

As of late, a resurgence of cultural pride among cultural groups has resulted in shows of traditional art, theater and dance.

Mexican art includes everything from painted wild fig tree bark to black Oaxaca pottery. Silver and gold have always been a popular medium and the quality of workmanship now found in Mexico is world class. Weavings and carpets have been finding their way into visitors' homes for half a century and the embroidered pieces that can be used as place mats, pillowcases or framed pictures come in colors and designs to accent any décor. Prices for these art pieces are less than half of what you would pay for comparable art in the States.

Embroidery & Weavings

Cotton *rebozos* (ray-BO-zoz), which are handwoven shawls, originated in the Oaxaca area, but can be purchased throughout the western states. This style of weaving, which is rather loose and usually of cotton, is now also being used to make dresses and skirts in fashionable designs that are especially attractive to visitors. In areas where Maya live, such as the villages near the ruins of Monti Alban and Mitla, you can find *huipiles* (wee-PEEL-ays), women's ponchos that are handwoven and then embroidered around the neck and shoulder areas in geometric, floral or animal designs. *Huipiles* are colorful and are often taken home by tourists to adorn the walls of their homes. Some people mount them on the wall with a mirror behind the neck hole.

There are also embroidered pillowcases or dresser scarves. Some are unique and of high quality, but you must usually hunt for those. Factory-made pieces are far more common and cost much less.

Wool and cotton are used to make the Zapotec handwoven **carpets**. The better ones are made with natural dyes that come from pomegranate, bark, nuts and flowers. They feature intricate geometric designs similar to those on Navajo rugs. The ubiquitous cotton **blankets** woven in simple stripes come in every color and quality.

The weaving of reeds, straw, needles and leaves has been tradition for about 5,000 years. Weavers make things like small mats that are far better for lying upon in the sand than towels. Panama hats made here last for centuries. Their soft quality allows them to be rolled into a tube for storage; when taken out, they retain their original shape.

Pine needle **baskets** have been used as containers for everything from food to babies and can be plain, or with geometric, floral or other intricate designs. Though these pieces are not colorful, their beauty lies in the design. Reeds, on the other hand, are often colored and woven into geometric designs, usually for baskets.

Huichol Art

Huichol art, made with beads, is seen in the shops throughout western Mexico. Some pieces are life-size replicas of animals; others are small. The work is colorful and intricate and depicts images representing stories and deities from Indian myths. Each piece is made by carving the desired shape out of wood or by using a gourd and covering it with a beeswax and pine resin mixture. The colored beads are then placed, one at a time, onto the wood or gourd to create the design.

▸▸ **AUTHOR TIP:** *If you purchase a piece of Huichol art, don't leave it in the sun, as the wax can melt.*

There are many imitations of this art form made in factories with the profits going to the industrialists, rather than artists. To avoid buying factory-made ones, ask if you can purchase another piece exactly the same. If you can, it's a sign that the piece is produced en masse.

HUICHOL BELIEFS

The Huichols, descendants of the Aztecs, are an indigenous group numbering about 18,000 who live in the mountains of Jalisco and Nayarit. They take a pilgrimage each year to the holy spot where the peyote cactus grows. There, they eat the plant and relive stories from the past or communicate with their gods. They sing and dance and see images that they reproduce in their art.

The deer, corn and peyote are the most sacred of all Huichol symbols. The deer represents the people, humorous and easygoing, never practicing open conflict. The peyote is the center of their religion and the vehicle with which they are able to communicate with their gods. They believe that humans are made of corn and corn is their sacred food. Before a field is planted, it is blessed with the blood of a deer. This ensures a good crop. Flowers that bloom during the corn's growing season are also sacred and the best of these is the white Toto, a solanaceous plant that belongs to the nightshade family and includes potatoes, tobacco, chili peppers and tomatoes.

Leather Goods

There is a **shoe store** on every street in Mexico. Although you can see the cheap offshore imitations of good quality shoes taking their place on the shelves, there are still many shops that sell the best. Prices are usually a third of what you'll find at home.

And the market isn't restricted to shoes. For reasonable prices, you can purchase purses, belts, jackets, pants, boots, hats and almost anything else that can be made out of leather. The best thing to do if shopping for leather is head to the closest highland town on market day. For example, if staying in Puerta Vallarta, take a trip to Guadalajara; if staying in Mazatlan, try Tepic. Both cities are only four hours from the coast.

Masks

Masks have been worn by traditional dancers for centuries. They can be made out of ceramic, wood, leather or papier mâché and decorated with paint, stones and metals.

As long as 3,000 years ago, masks were used to imitate gods that had reincarnated into exotic animals. During the conquest, masks were used to depict oppressors and to emphasize a specific aspect of a story. Now they are used in religious ceremonies and for artistic expression. No matter which mask you purchase, it will be an original.

Today, masks can be found in museums and in private homes. Some of the more complex ones are made by the Huichol artists (see above). For an interesting display and brief description of collectors' masks, visit www.mexicanmasks.us.

Pottery, Glass & Ceramics

Pottery and ceramics have been a part of Mexican culture since ancient times, even though many of the religious beliefs that inspired specific works of art have not. Indigenous styles are popular, but the most popular style is **Talavera**, from Arabia via Spain. Talavera pottery is produced only in Puebla. The more Persian-styled works come from Jalisco state. These pieces are usually decorated with gold and silver. If you're in search of something more Mexican-looking, you will be able to find finely decorated ceramic pieces called the "tree of life." They are very ornate and come from post Catholic times.

The **black pottery** from Oaxaca is famous. The most common vase shape has a round bottom and, because it cannot stand on its own, comes with an extra piece to support it.

The most famous master potter is **Juan Quezada**, who does work in the Mata Ortiz style. His exquisite pieces are decorated with ancient symbols combined with contemporary style that gives them a feel of sophistication.

Stoneware is also common. The most popular piece is a **chess set** made with Aztecs facing conquistadors as opponents. The pieces are usually made of obsidian or onyx.

Many **blown glass** pieces are also available. Occasionally, you can watch your selected piece being made.

There are numerous shops in all the tourist areas that sell top-quality works of art. The best guide is to purchase what you like and believe the story the sales person tells you about its origin.

■ Dress

Woman in traditional dress.

 Most mestizo dress like you, in comfortable pants or skirts of the latest fashions (although the women tend to dress on the conservative side). Shorts are worn in the country's western states. Down jackets help keep people warm in the highlands of Mexico.

Although there are some Amerindians who still wear traditional clothing, they are not usually found in coastal regions of Mexico. In the highlands, on market day or during a fiesta, it is common to see hand-embroidered clothes in myriad colors adorning the Amerindian people.

■ Music

Mexican music has been popular in European countries as well as the US and Canada since the beginning of the last century. This is probably because of the huge Mexican population in the southern US, especially Texas and California areas, which were once part of Mexico. In recent times, artists like Joan Baez and Linda Ronstadt sang for a large Hispanic audience and popularized Mexican songs like *Gracias a la Vida*.

Mexican music isn't only mariachi. **Corridos** are stories put to music that tell about mountain people who are in conflict with drug traffickers, vengeance killers, and robbers and bandits. They tell historical stories about the revolution or about revolutionaries fighting for peasant rights. There are also the **boleros** and **baladas**, Mexican love songs. If you don't know the meaning of *corazon* (heart), you'll never get the meaning of the love songs that cover the romance around past, present and future loves.

Mariachi

Although I often listen to the music of Ronstadt and Baez, for me, Mexican music is the traditional mariachi band. Before the Spanish came, locals used five different instruments to play mariachi. These consisted of various styles of wooden drums and rattles.

After the Spanish arrived, they used music to draw the locals into the Catholic religion. They opened a music school as early as the mid-1500s and introduced such string instruments as the violin, harp and guitar. It didn't take long for the Mexican musician to combine these sounds and make new music not only for the church, but also for fiestas.

By the revolutionary period in the early 1800s, the music had blended traditional Indian tunes with Spanish and Negro tunes. The instruments commonly used were a harp, a violin, a guitar, a drum and a flute. During the battle for independence, music became a unifying symbol. At that time, musicians wore peasant clothing; it wasn't until after independence that they started dressing in what we associate with the Mexican musicians today – tight pants, a black jacket fitted tightly at the waist, an embroidered belt and a wide bow tie. (See Antonio Banderas in the movie *Desperado*.) On their heads are huge sombreros that were not so much a symbol of music, but a symbol of wealth (sombreros were once worn only by wealthy hacienda owners).

Before the conquest, the Coca Indians called their five-tone music "mariachi" and, when **Amado Vargas** put together his five-piece band consisting of a guitar, violin, drum, harp and flute, it became a natural word to describe the music. Vargas's son and grandson were the ones to solidify the style and continued to make it famous. However, it wasn't until 1920 that **Cirilo Marmolejo**, another passionate player of mariachi music, moved his band to Mexico City. They added a trumpet and started playing for radio stations so people across the country could hear them. The Salon Tenampa opened and Concho Andrade and Cirilo Marmolejo performed there on a regular basis. The Tenampa became the center of mariachi activity.

Motion pictures of the 1940s and 1950s helped promote the image and the band of Mariachi Vargas de Tecalitlan appeared in more than 200 movies. It became the most important group in the history of mariachi. As bands formed around the country, they added more musicians until the group consisted of 20 or more players. Today, however, the bands have become rather small again and usually have just four musicians. Of these, two play violins, one a guitar and a *vihuela*, a small, guitar-like instrument with a convex back and five strings. Some bands also use the *guitarron*, which has six strings instead of five like the *vihuela*.

Aspiring musicians formed bands and roamed the streets and bars looking for an audience. Also by the 1960s, Nati Cano formed Los Camperos, an American group that popularized the music among non-Hispanics. The prominence of this group resulted in mariachi schools opening and, in 1979, an international conference celebrating the music was held in Texas.

Finally, in the 1980s, Linda Ronstadt mixed a bit of mariachi with the corridos style of music and popularized it with her album *Canciones de Mi Padre*.

THE CLAIM ON MARIACHI

The word "mariachi" comes from the no-longer-used Coca language of central Jalisco state. However, the French like to think that it comes from the French word *mariage*, and that they gave the word to Mexico. Historical documents indicate that the Coca, not the French, are responsible for the word.

■ Dance

Mexican dance is a sensual expression often performed with masks. Before the Spanish arrived, dances depicted the relationship between the gods and mankind. However, once Christian priests saw the advantage of the enactment, they used dance to stress good and evil in the world according to Christ. However, the Mexicans occasionally used dance as a mockery and to poke fun at the all-powerful forces. The Christians were much too serious to do this.

Each area has its own style of dance. For example, residents of Jalisco dance the jarabe, a romantic display about love and courtship. "Jarabe" means syrup. The dances of Nayarit show the joy of a party and the excitement of becoming an adult. Those in the state of Colima dance after the harvest and their exuberance often includes the throwing of knives. Not, I hope, at one another.

There are numerous **folklorica** shows in all major tourist centers. The acts are usually colorful and fun, and also give an interesting history of the culture and its relationship to the dances you see.

The Land

Mexico has almost 772,200 square miles/two million square km of land and is bordered by Belize, Guatemala and the US. It has 5,831 miles/9,330 km of coastline.

■ Geology

The land forms a bridge between North and South America and consists of high rugged mountains, plateaus, deserts and low coastal plains. Of these lands, 12% is farmland, 40% is pasture and 25% is forest and woodland.

There was once a lake that covered most of the state of Jalisco, part of Michoacan and Aguascalientes. Today, lakes Chapala, Cajititlan, El Molino, Atotonilco, Zacoalco, San Marcos, Atoyac, Sayula and Zapotlan are remains of the giant lake. Many of these smaller lakes have water in them only during the rainy season, but others, like Lake Chapala, have shallow water all year. When the great lake was in existence, research shows that it was anywhere from 700 feet/215 meters to 900 feet/275 meters deep.

Before the lake was formed, fossils indicate that mammoths and mastodons roamed the area. Volcanoes, many of which are now vegetated hills, were active at the time. Volcán de Colima is still active and easily accessible. Within the vegetated hills are plateaus and basins that form rich valleys like the Atemajac Valley near Guadalajara. A number of rivers drain these valleys into the Pacific Ocean.

The American Pacific coast from Alaska down to Tierra del Fuego is rock interspersed with sandy beaches. Just offshore most bays are dotted with tiny islands that rich with wildlife. There is a limited amount of coral off the coast.

■ Environmental Concerns

Environmental issues have been a big problem in Mexico. Hotels and cities along the oceans often dump their raw sewage into the ocean. Water purification plants are inefficient and below standard. Wildlife has been hunted almost to extinction. Air pollution is extreme and deforestation has resulted in erosion. However, there is a good side. Tourism is creating a market that demands clean air, clean water and lots of wildlife. The Mexicans are realizing this and their environmental practices, although still not up to the standards of places like Switzerland, are improving. People in the tourist industry are starting to insist on catch-and-release fishing and no-touch viewing of animals. More people are hiking rather than taking all-terrain vehicles into the jungle and Mexicans are putting emissions controls on their vehicles.

The best you can do, as a visitor, is insist on traveling only with tour companies who are environmentally sensitive. Below are a few examples of environmental groups working in Mexico. All are open to enlarging their membership and their bank accounts.

- La Systema Nacional de Areas Naturales Protegidas (Sinap) – type in "sinap Mexico" on the Internet and you'll see many references to their programs in Mexico. Click on one that appeals to you.
- Audubon Society, www.audubon.org.
- Greenpeace, www.greenpeace.org.
- Cetacea Defence, www.cetaceadefence.org.
- Sea Turtle Survival League, www.cccturtle.org/ccctmp.htm.
- Earthjustice, www.earthjustice.org.
- Sierra Club, www.sierraclub.org.
- World Wildlife Fund, www.panda.org.

■ Parks

 There are numerous categories for protected public land, but the ones of most interest to us are the national parks and reserves. National parks are used for recreation or have historical value. These can be large, wild areas with few trails or small parks that are used mainly for strolls. Reserves are wildlife sanctuaries or areas set aside for scientific study. Below are brief descriptions of the national parks and reserves in Mexico's Pacific Coast region.

NATIONAL PARKS & RESERVES

Isla Isabel National Park, Nayarit State, is a tiny island in the Sea of Cortez that has a volcanic crater lake in the center of its 479 acres of land. It is alive with birds. Camping is allowed on the island. See page 227.

Cumbres de Cuixmala Reserve, in the state of Jalisco, runs from the ocean into the mountains. It covers 32,500 acres and encompasses eight vegetation zones, each with its special communities of animals and birds. See page 330

Sierra de Manantlan Biosphere Reserve, also in Jalisco, is a cultural reserve, rather than a natural one. It features gargantuan stone carvings. In the reserve, the most traditional town is **Ayotitlan**.

Nevado de Colima National Park, in the state of Colima, has two volcanoes. **Volcán de Colima**, the higher of the two, is almost 14,000 feet/4,300 meters high. The other one, **Volcán de Fuego**, is still spewing fumes. There is hiking, climbing and camping in the park. See page 386.

Lago de Camecuaro National Park in Michoacan state is just 22 acres of bush set around a lake. The park is good for birding, camping and swimming.

Volcán Aacuten Park in the state of Michoacan has a new volcano that started rising above the surface of the earth in 1949. Today it stands at 1,300 feet/410 meters. You can hike or ride horseback to the top of the cone.

Pico de Tancitaro National Park has 72,500 acres of non-maintained parkland featuring **Tancitaro Peak**, a 12,670-foot/3,860-meter mountain where visitors can explore.

El Veladero National Park, in the state of Guerrero, covers almost 8,000 acres of hills above Acapulco. Wildlife is limited, but it is a good place to head for a refreshing walk.

Benito Juarez National Park in Oaxaca state, has almost 7,000 acres of forest with both deciduous and coniferous trees. Camping and hiking are encouraged in this area.

Bahias de Huatulco National Park, has wildlife galore, including rats, armadillos, squirrels, deer, salamanders, frogs, toads, iguanas, turtles and snakes. The bird population is huge, with hawks, owls, gulls, hummingbirds and gulls. See page 472.

Los Arcos Underwater National Park, near Acapulco, has great diving. See page 259.

Lagunas de Chacachua National Park, also in Oaxaca, is a jungle area west of Puerto Escondido that has lagoons, alligators, turtles, a mangrove swamp, mahogany trees, orchids and tropical birds.

Climate

The climate varies from tropical to desert and is dictated the most by elevation. Between November and March, it is warm and dry along the coast. Temperatures run around 26-28°C/80-85°F during the day and drop about 16°C/60°F at night. If you go up to Guadalajara (5,000 feet/1,500 meters), the temperatures average16-21°C/ 60-70°F, with 60% humidity during the day. Nighttime temperatures drop as they do along the coast.

In the wet season, from April to the end of October, the coast experiences around 90% humidity that, coupled with temperatures of over 30°C/90°F, makes walking more than three minutes a huge effort. Guadalajara temperatures average 21°C/75°F during the day, with 80% humidity. This is what locals call the eternal spring climate.

■ Hurricanes

 Because of high temperatures during the wet months (May to November), the water in the ocean heats up, causing a draft sometimes strong enough to create a hurricane. A hurricane forms when there's an area of low pressure in the upper atmosphere and the tropical waters warm to over 26°C/80°F to a depth of 200 feet/60 meters. The heat of the water causes circulation of the winds to accelerate.

The good news is that the west coast does not have as many hurricanes as the Caribbean because most hurricanes move northward in an east-to-west direction. This means that those over the Pacific often miss the mainland because they move toward the ocean. As they move north, the colder temperatures decrease the velocity of the winds. However, the winds and water currents on the swimming and surfing beaches during hurricane season are dangerous.

Hurricanes are categorized by the speed of the wind. This scale is called the Saffir-Simpson Scale and was designed by two Americans, one an engineer with a specialty in wind damage and the other the director of the National Hurricane Center. The scale was developed in 1971 and has been refined over the years.

SAFFIR-SIMPSON HURRICANE SCALE		
Category	Wind speed	Expected damage
One	74-95 mph/ 120-150 kph	Minimum damage caused mostly to vegetation.
Two	96-110 mph/ 150-175 kph	Moderate damage to vegetation and minimum damage to structures.
Three	111-130 mph/ 176-210 kph	Severe damage to vegetation, structural damage to small buildings and flooding along the shoreline.
Four	131-155 mph/ 211-250 kph	Excessive damage to vegetation, moderate damage to small buildings, major erosion along the shoreline.
Five	over 155 mph/ 250 kph	Total destruction of small buildings, excessive flooding three to five hours before the storm hits and catastrophic destruction to land.

■ Tsunamis

 Since Mexico sits on a tectonic plate, the country is subject to frequent tsunamis. The last one to hit the west coast of Mexico was in 1995, when Manzanillo was struck. Tsunamis can be expected after an earthquake or any other underwater volcanic activity. Occasionally, an underwater mountain will collapse or a landslide will occur and start a wave.

Tsunamis consist of huge waves that are formed far out at sea and can measure up to 90 feet/30 meters in height when they finally hit land. Moving toward land, they can travel as fast as a jet liner, up to 500 mph/ 800 kmph. They can move back and forth across the ocean for hours, over distances of up to 12,000 miles/16,000 km, before they finally peter out.

FACT FILE: A 1960 tsunami that started near Chile killed 150 people in Japan 22 hours later.

Tsunamis, when they reach land, throw the sediment from the ocean floor over a half-mile/one km inland; once the water subsides, this sedimentation can be over three feet/one meter deep. Tsunamis cause terrible destruction to the vegetation along the coast and often destroy entire villages.

As a tsunami approaches shore, it appears as a wall of water. A tsunami wave does not crest.

DEADLIEST RECORDED TSUNAMIS IN THE AMERICAS		
Location	Date	Lives lost
Chile	May 22, 1960	1,260
Colombia/Ecuador	Dec. 12, 1979	500
Venezuela	Jan. 31, 1906	500
Guatemala/El Salvador	Feb. 26, 1902	185
Nicaragua	Sept. 2, 1992	170
Aleutian Islands	Apr. 1, 1946	165
United States (Alaska)	Mar. 28, 1964	123
Chile	Nov. 11, 1922	100
Mexico	June 22, 1932	75
Canada (Newfoundland)	Nov. 18, 1929	51
Solomon Islands	Oct. 3, 1931	50

■ Earthquakes

Earthquakes in the central and south region of the country are common. The one that hit Mexico City on September 19, 1985 had a magnitude of 8.1 on the Richter Scale and was the worst to hit since the Great Jalisco quake of 1932. Quakes occur when tectonic plates under the earth's surface move. When the quake hit Mexico City, the tectonic plate moved seven feet/2.5 meters across and 32 in/80 cm in a vertical direction. When an earthquake occurs under manmade structures, the damage is immense. The 1985 quake covered an area of almost 5,405 square miles/14,000 square km. It caused a tsunami that hit the coast from Manzanillo to Acapulco, causing most damage in the town of Zihuatanejo, where the wave was 10 feet/three meters high.

The aftershock of the Mexico City earthquake hit two days later and measured 7.5 on the Richter Scale, but that occurred 60 miles/100 km from the main site. It too, caused some tsunami activity.

Plant Life

When we think of the Pacific coast of Mexico, we see swaying palms along sandy beaches and bougainvillea hanging over stone fences. Panning the landscape a bit farther inland we see giant cactus and spiked shrubs; lizards and snakes skitter around the dry ground. In the higher elevations, we see lush rainforest with canopies so solid they hide the sun and the parrots, monkeys, scorpions and snakes that live there.

■ Ecological Zones

The flora can be described in terms of seven distinct ecological zones between the Pacific coast and the highlands of Guadalajara or Mexico City. Each zone supports a huge variety of plants, animals, birds, amphibians and reptiles. The ocean has a vast array of vegetation, corals, mammals and fish. It is beyond the scope of this book to describe the entire natural habitat of western Mexico but, for the beginner, below are a few of the common characteristics of this unique environment.

Tropical Deciduous Forest

Tropical deciduous forest follows the west coast from the north to the south. It contains such plants as the palm tree (of which there are about 3,000 species worldwide), strangler fig or *mato palo* (in Spanish), pink trumpet tree (highly poisonous), cardinal sage, spider lily and the *mala raton* (bad rat). These plants usually lose their leaves during the dry season and flower between May and September, during the rainy season.

The **palm tree**, so common in the tropical deciduous forest, has been used for everything from baking ingredients to home construction to basket weavings to the promotion of paradise. The ones seen on the coast are usually the coconut or fan palm. The coconut palm is tall, with green-husked fruit clustered near the base of the fronds. You can recognize the palm that produces palm oil by the thousands of crab apple-sized nuts hanging below the fronds. On the fan palm, each leaf looks like a huge fan. The **strangler fig** is often associated with Tarzan and the deep jungle. This plant is a parasite that winds itself around a host tree and eventually sucks all the nutrients out of its captive. The strangler has numerous aerial roots that hang down from the host. Some of these roots can be quite thick and are strong enough to swing upon.

The **pink trumpet**, with its huge bell-shaped flowers that hang from every limb, is beautiful to look at but deadly to eat. **Cardinal sage**, also known as *Salvia fulgens*, should not be confused with *Salvia divinorum*, a hallucinogenic plant that was once used by shaman of the Oaxaca region for religious purposes. The cardinal version grows about three feet (one meter) in height, has red flowers and seems to be especially attractive to hummingbirds. When the Spanish arrived, the **spider lily** could be found growing near the swamps of Mexico City and has since spread to the swamps of the Pacific coast. The flower clusters grow in all shades of red, from light pink to deep maroon, and are found on leafless stems. The bulbs are poisonous. A sister plant to the Mexican variety grows in Japan and is planted at the entrances to temples.

Pacific Thorn Forest

The Pacific thorn forest is located around Mazatlan, south of Puerto Vallarta and between Manzanillo and Ixtapa. This vegetation zone, located in a fairly dry environment, includes such plants as the morning glory tree, the acacia, the mimosa, the fishfuddle tree and the candelabra cactus. Because of the climactic dryness, these plants are generally scrub or cactus-like in appearance.

The **morning glory tree** grows to about 30 feet/10 meters in height. Its cream-colored flowers are about two inches wide with bright red centers.

THE ROOT OF THE PROBLEM

The morning glory tree is also called *Palo del Muerte* (Tree of Death) or *Palo Bobo* (Fool Tree) because it was believed long ago that if one drank the water that flowed near the roots of the tree, he would either die or go crazy.

The **mimosa**, of which there are about 2,500 varieties, is often associated with the dry lands of Africa. However, some types can be found along the Pacific coast of Mexico. They can grow as high as 35 feet/10 meters, with a foliage spread of about the same. In some places the mimosa is known as the shaving brush tree because of its delicate thread-like flowers that resemble the edge of a shaving brush.

The **acacia** is similar to the mimosa in that its leaves are six to 12 inches long with anywhere from 11 to 23 leaflets attached symmetrically to a single stem. The thorn acacia has a double thorn at the base of the leaf stem and houses ants that bite any possible intruders. In return for this protection, the plant provides nourishment to the ant. The thorns were once used as sewing needles by those living in the area. The yellow clusters of flowers that appear in May are highly scented and leave a seedpod that is often eaten by birds.

The **fishfuddle's** real name is the **Jamaica dogwood**. This majestic tree grows to 50 feet/15 m high with a trunk that's two-three feet/one meter in diameter. The wood is hard and durable and was often used for building ships. The bark is gray, with dark patches, and the leaves are four to nine inches long with five to 11 shiny leaflets on each stem. The flowers are white with pink or red centers. Early fishermen used various parts of the tree to make a poison that would stun fish and make picking them out of the water easy. The **candelabra cactus** looks like its name suggests, except it always has more than the seven branches (the candleholders). The plant grows three-12 feet/one-four meters high. Its branches have six to eight ribs and a long central spine. When the skin is ruptured, the plant oozes a milky sap that is poisonous to humans.

Savannah

The savannah or plains grasslands are common in the state of Sorora and farther east. These semi-desert areas are often called *pastizales* (pastures) and are characterized by the abundant grasses (usually bunchgrass) that grow there. However, shrubs and small trees also flourish. The hot, dry climate receives less than 12 in/30 cm of rain a year and often has daytime temperatures of over 100°F/38°C. Over 700 invertebrate species make this environment their chosen home.

Two plant species common to this area are the gourd tree and the sandbox tree. The **sandbox tree** is also called the *habilla* or *quauhtlatzil* (meaning "explosive" in Spanish) and is characterized by the spikes on its trunk. The seeds come in circular sectional pods and, after being shed from the tree, they start to dry. This causes pressure that, in turn, causes the pods to explode (hence the name) and shoot individual seeds as far as several meters. The tree's sap is poisonous and has been used for dart tips in the past. The **gourd tree's** official name is the **cirian**. From a distance, it looks as though it has a number of grapefruit hanging from strings on the branches. This is the same fruit that is used to make bowls, often with local scenes cut into the skin. Some people use the flesh of the gourd to make a concoction that relieves bronchitis.

Mesquite Grassland

Generally, this land has been overgrazed, causing damage to the grassland. Mesquite grassland is where the **mescal cactus** is grown. There are numerous species of mescal grown and used in Mexico, but the most famous is the one from which tequila is made. It comes in two varieties, the agave tequelana and the aguey azul. In and around Guadalajara, Tequila and Tepatitlan huge plantations (a total of 62,000 acres is presently under cultivation) produce the aguey azul. These plants ripen in about six years, at which time the leaves are hacked away and the heart of the plant is chopped and roasted. It is then shredded and pressed, sugars and yeast are added and it is left to ferment. After fermentation, the liquid is distilled and we get to enjoy a delicious margarita.

Other agaves also grow in the area. Most have long spiked leaves and look similar, except for their colored markings. The **sisal** is fibrous and produces hemp for making rope. The **lechuguilla** is also a hemp-producing plant; sandals and baskets are made from it. This plant has a sharp needle on the tip of each spike. The **candelilla** is a shrub-like grass that produces a wax that was used at one time in the making of phonograph records and cosmetics. One of the most interesting cactuses is **sangre de drago** (blood of the dragon), which produces a red sap used for centuries as an antiseptic on wounds, rashes and sores. The plant grows 50-60 feet/ 15-20 meters tall and has a creamy white flower on a long stalk.

Pine-Oak Forests

The pine-oak forests of the Sierra Madres hold many endangered species. This ecosystem lies between 4,500 and 7,500 feet/1,400 and 2,300 meters in elevation and trees here grow to a height of 75-125 feet/25-40 meters. Pine-oak regions usually have a thick undergrowth that includes ferns and water lilies, many of which are endangered.

 FACT FILE: Forty percent of vertebrates known to live in Mesoamerica make the pine-oak forests their home, including the canyon tree frog. This is one of the most endangered ecosystems in Mexico at present.

Cloud Forests

Cloud forests or rainforests are defined as areas that receive 160-400 in/ 400-1,000 cm of rain annually and have little temperature change throughout the year.

FACT FILE: All of the world's rainforests lie between the Tropic of Cancer and the Tropic of Capricorn and are on land that has never been glaciated. This long period of consistency may be the reason that rainforests play host to such a huge number of different species.

Typically, trees in the rainforest grow over 150 feet/45 meters and their branches spread out, forming a lush canopy over the creatures living below. This canopy prevents most of the sunlight from reaching the forest floor, leaving the ground with few nutrients. Since the root systems of these trees must compete for the small amount of available nutrients, roots spread out sideways rather than heading deep down into the ground. This type of growth leaves trees somewhat unstable. To counter this instability, many trees, such as the ceiba, have developed buttresses at the base of their trunks that act like stabilizing arms. Long woody vines called **lianas** are common in the cloud forest, as are orchids and bromeliads, or air plants. **Orchids** are members of the most highly evolved plants on the planet. There are about 25,000 species worldwide. Their evolution has developed thick leaves that hold moisture for the plant. Some of the flowers are highly perfumed to attract creatures for pollination. The vanilla is the most aromatic of the orchids.

Similar in appearance to the orchids are **bromeliads**, plants of the pineapple family. Unique to the Americas, bromeliads will grow in any elevation up to 8,000 feet/2,500 meters and anywhere from rainforest environment to desert. Also like orchids, these plants gather nutrients and moisture in their leaves; their roots serve only as anchors and are not used to gather food. Some bromeliads are as small as one inch across, while others grow to three feet. The pineapple is the most commonly known bromeliad. Pineapples originated in Brazil and Paraguay and were spread by the local Indians before Columbus arrived. He took the plant to Europe, where it was planted and taken to other countries. This perennial grows up to five feet/1.5 meters high and has long pointed leaves that measure 72 inches/185 cm long. The edges of the leaves have sharp needles. Normally, each plant produces only one fruit. To find if the fruit is ready to be eaten, snap your finger against it. If you hear a solid dull sound then it is good, but if the sound is hollow, the fruit is of poor quality.

Tropical Regions

This moist environment below 1,500 feet/500 meters has many **heliconias**, plants like the ginger, bird of paradise, prayer plant and banana. These plants all have large leaves and brilliant flowers. Banana trees (not actual trees, but heliconias) are abundant in Mexico. The fruits of different species vary; some are tiny, some large, some sweet and some bitter. You'll often see banana stalks hanging from trees wrapped in blue plastic bags designed to protect the fruit from insects. After the fruit stalk is removed from a tree, the treetop is chopped off and left at the base as fertilizer. New shoots grow and, eight months later, a new stalk of bananas is growing on the new tree.

NOPAL CURES

Nopal is a plant that has been eaten for thousands of years. Its fruit comes in different colors and tastes like watermelon or raspberries or pears, depending on the color. The green leaf is used in herbal medicines to cure diabetes, kidney infections and burns. The fruit is also used in salads and soups.

Animal Life

The wildlife in Mexico is making a comeback after years of abuse – over-hunting of animals, over-grazing of grasslands, over-logging of forests and over-fishing of waters. Because tourists are more interested in whales and dolphins than in marinas, Mexicans are cashing in and again trying to give the tourists what they want. Parks and reserves are numerous and locals are relentless in their attempts to educate people about the environment.

Mammals common to the country are armadillos, coatis, spider monkeys and jaguars. Coyotes are numerous, as are rabbits, squirrels and deer. Reptiles include crocodiles, turtles, snakes and lizards. There is no greater thrill than to walk alone in the jungle and see a huge reptile slither away to the safety of the bush as you pass by. On the other hand, there is nothing more frightening than to come across the aggressive fer-de-lance snake while walking in the jungle.

Marine life is also rich, with gray and humpback whales, dolphins, swordfish, sailfish, marlin and roosterfish. There are many sportfishing operators who practice catch and release. The photos so common a few years ago of a dozen sailfish next to the proud white hunter are no longer popular.

■ On Land

Rodents

 There is the usual array of rodents, including the **squirrel, gopher, rat, rabbit** and **porcupine**. Distinct for their gnawing abilities, these animals have teeth that never stop growing and must be worn down in order for the animal to survive. Rodents are generally small and eat mostly vegetation, although their diets are often supplemented with eggs, birds and insects. Rodents are also a highly reproductive group, having at least one and sometimes numerous litters every year. Audubon's ground squirrel is seen near the beaches. Yellowish-brown in color, these two-foot-long, short-necked rodents live underground and are both gregarious and social. They live in underground communities, eat insects, fruits and grasses and usually have five kids per litter. They store food in ground holes and their keen sense of smell allows them to find the food again. The Colima squirrel is gray, with large eyes and small flexible ears. It grows up to three feet/one meter long, including the tail. Colima squirrels like to live in mango plantations and palm groves, where they feast on the fresh fruits. These sociable animals live in groups of 10 to 12 adults. Each female will give birth to about five kids, which she keeps close for eight to 10 weeks.

Bats

Bats are the only mammals that fly. In the Americas, bat wingspans range in size from a tiny three in/seven cm to six feet/two meters. There are over 1,000 types of bats in the world and Mexico has its fair share.

The wing of the bat is like a webbed hand, with a thumb and four fingers. It is used to scoop up food, cradle young or hug itself for warmth. Bats like their own homes and live an average lifespan of 30 years in the same cave, near the same hanging spot. All bats in a cave are related, except for one reproducing male who always comes from another family and area. The females give birth to one baby a year, but the infant mortality rate is high, up to 60%. During the first year of life, the mothers leave their babies only when hunting for food. When they return to the cave, they call to their young, who recognize their parent's sounds and answer. Following the sound, the mother joins her youngster.

 FACT FILE: Bats can eat up to 3,000 insects in one sitting and up to 1,000 mosquitoes in an hour. I don't know who does the counting but, if the figures are correct, I really like bats.

The vampire bat doesn't suck blood. Instead, it exudes anti-coagulating saliva that keeps the blood of its victim flowing (rather than clotting) from the spot where the bat has bitten. It then laps the blood up with its tongue, drinking as much as its body weight during one feeding.

Two bat caves under protection are the Boca Cave near Monterrey and La Gruta near Ciudad Hidalgo. The Boca Cave is thought to be the largest in the western hemisphere.

Cats

JAGUAR: Jaguars are the largest and most powerful cats in the Americas. Often referred to as *el tigre*, the jaguar stands 20-30 in/50-75 cm at the shoulder and has an overall length of six-eight feet/two-three meters. The jaguar's slender but strong body can weigh 250 lb/115 kg. The jaguar is built to hunt, with strong shoulders, sharp teeth, good eyesight and hearing, and claws that can rip the hamstring of a deer with one swipe. The jaguar's short fur is usually yellow with black spots, or black circles with a yellow dot in the center. Some jaguars appear all black, but it is just that the black circles are so big they override any trace of yellow. There is no specific breeding season for the jaguar. Both parents care for the kitten for about one year after birth, at which time everyone splits and fends for themselves. With good luck and lots of food, the jaguar lives about 20 years. Food is usually obtained at night; the meat-eating jaguar will kill large animals like deer, peccaries and tapirs. It also likes birds, monkeys, foxes and turtles. It is a great swimmer and can kill a sleeping alligator. It also loves to fish. As for eating man, this is a myth. There are stories of jaguars following humans for miles through the jungle, but the belief is that the jaguar likes to escort man out of its territory rather than attack him.

PUMA: The red tiger, or puma, is also called the mountain lion, cougar or panther. Just a bit smaller than the jaguar, this animal lives throughout North and South America wherever deer, its main source of food, is found. Comparable in strength to the jaguar, the puma can haul an animal five times its size for a considerable distance. When hunting, it strikes with lightening speed and can spring forward 25 feet/7.5 meters in one leap and jump down 60 feet/18 meters to land safely. Like the jaguar, the puma can mate at any time of year and both parents help look after the young. The puma's life expectancy is 15 years.

MARGAY, OCELOT: The margay and ocelot both have black spots or rings and broken stripes on their fur. An ocelot may weigh in at 35 lbs/16 kg, while the margay is not much bigger than a domestic cat. These cats hunt rabbits, rats, monkeys, birds, snakes and deer.

COATI: The coati is a tree-climbing mammal related to the raccoon. It has a long snout (tipped white) and an even longer tail that is usually the same length as its body. It keeps its striped tail high and, as it walks, the tail swings from side to side. Coatis are sociable animals and the females often travel with their young in groups of up to 20. When a group of these animals attacks a fruit tree, they often devour the entire crop in a few minutes. A full-grown male stands 10 in/25 cm at the shoulder and will grow to two feet/50 cm long. As this omnivore hunts both in the day and at night and eats just about anything, you have a good chance of seeing one moving along in tall grass or along rocky hillsides.

Monkeys

Spider monkeys have grasping hands that have no functional thumbs and a grasping tail that is hairless at the end. These five "hands" make the spider monkey efficient in maneuverability. They travel in bands of 20 to 30 and will attack threatening invaders. They use fruits and branches as weapons and have been known to urinate on enemies walking below. There are signs in Manuel Antonio Park, Costa Rica, warning tourists of this possibility.

Amphibians

Amphibians include **frogs**, **toads**, **newts**, **salamanders**, **sirenians** (sea cows) and **caecilians** (creatures that look like earthworms). Although amphibians have lungs, they also do some air exchange through their skin. They are found worldwide, except on the poles and in extreme deserts. Amphibians are hatched from eggs and usually go through a tadpole or larvae stage, where breathing is done through gills. They metamorphose and then use lungs. Their skins are moist, glandular and pigmented, although if living away from light, pigmentation is minimal. Some, like the salamander, are able to rejuvenate lost body parts (for some reason, the back end of the creature is quicker to respond to regrowth than are the front limbs). The most endearing feature of the amphibian is its ability to consume large amounts of insects, especially mosquitoes.

Reptiles

Reptiles are prominent in Mexico and it would be a rare visit if you didn't see at least one iguana, snake, turtle, or gecko while there. Reptiles control their temperature by moving in their environment. If it is too hot in the sun, they move to the shade. They all have a tough dry skin that is used primarily to preserve body moisture. Reptiles are the first creatures along the evolutionary ladder to have developed lungs. Reptiles have developed a number of protection devices. Some have hard shells or scales, while others inflict venom. Some change color so they blend into their environments. Reptiles always live in vegetated areas and prefer warm climates. There are more reptiles living on land than in fresh water and more in fresh water than in salt water.

SNAKES: The **fer-de-lance** is the most dangerous of Mexico's snakes and its bite is usually fatal. It is an aggressive, nocturnal viper that can be found almost anywhere – in a tree, on the jungle floor, in the grass or out in the open. Its markings are not distinct, so it is hard to identify. It has an arrow-shaped head and a mouth with two retractable fangs appearing too big for the snake's head. The fer-de-lance comes in many colors, from dark brown to gray to red, and has a row of dark-edged diamonds along its sides.

> **WARNING:** If you are attacked by one of these snakes, you must get to a doctor immediately. Twenty-four hours is too long to wait; some people say that you have only 20 minutes to receive treatment before you die.

The **rattlesnake**, found only in North America, is in danger of becoming extinct. Identified by the rattle sound made by the animal shaking its tail, rattlers are not as dangerous as the fer-de-lance, although their bite can be fatal. If bitten, you should see a doctor who will administer some antivenin, a drug obtained from horses that neutralizes the snake's venom.

Rattlers live in communities of 30 to 40 adults with between eight and 12 reproducing females. The females do not mature for nine to 11 years and they breed only once every three or four years. This means they reproduce only three to five times in their lives. Other than humans, hawks, owls, foxes, coyotes and raccoons are the snake's most common predators.

 FACT FILE: More people die every year in the US from bee and wasp stings than they do from snake bites.

Coral snakes are nocturnal, but are far less aggressive than the fer-de-lance and are hard to find as they like to hide in ground vegetation. They also prefer eating other snakes, rather than sharpening their teeth on you. However, if you step on one and are bitten, get to a doctor immediately as they are one of the most poisonous snake in the tropics.

The yellow-bellied **sea snake** is a carnivorous snake that seldom grows over 45 in/113 cm. It hunts fish during the day. When it spots a fish, it chews poison into the fish and then swallows it. The snake sleeps on the ocean floor, rising to the surface once every one to three hours to breathe. It is mild-mannered and often swims in groups of up to a hundred. If washed ashore by wave action, it has a hard time getting back to the water and it dies. Sea snakes expel only a small amount of poison when they bite. If bitten, your life is not in danger, but you should still see a doctor.

TURTLES: The **green turtle** is so named because of the color of its fat. The **black turtle** is a subspecies of the green. These slow-growers do not reach sexual maturity until 20 years of age, and some take up to 50 years. The green turtle will grow to 39 in/one meter and weigh about 330 lb/150 kg. In the recent past, these creatures would grow to twice that size. Today, we harvest them so rapidly that they no longer have time to grow.

The green turtle is vegetarian and likes to graze on meadows of sea grass that grow in warm ocean waters. However, immature greens are known to eat a bit of meat. The females nest once every two to four years. Each nesting season results in two or three breeding sessions that are about 14 days apart. The female lays about 100 eggs each time and the young hatch 60 days later. The largest known nesting beach is at Colola in the state of Michoacan.

Leatherback turtles are in great danger of extinction worldwide. This is the largest living turtle, growing up to 110 in/270 cm long and weighing up to 2,000 lb/900 kg. The leatherback is so named because it has a flexible shell that resembles leather. There is no separation from the sides of the shell and the underbelly, so it appears a bit barrel-shaped. An old study from the early 1980s found that of all the leatherbacks known to exist worldwide, almost half of them nested on the western shores of Mexico. However, more recent studies have indicated that the turtles travel to Japan to nest and, when the young hatch, sea currents return the babies to the western shores of America. One of the greatest threats to the leatherback is that it mistakes plastic bags and Styrofoam pollutants for food. Once the garbage is ingested, the turtle's gut becomes blocked, nutrition is limited and death is close.

The **Olive Ridley turtle** is the most abundant turtle in the Pacific Ocean. It is small, merely 22-30 in/56-76 cm long. Some of the females nest in arribados, or groups. The grouping of turtles is believed to have evolved so they can help each other protect their eggs.

THE WAITING GAME

Some turtles have been known to stay in the water waiting for a safe moment to lay their eggs and, while waiting, the eggs develop hard shells. When the turtle eventually tries to lay her eggs, they are very difficult to pass and, because of the rigidity, they break.

The Ridley Turtle nests every year, three to four times during each season, as opposed to the green turtle who has a nesting season only every two to four years but nests three times each season. It takes 14 days for eggs to hatch from the females who nest alone, and up to 28 days for the arribado nesters. Only 5% of eggs actually produce offspring. One scientific theory for this is that 90-95% of the eggs produced are unfertilized (without a yolk) and left at the top of the nest so predators will eat them and not bother with the fertilized eggs lying below. Olive Ridley turtles are omnivorous and include crab, shrimp, lobsters, jellyfish, algae and sea grasses in their diets.

Insects

Insects and arachnids include mosquitoes and cockroaches, botflies and butterflies, houseflies and fireflies, fire ants and leaf-cutter ants, termites and scorpions. Some bite and others don't. Some are good to eat (like ants, which you can cover in chocolate) and some are not even wanted by birds, toads or frogs (like fireflies). Below I have mentioned just a few of the more interesting ones.

Scorpions should be avoided because they do bite; shake out shoes and clothes before putting them on when in the jungle. Apparently, the smaller the scorpion the more lethal its bite.

For the most part, **ants** work in the service industry, cleaning up garbage left around the jungle floors (and your room, if you are careless). Highly organized, their hills can measure many feet across and be equally as high. A colony of leaf-cutter ants (also called wee-wee ants) can strip a full-grown deciduous tree within a day. These ants chew and swallow the leaves, which they regurgitate shortly after. The vomit grows a fungus, which the ants then eat for nutrition. The excretion left by the ants helps to fertilize the jungle floors. The ants' colonies consist of females only and the queen is the size of a small mouse. Her job is to lay eggs; she has workers to clean and feed her.

There are hundreds of species of **butterflies** and **moths** in Mexico and their colors and designs are fascinating. Some have eye markings at their tail end (to fool predators as to the direction they will be going), while others are so bright they attract the attention of all. Butterflies and moths have no jaws, so they don't bite. Instead, they suck up nutrients in liquid form. For protection from rain, high winds and extreme heat, they sit on the undersides of leaves.

Other Beasts

Skunks are often incorrectly referred to as polecats. A polecat is native only to Europe and Asia; skunks are found in America anywhere from northern Canada all the way down to Patagonia. Related to the weasel, the skunk is able to spray a foul-smelling substance a distance of 12 feet/ 3.5 meters. The skunk actually aims for the eyes of its enemy. The liquid produces temporary blindness in the recipient. A night hunter, the skunk comes out of its den when the temperatures cool and it forages for insects, larvae, mice and fallen fruits. Skunks mate in spring and have litters of five or six young that are ready to look after themselves after about two months. Their life span is around 10 years.

The **peccary** is a pig-like creature that has been around for about 40 million years (according to fossil finds). Not very big, it weighs about 65 lbs/30 kg and travels in herds of a few individuals to as many as 300. The peccary has two distinct features. One is the smell it exudes from a musk gland on its back whenever it is irritated. The second is its amazing nose, the tip of which is flat and reinforced with a cartilaginous disk that can lift logs and dig underground for roots and insects. A true omnivore, the peccary will eat anything from poisonous snakes to cactus. There is no fixed mating season and the female usually gives birth to one or two young about the size of a full-grown rabbit. By the time the young are two days old, they are ready to take their place in the herd.

The **armadillo** is an insect-eating mammal that has a bony-plated shell encasing its back. This shell is the animal's protection. The armadillo has teeth that are simple rootless pegs in the back of its mouth. Because of these teeth, the armadillo is able to eat snakes, chickens, fruit and eggs. It also likes to munch on the odd scorpion. The female gives birth to a litter of young that are all the same sex; the theory is that they develop from the same egg. The young are born with shells, but the shells don't harden until the animal is almost a year old. This is when it leaves its mother.

The **tapir**, or mountain cow, is related to the horse and rhinoceros, but it is unique in the fact that it is the last surviving ungulate (hoofed mammals) with an odd number of toes that bears its weight on the middle toe. It is named because of its thick hide from a Brazilian Indian word meaning thick. This short-haired animal stands four feet/1.2 meters at the shoulder and weighs in at around 600 lb/275 kg when fully grown. It has a trunk-like snout that grabs leaves from aquatic plants or forest foliage for food. An excellent swimmer, the tapir can stay underwater for long periods of time, especially when hiding from its worst enemies, the jaguar and puma. Also, it pees straight back, so when visiting the zoo, stay back!

■ Airborne

Birds

Because Mexico lies on the migratory path, seeing both common and rare bird species is possible, often in larger numbers than elsewhere. Numerous bird tours come to this area from the United States. Many environmental groups are involved in preserving areas that the birds use so their numbers are again increasing. If you have more than a passing interest in birds, bring your favorite identifying book and binoculars with you.

Parrots are brightly plumaged, gregarious creatures that have no problem imitating human speech. They will be the most ubiquitous bird (next to the frigate and pelican) you will see. In total, there are 358 parrot species worldwide. Along with bright colors, all parrots have strong hooked beaks with moveable upper jaws and thick tongues. They eat fruit and seeds. Captive parrots make strong bonds with their owners and are known to become physically ill if abandoned. The species most commonly seen on Mexico's west coast are the tiny (four-six inch/10-15 cm) Mexican parakeet, the orange-fronted parakeet, the lilac-crowned parrot and the military macaw.

The **frigate** is the big, black bird you see soaring over the water with a "W" shaped wing. It can soar for hours over the sea, although it seldom goes more than 50 miles/80 km from its home island. Because it does not lift off from water very well, it doesn't fish much. Instead, it steals from other birds or swoops down and catches fish swimming near the surface.

Pelicans come in eight varieties, the most common of which is the brown pelican. Their pouch bills could easily hold a newborn human. Their bodies are about 40 in/100 cm long and their wingspan is a mighty 90 in/ 228 cm. These birds, when fishing, torpedo into the water from great heights. Their ancestors can be traced back about 40 million years, but in the 1950s and 1960s pelicans almost disappeared from earth due to DDT poisoning. They are now making a comeback. Each female lays about three eggs per year and the hatchlings are born after four weeks. You will see many pelicans along the shores of Mexico.

An indiscriminate scavenger, the **cara cara** is a raptor with black and white plumage and a featherless face. It is Mexico's national bird. Its legs are bare and its tearing beak is hooked like an eagle's and long like a vulture's. It will eat garbage, dine with both eagles and vultures, or kill its own mammal for dinner. Cara caras love to eat anacondas, boa constrictors and caimans. When they leave the nest, young cara caras are 21 in/ 55 cm long, with a four-foot/1.3-m wingspan. Due to loss of savannah and wetlands, the cara cara is endangered. But loss of habitat is just part of the problem. Throughout Central and South America, their claws were used for jewelry and their feathers used to make ceremonial robes for priests and kings. More recently, the claws and beaks have been ground and sold as aphrodisiacs. The use of DDT in the last 25 years has also taken its toll on the development of eggs. Cara caras are slow reproducers.

Introduction

RECOMMENDED BIRDING BOOKS

The most comprehensive tome available is the *Field Guide to the Birds of Mexico and North Central America*, by Steve Howell and Sophie Wedd, published by Oxford Illustrated Press. It has color plates and black-and-white drawings that illustrate 750 species. It has 1,010 pages and is heavy to carry.

Mexico: A Hiker's Guide to Mexico's Natural History, by Jim Conrad, was published by Mountaineer Books in 1995. This 220-page book combines wildlife information with 20 trail descriptions.

Bird-Finding Guide to Mexico, by Steve NG Howell, Cornell University Press, 1999. The book's 512 pages describe 100 sites where birders may see more than 950 species.

Birds of Mexico and Adjacent Areas, by Ernest Preston Edwards, University of Texas Press, 3rd edition, 1998. Lists 870 species, with 300 that are not included in other guides. The names include English, Spanish and the scientific names.

■ In the Ocean

Dolphins are playful and intelligent. They mature between five and 12 years and a female gives birth to one calf every two or three years. The life span of a dolphin is up to 48 years. Dolphins travel in pods and it is suspected that each member of a pod is related. They like to stay near their home waters for their entire life. They hunt for fish using the echolocation method similar to bats. A dolphin will eat up to 150 lb/68 kg of fish a day.

Hammerhead sharks are one of nine species of sharks. They grow anywhere from three feet/one meter to 20 feet/six meters, but most average 11.5 feet/four meters long. They weigh around 500 lb/230 kg, but can weigh up to 1,000 lb/450 kg. They kill their prey by smashing them with their heads and they especially like to eat squid, rays, crustaceans and each other. They generally swim at a depth of 250 feet/75 meters, migrating north in summer and south in winter. Females give birth to 20 to 40 live pups that are about 27 in/70 cm long.

WHALES: Great gray whales migrate down the Pacific coast from the Arctic waters each year around October and return the following spring around May. The gray whale belongs to the baleen whale classification because it has baleen, a substance made of keratin similar to fingernails, instead of teeth. The baleen grows in strips down from the upper jaw.

FACT FILE: There can be up to 180 plates of baleen on each side of a whale's or shark's jaw. The strips grow two-10 in/five-25 cm and, since the ends wear down from eating, they must continue to grow during the animal's entire life.

Baleen is used to filter amphipods from the ocean bottom. Land deposits due to erosion of the earth along the oceans cause death to these tiny bottom growers and results in the grays having to go farther afield in search of food. An average-size gray measures 40-50 feet/12-15 meters long and weights up to 40 tons. Grays are known to live about 50 years, are gray in color and have scars caused from barnacles. It is also common to see orange whale lice growing on their skin. Gray whales have 10-12 dorsal nodules rather than fins and their tails are 10 feet/three meters across. Grays have hair, are warm-blooded and suckle their young for six months. During the suckling period, babies drink around 50 gal/200 liters of milk a day, gaining 50 lb/23 kg of body weight per day.

THE MOTION OF THE OCEAN

The courting ritual of the gray whale is, in my opinion, one that humans should adopt. A female will attract two males while on her southern migration. The first male swims beside her and rubs himself against her. This helps stimulate hormone secretion. Awhile later, a second male joins them and the three swim together, a male on each side of the female. They rub and bump along until she is ready to choose the winner. She flops to her side and the chosen male impregnates her while the second male (the loser) helps to support her enormous body. There is no aggression between the males.

A female must be 36-39 feet/nine-10 meters in length before she is mature enough to mate. A 15-foot/five-meter), one ton/1,000 kg calf is born a year later. During delivery, a second female may help with the birthing by holding the mother up near the surface so she can breath. After birth, the youngster does some practice swims back and forth against the current in preparation for the 10,000-km/6,000-mile migration north.

Humpback whales also belong to the baleen classification of mammals. They, too, have patterns on their dorsal fins and tails that are as unique as fingerprints on humans. Humpbacks are black on top and white on their bellies, have irregular-shaped dorsal fins and tails that can be up to 18 feet/5.5 m wide. They are usually 40-50 feet/12-15 meters in length and weigh 25-40 tons. They feed on small crustaceans and fish. Humpbacks consume around a ton of food every day.

Humpbacks reach maturity when they are 36-39 feet/11-12 meters long, which is usually reached by six to eight years of age. Females have a calf once every two to three years and the gestation period is one year. The calf weighs around a ton at birth and suckles for a year. Humpbacks, like gray whales, migrate north in summer and return south to mate and give birth in winter.

SPORTFISH: Swordfish are part of the billfish family and are identified mainly by their long sword-like upper jaws. They have large eyes, brown bodies with white bellies and have no scales or teeth. They have been known to grow up to 200 lb/90 kg but, due to over-harvest, are now much smaller. They like to eat other fish, squid and octopus.

Sailfish are also part of the billfish family and have a large upper jaw that looks like a spear. But it is the enlarged dorsal fin that gives the fish its name. Sailfish grow to four-five feet/one-two meters in their first year of life and usually reach seven feet/two meters and 120 lb/60 kg at maturity. The sailfish is a fast swimmer, often traveling up to 50 knots.

Blue and **black marlin** are more often found in the Atlantic than the Pacific. However, those in the Pacific grow to 14 feet/four meters and can weigh one ton/900 kg. The largest marlin found in the Pacific was 1,376 lb/624 kg. Marlin eat dolphin, tuna and mackerel. Spawning season is May to November, and the eggs hatch about one week after being deposited. The marlin's biggest predator is the white shark, but man, too, has over-fished this species. The catch-and-release practice of fishing has not been so good for this group because the damage occurred during the catch usually kills the fish.

The **rooster fish** has a spiked dorsal fin with eight thorns. It is gray-blue in color, with a silver underbelly and two dark spots, one on the nose and another on the nape of the neck. It likes to swim near shore where there is a sandy bottom and is also found around reefs. Rooster fish usually grow to 10 in/25 cm long and weigh about 115 lb/55 kg. Because of their great fighting ability, they are a desired sportfish.

The **crevalle jack** is copper and yellow, with large eyes and no scales except for a small patch just in front of the pelvic fin. Its color helps the fish blend with the environment as a form of protection. Jacks usually grow to 25 in/60 cm and can weight up to 50 lb/20 kg. They spawn from March to September and eat crustaceans and smaller fish.

Surf perch come in 23 varieties. All have short deep bodies, large eyes and forked tail fins. They grow four-18 in/10-45 cm long and weigh two-four lb/one-two kg. They mate in the spring and the female keeps the sperm for five or six months before she allows fertilization of the eggs. She carries the developing young for one year before giving birth to a batch of five-40 live look-alike babies. Perch live up to six years of age and like to eat worms, muscles, eggs and crustaceans in the estuaries, bays and shallow areas near shore.

Dorado is also called mahi mahi or dolphin. It has a flat face, large dorsal fin and is a metallic blue-green in color with orange-gold specks. It is grows from 15-30 lb/five-12 kg and eats mainly smaller fish. The dorado is known to travel in pairs.

The **king mackerel** is a long, narrow fish with a dark thin stripe along its side and spots below the stripe. The largest of the mackerels, it grows to 35 in/90 cm; the largest ever found measured 72 in/180 cm and weighed 100 lb/45 kg. king mackerel usually live to be 14 years old, although some studies show them to live almost twice that long. Size determines sexual maturity and they spawn from May to September.

Tuna are found around the world between the cold northern or southern waters to the equator. The bluefin tuna, the largest of this group, can reach 180 in/455 cm and can weigh 1,500 lb/680 kg. However, the most common size is about 75 in/200 cm. Because of the quality of the meat, these fish can sell for up to $45,000 each in Japan. Tuna become sexually mature at about four or five years and live to 15 years on average. They travel in schools when young. The schools are often a mixed bunch of students determined by size rather than species.

FACT FILE: Tuna like to swim as deep as 3,000 feet/1,000 meters and can cross the Atlantic Ocean in 60 days, swimming an average speed of 45 mph/75 kph.

National Emblems

■ National Anthem

The lyrics of the national anthem were written by **Francisco Gonzalez Bocanegra** and the music was composed by **Jaime Nuò**. It was declared the national anthem in 1854. The words below are translated from the Spanish.

Mexicans, at the cry of battle, prepare your swords and bridle;
and let the earth tremble at its center at the roar of the cannon.
O Fatherland! Your forehead shall be girded with olive garlands, by the
divine archangel of peace. For in heaven your eternal destiny
has been written by the hand of God.
But should a foreign enemy dare to profane your land with his sole.
Think, beloved fatherland, that heaven gave you a soldier in each son.

*War, war without truce against who would attempt to blemish the honor
of the fatherland!*

War, war! The patriotic banners drench in waves of blood.

*War, war! On the mount, in the valley, the terrifying thunder of the can-
non and the echoes nobly resound to the cries of the Union! Liberty!
Fatherland, before your children become unarmed beneath
the yoke their necks in sway, and your countryside
be watered with blood, on blood their feet trample.
And may your temples, palaces and towers crumble in horrid crash
and ruins remain saying: the fatherland
was made of one thousand heroes.*

*Fatherland, fatherland, your children swear to exhale their breath in
your cause if the bugle in its belligerent tone should call upon them to
struggle with bravery.*

*For you the olive garlands!
For them a memory of glory!
For you a laurel of victory!
For them a tomb of honor!*

■ Coat of Arms

The coat of arms is designed after the legend of the Mexican people. The gods told them to find a place where an eagle, eating a snake, landed on a prickly-pear cactus. After years of wondering, the people found the site and in 1325 started building a city on the island in the swamp where the eagle was found. The place became the center of religion, politics and commerce until it fell under the cannons of Hernando Cortez. To the Mexican people, the eagle was a symbol of war and in other pieces of art it can be found attacking a snake or a jaguar.

The first coat of arms was adopted in 1821 and was designed by **Francisco Eppens Helguer**a, an architect from San Luis Potosi. It has an eagle exposing its left profile and its wings spread as if in battle. The snake in the eagle's mouth faces the bird and has diamonds and stripes on its skin. The eagle stands on a prickly-pear cactus that seems to be growing out of a rock that is sitting in a small lake. The bottom of the shield has a semi-circle made of laurel and encino plants tied by a ribbon divided into three stripes of the same colors as the national flag. There have been five different coats of arms, but the basic theme has always been the same. The stance of the eagle is mostly what changes.

When the National Shield is placed on the reverse side of the flag, the eagle stands looking in the opposite direction.

■ National Flag

The national flag has three vertical stripes of equal size. The colors are green, white and red, with the white center stripe holding the coat of arms. The present flag was adopted in 1968 to update it for the Olympics being held in Mexico that year.

The original design was decreed the official flag on November 2, 1821 and confirmed in January, 1822. That design was abolished in April of 1823 and replaced with a second one that lasted until 1863. The following year, a third flag was adopted. This ornate flag, with crowns around its edges and also around the coat of arms, lasted until 1867.

■ National Prayer

National prayer, or the Initial Prayers for Mexico, are the traditional devotions of the Roman Catholic Church. During an Act of Contrition (during confession) a Mexican will recite:

O my God I am heartily sorry for having offended you, and I detest all my sins because I fear the loss of heaven and the pains of hell, but most of all because they offend you my God, who are all good and deserving of all my love. I firmly resolve, with the help of your grace, to sin no more and to avoid the near occasions of sin. Amen.

■ National Bird

The national bird is a raptor, a scavenger and, sadly, now on the endangered list. To learn more about the **cara cara**, see page 39.

Travel Information

Facts at Your Fingertips

AREA: 742,474 sq miles/1,923,000 sq km of land, with 19,112 sq miles/49,500 sq km covered by water.

BORDERS: USA, 2,414 km/1,500 mi, Guatemala, 800 km/500 mi and Belize, 200 km/125 mi.

CAPITAL: Federal District of Mexico (Mexico City).

COAST: 450 miles/725 km of coastline, more than half of which is on the western shore.

CURRENCY: The peso, the value of which fluctuates. At time of writing, it was 9.6 pesos for US $1.

ETHNIC GROUPS: 60% mestizo (American Indian and Spanish mix), 30% American Indian, 9% white and 1% other.

GDP: US $9,000 per person, but 40% of the population is under the poverty line. There is a labor force of 40 million people.

HEAD OF STATE: President Vincente Fox Quesada. The president is head of state and head of the government. He was elected with a 42.5% majority in 2000 and is the leader of the PAN political party. He will serve a six-year term.

HIGHEST/LOWEST POINT: Pico de Orizaba, 17,500 feet/5,350 meters; Laguna Salada, at 30 feet/10 meters.

LANGUAGES: Spanish, Mayan, Nahuatl.

LIFE EXPECTANCY: Average is 69 for males and 75 for females.

POPULATION: 105 million (estimated), with a growth rate of 1.43% and 2.53 children per family.

RELIGION: 89% Roman Catholic, 6% protestant and 5% other religions, including Buddhism, Hinduism, Sikhism and Taoism.

RESOURCES: Petroleum, silver, copper, gold, lead, zinc, natural gas and timber.

TRANSPORTATION: 10,000 miles/16,000 km of railway; 175,000 miles/282,000 km of highway; and 1,500 miles/2,400 km of navigable rivers and coastal canals. There are 231 airports with paved runways and 1,592 without.

When to Go

Mexicans travel within their own country a lot, so be certain to have your room booked during the peak seasons like Christmas, Easter and summer vacation, from June to mid-August.

At Easter and Christmas, most Mexicans close shop and spend time with their families. During these holidays, the large hotels will serve meals, but almost everything else will be closed. During any other festival, everything remains open. This is especially true in tourist areas. Only in the smaller villages may you find things closed; if you need anything, seek out the local proprietor.

■ National & Religious Holidays

■ January
1st – **New Year's Day**

6th – **Dia de los Santos Reyes** is when Mexicans exchange Christmas presents. The day corresponds to the day the Three Wise Men brought Jesus gifts.

17th – **Feast Day of San Antonio de Abad** is when animals are blessed in the church.

■ February
5th – **Dia de la Constitución** is when the constitution was inaugurated.

24th – **Flag Day** honors the national flag.

■ March
Carnival is the weekend before lent, 40 days before Easter. The date changes every year. Carnival is celebrated with parades, street dancing, partying and feasting. Mazatlan is the best town on the west coast in which to enjoy this celebration.

21st – Birthday of **Benito Juarez**, a national hero and one of the early presidents.

■ April

Semana Santa is the week of Easter and includes Good Friday and Easter Sunday. To celebrate, Mexicans like to break eggs filled with confetti over the heads of friends and family.

■ May

1st – **Primero de Mayo** is equivalent to Labor Day in the US.

5th – **Cinco de Mayo** honors the battle and victory over the French at Puebla de los Angeles in 1862.

10th – **Mother's Day** is especially important in Mexico.

■ June

1st – **Navy Day** is when coastal cities celebrate the importance of the Navy for defending the country. They have regattas and parades with decorated ships.

■ September

The annual **State of the Union**, when the president addresses the nation, is held at the start of September; the date changes.

16th – **Independence Day** is the day Miguel Hidalgo announced the revolution against the Spanish.

■ October

12th – **Dia de la Raza** commemorates the arrival of Columbus in America.

■ November

1st & 2nd – **Dia de los Muertos** is when Mexicans honor the spirits of their ancestors by visiting their graves, decorating them and feasting.

20th – **Revolution Day** commemorates the Mexican Revolution of 1910.

■ December

12th – **Dia de Nuestra Señora de Guadalupe** honors the patron saint of Mexico.

16th – **Las Posadas** starts the Christmas celebrations with a candlelight procession and commemorates the search for shelter by Joseph and Mary.

25th – **Christmas Day**

■ Seasonal Considerations

 Head to the Pacific coast between November and February if you want ideal weather. If you don't mind high heat and humidity, you can go at other times. The farther north you are, the longer the "winter season" of warm days and cool nights. During this season, daytime temperatures at northern beaches hover around 70°F/21°C, while evenings are cool, sometimes as low as 50°F/10°C. The humidity is between 30 and 50% and the rains have generally stopped. However, during the summer months, humidity is often around 80%, and temperatures are quite a bit higher than in winter.

From December to March, the central coast has warm weather, with daytime temperatures in the low to mid-80s and evenings in the mid-60s to 70s F (15-21°C). Summers are oppressively hot and hurricanes threaten between June and September. This is also rainy season.

The southern coast has much less rain than the north, and the humidity is generally never below 50%. Coupled with temperatures between the mid-70s and low 90s F (21-32°C), this makes for a hot visit. The best months to visit are between December and February. The rest of the time, the high temperatures and humidity can be too much to bear.

What to Take

■ Required Documents

 It is always advisable to travel with a valid **passport**. However, in Mexico, American and Canadian citizens need only a government-issued birth certificate or photo identification card, such as a valid driver's license. You may also enter with a notarized photocopy of your birth certificate and a photo identification card.

 FACT FILE: Your passport is the only document that shows valid proof of citizenship.

Children under 18 who are citizens of Canada or the United States may travel with a birth certificate but without a photo identification card. However, it is advisable to have a photo ID also. Children not traveling with both their legal guardians must have a notarized letter of consent from the non-traveling parent with permission for the child to cross international borders. A child too young to have received his birth certificate must have a notarized letter from the pediatrician or hospital identifying the child as belonging to the adult.

▶▶ **AUTHOR TIP:** *In our technological age you can scan your passport and e-mail the scan to your traveling e-mail address (i.e., Yahoo, Hotmail). This way, you always have a copy.*

> *You can do this with your postcard or e-mail address list also.*

Mexicans residing in the US may travel one way with a Mexican passport (even if it is expired) or they may present a Matricula Consular that is a Certificate of Nationality issued by the Mexican Consulate. Those using the Matricula Consular must have a photo identification card and birth certificate. If this is not possible, the Matricula Consular may be presented with a Mexican voter registration paper and a photo identification card. An American green card will not allow Mexican citizens permission to enter into Mexico, but the green card will get them back into the US.

Once in Mexico, and if staying more than 72 hours past the border zones like Tijuana, you will receive a **tourist card**. Do not lose this card as it will take a lot of complicated bureaucracy and a bit of money to get another. There is no charge for a tourist card when it is first issued.

Depending upon your reasons for traveling to Mexico, as well as your country of citizenship, you may be required to obtain a **visa**. Residents of some countries must apply for a visa to the Mexican consulate or embassy in their own countries before they arrive at the Mexican border. If there is no embassy or consulate, you must apply by mail to the immigration authorities in Mexico City (Mexican Ministry of the Interior, National Institute of Migration, Ejercito Nactional #862, Col. Los Morales/Sección Palmas, Mexico, DF, 11540). For more specific information, visit www.embamexican.com. It takes six to eight weeks to process this type of visa and only those applying for a visa may enter the Mexican consulate or embassy in their country. The cost is US $37 and must be paid in cash or money order.

VISAS, PLEASE

Citizens of the following countries are not required to show a visa to enter Mexico for tourist purposes, but they must have a valid passport: Andorra, Argentina, Australia, Austria, Belgium, Bermuda, Brazil, Costa Rica, Chile, Czech Republic, Denmark, France, Finland, Germany, Great Britain, Greece, Hungary, Ireland, Iceland, Israel, Italy, Japan, Liechtenstein, Luxembourg, Monaco, Norway, New Zealand, Netherlands, Poland, Portugal, San Marino, Singapore, Slovenia, South Korea, Spain, South Africa, Switzerland, Uruguay, Venezuela and Sweden.

Citizens of the following countries are required to obtain a visa, as outlined above: Afghanistan, Albania, Angola, Armenia, Azerbaijan, Bahrain, Bangladesh, Belarus, Bosnia-Herzegovina, Cambodia, Congo, Croatia, Estonia, Georgia, Haiti, India, Iraq, Iran, Jordan, Kazakhstan, Latvia, Lebanon, Libya,

Travel Information

Lithuania, Macedonia, Mauritania, Moldavia, Mongolia, Morocco, Niger, North Korea, Oman, Pakistan, Palestine, Qatar, Russia, Sahara Democratic Republic, Saudi Arabia, Somalia, Sri Lanka, Sudan, Syria, Tunisia, Turkmenistan, Turkey, Ukraine, United Arab Emirates, Uzbekistan, Vietnam, Yemen and Yugoslavia. Citizens of the following countries must also apply for a visa to visit Mexico, but they need not pay the US $37 consular fee: Bolivia, Colombia, Dominican Republic, Jamaica, Nicaragua, Peru, Ecuador, Rumania, Belize, Panama, Guatemala and Malaysia.

People who want to retire or reside in Mexico must have a special visa. For this one-year, multiple-entry visa you must present a valid passport, application form, photos, health certificate, letter from your local police department stating that you are free of a police record, letter from the bank stating that your monthly income exceeds $2,000 plus $1,000 for each dependent. And finally, you must pay a consular fee of $136 in cash or money order. This type of visa takes three days to process and can be extended on a yearly basis for a period of five years, after which permanent residence status must be obtained.

FACT FILE: If you make money in Mexico, you are subject to Mexican taxes and are eligible for social security.

For more information about immigration laws for retirees, contact the **Mexican Ministry of the Interior**, National Institute of Migration, Ejercito Nacional #862, Col. Los Morales/Sección Palmas, Mexico, DF, 11540. Specific information about becoming a Mexican resident is offered at www.embamexican.com/consular/resident.html.

Canadian and American journalists traveling in Mexico for a special event (or to write a book like this) must get an FM-3 migratory form from the nearest consular office in their country. This document allows the journalist to remain in Mexico for 90 days and to make multiple entries.

Working in Mexico requires a special visa. Workers may fill positions in the country that cannot be filled first by Mexicans. Companies big enough to require a foreign president, treasurer, general manager, and so on, must comply with the 90% Mexican employee to 10% foreign employee ratio. Professionals such as doctors, lawyers and engineers may receive immigrant status if they have their degrees and a special license to practice in Mexico. Investors must have 26,000 times the current daily minimum wage (43 pesos) to invest in Mexico before opening a company. At today's exchange rate, that's US $2,600, but the peso value fluctuates regularly. This money must be in the Mexican Development Bank guaranteeing that investment will be made within a specific time period. This time period is determined by the National Institute of Migration.

■ Traveling with Pets

You can bring pets into Mexico as long as you have a certificate from a veterinarian, issued within the last seven days, stating the animal is free of communicable diseases. You also need a rabies vaccination certificate showing that the pet was vaccinated at least one month and less than one year before crossing the border. It is advisable to have pet travel insurance. Taking any exotic or endangered pet like a macaw into Mexico is not permitted and the animal could be confiscated at the border.

Returning to the US with a traveling pet, you must have a vet's certificate saying the pet had a rabies shot within the preceding three years.

■ Packing List

Binoculars are a must if you are a birder. There is an abundance of exotic and migratory birds that are well worth scouting out. Binoculars are also fun to use on the beach to watch boats (and those on the boats) as they pass by. I even use mine on bus trips to look at distant hills and volcanoes.

Shorts and **t-shirts** are great. Everyone wears shorts, but a skirt or pants are acceptable too. Keep your clothing loose and comfortable – let the heat determine your attire, but keep in mind that revealing outfits are not acceptable. If you are a touch stodgy (like me) be prepared to be shocked by some of your fellow tourists as you wander the beach.

If going during the rainy season, May to September, pack some type of **rain protection**. **Sandals** are good at the beach, but **running shoes** or light **hiking boots** are needed for jungle walks, playing golf or touring the museums.

You will need at least one **bathing suit** and two would be better. A beach towel or grass mat is good for lying on the sand. Mats can be purchased along the beaches for less than $5.

Cameras are a great way to record memories. Bring one that you are familiar with so that you don't make mistakes on critical images. Humidity is high, so keeping your camera dry is an issue. I use a foam-padded carrying bag. Putting cameras in plastic bags is not advisable as the moisture condenses inside the bag. Non-expired film, camera batteries and flashes are readily available. Because there is so much intense sunlight, a slow-speed film is recommended (ASA 50 to 100). A flash should be used when photographing people during the day so that the harsh shadows are eliminated.

> ▶▶ **AUTHOR TIP:** *If you're interested in underwater photography, I suggest that you take an introductory course before leaving home. One lady I spoke with threw out the first 100 images she took because they were so bad. The second hundred were great photos of sand and water and blurred sand and blurred water. That is a lot of money wasted.*

Money belts are a necessary item if you plan to roam the area. (Those staying at an upper-end hotel do not need them as safes are usually made available.) Belts should always be of natural-fiber, pouch-style worn around the midriff and under clothes. I say natural fiber because it is far more comfortable in the heat than synthetic fiber. Keep documents and money in plastic bags inside the belt so the documents won't be soaked and damaged by sweat. Always place some money and/or travelers' checks in different places, so if you are robbed you will have some mad money to live on. There are belts sold today that have zippered pockets sewn on the underside. Money must be folded lengthwise to fit into the pockets.

> ▶▶ **AUTHOR TIP:** *Tiny pockets can be sewn into your clothing, in the hem of your skirt, or the cuff of your shirt. A few bills can also be placed in a plastic bag, under the inner sole of your shoe, but check this money regularly for wear. If it is worn through, no one will take it.*

Daypacks are far more convenient to carry than handbags or beach bags. They are also harder to pickpocket or snatch. In cities, on buses or crowded places like markets, wear your daypack at the front, with the waist strap done up. That way, your hands can rest on the bag while you walk. In this position, it is almost impossible for pickpockets to access the pack. Keep only the amount of money you need for the day in your daypack and the put the rest somewhere secure, like in your hotel safe or your hidden money belt.

Maps are essential. The best I have found is published by International Travel Maps and Books, 530 West Broadway, Vancouver, BC, ☎ 604-879-3621, www.itmb.com, and sells for less than $20 each. Their maps, Mexican Pacific Coast and Mexico Northwest, are easy to read, but do not have every village and pueblo included.

It seems to me that a map is really hard to follow if you don't have a **compass**. They are not heavy and you need not buy one that can do triangulation measurements. A simple one will do.

Tennis players should bring their own rackets because they, like other sports gear, are quite personal.

Golf clubs are also personal and should be brought with you. However, for those able to adapt to any clubs, rentals are most convenient.

Diving gear like wet suits and face masks can be brought from home or rented from dive shops. You will need your PADI diving certification ticket. The tour operators check this certificate every time you go out. You should also check their qualifications before heading into the depths.

Snorkeling mask and **flippers** can be carried with you from home or rented in Mexico. If going to only one resort, bringing your gear is not a problem but if traveling around, you may find it easier to rent.

Surf boards can be taken as a piece of luggage on the plane. Hardcore surfers should definitely bring their own board, but if you are interested in learning this sport, you can get away with renting.

Camping equipment should be brought with you if you are traveling around from beach to beach, sleeping in the campgrounds. Sleeping on secluded beaches is not recommended, although I know people do it. You will need a tent with mosquito netting, sleeping pad and a light cover. Cooking stoves should be able to use gasoline rather than white gas because of the availability of these fuels. The extent of your camping will determine what you will bring with you.

Use of a **sleeping sheet** is advisable if staying in the cheaper places or camping out. Because the climate is hot and humid, anything warmer than a sheet is not necessary.

An **umbrella** is good if you plan on doing any walking. It keeps off the sun or rain. These can be purchased in Mexico for about the same price or a little less than those at home.

Your **first aid kit** should include things like mole-skin, Advil (hikers' candies), tenser bandage, antihistamines, topical antibiotic cream and Band-Aids. All prescription medications and things like batteries for hearing aides or extra eyeglasses should be carried with you. A band that

Travel Information

attaches to your glasses and goes around your head to keep glasses from falling off is a good idea if you are even a little bit active.

Reading material is available in English at the magazine stands or bookstores. In addition, many hotels have book-trading services. But for the most part, you need to bring the really good books with you. Leaving them behind when you return home is a good idea. There are some places, like the Mazatlan Reading Library, Sixto Osuna #115, MazLibrary@ mexconnect.com, where you can borrow books and leave any that you have already read.

Sunglasses and **sun hat** should be brought and worn all the time you are in the sun because the intense ultraviolet rays can damage your eyes. If you forget to bring these, they are readily available in all the markets.

FACT FILE: Paul Theroux, author of *Patagonia Express* and other travel books, has problems with his eyes due to the damage caused by the ultraviolet rays. He often kayaked without sunglasses.

Sunscreen is necessary. Do not let yourself become cancer red because you don't like chemicals. If spending time in the jungle, you should bring **insect repellent**.

Health Concerns

General health should be kept at optimum level when traveling. Make certain you have rest, lots of clean water and a well-balanced diet that is supplemented with vitamins. This is not difficult to do. Salt intake is important in the heat to help prevent dehydration. Carry some powdered electrolytes in case you do become dehydrated, especially if you are planning some off-the-beach trips.

Bring with you anything you may need in the way of prescriptions, glasses, orthopedics, dental care and batteries for hearing aids. Things like vitamins, bandages, antihistamines and topical creams are readily available.

■ Medical Insurance

Mexico now has almost the same quality medical services as North America and Europe, but it is still advisable to travel with medical insurance. The cost is far less than any medical bill would be and many policies include ticket cancellation insurance and coverage against theft.

In the event of a serious illness or accident, you will want to get to your own country fast. Without insurance, the cost could be prohibitive.

Good insurance includes emergency evacuation, repatriation, emergency reunion, trip interruption, lost baggage, accidental death and trip cancellation.

For US citizens, the following table gives you an idea of what it will cost for $50,000 coverage with a $100 deductible. For each additional month but under a year, multiply the monthly premium cost by the number of months you will be staying. Those staying longer than three months are usually eligible for a 10% discount. Groups traveling together are often offered a lower rate, so ask first.

INSURANCE COST GUIDELINES		
Individual	15-Day Premium	30-Day Premium
Age 18-29	$24	$48
Age 30-39	$31	$62
Age 40-49	$47	$94
Age 50-59	$67	$134
Age 60-64	$79	$158
Age 65-69	$90	$180
Age 70-79	$122	$244
Age 80+	$212	$424

It is recommended that anyone traveling for longer than a month take out a higher insurance of up to a million dollars.

I worked with Patricia Romero Hamrick from **International Insurance-Seguros**, 1047 W. Madero Mesa, AZ 85210-7635, ☎ 480-345-0191, www.seguros-insurance.net. I found her helpful and quick to answer any questions. She also works through **Global Travel Insurance**, ☎ 800-232-9415, www.globalmedicalplans.com. The best thing about this company's insurance is that it covers emergency evacuation and reunion, which means a loved-one can be brought to your bedside in the event that you are in hospital away from home for a long time. Moderate expenses for this loved-one are included. Global Travel also carries a Hazardous Sports Rider for those partaking in sports such as mountain biking or rock climbing. This is especially important for the serious sportster.

Travel Information

■ Water

 Tap water, called purified water, is considered safe to drink in luxury hotels. If you feel uncomfortable with this, bottled water is available throughout the country. It comes in sizes from half a liter (pint) to four liters (one gallon). When there is no sign, water is considered drinkable. If there is a W1 or W2 sign, it means the water is untreated and not drinkable.

Use your common sense to avoid illness. Eat at places where locals are eating. If they remain healthy, you should too. An empty restaurant usually means a bad stomach. If the sanitation looks dubious, don't eat the salad; have some hot boiled soup instead.

If traveling where creek/lake water must be consumed, I suggest using a chemical such as iodine for purification. There is also a tablet available that has a silver (as opposed to an iodine) base that is far more palatable than the iodine. Chlorine bleach can also be used as a purifier, but it is the least effective of chemicals.

Mechanical filters take a long time to process the water and they do not filter out all organisms that could cause problems. They are also much heavier to carry than chemicals.

■ Common Ailments

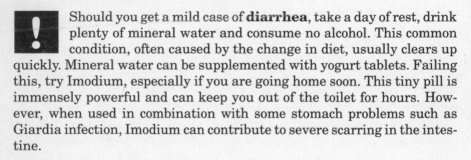 Should you get a mild case of **diarrhea**, take a day of rest, drink plenty of mineral water and consume no alcohol. This common condition, often caused by the change in diet, usually clears up quickly. Mineral water can be supplemented with yogurt tablets. Failing this, try Imodium, especially if you are going home soon. This tiny pill is immensely powerful and can keep you out of the toilet for hours. However, when used in combination with some stomach problems such as Giardia infection, Imodium can contribute to severe scarring in the intestine.

Fevers & Worse

According to the World Health Organization, contacting **malaria** is a possibility all year at elevations below 3,000 ft/950 meters anywhere from Guaymas in the north all the way south to the Guatemala border. The states of Sonora and Sinaloa are free of malaria except for the months between May and October, during rainy season.

People staying at major resorts need not use a prophylactic against malaria, but should use mosquito repellent after sunset or if going into the jungle. Anyone traveling around the country – especially those staying in lower-priced hotels – will need to use a prophylactic. Chloroquine is the prophylactic of choice. It should be taken for one week before entering the country, once a week while there, and for four weeks after returning home.

In the event that you develop a fever for no explicable reason like a cold or flu, especially if you are in mosquito country or have been bitten, you should see a doctor as soon as possible. The possibility of malaria should be considered for up to three months after leaving an infected area.

PROTECTION IS BEST
Keep exposed skin covered early in the morning or at dusk when the mosquitoes are most active. Using repellent laced with deet is also recommended. Although traces of deet have been found in the livers of users, this problem is still better than malaria. Use a sleeping net in infected areas.

Dengue fever and **dengue hemorrhagic fever** are caused by four related, but distinctly different, viruses that are spread by daytime-biting mosquitoes. Infection from one of the viruses does not produce immunity to the other three. Dengue cannot be transmitted from person to person.

Symptoms of dengue are high fever, headache, backache, joint pain, nausea, vomiting, eye pain and rash. There is no treatment except to take painkillers with acetaminophen in them rather than ASA (acetylsalicylic acid decreases you blood's clotting abilities, thus increasing the possibility of hemorrhage). Drink plenty of fluids and rest. If dengue hemorrhagic fever is contacted, fluid replacement therapy administered by a medical practitioner may be necessary. The illness lasts about 10 days and total recovery takes between two and four weeks.

Dengue is now on the rise worldwide. In 1960s, the WHO stated that there were about 30,000 cases worldwide. By 1995, this number increased to 592,000, with 240,000 cases in Mexico. Today, with the increase in urbanization and decrease in eradication programs, the WHO believes there are 20 million cases worldwide. This means that mosquito bites are potentially dangerous when traveling in the tropics. For more information, visit the website of the World Resource Institute at www. wri.org/wr-98-99/dengue.htm.

Yellow fever is present in all the jungles of Central America. Though inoculation is not required for entrance to Mexico, it may be required for reentry to your own country. Inoculation, good for 10 years, is recommended if you want to avoid a lengthy stay in quarantine. Children must also have a certificate of inoculation, but it is not recommended to inoculate children who are less than one year of age.

Routine inoculations common in your home country should be up to date. Besides these, **immune globulin** is recommended against viral hepatitis; the shots are good for about six months. If you have had viral hepatitis, you are already immune. Inoculation against **typhoid fever** is highly recommended. This inoculation is good for 10 years.

Bugs

Worms and **parasites** can be a problem anywhere in the tropics. To name and describe them all would be impossible. Keep your feet free of cuts or open sores so that worm eggs or parasites cannot enter. Use sandals in showers where cleanliness is a question. Wear closed shoes such as runners or hiking boots when in the jungle.

The **bot fly** and the **New World screw worm** are insects that cause a boil-like sore after the larvae (maggot) has started to grow in its host (you). Botflies transport their eggs by way of the mosquito and the screw worm in the fly stage drops its eggs near an open sore or on mucus membranes. Once the egg is in its host, it hatches and lives under the skin. However, the fly must have air. If you have a red, puss-filled swelling that is larger than a mosquito bite, look closely. If you see a small hole in the swollen area cover it with petroleum jelly to prevent the fly from breathing. Without air, it dies. It takes four to eight days for the botfly larvae to hatch and five to 12 weeks for the screw worm.

Chagas, also known as the kissing bug, exists in Latin America and infection can become either chronic or acute. The parasite enters the blood stream when the infected oval-shaped insect inserts its proboscis into your skin. As it sucks your blood, its excretion is forced out and into the opening it has formed in your body. It is the excretion that carries the larvae of the parasite.

Once planted, the larvae migrates to the heart, brain, liver and spleen, where it nests and forms cysts. If you wake up one morning after sleeping under a thatched roof and you have a purplish lump somewhere on exposed skin, you may have been bitten. If fever, shortness of breath, vomiting or convulsions occur, see a doctor immediately. Mention your suspicions.

Jellyfish Stings

These are a possibility for anyone who enters the water. There are often flags along the beach indicating that jellyfish are present and what their parameters are. Some stings can leave a welt for weeks, but most last only a few hours. When a jellyfish stings you, it is actually the nematocysts attached to the tentacles that touch your skin and release a toxin. This is what burns. If you do get stung, douse the area with vinegar and cover with ice to relieve the pain. A product available in the United

States called After Sting Gel, which sells for about $4, can be used for jellyfish and bee stings. For more information on jellyfish, see www. diversalertnetwork.com.

■ Treatment Options

 If you become sick, contact your own consulate for the names of doctors or medical clinics. The consulates can usually recommend doctors who have been trained in your place of origin.

An alternative is to contact the **IAMAT** (International Association for Medical Assistance to Travelers) clinics. The doctors speak English or French and Spanish (in Mexico) and charge between $55 for an office visit to $95 for an emergency call-out at night or on Sundays.

The information reported in this section is taken from either the IAMAT's or the World Health Organization's publications. You can become a member of IAMAT and/or send a donation to them at 417 Center Street, Lewiston, NY 14092, ☎ 716-754-4883, or 40 Regal Road, Guelph, Ontario, Canada, N1H 7L5, ☎ 519-836-0102, www.sentex.net/~iamat. com. Their services are invaluable. Some of the money they raise goes toward a scholarship program that assists doctors in developing countries to go for medical training in more advanced parts of the world. They also sell, at cost, a portable mosquito net that weighs about five lbs/two kilos.

SAFE INDEED

IAMAT was started when Vincenzo Marcolongo, a graduate of medicine from McGill University, was working in Rome in 1960 and saw an ill Canadian who had previously seen a local doctor. He had been given a drug that was banned in North America because it destroyed white blood cells. Blood transfusions and antibiotics saved the patient's life. Realizing the problems of language and culture for foreign visitors, Dr. Marcolongo started a worldwide list of North American- and European-trained doctors that could be available for travelers. Over 200,000 contributing members now receive the directory containing 850 doctors working in 125 countries.

IAMAT Clinics

Remember, no area code is needed when making a local call.

■ Acapulco
Medical Dept., Fairmont Acapulco Princess and Marques Hotels, Playa Revolcadero, ☎ 744-469-1000, ext. 1309/1310 or 744-484-2108.

▪ Bahias de Huatulco

Clinica Medico, Quirurgica, Sabali #403, La Crucecita or Barcelo Huatulco Beach & Resort, ☎ 958-587-0687, 958-587-0600 or 958-581-0005

▪ Guadalajara

IAMAT Center, Francisco Zarco #2345, Col. Ladron de Guevara, ☎ 33-166-9616 or 33-615-9542.

▪ Hermosillo, Sonora

Clinica de Praga #1 Altos, Juarez y Jalisco, ☎ 662-213-2280

▪ Mazatlan

Clinica Mazatlan, Zaragoza #609, ☎ 669-981-2917 or 669-985-1923

▪ Oaxaca

Clinica Hospital Carmen, ☎ 951-516-4701 or 951-514-7545.

▪ Puerto Vallarta

IAMAT Center, Lucerna #148, Col. Versalles, ☎ 322-223-0011.

KB3 Blvd, Francisco Medina Ascencio, Plaza Neptuno D-1, ☎ 322-221-0023

IAMAT Center, Rio Nilo 132, #8, Col. Mariano Otero, ☎ 322-293-0036.

▪ Zihuatanejo

IAMAT Center, Cuauhtemoc #299, ☎ 755-312-0573 or 755-312-3010.

Alternative medicines are popular and as North Americans get more and more into natural health, herbal treatment for minor ailments may be a priority. There are some locals who learned from their ancestors the art of medicine using jungle plants and they are willing to treat or share information with visitors. However, for more serious ailments like a burst appendix or a broken leg, I recommend the use of traditional scientific medicine that uses strong drugs or surgery.

For official government updates on outbreaks, advisories and more, visit the **Centers for Disease Control & Prevention** run by the US Health Department at www.cdc.gov.

Medic Alert is an emergency response service that has been in business since 1956. Members get a bracelet that has their membership number on the back. If you have a medical condition that could result in your hospitalization while you are in an unconscious state, the medical staff contacts the 24-hour service at Medic Alert, providing your membership number. Medic Alert relays your medical conditions and any necessary precautions that must be taken. They also call your family. Medic Alert can be contacted at ☎ 888-633-4298 in the US or 209-668-3333, from elsewhere, www.medicalert.org.

Critical Air Ambulance, ☎ 800-247-8326 in the US or 800-010-0268 in Mexico. This is a team of medical experts who transport patients with multiple injuries, cardiac failure, severe head injuries, cerebral bleeds, and so forth, to the nearest fully equipped hospital in the United States. If your medical insurance handles air evacuation then they may well use this company. If not, keep the number handy in case you or a member of your group needs to get home quickly. The cost would be around US $10,000.

Sky Med, ☎ 800-475-9633 in US and Canada, 866-805-9624 in Mexico, www.skymed.com, is another company that will take you home in the event of an emergency. They go one step farther by insuring that your vehicle and all belongings also get home. They will allow a companion to travel at your bedside during the trip. Sky Med will take Canadians to a Canadian hospital if time permits, rather than an American one. This is not an expensive insurance, especially for anyone doing extreme sports where chance of accident is high. An evacuation could cost up to $30,000 from Mazatlan to Chicago (for example), so some type of insurance is advisable.

Money Matters

Mexico is a good deal even though prices have risen with the signing of the North American Free Trade Agreement. You can expect to pay about half of what you would in the United States for a comparable vacation. All-inclusive packages are often almost as cheap as airfare alone and those on a strict budget can almost always find a clean hotel for about $20 a night. The cost of an average vacation in a three-star hotel with restaurant food and at least one activity a day will run about $100 per person, per day. If sharing a room, the cost drops to half for every additional person.

■ Banking/Exchange

The local currency is the **peso** and it is indicated by the $ sign. Each peso is divided into 100 **centavos**. Coins come in denominations of 10, 20 and 50 centavos and one, two, five, 10 and 20 pesos. Notes come in the two, five, 10, 20, 50, 100 and 200 peso denominations. At time of writing, the exchange rate was about 10 pesos to US $1 and 13 pesos to one Euro.

Foreign money can be exchanged at the banks or Casas des Cambios. Banks are open 9 am-1:30 pm, Monday to Friday, and a few banks are open on Saturday afternoons. Casas are open later in the day, but seldom

BANKS OPERATING IN MEXICO	
A visit to the bank websites will enable you to monitor the exchange rate for the day.	
Banamex/Citibank	www.banamex.com
Banco de Mexico	www.banxico.org.mx
Bancrecer	www.bancrecer.com.mx
Bancomext	www.bancomext.com
Cancomer	www.bancomer.com.mx
Banorte	www.banorte.com
Bital	www.bital.com.mx
Santander	www.santander.com.mx

on Sundays. The exchange rate for cash is always higher than that for traveler's checks.

Traveler's checks issued by Visa, American Express or Thomas Cook are accepted throughout the country. The preferred currency is the American dollar.

There are over 9,000 ATMs in Mexico and, although there are plenty, finding one can sometimes be tricky as they are usually not open to the street. Occasionally, you will have to ask a local. Grocery stores are a good place to access these machines because, as a foreigner, you have the protection of a crowd and a gun-wielding guard. You can usually withdraw US/CAN $500 per day from your account (as long as the cash is in there to begin with), more than enough for your travels in Mexico.

■ Credit Cards

 Credit Cards are acceptable anywhere in Mexico except at the tiniest food stall or market merchant. The most common are **Visa**, **MasterCard**, **Diner's Club Card** and **American Express**.

If you need money wired from home, contact **Money Gram**, www.moneygram.com, or **Western Union**, www.westernunion.com. Visit their websites to obtain local office numbers (Moneygram has 21 agents in Acapulco and Western Union has over 130 agents in Guadalajara).

■ Planning Expenses

 If you make all your own arrangements, your cheapest day could run about $50 per person. This would include a basic room with a fan, two meals in the market or one of the smaller restaurants and the entrance fee to one attraction, like a museum. Your main entertainment would be sunning on the beach and reading a book which you brought with you. Should you want to do more – whale watch, scuba dive or play golf – the price goes up substantially. A better hotel will cost another $50, and drinks with dinner raise the price quite a bit.

To go first class – enjoy a piña colada at your hotel while watching the sun set over the Pacific and rent a car – will run between $250 and $500 per day. Most people budget for somewhere between the two extremes. There are, of course, a few places that offer even more than first class; prices at such resorts run around $1,000 a day.

Hotel Price Scales

For each hotel reviewed in this book, I give a price range rather than a fixed rate. The price for a single and double room is the same unless otherwise stated. Use these rates as a guideline only; always call and verify current prices.

For each establishment, I give my personal impression, followed by a brief review. My impressions may have been influenced by whom I saw and how they treated me. Once you have used the book for a while, you will have an idea as to what events and experiences interest me and what level of service I expect.

HOTEL PRICE SCALE	
Price for a room given in US $.	
$	Up to $20
$$	$21-$50
$$$	$51-$100
$$$$	$101-$150
$$$$$	$151-$200
Anything over $200 will be specified.	

■ Taxes & Tipping

% There is a 15% **Value Added Tax** (VAT) on everything for sale, except food purchased at a grocery store and medicines. Hotels have a 12% tax and you may also be charged 10% service charge over the quoted price for the room. Ask before booking.

Tipping is expected in restaurants and hotels. However, if a service charge is added to the bill, I fail to see why a tip would be expected; I don't tip. Taxi drivers appreciate a tip, although it isn't necessary. The average tip is between 10% and 15%, depending on the service.

Travel Information

Measurements

Mexico is metric, distance is given in kilometers, gas is sold in liters, and the temperature is read in Celsius (although, to accommodate the North American tourist, it is often quoted in Fahrenheit).

Going Metric?

To make your travels a little easier, we have provided the following charts that show metric equivalents for the measurements you are familiar with.

GENERAL MEASUREMENTS

1 kilometer	=	.6124 miles
1 mile	=	1.6093 kilometers
1 foot	=	.304 meters
1 inch	=	2.54 centimeters
1 square mile	=	2.59 square kilometers
1 pound	=	.4536 kilograms
1 ounce	=	28.35 grams
1 imperial gallon	=	4.5459 liters
1 US gallon	=	3.7854 liters
1 quart	=	.94635 liters

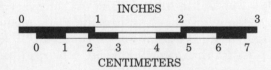

INCHES

0   1   2   3

0 1 2 3 4 5 6 7

CENTIMETERS

TEMPERATURES

For Fahrenheit: Multiply Centigrade figure by 1.8 and add 32.

For Centigrade: Subtract 32 from Fahrenheit figure and divide by 1.8.

CENTIGRADE		FAHRENHEIT
40°	=	104°
35°	=	95°
30°	=	86°
25°	=	77°
20°	=	64°
15°	=	59°
10°	=	50°

Dangers & Annoyances

Some houses in Mexico are secured by high concrete walls that have glass shards or razor-wire cemented along the top and steel bars on the windows. Inside, there are either vicious guard dogs or security guards armed with machine guns. Banks, too, have armed guards, as do some of the high-end restaurants.

This high security is not an environment that nurtures a trusting personality. Instead, it produces a "get him before he gets me" attitude, which results in many rip-offs for the unsuspecting visitor. To help prevent this, always ask the price, especially if the item you want is not on the menu or if the taxi you are using has to wait while you check out of a room. If you are not comfortable with this kind of clarification, then you may want to book into an all-inclusive package and never venture into the streets. If this also is not what you want, then Mexico may not be for you.

Even with all my experience traveling in Latin American countries, I still get royally annoyed when I get taken. To avoid this, always clarify.

SCAM ALERT – THEY GET A CHARGE OUT OF THIS

The latest scam is at the airports, particularly Puerto Vallarta and Acapulco. The workers at the security desks are now confiscating batteries, but only those still in packages. They tell the traveler that it is illegal to carry them on board. In fact, they are selling the batteries in the markets to supplement their incomes. You can take packaged batteries onto a plane.

■ Airport Security

Since 9-11, airport security has increased. Cameras and laptop computers are checked for explosives. People are asked to remove their shoes. I have even seen security guards demand that metal earrings be removed.

However, there are some things that most people would never think of. For an example, the explosive powders from firecrackers can set off alarms, as can the residue of explosives from those who have been at firing ranges or those who set off explosives for avalanche control. It is illegal to transport firecrackers and, if caught with them, you will be subject to a $25,000 fine and/or up to five years in prison. Fertilizer on the shoes of golfers and nitroglycerin for heart patients can also set off alarms. The most recent alarming substance is the glycerin in some hand lotions.

Doing your part in avoiding these substances before going to the airport will speed up your trip through the security monitors.

Travel Information

For those with a common last name, especially one like Garcia or Martinez, be aware that you may be stopped at American immigration for questioning. The interrogations usually last no longer than 10 or 15 minutes, but they are irritating. Keep your humor and matters will be dealt with much quicker.

If you are a frequent flier you should get a letter from Customs declaring that you are not "the Garcia" or "Martinez" who has a criminal record or direct links to Osama.

■ Common-Sense Precautions

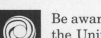 Every country in the world has robbers and petty thieves, whether you are in the polite society of Japan or the northern wilds of Canada. If you hang out in very poor sections of a city where you are unknown, if you are staggering drunk in a back alley, if you trust a stranger to hold your cash while you run to the washroom, you are going to have a sad tale to tell.

When out, be aware of what is around you. If it seems like you are being followed, go into a store or knock on someone's door. Make certain that expensive items like your camera or Rolex watch are out of sight.

Be inside at night and take a taxi back to your room if you have been out late. Don't be drunk in public. A drunk is a great target. Don't get mixed up in the dope trade. Save booze and dope for home. If you do get into trouble at home, you know the rules, you have friends to help and the prisons are far more comfortable than they are in Mexico.

Women should walk with confidence. If you appear frightened or lost, you are a target. Don't walk alone in non-populated places like jungles or secluded beaches. In the event that you are grabbed or accosted in any way, create a scene. Holler, scream, kick and fight with all your might. However, if you are approached by someone with a weapon, let them have it all. Being dead or seriously maimed isn't worth any possession you have, including your virginity.

■ Toilets

Be aware that the sewer systems in Mexico are not like those in the United States. Except for in the newer, up-market hotels, used toilet paper should be placed in a basket beside the toilet, rather than in it. It is a huge problem when those unaccustomed to this method of disposal refuse to follow the rules. Please be sensitive to the needs of the Mexican Public Service Department and put your paper in the basket.

Tourist Assistance

■ Police & Other Agencies

 Mexico has almost more types of police than it has beaches. There are the Federal Police and the Federal Traffic Police. The **Federal Police** have no jurisdiction over immigration documents or other tourist-type matters. If you are stopped and asked to show documents by these people, tell them to come to your hotel. Once there, have the manager call your consulate. Because of low wages, these police have a reputation of being corrupt.

The **Tourist Police**, on the other hand, patrol areas where tourists gather. To my knowledge, they are fairly good, and I never felt threatened or unsafe when dealing with them. If you are robbed or harmed in any way, report all instances to the Tourist Police (numbers are given at the start of each town section in this book).

Green Angels (Angeles Verdes) is Mexico's national road emergency service that is in place to help motorists on major highways. They have a fleet of 300 trucks that patrol fixed sections of major highways twice a day. Drivers speak both English and Spanish, can help with mechanical problems, have first aid, radio-telephone communications and can tow a broken-down vehicle into a garage. Although this is a free service, a tip is always appreciated. They can be reached at ☎ 800-903-9200.

The **Consumer Protection Service**, known as the Secreteria y Fomento Turistico (SEFOTUR), is in place for complaints about businesses in Mexico. They are located in all major centers. If you have problems with a merchant, report it to this agency.

Communications

■ Telephone

Most public phones require a calling card. **Ladatel cards** are sold in 20 or 50 peso denominations and are available at stores, restaurants and automated machines at the airport and bus station.

To make international calls, you must dial the international access code (98), then dial the country code (1 for the US and Canada, 44 for England), the area code and the local number. To reach Mexico from overseas, you must use the country code (52), then the city code and the number you wish to reach.

Some common city codes are: Acapulco, 744; Guadalajara, 33; Oaxaca, 951; Puerto Vallarta, 322. Codes for cities not listed here are provided at www.telmex.com. Click on English Version, then on Area Code by State. There you can type in the name of the town and get the area code. If you are placing a city-to-city call, dial 01 (for long distance), the city code and then the number. No city code is needed when making a local call.

The following numbers are used throughout Mexico.

24-hour Tourist Assistance, ☎ 800-9-0392

Emergency Assistance, ☎ 060

Operator-assisted international calls, ☎ 090

Operator-assisted national long distance, ☎ 020

Automatic national long distance, ☎ 01

Automatic long distance to Canada and the US, ☎ 001

Information, ☎ 040

To call a toll-free number from Mexico, dial, 01-8XX (numbers are usually 800, 888, 877, etc.) then the seven digits. You may find the following numbers useful.

Sprint, ☎ 01-800-877-8000

AT&T, ☎ 01-800-288-2872 or 01-800-112-2020 for Spanish.

Teleglobe Canada, ☎ 01-800-123-0200

You can also become a customer of companies like **World Wide Callback**, www.worldwidecallback.com, where you call a number that has been given to you by Callback from anywhere in the world. Once you hear the ring sound, you hang up and they call you back. From there you place your international calls. You are charged to a credit card at American rates. This system must be set up before you travel.

■ Mail

 It is easy and safe to send and receive mail. It takes from five to seven days for a letter/postcard to reach the United States from anywhere in Mexico. The cost for a letter is about 40¢ for up to 20 grams. Parcels don't have to be inspected before being sent out of the country, so they can be wrapped before taking them to the post office. Insurance is highly recommended for parcels.

You can receive mail at the ***post restante*** in any town. You will need your passport for identification to pick up your mail.

International courier services are also available: **Federal Express**, ☎ 5-228-9904 (in Mexico) or 800-900-1100, www.fedex.com; **Airborne Express**, ☎ 5-203-6811; **Aeroflash**, ☎ 5-627-3030; **DHL**, ☎ 5-345-7000, www.dhl.com; **UPS**, ☎ 5-228-7900 or 800-902-9200, www.ups.com.

■ Mexican Newspapers

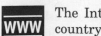

English-language newspapers published for tourists are mentioned under the specific cities where they are published.

Reforma, www.reforma.com, is in Spanish and covers both national and international news. You must subscribe to the paper before you can read anything but the headlines.

El Financiero, www.elfinanciero.com.mx, gives a summary of the financial status of Mexican economics.

La Jornada, www.jornada.unam.mx, seems to be a left-wing Spanish publication.

Excelsior, www.excelsior.com.mx, is an online magazine that you must subscribe to. You can subscribe to only the sections that are of interest to you, be they TV information, articles or tidbits.

El Universal, www.eluniversal.com.mx, is a mainline newspaper with everything from headlines to horoscopes.

Milenio, www.milenio.com/mexico, has both national and international news, plus a good general interest section.

El Economista, www.economista.com.mx, leans more toward finance than news and covers international finance too.

Cronica, www.cronica.com.mx, offers general news daily.

El Norte, www.elnorte.com, has full coverage daily.

Proceso, www.proceso.com.mx, also has full coverage daily.

Expansion, www.expansion.com.mx, makes American news a top priority.

■ Internet

The Internet is the best way to communicate in Mexico; the country has over 3.5 million users. Internet cafés are almost as common as shoeshine boys. Prices are $1-2 an hour – the rate seems dependent on whether there is air conditioning in the café or not.

Travel Information

Culture Shock

■ Public Affection

Once away from the beach resorts, you will find that Mexico is still a conservative country. Physical affection in public is not common. Holding hands seems to be okay, but passionate kissing, especially by same-sex couples, is still not acceptable. Mexico is a Catholic country where most people still follow the laws of the church. However, there is one nude beach at Zipolete, south of Acapulco, that the locals tolerate.

■ Gay & Lesbian Travel

There are numerous gay- and-lesbian-friendly bars and hotels along the coast. Cancún even held a gay festival. Although the possibility of finding a same-sex relationship with a Mexican exists, you must be careful not to think that because a Mexican has sex with you that she or he is gay. Some Mexicans look at having same-gender sex as entertainment, not a way of life.

The magazine *Ser Gay* is a good source of information for those who read Spanish. It can be found online at www.sergay.com.mx.

■ Special Needs Travelers

Special needs persons are now considered in the tourist areas of Mexico and some hotels have wheelchair accessibility. The streets are still pretty shoddy in places, but taxis are plentiful. Taking a small wheelchair from a hotel to a restaurant that is on street level would be possible. Blind or deaf people should have an assistant.

■ Human Rights

Since Fox took over leadership of the country he has tried to establish some accountability for those who committed serious human rights abuses in the past, especially during the 1960s and 1970s "Dirty War" period. There is a Freedom of Information law and 80 million files pertaining to the abuses between 1952 and 1985 have been released.

A special government office has been opened to look into past abuses but, due to lack of money, it so far has been ineffectual. As a result, the military and the police have not been made accountable for their abuses. So even now, those opposing the government or the police are sometimes killed or sentenced to long prison terms for minor crimes. Often, confessions are obtained under torture. At present, the government is trying to cease the practice of arbitrary detentions without access to a lawyer or doctor.

Prisons are for the most part overcrowded due to prisoners awaiting trial. The state of the prisoner usually depends on how much money the family can provide so the prisoner may purchase his daily needs. Paying bribes to the guards is often necessary for prisoners to receive goods from their family. Some prisons have cells measuring 10 by six feet (three by two meters) that house three men. Often, men are forced to sleep on benches, use only cold water for washing and open buckets as toilets. Female prisoners are frequently held in the same building as males. Females are permitted, in some prisons, to keep their children up to the age of three. However, this is not consistent throughout the country. All in all, prisons are not pleasant places.

Food

Mexican food needs no explaining to most people in North America and Europe because those countries have as many Mexican restaurants as they have hamburger and pizza joints. Mexican food is usually made up of onions, tomatoes, rice, beans, corn, eggs, cheese and *pollo* (chicken). These foods are accompanied by some kind of corn tortilla.

However, with the proliferation of tourism, today you can get any kind of food in Mexico, from Chinese to Japanese to Bavarian and Thai. Along the coast, of course, seafood or fish is the most popular meal. Be certain to try some ceviche, a raw fish or sea food pickled in lime juice, or *pescado* Veracruz, a fish smothered in fresh tomato and onion sauce.

Because you are in the tropics, seasonal fruits are abundant. Try guanabana, a slimy white substance that is succulent beyond belief. Taste some guava, especially if your stomach is a bit queasy as it is supposed to slow down peristaltic action in the gut. Try the mango; when fresh there is nothing like it. Banana *con leche* (banana with milk) or fresh-squeezed orange or grapefruit juice will always refresh you when you are hot or tired. Other fruits to try are avocados, grapes, papayas (larger than those found in North America), peaches, fresh-picked peanuts, pears, pineapples, strawberries, watermelons and prickly pears.

Travel Information

■ Favorite Dishes

An **enchilada** is a tortilla stuffed with ground meat, beans and cheeses. A **tostada** is the same thing, only the tortilla is toasted and left flat on the plate.

Guacamole is made with avocado that is mashed and mixed with onion, tomato and lime juice. It is often served as an appetizer or included as one of the sauces for your meal.

FACT FILE: Avocado is one of the few vegetables that has a lot of calories.

Mole de pollo or **mole poblano** is considered the national dish. It consists of *mole*, a tasty brown sauce, that is cooked with either chicken or turkey. However, the *mole* sauce can be served in many ways, including as a dark thick soup. The word "mole" comes from the Aztec word meaning "sauce." When you are offered a red mole with your chicken, you should ask how spicy it is. Chances are, it probably has a lot of red chilies. A brown mole will have a chocolate base and be less spicy.

Chilmole is occasionally called *relleno-negro*. It is made using a sauce that incorporates orange juice, chiles, cloves, allspice, black peppers, oregano, cumin and garlic. This is cooked with either chicken or turkey.

FACT FILE: Prior to the arrival of the Spanish, the locals made tamales for the gods, as well as for themselves. Some were made in special designs like spirals, while others were huge, weighing up to a hundred pounds.

Tamales are a feast dish that take hours to make and only minutes to devour. They are made with a corn flour paste filled with things like meat, chiles, fish, frogs, beans, turkey, squash seeds or any combination of these foods. Most are rolled into banana leaves and steamed or roasted.

CHEF'S SECRET

Should you decide to make your own tamales once you are back at home, the one secret I can pass on to you is that a tamale, no matter how much care is taken in the making, will not turn out unless the cook has music blaring in the background.

Quesadillas are made with wheat-flour tortillas and are the same as *tostadas*, except these have tons of melted cheese on top.

Frijoles refritos, or re-fried beans. In Mexico, it matters not if you are having breakfast, snack, meal of the day or beer – *frijoles* will appear. Served with sour cream, they are delicious and an excellent source of protein.

Bread has, with the demands of tourism, become more common in Mexico. Now it is possible to purchase other pastries, including a torte similar to one you might find in France. Quality fruit tarts and pies are also available. Mexican pecan or key lime pies make the fat under your skin bubble on the first bite. You can find these foods in cafés and pastry shops.

For a good glossary of Mexican foods, as well as recipes and interesting historical tidbits, go to the TexMex website at www.texmextogo.com.

Booking a Room

Many people book their accommodations over the Internet. This is okay, but be aware that not everything on the Web is true. Photos probably show only the best side of an establishment, and lighting plays a big part in making something look far more attractive than it is. You will not see the cockroaches in the corners or hear the bus terminal next door. Rates quoted may be off-season, with no indication of what in-season rates are, and taxes may not be mentioned. Ask some questions before turning over your credit card number.

- *Is there air conditioning or a fan?* In a thatched-roof hut, air conditioning is useless because the cold air goes out through the roof.

- *Is there hot water? How is it heated?* Water heated on the roof by the sun is far cooler than water heated in a gas water tank.

- *What does "all-inclusive" mean?* Is it rice and beans for three meals a day and a lawn chair around the pool, or does it include excursions around the area?

- *Do the prices include taxes and service charges?* Tax is an additional 25%; it makes a huge difference on your bill.

- *Does the hotel accept credit cards and do they add a fee for this?* Charging for this service is against their contract with the credit card companies, but some places add this anyway.

- *How close to other places is the hotel? Will you be able to move around easily without having to pay for taxis?*

Travel Information

If you do book ahead, print out all correspondence and bring the documentation with you. Some proprietors have been known to offer one rate, but charge another after the customer has arrived. Make certain you read all the fine print.

See page 65 for a guideline to hotel prices.

Getting Here

There are many options. For a luxurious stay near the beach, you can have a tour agent from your own town book your flight and hotels so all you need to do is pack, grab your cash and credit cards, and get yourself to the airport. Or you may be on a long trip and arrive by traveling overland from the US, Guatemala or Belize. You may want to do nothing but visit one beach after another or stay on the same beach for the entire vacation. If you have specialized activities you would like to pursue, like kayaking or horseback riding, consider working with one of the companies that focuses on these activities. You may want to fly with a charter and return on a non-changeable date. These tickets are usually the best deal, especially if you can negotiate the flight without hotels. Be certain to confirm your return schedule at least 72 hours before departure.

The following airlines are the most common ones dropping into the west coast of Mexico. For more information about them, go to their websites or call them direct.

■ By Air

 Aero California, ☎ 800-237-6225 (Mx), www.aerocalifornia. de, flies from Los Angeles and Tucson to Manzanillo, Mazatlan, Guadalajara, Puerto Vallarta, Colima and Tepic.

AeroMexico, ☎ 800-237-6639 (US), 800-021-4010 (Mx), www.aeromexico.com, flies from Los Angeles, New York, Tucson, San Diego, Dallas-Ft. Worth, Atlanta and Miami in the States and Ontario in Canada. They have flights to Guadalajara, Mazatlan and Mexico City.

Alaska Airlines, ☎ 800-252-7522 (US), 800-468-2248 (US for packages), 55-5282-2484 (Mx), www.alaskaair.com, serves 80 cities in the United States, Canada and Mexico, and has flights from Europe and Asia. I flew with them and found their prices the best, their planes full and their service exceptional, especially at the airport in Puerto Vallarta. I recommend this company.

American Airlines, ☎ 800-433-7300 (US), 800-904-6000 (Mx), www.aa. com, was one of the first airlines to fly passengers and cargo into Mexico.

They fly from Dallas-Ft. Worth, Miami and Los Angeles to Mexico City, Guadalajara, Puerto Vallarta and Acapulco.

America West, ☎ *800-363-2597 (US), 800-235-9292 (Mx), www.americawest.com*, leaves from Phoenix and Las Vegas and flies to Acapulco, Ixtapa-Zihuatenejo, Puerto Vallarta and, through an affiliate, to Guaymas and Guadalajara.

Aviacsa, ☎ *800-735-5396 (US), 800-711-6733 (Mx), www.aviacsa.com.mx*, flies between Houston or Las Vegas and Mexico City. They also offer many flights inside Mexico.

British Airways, ☎ *800-AIRWAYS (US), 55-5387-0300 (Mx), www.ba.com,* offers three flights a week between London and Mexico City.

Continental Airlines, ☎ *800-231-0856 (US), 800-900-5000 (Mx), www.continental.com,* flies from Houston and Newark to 21 destinations in Mexico, including Manzanillo and Colima.

Delta, ☎ *800-241-4141 (US), 800-123-4710 (Mx), www.delta.com*, flies from many US areas, including Los Angeles, Dallas-Ft. Worth and Atlanta, to Mexico City, Acapulco, Puerto Vallarta and Guadalajara.

Frontier, ☎ *800-432-1359, www.frontierairlines.com*, flies from select US cities to Mazatlan, Puerto Vallarta and Ixtapa/Zihuatenejo.

Mexicana, ☎ *800-531-7921 (US), 800-509-8960 (Mx), www.mexicana.com*, leaves from Los Angeles, San José, San Francisco, Oakland, Chicago, San Antonio, Newark, Miami, Denver, Montreal and Toronto. There are numerous cities in Central and South America from which it operates. It flies to Mexico City, Puerto Vallarta, Guadalajara and Mazatlan. Mexicana has been in business since the 1930s and has a good safety record.

United Airlines, ☎ *800-538-2929 (US), 800-003-0777 (Mx), www.united.com,* flies from San Francisco, Chicago, Los Angeles, Washington, DC and Miami to Mexico City.

Travel Information

SPECIAL OFFERS

At the time of writing, **Funjet Vacations**, ☎ *888-558-6654, www.funjet.com,* was offering a vacation to Puerto Vallarta from Seattle for $530 that included airfare (Alaska Airlines), airport transfers and three nights' accommodations. The offer also included your food, drinks and hotel services at the Occidental Nuevo Vallarta. This is a good deal. They offer stays at other hotels too, with most deals being mid-week travel. Check their website for current vacation deals.

Arriving at the Airport

When you fly into any Mexican airport, the procedure is simple. First, you go through Immigration, where you will receive a 90-day (usually) visitor's permit. You then pick up your bags and head for Customs inspection. You will be asked to push a button. If the light above the button turns green, you and your party are free to walk through. If it turns red, the inspectors will check your bags for any forbidden substances.

There are banks at the airports, along with some souvenir shops and places to eat, though the food is usually terrible.

To get to town, if you haven't arranged for a pick-up by one of the bigger hotels, you can take a taxi to the center. Fares are lower if you hop a cab from out on the street; taxis with ticket wickets at the airport are up to four times as expensive. When taking a taxi from the street, be certain to establish the price beforehand.

A bus is an option if you don't have too much luggage. Ask at the information booth in the airport which bus will take you where you want to go. Usually, the bus stops are just outside the airport, beyond the taxis on the street.

■ Overland by Bus

 Buses from other countries do not cross the border into Mexico. They leave you at the border and you must either walk across or take a local bus or taxi to the nearest bus terminal and catch a Mexican bus.

Bus travel in Mexico can be first class, second class or peasant class. The first-class buses are roomy, air-conditioned vehicles that often come with an attendant to look after your needs. The 44 seats found on each bus are soft and recline. Your lunch and a drink may be included in the price of the ticket and handed to you as you board the bus. There are toilets available and, often, you can even make yourself a tea or coffee. Videos are played, usually not too loud, and they are often fairly decent and in English. Some of the companies have private waiting rooms at the bus stations, where only their passengers may sit. These companies also offer bathrooms not used by the general public in the main terminal. Second-class bus service is almost as luxurious as first class, except you don't get lunch and the bus stops at some towns on the way to your destination. They are more like the buses found in North America. Peasant-class bus travel in Mexico is most interesting, although the least comfortable. You never get a lunch or an attendant and the buses stop at many towns. No matter what class service you use, no longer do buses go only when full and carry everything, including the chicken going to market.

Ticket prices run about $5 per hour of travel for the best class and drop to just over half that for second class (usually) and even less for peasant class. It is only the peasant-class tickets that do not have reserved seats. Bus drivers are the bosses of the road and of the bus. They know their job and do it well.

Bus stations are generally large buildings on the outskirts of bigger cities. You must pay a 25¢ tax if using buses from the terminals and occasionally your carry-on luggage will be searched by security. The following companies service travel from the US border down into central Mexico.

The Estrella Blanca (Elite), ☎ *221-0850, 290-1001 or 290-1014.* Buses leave for Guadalajara, Mexico City and all major stops in-between.

Primera Plus, ☎ *221-0095, www.flecha-amarilla.com.* The ticket price includes a sandwich and juice. The air-conditioned bus is a luxury liner and comes recommended for any trips in the area if their schedule is right for you. I traveled with them and was quite pleased.

ETN, ☎ *223-5665 or 223-5666, www.etn.com.mx*, has buses going to most major destinations. This, too, is a luxury liner, but I found them less than caring about their passengers.

Transportes del Pacifico, ☎ *222-1015 or 222-5622,* has buses going around the country often, usually once every hour to major destinations.

TAP, ☎ *290-0119*, has buses going to 24 destinations around the country. I found the workers at the PV office helpful and honest. I would not hesitate traveling with them. TAP also covers many destinations to the north like Tijuana and Guaymas.

■ Overland by Car or RV

 Before entering Mexico with a vehicle you must have an American, Canadian or international driver's license. At the border you must apply for a temporary **vehicle importation permit**. For this you need proof of ownership, registration, proof of citizenship and an affidavit from lien holders allowing this temporary importation. (If you take a rental car from the US or Belize into Mexico, the rental company will provide all necessary documents.) This permit is good for six months and can be used for multiple entries. The fee ($15) must be paid by Visa, MasterCard or American Express. The permit must be pasted onto the windshield. It proves that you paid to bring the vehicle in and shows the date when you must have the vehicle out of the country. If you overstay, your vehicle will be confiscated. RVs require an additional permit. It is illegal to leave your vehicle in Mexico unless you pay a 30% tax levied on the value of the vehicle.

The main roads between the American and Guatemalan border are all paved, double-lane highways. Secondary roads that follow the coast are also paved, but narrow and winding, with almost no shoulders. The speed limits, measured in kilometers, are reasonable (40-60 mph/65-100 kmh) and there are Green Angels around should you run into any mechanical problems (see page 69). Maps are accurate and signs well posted. RV parks are dotted along the coast; most allow tenting. Hotels often offer some sort of off-street parking, which is necessary if leaving the vehicle overnight.

If you have decided to bring your car, be certain it is in top shape, with good tires, a tuned-up motor, a recent carburetor overhaul, and so on. Paying for repairs at gringo prices would make this an expensive vacation. If taking a motor home, don't overload it. You can purchase anything you may want or need in Mexico and often the price will be less than at home.

Insurance

Mexican car insurance is essential. Foreign insurance is of no value. Offices of insurance companies line the borders for your convenience. There are two components to consider if you are involved in an accident. First, damage to the car, the property, the person, medical expenses and loss of wages must be considered. Then the moral damages are calculated. This is the pain and suffering incurred by the injured and, in Mexico, this is usually about one-third of what the actual damages are. You then have the choice of a civil or criminal case. In a criminal case, the victim receives an appointed lawyer and the liability is not limited like it is in civil cases. In the worst-case scenario, should you kill a person in an accident that you caused, you would have to pay for the damaged vehicle, the medical expenses incurred, funeral expenses and loss of wages. This would be calculated at the minimum daily wage of the person killed for a period determined by the courts. Moral damages would be added to all this. For an average person, $100,000 liability coverage should be adequate.

In the event of an accident, first and always, contact your insurance company. They know what to say and do. Do not sign anything or answer questions until you have a legal representative with you. This is your right as a driver in Mexico. If you are arrested, you have the right to be released on bail; the amount of bail is determined by a court official, not by the police. Should you be under the influence of drugs or alcohol, you may be detained for a long time.

Most of the car insurance information I used came from DriveMex.com (see below).

Insurance Companies

There are numerous companies selling car insurance in Mexico. I recommend the following because they have built a good reputation. If you fall in with a fly-by-night company, you could lose some cash. Take the recommendations given here or those of a trusted friend.

International Insurance-Seguros, *1047 W. Madero, Mesa, AZ,* ☎ *480-345-0191, www.globalmedicalplans.com*, sells car, boat and medical insurance. They are responsive and knowledgeable. The company's owner, Patricia Romero Hamrick, is a Mexican lady with a lot of experience with insurance in Mexico. Patricia has many Mexican clients. Whenever I dealt with her, I was always satisfied. It is important to know that Mexican insurance claims can end up in court for years, whereas American claims are usually settled quickly. With this company, you can purchase insurance (dealing in English) before you head to Mexico and, since this is a Mexican company, the insurance is acceptable over the border. Their medical insurance includes emergency evacuation and reunion. That means a loved-one can join you should you be in hospital for a long time.

Sanborn's Insurance, ☎ *800-222-0158, www.sanbornsinsurance.com*, is a large company stationed in Mexico. It has been around for a long time.

Seguros Tepeyac, ☎ *800-837-3922*, was founded in 1944. It belongs to the MAPFRE system from Spain and operates in 26 countries.

DriveMex.com, ☎ *866-367-5053, www.drivemex.com,* is operated by Comerco Courtage Inc. I have worked with this company and I was pleased.

■ By Sea

You can come to Mexico by private boat, public ferry or cruise ship. If taking a cruise, your agent will look after all necessary documents. All you will need is this guidebook, clothing, some money and your passport. If going by ferry between La Paz, Baja California and Mazatlan, you may find that some boats offer poor service. The business has been privatized.

The **Sematur Transbordadores Ferry** transports people and vehicles between La Paz, Baja California and Mazatlan, on the mainland, twice a week. The boat leaves at 3 pm from La Paz and the journey takes 19 hours. This was once the government-owned Caminos y Puentes Federales de Ingresos y Conexos, but the line was sold in 1989 and, since then, services have dropped. This company also runs a ferry from Santa Rosalia to Guaymas on Sunday, Tuesday and Friday, leaving from Santa Rosalia at 10 pm and returning Monday, Thursday and Saturday at

10 pm. This is a tourist-class run that takes between seven and eight hours. The cost is about $40 for adult, $20 for children, $200 for a pick-up truck and $135 for a motorcycle. The company has numerous telephone numbers in each city they service. Visit the website, www.simplonpc.co. uk/SEMATUR.html.

Baja Ferries, ☎ *800-718-2796 or 800-012-8770, www.bajaferries.com,* has a high-speed catamaran that travels between La Paz and Topolobampo (Los Mochis) every day. Vehicles can be transported and passenger service is either first or second class. Travel time is five hours. Check at the docks for departure times. The salon-class lounge offers bus-style seats that recline. A tourist cabin has either two or four bunks and the cabin is shared with others. However, males and females are segregated. Private cabins hold two people and have a bathroom. There is a restaurant, bar and cafeteria on the boat.

Private Boat

If you are sailing your own vessel into Mexico, you will need to stop first at the Immigration office at the port of entry to get a **tourist visa** and a **temporary import permit** for your boat. You will need ownership papers proving the boat is yours or the lease agreement if the vessel is rented. You will need proof of citizenship so you can obtain a tourist visa and an arrival and departure clearance document. You must post a bond (for the value of the vessel, plus an added $10 processing fee) using a major credit card at the Banjercito bank.

You must then register your boat at a marina. If you plan to sail from one port to another, you must obtain a document specifying your arrival and departure clearances. For more specific information on sailing in Mexico, go to www.mexonline.com/boatmex.htm.

Boat Charters

Orca Sailing, *1017 15th St., Bellingham, WA,* ☎ *800-664-6049, www. orcasailing.com,* has a number of different yachts that can be rented by the week. They run between $4,000 per week for six people up to $175,000 for 12 people in a luxurious liner. The per-person cost is lower if you join a group, rather than hire the boat privately. For one person to rent the boat will cost $500 a day, but with a group of six and a full hired crew, the cost goes down to about $200. On their prescheduled trips, rates run under $200 per person, per day, even less if you share a bathroom. With this company, once two people have confirmed their trip, the deal is a go. The prices include everything after you arrive at the boat's dock, even the wine with your gourmet dinners. You will be expected to help with the sailing by taking your share of the watch, monitoring weather, getting cyclone updates, studying the ocean currents, using SSB & VHF radios and helping with chart selection. Your route can be tailored to your specs. Equipment for high-speed watersports is included. This is a great way to see Mexico.

Cruise Ship Centers, ☎ *866-358-7285, 800-707-7327 (Canada) or 877-791-7676 (US), www.cruiseshipcenters.com,* offers three- to eight-day cruises in the Pacific, stopping at places like Puerto Vallarta, Mazatlan and Acapulco. If you wish to have your every need catered to, eat more exotic foods than your encyclopedia could list, and still enjoy the best of Mexico, this is one option. The ships have a climbing wall, jogging tracks, mini golf, fitness and dance classes, spa facilities, pools and hot tubs, deck games, casinos, lounges, art auctions, duty-free shopping and facilities for children. The different restaurants are too many to name. The cost for one of these cruises starts at about $750 per person. I have worked with Carrol Johnson (cjohnson@cruiseshipcenters.com) for years and she has always managed to get me what I want, when I want it, for a price close to what I can afford.

Royal Caribbean, ☎ *800-511-4848,* has a three-day trip to Ensenada where you can ride horse through the hills or just sit on the beach. The ship leaves from Los Angeles. Luxurious staterooms start at $530 a day, while regular rooms cost $220 a day. This is all-inclusive. The boat has two pools, nine bars, a cinema, a fitness center, a spa, a casino and children's facilities.

Getting Around

■ By Plane

 There are numerous companies working in Mexico. AeroMexico and Mexicana are the biggest. However, Alaska Air, Aviacsa and Aero California also offer service to many destinations at competitive prices.

Note that ticket changes are costly in Mexico, usually running 25% of the original fare. When traveling, arrive early as your seat could be sold to someone on the standby list. Carry on as much as possible. Lost luggage is not fun. I once had all my baggage lost and it took three days to be found. During that time the airline refused to supply even a toothbrush. It was an American couple listening to my arguments with the company representative who finally produced the needed items.

See *General Directory*, page 87, for airline contact information.

■ By Bus

 Unless you are in a hurry to get from one place to another, I suggest taking a bus. This way, you can watch the countryside, talk to locals and get to your destination feeling relaxed. Not that air travel is stressful, but bus travel is more comfortable in Mexico than it is in the US and Canada. After all, you did come to see the country.

Usually, you will find numerous bus companies going to your destination at different times during the day. If there is no direct bus, you may need to travel to the nearest city en route and connect to another bus going to your destination.

Tickets may be purchased in advance, in person. Bus companies do not take credit cards, but every bus station except in the tiniest of villages has an ATM. Baggage is labeled when you hand it over and you get a ticket that you must present to get your bags back. It is customary to give the baggage handler a few pesos for his service when putting the bags on the bus. Occasionally, you will have to go through a wand-over-body security check. Theft of baggage is not a concern.

If traveling at night, buses are comfortable, children are quiet and there are no chickens in the carry-on baggage. You may find it easier to sleep on the right-hand side of the bus, without the glare of headlights from oncoming traffic.

■ By Car

 For details about entering Mexico with your own car, see page 79. You can rent a vehicle from many of the main car rental companies in the US and Canada (see page 87). Privately owned companies are listed in the cities where they are located.

Mexican car insurance is essential (see page 80) and you must have a valid driver's license to rent. You must be 25 years of age or older and hold a major credit card. Remember, if you get into an accident, call the insurance company/car dealer before you answer questions or sign any papers.

▶▶ **AUTHOR EXPERIENCE:** *On my recent Mexico trip, I dealt with National, although I spoke with most other companies. I found that National was far more interested in telling me about the road conditions, things of which I must be aware and general information about driving in Mexico than they were in renting me a vehicle. They also gave me very good service.*

See *General Directory*, page 87, for car rental company contact information.

Driving

Driving is on the right, as in the US. One problem, especially if you have a large motor home, is the congestion in the towns. This congestion makes walking a hazard, never mind driving. Also, driving along the secondary roads at night should be avoided as there are always animals, one-lane bridges and cars without headlights to negotiate. There are three times as many road fatalities at night than during the day. There are also speed bumps (silent policemen) at the entrance and exit of every town and village. These should be approached slowly. Avoid parking in secluded places.

Once you arrive, if you hire a car watcher while you go into a restaurant or any other place, the watcher should get about a dollar. If you hire a valet to park your car, tip about the same.

Some basic laws you should know include:

- It is the law for drivers to fasten their seat belts, but it is not required for passengers.
- Traveling in the back of a pickup truck is legal.
- Drinking and driving is prohibited, but passengers may drink in a vehicle.
- For motorcycles, there is no helmet law.

Gas

Gasoline is available from **Pemex**, the government-owned petroleum company. Some stations have a car wash and mini-mart and offer oil changes. They sell three grades of gas. Nova is the lowest grade and price and is sold from a blue pump. RVs should not use this gas as the octane level is less than anything sold in the US or Canada and can cause knocking in the motor. Magna sin is the mid-grade fuel that is sold from the green pump. The octane level of this gas is around 86 and is probably equal to regular gas in the US or Canada. Premium gas is sold only in larger centers and is the equivalent of premium gas anywhere. Diesel is also available and is praised by drivers of RVs, who claim it is superior to American fuel in cleanliness. It is commonly recommended that RVs have a pre-filter installed and fuel/water separators to protect their pumps and injectors. Gasoline costs about 55¢ a liter/$2+ a gallon.

Toll Roads

Be aware that most motor homes and pick-up trucks are classified as two-axle vehicles. There is always an icon beside the term describing how many axles your vehicle has and those illiterate in the language of axles can make out what they will have to pay by matching their vehicle with the icon. If you are towing a trailer or a boat, you will be charged according to the number of axles. The cost is $16 (158 pesos) for the 90 miles/147 km between Colima and Guatalajara. Go to www.mexperience.com/guide/essentials/toll_road_charges.htm and click on road charges for distances between places and the cost to travel on the toll highways. The site has other information, too. In my opinion, the amount one saves on gas, along with the savings in tranquilizers because of the better road conditions and the time saved, make the price of a toll highway well worth it.

Police/Tickets

It was at one time common to pay the police a bribe and be on your way. This, with increased tourism, is changing. Now, if a police officer stops you and accuses you of a violation, ask for the fine. Usually, the police officer will leave you alone. If he does give you a ticket, chances are you are guilty of the crime. If you are, he will probably take your driver's license and give you a ticket. You can pay the ticket and retrieve your license at the nearest city hall. If you pay the ticket within 24 hours, it costs less than if you wait. If you are not guilty of a crime, the police officer will probably send you on your way with a warning not to do what he charged you with doing. Smile, say thank you, and be gone.

■ Hitchhiking

Mexico is not a place to hitchhike. Although most Mexican families are friendly and willing to give you a ride, there is always the opportunist who will target a foreigner. Robbery or worse should always be considered. If for some reason you must hitchhike, go to a service station on the edge of town and ask for a ride from a family that is going in your direction.

Author's Top Picks

1. **Copper Canyon**, for hiking and a train ride.

2. **Bay of Guaymas**, for kayaking.

3. **Turtle Island Peace Camp** near Navojoa.

4. Hike to **Urique** from **Batópilas**.

5. Cycling around **Creel**.

6. Guadalajara, where you can poke around the plazas and museums or take the Tequila Express tour.

7. Walk in **Old Mazatlan**.

8. Visit the ruins of **Oaxaca**.

9. Bird at any of the sites around **San Blas**.

10. Puerto Vallarta, for the Canopy Tour and eating and drinking at the Cliff.

11. Deep-sea diving/snorkeling near **Manzanillo**.

12. Watch for whales and turtles anywhere down the **coast**.

13. Sighting monarch butterflies at **Anganguero**.

14. Acapulco, where you can raft the Papagayo River or watch cliff divers.

15. Sit on the beach all day with a beer in hand.

Directory

GENERAL DIRECTORY

■ MEDICAL & HEALTH CARE

Critical Air Ambulance . . ☎ 800-247-8326 (US); 800-010-0268 (Mx)

Sky Med. . . . . ☎ 800-475-9633 (US); 866-805-9624 (Mx) . . . . www.skymed.com

Medic Alert. . . . . ☎ 888-633-4298 (US) . . . . www.medicalert.org

■ CAR RENTAL COMPANIES

Avis . . . . ☎ 800-288-8888 (US); 5-558-8888 (Mx) . . . . www.avis.com

Alamo . . . . ☎ 800-462-5266 (US) . . . . www.alamo.com

Budget. . . . . ☎ 800-472-3325 (US) . . . . www.budget.com

Dollar . . . . ☎ 800-800-3665 (US) . . . . www.dollar.com

Hertz. . . . . ☎ 800-654-3030 (US). . . . . www.hertz.com

National . . . . ☎ 800-CAR-RENT (US) . . . . www.nationalcar.com

Thrifty. . . . . ☎ 800-THRIFTY (US) . . . . www.thrifty.com

■ AIRLINES

AeroMexico . . . . ☎ 800-237-6639 (US); 800-021-4010 (Mx) . . . . www.aeromexico.com

Alaska Airlines. . . . . . . ☎ 800-252-7522 (US); 55-5282-2484 (Mx) . . . . www.alaskaair.com

America West. . . . . . . ☎ 800-363-2597 (US); 800-235-9292 (Mx). . . . . . . www.americawest.com

Aviasca . . . . ☎ 888-528-4227(US); 800-711-6733 (Mx) . . . . www.aviasca.com.mx

Travel Information

GENERAL DIRECTORY

■ AIRLINES, CONT.

Continental . . . . ☎ 800-231-0856 (US); 800-900-5000 (Mx) . . . . www.continental.com

Delta . . . . ☎ 800-241-4141 (US); 800-123-4710 (Mx) . . . . www.delta.com

Frontier Air . . . . ☎ 800-432-1359 (US) . . . . www.frontierairlines.com

Mexciana Airlines . . . . ☎ 800-531-7921 (US); 800-509-8960 (Mx) . . . . www.mexicana.com

■ EMERGENCIES WHILE IN MEXICO

Tourist Assistance . . . . ☎ 800-9-0392

Emergency Assistance (any kind) . . . . ☎ 060

■ CONSULATES

For foreign consulates, see *Consulates*, page 491, in the *Appendix*.

■ CREDIT CARD ASSISTANCE

NOTE: The telephone numbers listed above can change without notice at any time. It is best to check the Internet site for the latest telephone numbers.

VISA . . . . ☎ 800-847-2911 (US & Mx) . . . . www.visa.com

MasterCard . . . . ☎ 800-MC-ASSIST (US); 800-307-7309 (Mx) . . . . www.mastercard.com

Diner's . . . . ☎ 800-234-2377; 5-258-3220 (Mx) . . . . www.dinersclub.com

American Express . . ☎ 800-992-3404 (US); 336-393-1111 (collect) . . . www.americanexpress.com

■ INSURANCE COMPANIES

International Insurance-Seguros. . . . . ☎ 480-345-0191 (US) . . . www.seguros-insurance.net

Global Travel Insurance . . . . ☎ 800-232-9415 (US) . . www.globalmedicalplans.com

■ USEFUL WEBSITES

www.mexonline.com

www.visitmexico.com

www.mexico.com

www.elbalero.gob.mx_kids.html. This is a great site for kids.

www.go2mexico.com

www.mexconnect.com

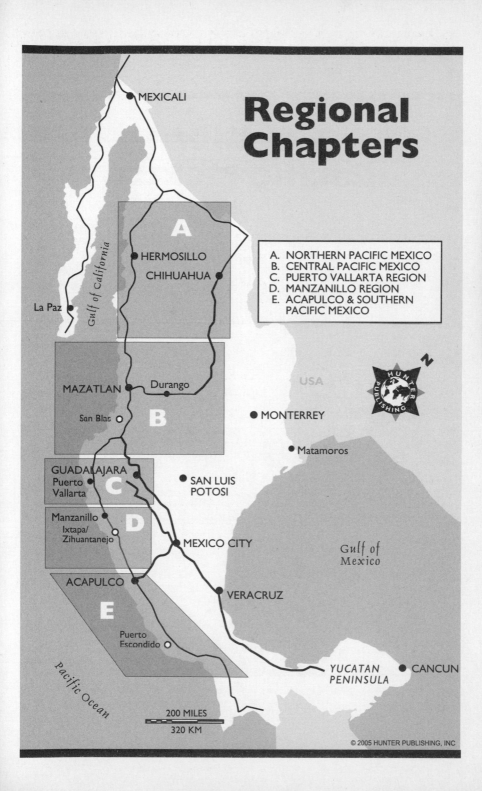

Regional Chapters

A. NORTHERN PACIFIC MEXICO
B. CENTRAL PACIFIC MEXICO
C. PUERTO VALLARTA REGION
D. MANZANILLO REGION
E. ACAPULCO & SOUTHERN
   PACIFIC MEXICO

Travel Information

MEXICALI

A

HERMOSILLO
CHIHUAHUA

La Paz

Gulf of California

USA

MAZATLAN   Durango
San Blas

B

MONTERREY

Matamoros

GUADALAJARA
Puerto
Vallarta

C

SAN LUIS
POTOSI

Manzanillo
Ixtapa/
Zihuantanejo

D

MEXICO CITY

Gulf of
Mexico

ACAPULCO

E

VERACRUZ

Puerto
Escondido

Pacific Ocean

YUCATAN
PENINSULA

CANCUN

200 MILES
320 KM

© 2005 HUNTER PUBLISHING, INC

Northern Pacific Mexico

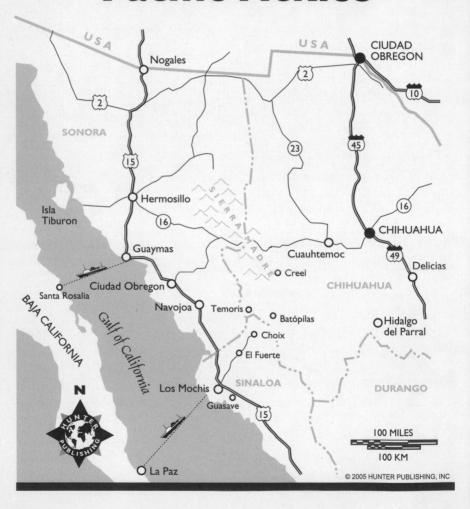

© 2005 HUNTER PUBLISHING, INC

Northern Pacific Mexico

Guaymas/San Carlos

Guaymas, also called San José de Guaymas, is set on the Sea of Cortez and is back-dropped by rust-colored mountains. This bustling port has a population of about 200,000. Just over the mountains is the town of San Carlos, with a population of about 7,000. San Carlos has more drive-down tourist traffic than any other Mexican mainland destination. It is a mere five-hour drive from Arizona and is the sister city of Mesa.

The two towns are located on a large bay with isolated beaches within walking distance of each town. San Carlos is starting to get luxury hotels, gourmet restaurants, coffee bars and discos, making a vacation here a true rest in an exotic setting. At present, 68% of the population of San Carlos is American or Canadian.

The 16 miles/24 km of highway between San Carlos and Highway 15 joins Algodones Beach, where accommodations are luxurious. The highway passes through a landscape that has desert on one side and beaches on the other. There are 2,200 palm trees lining the way. The road passes beside Tetakawi Hill, a distinct landmark between the two towns.

Because the towns are so close, I cover them together here. It is easy to get back and forth between the two, although visitors usually spend most of their time in San Carlos.

■ Getting Here

By Plane

 There are several daily flights from Phoenix, Los Angeles and Mexico City. AeroMexico, Mexicana Airlines and American Airlines fly into the Guaymas/San Carlos airport.

Note that all long-distance calls in Mexico must have the 01 before the city area code. No area code is needed when making a local call.

AIRLINE CONTACT INFORMATION		
AeroMexico	www.aeromexico.com	☎ 800-237-6639 (US); 800-021-4010 (Mx)
American Airlines	www.aa.com	☎ 800-433-7300 (US); 800-904-6000 (Mx)
Mexicana Airlines	www.mexicana.com	☎ 800-531-7921 (US); 800-509-8960 (Mx)

Taxis from the airport cost $30 for up to four people to either San Carlos or Guaymas. This is a unionized run and there is no bartering. Buses from the airport into Guaymas cost about 75¢ and pass the airport once every hour.

By Car

If driving from the US, follow the main highway, 200, from the Arizona border, just 263 miles/350 km from San Carlos. It is 325 miles/450 km from Tucson and 380 miles/600 km from El Paso. The four-lane road has four tollbooths between the border and San Carlos/Guaymas. You may pay in either US dollars or Mexican pesos, but not a mixture of the two. The cost is $3-6 at each booth, depending on the currency rates and vehicle type.

Budget, ☎ *800-527-0700*, and **Hertz**, ☎ *800-654-3001*, have offices at the airport. A small car will cost about $70 a day, plus insurance.

By Taxi

A taxi between San Carlos and Guaymas will run $15 for up to four people. It is $3 between downtown locations in either city and $6 out to Algodones Beach from San Carlos center.

> ▶▶ **AUTHOR TIP:** *In San Carlos, taxis stop operating at about 8 pm. If you need a cab after that time, ☎ 622-224-0466, in Guaymas.*

By Bus

Local buses between Guaymas and San Carlos can be caught at the Ley Shopping Center and cost a dollar. Buses are fairly new and in good condition. They run between the towns every 20 minutes from 6:30 am to 7 pm and then once every hour until 11 pm, excluding one at 10 pm. The cost is 40¢ for stops around town. Buses can be flagged down just about anywhere in either town or along the highway between the towns.

The long-distance bus station is on Calle Serdan and Guaymas Av, three blocks from the center of Guaymas. A few Greyhound buses come direct from Phoenix and Tucson. These are the only buses that travel from another country into Mexico. Buses servicing this area are **Norte de Sonora**, ☎ *622-222-1271;* **Transportes del Pacifico**, ☎ *622-222-3019;* **TUFESA**, ☎ *622-222-5453;* and **Transportes TBC**, ☎ *622-226-0006.*

By Sea

Baja Ferry, ☎ *622-222-3390*, goes from San Carlos docks to Santa Rosalia on the Baja peninsula and will carry both foot passengers and vehicles. Check to see if the ferry is running before you make the trip (it has a reputation of stopping service every now and then).

If you bring your own **boat**, see page 82 for information on arriving. For other sailing information about the San Carlos area, visit www. cruisecortez.com. This website is loaded with information for sailors and also maintains a message board.

■ History

 Originally occupied by the **Guaymenas Indians**, the area wasn't explored by **Europeans** until 1539, and the city wasn't established until the **Jesuit missionaries** came in 1617. Father Kino and Father Salvatierra worked with the tribes around 1680 and sent reports back to Spain about the natural resources in the area. This brought more adventurers.

In the early 1700s, **Captain Antonio Soto** came from Mexico City with a company of men. But they couldn't get along with locals, and the next 40 years brought nothing but rebellions and death for both groups. The Jesuits were then expelled from America and the Franciscan Fathers arrived to look after the souls of San Carlos. Due to lack of funding, they did poorly. Finally, the Spanish gave up and left the local people to themselves.

Americans were the next to invade during the Mexican War. In the early part of the struggle, the Mexicans captured two American ships, the *Eagle* and the *Reliant*, and took control of the port, although they had to contend with pirates now and then. This lasted until a French pirate by the name of **Captain Rousset** attacked the city with 400 men, in a battle that lasted four days. Once again, the locals won and they executed Captain Rousset. His followers retreated to the ocean.

The port of Guaymas became important once again during the American Civil War. At that time, it was used as a transfer post for supplies from the west coast of America, which came to Guaymas and then went overland on pack trains to Arizona, New Mexico, Nevada and Utah. After the Civil War, things didn't die down for long. The port became an important transfer post for the US Army, which was trying to stop Apache Indian attacks against settlers. Finally, the export of gold and silver from Sonora kept the place busy.

During the Mexican Revolution at the beginning of the 1900s, the port became a supply point for the famous **Francisco (Pancho) Villa** as he battled for the betterment of his people. Once all the overt fighting and greed subsided, the film industry invaded and San Carlos became an important backdrop for movies. Last came tourists, looking for something "undiscovered."

THE LIFE & TIMES OF PANCHO VILLA

Francisco Villa was born on June 6, 1878, as Doroteo Arango Arambula. He adopted his grandfather's name, Villa. His was a sharecropper family in San Juan del Rio, Durango. Francisco became responsible for his mother and four siblings after his father died. At age 16, Pancho came home one day to find his mother trying to protect his 12-year-old sister from being raped. Pancho killed the man and fled, afraid of the police. Unable to make a living, he joined the famous bandit Ignacio Parra. Pancho was arrested for numerous crimes, including the theft of mules, assault and robbery, and cattle rustling. He was sentenced to a year in the army for one crime, deserted and then went straight – sort of. Social justice seemed to be his life's ambition. He became a Robin Hood type of character, breaking up land holdings that he stole after killing the owners and redistributing them to orphans and widows. He stole cattle and traded the meat for arms to fight corrupt governments. Pancho, with his friend Emilano Zapata, became legendary in their fight during and after the Mexican Revolution. Zapata had helped Francisco Madero take control of the government, but when Madero refused to implement the land reforms he had promised, Zapata joined Pancho to fight against the ruling government under the presidency of Venustiano Carranza. Battles and struggles for power continued until, in 1920, they made peace with the government, then led by Alvaro Obregón. Villa, getting tired of battle, retired to an estate given to him by the government. But retirement was short-lived. Pancho Villa was assassinated by some of his old gang on July 20, 1923, just a year later.

■ Services

The following services are located in **Guaymas**.

Tourist Office, *Av 19 and Calle 6,* ☎ *622-224-4114, Monday to Friday, 8 am-2 pm.*

Post office, *Av 10 between Calles 19 and 20, Monday to Friday, 9 am-3 pm, Saturday till 1 pm.*

Police, *Calle 11 and Av 9,* ☎ *622-224-0104.*

The following services are located in **San Carlos**.

Tourist Office, *Calle Beltrones,* ☎ *622-226-1314, Monday to Friday, 9 am-5 pm, Saturday, 9 am-2 pm.*

Ambulance & Emergency Services, *Creston #68,* ☎ *622-226-0101;* **Fire**, ☎ *622-222-0010.*

Post office, *Calle Beltrones, next to the beauty parlor. Monday-Friday, 9 am-3 pm, and Saturday, 9 am-1 pm.*

Publications

El Imparcial, *www.elimparcial.com*, has general news in Spanish.

Cambio Sonora, *www.cambiosonora.com,* includes general news, but focuses more on events happening in the state. Spanish only.

Tribuna del Yaqui, *www.tribuna.com.mx,* has their headquarters in Obregón, so the news is focused more on the state of Sonora. Spanish.

■ Fiestas

Carnival in Guaymas follows the Italian tradition. It was started in 1888, which makes it the longest-running carnival in Mexico.

FACT FILE: The word *carnival* probably comes from the Latin medieval term *carnelevarium,* which meant abstinence from meat during Lent.

The festival is celebrated throughout Latin America for the three days before Ash Wednesday and, in some cases, it is celebrated for at least a week. Events in Guaymas include the crowning of a Carnival Queen, the Pyrotechnics Games (fire games) and colorful parades. Carnival is when breweries make a booming business – because 120,000 people come to help in the festivities and most of them drink beer.

■ Sightseeing

Walking Tour of Guaymas

Your tour should start at **San Fernando Church**, two blocks north of Av Seridan. This church, with its distinct double steeples, was built in the 1800s. It can be seen from anywhere on the bay. After touring the church, you can rest in the tree-shaded park next door before heading out for more sights.

San Fernando Plaza in the center of Guaymas has the famous statue of the Tres Presidentes (Three Presidents), located on the corner of Av Serdan and Calle 23. The statue honors three political leaders; Adolfo de la Huerta, Plutarco Elias Calles and Abelardo L. Rodriguez, all born in Sonora. Across the plaza, on Av Rodriguez, is the imposing **Municipal Palace** (City Hall) built in 1899. It still has most of its original structures. Just down from the main plaza is the neoclassic **Bank of Sonora** building constructed in the early 1900s. Also here is the **Guaymas City Jail**, built at the end of the 1800s and now being converted to a museum. Ask at the tourist office if it is completed (it was not, on my last visit).

Plaza del Pescador, located on the *malecón* (seafront) just east of the Municipal Palace by one block, has a statue of a fisherman holding his prized catch. The statue was carved from one piece of rock and it has become the symbol of the city. The *malecón* follows the bay for only a few blocks and is lined with numerous seafood restaurants. **Castro's Fish Market**, on the waterfront, is a great place to visit in the late afternoon when the fishing boats come in.

■ Adventures on Foot

Hiking

Tetakawi Hill is the double mountain you can see east of San Carlos and west of Guaymas. The name means "tits of a goat" in the Yaqui Indian language (although the Yaqui deny this). The mound is about 2,000 feet/600 meters tall. From its top, you can see the entire town, both bays, and far out to sea. A cave on the mountain has bats. Some of the plants you may encounter include the palm and saguaros cactus.

BIRD WATCH: *Birders may spot many species, such as cenzontles, woodpecker, cardinal and numerous seabirds.*

Approach Tetakawi Hill from either side and follow one of the many trails leading up and toward the saddle between the peaks. Some paths will end against a rock wall covered with scrub, while others seem to go around in circles. If you hit a non-passable wall, go back down a bit and try another trail that may go around or over the obstruction. These trails are not marked. It will take three to four hours to reach the saddle and then a little longer to climb one or both of the peaks. For the most part, the rocks and paths on the way up are solid, but the cliffs above the saddle are steep, so take care. The descent will take about two hours. Only those in good shape will reach the top. To date, the oldest person to have done this was 75 years old.

▶▶ **AUTHOR TIP:** *You should carry water with you on this hike. Wear sunscreen, a hat and long pants for the brush.*

Nacapuli Canyon is 15 minutes from San Carlos by car and, although mostly desert, it has a wet tropical climate in some parts. There are also caves and some of the rocks hide quartz crystals. The area is superb for reptiles and amphibians, and many scientists come here to find new species. The canyon may be visited on mountain bikes or horses or on foot. To get here you will need to hire some form of transportation. Directions are available from the tour office in town.

Golf

San Carlos Marina Country Club, *Domicilio Conocido,* ☎ *622-226-1116,* is between Guaymas and San Carlos. Open from 7 am to 8 pm daily, it is an 18-hole, par 72, 5,858-yard course. It was designed by Pete and Roy Dye and has Bermuda grass on both the greens and fairway. Carts are available. I have no information on green fees.

Campestre de Hermosillo Golf Club, ☎ *662-260-3095,* in the city of Hermosillo, is one hour north of Guaymas by car or bus. This is an 18-hole, par 72, 6,234-yard course. It was designed by Larry Hughes. Caddies are available, but carts are not. Call for fees.

Los Lagos Golf, *Calle Lago del Cisne #205,* ☎ *662-260-3119*, is also in Hermosillo. This is an 18-hole, par 72, 6,580-yard private course that's open to visitors. Caddies and carts are available. Green fees start at $35.

Tennis

Tennis courts are found in the bigger hotels and condo complexes. Some hotels will permit the public to play, but only if the courts are not occupied by their paying guests. There is no public court.

Bowling

Bowl San Carlos, *Plaza Los Jitos, Blvd Escenico, Km 10,* ☎ *622-226-0201*, has a number of lanes and is open daily. There is also a billiards room on site. It is in the same place as the 1910 Cantina.

■ Adventures on Water

Beaches

 Guaymas harbor is polluted due to the fact that it is an old port, used as a dumping ground long before the ecological movement got going. However, it doesn't take much of a walk along the shore to get out of the pollution and into clean waters. Near San Carlos, conditions improve tremendously.

Playa Miramar is north of Guaymas on Bacochibampo Bay and is where locals have built residences back from the water. To access the undeveloped beaches away from town, take the coastal road (not paved) and pick the cove that suits your fancy.

MOVIE SETS

Because of the beaches and complimentary sunsets, this area of Mexico has been used often by film production companies. The *Catch 22* film set, in part, is located west of San Carlos. This 1970s movie starred Alan Arkin as Captain John Yossarian and Martin Balsam as Colonel Cathcart. The set is about 900 feet/300 meters up from the beach. The old movie house is still standing, although it is not used for anything and the airplane runway is closed.

Segments of other movies have been filmed here. *The Lucky Lady*, directed in 1975 by Roger Christian, starred Liza Minelli, Gene Hackman and Burt Reynolds. *Mask of Zorro* was filmed in 1998, directed by Martin Campbell. It starred Antonio Banderas and Anthony Hopkins. Banderas stayed at the Hotel San Carlos while filming. The film *Camaroneros* was a Mexican production starring Erick del Castillo.

Playa Algodones (Cotton Beach) is also called *Catch 22* Beach because some scenes from the movie were shot here. The beach is west of San Carlos, across from San Carlos Plaza Hotel, and has miles of white sand with a backdrop of rust-colored mountains. The dunes at this beach often catch the foam from the gentle surf. The foam resembles balls of cotton, hence the name. The swells are smooth and snorkeling is good. The bay is also good for novices to try watersports, such as windsurfing.

Frenchies Cove is to the left of El Mirador RV Park. It's a nice little cove tucked in around some rocks and within easy walking distance of the center of San Carlos.

The areas to the north and south of the lagoon near Club Med (often used as a landmark) are great destinations and are often deserted.

Diving & Snorkeling

The bays offer about 800 species of sea life, 400 of which are shellfish. There is the possibility of seeing hammerhead sharks, whales, sea lions and manta rays. The temperatures seldom drop lower than 60°F/16°C and visibility ranges from 30 feet/10 meters to 100 feet/30 meters around Isla San Pedro, 17miles/25 km north of Guaymas. In spring, the large species of seaweed that grow here attract many species of fish. It is also the time when sea slugs, mantas and whales are quite active. Good dive and snorkel spots are **Window Rock** (which actually has a hole in the rock that is a great photo op) and **San Pedro Island**.

Two sunken vessels 15 miles/22 km northwest of San Carlos form an artificial reef that attracts many tropical fish, including starfish and sea anemones. One of the boats is a 120-foot/40-meter vessel and the other is a 350-foot/125-meter passenger liner called *Diaz Ordaz*. This boat is about 75 feet/25 meters below the surface, 1,500 feet/500 meters from shore. It is the largest accessible shipwreck on the western coast of Mexico.

To dive around these sites, you must have a guide. Lessons are offered in San Carlos and include everything from an introductory course at the junior age level to night dives and advanced certification by qualified instructors. A $99 special offered by El Mar includes a short classroom introduction, lessons, one ocean dive, all equipment and regulator tanks. For open-water certification, you do four ocean dives with an instructor. Classroom refresher courses included the "Scuba Tune-up" book and an ocean review (gear not included). Junior divers can take their PADI training with three pool dives and two open-water drops. Courses are available to suit almost all ages and skill levels.

Fishing

Fishing during the summer months will bring in the big-game species like marlin, sailfish, dorado and tuna. Because deep water is just a few miles offshore, even small boats go for the big fish. From late fall to spring, bottom fish are the desired catch. These include snapper, sea trout, yellowtail and the great-fighting sea bass. Winter will reward the fisher with yellowtail, grouper, pinto bass, snapper, skipjack and salmon.

Northern Pacific Mexico

WHAT & WHEN IN THE FISHING WORLD

The following list was provided by Tequila Sheila Fishing Charters.

- **January/February** – grouper, sierra, cabrilla (sea bass), barracuda, yellowtail, Pacific whitefish, red snapper.
- **March** – grouper, sierra, cabrilla and white sea bass.
- **April** – grouper, sierra, cabrilla, tortuava, dorado, skipjack tuna, white sea bass, yellowtail and red snapper.
- **May** – grouper, sierra, cabrilla, dorado, skipjack, tortuava, white sea bass, corvina, yellowtail, Pacific whitefish and red snapper.
- **June to September** – grouper, sierra, cabrilla, dorado, skipjack, corvina, sailfish, rooster and marlin.
- **October** – grouper, sierra, cabrilla, dorado, skipjack, sailfish, rooster, marlin, baracuda, yellowtail, Pacific whitefish and red snapper.
- **November** – grouper, sierra, cabrilla, yellowtail, whitefish and red snapper.
- **December** – grouper, sierra, cabrilla, baracuda, yellowtail, whitefish and red snapper.

The best place to fish is at **Rocky Point**; the marina there has 14 spaces and good inner harbor services. Trips run $35, a price that is controlled by the Fisherman's Union. The area offers catches of sole, grouper, yellow snapper, baqueta (Gulf coney), Gulf sierra mackerel and pompano. Rocky Point's huge tides (18 feet/six meters) leave mollusks and crustaceous creatures on the beach.

Tournaments

A fishing tournament is held in San Carlos every Labor Day weekend. Amigos del Sonora does the organizing; the tournament is conducted under the International Game and Fish Association rules and follows a point system. Billfish = 150 points, dorado/tuna = 1 point per pound over a minimum of 18 pounds.

The total catch entered in the competition in 2003 consisted of 38 marlin, 26 dorado and four tuna. Each year, after the weigh-ins are completed, there is a cocktail party and awards dinner, a raffle and a fund-raising auction. The tournament raised $14,000 for charity in 2002. To ensure honesty in the billfish category, a disposable camera was issued to each registered team to photograph their catch. For more information contact Bill Hammer in Mexico, ☎ 622-227-0114, www.sancarlosmexico.com/tournament.html.

For more general information about fishing in San Carlos, visit www.sancarlosbay.com/fishing.html.

The San Carlos International Billfish Tournament, ☎ *622-224-0082, 800-515-4321 (Canada & US)*, has been held for more than 50 years every July. The entry fee is $80 and the hotel host is Marina Terra, located just before Plaza las Glorias.

A **Ladies International Tournament**, ☎ *622-226-0343 or 622-226-1684*, is held every May around Mother's Day. The $50 entry fee includes dinner at the awards ceremony.

COMMON FISH	
English	**Spanish**
Tuna	*Atun*
Sailfish	*Pez vela*
Blue/black marlin	*Marlin azul / negro*
Striped marlin	*Marlin rayado*
Swordfish	*Pez espada*
Mahi-mahi	*Dorados*
Black bass	*Lobina*

Boat/Fishing Charters

La Sirena Charters, ☎ *928-925-2729 (US), www.cybertrails.com / ~jwbrown / lasirena / dive.html,* has a 34-foot Baja Power Cat with an experienced captain and crew. They supply Penn International tackle and a large assortment of lures and bait. For diving tours, they have a catamaran that cruises at 30 knots and can hold up to 14 divers and equipment. They have oxygen on board, changing facilities and freshwater showers. They run two- and three-tank dives, night dives and special trips to Tortuga Island. Bookings must be made via the US contact.

Sunset Fiesta Cruise, ☎ *622-226-1595, www.catsancar.com / musicat,* aboard *Musicat,* offers a boat for $80 an hour for one to 10 people, including crew (provided). They also run snorkeling and diving tours. The cost for a two-tank dive in the bay is $50; a trip to San Pedro Island is $75 per person. They have equipment for rent.

San Carlos Fishing Charters, *G Dock, Marina San Carlos,* ☎ *622-226-0403,* has a 24-foot/eight-meter Mako Walk Around and a 41-foot/12-meter sportsfisher with captain and crew for rent.

Surface Time, *1 edificio Villa Marina,* ☎ *622-226-1888 or 480-897-2875 (US), www.surfacetime.net,* is one block past the Marina Terra Hotel in Guaymas. This company specializes in small groups. They have a Mainship Pilot 30 that cruises at 20 knots and they offer both fishing and diving trips. They have a freshwater shower on board, a covered cockpit, and a full supply of diving gear and kayaks for rent. A two-tank dive to the island or the sunken boats is $85 and a night dive is $40 with a mini-

Northern Pacific Mexico

mum of four people. Snorkeling costs $65 for an all-day trip with a minimum of six people.

Tequila Sheila Fishing Charters, *L Dock, Marina San Carlos, no phone, www.geocities.com/fishsancarlos/*, attracts me just because of the name. They offer scuba diving and snorkeling trips, fishing trips and sunset cruises from the boat called *Tequila Sheila*. They also have ATV rentals. Stop by for rates.

Navegantes, *O Dock, Marina San Carlos*, ☎ *622-226-1448*, offers watersports and boat charters.

Sociedad Co-op Tetabampo, *L Dock, Marina San Carlos*, ☎ *622-226-0011*, does fishing tours and boat charters.

Dory Charters, *Plaza Las Glorias #12, San Carlos*, ☎ *622-226-0044*, runs fishing trips.

Cruises

Sunset Fiesta Cruise aboard *Musicat*, ☎ *622-226-1595, www.catsancar.com/musicat*, is a two-hour sunset cruise that runs daily. The $30 charge includes margaritas, beer, soft drinks, snacks and music. Children age seven-17 years pay only $15. The boat leaves at 6 pm and follows the San Carlos coastline from San Pedro Island and San Antonio Point to Miramar and Haystack Rock.

Other Watersports

Windsurfing is becoming legendary in these parts. The beach features prevailing offshore breezes that offer a long clean wave and the longest breaks on the west coast. The best seasons for this are fall, winter and spring. February is the best time, but it is also when the water is the coldest. The winds at that time are usually 15-35 knots. Kite boarding/windsurfing lessons are offered by Sonoran Sports (read my review of this company on page 105).

Kayaking around the bay and harbor of Guaymas can be done without a guide. Those looking for adventure should head north of San Carlos where the shore is rocky and dotted with caves and canyons, some with freshwater springs. This is best done with a guide (Sonora Sports has some good ones).

■ Adventures in Nature

San Pedro Nolasco Island, 17 miles/25 km northeast of San Carlos Bay, is a sea lion sanctuary. It's located in front of Las Barajitas Canyon. Because of its safe environment, San Pedro also has hundreds of birds living on it and an equal amount of fish in the waters below. The sea lions are playful and often dive under the water at your side. In the spring, gray whales pass here en route to northern waters. If you are not a diver, snorkeling is also excellent in the shallow waters near the island. The deeper waters have sheer cliffs, an underwater canyon and boulders that hide moray eels, puffer fish (that are so much fun to watch), parrotfish, manta rays and hammerhead sharks. Farther down are beautiful porcelain-like nudibranch (commonly called sea slugs) sparkling white with red trim, red sea fans, crown thorn starfish and gorgonian coral. While on the island, look for spiny-tail iguanas, whiptail lizards and side-blotched lizards.

Mirador Escenico is a bluff on the point just out of San Carlos on the way to Club Med. (*Mirador* means "lookout.") Mirador Escenico is where some scenes from *The Mask of Zorro* were shot.

BIRD WATCH: *Birders can spot some interesting species such as the brown- or blue-footed booby, Brandt's cormorants, frigates, terns and Pacific loons. Looking in the other direction toward the desert, broad-billed hummingbirds, flycatchers, orioles, and grasshopper and rufous-winged sparrows may be seen. The lagoon farther up the bay toward Club Med and less than a half-mile/one kilometer from the mirador has greater and lesser scaups, as well as ruddy ducks. Bring binoculars or a scope, as most birds are seen at a distance.*

Soldier's Estuary is near the Pilar Condos at the entrance to San Carlos Bay. It is a great spot to see numerous birds, including white herons, marine crows, doves, white-necked crows and ducks. Nearby is an oyster/pearl farm (see below).

Perlas del Mar de Cortez, *Bahai de Bacochibampo and Calle Frac. Lomas de Cortes,* ☎ *622-221-0136, www.perlas.com.mx.* This is one of the few pearl farms in the New World. The oysters were once exploited to almost extinction, but local farmers and scientists have started to revive the industry. At one time, Mexican pearls were the best in the world, but over-farming resulted in a shortage. In 2001, the farm produced about 4,000 loose pearls and 2,000 mabés (immature pearls). By the end of 2004, they hope to bring the production level up to 10,000 pearls. This farm uses the *Pteria sterna* genus, a rainbow-lipped oyster. They grow pearls that are amber, gray and purple with opalescent colors of green, blue and purple. A unique aspect of these pearls is that only about 5% are round, while the rest are oval.

The farm is associated with the university in Guaymas. There are guided tours offered every hour, Monday to Friday from 9 am to 3 pm and Saturdays from 9 am to 11 pm. No entrance fee.

Canyon Las Barajitas, 12 miles/18 km north of San Carlos, can be reached only by boat. The 2,000 acres of desert and canyon, with 1.5 miles/two km of shoreline, boasts three different ecosystems. Inside the canyon a semi-desert environment co-exists with a subtropical one. In addition to raccoons, coyotes, foxes, mountain lions and reptiles, you will see saguaros cactus, endemic to here and Arizona. If you want seclusion in a rugged sea cove, this may be your paradise. Hiking in the mountains can be done solo or with a guide, who will point out medicinal plants used for various ailments by the Seri Indians.

■ Adventures on Horseback

Horseback riding along the beach is great and there are even a few trails going off into the hills. To rent a horse for the hour or for the day, ask at your hotel or go to the stables next to the Club Med entrance located near the end of the main highway going through town toward the water. Rates are $7-10 per person, per hour and, should you need a guide, the cost for one is about $10 per hour. Also check out **Diane Smith's Riding** (see page 105), just out of town.

■ Adventure in Culture

La Pintada Cave Paintings are 43 miles/69 km north of San Carlos along Highway 15 in the National Archeological Park. The paintings depict animals and geometric designs, some with religious significance. They are set quite high on the walls, which suggests the caves at one time had water in them. To get here, take a bus going north toward Hermosillo and ask to be let off near the park. You must walk two miles/three km into the desert along a fairly well marked trail after leaving the bus. On the way you will pass a ranch. The owners speak English well enough to ask for an entrance fee and show you the way to the caves.

Club Deportivo, *www.vivasancarlos.com/deportivo.html*, is a nonprofit Mexican corporation that obtains its operational revenue through social dinners and the renting of storage units. With this money they organize things like fishing tournaments, square dancing, bingo, performing arts, hunting clubs, exercise groups and the welcome wagon. Their art league has brought together professional and amateur artists to learn from one another, offer classes and give general support. If you're an artist, touch base with these guys.

Geo Caching or **Stash Hunt**, *www.geocaching.com*, is a game for GPS users. There are caches all over the world, including San Carlos. To participate, go to the website and find out the coordinates for the cache in the city/town you are going to visit. Then, using your GPS, locate the cache. Take your loot and leave something else for others to find. Although this sounds easy, remember that the cache could be under a banana leaf or in the branch of a mango tree or in any of the trees within the 20-foot circumference, the range for GPSs. The rules are simple: take something, leave something and record it in the logbook located in the cache. Often, the items and book are inside a marked pail or container of some kind. Caches are often placed in a hidden viewpoint, an unknown campsite or some other unusual location not found in guidebooks. Suggested gifts for the cache are something like a bookmark from your town or a coin from your country.

You can start a new cache in your area. Read the rules and register online. After you set up your cache, leave the coordinates on the net and wait for visitors. Numerous languages are used for non-English speakers.

■ Outfitters/Tour Operators

Sonoran Sports Center, *Marosa Building #1 in San Carlos*, ☎ *622-226-0929, www.sailsancarlos.com*, has kayaks ($30 for half a day) and windsurfing boards for rent. They will also take you diving in the bay for $75, to the wrecks for $85 and to San Pedro overnight for $150 per person. The overnight trip is on the 40-foot/12-meter trimaran and includes three dives, use of kayaks, food and drinks (booze excluded). Full gear rental is $45. A double kayak costs $25 for half a day and $40 for a full day; singles cost a bit less. They also have new or used equipment for sale should you get hooked on one of the sports. They carry Naish Kites, Liquid Force, Sling Shot and Da Kine surf boards.

Diane Smith's Riding, **Horse Rentals and Trail Rides**, ☎ *622-226-0475 (local)* or *622-224-4776 (from the US)*, offers lessons and guided tours. I have no address for this company; all inquiries must be made by telephone.

Rent-A-Boogy, *along the main drag in San Carlos*, ☎ *622-226-0509*, has scooters, cars and vans for rent.

El Mar Dive Center, *263 Creston Av, San Carlos*, ☎ *622-226-0404, elmarmex@- prodigy.net.mx,* is open seven days a week from 7 am to 6:30 pm. They have been in business since 1963, originally working mostly with divers from Arizona. They are a five-star IDC (Instructor Development Center) and CDC (Career Development Center) agency and offer up to seven college credits for their courses. Those not certified for

Northern Pacific Mexico

diving can take lessons in one of two classrooms and use the heated pool on premises. El Mar will take you on night dives and sunken boat dives; they rent all equipment. They are PADI certified (bring your card). Their boat, the *Granny Slick*, is a 46-foot/15-meter Newton that can carry up to 36 divers and equipment for up to three dives per trip. It has a freshwater shower, camera tables and rinse buckets on deck. Lunch stops are made on Honeymoon Island. The cost of a dive is $75 with a minimum of two people, and a kayak excursion is $35 per person for three hours with a minimum of two people. The cost to rent equipment is $6 for a tank, $15 for a regulator, $12 for a wetsuit, $5 for rock boots, $1 for a snorkel, $3 for a mask and $3 for fins. They also offer a repair service if you have your own gear. For those wanting to rent a kayak and head out to the bay for a day of discovery, the cost is $30 per day and includes paddles, boat and lifejacket. This is a well-organized and competent company.

Gary's Dive Shop, *Blvd Escenico, Km 10*, ☎ *622-226-0049, www.garys-divemexico.com/index.html,* offers dive lessons, as well as numerous diving and fishing trips at various prices. They have been in business since 1971. For example, a two-tank dive with a divemaster and a minimum of eight divers to San Pedro Island costs about $85 per person. They will also do night dives. They rent all equipment on a 24-hour basis with a deposit. A scuba mask and snorkel will cost $5.50 with a $92 refundable deposit; a wet suit is $13.50 with a $520 deposit; and a Nitrox tank is $26.50 with a $422 deposit. Deposits can be made with a major credit card. They also sell old equipment at a great reduction from the purchase price. Pure air and Nitrox refills are available and a boat or shop air-fill costs $4.95.

Desert Divers, *Marina San Carlos,* ☎ *622-226-0696, www.desertdivers. com,* have dive shops here and in Tucson. In addition to diving tours, they have an equipment repair service and will find a buddy for those traveling alone. Their guides are PADI and SSI certified so they can take students with different skill levels. Free lifetime refresher courses are available after completion of any dive certification taken from Desert Divers. They are affiliated with Ocean Sports (below). For those addicted to San Carlos, they offer a free trip to San Carlos that includes two days diving and lodging at the Fiesta Hotel after you have been to San Carlos five times in 24 months and used their services each time.

Ocean Sports Scuba Center, *L-7, Marina San Carlos,* ☎ *622-226-0696, www.divecortez.com,* has a 46-foot/16-meter Newton boat and a 52-foot/18-meter DeFever live-aboard dive/fishing vessel. They also have a few pangas for small fishing charters. This company offers family excursions such as whale-watching trips, kayaking, water-skiing, wake boarding, mountain biking, hiking and horseback trips. Stop in and see them for more information. Their prices are comparable to others in the area.

■ Shopping

 Seri Indian ironwood carvings are unique and available only in this area of Mexico. Ironwood (*Olneya tesota*) is the second-heaviest wood that grows in the Americas. It likes dry areas from sea level to 2,500 feet/800 meters. The Seri have always carved things like toys, violins and yokes out of soft woods and things like musical rasps, bull roarers, yokes and oar blades from ironwood. But these were functional objects. In 1961, José Astorga made friends with an American visitor who was doing a lot of writing. José noticed that writing paper was always being blown away by the wind, so he made a paperweight. The only thing unique about this weight was that it was a bridge with reproductions of sea animals, birds, reptiles and people found around San Carlos. His friend was so impressed that he encouraged José to make more objects. José did, and eventually refined the art and expanded the subjects so that now you can get decorative items, bowls, hair barrettes, spoons and so on. José soon had more orders than he could fill, so members of his village started carving. Today, carvings are considered one of the best souvenirs a visitor can purchase. Look for them in the shops around the town.

BARTERING

The nicer the shop, the less the bartering. You will pay more, but probably get better quality. Bartering, especially in Spanish at the markets, is fun and will often reward you with not only an item you like, but improved Spanish and maybe even a friendship.

The John Ramos, *www.johnramos.com*, prints and calendars are gems to give as gifts. The prints (16 x 31 inches/40 x 75 cm) feature Mexican scenes that include donkeys or knurled trees. The script on the calendar is in English and Spanish. Prints sell for $25 each; limited-edition prints are available too, at a higher cost. John Ramos paintings are found at many of the shops in San Carlos, or you can order through the website.

Amparo Huaracheria, *El Creston #3, next to the post office in San Carlos, no phone,* has a large selection of leather sandals, some exquisite in design. They also have women's dresses, blouses and bags.

Antigua Casa Kiamy, *Main St. and Creston,* ☎ *622-226-0338,* has a lot of antique furniture that can be packaged and sent home. They specialize in antique silver.

The Bye Bye Shop, *Privada del Delfin #10,* ☎ *622-226-0022*, has a great selection of t-shirts. They also have shops in Hotel Posada and the Howard Johnson Hotel. Everyone likes t-shirts and there are some unique designs to be found here.

Northern Pacific Mexico

Casa de Palo Fierro, *Paseo del Ensueno # 156-3*, ☎ *622-226-1272*, across from the country club, has fine ironwood carvings. This is the place to get your most treasured souvenirs of Mexico. They will also do special designs for you and ship them to your house.

Kaimy Gift Shop, *M.F. Beltrones and Km 10*, ☎ *622-226-0400*, sells everything from ceramic figurines to t-shirts. They have leather bags and jewelry, clay figures and hats, ironwood carvings and bags. This is a fun place to hang out – it is air conditioned, too.

La Playa, *Creston #305*, ☎ *622-226-0503*, is where you should go for anything to do with the beach – from tanning lotion to glasses to suits.

La Tiendita, *Plaza Las Glorias and Marina Boardwalk*, ☎ *622-226-1332*, is open 9 am to 7 pm and sells beachwear and t-shirts.

Sagitario, *Villahermosa #132 and Escenico Bvd.*, ☎ *622-226-0090*, sells jewelry and fine arts and crafts. Their prices are reasonable.

■ Places to Stay

Guaymas

 When I visited, there were 24 hotels in Guaymas with a total of 1,800 beds. There are different levels of comfort; most upper-end options offer the equivalent of American standards. My suggestion is to always book only one or two nights for your vacation time and take a day to look around for something that better meets your needs. Most visitors spend their time in San Carlos. Public buses take just 20 minutes to travel between the two centers.

▶▶ **AUTHOR TIP:** *Always look for specials before making a reservation. Some deals offered on the Internet are too good to ignore.*

HOTEL PRICE SCALE
Price for a room given in US $.
$. . . . . .Up to $20
$$. . . . . $21-$50
$$$. . . . . $51-$100
$$$$ . . . . $101-$150
$$$$$ . . . . $151-$200
Anything over $200 is specified.

Del Puerto Motel, *Av Yañez #92*, ☎ *622-224-3408*, *$*, has 72 rooms in a stereotypical motel. They have private bathroom, air conditioning and satellite TV. There is free parking and the place is close to the center of town.

Flamingos Motel, *Main Highway, Km 198*, ☎ *622-221-0961*, *$$*, has 55 rooms with air conditioning and cable TV. There is a restaurant, bar and pool.

Ana Hotel, *Calle 25 #135 and Av Adolfo de la Huerta*, ☎ *622-223-3048*, *$$*, has 30 rooms that are clean and comfortable.

Impala Hotel, *Calle 21 #40*, ☎ *622-224-0922, $$,* has 58 rooms just one block from the main street (Serdan). This is not the hotel of choice; the tatters are showing. On the upside, there is air conditioning and a TV in every room.

Santa Rita Motel, *Av Serdan #590 between Calle 9 and 10,* ☎ *622-224-1617, $$,* has 40 spotless rooms with air conditioning, televisions and telephones. The place is comfortable and quiet – a good choice.

Hotel Armida, *Main Hwy, Salina North,* ☎ *622-224-3082 or 622-224-3035, $$$,* has 125 rooms with satellite TV, telephone, air conditioning and private bathroom. There is a bar and restaurant on site and parking is available. There is a gym, a pool and a tennis court, and golf is close by.

Playa de Cortes, ☎ *622-221-1047, www.hermosillovirtual.com/ganara, $$$,* is on Bacochibampo Beach, about 1.5 miles/three km west of Highway 15. This is also an RV park with 90 full hookup sites. The hotel is a two-story building with rooms set around a pool. There is laundry service and a restaurant, as well as a dock and tennis courts. Patios dotted around the property.

San Carlos

Marina San Carlos Resort, ☎ *622-226-0203, www.marinasancarlos.com,* is for those who need dock space, as long as their yacht is under 55 feet/18 meters. The resort has 340 slips with electricity, water, ramps, lockers, bathrooms, showers, radios, fax, telephones and dinghy service. The dock sizes range from 16 feet/five meters to 51 feet/17 meters. There is 24-hour security and a card key entrance to each dock. Parking is available near the marina. Unleaded fuel is available from 7:30 am to 4 pm daily. The office is open daily from 7:30 am to 5 pm. There are 30 moorings in the outer bay, protected from weather. Users have access to the dinghy dock, bathrooms and showers. The costs in 2003 were 45¢ per foot without electricity and 50¢ with; long-term stays are discounted. Moorings were $95 per month and dinghy service in the marina was $6 for each use and $9.50 from the outer bay. Visit the website for other prices on services specific to your needs.

Fiesta San Carlos, *Km 8.5 on the San Carlos Highway,* ☎ *622-226-1318, $$, fiestahotel@visto.com,* is set on the beach. It has 33 rooms with air conditioning, private bathroom and comfortable beds. There is a pool, a restaurant and a sports bar.

Los Jitos Hotel & Spa, *Paseo de Los Yaquis and Av de los San Carlos,* ☎ *622-226-0092, $$,* is past downtown San Carlos near Los Jitos Commercial Plaza, the bowling alley and the 1910 cantina. It is a motel-style, three-star hotel that has a pool, tennis courts and restaurant.

Motel Creston, *Blvd Escenico, Km 15,* ☎ *622-226-0020, $$,* is economical and clean. The 23 air-conditioned rooms are just 600 feet/200 meters

from the beach. There is a pool surrounded by trees in the treed courtyard and some of the furniture is held in place with chains so you can
count on some seats and benches being there. This is a family-owned establishment.

Hacienda del Desierto, *San Carlos #11*, ☎ *622-226-0072, $$,* is re-
ported to need a bit of spiffing up. If you happen to have your own sleep-
ing sheets and you aren't too concerned with décor, you may want to have
a look here. The rooms are inexpensive, have air conditioning and are
close to the beach.

Hotel Plaza Las Glorias, *Plaza Comercial Diez*, ☎ *662-226-1021 or
800-342-2644, $$$,* has 105 standard rooms, 18 suites and 87 deluxe
rooms with satellite TV, telephones, safe deposit boxes, hair dryers and
air conditioning. There is a restaurant, lounge and coffee shop on site.
For entertainment there is an outdoor pool, a heated pool, a Jacuzzi, a
sauna and a tennis court.

Hacienda Tetakawi, *Km 10 on the San Carlos Highway*, ☎ *622-226-
0220, $$$,* has just been redecorated. It is a Best Western hotel. Each of
the 22 rooms located on three floors has an air-conditioner, balcony, coffee
maker, hair dryer, ironing board, alarm clock, telephone and refrigerator.
The large pool is rimmed with palm trees, palapa huts and gardens. To
get here, travel along Highway 15 to the San Carlos Road and follow that
toward the ocean for six miles/nine km. The hacienda is across the road
from the ocean.

Paradiso, ☎ *622-227-0007, www.mex4fun.com/paradise.asp, $$$,* is six
miles/nine km from the center of town, tucked into the bay on Playa Los
Algodones. It is the old Club Med, a luxurious compound with 375 rooms
available for the wannabe rich and spoiled. The ranch-styled rooms sit
around an oversized pool, close to the bay. On the bay are two beaches.
There is a fitness center, nightclub, sauna, tennis area with 10 courts, a
theater, massage parlor and horse stables. You can play volleyball or bas-
ketball, push weights, kayak or snorkel. Windsurfing, scuba diving,
horseback riding, fishing and biking cost extra. Specials that include
meals and airfare allow for a luxurious vacation/rest at affordable prices.
You may want to consider this resort first.

Pilar Codominiums, ☎ *520-577-0645 or 800-868-0704, www.mexonline.
com/pilar.htm, $$$,* are privately owned and managed condos located
right on the beach near the entrance to the bay. The condos are white
stucco accented with red tile roofs, and the property is dotted with palm
trees. There is a pool, restaurant, laundry service, maid service and air
conditioning. The kitchens are furnished and have microwaves. A two-
bedroom suite that can hold six people costs around $125 a night. The
costs, of course, are dependent on the amenities, furnishings and view.
There is a two-night minimum stay. This is a good deal.

Club el Dorado, ☎ *622-226-0307, $$$,* is a privately owned condo establishment situated on the beach. It has a pool and patio, and the suites are furnished. There's a two-night minimum. I have no further information on this place except that it exists.

Sea of Cortez Vacation Club, *Paseo Mar Bermejo North #4,* ☎ *22-227-0377, www.seaofcortezrentals.com, $$$,* is a plush five-star hotel just two miles/three km from San Carlos. Its 31 rooms are located on four levels. Rooms, some of which are wheelchair-accessible, can sleep anywhere from one to six people. Overlooking the Sea of Cortez, the hotel is cozy and personal. Rooms have private patio, air conditioning, coffee maker, double bed, safe deposit box, telephone, cable TV and hair dryer. The tiled bathrooms are large. There are also studios and two-bedroom units available. The suites with kitchens are fully supplied for in-room meals.

Amenities include a heated pool, a game room, gift shop, tour desk, playground, poolside snack bar, free parking, restaurant, spa, ice machines in the halls and movie rentals. The lounge area features Spanish-style arches, soft couches, china cabinets, coffee tables, wood floors polished to a gleam and circular bar with a fireplace.

Hotel Loma Bonita, *Paseo de los Yaquis y Av de San Carlos,* ☎ *622-226-0713, $$$$,* is next to the golf course and across from the beach. The two-story hotel has 69 rooms and is tastefully designed in Mediterranean style. Condos have fully equipped kitchens and hold up to six people; they are perfect for a family. There are coffee makers, microwaves and fridges in the rooms. There is a pool, sauna, waterslide, playground and tennis court on site. This very attractive place is just eight miles/13 km from the airport.

Posada de San Carlos Hotel, *Paseo Mar Bermejo North #4,* ☎ *622-226-0077, $$$$,* is a five-star hotel with 173 rooms/suites, some wheelchair-accessible. The hotel is set right on Los Algodones Beach, which has calm water and sand dunes to hide behind when tanning. Rates range from $125 a night for a room up to $995 for the presidential suite. Suites run between $210 and $340. There are master suites, junior suites, deluxe rooms, standard rooms and the impressive presidential suite. The spacious rooms (not suites) have huge windows, writing desks, tables, bedside lamps, carpets and private, tiled bathrooms. Standard rooms have private bathrooms, satellite TV, air conditioning, mini-bars and first-class décor. There is lush vegetation decorating the courtyard and a large heated pool with a bar. The hotel also has an outdoor pool, a Jacuzzi, laundry service, child-care facilities, a bar, a lounge and two restaurants, a number of souvenir shops, two lit tennis courts and a fitness center. Next to the pool you can rent water bicycles and Jet Skis. Private parking is available. The hotel is located three miles/five km west of town off Highway 124.

Northern Pacific Mexico

FACT·FILE: The cast from the film *Mask of Zorro* stayed at the San Carlos while the movie's ocean scenes were being filmed.

Sanctuary on the Sea, *near the center,* ☎ *877-848-6124, www. sancarlosvilla.com*, is a plush villa perched on a cliff overlooking the bay. Up to 13 guests can stay here. Each room, done in heavy Spanish design, has a wood-burning fireplace and a post-and-beam ceiling. There are fruit trees shading the fountains and courtyards surrounding the property. Grass-covered palapas located in strategic positions offer good views. The décor is inviting. There is a pool, sauna, games room and reading room. There are three kitchens available for guests to use and a maid comes in four times a week. A minimum stay of two nights is required and the cost is $550 per night, $3,500 for a week. You must leave a $1,000 damage deposit. Meal service is available at a cost of $10 per hour, plus the cost of groceries and tips.

■ Places to Eat

There are more places to eat and drink than there are hotels in San Carlos and Guaymas. Below, I suggest a few of the more popular places in San Carlos, but you should explore and find more.

Evie's Simply Coffee, *across from Plaza las Glorias in the marina*, has user-friendly, crash-resistant Mac computers with Internet access. But the main reason to come here is the cinnamon buns, second to none between here and the Yukon in northern Canada. Evie's has good coffee, too.

Lung Fu's Chinese Restaurant, *across from Plaza las Glorias,* has both Chinese and international dishes. They also have Internet connection for public use. Prices for a meal run around $5.

El Arrecife, *Blvd Escenico # 156, across from the country club,* ☎ *622-226-1344,* is open 11 am to 8:30 pm. It specializes in seafood and is popular with German tourists.

El Bronco, *Blvd Escenico, Km 10,* ☎ *622-226-1130,* is open 1 pm to 11 pm. It specializes in grilled beef and salmon. The steaks are always done to perfection and the prices are reasonable.

The Beefeater, *Blvd Escenico near the Tononaka RV Park, no phone,* is a franchise that specializes in beef dishes. The restaurant carries a British motif, but don't worry about the reputation for tasteless British food. This place is good. Prices are moderate (over $5, but under $10 for a meal).

Bananas, *Creston #245 and Blvd Escenico, Km 10,* ☎ *622-226-0610*, is a good place to stop for breakfast and/or snacks. The coffee is excellent. This is a popular place with upper-crust vacationers, who arrive for late afternoon beers.

Blackies, *Blvd Escenico, Km 10.4,* ☎ *622-226-1525*, is located next to the gas station. It serves international cuisine with a Mexican touch. The specialty is seafood, which is fresh off the fishing boats. Every Wednesday features Mexican music, Mexican food and Mexican tequila at Mexican prices (about $5 for a meal).

Jax Snax, *Blvd Escenico, Km 10,* ☎ *622-226-0270*, is open 7 pm to 11 pm. Jax has the best hamburgers and pizza on the bay. Add a thick milk shake and you are ready to hike any mountain. A burger and shake will run about $4.

Piccolo Restaurant, *Calle Creston #305,* ☎ *622-226-0503*, prides itself in service. They serve Italian foods and their spaghetti with tomato sauce is spiced with lots of garlic. A glass of good Italian wine can also be had. Yum.

Pollo Feliz, *Blvd Escenico across from Kiamy,* ☎ *622-226-0111*. I find it difficult eating the happy chicken (I'd rather let him peck around the yard for a bit), but the fact is that this one is tastier than anything the Colonel ever cooked up.

Rosa's Cantina, *Calle Aurora #297,* ☎ *622-226-1000,* is open 6:30 am to 9:30 pm daily. They serve Mexican food and have daily specials. This is a popular restaurant.

San Carlos Grill, *Commercial Plaza #1,* ☎ *622-226-0509*, is open Tuesday to Sunday from 1 pm to 10 pm. Try the gringo lingo fillet or the shrimp tequila. The atmosphere matches the dish names – innovative.

■ Nightlife

Most tourists stay and play in San Carlos, so I've listed the best spots in that town.

Mexican Party Night, *held every Tuesday at the Plaza San Carlos Hotel,* ☎ *622-227-0077 (ext. 509/510),* has a lively performance of local music and dancing for $18 per person. This includes one drink.

Notche Mexicana is held at Blackies Restaurant, ☎ *622-226-1525,* every Wednesday. It features Mexican music, food and tequila.

Fiesta Bar, *Blvd Escenico, Km 8.5,* ☎ *622-226-0229,* is in the Fiesta Hotel. It is a popular bar with a quieter crowd.

Mai-Tai Bar, *Plaza las Glorias,* ☎ *622-226-0656,* is a sports bar complete with noise and funny (rowdy?) customers.

Northern Pacific Mexico

Neptunos/Ranas Ranas Discoteque, *Blvd Escenico #95, Km 8,* ☎ *622-226-0727,* is a sports bar with pool tables. The disco section has both DJs and live music. It is one of the more popular places to party. They have happy hour all week and serve the best margaritas in town. They boast that John Travolta slept here.

Tequilas Bar, *Calle Almirante and Marina Rd,* ☎ *622-226-0545,* is a very popular place to stop for a beer or two. They have live entertainment and a happy hour.

Cantina 1910, *Plaza Los Jitos, Blvd Escenico, Km 11,* ☎ *622-226-1413*, is another popular spot for a drink and a dance. There is a disco and live entertainment. When you've had enough of that you can go across to the bowling alley and pool hall located in the same building at Plaza los Jitos.

Ciudad Obregón & the Yaqui Valley

O bregón is a bird-hunting area that has hundreds of thousands of acres reserved for the sport. It is also a popular home base for fishing excursions. The city itself, with a population close to a million, has every amenity you could possibly want, from good international food to comfortable accommodations. The fishing lodges, too, are worth looking at.

■ History

 The city is named after **Alvaro Obregón**, an active member of the Mexican Revolution who lived from 1880 to 1928. The area along the Yaqui River was originally part of Yaqui Indian territory. The Jesuit missionaries were the first Europeans to settle in the area. They were soon followed by gold seekers and then by farmers.

Alvaro Obregón was born near Alamos, and when his father died, his family went to live with the Mayo Indians. After he grew up and was building his armies, many of Obregón's men were Mayo and Yaquis Indians. His claim to fame came when he joined forces with Pancho Villa and, together, they overthrew an unpopular leader by the name of Huerta. The monument to Alvaro Obregón is on the site where he was killed.

■ Festivals

June 24 brings the most interesting festival in the area. This is when everyone goes to the Yaqui River for a bath, in the custom of the Yaqui Indians. After your bath, you can celebrate.

■ Sightseeing

Obregón

Yaqui Museum, *Calle Allende and 5 de Febrero, Monday to Friday, 8 am-6 pm,* has a collection of ethnological objects, including historical photos, costumes, household utensils and a reproduction Yaqui dwelling. You can buy handmade items from locals.

Monument of Alvaro Obregón, *Calle Arenal and Abasolo in San Angel (a suburb).* This is where Obregón was assassinated by Leon Toral and Conchita, who is credited with planning the plot. The monument is in the place where the famous restaurant called the Light Bulb was located. The restaurant was frequented by politicians and the rich and is where Obregón was killed.

The church and monastery of El Carmen, built in 1615 in the churrigueresque style, is on the main plaza.

■ Adventures on Foot

Duck/Dove Hunting

From early November to mid-March, this area is known for its two million pintail, gadwall, green, cinnamon and redhead ducks, canvasbacks, Pacific-black brants and widgeons. There are 16 species in all, along with white-winged doves, a major draw for hunters.

Gabino's hunting area (see page 117) has an extensive network of man-made and natural blinds, accessed each morning by hunters in airboats. Decoys are set by the staff. Gabino has access to hundreds of thousands of acres of duck- and dove-shooting habitat that is managed in an environmentally sound manner. He also has experienced guides and spotters.

Golf

Club de Golf Obregón, ☎ *644-418-0044,* is an 18-hole course, five miles/eight km out of town along the main highway. Call for rates and reservations.

■ Adventures on Water

 Oviachic Dam, or Presa General Alvaro Obregón, is a recreation area 18 miles/24 km north of Obregón where you can camp, sail, fish and water ski. Oviachic Recreational Park, with the Sierra Madres standing guard in the distance, has grills, games and a large parking lot. To get here, take a bus from the center of town. The big fishing catch is the wide-mouth bass that run from three to eight pounds. The re-stocked lake is shallow, with rocky points, creeks and underwater islands with steep drop-offs. See Gabino's (below) for boats and guides if you would like to fish.

Nainari Lagoon is on the outskirts of the city and is accessible by bus from the center of town. It has a park for picnics, plus a children's zoo.

■ Adventures in Nature

 Isla Huivulai is 30 miles/45 km southwest of Obregón along a five-mile/eight-km stretch of coast that offers excellent birding. The island acts as a barrier that forces mud to collect near the shore, creating the Estero Tobari (Tobari Estuary) which, in turn, has led to mangroves and mudflats around the lagoon. Sand dunes can be found on the beaches between the lagoon and the ocean.

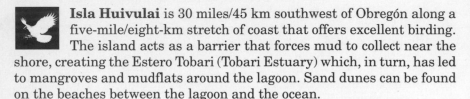
FACT FILE: The name *huivulai* means "long neck" in the Mayo language. The long neck refers to the shape of the island, which measures 10 miles/17 km long and one mile/1.6 km at its widest.

Walking along the mainland is enough, but taking a boat to the island makes the trip spectacular. There are frigates and terns, Swainson's hawks, boobies, turnstones, spoonbills, skimmers, waders, pelicans, cranes and gulls all around. What draws the birds are the shrimp, which thrive in the muddy plain. There are organizations, such as COBI (Comunidad y Biodiversidad) and AWA (Alamos Wildland Alliance) trying to manage the growth of both the estuary and shrimp populations. The freshwater well here is about 300 feet/100 meters deep. Its water enhances the growth of date palms in the vicinity. The entire area is protected by the government.

You will need to hire a car to get here. Follow 5 de Febrero out of town and turn toward the ocean (west) and to the left (south).

■ Outfitters/Tour Operators

Gabino's Yaqui Valley Hunting and Fishing Resorts, *1305 N. Grand Av, # 415, Nogales AR,* ☎ *644-415-0621, or Sinoloa and Yaqui #826, Obregón,* ☎ *614-413-4648, www.frankruiz.biz,* has probably the most luxurious operation for hunters and anglers in the country. Frank Ruiz, guide and tour operator for more than 20 years, goes out twice a day on guided hunts. The price includes your gun permit, Mexican hunting license, one case of shells and the use of his shotguns. Your luxury accommodations are in a hunting lodge with stuffed trophies enticing you to do better. Three gourmet meals a day are served and all beer and soft drinks are included. Frank even throws in an evening cocktail if you would like one. The cleaning and packing of game and all ground transportation after you arrive in Obregón, Guaymas or Los Mochis is included in the price, but please bring your own ice chests if you are planning on taking home your catch.

Anglers should bring gear that includes 6-6.5-foot/two-meter bass rods with 17-20# test line, as well as lures; recommended lures are eight-inch/25-cm plastic worms in black, red shad, motor oil and tequila sunrise. Also bring crank baits and rattle traps in fish colors, plus white and chartreuse spinner baits and jigs.

Frank has a number of packages that offer everything from duck hunting alone to duck, dove, quail hunting and bass fishing. All-inclusive trips run $2,255 to $3,200.

▶▶ **AUTHOR NOTE:** *Although I am against any type of hunting, I have included this information for those who think differently than me. I have been told that the hunting here is being scientifically managed, so over-hunting does not occur.*

Mark Pretti Nature Tours, *2915 Keeling Rd, Hereford AZ,* ☎ *520-803-6889, www.markprettinaturetours.com,* runs guided educational tours in Sonora, San Blas and Oaxaca. These bird specialists will do custom tours for individuals or families and they have environmental education programs for children. Mark also has an interest in natural history, conservation and identification of plants and knowledge of ecological relationships between species. He is a trip leader for both the Southwest Wings Birding and the Huachuca Audubon Society. He also has a degree in zoology. His trips are limited to eight persons and cost under $1,700 for 10 days. Mark also works with Bird Treks from the United States, www.birdtreks.com.

■ Shopping

 The things to shop for in the area are cotton weavings, straw baskets and pottery. Because tourism isn't a huge draw, there aren't the stalls and market shops that are found in tourist towns. However, if you enter any of the better shops, especially those in big hotels, you will be able to find something that you like.

■ Places to Stay

Remember, no area code is needed for local calls.

Hacienda La Escondida, *Sinoloa & Yaqui #826,* ☎ *644-413-4648, www.frankruiz.biz,* has seven bedrooms with bathroom, a lounge area, bar, dining room, exterior patio, satellite TV, Jacuzzi, telephone and Internet access. This is an all-inclusive resort. See Gabino's, page 117, for prices.

HOTEL PRICE SCALE
Price for a room given in US $.
$....................Up to $20
$$....................$21-$50
$$$....................$51-$100
$$$$.............$101-$150
$$$$$.............$151-$200
Anything over $200 is specified.

Posada San José, *Calle Veracruz # 413 South,* ☎ *644-415-1600, $,* is a basic place that is clean and in a good area.

San Alfonso, *Calle Chihuahua #425 South,* ☎ *644-415-0221, $,* has 58 rooms with private bathroom. There isn't much luxury here, but it's good value.

Continental, *Calle Chihuahua #628 South,* ☎ *644-414-7966, $$,* is 1½ blocks down from the Alfonso and has 21 rooms with private bathroom.

Kuraica, *Calle 5 de Febrero #211 South,* ☎ *644-415-1744, $$,* has 32 rooms and a three-star rating.

San Jorge, *Av Miguel Aleman #929,* ☎ *644-414-0040, $$,* is a three-star property with 90 rooms.

Suites Colonial, *Calle Tlaxcala #203,* ☎ *644-414-0187, $$,* is another three-star hotel with 13 rooms in all. This is a tiny but comfortable place. Every room has private bathroom and is clean.

Cuenca del Sol, *Av Miguel Aleman #141,* ☎ *644-414-1144, $$$,* is a four-star hotel with 24 rooms, air conditioning and private bathrooms. It is clean and comfortable and not a bad deal for the price.

Santa Ines, *Calle Veracruz #261, 644-413-6397, $$$,* has 15 rooms with private bathroom and air conditioning.

Ciudad Obregón Hotel, *Travelodge Hotel, Jalisco Norte #350 and Morelos,* ☎ *644-414-5044, $$$,* is a fairly new four-star hotel. There is a pool, restaurant, bar, laundry service and business center. Each room will hold up to three people, has air conditioning, cable TV and a hair dryer in the bathroom.

Motel Costa de Oro, *Av Miguel Aleman and Allende # 201 North,* ☎ *644-414-1775, $$$,* is a Days Inn chain hotel in the center of town. Each of the 145 rooms, located on three floors, has air conditioning, cable TV, desk, ironing board and iron, coffee maker and balcony and is wheelchair-accessible. There is also a coffee shop, hot tub, lounge, outdoor pool and restaurant. Safe deposit boxes and free parking are available.

Holiday Inn, *Av Miguel Aleman and Tetabiate,* ☎ *644-414-0940, $$$$,* has 135 rooms that offer no surprises for anyone who has stayed in other Holiday Inns. The rooms have coffee makers, irons and boards, air conditioning and mini-bars. There is free parking, a lounge and a restaurant.

San Jorge de Obregón, *Av Miguel Aleman # 929,* ☎ *644-414-4353, $$$$,* is a Best Western hotel that has rooms with air conditioning, TV and telephone. There is a restaurant and bar, pool and free parking.

Nainari Valle Grande, *Av Miguel Aleman and Tetabiate,* ☎ *644-414-0940, $$$$$,* has rooms with air conditioning, private marble bathrooms, cable TV, writing desks and tiled floors. There is a restaurant and pool.

Valle del Yaqui, *Av Miguel Aleman and Cajeme,* ☎ *644-414-1300, $$$$$,* is a five-star hotel with 86 rooms that have air conditioning, TV, telephone and private bathroom with hot water. There is a pool.

■ Places to Eat

Los Molinos Restaurant, *Av Miguel Aleman and Allende # 201 North,* ☎ *644-414-1775,* in the Costa de Oro Motel, serves breakfast from 7 to 10 am, lunch from noon to 4 pm and dinner from 7 to 11 pm. They specialize in steaks and seafood.

Sport Race Bar, *Av Miguel Aleman and Allende # 201 North,* ☎ *644-414-1775,* also in the Costa de Oro Motel, is open Tuesday to Sunday, 10 am to 2 am. They have music, Karaoke, and happy hour every day.

Navojoa

If the city of Obregón is too big and busy for you, maybe Navojoa, with its 200,000 people, will be more attractive. It has a couple of hotels, some non-descript restaurants, a university, theaters and a horse track close by.

■ History

It was the Mayo Indians who first lived in this valley beside the Mayo River. Outsiders came later, and it took until 1923 for the settlement to grow into a city.

✤ **LOCAL LINGO:** *The word* navojoa *means "house of the prickly pear" in Mayo language.*

Don Diego de Guzman came to the area for the first time in 1533 and was followed in 1593 by **Captain Diego Martinez de Hurdaide**, who fought with and conquered the Mayos. Then came the **Jesuits** in 1610, who left just over half a century later. The town remained a sleepy little place until the Spanish settled in the area in the 1700s.

■ Adventures on Water

Beaches

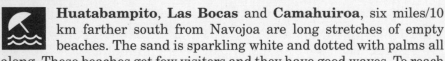

Huatabampito, **Las Bocas** and **Camahuiroa**, six miles/10 km farther south from Navojoa are long stretches of empty beaches. The sand is sparkling white and dotted with palms all along. These beaches get few visitors and they have good waves. To reach them, take a bus from Navojoa to Huatabampo and then another from there to the beach of your choice. While in Huatabampo, visit the Municipal Palace, built in 1928. Purchase water and something to eat before heading down to the beaches. Those with camping equipment and a car can find secluded spots to spend a few days/weeks.

■ Adventures in Nature

Turtle Island Peace Camp, *40 miles / 60 km south of Navojoa at Melchor Ocampo, www.geocities.com / navopatia / welcome. html, islat_mx@yahoo.com,* is three miles/ 4.5 km off the highway. This outdoor education program offers language study, solar energy outreach, organic agriculture and natural construction. They do kayaking, birding and ecological studies. The camp has a communal kitchen and five palapa huts that can accommodate 20 people. If they are full, stays can be arranged in neighboring places. TIPC offers workshops in weaving and dyeing of materials, star-gazing, or any activity that falls under the "cross-cultural exchange" umbrella. The camp has a dozen small watercraft that visitors may use for a cost of a few dollars per hour. You can stay one night, a week, or forever. People come from as far away as Switzerland to watch for birds and study solar technology. The cost is

$15 per person, per night, including basic board. There are many places to camp. Stay awhile and you'll meet Gracie the gray dolphin, who has hung out near the camp for the past eight years.

To get here, take a bus to El Carrizo. From there, catch a bus to Estacion Don and another to Juan Escutia. From there it is a three-mile/4.5-km walk to Melchor Ocampo. Ask for Kenny or Maggie. From Navojoa, take the bus directly to Juan Escutia or an Autoverdes bus to Melchor Ocampo. Los Mochis is 38 miles/60 km to the south.

■ Places to Stay

Best Western Hotel del Rio, *Pesqueira Prolongacion Norte (one mile/1.5 km from town near the Mayo River Bridge)*, ☎ 642-422-0331, *$$$*, is a new hotel with an attractive patio and pool that has resident parrots. The hotel features a gift shop, ice machines, cable TV, tennis courts, spa, restaurant and bar. The rooms are spacious, with mini-fridges and air conditioning,

HOTEL PRICE SCALE	
Price for a room given in US $.	
$.	Up to $20
$$.	$21-$50
$$$.	$51-$100
$$$$	$101-$150
$$$$$	$151-$200
Anything over $200 is specified.	

El Rancho Motel, *Main Highway, Km 1788*, ☎ 642-422-3231, *$$*, is along Carratera Internacional. Each spacious room has TV, telephone, mini-bar and private bathroom. There is a pool, bar and restaurant on site and the motel is wheelchair-accessible.

■ Places to Eat

Restaurant Los Arcos, *in the Best Western Hotel (see above)*, ☎ 642-422-0331, serves national and international foods (no surprises) at reasonable prices. Otherwise, choose any restaurant around the square in the center of town.

Copper Canyon

Although Copper Canyon is not actually along the western coast of Mexico, the starting point of the rail line that gets you to the canyon (Los Mochis) is. Many visitors to Pacific Mexico also visit the canyon. Its landscape is dramatic. For general information about Copper Canyon, visit www.coppercanyon-mexico.com.

This area is for those who want a mix of hiking, biking, climbing and rafting with their surfing, ocean kayaking and wildlife viewing. Also for those with anthropological interest, the Tarahumara tribes (semi-nomadic cliff dwellers) are interesting.

There are a number of ways to explore this area. You can join a tour company that does everything for you except click your camera or you can make your own arrangements. You can buy a train ticket and stop at the towns along the way or you can join a tour. If you are more an observer than explorer, then riding the train is your best bet. If you want to see all the most exciting places in the area, it will take up to two weeks on a guided tour. If you want to explore the area extensively, you'd better get immigrant status when you enter Mexico.

Copper Canyon (Barranca del Cobre) is the name of only one canyon out of six found along this strip of landscape. The six canyons have more than 200 gorges, four of which are over 1,000 feet/300 meters deeper than the gorges of the Grand Canyon in Colorado. The correct name for this collective group of canyons and gorges is the **Sierra Tarahumara**, named after the indigenous group who has lived here for centuries. The Sierra Tarahumara encompasses an area of 25,000 sq miles/64,000 sq km. Some of the lodges found along the way are perched one mile above the river (Uno Lodge, page 156, and Hotel Barrancas Divisadero, see page 157). The rivers swell each spring as they drain the snow-capped peaks and hack their way into the bedrock.

The dramatic landscape holds alpine lakes and is dotted with Ponderosa pine and oaks that are hundreds of years old. The rivers have enormous waterfalls that plunge through sub-tropical vegetation into the gorges below. The area has almost 300 species of birds and 90 species of reptiles, as well as bear, deer and mountain lions.

The people of this region are shy and gentle, living quietly as subsistence farmers growing vegetables, sugarcane, fruits and corn. The men of the Tarahumara (also called Raramuri) tribes are known for their running ability and often give displays of their skill. Some can run non-stop for over 100 miles.

FACT FILE: Tarahumara men were hired by Nike one year to run a marathon wearing Nike shoes. The men were miserable in the enclosed footwear and were losing the race. They dumped the Nikes for their own rubber-tire sandals and passed their opponents.

Chihuahua al Pacifico Railroad

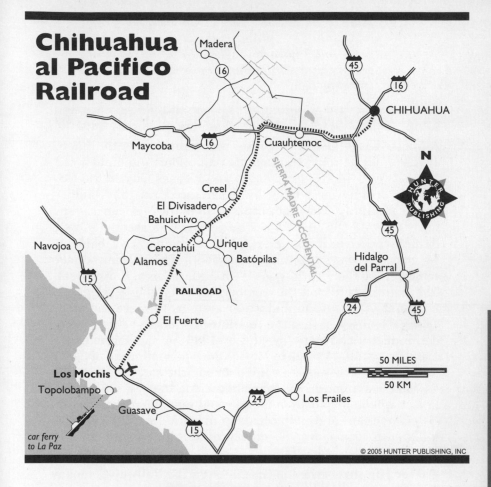

Madera
16
45
16
CHIHUAHUA
Maycoba
16
Cuauhtemoc
N
SIERRA MADRE OCCIDENTAL
Creel
El Divisadero
Bahuichivo
45
Navojoa
Cerocahui
Urique
Alamos
Batópilas
Hidalgo del Parral
15
RAILROAD
24
45
El Fuerte
50 MILES
50 KM
Los Mochis
Topolobampo
Guasave
24
Los Frailes
15
car ferry to La Paz

© 2005 HUNTER PUBLISHING, INC

Chihuahua al Pacifico Railroad

The most popular way to access the area is via the **Chihuahua al Pacifico Railroad** that goes from the sea at Los Mochis, through Creel, to the highlands of Chihuahua 395 miles/650 km away, passing through five climate zones and land as high as 8,000 feet/2,400 meters. You can stop along the way and do day hikes around canyon rims or you can hire a guide and do longer backpacking hikes into the deep gorges.

The best time to visit is in the fall, after rainy season and once the rivers have subsided. (Rainy season is July through September and the rivers subside by mid-October.) Although it is warm in the lower canyons, November to March can bring snow at the higher elevations.

▸▸ **AUTHOR NOTE:** *The section between Creel and Chihuahua is not very interesting for landscape and I have not included it in the book. If going on to Chihuahua, many people opt to travel by bus.*

CHIHUAHUA AL PACIFICO RAILROAD HISTORY

Albert Kinsey Owen came to Topolobampo from the US in 1872 so that he could create a utopian colony and build a rail line between the coast of Mexico and Kansas City in the US. Owen's dream was shared by experienced rail line builder **Cyrus Holliday**. They got a contract from the Mexican government to build the line. Once the permit was secured, Owen formed the **Credit Foncier Club**, a co-operative bank in which people wanting to become members of his utopian society could deposit their worldly goods (in the form of cash, of course). The dream was to have the members build a rail line, telegraph communication system and water systems to serve the area. Owen also insisted that the commune members believe in order, industry and courtesy, and by 1886 he had attracted 27 members. After 15 years in Mexico, he had a following of 2,000 members. But dissension spread among the congregation and an American named Ben Johnson decided that he and his followers who had split from Owen could make money in sugar. He planted cane and built a canal from Los Mochis to El Fuerte, a distance of just over 80 miles/120 km. The commune disbanded completely by 1900.

Foster Higgins of the Rio Grande & Pacific Railway Company took up Owen's dream and secured a contract and some money from the Mexican Government. He completed a line from Ciudad Juarez to Casas Grandes in Chihuahua state before running out of money. Enrique Creel saw the potential and continued the line as far as La Junta. This took until 1914. The Mexican Revolution that same year put a halt to all construction. By 1928 a line from El Fuerte to the coast was complete, but there was still over 150 miles between El Fuerte and Creel, the most difficult part, to be connected. No one seemed to have the money or the engineering skill to attempt this. It wasn't until the Mexican government took over the rail lines in 1940 that construction was again started to join the two sections. Finally, in 1961, just 90 years and 90 million dollars later, the 408 miles/600 km of track that passes through 86 tunnels and over 37 bridges was completed.

To learn more about the Chihuahua al Pacifico Railroad, check out the *Recommended Reading* section, page 486.

■ The Ride

The first hour after leaving the Pacific Ocean is uneventful, passing calm lakes and tiny villages. This allows you to have a coffee and wake up before the scenery begins. The drama starts shortly after El Fuerte with a run over the Chinapas Bridge that spans the river for 1,837 feet/560 meters. After the bridge, the grade

STATION STOPS & ELEVATIONS	
Los Mochis	300 feet/100 meters
El Fuerte	300 feet/100 meters
Témoris	3,600 feet/1,100 meters
Bahuichivo	5,250 feet/1,600 meters
Divisadero	7,550 feet/2,300 meters
Ojitos	8,200 feet/2,500 meters
Creel	7,900 feet/2,400 meters
Chihuahua	6,600 feet/2,000 meters

increases to 2.5% and continues like this for the next six hours as it winds through **Septentrion Canyon**. It snakes its way through other canyons and gorges, continuously gaining elevation. As the train climbs and circles, one often emerges from a tunnel believing that the train will plunge over the edge into the abyss below. The longest tunnel on the run, at **Chépe**, goes 5,966 feet/1,818 meters through the mountain. The second bridge, at the village of **Chinipas**, is only half as long as the one at El Fuerte, but it is 1,165 feet/355 meters above water. Note the railcar graveyard below. At **La Pera**, near Temoris, the track winds up a cliff face and enters a tunnel, where it makes a 180° turn while continuing up the mountain to a plateau 3,075 feet/937 meters above the canyon floor.

From Témoris, the train passes the mission towns of **Bahuichivo** and **Cuiteco**, both established in the late 1600s. By mid-afternoon the train arrives at **Divisadero**, where it stops for 15 minutes so passengers can get out and walk to the rim of the canyon. The canyon walls drop over 6,000 feet/2,000 meters and the opposite wall is 10 miles/15 km away. From this spot you can see the dramatic change in the color of the landscape and view how the canyons seem like a network of electrical wires, splaying out from one another from a thick cable at one end and a delta at the other.

Northern Pacific Mexico

FACT FILE: The change in elevation on this route is so extreme that you can see pine trees at the top, tropical jungle in the middle and desert at the bottom. The temperature difference between the top and bottom is about 25°F/ 14°C. It has been said that summer rain usually evaporates before hitting the bottom.

Between Divisadero and Creel the train passes the **Urique**, **Copper** and **Tararecua canyons**. Tararecua Canyon includes Piedra Volada (Flying Stones), a popular hiking destination. The train ride has 80 tunnels and 30 bridges.

▪ Organized Tours

The **Chihuahua al Pacifico Railway**, ☎ *614-439-7210 or 888-484-1623, www.chepe.com.mx (shows times and rates)*, is usually called the Chépe (CHAY-pay). It starts in Los Mochis, but most people get on at El Fuerte because the train leaves there at a more reasonable time of morning and the first section between Los Mochis and El Fuerte isn't very interesting. The train continues to Chihuahua in the east and offers first- and second-class trains once a day. By starting in El Fuerte, you will see more canyons during daylight hours. Take a seat on the south (right) side of the train for the best views. This train line was privatized in 1998 and is one of only two passenger trains still operating in Mexico. Both travel classes are air-conditioned. First-class seats are softer and recline. The aisles are carpeted. But second-class travel is also comfortable. First-class trains stop only at places of interest to tourists, whereas second-class trains may stop anywhere from 15 to 60 places along the way and, of course, take a few hours longer. The trains leave from either end around 6 or 7 am daily and arrive at their destination at 8 or 9 pm. You may purchase tickets ahead of time at the station or on the train. You pay only to your destination (rather than the entire distance), but if you get off before Chihuahua (except at Divisadero, where there is a 15-minute break to walk to the rim of the canyon), you are not allowed back on for 24 hours. There are numerous passenger cars, one dining car, one lounge car and bathrooms on each train. A first-class ticket from Los Mochis is $85; second class is $45.

Banana Fish Tours, *2609 Grant #C, Redondo Beach, CA 90278,* ☎ *800-462-6773 or 508-264-5078, www.traintraveling.com/latam_carib/ latamcarib_tours.html (click on Banana Fish Copper Canyon)*, offers a five-day trip from Los Mochis or El Fuerte to Creel and back. The cost is about $150 a day, all-inclusive. They have a private passenger car that allows for open-air viewing without obstructions. If you don't want the wind in your hair, you can sit in the lounge, enjoy a drink and watch the scenery out of the panoramic windows. If quiet contemplation is what you need while passing through this landscape, head for the comfortable sitting area. This company is reported to have the largest windows of all the trains running this line. The train travels at 25 mph/40 kmh, so you can take moving pictures. A knowledgeable guide is provided. There are a few options with this company as to length of trip and places visited. Give them a call or e-mail. I found them exceptionally cooperative and helpful.

Sierra Madre Express, *PO Box 26381, Tucson AZ, 85726-6381, ☎ 800-666-0346, www.sierramadreexpress.com*, was founded by Peter Robbins in 1986. Peter's company offers soft adventure with a feeling of security. His trips start in Tucson and you travel by van and train through the canyon and back again. The company has five historical cars that have been restored and upgraded to today's standards. The Arizona Car, built in 1946 by Pullman, was used by the Northern Pacific between Chicago and Seattle until the mid-1950s. This is now the lounge car that has a glass observation area. It can also hold 22 guests in the four compartments that have both upper and lower berths, with a sink and a toilet in each compartment. The Chile Verde has the same history as the Arizona except, after it ran from Chicago to Seattle, it was purchased by the Chicago, Burlington and Quincy before it went to the Sierra Madre. This car has little roomettes for single guests; the rooms do not have bathroom facilities. The Ing. Ballesteros car was built in 1949 and used by the Union Pacific as a baggage car. It has been remodeled to hold eight staterooms that have lower berths and private bathrooms. The Divisadero was built in 1949 by the American Car and Foundry Co. and has an open-air observation section where passengers can take great photos. There are also eight staterooms with lower berths and private toilets in this car. The Tucson was built in 1965 and was used by Amtrak and later by the Entertainment line as a dinner car in Maryland. The all-inclusive (including drinks), one-week trip from Tucson is $3,400 per person, based on double occupancy. The trip includes four nights in first-class hotels along the way. Sierre Madre offers a substantial discount if you can pay six months in advance. They have over a dozen trips a year with some special tours like the New Year's Tour.

Canyon Travel, *900 Ridge Cr, Bulverde, TX 78163-2872, www.canyontravel.com*, are the people to use if you want to go first class. Once you arrive in Los Mochis, they wine, dine and entertain you. They have special birding treks and a waterfall hike that is superb. Their secluded eco-friendly lodges are comfortable. They offer many options, such as the seven-day Western Canyon Expedition that starts in Los Mochis. It spends one day exploring the colonial town of El Fuerte, where a Spanish fort and the Camino Real (not the hotel chain, but a historical cobbled road) are located. Sadly, the recent road construction has destroyed some of the Camino Real, making hiking and horseback riding trips less pleasurable. The second day includes a boat trip down El Fuerte River to some Nahuatl petroglyphs.

 BIRD WATCH: *On the way down the river, birders may spot a bare-throated tiger heron, a rufous-bellied chachalaca or a social flycatcher.*

Participants watch a performance of the traditional Dance of the Deer, get to see the deepest gorge in the area, and hike to secluded waterfalls. The accommodations are all first class and the meals, which include wine or beer, are gourmet. For a mere $200 a day, you will be treated like Aztec royalty. After you have booked your trip and given a deposit, this company sends its clients a 100+ page book describing the area.

Copper Canyon Guides, *www.coppercanyonguide.com,* ☎ *406-587-3585 in Montana,* is a cooperative of Tarahmuara guides who work with Santiago Tours. The guides know the backcountry and will take you hiking, horse riding or canyoning. For the canyoning trips, you must have experience and your own gear as the travel is considered difficult. They will travel into Batópilas, Urique, Sinforosa and Oteros canyons and have pack animals for hire. They like to take children, especially on the Batópilas-to-Urique hike. For a village home-stay visit, contact Martha Garcia in Norogachi or call Santiago Tours. If you are in one of the villages where the hikes start (Batópilas, Urigue, etc.), you can usually find these guides and join their group. Ask at the local tourist office.

Buses also pass through parts of the area and are the best way to get from Creel to Chihuahua or from one village to another. There is no road that goes all the way from Creel to El Fuerte, as the train does, but there is one that goes from Creel to Cuiteco, just south of Divisadero. First- and second-class buses are available. The fare from Creel to Chihuahua is about $15 per person.

NIGHTLIFE IN THE CANYON

Nightlife in any of the Copper Canyon towns is what you make yourself. Find a place that serves the drinks you like, sit beside someone who looks/sounds interesting and hang out. You could also use this time to rest up before hitting an area (like Mazatlan) with a more lively nightlife. If camping, buy a bag of beer and sit around your tent watching the other campers walk by. In Creel, you can always hit the bike-race people; they know where everything is.

Los Mochis

Located 10 miles/16 km from Topolobampo on the Pacific Ocean, the town of Los Mochis was founded in 1894 by Ben Johnson, an American farmer who came to Mexico in search of a better life. He worked, cultivated land, grew sugarcane and eventually started the Ingenio Azucarero (Sugar Mill) that is still in operation today. The town has wide streets lined with palms, and is home to almost half a million people, many of them Tarahumara Indians.

> ✤ **LOCAL LINGO:** *The name* Los Mochis *means "Place of the Land Turtles" in the Tarahumara Indian language.*

Most travelers don't spend much time in Los Mochis, preferring to head out to El Fuerte. However, if you are interested in shrimp fishing, the nearby town of Topolobampo will attract your attention.

> ✤ **LOCAL LINGO:** *Tarahumara Indians call themselves the Raramuri people, which means "men of light feet." It was the Spanish who called them Tarahumara, after the mountains they live in.*

The highly religious Tarahumara people were introduced to the Catholic faith through the Jesuits, who lived in the area for about 150 years. After they were expelled in 1767, the Indians modified the religion to suit their tastes. This blending of faiths can be enjoyed during festivals such as Semana Santa.

> **FACT FILE:** Tarahumara men at one time played a game where opposing teams raced a distance of about 60 miles/100 km, all the while kicking a ball ahead of them. Their running abilities were so refined that, while hunting, they could run down deer.

▪ Getting Here

By Plane

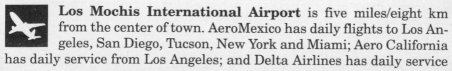

Los Mochis International Airport is five miles/eight km from the center of town. AeroMexico has daily flights to Los Angeles, San Diego, Tucson, New York and Miami; Aero California has daily service from Los Angeles; and Delta Airlines has daily service from all major US cities. A taxi from the airport to the town center costs about $5.

AIRLINE CONTACT INFORMATION		
Aero California	www.aerocalifornia.de	☎ 800-237-6225 (Mx)
AeroMexico	www.aeromexico.com	☎ 800-237-6639 (US); 800-021-4010 (Mx)
Delta Airlines	www.delta.com	☎ 800-241-4141 (US); 800-123-4710 (Mx)

■ Getting Around

By Car

 You can rent a car at the airport or at the larger hotels in town. If you book ahead, be certain to bring all documentation and proof of quotes with you. **Budget,** ☎ *800-527-0700,* and **Hertz,** ☎ *800-654-3001,* both have offices at the airport.

By Bus

Buses go to El Fuerte (every hour), leaving from Zaragoza and Ordoñez streets, and to Guaymas (four a day) from the Transporte de Sonora station 10 miles/16 km from the center of town. The cab fare out to this station is $5; city buses cost much less. You can catch a city bus at any bus stop along the main street. This is not a huge city, so finding a bus is not difficult.

By Taxi

Taxis come in two colors, green and yellow. The green are cheaper and supposed to be more ecologically sensitive. What this means, I am unsure.

By Ferry

Ferries run daily from Topolobampo, on the ocean, over to the Baja. The **Baja Ferry,** ☎ *800-718-2796 or 800-012-8770, www.bajaferries.com,* departs several times a week (see page 82) and it takes about nine hours to reach La Paz. An express speedboat takes five hours, but it does not operate all the time. The problems seem to be financial, so it is an on-again, off-again service. On the ferry, cars and trucks can be transported. There is a restaurant and bar on the boat.

By Train

See *Chihuahua al Pacifico Railroad*, page 123.

■ Services

i **Tourist Office**, *Calle Ordoñes and Allende, next to the government office,* ☎ *668-812-6640, Monday to Friday, 9 am-4 pm.* It has free information and brochures and the staff genuinely like to see tourists.

Post office, *Ordoñez #226, Monday to Friday, 9 am-3 pm.*

Police, *Degollado y Cuauhtemoc in the Presidencia Municipal,* ☎ *668-812-0033.*

Hospital Fatima, *Jiquilpan #639,* ☎ *668-812-3312,* or call the **Centro de Salud,** ☎ *668-812-0913.*

■ Festivals

The spring festival, or **Samana Santa**, occurs during the week of Easter that takes place 40 days after the beginning of Lent. The date changes yearly, but it is always in March or April. Indigenous people wear traditional clothes, play traditional music on traditional instruments and drink tons of *tesquiño*, a fermented corn drink. May has the **Expo of Los Mochis**, and in December there is a **commercial fair**. The spring festival offers most entertainment for tourists. If you are here in spring, check with the tourist office for details.

> **DANCE OF THE DEER**
>
> The Dance of the Deer is performed during special fiestas to honor hunting rites. It features a man with the head of a deer placed on his head. He is usually bare-chested and keeps beat to the music with rattles made from dried gourds. This is a high-energy dance, often performed for the benefit of tourists.

■ Sightseeing

Regional Museum of the Valle del Fuerte, *Calle Obregón y Antonio Rosales,* ☎ *668-812-4692, Tuesday to Sunday, 10 am-1 pm and 4-7 pm. Entry fee is 50¢ per person and Sundays are free.* The museum, housed in the residence of a former citizen, Dr. Chapman, has his old guns and diaries on display. Occupying six rooms, the museum has artifacts from Valle del Fuerte, including petroglyphs from the

Yoreme or Mayo culture, as well as photos showing the history of Los Mochis. There are guided tours in English and a bookstore on site.

Casa del Centenario, *Blvd Juan de God Batiz y 20 de Noviembre,* ☎ *668-812-5858 or 812-5959,* is one of the original colonial houses that were built in Los Mochis over a hundred years ago and is now used as an art center. Besides regular performances, it features temporary art pieces and some permanent local work. Stop by the tourist office in town for performance schedules.

Church Sagrado Corazon is just off the Plaza 27 de Septiembre. It is a white plaster building with a four-story bell tower. Built by the Protestant wife of sugar baron Ben Johnson, it is a must to visit while in the town.

Memorial Hill is the hill seen from the center of town. On the top is a sculpture of the virgin. A legend associated with the hill says if you climb up and ask the virgin for something special, your wish may be granted. It is the "may" that makes me wonder about her. However, the climb is good exercise, and I think it will contribute to a longer life if that's what you wish for.

■ Adventures on Water

 Nature tours in the bay and to **Isla de los Pajaros** (Bird Island) on the river will reward the birder with huge numbers of sightings. The **Island of Farallon de San Ignacio**, where sea lions and seals hang out, is an ecological preserve only 45 minutes by boat from the port of Topolobampo. Dolphins that like to play in the bay may accompany you on your voyage.

■ Adventures in Nature

 Sinoloa Park and Botanical Garden (no phone) is on Rosales and Castro in Colonia Americana district, the old residential district that has plantation-styled mansions surrounded by manicured yards. The gardens, located on 32 acres, have the largest collection of palms in Mexico. They also have a number of plants collected by the original land owner, Ben Johnson, brought from places like India, the Philippines, Indonesia and Java. The plants are all labeled. There is also a good display of local plants. Although the park and garden are open all the time, the plants do get a bit wilted in dry season.

BIRD WATCH: *Birders may be lucky to spot some new birds in Sinoloa. There are vultures, swainsons, violet-crowned and blue-gray gnat-catchers, lesser goldfinches, Euro-rash, white-winged and Inca doves, house finches, kiska-dees, groove-billed anis and Western tanagers. Also, look for great-tailed grackles that are said to love the park. If you go farther into the park, you may see an elegant trogon, the golden prize for birders in Mexico.*

■ Outfitters/Tour Operators

Flamingo Tour Operator, ☎ *668-818-7046 or 800-896-8196, www.mexicoscoppercanyon.com/flamingo,* has been in business since the 1960s. They offer tours to the islands, river cruises, bike tours and kayaking in the area. For birders, they also have knowledgeable guides, some who can imitate different calls. Prices vary according to the time and activity.

Sierra Madre Tours, *Leyva y Hidalgo,* ☎ *668-247-3464,* in the Santa Anita Hotel, has four- and seven-hour boat trips out to the islands to watch the sea lions, birds and dolphins. The seven-hour trip includes snorkeling. They will also take out sportfishers who would like to catch a marlin, dorado, sailfish, yellowtail or wahoo. Rates depend on numbers, location and itinerary. Bait, tips, food and drinks are not included.

■ Places to Stay

Los Mochis Trailer Park, ☎ *668-812-0021, $,* has laundry facilities, flush toilets, a lounge and a night watchman. The park is set on five acres of land. Tenting is an option.

Rio Fuerte Trailer Park, *Calle Jon Rubi #637,* ☎ *668-812-9686, $,* is on 10 acres of land overlooking Rio Fuerte. The resort has a pool, lounge, grocery store, laundry facilities and flush toilets.

HOTEL PRICE SCALE
Price for a room given in US $.
$.................Up to $20
$$.................$21-$50
$$$.............$51-$100
$$$$ ....$101-$150
$$$$$ ....$151-$200
Anything over $200 is specified.

Hotel Hidalgo, *Calle Hidalgo #260,* ☎ *668-812-3456, $,* just up from the Beltran, has 46 rooms. Although the rooms are small, the Hidalgo is one of the better cheapies. There are ceiling fans in the rooms and, for a bit more cash, you can get air conditioning.

Hotel Del Valle, *Guillermo Prieto # 302, $*, has 26 rooms and is a one-star hotel. All rooms have private bathroom and satellite TV. The place is clean.

Hotel America, *Calle Allende #665 South,* ☎ *668-812-1355 or 812-1356, $$,* has 49 rooms with large windows and tiled floors. There is cable TV, purified water and an ice machine in the hallway. Try to get a room that does not face Calle Allende, which can be noisy, especially early in the morning. There is a restaurant on site.

Hotel Fenix, *Av Flores #365 South,* ☎ *668-812-2623, $$,* has large rooms with private bathrooms, color TVs, air conditioning, hot water and telephones. This is one of the better lower-end hotels.

Santa Rosa, *Lopez Mateos #1051,* ☎ *668-812-2918, $$,* is a small place. Each room has color TV, hot water in the private bathroom and air conditioning.

Hotel Beltran, *Hidalgo #281,* ☎ *668-812-0710, $$,* is a two-star hotel with 55 rooms. Each room has air conditioning, telephone and color TV.

Hotel Monte Carlo, *Angel Florex #322 South,* ☎ *668-812-1818, $$$,* has 50 rooms with color TV, private bathrooms, telephones and air conditioning. There is a restaurant, bar and free parking.

Hotel Lorena, *Av Obregón #184,* ☎ *668-812-6846, $$$,* has 50 rooms with private bathroom, air conditioning and TV. The hotel has purified water and sparkles with cleanliness. There is a restaurant and bar.

Hotel El Dorado, *Calle Leyva #525 North and Main St.,* ☎ *668-815-1111, $$$,* is in the heart of the shopping area. This sparkling white hotel has 93 rooms on three floors (there is an elevator), pool, restaurant, cable TV, free local calls and air conditioning. Some rooms are interconnected to accommodate larger groups. They also have a currency exchange and babysitting service, tour office, business center, tennis courts and laundry service. They offer a shuttle to the airport for $5.

Corintios, *Av Obregón #580,* ☎ *668-818-2300, $$$,* is a four-star hotel with all the amenities of a good place. Built in 1993, the three-story building with 35 spacious rooms with carpeted floors, double beds and a luggage rack is set around a central courtyard. Bathrooms are marble. Greek columns stand in the well-decorated lobby. There is a bar and restaurant on site. Purified water is supplied and a breakfast of juice, coffee and bread is included in the price. There are also laundry facilities and free parking.

Hotel Taj-Mahal, *Av Obregón #400, $$$,* has 40 rooms with private bathroom, satellite TV, air conditioning and coffee maker. There is parking and a restaurant on site. The place is decorated inside and out like the Taj Mahal and is kept clean. The floors are mostly tile, with the exception of a carpet around the king-size beds.

Hotel Santa Anita, *Calle Leyva y Hidalgo #159,* ☎ *668-818-7046, $$$ / $$$$,* has 120 rooms on four floors and each large room has a double, king or queen-sized bed, dresser, chair, cable TV and a purified water system. The bathrooms are large and have hair dryers. There is a restaurant, tour desk, currency exchange, laundry service and parking on site. This is the most popular place to stay because it is comfortable and quiet and the early transportation to the train is reliable.

Hotel Plaza Inn, *Calle Leyva y Cardenas,* ☎ *668-818-1043, www. mexonline.com / plazainn.htm, $$$$,* is in a large building with over a hundred single and double rooms on its five floors. There is a beauty salon, a swimming pool, a Mr. Owens Coffee Shop, a dining room that offers live entertainment, and a bar. Parking is free. Each room has one or two queen-sized beds, air conditioning, cable TV, full bathroom, hair dryer, alarm clock, coffee maker, fridge, ironing board and security box. Some rooms have a kitchenette. For the duck hunter, this is the place to come for good guiding service. Ask at the tour desk. The hotel is two miles/ three km from the train station, 10 miles/16 km from the bus station and 15 miles/25 km from the docks.

Posada Real, *Leyva y Buelna,* ☎ *668-812-2363 or 812-2179, $$$$,* has 35 rooms with private bathrooms, TVs and telephones. There is a pool.

Villa Cahita, *Ramirez y Leyva #400,* ☎ *668-812-1200, $$$$,* is a three-star hotel that has 66 rooms with private bathroom, air conditioning and cable TV. There is a restaurant, bar, beauty salon and travel agency.

■ Places to Eat

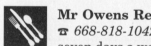 **Mr Owens Restaurant and Coffee Bar**, *Leyva y Cardenas,* ☎ *668-818-1042,* in the Plaza Inn, is open 6 am to midnight seven days a week. Breakfast is the big draw, because this place is open before the train leaves; the coffee is good. The cuisine is international. Prices are mid-range – a snack costs about $5.

Cazadores, *Leyva y Cardenas,* ☎ *668-818-8696,* also in the Plaza Inn, is open 10 am to 11 pm. The specialty is steak cooked to perfection and served with your choice of seafood. This is one of the more popular places in town.

Bueanero, *Leyva #525 North and Main St,* ☎ *668-815-1111,* in El Dorado Hotel, is open 10 am to 11 pm. The specialty is seafood done Mexican style, which means lots of onions and tomatoes. Meals run $10-15.

Chino Palacio, *Blvd Rosales Sur #330,* ☎ *668-818-1419,* open 10 am to 11 pm, has good Chinese food for less than $10 per serving. Another good Chinese eatery is the **Tong Wah**, *Venustiano Carranza #172,* ☎ *668-812-3873,* open daily from noon to 11 pm. An average meal costs $10.

El Farrallon, *Angela Flores y Alvaro Obregón,* ☎ *668-812-1428*, open 9 am to 11 pm, is known for its huge variety of seafood. It's cooked mostly Mexican style, with lots of garlic and/or chilies. Most of the dishes are huge; some are cold, while others are hot. The squid is exceptional and is the cheapest thing on the menu – it comes recommended. But then so does the marlin. Meals run between $5 and $10 per serving.

El Taquito, *Leyva y Barrera,* ☎ *668-812-8119,* is open 24 hours a day so you can get breakfast as early as you wish for less than $5. A Mexican dinner will run around $6-$8 for a large serving. The tortilla soup is recommended.

Restaurant España, *Obregón #525,* ☎ *668-812-2221,* is the place to hang out with the upper crust in Los Mochis. Their favorite dish is seafood paella or steak, usually for under $10. The atmosphere is pleasing, with carved wooden tables and a fountain in the room. The servers are pleasant and quick to produce a meal.

Sushiko Japanese Cuisine, *Heriberto Valdez 1300, at Plaza Campañario,* ☎ *668-812-2043,* has good sushi for less than $10 a meal. For a change, this is a good choice.

■ Nightlife

International Sugar Company, *Leyva y Cardenas,* ☎ *668-818-1043, in the Plaza Inn, is open 11 am-2 am daily.* Although not the cheapest bar in town, it is one of the better places.

El Fuerte

This tiny town of about 30,000 people is 45 miles/80 km northeast of Los Mochis and is far more popular with tourists, perhaps because of its size and its location on El Fuerte River, where the Septentrion Gorge begins.

■ History

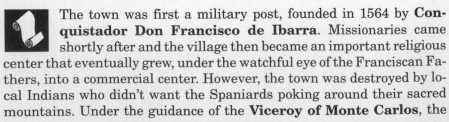

The town was first a military post, founded in 1564 by **Conquistador Don Francisco de Ibarra**. Missionaries came shortly after and the village then became an important religious center that eventually grew, under the watchful eye of the Franciscan Fathers, into a commercial center. However, the town was destroyed by local Indians who didn't want the Spaniards poking around their sacred mountains. Under the guidance of the **Viceroy of Monte Carlos**, the town was rebuilt in the form of a fort. Because of the precious metals the Spanish hoped to pull out of the canyons, the Camino Real trade route was designed to run past the village. The fort was completed in 1610 to securely hold the valuables en route to the Pacific.

The town, in 1824, became the capital of the area now known as Sonora and Sinaloa states and remained so for many years. Then the region was divided into separate states, each with its own capital. Now the town is a tourist center at the gates to the greatest canyon area in Mexico.

■ Services

Tourist Office and **post office** are at *5 de Mayo in the Government Building,* ☎ *698-893-0810.*

Police, *on the road between El Fuetre and Los Mochis at Km 78,* ☎ *698-893-0594.*

Medical Clinic of the Good Samaritan, *Calle Melchor Ocamp and Antonio Ceceña, #716,* ☎ *698-893-0688.*

■ Sightseeing

The **fort**, located on El Fuerte River, was built in 1610 to protect Spanish settlers from Indian attacks. It was built by Diego Martinez de Hurdaide during the Viceroy-ship of Don Juan de Mendoza. Once peace was made between the two cultures, the area became a prosperous agricultural center and stop-over for the miners taking the silver and gold from the mines in the mountains out to the coast for shipment. As the mining industry declined, the fort was no longer needed and it fell into disrepair. Recently, restoration began and the fort is now a museum. Ask at the Tourist Office for directions.

■ Adventures on Foot

Cerro de la Mascara (Mask Hill) is above the town. To get here, walk down Calle 5 de Mayo to the river and head up the hill. This is where local people hundreds of years ago came to carve their history in stone. Some of these glyphs, still visible today, are circles, while others are lines that form a square. The deep carvings, believed to be anywhere from 800 to 2,000 years old, are numerous enough to make the climb worth your while. The hill is dotted with vegetation, some of it deciduous and some cactus like. From town, the walk is about 1.5 miles/2.5 km one way.

■ Adventures on Water

 Travel on **El Fuerte River** by motorboat or river raft will be rewarded with sightings of turkey vultures and herons. There are locals fishing with nets and lush jungle vegetation hiding lizards and snakes, butterflies and bugs. The trip passes through an agricultural area before it hits the marsh and then the mangroves that hold a large number of birds. Past the mangroves are lagoons and estuaries, where crocodiles live. They can be anywhere from three-10 feet/one-three meters long, and the big ones weigh well over 500 pounds/200 kg.

Lake Dominguez, a man-made lake 10 miles/16 km northwest of El Fuerte, sits at 308 feet/94 meters above sea level. It is good for birding and bass fishing. Bass are big here, with many "double digit" fish being caught. Because bass are such good fighters, they attract many anglers.

 LOCAL LINGO: Lobina *and* robalo *are the words for bass in Spanish.*

Anglers need to purchase a permit either in town or off the web at www.mexicanlakes.com. The costs are $24 for a week, $35 for a month and $45 for a year. Use of 80# spider line is recommended so that you don't lose too many lures. The "Go-Get-It" lure retrievers sold by Parey Products, ☎ *270-384-7865, www.mygogetit.com*, work well. **Hotel Villa Dominguez**, ☎ *698-893-0802*, is on the lake.

■ Adventures in Nature

El Fuerte is surrounded by dry tropical deciduous thorn forest that is good raptorial habitat. Just north of El Fuerte River in the **Sonoran Desert**, the birder will be rewarded with unique landscapes along with endemic species. The areas between the desert and the forests offer even more for you to explore.

 FACT FILE: The El Fuerte area has evolved so that some pockets of land, called centers of endemism, have birds and animals that are native only to that area. This part of Mexico has 22 endemic bird areas (EBAs). Seven other countries are known to have 10 and only Brazil and Indonesia have more than Mexico.

On El Fuerte River is **El Mahone**, where there is a bird rookery. Some of the birds that you may see on the way out here are the bare-throated tiger heron, the russet-crowned motmot, the great black hawk, the white-fronted parrot and the rufous-bellied chachalaca. There are over 60 species that can be identified along this stretch.

On the eastern side of the mountains, accessible by car, is the **Sierra Madre Occidental EBA**, characterized by pine oak, pine and fir forests. This area is commonly called the Madrean pine-oak forest. This area has the most numerous species of oaks located in one spot in the entire world.

Emilio Kifuri of **Canyon Travel**, ☎ *800-843-1060*, provided the above information about birding. Canyon Travel offers one-week trips especially designed for birders or botanists (see below).

■ Adventures in Culture

 Tehueco Mayo Indian Mission is nine miles/15 km from El Fuerte and takes about half an hour by bus to reach. The village was founded in 1648 and the mission was built in 1650. However, it was left to go to ruin after the Jesuits were expelled from the New World and the present mission wasn't built until 1811. The new building sits beside the old.

 LOCAL LINGO: *The Mayo Indians speak Cahita, which is similar to Tehuec and Yaqui. All of these are part of the Shoshonean language group.*

When the Mayo were first seen by the Spaniards in 1532, it was not love at first sight. Diego Hertado de Mendoza and his crew were killed in their sleep by locals. The following year, Diego de Guzman went through safely. Then in 1610, the Mayo and the Yaqui, after some bitter battles, signed a peace agreement that was negotiated with the help of the Spanish. The first Jesuit, Father Pedro Mendez, arrived in 1613 and he is noted for performing over 3,000 baptisms within 15 days of his arrival. Seven missions were built in the area in the next few years.

The tribes lived peacefully until about 1740, when they revolted against each other because one town had a better church than another. Rumor has it that the revolt was instigated by the Spanish. The reputation of the missions declined after this until the Jesuits were expelled from Spanish America in 1767.

Nahuatl Petroglyphs are nine miles/15 km from town, so you will need either a taxi or hired van to get here. Another option is to take a boat across the river and hike for a mile or so to the stones. This crossing passes Bird Island, where you also can do a bit of birding. For me, getting there was far more exciting than viewing the glyphs, which are believed to be about 1,500 years old.

Northern Pacific Mexico

■ Outfitters/Tour Operators

 El Fuerte Eco-Adventures, *Av Hidalgo #260 and 5 de Mayo, Los Mochis*, ☎ *668-818-3456, www.mexicocoppercanyon*.com, offers horseback riding trips, rafting excursions, river crossings and tours to the petroglyphs and the Mayo Indian village of Tehueco. There is also a walking tour of the city, which I highly recommend.

Nature Treks & Passages, *PO Box 64805, Tucson, AZ 85728,* ☎ *520-696-2002, www.naturetreks.net/birding.htm*, is affiliated with the Tucson Audubon Society and has Audubon guides. One, Larry Liese, is the author of *Dastardly Duos* in the *TAZ Flycatcher*, a magazine put out by the Tucson Audubon Society. A nine-day trip costs $2,000 per person, based on double occupancy. This is all-inclusive, except for airfare to Los Mochis and booze. If you book the trip with **Aero California**, $150 of the airfare to reach Los Mochis from Tucson will be donated to the Tucson Audubon Society. Each tour is limited to 12 people, with a minimum of eight. You must be a member of the Tucson Audubon Society ($20; $15 for seniors over 62) to participate.

The California Native, *6701 W. 87th Place, Los Angeles, CA 90045,* ☎ *800-926-1140, www.calnative.com/index.htm,* has a seven-day deluxe tour that runs just under $2,000. Their 14-day trip costs $3,000, all inclusive from Los Angeles, Tucson or El Paso in the US. This package incorporates a train ride to Creel and return to Los Mochis.

Copper Canyon Tours, *Donato Guerra #209,* ☎ *698-893-0915,* is the company to see if you have arrived in the area without first pre-booking all your accommodations, meals, transportation and tours. I appreciate a company that can get me onto a tour without lots of preplanning.

You can purchase **train tickets** from the office on Av M. Hidalgo #101, ☎ *698-893-0242*.

■ Places to Stay

Castillo Campground, ☎ *698-893-0836*, is six miles/10 km west of town near the Dominguez dam and lake. There are basic services and hookups for motor homes.

Hotel Herradura, *Av Hidalgo and 5 de Mayo, behind the church and next to Posada del Hidalgo, no phone, $$*, has eight clean rooms on the main floor with private bathroom, hot water and air

HOTEL PRICE SCALE		
Price for a room given in US $.		
$		Up to $20
$$		$21-$50
$$$		$51-$100
$$$$		$101-$150
$$$$$		$151-$200
Anything over $200 is specified.		

conditioning. New rooms on the second floor are now available. The owner, Julian, always has a pot of coffee in the lobby ready for early risers.

Rio Vista Lodge, *Cerro de la Pilas*, ☎ *698-893-0413, $$$*, is owned by Chal Gamez and run by Canyon Travel (see *Los Mochis Tour Operators*, page 133). The hotel gives guests a feeling of seclusion as it sits on the hill overlooking El Fuerte River. The stone and plaster building is decorated with potted plants and local arts from the Yaqui and Mayo Indians. The 13 rooms have tiled floors with scatter rugs, air conditioning and private bathrooms. There is a parking area. The best feature is the dining area overlooking the river and valley with hundreds of hummingbirds buzzing around as you enjoy your meal or a drink. The owner is a knowledgeable guide for the area.

Hacienda San Francisco, *Obregón #201*, ☎ *698-893-0055, $$$*, is a colonial-styled building that has 18 rooms built around a pleasant garden. Each room comes with private bathroom and air conditioning. There is a pool on site and tour guides are available for hire.

Villa del Pescador, *Rodolfo Robles #103*, ☎ *698-893-0106, www. go2coppercanyon.com/pescador, $$$*, is a small lodge with only eight rooms, each with private bathroom. There is also a pool, bar and dining area on site. If staying here, your meals are included in the price.

Posada del Hidalgo, *Av Hidalgo #260 and 5 de Mayo*, ☎ *800-896-8196 (US) or 668-818-3456 (Los Mochis), www.mexicocoppercanyon.com, $$$$*, was constructed in 1890 by Rafael Almada, a town mayor who spent five years and 100,000 gold pesos building the hacienda. It has 46 rooms built around a central courtyard that has a garden with a fountain. The wood beams are made from Canadian red pine brought into the area when Albert Owen was trying to build his utopian community. The brick is four layers thick and the ironwork around the building was brought from Mazatlan. Numerous presidents have stayed in this hotel and there are a number of historical documents on display. I don't know if Rafael Almada was flaunting his wealth at the Owen crew or if this was what Owen was trying to accomplish for his followers, but I would certainly join an organization if I was guaranteed this kind of residence.

The rooms are old or new. The old ones have high ceilings with wood beans and balconies. These are in the original mansion. Newer rooms face the garden and are similar in design, although modern in construction materials. Each room has a private bathroom, TV, alarm clock, safe deposit box, wood floors and air conditioning. There is a swimming pool, souvenir shop, car rental desk, currency exchange, tour office and dining room. The restaurant's best meal is the buttered bass filets, which cost less than $10 for a large portion.

El Fuerte, *Montesclaro #37*, ☎ *698-893-0226, $$$$$*, is a colonial mansion that has been restored and modernized. The 31 rooms have a double bed, tiled bathroom, air conditioning and colonial furniture. A gift shop carries local pottery and the gallery sells paintings of local scenes. There is also a bar and a restaurant, where the international food is said to be excellent.

Rio Fuerte B & B, *Calle RG Robles #105*, ☎ *698-893-0308, $$*, is a popular place and more personal than a hotel. Phone before you go over as they are often full.

Hotel Villa Dominguez, ☎ *698-893-0802, $$$$$*, is on the man-made Lake Dominguez, just nine miles/15 km out of El Fuerte. This rustic hotel is set in a well-tended garden with a patio overlooking the lake. You can go out on the water at any time. Bass anglers seem to be the most common clients. Meals are included in your room rate.

■ Places to Eat

Mesa del General just off the plaza is a clean restaurant with brightly painted walls and tiled floors. The specialty dish is bass in oyster sauce, done Oriental style. It is good and costs $7 per plate.

Restaurant Supremo, *Constitución and Rosales #108*, ☎ *698-893-0021*, is on the main street into town. It has excellent meals for reasonable prices; beef enchiladas are less than $5 per serving. If you opt for the meal of the day, it will no doubt cost less but still taste good.

Burger Mania, *Av Juarez # 110*, ☎ *698-893-0555*, has great burgers and comes highly recommended. Even if you are vegetarian, try them out; their taco salad is superb.

Témoris

To get here, you must ride the train or drive a 4x4 vehicle. The village is located at Km 225 (Mile 150) on the rail line and El Fuerte is at Km 430 (Mile 200). It should be noted that the train station and the town have about 2,000 feet/ 650 meters of elevation between them. The village is in the Septentrion Gorge and close to the river flowing at the bottom of the valley. It is advisable to bring a bicycle if you would like to explore this area (second-class trains will carry bicycles).

The village's only **hotel**, ☎ *635-456-0750, www.fippless.org / Hotel, $$$*, is the place to stay if you want to explore the area around El Fuerte.

FACT FILE: Near Témoris is the **longest tunnel** and the last one to be built along the Chihuahua el Pacifico line. A 180° loop is made inside the tunnel. This is the most interesting and difficult engineering feat on the line.

Témoris has electricity for a few hours in the evenings only, most people don't speak English and many still like the four-hoofed style transportation over the four-wheeled style. Fax and e-mail are also a long way in the future for most people living here. The phone number for the hotel above will connect you to the town operator. Ask for Oscar Alvarez and you will be put on hold for about three minutes while someone gets Oscar, who speaks English.

▪ Adventures

Other than hang out, drink margaritas and eat, you can do **horseback riding** or **hiking trips** from Témoris. Ask Oscar at the hotel. The costs run around $50 a day for middle-class travel (not luxurious and not terrible). If you are adventuresome and like out-of-the-way places, this may be a good place to stop and explore in an area never visited by the tour groups.

Choix

This tiny mining town located near the Mocorito River is off the rail line, but along the highway just 70 miles/123 km northeast of Los Mochis. The elevation is a bit higher than El Fuerte, so the climate is pleasant for almost everybody. There are sportfishing lodges, one hotel and a few restaurants, but the big draw is the hot springs just a few miles from town.

▪ Adventures on Water

Lake Huites is another hydro dam reservoir that is used for recreation and catch-and-release bass fishing. The stocked lake has fish that weigh 16 pounds/seven kilos, but most are around 10 pounds/five kilos. Motorized craft are permitted on the lake. To get here, you'll need to take a bus or hire a vehicle.

The lake is tucked into the foothills of the mountains and features an interesting geometric sculpture at its side, called the Guardian of the Dam.

A fishing camp on the lake, www.wetaline.com/bass-mexico.htm, built in 1998, can accommodate 26 guests. The rooms are large, with tiled floors and private bathrooms. An all-inclusive stay with boat use, a bed, some booze, food and transport from the airport in Los Mochis runs just over $200 a day. The boats are Skeeters, equipped with fish finders, 150 hp Yamaha dual-trolling motors, GPS and water thermometers. If you want to use the boats only, the cost is $100 per day; guests at the lodge get first dibs on them.

The **hot springs** of Chuchaca, Apuche, Agua Caliente de Baca and Agua Caliente Grande can be reached from the village by bus or hired vehicle. Chuchaca and Apuche are closest to town.

■ Places to Stay

Real de Minas, *Obregón #28*, ☎ *635-866-0400, $$*, is a basic establishment with rooms at economical prices. I have no information on this hotel because I never made it to Choix.

Club Hidalgo Lodge, *Calle Zaragoza #820*, ☎ *635-893-0657, $$$*, is the up-scale place in town. However, I have no further information on this lodge.

HOTEL PRICE SCALE
Price for a room given in US $.
$.................Up to $20
$$..................$21-$50
$$$...............$51-$100
$$$$ ....$101-$150
$$$$$ ....$151-$200
Anything over $200 is specified.

There are a number of lodges on the lake, catering mostly to anglers.

■ Places to Eat

Restaurante Cuauhtemoc, *Obregón #37*, ☎ *635-866-0350*, serves Mexican dishes. **Pollos Mayos**, *Obregón and Guerrero*, ☎ *635-866-0324*, serves chicken (but not the happy ones) and **Restaurant Anita**, *Guerrero #2*, ☎ *635-866-0404*, is best for breakfast. There are other places in town; be adventurous and scout them out.

Bahuichivo & Cerocahui

Bahuichivo Station serves the colonial villages of Cerocahui, home to about 1,500 residents, and Urique, a little closer to the south end of the canyon. Cerocahui is about six miles/10 km from the train station; the road is mud. The owners of Paraiso del Oso will take you to their hotel if you let them know ahead of time, and a bus that meets the train goes down to the village if you would rather look around town for other accommodations.

Cerocahui is a tiny mission town with little to do except take a trip to Cerro Gallego overlooking Urique Canyon, walk/ride to the waterfall for a day trip or take a horse/hiking tour down to the mining town of Urique. Cerocahui has a colonial church and is one of the oldest communities in the mountains.

■ Adventures on Foot

A hike along **Urique River** takes you down the canyon 5,500 feet/1,800 meters and then, at the end of the day, back up again. Since the town sits on the rim of the canyon, you need to walk to the rim from your hotel and take any of the trails going down; they all join before long, and you can't get lost. Along the way are the remains of an old mining site where gold, silver and copper were once extracted. There is also a colonial house, a cemetery and a church. This hike takes approximately 10 hours to complete. Water should be carried.

The Cave of the Crosses, an old Raramuri cave dwelling, is easy to hike to in an afternoon. Ask in Cerocahui or at your hotel for directions.

The hike to **Urique** is a popular three-day excursion for those with stamina and experience. From Cerocahui, you head to San Ysidro, five hours by foot. Along the way you will pass through El Cajon Box Canyon. The next day features a walk to Naranjo, a village surrounded on three sides by canyon walls. From there, it is just another four hours to Urique – located at the bottom of the second-deepest canyon in North America – where there is a great campsite on the sandy beach of the river. Crossing the river on a long suspension bridge requires some nerve. The town of Urique itself has two basic hotels along its main street.

Cerro Gallegos is a dramatic lookout point that has a 500-foot drop straight down. Along the trail there are a few spots with guardrails, but not many. The dry twisted trees that eke out an existence are a photographer's delight. The hill is 20 miles/38 km from Cerocahui, so you will need to hire a vehicle to get here. There are no car rental outlets at Cerocahui or at Bahuichivo. You must hire a vehicle and driver or you must bring in a rental from a larger city like Creel or Los Mochis. Look for military macaws and trogons here.

Yeparavo Waterfall is two miles/four km south of town and the journey to reach it is a good walk. However, you should have a guide as there are so many trails where you can branch off that you will get lost. See any of the locals in town for guiding service. The cost should not be more than $10 for the trip. The falls themselves are okay, but it's the birding that is the real draw.

Northern Pacific Mexico

■ Adventures on Water

Those in search of exciting river exploration in the safety of a raft can paddle the 40 miles/65 km of the Urique River as it passes through the 6,000-foot/2,000-meter walls of Urique Canyon to the mission town of Tubares on El Fuerte River. This run takes three days and can be done only during rainy season, July to October. At this time, the water is laden with debris pulled from the mountains during run-off. This trip is exciting and remote, so remote that Tubares isn't yet on maps of Mexico. Those experienced in whitewater kayaking and who have their own boats can do the run. They should, however, be accompanied by a raft for safety reasons. There is the option of doing a half-day run on the river for a cost of $45 per person. See Hotel Paraiso del Oso (below) for details or e-mail doug@mexicohorse.com for prices on your custom trip.

■ Adventures on Horseback

Horse trips, arranged through the Paraiso del Oso Hotel (page 148) can be for a few hours or for a week. The owner, a former guide, has a dozen horses that are well cared for, well trained and well equipped. They are also gentle (even I can handle them) and Western saddles are used. Trips can be had in various terrain and go into wild country or along steep rocky trails. The days are long, and you are expected to help with camp chores. Campsites are exclusive so other groups will not be there.

You can ride to the canyon floor on a day trip and then return to the hotel by vehicle. Those in the area for Samana Santa could have an extraordinary experience by joining locals in their celebrations where they eat traditional foods, drink homemade beer, dance ancient dances to the beat of traditional music and dress in costumes not seen elsewhere.

You can also ride to **Batópilas**, which entails riding through the canyon to reach the town.

> **BIRD WATCH:** *For birders, Batópilas has broad-billed, beryline, violet-crowned and lucifer hummingbirds, orioles and tanagers. Farther along the river are white-fronted and lilac-crowned parrots and elegant trogons.*

You can also opt to ride a mule, which is more sure-footed than a horse. The ride, however, is more bumpy for the inexperienced rider. Paraiso del Oso Hotel will do a cross-country trip from El Paso down to Cerocahui for experienced riders who can take 12 hours a day in the saddle and then a few hours of camp chores after that. To arrange such a trip, contact the owners and make arrangements well in advance. All equipment is provided. You need only your clothes, sleeping bag and pad. If you share a tent, the cost, including all meals, is $1,200 per person, per week. This includes familiarizing you with the horse before the trip and visits to especially interesting and out-of-the-way places.

A more interesting ride is on the **Silver Trail** that follows part of the Camino Real, built originally under the watchful eye of Alexander Shepherd so that the silver and gold he mined could be transported to the Pacific Ocean. After a day of rest in Batópilas, you continue to the village of Creel by truck. From there, the trail starts along the canyon bottom where cactus stand 12 feet/four meters above your head and desert-like flowers abound. You will pass through El Cajon Box Canyon.

✤ **LOCAL LINGO:** El Cajon *means "big box" in Spanish. This is a perfect description for the canyon, which has narrow walls and ladders perched at slightly less than 90° angles. The Raramuri collected honey from the hives along these cliff walls. You will see the hives from the comfort of your saddle.*

The Silver Trail (it can also be done as a hike) has an elevation change of of 4,200 ft/1,300 meters in four miles/six km, and covers a distance of 70 miles/110 km. Those not crippled with butt blisters when they arrive in Batópilas can return by horse to Cerocahui. There is an additional $400 charge for this torture. Others will be taken by vehicle to Creel. This trip may be done only between October and June (dry season) and costs $1,500 per person, with a minimum of three riders.

BIRD WATCH: *Birders should look for such species as black-throated magpie jays, mourning and white-winged doves and Vermilion flycatchers.*

■ Outfitter/Tour Operator

Hotel Paraiso del Oso, ☎ *421-3372, www.mexicohorse.com,* offers many different tours, but horse tours are the specialty. Doug, the owner, loves the animals, treats them well and knows where they can go to make your trip exceptional. He also offers river rafting when water levels allow.

■ Places to Stay & Eat

 Cerocahui Wilderness Lodge, ☎ *800-843-1060, $$$$, www.canyontravel.com/lodgecero1.htm,* is close to town and managed by Canyon Travel. The hotel is perched on the edge of a canyon so it has great views. The interior of the main building where guests eat or relax is made of wood beam and stone and decorated with traditional Mexican furniture. The rooms are

HOTEL PRICE SCALE	
Price for a room given in US $.	
$	Up to $20
$$	$21-$50
$$$	$51-$100
$$$$	$101-$150
$$$$$	$151-$200
Anything over $200 is specified.	

brightly colored, with tile floors and fireplaces. Each room has a sitting area and large closet for clothes and luggage.

Hotel Paraiso del Oso, ☎ *614-421-3372 in Chihuahua or 800-884-3107 in the US, $$$$ (including meals), www.mexicohorse.com,* opened in 1990 and is one mile from Cerocahui. It has 21 rooms with kerosene lamps, wood-burning stoves, plush comforters and lots of hot water in the shower. The staff offers as much pampering as you can take. Electricity is generated from solar panels. There is a covered walkway around the hotel dotted with willow furniture for guests to use, plus a bar and restaurant and a reference library, complete with maps. Owner Doug Rhodes is an adventuresome horseman who takes guests into the backcountry on trips from half a day to one week. He will also provide transportation from the train station to the hotel.

 LOCAL LINGO: *The name of the hotel,* Oso *or* bear, *comes from a rock formation located behind the building that looks like Yogi Bear wearing his hat.*

Those with **camping** gear can pitch a tent at the campsite next to the hotel. The grounds are tucked under stone pillars, one of which is Oso (Yogi Bear). There is a fire pit with grill, an outhouse and hot showers. Campers can eat some meals at the hotel.

Hotel Mision Cerocahui, *located on the plaza, Calle 20 de Noviembre #141,* ☎ *635-543-0089, $$$$$,* offers spacious rooms with private bathrooms, hot water, electricity until midnight, wood-burning stoves and kerosene lanterns for use after the electricity is shut down. The price includes all meals. They also provide guides and transportation for any tours you may wish to do, including mountain biking.

Garden Hotel, *20 de Noviembre, #46,* ☎ *635-543-0090, $,* is a basic place just up from hotel Mision Cerocahui.

Hotel Viajero, *Vincente Guerrero # 302*, ☎ *635-543-0074*, *$$*, is a budget hotel in town. I didn't check it out, so I have no other details.

Hotel Chaparro, *Calle Francisco Villa #1*, ☎ *635-543-0210*, *$$*, in the center of town, is a two-star place. Rooms have private bathrooms and the hotel is clean.

Urique

U rique was founded in 1691 by a Spanish prospector. It lies in the deepest gorge of the Copper Canyon maze and takes a lot of work to reach. If you want to do things after getting down there, you need to stay overnight. The town is basically one main street (that is being paved this year) and has a new hotel (see below). The gorge has numerous columns and spires dotted with tropical plants that make the town picturesque.

■ Adventures on Foot

The enormity of the gorge intimidates even the most avid hiker. However, going on a hike is a must. Trails are clear and often have barricades along the edge to keep you from falling over. The cliffs have vegetation clinging to every stone.

■ Places to Stay & Eat

The new hotel and restaurant (unnamed, as yet) in town is owned by Elena Acosta. I have not seen it so I can't give a firsthand opinion. I have been told that it is fairly plush for Urique.

HOTEL PRICE SCALE		
Price for a room given in US $.		
$		Up to $20
$$		$21-$50
$$$		$51-$100
$$$$		$101-$150
$$$$$		$151-$200
Anything over $200 is specified.		

Cañon de Urique Hotel, *main street*, *$*, is the one basic hotel in town. Each room has a private bathroom and a bed.

There are **home stay** programs in this village. The great thing about a home stay program is that the locals (rather than hotel chains) get your cash in exchange for a cultural experience. Ask at the store in town.

There is a **campground** in town, but during the last rainy season the river washed away the bunkhouse, outhouse and showers. If you stay here, you will have to be fully independent.

Tita's Restaurant Plaza is in a garden just off the street. The portions are large and the prices are small. Because Urique is technically a dry town, beer is costly when purchased at a restaurant. However, many locals make *tesquiño* (corn beer) that you can purchase; ask around. Distilled alcohol is best brought with you, as illegal stills can and often do produce booze that will kill you.

Batópilas

Batópilas is 70 miles/120 km south from Creel and occupies one narrow street that runs along the river. Coming into town by car you'll have the canyon wall on one side and the river down below on the other. The canyon walls go up from every direction in town, keeping the heat in and the humidity high. Because of the accommodations, the setting and the remoteness, this town has become a destination in itself and everyone who visits should consider spending at least three days here.

Batópilas was once a wealthy mining city reminiscent of Potosi in Bolivia. The first mines were opened in 1632 and, during the colonial years, over 300 mines were explored and worked. The most notorious miner/developer of the area was **Alexander Shepherd**, who had quite a history before coming to Mexico.

ALEXANDER SHEPHERD

In 1871, Alexander Shepherd became the territorial governor of the District of Columbia. During his time in office he constructed roads, built sewer lines and put in gas and water mains. He was expelled from office after congress discovered that he had overspent by $15 million. He moved to Batópilas in 1880 just after John Robinson discovered a rich silver vein that he was unable to work due to lack of funds. Shepherd purchased the mine for $600,000 and, always the profiteer, filed over 300 claims and consolidated the Batópilas Mining Company. El Peñasquito Silver Mine, owned by Shepherd, became one of the richest in the world.

There are places along the Camino Real where wooden support beams hold up huge boulders that you must pass around or under, but in other spots you can walk on the stone path with no problem.

The area has so many old houses, schools, churches, bridges, tunnels and mills that it is impossible to describe them all. If you are adventuresome and want secluded places, then try this area.

■ Getting Here

If you arrive by train, you can walk to the town square from the station.

You can drive here only if you have a 4x4 with standard transmission. At Km 70 along the southern road from Creel, turn onto the signed road to Samachique. This road is paved only to San Rafael. You must follow the steep road from the turnoff into the Batópilas Canyon for 80 miles/55 km (about four hours). This is a treacherous route that should be attempted only by drivers experienced in this type of terrain.

■ Adventure on Foot

The Lost Mission, also known as Satevo, is a colonial cathedral set on the Batópilas River five miles/eight km downstream from town. It once had over 7,000 residents; today fewer than 1,000 people call it home. The mud brick church has numerous Moorish-styled ceilings covered with rust-red finishing. The building is about 250 years old, and the lit candles on the altar are an indication that the church is still in use. This is a good half-day hike (two hours, one way) from the village along a path that runs beside the river.

BIRD WATCH: *Birders who visit the Lost Mission may see tufted flycatchers, brown-backed solitaires, scrub euphonias, ivory-billed wood-creepers and slate-throated redstarts.*

A trip to the **Ruins of Alexander Shepherd's House** at San Miguel, just down from Batópilas, is a good half-day hike. The building is without a roof but the main structure, an imposing mansion, is still intact. Just before you reach the ruins there is a un-named B&B overlooking the river. A prominent sign on the east side of the bridge going into town points the way. I have no idea of the cost or amenities offered.

You can hike to **Urique** in four days, but you must be fit to do so. The first day requires an ascent of 3,800 feet/1,300 meters within six miles/nine km. (Remember, this is with full packs.) After crossing the plateau, you descend into Urique Canyon 4,200 feet/1,400 meters within six miles/10 km. That is steep. However, the latest I heard is that someone around 75 years of age completed the trip and was able to boast about it. This hike can be arranged before you come to Mexico or it can be set up in Batópilas. See next page for tour agents.

CANYON RUN MARATHON

Canyon Run is a race from Batópilas to Urique. The event occurs once in the fall and once in the spring, going in the opposite direction. If you want a marathon that will make the Boston look like a stroll in the park, this may be for you. The entry fee is $100 (money goes to the Tarahumara runners and those working at the stations along the route). There is a limit of 30 non-local runners. The race was first started by an American called Caballo Blanco (white horse) and, at the time of writing, was still being organized by him. There is a mandatory pre-race briefing at the starting point. Camping is available near the race start/ finish lines. The run includes a 3,000-foot/1,000-meter incline and an 1,100-foot/350-meter decline, plus miles along the riverbank and through oak and pine forests above the canyon. Learn more at www.caballoblanco.com/raceagain.html.

■ Guides

A guide for the day should cost anywhere from $25 to $35 for him and his horse (I haven't heard of any women guides – yet). A second horse will be another $15 to $20 a day. **Manual Gil** is a good hiking guide who has been recommended to me by a fellow trekker, but ask in town for others. Numerous people are knowledgeable and can help.

■ Places to Stay

Hotel Mary, *Juarez #15*, ☎ *649-456-9031*, $, in the center of town, is a basic place with communal bathrooms. The patio has good food that is cooked after you order. This is a popular place to eat and stay.

Hotel Batópilas, ☎ *649-456-9002*, $, is basic but clean. It is popular with back-packers.

HOTEL PRICE SCALE	
Price for a room given in US $.	
$	Up to $20
$$	$21-$50
$$$	$51-$100
$$$$	$101-$150
$$$$$	$151-$200
Anything over $200 is specified.	

Monses Hotel, ☎ *649-456-0624*, $$, is between the river and the town square. There are old mango, avocado and papaya trees in the central courtyard that give shade during the heat of the day. The four rooms are set around this area. Each room has a private bathroom, but you must have the owner start a fire in the stove before you get any hot water. The owner knows more about the area than I could write in this guide, so chat with him.

Casa Real de la Mina, ☎ *649-456-0632, $$*, is in the center of town and is more upscale. Rooms are built around a courtyard with a fountain in the center. They have private bathrooms and hot water. There is also a place to eat. The colonial building housing the hotel was built over 100 years ago.

Riverside Lodge, *across from the park, $$$$*, has Arabian Nights décor – white plaster buildings with blue domes and decorative tiles. There are many terraces, passageways and stairs connecting the different levels. Each room is like a private condominium with its own personality. The high ceilings keep the rooms cool and the tile floors help too. Because of their beauty, rooms are named after women, of course. They have private bathrooms and open onto private balconies. The minarets around the property can be climbed for views of the surrounding mountains. This is the gem of the town and highly recommended. Meals are also available and are reported to be excellent.

■ Places to Eat

 Reyna's Restaurant is down by the river. Fresh juice costs between 50¢ and $1.25, depending on flavor and size. A fish or steak dish runs $4.50, but it is the enchiladas that are recommended. They cost less than $3 for a full meal.

Doña Mica's is a good place for dinner when Reyna's becomes boring. This wonderful lady makes the best *sopa de papas y queso* (cheese and potato soup) in the country. The coffee is also delicious – strong, flavorful and full of sweet cream. This is not a certified restaurant, but rather Doña's home, and you are more than welcome to sit on her porch for meals. There are others who will feed you from their kitchens. **Señor Che's** has also been recommended.

Caroline is reported to be the newest and the best restaurant in town. They offer real coffee – always a draw for tourists. The food is reported to be excellent, although I have not tried it myself.

El Café has an expresso machine and is the best place for your afternoon picker-upper. It is located across from Riverside Lodge.

Casa Morales is a little store that gives good exchange rates for the dollar. It is just before Doña's place.

Divisadero

Divisadero gets its name from the blue/green lichen that clings to its rocks. It has the most famous viewpoint for looking down into the Copper Canyon. The town is good for market foods and crafts. For those doing the one-day ride, the train stops here for 15 minutes and everyone is permitted to get off, walk to the canyon rim just a minute away, take a photo or two and get back on the train. If you are quick, you may even purchase a few things from the locals selling their wares along the tracks.

If you want to stay in the area, head to the nearby town of **Areponapuchia**, which has hotels, inns, restaurants and places to explore. Anyone staying at the big Barranca Divisadero Hotel or in Areponapuchia can take a bus from the train station.

■ Adventures on Foot

Hiking

 Candameña Canyon is also called the Canyon of the Waterfalls. This area holds the famous Basaseachic Falls, the second-highest in Mexico. This hike – taking in the falls, the famous climbing wall and Flying Rock view point – can be done in three days and requires a guide. For the really fit and fast, the walk can be done in two days. Just before the Basaseachic Falls is a cave where Padre Glandorff, a missionary, lived during the 18th century. Have your guide point out his cave. The hike through these canyons will also take you past old mining settlements featuring homes called *larga*. These brightly painted, two-story mansions with wooden balustrades are made of adobe brick. Some of the missions in the area are also worth stopping to see.

Basaseachic Waterfall has a viewpoint 812 feet/246 meters above the canyon floor where the water comes tumbling down, taking with it any vegetation that may be clinging to a crack in the rock. These falls should be viewed from both the top and the bottom. A path leads down to the canyon floor and the pool at the bottom of the falls. During the end of dry season, these falls are not as impressive. Some cliff-dwellers' caves can be found near here.

 BIRD WATCH: *Barn swallows, white-throated and black swifts, blue-throated hummingbirds, zone-tailed hawks and hairy woodpeckers are common sightings. Rare and endangered thick-billed parrots are also found in the area.*

Piedra Volada (Flying Rock) is not for the faint-hearted. The four-mile/seven-km hike from Basaseachic Falls to the rock takes you to the edge of a gorge, across cracks in the rock that go hundreds of feet down and a canyon edge where the bottom is 1,500 feet/450 meters below. The red rocks are rugged and breathtaking. In wet season (May-September), water cascades over Piedra Volada, turning it into a waterfall. On the walk to the precipice you will pass the Huajumar and Cerro de la Corona lookout points. Huajumar is the best place to look at the Peña del Gigante climbing wall.

Rock Climbing

Peña del Gigante, on the Candameña Canyon hike, is a 2,290-foot/885-meter vertical rock wall that shoots upward from the Candameña River.

 FACT FILE: Peña del Gigante is the highest rock wall in the country. Prior to 1997, it was believed that El Portrero Chico was the tallest.

Peña is just becoming recognized in the climbing world, so many routes are still unrecorded. This wall is located in front of the Piedra Volada and is best seen from the Huajumar lookout point. It takes one day to reach on foot from Basaseachic Falls. If you have climbing gear, it's essential to hire donkeys to carry the load.

THE HUMMINGBIRD ROUTE

Two Spanish climbers, Cecilia Bull and Carlos Gonzales, and two Mexican climbers, Bonfilio Sarabia and Higinio Piñeda, spent 39 days climbing the wall in 1998 and received international recognition for their exploits. It was so difficult that one day they ascended only 75 feet/25 meters. The difficulties they encountered included humid rocks that didn't offer much grip and weak fixing points. For experienced climbers, the degree of difficulty is rated as 5.11. The route these teams took is now called Simuchi, which means "hummingbird" in Tarahumara language. The team saw a hummingbird every day that they were climbing.

From my limited experience in climbing, the area to me looks much like the Cirque of the Unclimbables in northern Canada, except this has a much more conducive climate for climbing.

An alpine lake, **Lago Pilares** (Pillar Lake), is tucked into the woods near here. On the trail going to the bottom of the canyon is **Las Escaleras**, an outlook.

■ Places to Stay

Trailhead Inn, ☎ *635-578-3007, $$, www.trailheadinn.com,* offers good clean rooms with private bathrooms for reasonable rates. The hotel is small and has just five rooms, all leading to a porch lined with comfortable chairs where you can sit and enjoy the views. Each bathroom is tiled and there is a heater for the colder season. Meals are available from

HOTEL PRICE SCALE	
Price for a room given in US $.	
$	Up to $20
$$	$21-$50
$$$	$51-$100
$$$$	$101-$150
$$$$$	$151-$200
Anything over $200 is specified.	

the family that owns the hotel. They also offer area tours and have burros for rent ($10 a day). To get here, take the trail leading to the canyon, across from the main store and the church. The inn is about 300 feet/100 meters along the trail.

Cabañas Areponapuchia, *no phone, $$$,* is two miles/four km from Divisadero, at the junction of three canyons. Signs point the way. The owners of this hotel have a van with Turismo Barrancas Tours painted on the side; you'll see it at the station whenever the train arrives. The hotel is clean and has everything you need: hot water showers, meals ($5 each) and a location from which to explore. You can also hire a guide and mule here.

Uno Lodge, ☎ *800-843-1060 (Canyon Travels), $$$$,* is nine miles/15 km out of Divisadero, perched on the edge of an outcropping that overlooks the canyon and river one mile below. From the front deck, visitors get 180° view of the landscape. It was this lodge and its view that made me decide to include the canyon area in this book. A spotting scope is mounted on a tripod at the lodge so people can spend their entire vacation watching for wildlife if they wish. In the evenings, the owners often have a campfire for guests to enjoy. The lodge itself has rooms with private bathrooms complete with terrycloth bathrobes. Electricity is solar powered. Local guides are available for hiking trips. The Uno Lodge is owned by the Tarahumaras and is operated with the help of Canyon Travels.

Hotel Tejaban, ☎ *635-462-4442, $$$$/$,* is between Batópilas and Creel on a side road that is winding and steep in places. It takes 1½ hours by car to reach this hotel that is perched on a cliff overlooking Copper Canyon and the Urique River below. There are signs indicating the turn-off if you are driving. Tejaban has a deck around the front that faces the mountains and a huge fireplace in the foyer. Each of the 21 large rooms has its own fireplace, purified water and cable TV (can't live without that!). Some rooms have stone decorating the walls and all have soft double beds. There are ping-pong tables and all-terrain vehicles are available for rent. From the dining room you look out over mountains. Rates include three meals a day and, if four people are sharing one room, the price becomes quite affordable. There is also a dorm ($) that will hold up to 40 people. This room has bunks and a fireplace. Dinner and breakfast is $20 if staying in the dorm.

Hotel Barrancas Divisadero, ☎ *800-359-7234, $$$$$*, is located on the canyon rim, but it is just under 2.5 miles/four km from the train station; a bus will take you out to the hotel. This 50-room hotel overlooks the Tararecua, Urique and Copper canyons and the view you get is worth the bucks you pay to stay here. Each room, decorated in the designs of the Tarahumara people, has a frigobar, two double beds, a bathroom with a shower, a balcony, telephones and an iron. There is a restaurant, tour office, laundry service and gift shop on site. Room rates include all meals. You can rent bikes and horses or sign up for a mini-bus tour. This hotel books through agencies only – the phone number listed here is an agency in the States.

Mansion Tarahumara, ☎ *635-415-4721, $$$$$, www.mansiontara-humara.com.mx,* is tucked into the trees close to the canyon rim. This plush, five-star hotel has 50 cabins, each with private bathroom, porch, fireplace, tasteful décor and a telephone. The cabins are near a private lake where ducks swim. There is a restaurant and bar, disco, Jacuzzi, indoor pool, tour office and games rooms. Horseback riding is available. The tour office building looks like a Cinderella castle. The hotel is set on 30 acres and was first started as a modest restaurant with a few cabins. It became very popular and can now accommodate 120 people.

■ Places to Eat

There are food stalls where the train stops, but most people eat at their hotel.

La Bufa

This village is south from Creel about 60 miles/100 km along the road toward Batópilas. It has a splendid lookout down into Urique Canyon. Across the canyon is the Cerro de Siete Pisos (Hill of the Seven Floors) that has seven layers of earth visible along its walls. In the right light, photographic possibilities are endless.

Casa La Cancha, ☎ *635-346-0248 in Creel or 649-456-0624 in Batópilas, $$$,* has a guesthouse with private rooms, camp cots on the verandas and a campground with water and a toilet. The guesthouse includes a kitchen that has tiled floors and counters. The rooms are sparkling clean and comfortable, decorated in a simple style. The hotel is littered with clay artifacts, wood tables and plants enough to keep any horticulturist busy for days. The water comes from a natural spring in the mountains and meals can be included in the price. Camping is $5 per person. If you want to explore from this hotel, jeeps, drivers and guides are available. If you want to be sure of a room, book in advance. Casa La Cancha sits on a hillside above the only store in town. There is a sign. The down-side is that this place is now for sale.

Creel

Creel sits at 7,600 feet/2,200 meters above sea level and is surrounded by pine forests. The climate is cool. July and August are rainy months when biking and climbing are not good activities. By September, things start to dry out, and by November you can expect frost at night.

■ Getting Here

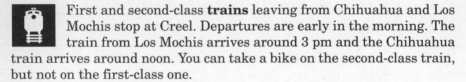

First and second-class **trains** leaving from Chihuahua and Los Mochis stop at Creel. Departures are early in the morning. The train from Los Mochis arrives around 3 pm and the Chihuahua train arrives around noon. You can take a bike on the second-class train, but not on the first-class one.

> ▶▶ **AUTHOR TIP:** *When you arrive at the station, numerous hawkers will try to sell you a room, a meal or a souvenir. If you go with them, they get a commission for taking you to a particular establishment, and that commission is added to your bill.*

Buses go from Creel to the south every other day. On the opposite days, there is a van at the Los Piños Hotel that will take you to Batópilas ($15, seven hours) – but only if it is not full with hotel guests.

■ Adventures on Foot

Hiking

Cusarare Village, a mission, has a little church built in 1733 that was restored in 1967. Prior to restoration, when the bell tower collapsed and nearly destroyed the church, the priest took out a set of paintings. They were sent to Europe and restored by profes-

sionals and are now back in the village museum, along with other artifacts from the local culture.

About a half-mile/one km east of town are some **rock paintings** depicting hunting scenes. Ask a local to take you to them. There is a lovely **waterfall** formed by the Cusarare River near the center of town that drops
90 feet/30 meters into a pool that's great for swimming. The trail from
town down to the waterfall and pool is easy to follow. There is a $1.50 en-
trance fee to see the falls.

> **BIRD WATCH:** *Birders in the Cusarare area
> will likely see eagles, Mexican chickadees, red-
> faced warblers, brown creepers, white-eared
> hummingbirds, dippers, belted kingfishers and
> eared trogons.*

Cusarare is 14 miles/22 km from Creel along the road to Guachochi. A
sign marks the turnoff, then it is two miles/three km down to the village.

> **LOCAL LINGO:** *The canyon in which
> Cusarare Village sits is a finger off the main
> Copper Canyon. The word* cusarare *means
> "place of the eagles" in Raramuri.*

Rock Climbing

The area offers volcanic terrain with vertical and overhung walls. Some
of the rock is soft and without many cracks, which makes it difficult to
place leads. Although a few leads are bolted into some spots, I suggest
that you check with locals before drilling. Also, bring glue-ins or ½-inch
bolts. Some climbers have used removable bolts. There is good bouldering
on the east side of the sewer plant.

Other areas recommended by Outpost Wilderness Adventures are along
the trail to Cusarare and the area around Basaseachic Falls. Serious
climbers should contact **Outpost Wilderness Adventure,** ☎ *830-238-
4383 in Texas, 719-748-3080 in Colorado, www.owa.com/copper-
schedule.cfm.*

Cueva de Leones is about a mile west of town and is only for those enjoying a hard climb. This cave area is found up a creek drainage and can
be reached by walking. There are many 5.10/5.11 climbs up the solid rock.
Cabins here have hot water, fireplaces and electricity. The cost is low, $$.

Valley of the Monks is six miles/nine km from Creel, past San Ignacio.
It has some excellent freestanding rock spires, some with anchors in
place. There is a $1.50 fee to enter this valley. Take the road going to San
Ignacio. The spires can be seen from San Ignacio – continue along the
road toward them.

■ Adventures on Water

 Located at the bottom of the Tararecua Canyon about 1,600 feet/ 500 meters below the village, **Recohuata Hot Springs** maintain a temperature near 98°F/37°C. The springs are in their natural state; no work has been done on the numerous pools lying in natural rock formations that are just made for soaking. There is a $1 entry fee.

To reach **Lake Arereko** you'll need to hire a vehicle, plus do some walking. The cost of transportation from hotels in town is about $15 per person. Lake Arereko is an alpine lake that sits at 8,000 feet/2,400 meters and is close to San Ignacio. It has the remains of an old mission and some interesting rock formations that look like mushrooms. The nearby mountains hold caves once used as homes by the Raramuri people. People living at Mission of Arereko on the lake sell handicrafts. The entrance fee to the lake is $1.50 per person.

 BIRD WATCH: *The lake is good for birders. Buffleheads, ring-necked ducks, blue-winged teals and osprey live here. Also rose-throated becards, squirrel cuckoos, buff-breasted flycatchers, military macaws, white-fronted parrots and trogons have been spotted.*

■ Adventures on Wheels

 You can pedal around on your bike for days without ever seeing the same rock, canyon or gorge twice. Or you can join in a race or guided trip. See Umarike Expeditions (page 162) or Outpost Wilderness Adventures (page 161) or visit www.yonke.org for details.

Bike Races & Guided Bike Tours

Cristo Ray Bike Race is held during the September 16th (Independence Day) celebrations. Everyone is welcome.

The **Dirt Crit Race** takes place at the KOA grounds every Friday afternoon. It is inexpensive to enter this BMX-style race, where each lap takes two to three minutes to complete. However, it is strenuous.

The Cross Country Race has numerous classes – expert, advanced, intermediate, beginner and juniors – all with specific age groupings. The race starts in the plaza, goes down the main street and up a dirt road to San Ignacio. It then climbs along a single track to the mesa overlooking town. The fun part is returning down the slippery trail that brings you back into town just so you can do it all over again. Depending on your class, you will do this circuit two to four times per race. The entry fee is about $10. This is becoming a popular run; in 2001 there were 350 competitors.

The Downhill Race is a head-clearer (after Saturday night at the bar) that takes place every Sunday morning. This steep downhill run starts at the highest point overlooking town and goes through switchbacks into the village. The course gets steeper as you go down; near the bottom it seems to be a corkscrew.

On Thursdays a single-track **guided ride** is held. It's a great opportunity for those new to the area.

La Onza Bike Race, held in July, is becoming a big event. It is the Mexican version of the Tour de France. In 2003, 450 racers completed this three-day course. The entry fee is $10 per person, making it affordable for most Mexican cyclists, the strongest competition. The race starts in the town square.

■ Outfitters/Tour Operators

Canyon Travels, *900 Ridge Creek, Bulverde, TX 78163-2872,* ☎ *800-843-1060, www.canyontravel.com.* These people work directly with the Tarahumara Indians in three lodges owned by the Indians. They also work with the Tarahumara Children's Hospital Fund and the Sierra Madre Alliance. They are underwriters for the Colibri Ecotourism Award and members of the International Eco-Tourism Society, The Adventure Travel Trade Association and the American Outdoors Association. They offer custom or pre-designed trips, specializing in day hikes, overnight camping treks and cultural, archeological and birding tours. They have guides trained in specific fields like birds or local history. Most of the guides are locals and, if they can't answer your question, will research the answer. The hotels are ecologically sound and offer first-class meals.

Outpost Wilderness Adventure, ☎ *830-238-4383 in Texas or 719-748-3080 in Colorado, www.owa.com/copperschedule.cfm*, is for anyone wanting to mountain bike or hike from Creel. This company of high-energy guys organizes a lot of biking events in the area. They have regularly scheduled rides from Creel toward Divisadero and each day they set up a classic single-track or logging road whirlwind run. If the weather is too cold, then a drop down to Rio Conchos will be their solution. OWA takes intermediate and advanced bikers only. Each day entails substantial climbing and descending and lots of technical maneuvering that translates into long hard days. Some rides will take in Recohuata Hot Springs, La Estrella outlook over Batópilas Canyon or the mesa single tack. Some routes even plunge into the Batópilas Canyon and then climb back out. This company takes small groups, usually around a dozen peo-

Northern Pacific Mexico

ple, and the cost (including food and accommodations) is $1,150 for eight days. You must be 18 or older for most runs, but they do have easier runs for younger people. If you have a bike and are interested in some of the local runs, contact OWA. But biking is not all they offer. They also give climbing lessons and take trips to climb some of the most challenging walls in Mexico. Their hiking excursions challenge even the most experienced trekkers. Outpost Wilderness Adventures is number one for outdoor adventure taken to the limit in the canyon area.

Umarike Expeditions, *Av. Francisco Villa,* ☎ *635-456-0248 or 406-5464, www.umarike.com.mx,* offers a long hike down to Batopolis and back. You must be in good shape to do this trek. They also do custom tours. They have an office in town, so stop by and talk to them if you have not made previous arrangements. Umarike also runs biking tours, is involved in the bike races in town and rents bikes ($12, four hours; $18, eight hours; $50, full day) if used in a race.

Best Western, *Lopez Mateos #61,* ☎ *800-716-3562 (Mexico) 635-456-0071 (local), 877-844-0409 (US), www.thelodgeatcreel.com/english.html,* offers numerous trips in a vehicle to places like the Valley of the Mushrooms and Frogs, Arareko Lake and the Tarahumara Caves for a mere $13 per person. These are half-day trips. There are over a dozen trip options, some of which take all day and cost $50 per person. Talk to them.

Copper Canyon Adventures, *PO Box 91123, Sioux Falls, SD 57109,* ☎ *800-530-8828, www.coppercanyonadventures.com.* This company offers either guided tours with a group or custom tours to suit every taste. However, they do suggest their guided tour, for three reasons. First, so that you can learn things that you wouldn't learn from books, such as local stories, beliefs and gossip. Also, the guides can do the translating for you when the locals can't speak English or Spanish. Finally, their guides will take you to places seldom visited. The cost is around $200 per day, depending on how many people book and what you do.

> ▶▶ **AUTHOR NOTE:** *The Copper Canyon Adventures website asks that you pay an extra $100 if paying by credit card. I didn't check with them on this, but it seems to me it would be against their contract with the credit card company. If they insist on this charge, report them.*

■ Places to Stay

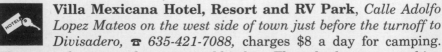

Villa Mexicana Hotel, Resort and RV Park, *Calle Adolfo Lopez Mateos on the west side of town just before the turnoff to Divisadero,* ☎ *635-421-7088,* charges $8 a day for camping. There are showers and a communal kitchen. They also have some cabins with private bathrooms and kitchenettes that cost $65-$85 a day. There is a restaurant, bar and grocery store.

Los Piños, *on the main street, across from Restaurant Lupita, no phone, $,* has rooms with private bathrooms that are so clean you feel you must disinfect yourself before entering. This is a great place, but I have heard that the friendliness for which it was so famous has declined. The service is still considered good.

HOTEL PRICE SCALE	
Price for a room given in US $.	
$	Up to $20
$$	$21-$50
$$$	$51-$100
$$$$	$101-$150
$$$$$	$151-$200
Anything over $200 is specified.	

Best Western Lodge, *Lopez Mateos #61,* ☎ *635-456-0071, www. thelodgeatcreel.com/english.html, $$$,* has lakeside log cabins, some of which can sleep up to 10 people. Each cabin has a kitchenette, satellite TV and stone fireplace or heater. There are two double beds in each cabin and a spacious private bathroom. The stonework in the cabins is accented by the wood beam structure. The hotel offers laundry service, purified water, VCR movies, safe deposit boxes, telephones, Internet access and a doctor on call. English, French and Spanish are spoken. They also have bicycle and horse rentals. This is probably the best place in town.

Casa Huespedes Margarita's, *on the square,* ☎ *635-456-0045, $/$$$,* has dorm-styled rooms as well as private rooms with bathroom. The cost includes breakfast and supper. Delicious meals are served at huge tables and everyone gets the same. This is the most popular place for backpackers.

Parador de la Montaña, *Mateos #44,* ☎ *635-456-0075, $$$,* has large rooms with TV and private bathroom. The rooms are beautifully decorated and warm. The hotel is on the main street.

Margarita's Plaza Mexicana, *on the plaza,* ☎ *635-456-0245, $$$$,* is an upscale place with rooms around a central courtyard. They have a private bathroom, air conditioning and TV, and the price includes two meals a day. The bar here is patronized mostly by foreigners.

Nuevo Barrancas del Cobre, *Calle Francisco Villa across from the train station,* ☎ *635-456-0022, $$$$,* has beautiful old rooms with high comfort levels. There are also cabins that sleep up to four people and come with air conditioning, TVs, private bathrooms and nice sitting areas.

■ Places to Eat

 La Torje, just up from the train station and across from Umarike Office, is the first coffee shop in Creel to use organic Oaxaca coffee. The desserts are excellent. They are open from 5 to 10 pm daily.

The Lodge at Creel in the Best Western Hotel has their restaurant tucked behind the floor-to-ceiling stone fireplace. The atmosphere is warm and the food is excellent.

The Tungar is a small café next to the tracks between the train station and the Mission store. This little café is known as *Hospital de Crudos* (Hangover Hospital). If this diagnosis is correct for you, the seafood done Mexican style (spicy) is sure to be the remedy. Actually, it's good whether you have a *crudos* or not.

Veronica's on the main drag is highly recommended and patronized by most backpackers (*muchileros*).

Parador de las Montañas, *Calle Alfonso Lopez Mateos #44,* across from Tarahumara Hotel. They open late in the afternoon and stay open until midnight. This is the most upscale place in town. Enchiladas cost $3, chicken in a mole sauce is $4, and a coke costs less than a dollar.

Todo Ricos is the most popular place in town to have a beer and hamburger. It is on the main drag and open 9 am to 11 pm. A burger is priced at $2.50 and comes with cheese and lettuce that is safe to eat.

South of the Copper Canyon

Guasave

This attractive little city of 100,000 people is just 25 miles/50 km from the ocean. Located on the Sinaloa River, the town supports an agricultural population, one that grows corn, wheat, sorghum, soy, cotton and beans. The biggest draw for visitors are the Nio Ruins, which date back 800 years, and the birdlife on the islands at Las Glorias.

■ Services

Contact the **Police** at ☎ *687-872-1232*.

There's a **medical center** on *Av Lopez Mateos #643,* ☎ *687-872-8283.*

▪ Sightseeing

 The **Church of the Rosary** near the plaza has a statue of Mary with the Christ child in one arm and a rosary dangling from the other. The statue is paraded through town on the first Sunday every October and the last Sunday every November. The church itself is not overly ornate.

▪ Adventures on Water

 Playa Las Glorias is known for its sunsets and its abundant bird population. To get to Tamazula and Las Glorias, south of Guasave, follow the signs and the paved highway for six miles/ 10 km to Cubelete. Turn south (left) and follow the road for 4.5 miles/ eight km to Tamazula. Take the dirt road across from the church in Tamazula and follow it past Zerote and Brecha. Las Glorias is eight miles/13 km past Brecha.

 **BIRD WATCH:** *There are Swainson's hawks, forest falcons, finches, verdins, terns and pelicans. Those with a bit more birding knowledge should keep an eye out for colima warblers, blue, black and gray gnatcatchers, laughing gulls, ring-billed gulls, Hermann's gulls, herring gulls and snowy egrets.*

Just south of Las Glorias is a 50-mile/80-km bay dotted with islands and inlets. Both the Mocorito and Evora rivers drain into this stretch of water, creating a rich estuary. The most important areas for birding are **Red Beach Bay** and the **Bay of Santa Maria the Reformation**. The islands of interest are **Saliaca**, **Altamura** and **Tachichilte**. The island of Altamura is especially interesting because of its large sand dunes. You will need to hire a boat to take you out. The fishing villages of La Reforma or Las Glorias have people who will rent you a barge. Ask around. Besides Mr Moro's Place on the beach just south of Las Glorias, the villages of Guasave, Angostua and Navolato have comfortable places to stay and numerous places to eat. Angostura and Navolato are along Highway 15 (also referred to as the main or interstate highway) heading south toward Mazatlan.

Navachiste Bay is a long bay (one mile/two km) that is part of a 30-mile/ 50-km stretch of inlets and islands. Just south of that stretch there is a peninsula and another 50 miles/80 km of the same. The entire shore has white sand interspersed with rocks. The area is enjoyed mostly by birds and a few Mexican fishermen. The bay is protected by the islands of San

Ignacio and Macapule (15 miles/23 km long and two miles/2.5 km wide) to its north and is dotted with mangroves (where rivers drain into the ocean) that house numerous varieties of birds. White storks and plovers are the most common birds in the area. Inland, mountains rise at least 600 feet/200 meters and those that reach the shore often stop abruptly, leaving high cliffs.

The islands south of Navachiste Bay are filled with wildlife and some have ancient rock sculptures. All are good for photographers. One of the islands is called the **Island of the Poets**. It got its name when an international group came here every year to write poems. The landscape offers inspiration for literary creations. Another island is called **White Hill**, because of the guano that sparkles against the red rock. **The Windows** is another island where rocks have been used for recording history. Some of the petroglyphs represent sea creatures and are fairly large, standing up to three feet/one meter.

Bird Island is a must for birders. Surrounded by mangrove swamps and dotted with spiny underbrush, it is a haven for feathered friends. There are numerous species in plentiful numbers. To find a boat to take you to the islands, stop by Mr. Moro's Place at the hotel/RV site in Las Glorias.

 BIRD WATCH: *Bird Island has cormorants, storks, pelicans, seagulls, frigates and osprey. Farther inland you will find ibis, storks, vultures, and numerous songbirds. Even during non-migratory periods, birds abound. Records show that 117 species live on this island.*

Fishing is good at the mouth of Sinaloa River, but the rocks are steep and take a bit of clamoring around before you find a good perch.

■ Adventures in Culture

Nio Ruins archeological site is less than six miles/10 km west of town on Sinaloa River. There are also a number of old missions farther up the river. Nio has a necropolis that was in use between 800 and 1,200 years ago. At that time, this farming community made ceramics that were superior to those of other villages. Found at the site were burial jars, plates, bowls and pots. The ceramics indicate to archeologists that residents traded with people as far away as Oaxaca and Mexico City. One of the vases, made of alabaster, is similar to some found in the Veracruz area. Once the Jesuits arrived, they converted people to Catholicism and built structures in the European fashion. Walls and two complete arched entrances from the early Jesuit missions still stand. The mud brick buildings that served as the monastery and church are also in fairly good condition. Only one of the buildings has a roof on it.

Tamazula is 11 miles/18 km south of Guasave and is the last mission town along the river. The mission was founded by Father Clerecis. It was built in the 16th century but was later destroyed by cyclones. The present church was built in 1820 in the Franciscan style with baked bricks. The museum attached to the church shows religious artifacts. The route to the mission is also a good way to reach Las Glorias Beach, one of the best along the coast. To get to the mission, turn off Highway 15 at El Cubilete and follow the signs to Tamazula. To get to Playa Las Glorias, follow the dirt road opposite the church.

■ Places to Stay

 San Enrique Motel, *Blas Valenzuela #42*, ☎ *687-872-0040*, *$*, has 48 rooms with private bathrooms. Free parking.

HOTEL PRICE SCALE
Price for a room given in US $.
$.................Up to $20
$$..................$21-$50
$$$...............$51-$100
$$$$ ....$101-$150
$$$$$ ....$151-$200
Anything over $200 is specified.

Hotel Mission, *at Km. 144 on Highway 15, no phone, $*, prefers to rent rooms by the hour. It is very basic but includes porno flicks.

Hotel El Rosario, *Corregidora #150*, ☎ *687-872-0003*, *$$*, is a three-star hotel with 30 rooms, all with private bathrooms and air conditioning.

Mr Moro Hotel and RV Park, *Blvd El Tiburon #1000*, ☎ *687-873-7007*, *www.mrmoro.com.mx*, *$$$*, has 20 rooms and 80 RV sites right on the beach at Las Glorias. The rooms have air conditioning, great views, private bathrooms and comfortable beds. Rooms are clean and pleasantly decorated. There is a pool surrounded by palapa huts and a children's play ground. The RV sites all have full hookup. A restaurant on site serves international and local dishes with specialties like shrimp, calamari, onion rings and salads. The bar makes excellent margaritas. Mr Moro also rents boats with guides so you can fish or visit the islands.

Hotel El Sembrador, *V. Guerrero and Emiliano Zapata*, ☎ *687-872-4011*, *www.hotelelsembrador.cjb.net/*, *$$$*, has 85 rooms and 10 suites. All have air conditioning, carpets, cable TV, private bathrooms, purified water and soft beds. There is laundry service, a money exchange, a travel agent and free parking. A restaurant, bar and disco are also on site. The disco has music every night but the bar has it only on the weekends. The restaurant has a breakfast buffet on Friday, Saturday and Sunday that is popular.

Northern Pacific Mexico

■ Places to Eat

 Retaurante El Granero, *V. Guerrero and Emiliano Zapata,* ☎ *687-872-4011, www.hotelelsembrador.cjb.net,* in the Sembrador Hotel is about the best place to have a meal unless you head out to the beaches and eat seafood from one of the palapa huts.

Restaurant La Pizzeta, *Blvd Central #115,* ☎ *687-872-7777,* has pizza for reasonable prices. This is always a safe bet.

Central Pacific Mexico

Mazatlan

Herman Melville, the author of *Moby Dick*, was in Mazatlan in the late 1800s for a period of two weeks. There is a plaque commemorating his visit. He loved the place. Since his visit the area became first a tourist draw and then an ideal retirement community. The town is

in close proximity to places of interest where one can ride horses, watch whales, photograph birds, swim with dolphins or surf the waves. Those seeking other forms of entertainment won't be disappointed, either. Mazatlan has everything from a Hooters bar to the symphony, golf courses to art museums, sandy beaches with good surf to quiet bays for kayaking.

Mazatlan is divided into three sections. **Old Mazatlan** is at the south end of the bay where the town started to develop for tourism in the 1950s. The center part, **New Mazatlan**, which starts east of Del Mar Avenue, is where new homes, shopping centers and industrial parks have sprouted. The *Zona Dorada*, or **Golden Zone**, is north of Rafael Buelna Avenue, and it's where you'll find big hotels, restaurants, discos, bars and souvenir shops.

■ Getting Here & Around

By Plane

 The city is served by Aero California, AeroMexico, Alaska Airlines and Mexicana Airlines. The airport is 11 miles/18 km south of the city. A **taxi** (car) to the city center costs about $25. The more affordable taxis, called *pulmonias* (pneumonia!), cost about $5 and are actually made-over golf carts.

AIRLINE CONTACT INFORMATION		
Aero California	www.aerocalifornia.de	☎ 800-237-6225 (Mx)
AeroMexico	www.aeromexico.com	☎ 800-237-6639 (US) 800-021-4010 (Mx)
Alaska Airlines	www.alaskaair.com	☎ 800-252-7522 (US) 55-5282-2484 (Mx)
Mexicana Airlines	www.mexicana.com	☎ 800-531-7921 (US) 800-509-8960 (Mx)

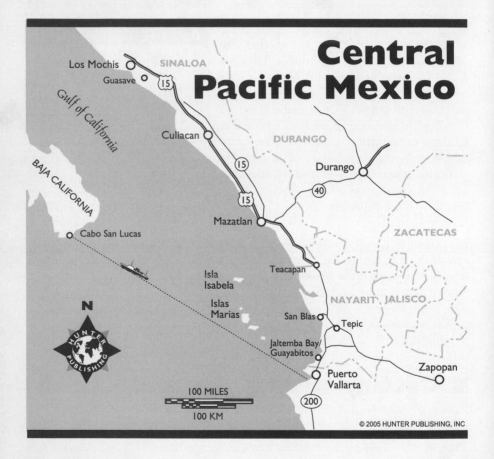

By Bus

The bus station is three km/two miles north of the city along Highway 15. It is a large terminal with first- and second-class areas. There is a baggage storage desk, a couple of food stalls, some souvenir shops and lots of companies vying for your business.

PULMONIAS

Pulmonias were first invented by Miguel Ramirez-urquijo in the early 1960s as a cheap method of transportation. He called them pneumonia (tongue in cheek), in Spanish. Considering the climate in Mazatlan, that is the last thing these delightful taxis would cause. They are brightly painted with things like streaks of fire, exotic birds or anything else that will make the look unique and distinct.

Pulmonias sport unique paintwork.

By Car

There are numerous places to rent vehicles in Mazatlan. The highway is not as busy as the streets in town, and Highway 15, going both north and south from Mazatlan, is a four-lane toll highway that is in excellent condition.

CAR RENTAL COMPANIES

They are all here: Budget, Hertz, Avis, National and so on. If you book from one of the large hotels, you will have to use the company they work with. I mention just a couple here to give an idea of prices and types of cars available.

AGA Rent-a-Car, *at the airport,* ☎ *669-981-3580, or on Av Culiacan and Mochis,* ☎ *669-914-4405, www.agarentacar.com. mx*, has small cars for rent. Smaller vehicles are a good option here because they are easier to maneuver around the maniac city drivers. The approximate price for a Volkswagen is $400 a week and a Jetta Stratus is about $950. Insurance is extra.

Budget Car Rentals, *Av Camaron Sabalo #402, Zona Dorada,* ☎ *669-913-2000, or at the airport,* ☎ *669-982-1220*, has cars with unlimited mileage, automatic transmission and air conditioning. They can be rented from the airport for $200-$400 a week, depending on the size of the vehicle. Insurance is extra.

Rent-A-Ride, *Av Camaron Sabalo #204, Lomas Plaza (next to Kelly's Bike Shop),* ☎ *669-913-1000*, has 150 to 1500 cc motorbikes. You can rent them for four hours or up to a week, or take a guided motorcycle tour to Copala, Concordia or La Noria. You must have a motorcycle license to qualify. I have no prices for the bikes, which all appeared to be in good condition. However, be aware that I know zip about motorbikes.

By Ferry/Boat

The **Baja Ferry Company**, ☎ *669-622-3390*, runs between Mazatlan and La Paz on the Baja California Peninsula, leaving Mazatlan every day at 3 pm. The terminal is at the harbor on Av Carnaval. The cost to bring a vehicle over is $250-$400, depending on size. Passengers willing to sit up all night in fairly comfortable seats pay $30; cabins with private bathrooms are available for about $60 per person. The crossing takes 12 to 18 hours.

If arriving by private boat there is an immigration and customs office at the ferry slip. Should you need to extend your visa, the staff is all too willing to help.

■ History

 The **Nahutal people** lived on the bay and fished. Some of the petroglyphs found on the islands along this strip of coast go back 10,000 years, so we know that the worship of sun and sand is not a new phenomenon with the coming of the Europeans.

Nuño de Guzman and his 25 sailors are credited with being the first Europeans to settle on the bay. That was in 1531. When Guzman left with his boats full of gold that was taken from the mines inland, the bay was left to the locals again. However, it didn't take long for the French and English pirates who sailed the waters playing rogue with each other to

Toys for All Soul's Day

Couple snorkeling, Puerto Vallarta

Above: Sugarcane flowers

Below: Dawn mist on lagoon in Southern Mexico

Painted wooden furniture, Patzcuaro

Above: Elderly woman on cobblestone street

Below: Sunset with palm trees

Cathedral, Mazatlan

Above: Guaymas marina at sunrise

Below: Dolphin statue, Mazatlan

Man in traditional dress

Mazatlan has something for every traveler.

take advantage of the hiding places along this shore. Finally, in the late 1800s, the Spanish government built watchtowers on the hills around the bay so that they could send their navy out and get rid of the pirates.

Mazatlan then became an important port. The Americans occupied it during the Mexican American War and Confederates took over during the American Civil War. In 1871, the British Navy occupied the area. This seemed to draw criminals of all sorts and the streets became dangerous. It was during this time that residents started putting bars on their windows and doors, a practice still followed today, although the dangers are almost nonexistent.

Mazatlan was the state capital from 1859 to 1873. The dictator **Porfirio Diaz** became president between 1876 and 1910, at which time a railway arrived at the port, the waterfront and the lighthouse were modernized, the cathedral was finished and the arts flourished. The Teatro Rubio was completed by the late 1890s. There were up and down periods during the next 75 years, and then the final invasion began. It was that of the tourist.

■ Services

i **Police Station**, *Calle Ruiz and Santa Monica, Zona Dorada,* ☎ *669-903-9200.*

The **Tourist Office** *is on the 4th floor of the Banrural Bldg, Av Sabalo and Tiburon,* ☎ *669-916-5166,* two blocks past El Cid Resort.

The **post office**, *Calle Florez and Juarez,* ☎ *669-981-2121, Monday to Friday, 8 am-5 pm, Saturday until 1 pm.* Red mailboxes are along sidewalks everywhere in town.

Head to **Hospital Sharp**, *Calle Kumate and Bueina near Zaragoza Park,* ☎ *669-986-5676 or 986-7911,* if you have an emergency. There is a lab, X-ray and intensive care services available here. English is spoken.

Polimedica, ☎ *669-913-9984, annachangmd@red2000.com.mx,* is a plastic surgeon should you want a tummy tuck, breast enlargement, face lift or any other type of reconstruction. Mazatlan is a choice place to recover from something like this.

The **Tourist Emergency Hotline**, ☎ *078,* is for tourists who run into problems. The line features bilingual operators who can provide information or transfer emergency calls to the appropriate agency. This is a 24-hour, seven-day-a-week service.

Publications

Pacific Pearl, *www.pacificpearl.com*, lists lots of event times and dates and also has a want-ad section.

Mazatlan Interactive has information about events, such as the annual triathlon, and columns with Mexican recipes.

Complete Guide to Mazatlan, by Oses Cole Isunza and written in English, is a little red pamphlet you'll see at tour offices and some hotels. For those wanting more history than my book can supply, Isunza's book is the one. It is not expensive ($10) and the proceeds go to the Red Cross of Mazatlan. The book is very well researched and has an infinite amount of historical details about the city. There is also a map at the back indicating where all the important buildings are located in Old Mazatlan.

■ Sightseeing

Old Mazatlan

 This area was in total disrepair until the 1980s when a group of wise citizens realized that the old buildings were, in fact, cultural history and needed to be salvaged. Today, the transforma-

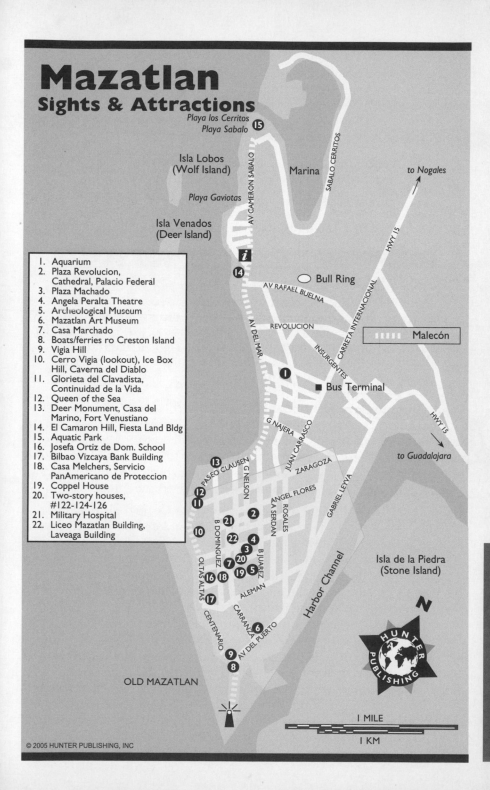

Mazatlan
Sights & Attractions

Playa los Cerritos
Playa Sabalo ⑮

Isla Lobos
(Wolf Island)

Marina

to Nogales

Playa Gaviotas

Isla Venados
(Deer Island)

AV CAMERON SABALO

SABALO CERRITOS

HWY 15

i

⑭

Bull Ring

AV RAFAEL BUELNA

CARRETA INTERNACIONAL

REVOLUCION

AV DEL MAR

INSURGENTES

❘❙❙❙❙ Malecón

❶

■ Bus Terminal

HWY 15

G NAJERA

to Guadalajara

1. Aquarium
2. Plaza Revolucion, Cathedral, Palacio Federal
3. Plaza Machado
4. Angela Peralta Theatre
5. Archeological Museum
6. Mazatlan Art Museum
7. Casa Marchado
8. Boats/ferries ro Creston Island
9. Vigia Hill
10. Cerro Vigia (lookout), Ice Box Hill, Caverna del Diablo
11. Glorieta del Clavadista, Continuidad de la Vida
12. Queen of the Sea
13. Deer Monument, Casa del Marino, Fort Venustiano
14. El Camaron Hill, Fiesta Land Bldg
15. Aquatic Park
16. Josefa Ortiz de Dom. School
17. Bilbao Vizcaya Bank Building
18. Casa Melchers, Servicio PanAmericano de Proteccion
19. Coppel House
20. Two-story houses, #122-124-126
21. Military Hospital
22. Liceo Mazatlan Building, Laveaga Building

PASEO CLAUSEN

⑬

JUAN CARRASCO

ZARAGOZA

G NELSON

⑫
⑪

ANGEL FLORES

ROSALES

A SERDAN

GABRIEL LEYVA

⑩

㉑

②

B DOMINGUEZ

㉒

④

③
⑦

B JUAREZ

⑲ ⑤

Isla de la Piedra
(Stone Island)

OLTAS ALTAS

⑯ ⑱

ALEMAN

⑰

Harbor Channel

CENTENARIO

CARRANZA

⑥

AV DEL PUERTO

⑨
⑧

N

OLD MAZATLAN

HUNTER PUBLISHING

1 MILE

1 KM

Central Pacific Mexico

tion has occurred and walking, sitting, eating or touring in this area is a must for at least a few days. It will appear you have entered a time warp and gone back a hundred years; the modern conveniences incorporated into the restorations are non-intrusive. The buildings are pastel-colored with wrought iron bars decorating the windows and plaques identifying where you are. The streets are narrow and the plazas usually have restaurants with tables on the street.

 Viejo Mazatlan is a locally produced paper that features historical stories about things like the coming of the Japanese after World War II or the first writers to the city and what they said about the place. Be certain to read this and patronize some of the events listed.

SINALOA TAMBORA

The Sinaloa tambora is the type of band you'll hear playing around Mazatlan. It was first started in the early 1900s when a group of Germans came from Bavaria to start a brewery. Being typical Bavarians, they couldn't live without their "oompah-pah," so the music was quickly adopted and incorporated into Mexican music. Today it is a unique sound that is part German, part Mexican.

Plaza Revolucion, has *Calles Angel Florex, Guillermo Nelson, 21 de Marzo and Benito Juarez* along its four sides. This was once the site of the city's market, but now it has numerous laurel trees interspersed with park benches. These surround a kiosk built in 1909 with 4,000 pesos left by a German merchant commemorating his own 50th birthday. The kiosk was built 13 years after the municipality received the funds.

Building of the **Cathedral of the Immaculate Conception**, at one end of the square, was started in 1856 but not completed until 1899. It was delayed because the Laws of the Reform caused confusion as to the allocation of funds. It was under the pressure of Father Miguel Lacarra, who wanted the building finished, that the work was completed. The two towers weren't finished until the mid-1890s. This was because of politics between the designer and the priests of the parish. Inside, the cathedral has three naves and a gothic altar. There are statues of saints and angels carved from white Italian marble. There are four side altars in the church and the tomb of Miguel Franco, the first Bishop of the dioceses of Mazatlan. The main altar is made from Carrera marble and crystal chandeliers light the main aisle. The pipe organ came from Paris and was first played in the church in 1889. The stone that is so prominent in the arches and columns is from a nearby quarry. The cathedral, like many parts of Old Mazatlan, is being restored to its original grandeur.

Palacio Federal, *east side of the plaza*, is a modern two-story building that was constructed in the 1940s. It has the post office inside. **City Hall**, built in the 1850s, is also on the plaza. It houses most of the elected municipal representatives. In the mayor's office is an exceptional portrait of Miguel Hidalgo, the father of Mexican Independence. The balcony overlooking the square is where the Grito ceremony takes place every September 15. The ceremony commemorates the call to arms made by Hidalgo in 1810 that finally resulted in independence.

Plaza Mochada, *Av Miguel Aleman,* is the oldest plaza in the city. Today it is lined with restaurants, most of which have seating on or near the street. There is only one road past the plaza so traffic is low, the square unpolluted and quiet. This is a very bohemian place to sit at any time of day. Nearby restaurants are Pedro and Lola, Altazor Arz, El Cielo, Nikoy Suchi and Café Pacifico.

The land holding the plaza was originally a swamp, but city officials in the early 1800s closed a saltwater channel that fed the area and let the land dry. The land was donated to the city by Juan Nepomuceno Machado, a rich merchant originally from the Philippines who made his fortunes in Mazatlan. Just off the plaza is the bust of Romana de la Peña de Careaga, the founder of the city's orphanage. Across from the bust is the Angela Peralta Theatre, an active performing and visual arts center.

Angela Peralta Theatre, *Calle Carnival #47, just off Plaza Mochada, no phone,* was the dream of Manuel Rubio who, in 1869 bought the property and started the construction. He died when the ship he was traveling on sank, so his widow had the theater finished and, in 1874, it opened. However, due to financial difficulty, she couldn't keep it running, so she sold it to Martin Mendia, who did some work to the building and again sold it, probably at a handsome profit, to Juan Bautista. Under that directorship the theater flourished and became the best performing arts center in western Mexico. In 1943, its name was changed to honor the singer who never managed to sing on its stage. Angela Peralta and her entourage of 76 people came to the city to perform but died during Mazatlan's yellow fever epidemic.

THE MEXICAN NIGHTINGALE

Soprano Angela Peralta was dubbed the Mexican Nightingale when she mesmerized European audiences with her voice. She was just 16 years of age. In 1873 she did a second tour of Europe and sang with Aida with Verdi as conductor. She not only sang, but she also composed operas. After a famous life peppered with scandals, Peralta died in Mazatlan in1883 at the age of 38.

During a hurricane in 1975, the building was destroyed and lay in ruin until the mid-1980s, when all of Old Mazatlan was under restoration. It took from 1987 to 1992 for the building to be reconstructed.

Before entering the theater, visit the exhibition gallery to view temporary exhibits and old photos showing the building's history. There is also an extensive display of carnival costumes. There is a $2 charge to tour the theater if you are not attending a concert.

The theater seats 840 people and you can get cubicles where your party can sit separate from the rest of the audience, much like they did 200 years ago in theaters across Europe. These cubicles are complete with red velvet curtains held in place with gold ropes and tassels. Elegant! The theater is open about an hour before public performances. Check the posters outside or with the tourist office for performance times.

The **Church of San José**, *Calle Neveria and La Campaña*. Constructed in 1835, this is the oldest church in town. Although tiny, it is one of the nicer churches in the area.

The **Archeological Museum of Mazatlan**, *Sixto Osuna #72,* ☎ *669-985-3502, 10 am-6 pm daily, except Mondays, Sunday until 3 pm, $5*. The museum is in a restored building constructed in 1904 as the home of Marcos Elorza. There is a small collection of Indian artifacts and some collected items of the city's chronicler, Miguel Valdes. Of the three salons, the first holds mostly ceramics from around the state. The second has clothes made from cotton and animal skins, lace collars and ornaments used to decorate the body. The third has mostly funereal objects, including urns and objects needed while traveling in the afterlife, such as jewelry and personal belongings that were precious to the deceased. The displays are well organized and there is a bookstore with English publications about Mexican art and history.

Mazatlan Museum of Art, *Calle Venustiano Carranza #1, no phone, open daily except Monday, 10 am-6 pm, and Sunday until 3 pm,* is located in a historic building constructed in 1896 by an old ship-owning family. The building was taken over by the government, restored and made the cultural center in 1998. Today you can see paintings from well-known artists such as José Luis Cuevas, Rufino Tamayo and Francisco Goitia. There is also a room dedicated to local artists.

Casa Machado, *Calles Heriberto Frias, Sixto Osuna, Belisario Dominguez and Constitución, no phone, 9 am-6 pm daily,* contains furniture and artifacts from Old Mazatlan. This huge building, also called Portales de Canobbio, is named after the family who owned it for about 150 years. It was Benito Machado and his brother Juan Nepomuceno (I too don't see the connection in family names) who ran a trading house in the building. It changed hands occasionally until 1830, when Tomasa Ostuna got hold of it and became the only legal seller of footwear in the city. The *casa* was expanded and thus started the world-famous shoe store business. Eventually, the house was willed to the wife of Luis Canobbio (aha – the connection) and they opened a pharmacy in part of the building. This family also developed some medical remedies that earned them a fortune.

There's a **bullfighting** ring at Av Rafael Buelna at the Plaza Monumental. Bullfights are held every Sunday starting at 4 pm sharp from Christmas to Easter. This is an old Latin spectator sport that is distasteful to some but should be viewed with an open mind at least once. The bull, once killed, is used meat. The cost for this event is $25 per person and usually three bulls are killed each week.

Matadors challenging el toro.

A fight has three stages. The first is when the bull is rushed into the arena to display his powers and two *picadors* thrust lances into its shoulders. The second stage is when the *banderilleros* stick long darts into the shoulders to debilitate the animal. The final stage is announced by trumpets. This is when the *matador* dodges and taunts the dying bull.

> ### TERMS OF BULLFIGHTING
>
> ■ *Banderilleros* are the men who assist the matador in positioning the bull in the ring.
> ■ *Banderillas* are the short swords used by the *banderilleros* to stab the bull.
> ■ A *corrida* is a bullfight.
> ■ The **matador** is an experienced bullfighter who is always dressed in an elaborate outfit.
> ■ The *picador* is the fighter who, from the back of a horse, stabs the bull in the neck and shoulder muscles.
> ■ *Sorteo* is the process of choosing a bull for a *matador*.
> ■ *El toro* is the bull.

■ Adventures on Foot

Along the Malecón

 The *malecón* is one of the nicest in Mexico, starting in the old city and working 12 miles/20 km up the coast to the big hotels. There are historical viewpoints, statues and palapa-hut restaurants along the way. Some of the beaches are great for cooling off, while others are best for surfing. It is a good day's easy exercise to walk from one end to the other and then take a bus/taxi back.

I will start my description of the town at the south end of the *malecón* in Old Mazatlan where the ferry crosses over to **Creston Island**. The island has **El Faro**, set on a hill just over 500 feet/150 meters high. Many consider this the tallest working lighthouse in the world. Light projected from the lighthouse can reach 36 miles/45 km out to sea. There are restaurants at the jetty, along with numerous boats ready to take you to the islands just offshore.

Following **Centenario Blvd**, named so because it was finished during the 100-year anniversary of Mexico's independence, climb Vigia Hill on the opposite side of the road to the ocean. On the hill is an old British canon manufactured in the 1800s. This lookout is where the colonists kept vigil for pirates coming into the bay, and used the cannon on them. Looking from the top of the hill, the two white islands covered in guano, called the Two Sisters, are impressive. The third island, from November to May, holds a colony of sea lions.

Where the *malecón* turns into **Olas Altas Blvd** and joins Olas Altas Bay (means "big waves") is the Shield of the State. The bay here is good for surfers and you will often see surfing classes taking place in the waters protected by the huge rock forming the barrier between the two bays.

The oval **shield** has the Mexican eagle on top with a snake in his mouth. Under the snake, in the oval area, is the name of the state and on the bottom is the date of independence for the state. The oval is divided into four equal sections and represents the cities of Mazatlan with the deer, El Fuerte with the fort, Culiacan with the anchor and Rosario with the sheep. The shield is made of ceramic tiles.

Olas Altas in 1862 was victory square when the Mexicans expelled the French. The celebrations lasted 15 days, during which time tents were put along the street to hold restaurants, saloons and ice cream parlors. There were street musicians, fireworks and betting games. Tourism in the 1960s caused the transformation of the area, and now the street is full of hotels, restaurants, marinas and commercial housing developments.

Continuing along the avenue, but before Calle Angel Florez, are two old mansions. One, built in 1904 by Marcos Elorza, is now the archeological museum (see page 178), and the second is the Angela Peralta theater started in 1869 and completed in 1874 (see page 177).

After the next small point in the bay is **Ice Box Hill**, on the opposite side of the road to the ocean. This is where city residents once kept ice imported from San Francisco. The coolness of the inner mountain kept the ice solid for a long time. At the base of the hill is a barred-off entrance called the **Caverna del Diablo** (Devil's Cave), where colonists kept ammunition in the days when the cannon on Vigia Hill was in full use. Across from the hill is the bronze monument to the **Women of Mazatlan**. They appear to be sea nymphs, and look very sexy with their outstretched arms and clinging robes.

Just beyond the monument is the **Glorieta del Clavadista**, the cliff where divers plunge into the swirling waters below. The trick is to dive just when the waves are at their highest below the cliffs. If they miscalculate, the water won't be deep enough and they will crash onto the rocks. At one time this was a trade where divers went into the water for coins thrown by spectators, but now they do it for entertainment and collect the coins personally. To watch them is breathtaking. They perform twice daily, once at 11 am and once at 1 pm. Next to the cliff is the **Continuidad de la Vida** (Continuation of Life) statue with plunging and diving dolphins representing life. Up from the dolphins is the **Queen of the Sea**, a little mermaid with cupid beside her.

The *malecón* turns east at this point and the name changes to **Claussen Blvd**. Just before it turns is the monument to the deer.

 LOCAL LINGO: Mazatlan *means "Place of the Deer" in local Nahuatl language.*

On the point across from the deer are two mansions standing alone. One is the **Casa del Marino**, House of the Sailors, where visiting sailors could stay as guests of the city. The second one is **Fort Venustiano Carranza**, built after the French left. There is a sheltered cove along the beach called Playa Los Piños, another surfing beach. The second cliff forming this cove is Punta Tiburon, where the University of Sinaloa has its marine sciences building. You will often see students on the rocky shore working on projects.

The next stretch follows Av del Mar. This is the longest bay in Mazatlan; it starts at Tiburon and goes all the way to **El Camaron Hill**, five miles/ eight km away. Long ago this bay was called San Felix Bay and the port at one end was called Puerto Viejo, but now the beach is simply called North Beach.

CITY SYMBOL

Part way along Av de Mar, at Av Gutierrez Naiera, is the **Fisherman's Monument**, built in 1958 by sculptor Rodolfo Becerra. The fisherman is throwing a net while his naked woman waits nearby and a marlin swims below. This is the symbol of the city. Who ever said the Mexicans were conservative? The tall column entwined in the sculpture represents the lighthouse. The plaque with the poem on it is the work of Charles MacGregor.

This stretch of beach is where the more expensive hotels and trendy restaurants are located. It is also where joggers, entertainers and fishermen congregate once the sun falls below the waters.

Near the far end of the *malecón* is Punta del Camaron with the **Fiesta Land** building, a Moorish-styled complex with hotel, restaurants, discos and bars. It is a landmark that is easily seen from most parts of the city. You have now entered the Golden Zone, where **Playa Las Gaviotas** and **Playa Sabalo** offer their clean beaches and soft surf for swimming. North of Camino Real is **Playa Los Cerritos** (Little Hills Beach), where the sand and sea stretch for six miles/10 km. This is one of my favorite areas because it is isolated and exceptionally clean.

Historical House Tour

This may be the only city in the country that boasts a walking tour of historical houses, all researched and recorded by Oses Cole Isunza in his book (see page 486). There are almost 40 buildings mentioned in the book; I describe only a few here. Unless there is a sign and ticket box outside the house, it is not open to visitors. Those that are open charge $2-$5 per person. Whether you enter or not, the houses are interesting to look at and to photograph. I like to speculate on what life was like over a century ago in Mexico and these buildings give me lots to think about.

Josefa Ortiz de Dominguez School, *Olas Altas at the ocean*, was built by Natividad Gonzalez at the end of the 1800s. The man's initials are still visible in the wrought iron of the upper windows. The building covers an entire city block and was regarded as decadent even in pre-Revolutionary times. It was confiscated during the revolution. You can enter the halls and look at the basic construction of the building but, since this is an operating school, you cannot enter the classrooms.

Bilbao Vizcaya Bank Building, *Olas Altas #67,* has been a bank since the 1920s. The building was originally constructed in 1870, as a private residence by John Kelly, the British Consul to Mazatlan. In 1910 Grandfather Rico, ancestor of the present owners, bought privately issued bank notes belonging to this banking company. Due to political upheaval, the value of the notes depreciated.

SMART DEAL

As the value of the bank notes dropped, Señor Rico was able to purchase enough of the money to exchange it for the deed of the property. The bank owners originally believed that Mr. Rico would pay in silver.

Telleria House, *Calles Malpica and Olas Altas,* was built in the early 1900s as a private residence. The unique aspect of this building is that it appears to have a basement, something not built in homes around Mazatlan. Two granite support beams hold the roof of the terrace.

Casa Melchers, *corner of Constitución and Venus*, was built in 1846 for the German Merchant Company. The two dwellings were for the manager and the clerks, who were brought from Europe during those days. This company flourished and by the 1900s offered the first automobiles for sale in Mexico. Locals would go out of their way to pass the building so they could gawk at the new form of transportation. John Bradbury bought the first vehicle and he transferred it on carts drawn by oxen to Rosario, where he lived. After the 1929 market crash the building became a warehouse that finally burned down. It was rebuilt as a truck assembly plant and then it was abandoned. Tunnels under the buildings were used by the merchants, during political upheavals, to transfer smuggled merchandise from one hiding spot to another in order to escape taxation from the new authorities.

Servicio Panamericano de Proteccion Bldg, *Constitución and Venus, opposite Casa Melchers,* is the two-story building built in the early 1900s. It was originally the Bank of London and Mexico. After the revolution it became the Bank of Mexico and then the Mexican version of Brinks, the Servicio Panamericano de Proteccion.

Coppel House, *Calle Constituccion #118,* was built by Luis Fontana between 1865 and 1870 as his primary residence. He sold it in 1878 to a man called Juan B. Acosta, who changed it to its present design. The design of the balcony with its massive cornices is of special interest.

Two-story Houses, *Calle Mariano Escobedo, numbers 122-124-126,* were built in 1865 for Federico Ymaña, who owned the local hat factory. The gargoyles on the ironworks are interesting.

 FACT FILE: The rust on the iron at the two-story houses is an indication that the pieces are from Europe, because the ones made in Mexico are alloyed so that they don't rust.

Military Hospital, *Calles Venus and Angel Flores,* was built in the mid-1850s and is one of the oldest hospitals in western Mexico. Part of the present structure is new, but was built in the old architectural style. Along one side of the building you can see tree roots imbedded into the wall. This is a fascinating building and, if you have a special interest in architectural design, ask permission to enter. You may be granted entrance to the vegetated courtyard.

Liceo Mazatlan Bldg., *Calle Constitución and Niños Heroes,* was a trading house constructed by prosperous merchant Elorza, Lejarza and Compañia and finished in 1900, It remained a trading house until the 1960s when the company relocated. The iron balconies and window frames along the second floor are of special interest.

Laveaga House, *Constitución and Niños Heros, across from Liceo Bldg.,* was built by José Vicente de Laveaga, a rich mining baron of the 1850s. After he built it as his residence, he made himself into a private banker and conducted his business on the lower level of the house. When the French arrived in 1862, he liquidated his assets and headed for California to live (and die).

Golf

Estrella del Mar Golf Course, *Isla de Piedra,* ☎ *669-982-3300, www. estrelladelmar.com/location.htm,* is an 18-hole, par 72 course designed by Robert Trent Jones. It sits on 175 acres of prime real estate right on the beach on Isla de Piedra (Stone Island) and is said to be better in price, service and scenery (most holes overlook the ocean) than any course in Puerto Vallarta. They offer a special twilight rate (18 holes, $69) and a "discount Wednesday" (18 holes, $82.50, 25% off regular cost). Golf lessons are available from the John Jacobs' Golf School.

Campestre Mazatlan Golf Course and Country Club, *Camino International South at Km 1195*, ☎ *669-980-1570, 7 am-6 pm daily*, is an older, nine-hole course that costs about $15 per person to play a round. Caddies are available.

El Cid Country Club, *7 am-5:30 pm,* was designed by Larry Hughes and Lee Trevino. This course is available only to El Cid guests. Some of the greens are slick, while others are a bit shaggy. The tee boxes are poor. You must use a caddy provided by El Cid (and pay for him). All reports I have gotten indicate that this isn't the best course in town. However, the annual tournaments held here every March and November offer thousands of dollars in prizes as well as carts and vacation packages. There is also a driving range, putting greens and a short-game area.

Tennis

Sports World Kaoz, *Av Rafael Buelna, behind the bullring,* is in the sport complex. Three hard courts are open to the public, plus there is a pool with water slides, a squash court, a football and soccer field, a snack bar and a lounge.

■ Adventures on Water

Aquarium, *Av de Los Deportes #111*, ☎ *669-981-7816, 9:30 am-6 pm daily, entry $5 for adults and $2 for children.* The aquarium has a botanical garden at its entrance and is guarded by a few old crocodiles. The aquarium has over 250 species of fish from around the world, a marine-life presentation area where you can watch films about the ocean, and a sea lion show that is a big attraction to youngsters. The shows are three-in-one: the first starts at 10:30 am when the diver feeds the shark; at 11 am the sea lions perform; and at 11:30 parrots do their entertaining. This is repeated two more times throughout the day. There is also an art gallery. The gardens have an aviary with eagles, hawks, peacocks and turtles. A tour and show takes about three hours. At the entrance to the aquarium is a statue of three kids. They are on each others' shoulders, trying to feed a dolphin that is jumping out of the water.

The aquarium is the home of the rehabilitation center called Friends of the Aquarium, www.mexonline.com/acuario.htm. This non-profit organization takes and cares for injured or mistreated parrots, birds of prey, ducks and pelicans. It was started by biologist Sandra Guido and American Kittie Jepsen, and has attracted veterinarians, educators and marine biologists to help with the work. To visit them and offer help of any kind (the best is always financial) will help a few more birds survive.

Across the street is the statue of Don Cruz Lizarraga, founder of the famous band El Recordo. The statue has Lizarraga standing with a clarinet in his hand and a tuba and snare drum at his side.

Aquatic Park Mazagua, *at Sabalo Cerritos,* ☎ *669-988-0041, from 10 am-6 pm daily.* There are water slides, a wave pool and a shallow river for youngsters to float through with their safety devices well in place. There are diving boards and a waterfall. First built in 1989 with kids in mind, the park is a toddler-friendly place with numerous climbing areas shaped in the forms of different animals.

Offshore Islands

Deer Island is reached by boat from the waterfront at El Cid. The boat is a World War II amphibious landing craft called the Duck and painted to look like a shark with its mouth open. It leaves the dock at 10 am, noon and 2 pm and costs $8 round trip. The last boat back is at 4 pm. You can also rent a kayak ($10 an hour) or Hobie Cat ($30 an hour, up to four people) from numerous places along the beach and paddle or sail over to Deer Island (the distance is very short). El Cid can provide a tiller-man with their Hobie Cats. The island itself has volleyball nets on the beach. Snorkeling is best to the left when facing the water. Where the rocks start getting big you will see red sea fans, sponges, conch and tropical fish. There are also some turtles, eagle rays (rare) and tons of tropical fish. As you pass the point, the water gets rougher, the rocks bigger and the fish larger. In the opposite direction, to the south, there is a rock shelf with sea urchins. In the center of the island are rock paintings of historical value. Ask directions from your boatman. Two other islands – Bird Island and Wolf Island – also have nice beaches and can be reached on the Duck.

Stone Island is accessed by water taxi ($1, round trip) that leaves from the ferry slip at the end of the bus line. Take the bus marked Sabalo Centro. On your way over, dolphins will often follow the boat. The island has nine miles/15 km with beaches, trees and open-air restaurants. When you arrive, go straight ahead for the restaurant area and go to the right for a bay that offers good snorkeling and gentle waves. On a mild day, going to the deeper water where the rocks are bigger and the swells stronger is advisable. There is a coconut plantation on the island (turn left from the boat landing) where you can rent horses for an hour or two.

▶▶ **AUTHOR NOTE:** *All the restaurants near the boat landing serve delicious food. Please do not bring your own lunch, as the economy of the island is delicate and your contribution by way of buying a meal is greatly appreciated. You will find the prices less than those along the* malecón *in town.*

Wooden boats line Mazatlan's harbor.

Tourists from the hotels and cruise ships arrive on Stone Island in the morning and usually leave by 5 pm.

Also on the island is the **Estrella del Mar Golf Course**, *Isla de la Piedra*, ☎ *669-982-3300, www.estrelladelmar.com/location.htm,* an 18-hole, par 72 green designed by Robert Trent Jones. See page 184. The same beach resort has 26 suites and 22 villas, all with air conditioning, dishwashers, BBQ grills, stereos, king-sized beds, toasters, ceiling fans, cable TV, cooking utensils and coffee makers. High-season rates run $115-$249 per person, per day, with a substantial discount for bookings of a week or more. There is a minimum stay of three nights. Also see *Places to Stay*, below, for details about the Hilton Estrella del Mar.

El Patio Restaurant, along the strip near the boat landing, has both international and Mexican dishes for reasonable prices.

Sportfishing

Fishing is popular around the bay. The big catches are marlin, sailfish, dorado and tuna. Catch and release only. You might also find mahi-mahi, sea bass, wahoo and rooster fish. See the chart on page 100 for information on what can be caught each month.

Beaches

Playa Olas Altas in the Old Town is good for surfers because the waves are consistently high. Boogie boarding and body surfing for experienced swimmers is good here. It is not a recommended area for swimming or snorkeling.

Playa Los Piños is also a surfing beach. It is rocky, so it has some eddies where you can get calmer water; the surfing section starts at the cliff where the water is calm. You will often see surfing classes in this area. Some anglers cast from the rocks on the north side of this beach.

BEACH DANGER FLAG SYSTEM

There is a system of red, yellow and white flags that indicates possible dangers in the water.

- RED – The undercurrent is dangerous to swimmers and under no circumstances should you go into the area between the two red flags. Undertow is not to be ignored; it has caused many deaths.
- YELLOW – Jellyfish are in the area. To avoid being stung, do not go into the water between the two yellow flags.
- WHITE – The white flags mean there is some soft surf, but have fun.

Playa Norte is the long (five miles/7.5 km) stretch along the *malecón*. Once past the fishing-boat area at the south end, the sand is kept fairly clean. There are many palapa-hut restaurants along this beach. The swells in the water are gentle and good for swimming. The waves at the north end of this beach are good for beginner surfers.

Playa Camaron in Zona Dorado starts around Valentinos, also where the luxurious hotels start. The water at Camaron is rough and not for swimmers or surfers with average skill. The beach is narrow and consists mainly of crushed shells.

Playa Las Gaviotas starts where the beach levels off and becomes much wider, and the water becomes gentle. This stretch is exceptionally calm because it is protected by offshore islands. This beach is good for swimming, but the waves are not strong enough for surfing.

Playa Sabalo goes past the Camino Real to the tidal lagoon on the north end. The beach lagoon is good and the lagoon itself is a popular birding spot. The waters between here and Los Cerritos are often dotted with windsurfers.

Playa Los Cerritos is beyond Camino Real. Here, the tourists thin out. Although there are a few palapa huts, it is mainly undeveloped and good for beachcombing. This is a long walk from the center of town.

■ Adventures in Nature

Teacapán can be visited as a day trip from Mazatlan. It is an expanse of palm groves, mangroves, estuaries and lagoons, called the lungs of Mexico. About 95 miles/140 km of wetland can be traveled by boat. People do so in search of birds mainly, but also lizards, iguanas, snakes and insects. For the botanist, the interesting vegetation is limitless. You can also rent bikes, horses and kayaks, or take a boat to Isabel Island to see sea lions and whales during their migratory season. You can also visit Bird Island and, en route, pass by Sea Shell Hill, an odd piece of land made entirely of crushed shells.

Playa/Laguna Caimanero area is now under environmental control because of the vast numbers of migratory birds that pass through. During wet years, the numbers increase from hundreds to thousands. The town of Caimanero is at the south end of a huge sand dune that separates Laguna Caimanero from the beach. The lake is about 50 miles/75 km long and five miles/eight km wide, but only three inches/eight cm deep. This lake in the past was used for hunting, but that sport has been abolished.

BIRD WATCH: *The thorn bush beyond Caimanero Lake is known to hold the rare chuck-aucka. This bird closes its eyes while it sings, making it easy to hunt.*

There are small palapa-hut restaurants at the south end of the lake where you can eat, but there is no place to stay unless you have your own tent. Water must be carried in, as there are no freshwater streams along the beach.

■ Adventures of the Brain

Centro de Idiomas de Mazatlan, *Belisario Dominguez #190, ☎ 669-985-5606, www.spanishlink.org,* offers courses designed for serious participants who need a working knowledge of conversational Spanish in a short period of time. There are a maximum of six students per class, and the main focus is on speaking and listening. Opened in 1973, this school has won the International Committee of Quality Award twice, plus the Quality and Prestige Award from the Mexican National Chamber of Commerce. Courses start every Monday and you should enroll by the Saturday before. There is no compensation if your classes fall during national holidays. The cost is $30 to register, plus $150 per week for four hours of intensive study per day. Private lessons cost $330 a week for four hours a day. Books are $20 extra. Should you study longer than a week, a discount is offered.

Mazatlan Reading Library, *Sixto Osuna #115, corner of Carranza, next to the Archeological Museum, MazLibrary@mexconnect.com*, is run by an energetic and knowledgeable man by the name of Joe Ketchum. If there is anything you want to know that I have not included in this book, ask Joe – he'll know the answer. You can borrow from the fairly extensive non-profit library designed to gather and maintain a collection of writing in English or Spanish. The library cooperates with schools to promote reading and will provide information to anyone. It has over 4,000 titles, most in English, mostly fiction. You can become a member for $25 a year, which would include two adults and minor children of the same household. Additional adults in the same family pay just $5 extra per year. Short-term visitors pay $5 per month. The library is run by volunteers and they encourage you to borrow books, offer a few hours of work or just donate money and books. It's a great place to sit around and talk.

■ Day Trips

 Below, I have listed villages that can be visited as a day trip from Mazatlan. However, you can also go to many of them and stay for more than a day. This is recommended so that you get a better idea of what Mexico is really about. Plus, you get to spread the buck a bit, so more people benefit from your visit.

Estacion Dimas

Estacion Dimas is just 45 miles/60 km north of Mazatlan, where there are the **Piedra Labradas**, ancient stone carvings lying on the beach. These huge, black volcanic rocks have numerous designs and are considered some of the best examples of rock art in Mexico. Some believe that the carvings are from the Toltec civilization. Near the stone carvings is **Barra Piaxtla**, natural stone arches in the sea. Because of the proximity of the two, it is thought this may be a holy place. Archeologists believe these stones were carved about 1500 BC. Occasionally, they are covered by a high tide; this is, evidently, one of the reasons they are in such good shape.

PETROGLYPHS 101

The earliest petroglyphs were carved about 40,000 years ago in Australia. Eventually, about 17,000 years ago, the work evolved and teachers used carved slates so they could carry their works with them. This development happened throughout the world, including Mexico.

There are five subjects that are used in 80% of all rock art. They are warriors (as single soldiers or armies), animals (either real or mythical), wood-and-stone houses, symbolic inscriptions and weapons. Some of the stones at Piedra Labradas have two holes that were used to hold burning incense when honoring the gods. Other holes feature engraved serpents.

Near the village of **Piaxtla,** a few miles north of Dimas, are caves with ancient paintings inside.

It is possible to access the stone carvings without a tour guide, but the cave paintings are a bit more difficult to reach, unless your Spanish is excellent and you can ask directions from the locals.

El Quelite

El Quelite is 20 miles/33 km north of Mazatlan across the Tropic of Cancer and on El Quelite River. This tiny colonial town can easily be reached by local bus or car. There is a nice walk, up the hill that has the stations of the cross, for views of the area. The **church** on the plaza has some paintings from the 1600s. This is an excellent place to get the flavor of "Old Mexico," have a bite to eat, and take some good photos. If you want to stay the night, there are two small hotels in town – **Meson de los Laureanos** and **Meson de Doña Mercedes**. You will have to look at both and see which one you prefer.

Concordia

Concordia, 30 miles/45 km southeast of Mazatlan, is a mining village of 26,000 people known today for its ceramics and wood furniture. **San Sebastian Church**, located on the town plaza, was built between 1705 and 1785 and is the state's oldest church. Constructed of stone with a single tower, the building is still in perfect shape. The carved column at the other end features St. Barbara, Lady of Guadeloupe (the patron saint of Mexico) and St. Sebastian, the protector of the village. Across from the church is the sacristy with a sculpture of a man and his son (both missing their heads).

A **giant rocking chair** in the square makes one look like an elf when sitting in it. If you are here on January 20, you will be able to partake in the town's greatest **festival**, which celebrates liberation from the French.

QUEST FOR RICHES

Basque national Francisco de Ibarra came looking for silver and settled in Concordia, then called San Sebastian. He never did find the rich mother lode, but he did establish Concordia and Copala, a bit farther east. He died in Panuco, at the bottom of a canyon, in 1575. In the 1800s, a German traveler called Alexander von Humboldt wrote about the 500 mines he found in Mexico that were rich in precious metals. Among the towns he mentions are Concordia, Panuco and Copala.

Copala

Copala is 14 miles/21 km east of Concordia, and just 10 minutes walking off the main highway. The village can be reached by public buses (get off on the corner and walk the last section) or by your own vehicle. The town, a colonial silver-mining village with white houses topped in red clay tiles, was founded in 1565. Today it has 650 residences, narrow cobblestone streets, a quaint **plaza** with an austere **church** just a block away. The church is dedicated to St. Joseph and has one tower. The numerous plaques on the outside of the church could take an entire afternoon to read. If you decide to stay here, **Daniel's Hotel** costs $30 a night for two people. Daniels also has a restaurant that serves banana cream pie that comes highly recommended. There's also the **Copala Butter Company**, a café. I don't know anything about it, but the name alone is intriguing.

The **Tequila Factory** at **Hacienda Las Moras** is six miles/10 km past La Noria and along the same road. You'll need your own transportation to get here. The 150 year-old former tequila distilling plant has been converted, in part, to a restaurant. There are few of the old factory workings left, but many people come to gawk at the rich environs and have a beer and lunch before heading on. Others stay awhile, whether there is tequila available or not. The factory is part of a guest ranch located on 2,000 acres that has a pool, chapel, tennis courts and horses for rent. There are reports that claim the horses are not well cared for here. You will have to judge for yourself. If you can see their ribs or if their hoofs are split, do not ride them. The grounds are home to birds, including peacocks, which roam freely through the rich vegetation. Note that you will not be allowed into the grounds unless you give advance notice. There are 11 villas, decorated in old Spanish hacienda style, but with modern bathrooms and air conditioning. The villas cost $280 for two, per night, including all meals. To tour or stay at the factory, contact them in Mazatlan at *Cocoteros #1, Rincond de las Palmas, in Zona Dorada,* ☎ *669-914-1346, www.lasmoras.com/english.htm.*

Aguacaliente

Before Rosario, along the highway, is the village of Aguacaliente. It has numerous little **hot pools** that have curative powers, but they are used mostly for washing clothes. However, the hot springs are not the draw to this town. Rather, the **piñatas** made here are the attraction. If you are at all artistic and would like to know how to make one of these items specific to Mexico, see if you can join a class.

PIÑATAS

Piñatas were originally used by the Franciscan Fathers to portray the idea of the devil hiding treasures of goodness. The Franciscans made the piñatas of papier mâché in the shape of the seven-pointed star with each point representing one of the seven deadly sins. Cumulatively, they symbolized the devil. The treats inside represented good and the resistance to sin. The mythical idea was that if you hit the devil hard enough, he would release all the good things he held. Today, the piñata has developed into every shape and size possible and is usually full of candy that falls onto the floor when the piñata is broken. During Semana Santa, some Mexicans make a Judas and fill him with firecrackers that are ignited, then blow up the Judas, much to the delight of the watchers.

Rosario

The colonial village of Rosario is 47 miles/65 km from Mazatlan on the way to Tepic. First established in the mid-1600s, it now has a population of about 75,000.

 LOCAL LINGO: *The town name comes from a legend. A herdsman was coming home after finding a lost cow. He was playing with the beads of his rosary and, just before dark, the beads broke. Not wanting to lose them, he made a fire to cook some dinner and then spent the night so that he could look for the beads in the morning. Instead, he found a very rich vein of silver, smelted out of the ground by his fire.*

Our Lady of the Rosary Church is the main attraction in town. The golden baroque altar dates from the 18th century. Of the statues, the Virgin of the Rosary is the most distinguished. There are wooden sculptures of saints around her. This church had to be moved from its original site because silver mining tunnels below it were causing structural damage.

The **Lola Beltran Museum**, on the street of the same name, is located in a house that was originally the family home. Born in 1932 in the village, Beltran was called the Queen of Mexican Ranchera music. She appeared in over 50 movies and recorded over 100 music albums. Lola started her career by singing in the church – it must have been the gold of the altar that inspired her. It was her teacher, Señor Gallardo, who encouraged her to sing elsewhere. She started to perform with mariachi groups; her popularity was, in part, due to the subject of her songs, which told of the downtrodden Mexican and the hardships he suffered. She became a world-renowned singer, and performed for people such as Eisenhower, Nixon, De Gaulle and Haile Selassie. Lola Beltran died of a stroke in 1996 and her body was laid to rest in Rosario.

■ Outfitters/Tour Operators

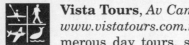 **Vista Tours**, *Av Camaron Sabado, # 2 and 3*, ☎ *669-986-8610, www.vistatours.com.mx,* is in the Zona Dorada. They offer numerous day tours, such as the Tequila Tour or a trip to La Rosario. Both include lunch and cost $35 and $45 per person, respectively. They also offer a sightseeing dinner tour, an afternoon Copala tour, or will take you on an all-day excursion into the jungles of San Blas for less than $100, including breakfast and lunch. Most of these tours include transportation, beer, water and soft drinks.

Marlin Tours, ☎ *669-913-5301, www.toursinmazatlan.com*, offers an excellent city tour that everyone should do at least once. City tours always give visitors a much better insight into an area not visited before. They will take you through Zona Dorada and the Aquarium, then go downtown and visit city hall, the cathedral and the local market. In the old town you get to visit the art school, the Angela Peralta theater and museum, as well as a number of historic houses. Also on the tour are El Mirador, where the cliff divers plunge into the sea, Lookout Hill and the lighthouse. This is a 3½-hour tour; it costs a mere $20, well worth every penny. Marlin does other tours too, like trips to Rosario, Teacapán and the Tequila Factory. The open-air, street car-styled trolley that you see around town belongs to Marlin.

Pronatours, *Av Camaron Sabalo in El Cid commercial area*, ☎ *669-913-3333, pronatours@mazatlan.com.mx,* offers tours to the Marine Turtle Hatchery. The hatchery is sponsored, in part, by El Cid. They also have bird-watching excursions, Deer Island kayak and snorkel tours, mountain bike trips and whale-watching boats. They raise money to support the environment by selling t-shirts, arts and crafts, books and calendars. Although prices are unavailable for the tours mentioned above, their yacht rentals are $35 an hour or $210 a day for up to four people. Larger ones cost up to $450 a day for up to six people. This includes tackle, ice, insurance, captain and crew. Transfer from the airport to the city is $25 for up to four people.

Viajes El Sabalo, *Rodolfo Loaiza #200*, ☎ *669-914-3009*, offers a half-day catamaran trip to Adventure Island, where you can snorkel, ride horses, kayak, windsurf, or ride a banana boat or Jet Ski. The boat has music, an open bar, bathrooms and a sundeck. As you travel, keep an eye out for seals and other marine life. Viajes El Sabalo also have city tours, tours to Copala and Concordia, booze cruises and deep-sea fishing tours. Their costs are comparative to those of others operators.

■ Shopping

Prices are fixed in stores and galleries. However, in the market you can barter; about 25% discount should be expected.

Joyeria El Delfin, *Edificio Balboa, Av Camaron Sabalo #1600*, ☎ *669-914-3209, www.isabelmatiella.com*, carries jewelry designed by world renowned Isabel Matiella, who incorporates Mexican petroglyphs into her work. If you would like a special souvenir of the highest quality, consider one of these pieces.

Madonna's, *Av Las Garzas and Laguna*, ☎ *669-914-2389, or Playa Gaviota #401*, ☎ *669-913-1467, www.madonnajewelry.com*, has an extensive selection of pottery and blown glass pieces at reasonable prices. These include Huichol Indian art, Mayolica ceramics and Talavera art, all made by Mexican artists. These are high-quality, intricately-designed products. You can get copies (of lesser quality and at lower prices) in the market in the old town.

Sea Shell City, *Calle Rodolfo Loaiza between Las Garzas and Av del Mar*, ☎ *669-913-1301, open 9 am to 8 pm*, has some of the rarest specimens of shells found in the Pacific, but it also has some of the tackiest shell-covered pieces in Mazatlan. This is where to shop if you want to get even with your mother-in-law.

Constantino's Leather Factory, *Av Camaron Sabalo, #1530*, ☎ *669-914-6434, and Av Playa Gaviotas #425*, ☎ *669-916-5550*, has high-quality leather goods, from jackets and pants to cowboy hats.

Gallery Michael, *Av Las Garzas #18, no phone*, is open Monday to Saturday, 9am-9 pm, Sunday until 4 pm. They have a huge selection of items from Tlaquepaque art centers in Guadalajara. Credit cards are not accepted here.

Pardo Jewelry, *Av Playa Gaviotas # 411*, ☎ *669-914-3354*, offers mostly bracelets, necklaces and rings that feature diamonds.

▶▶ **AUTHOR TIP:** *Diamonds in Mexico are tax-free, so if you need that engagement ring or a present for mom, this is where to look.*

NidArt Galeria, *Av Libertad and Carnaval*, ☎ *669-981-0002*, *next to the Angela Peralta Theater*, is open Monday through Saturday, 10 am-2 pm. It specializes in masks, faces and sculptures of leather. The pieces for sale are all made by local artists, many of whom have studied in Mazatlan. If you want something different, stop by.

Mercado Central is in the center of town, near the cathedral. The market is full of tiny stalls selling everything from meat to t-shirts. Originally, this was a bullring that was purchased in 1895 to be used for a market. The prices aren't that much lower than in the shops and I found the quality to be average, rather than exceptional.

■ Places to Stay

Like most tourist cities, Mazatlan has a plethora of hotels from which to choose. I can't possibly mention them all (60 are registered with the tourist office), so I have profiled only a few. Remember, no area code is needed when making a local call.

HOTEL SAVVY

Never book the room for your entire vacation unless the deal is too good to ignore. Should the hotel you book with turn out to be a roach-infested dive, you then have the option of moving on. Also, you may not want to spend the entire time in the city, but instead head into the hills and explore. Always leave your options open.

Hotel Emperador, *Calle Rio Panuco*, ☎ *669-982-6724, www.mazatlan.com. mx/emperador, $,* is located across from the bus station and is cleaner than the Fiesta (reviewed below). Each room has two beds, private bathrooms, air conditioning and hot water. There is also a restaurant that offers breakfast ($2.50) as well as lunch ($3). Parking is available on site.

HOTEL PRICE SCALE
Price for a room given in US $.
$.................Up to $20
$$..................$21-$50
$$$................$51-$100
$$$$ ....$101-$150
$$$$$ ....$151-$200
Anything over $200 is specified.

Mazatlan
Places to Stay & Eat

PLACES TO STAY
1. Hotel Emperador
2. Hotel Fiesta
3. Santa Maria
4. Hotel del Rio, Hotel Santa Barbara
5. Hotel Bel Mar
6. Hotel Centro
7. Hotel Central
8. Hotel La Siesta
9. Hotel Plaza Gaviotas
10. Royal Dutch B&B
11. Playa Mazatlan
12. Fiesta Inn
13. Royal Villas
14. Posada Freeman
15. Las Flores
16. Aguamarina Hotel
17. Costa de Oro
18. El Quijote Inn
19. Holiday Inn
20. Hotel Plaza Marina
21. Faro Mazatlan
22. Los Sábalos Resort
23. Pueblo Bonito Resort
24. El Cid

PLACES TO EAT
25. El Parral
26. El Marismeño
27. Shrimp Bucket
28. Restaurant Bar del Pacifico
29. Machado, Pedro & Lola
30. Señor Frogs
31. Panama
32. Señor Pepper
33. Vittore Italian Grill, Joe's Oyster Bar
34. Casa Loma
35. Panchos
36. No Name Café
37. Valentino's Disco, Bora Bora Bar
38. Ambrosia Vegetariano
39. VIP
40. Angelos
41. Soho
42. Club Mia
43. Mundo Bananas
44. La Taberna
45. Tony's Bar & Grill
46. Muralla China
47. Bahai Mariscos
48. Fiesta Mexicana

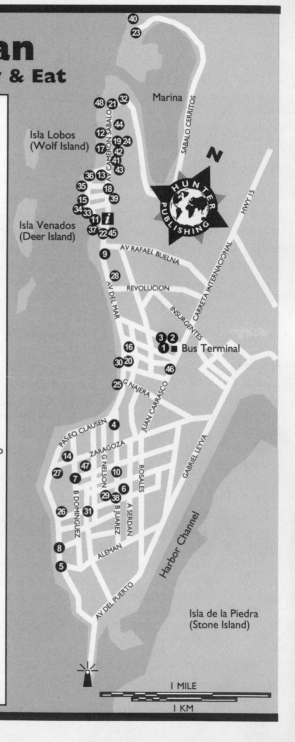

Marina

Isla Lobos (Wolf Island)

Isla Venados (Deer Island)

AV RAFAEL BUELNA

REVOLUCION

AV DEL MAR

INSURGENTES

CARRETA INTERNACIONAL

HWY 15

SABALO CERRITOS

Bus Terminal

G NAJERA

JUAN CARRASCO

PASEO CLAUSEN

ZARAGOZA

G NELSON

B DOMINGUEZ

ROSALES

A SERDAN

B JUAREZ

GABRIEL LEYVA

ALEMAN

AV DEL PUERTO

Harbor Channel

Isla de la Piedra (Stone Island)

1 MILE

1 KM

Hotel Fiesta, *Ferrosquila #306*, ☎ *669-981-7888, $*, in front of the bus station (not to be confused with Fiesta Hotel on the beach). The hotel has a coliseum façade. The rooms are clean, with private bathroom and purified water. Those with air conditioning and TV are a bit more expensive than those without.

Santa Maria, *Calle Rio Panuco*, ☎ *669-982-2308, $*, on the main street across from the bus station, is the best of the three in the area. Each room has two beds, private bathroom, air conditioning and hot water. The owners are friendly and the prices do not change from summer to winter.

Hotel del Rio, *Av Benito San Suarez, no phone, $*, has some very tiny rooms that cost $12 for a double bed. The rooms with air conditioning for $18 are much better, although you couldn't hold a party in them. The hotel is exceptionally clean and the staff is friendly. There's an area where you can store some of your things when out on trips.

Hotel Santa Barbara, *Benito San Suarez and 16 de Septiembre, (no phone), $*, has rooms for $12 a single and $38 for four people. I couldn't get the correct prices for two or three people, but they are somewhere in-between. The place is fairly decent. If the Hotel del Rio up the street is full, try here.

Hotel Bel Mar, *Olas Altas, no phone, $$*. This was the first hotel ever built in Mazatlan and the old doors at the entrance certainly attest to this fact. The original area still has its old tiles and some wall paintings, but is now used as the car park. The newer section was built around a pool and all rooms have air conditioning. The place is a bit battered, but the charm makes up for it and the service is exceptional. It is also on the beach and in Old Mazatlan. Hotel Bel Mar was originally built in the 1920s by Louis Bradbury, an American mining entrepreneur. He filled the back garden with exotic plants from around the world; the restaurant was notorious for its fine cuisine throughout the northwest. Two scandals occurred at the hotel.

SCANDALS AT HOTEL BEL MAR

In 1922, General Abelardo Rodriguez's wife committed suicide in one of the rooms. He later became president of Mexico. The second scandal occurred during Carnival in 1944, when State Governor Rodolfo T. Loaiza was murdered in his room after attending the Queen's ball. Today, the place seems *tranquilo*. At least, I came out of it alive.

Hotel Centro, *José Ma Canizales #705*, ☎ *669-981-2673, $$*, is dark and dreary, although the rooms are a fair size and have a private bathroom, air conditioning and TV. The staff is pleasant.

Hotel Central, *Belisario Dominguez #1607*, ☎ *669-982-1953*, *$$*, has central air conditioning and large rooms that are clean. The 20-year-old building is in the center of the old town and the staff is both friendly and helpful. There is a restaurant on the top floor that is a good coffee/meeting place.

Hotel La Siesta, *Blvd Olas Altas #11*, ☎ *669-981-2334*, *www.lasiesta. com.mx*, *$$*, has rooms around an open central courtyard that is adorned with ancient trees. The rooms all have air conditioning and TV, and are clean and well kept. The cost is $35 for a double without a view of the ocean and $47 for a room with a view. This is one of the best deals in town if you go for old and charming. The on-site Shrimp Bucket Restaurant, opened in the 1950s, was so successful that it was the start of what is now a fairly large chain around Mexico.

Hotel Plaza Gaviotas, *Rodolfo Loaiza*, ☎ *669-913-4322*, *www. plazagaviotas. com*, *$$*, across from Playa Mazatlan, has 67 rooms with air conditioning, telephones, cable TV and private bathrooms. Parking is available. The hotel is across the road from the beach. There is a bar and the Green Chile Restaurant on site. When I was here, the restaurant was a popular place for Mexican families. I interpret this as a sign that the Mexican food is good.

Royal Dutch B&B, *Calle Juarez #1307 and Av Constitution*, ☎ *669-981-4396*, *$$$*, has two rooms at present and they have plans for two more in the near future. The cost is $65, including a huge breakfast of almost anything you could want. Often, tea and goodies are offered at night. Rooms are in a restored house in the old section of town. This place is run by a Dutch man married to a Mexican woman, who operate a clean and comfortable establishment. If you are into the quiet and small, try them. Royal Dutch is closed every summer from June to October.

Playa Mazatlan, *Rodolfo Loaiza #202*, *www.playamazatlan.com.mx*, *$$$*, has over 400 rooms on five floors and the reports I have seen make this one of the better places to stay in this price range. The service is excellent, the Mexican hacienda-style hotel is exceptionally clean. From the front-facing rooms that are now being remodeled, the surf can be heard hitting the seawall. There is a pool, a fitness center, laundry service, childcare, parking, a restaurant and a snack bar on site. Each room has a hair dryer, cable TV, iron, coffee maker, data port, alarm clock and air conditioning.

Fiesta Inn, *Av Camaron Sabalo #1927*, ☎ *669-989-0100 or 800-FIESTA-1 in the US*, *$$$*, has 117 tiny rooms with two beds, a dresser and a nightstand. There is a hair dryer in the bathroom and a coffee maker in the bedroom. All rooms have cable TV and air conditioning. The views of the ocean are a big draw. English is spoken and the pool and beach areas are clean. There is a business center and babysitting services.

Central Pacific Mexico

Royal Villas, *Av Camaron Sabalo #500*, ☎ *669-916-6161, www. royalvillas.com.mx/*, *$$$*, has large, well-decorated rooms with tiled floors and private balconies. Many overlook the ocean. The suites all have fully equipped kitchenettes and eating areas, and the deluxe rooms are big enough for eight people, with two bathrooms and two balconies. There is air conditioning, parking, a purified water system, laundry service, satellite TV, wheelchair access, a money exchange, safe deposit boxes and a business center. This large hotel is right on the beach. The rate for the penthouse, which holds six people, is less than $100 per person, per night. Before booking, be sure to ask about special promotions. La Hacienda de la Flor restaurant at Royal Villas is one of the best in town.

Posada Freeman, *Av Olas Altas #79*, ☎ *669-981-2114, $$$*, is an old classic built in 1944 and named after the designer Guillermo Freeman. It was Mazatlan's first skyscraper. The hotel was closed in 1985 due to lack of business, but has since been purchased and remodeled by Best Western. It has become a popular spot in the old city. It has 64 rooms, done in typical Best Western style, with coffee maker (coffee included) and an Internet connection in the rooms. Breakfast is included in the price. There is a rooftop swimming pool that is very attractive.

Las Flores, ☎ *800-452-0627 (US), 877-756-7529 (Canada), www. lasflores.com.mx/english/indexENG.htm, $$$/$$$$*, is a small hotel with just over a hundred suites, studios or standard rooms. Suites can hold up to six people and have fully equipped kitchenettes; studios and standard rooms hold up to four people. The rooms have tiled floors, beamed ceilings, air conditioning, sitting areas and cable TV. Located with a view out to Deer Island, the beach has gentle waves. Las Rejas bar here is famous for its happy hour.

Aguamarina Hotel, *Av Del Mar # 110*, ☎ *669-981-7080 or 800-537-8483 (US), www.aguamarina.com, $$$/$$$$*, has smallish rooms and larger suites complete with kitchenettes. The hotel is small and not right on the beach (you must walk across the *malecón*), but it has a nice pool and is clean. Rooms have tiled floors, private bathrooms, air conditioning, satellite TV and telephones. This is a popular place with Mexican people. There is a restaurant and bar.

Costa de Oro, *Av Camaron Sabalo #710*, ☎ *669-913-2005, www. costaoro.com, $$$/$$$$*, is an older hotel, right on the beach, with 180 rooms and 110 suites. Rates are often discounted for promotional purposes. Rooms have double beds, air conditioning, satellite TV, bathrooms and phones. Suites have all of the above, plus a kitchenette and balcony. There are three tennis courts, a snack bar, two restaurants, two bars, safe deposit boxes, a travel agency, car rental and shopping on site. There is also laundry service and free parking.

El Quijote Inn, *Av Camaron Sabalo and Tiburon*, ☎ *669-914-1134 or 800-699-7700, www.gomazatlan.com/english/d_lodging/quijote/*

quijote.asp, *$$$/$$$$*, has Mexican décor throughout. The 67 clean rooms have cable TV, private bathrooms, comfortable beds, equipped kitchenettes and sitting areas. There is a pool with very cold water, a Jacuzzi, business center, parking area, beauty salon, bar and lounge, safe deposit boxes and tennis courts. This is a safe place where the staff gives green gringos assistance and good advice. The hotel is on the beach.

Holiday Inn, *Av Camaron Sabalo #696*, ☎ *669-913-2222 or 800-716-9707*, *www.holiday-inn.com*, *$$$/$$$$*, has 183 rooms that have recently been remodeled. Each room has air conditioning, kitchenette, satellite TV, telephone, radio, fridge, hair dryer and tiled bathroom. The hotel is on the beach and has private palapa huts for guests. There is an indoor and outdoor pool, a tennis court, a racquetball court, babysitting service, a playground, and a restaurant and bar. All the reports I have say that staying here is a great deal for the money.

Hotel Plaza Marina, *Av Del Mar #73*, ☎ *669-982-3622 or 800-711-95465*, *www.hotelplazamarina.com*, *$$$/$$$$*, has over 100 rooms and suites, all of which are a fair size. Although not elaborate in their décor, they do have balconies, air conditioning, cable TV and private bathrooms. The pool is at the back of the hotel, rather than at the front facing the beach. The palapa huts on the beach are serviced by the hotel's waiters.

Faro Mazatlan, *Punta del Sabalo*, ☎ *669-913-1111*, *$$$/$$$$*, is a large hotel on the ocean. Half the rooms have balconies overlooking the ocean, while the rest overlook the marina. This was formerly called the Playa Real Beachfront Hotel. It was built in 1972 and renovated in 1987. Rooms have air conditioning, tiled bathrooms, cable TV and coffee makers. There is a business center, babysitting service, outdoor pool, fitness center, bar and lounge.

Los Sábalos Resort, *Av Playa Gaviotas #100*, ☎ *669-983-5333 or 800-528-8760 (US)*, *877-756-7532 (Canada)*, *www.lossabalos.com*, *$$$$*, is a five-star, Mediterranean-style hotel located on Las Gaviotas beach. It has 200 rooms and suites, some with ocean views, all with balconies. Suites and standard rooms have one or two queen-sized beds, satellite TV, telephones, tiled bathrooms, coffee makers, hair dryers, safe deposit boxes and air conditioning. An all-inclusive deal runs $100 per person, per day, double occupancy, and includes all meals. The hotel has a spa, steam room, sauna, Jacuzzi, massage room and beauty parlor. The treatments offered include a facial ($38), manicure ($11), pedicure ($15), full body waxing ($22) and body peeling ($38). For the peeling, I hope the knife is sharp. There are five restaurants on site that go from the casual Joe's Oyster Bar to the elegant Vittore Italian Grill.

Pueblo Bonito Resort, *Av Camaron Sabalo #2121*, ☎ *669-914-3700*, *www.pueblobonito.com/mazatlan/junior.html*, *$$$$/$$$$$*, has 247 suites that are tastefully decorated with the sitting area separated from the sleeping area by arches. The tiled floors add a coolness to the breeze coming in off the ocean. Each suite has 575 square feet that gives you ample room for a long-term vacation. Each kitchenette is fully supplied with a fridge, stovetop, coffee maker, toaster, microwave and dishes. The dining areas seat four. There are ceiling fans and air conditioning, telephones, satellite TV, hair dryers in the bathrooms, private safes and irons and ironing boards. The hotel has parking, daily maid service, laundry service, bilingual staff, a tour office, auto rental, currency exchange and baby sitting service. The hotel is wheelchair-accessible. Rooms hold four or six people (two kids) and cost between $165 and $300 per night. The Royal and Presidential suites run more than double that. The hotel is on the beach and tucked into the bay, beside a nice rock outcrop.

El Cid, *Av Camaron Sabalo,* ☎ *669-913-3333 or 800-525-1925 (US), www.elcid.com, $$$$ / $$$$$ (high season up to $680 per room)*, is four hotels and a shopping center rolled into one city within a city and is so distinct that it has become a landmark. It is one of the largest resorts in Latin America and has a fully equipped marina and sailing fleet, 27-hole golf course, squash, racquetball and tennis courts (instruction is available), spa, fitness facilities, tour desk and dive shop. The tennis courts have ball machines, video analysis and rental rackets. You can get lessons and clinics that run from a half-day to four days from November to May. The hotel has 1,086 rooms, eight swimming pools, eight restaurants, three bars and a private beach. Each room has a balcony, private bathroom, satellite TV, air conditioning, ceiling fans and telephone.

Teacapán

In the village there is **Hotel Denisse**, *Calle Morelos and R. Buelna, right on the square,* ☎ *695-954-5266, $$,* that has only six rooms around a courtyard dotted with plants. The rooms have private bathrooms and air conditioning and the place is clean. For food, there are two places that are recommended; the **Playita** near the laguna and **Mr. Wayne's** in town. Both specialize in fried fish for about $5 per serving.

Just out of town is the **Villas Maria Fernanda**, ☎ *695-953-1343 or 954-5393, www.villamariavernanda.com, $$$,* that has an eco-lodge on the beach near the largest estuary in Mexico. The cabins, which can hold four or eight persons, are white-plaster buildings with palm-fond roofs, tiled floors inside and bamboo railings on the porch. The beds are soft and the place is clean. Cabins have an air-conditioning unit, TV, stove and fridge. Outside, the huge grounds contain a pool, hot tub and palapa huts for shade. There are over a million palm trees, banana trees, bougainvillea and other colorful flowering trees on the property to help shade the environment that holds 55 species of tropical birds. There are also barbeque pits available for each residence and a children's playground. The hotel has kayaks and bikes for rent and they can arrange for horseback riding, snorkeling or deep sea diving. But mostly they take people on bird/plant tours of the wetlands. Kayaks cost $6.50 per hour and bicycles cost $3.50 an hour. Although they don't have horses on their property at the moment, there is some whispering that they will in the near future. There is English spoken at the villas and the owners are extremely friendly. This is a great place to stay.

Your final option is the **Rancho Los Angeles**, ☎ 665-953-2550, $$$, which has 21 rooms in all with the best being in the main building rather than those facing the highway. The adjacent trailer park has room for 40 motor homes. There is a restaurant and pool on site.

Isla de la Piedra

Hilton Estrella del Mar, *Isla de la Piedra*, ☎ 669-982-3300, *www. estrelladelmar.com*, $$$$$, is a hotel and resort community with condos for sale. The compound has 3.5 miles/six km of private beach and an 18-hole golf course designed by Robert Trent Jones, Jr. Hotel accommodations include air conditioning, hand-carved wooden furniture, and either ocean or garden views. The hotel has a formal restaurant and a bar, swimming pool, Jacuzzi, volleyball courts and beach palapas. There is also a commercial area and ambulance service to Sharp Hospital in Mazatlan or "Life Flight" to the US.

RV Parks

There are six RV parks in the Mazatlan area. Prices run $20 to $25, depending on services.

San Fernando Trailer Park, *Av Tiburon*, ☎ 669-914-0173, has 57 sites with water, electricity, sewers, bathroom facilities, laundry, pool, cable TV, telephone, green areas, mail service, social center and Jacuzzi.

Mar-A-Villas, *Av Sabalo Cerritos*, ☎ 669-984-0400, has 35 units with water, full bathrooms and a social club. The park is on the beach.

La Posta, *Av Rafael Buelna #7, Laguna del Camaron*, ☎ 669-983-5310, *www.mazatlan.com.mx/servicesandadvice/trailerparks.htm*, has 180 sites with water, electricity, sewers, barbeque pits and cement pads. The park has full bathrooms, laundry, pool, telephone, green areas, mail service, ice, purified water and a social club.

San Bartolo, *Av del Pulpos*, ☎ 669-913-5755, has 48 sites with water, electricity, sewers, barbeque pits and cement pads. The park has full bathrooms, laundry, cable TV, telephones, green areas, mail service, a social center and a Jacuzzi.

Mar Rosa Park, *Av Camaron Sabalo #702*, ☎ 669-913-6187, has 82 sites with water, electricity, sewer hookup and cement pads. The park has full bathrooms, cable TV, telephones, green areas, mail service, a social center and purified water. The park is located on the beach.

Central Pacific Mexico

Las Palmas, *Av Camaron Sabalo #333,* ☎ *669-913-5311,* has 66 sites with water, electricity, sewer hookup and barbeque pits. The park has full bathrooms, a pool, cable TV, telephones, a money exchange office, green areas, mail service and a social center.

■ Places to Eat

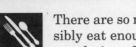 There are so many restaurants in Mazatlan that I couldn't possibly eat enough in a year to try them all. I have taken recommendations from others to add to my own personal list. Most meals in average restaurants cost around $10 per person. Coffee shops are much cheaper and the fine dining places cost $15 to $20 per serving. Some portions are very small, most are average, and a few eateries offer a decent-size plate.

El Parral, *on the* malecón *next to Hotel Amigo,* ☎ *669-990-1368,* may be okay for some things, but I was charged US $8 for a small jug of lemonade. It wasn't listed on the menu so the waiter charged about three times the price in other cafés. My mistake was not confirming the price before ordering.

Restaurant El Marismeño, *Olas Altas #1224 on the* malecón, ☎ *669-912-2612,* has okay coffee and exceptionally good cheese omelets served with fried potatoes. The French toast is coated with sugar and cinnamon so, if this is not to your liking, let them know. Their specialty, as with many restaurants here, is seafood. This restaurant uses its own boats to bring in the fish to ensure freshness. It is usually excellent.

Shrimp Bucket, *Av Olas Altas #11-126,* ☎ *669-981-8019, open 7 am-11 pm,* has a decent breakfast, but the coffee leaves a lot to be desired. However, their specialty is dinner, notably shrimp. They have things like *camarones escabeche* (pickled shrimp), *ensalada atun* (direct translation is nitwit salad, but it really means tuna salad), *empanadas* (pastry filled with seafood), *pescada* Veracruz (fish in a tomato sauce) and *sopa verde* (green soup). Servings run $5-$10. The first Shrimp Bucket was opened on this site in the 1950s and its popularity grew so that it is now a leading Mexican chain.

Restaurant Bar del Pacifico, *Av Del Mar #1910,* ☎ *669-981-3150,* is along the *malecón* on the far side from the beach. It serves some of the best food in Mazatlan for around $8 a plate. I had fish done in a special Mexican hot sauce. The waiter was attentive, but not hovering, and the drinks were not watered down. I suggest you try this restaurant at least once.

Ambrosia Vegetarian Restaurant, *Sixto Osuna #26,* ☎ *669-985-0333,* is open 7 am-10 pm, with specials offered at each meal. The prices are excellent, the service good, the food delicious.

La Taberna D. Miguel, *Av Camaron Sabalo*, ☎ *669-916-5628*, open 5-10 pm. This taco bar is great for a drink and tacos or a quesadilla. Costs are $1 for a small beer, $3 for a tequila and $4.50 for the special that includes a glass of wine or a beer, re-fried beans, a sausage, tortilla and salad.

Machado Restaurant and Bar, *on Machado Square in the old town,* open 8 am-11 pm, is a great place to sit and watch life pass by. It offers good seafood and live music on weekends.

VIP's, *Camaron Sabalo and Albatroses,* ☎ *669-914-0754*, has air conditioning and a magazine store attached. For English-language readers, I saw *Time, Newsweek, Scientific American* and *Reader's Digest* for sale. This is an American chain, so the food is American chain food – frozen fries, cheap buns, tinned soup and ketchup. At least it's familiar. You can get a good burger here.

Pedro and Lola, *Constitución and Carnaval on Machado Square,* ☎ *669-982-2589*, has street-side tables. The food is excellent, as it is at the other four restaurants on the square.

Restaurant Casa Loma, *Av Gaviotas #104*, ☎ *669-913-5398*, is open daily from 1:30-10:30 pm. They opened their doors in 1976 and offer a quiet Mexican (oxymoron?) atmosphere for those who like out-of-the-way places. The food is international and the prices are around $15 for a meal.

Joe's Oyster Bar, *Av Playa Gaviotas #100*, ☎ *669-983-5333, www. lossabalos.com,* is open 11 am-2 am and is located in Los Sabalos Resort. Joe's is a fun place on the beach, and their specialty is fresh oysters and shrimp tacos served with exotic drinks. If you are not into exotic, have a beer. It is also an open-air disco.

Vittore Italian Grill, *Av Playa Gaviotas #100*, ☎ *669-986-2424, www. lossabalos.com,* is open noon-1 am and is in Los Sabalos Resort on Las Gaviotas beach. This is an exquisite restaurant, complete with white linens and black-jacket waiters. Their pizzas are baked in a wood-fired oven, the pastas are homemade fresh every day and the desserts are made by an Italian cook. They also serve lamb chops, a rarity in Mexico. Most of the wines are imported.

Tony's Bar and Grill, *Av Rodolfo Loaiza and Camaron Sabalo,* ☎ *669-983-5700,* has the mix of great burgers and live music.

Muralla China, *Juan Carrasco #518 and Aguascalientes,* ☎ *669-985-3914,* specializes in Szechuan and Hunan cuisines in a small and informal setting. The Szechuan cooking consists of light food that is really hot and delicious.

Central Pacific Mexico

Angelos, *Av Camaron Sabalo # 2121 at the Pueblo Bonito Hotel,* ☎ *669-914-3700,* open 6-11:30 pm, is a quiet piano bar decorated with polished wood and crystal chandeliers. The best gourmet dinners include shrimp, pasta and scampi that should be enjoyed with a good bottle of imported wine. The wine selection is large. The average cost of a meal is $15. There is a dress code; beachwear, jeans and flip-flops are not permitted.

No Name Café, *Av Playa Gaviotas #417,* ☎ *669-913-2031,* is open for meals from noon to 12:30 am. This sports bar has good barbeque ribs, although the steaks are not the best in town. They also serve pork chops, hamburgers and barbequed chicken that is very tasty. Happy hour runs from 5-6 pm and again from 10-11 pm. Watch the "happy hour" prices, as they are often higher than the regular prices. No Name is also open for breakfast at 8 am. The sports section has 30 large-screen TVs and two giant screens, and is decorated with tons of posters, pennants, photos and baseball cards.

Panchos Restaurant, *Av Playa Gaviotas #408,* ☎ *669-914-0911,* overlooks the ocean. They serve seafood Mexican style.

Señor Pepper, *Av Camaron Sabalo,* ☎ *669-914-0101,* open 5 pm-midnight, is located across from Hotel Playa Real. The attached bar is open 5 pm-2 am. This eatery belongs to the same chain as the Shrimp Bucket – a company that knows what the average Jill and Joe want. Their specialty is prime rib steak or lobster (in season) for about $25. All meals are served under candlelight in an elegant setting with potted plants and polished crystal. There is live entertainment and dancing.

Pura Vida, *Bugambilia #100 and Laguna,* ☎ *669-916-5815,* is open 8 am-10 pm and offers decent-sized servings. For breakfast, you can get coffee, juice, whole-wheat pancakes or omelets. Lunch has soy burgers, vegetarian pasta dishes or sandwiches – all are excellent. Soups are recommended. Prices never exceed $7 per person.

Jungle Juice, *Av de las Garzas,* ☎ *669-913-3315,* open 8 am-10 pm, is located on an open terrace. The music is loud but the atmosphere is appealing. I love the name. They specialize in grilled meats and juice and smoothies. It was the smoothies that gave them their reputation. They also have some very good vegetarian dishes.

Bahai Mariscos, *Av Mariano Escobedo #203,* ☎ *669-981-2645,* open 10 am-8 pm, has the best fried fish in town. They also serve their famous seafood stew. Meals are average in price and size. The restaurant is located in a restored old house; the owner will take you on a tour. This restaurant was opened in 1950 by Alejandro Flores Curlango; his specialty was ceviche. If you are stopping here for an afternoon beer, try a ceviche snack.

Soho, *Av Camaron Sabalo #312,* ☎ *669-913-1300,* is a traditional sushi bar that serves other Japanese foods, including their specialty,

Yakimeshi (a fried rice dish that has ham, onion, ginger, sesame oil, eggs, dashi sauce, sugar and pepper).

Panama, *Calle Dominguez and Sixto Osuna*, ☎ *669-981-7517*, is another popular chain where you can get mostly Mexican dishes, but also things like a ham and cheese sandwich or a cheeseburger for $3. Their fresh juices are excellent and their milkshakes (*liquido de fruta con leche*) are not to be missed. They cost under $2 for a large glass. Panama is also a pastry shop. If you need some cake and coffee, this is the place to stop. It is always busy, an indication that the food is good.

■ Nightlife

Mazatlan is known as the party city, so finding action after sunset is no problem. The city is safe, so having a drink or two should not hamper your personal safety. However, do not get loaded and then stagger down a dark alley with all your money in your back pocket (or your front one, for that matter). It is also best if you travel in a group after being at the bar, because a person alone is an easy target.

Valentinos Disco, *Punta Camaron*, ☎ *669-984-1666*, is the huge Moorish-looking structure that can be seen a long way down the beach. It is a definite draw for the young. There is a $5-$10 cover charge. The light show here is definitely 21st century in style and sound. To get away from the modern disco, you can have a game or two of pool in the next room. The **Bora Bora** bar, also in this building, has a volleyball court and a surfing simulator.

Cuba Mia, *Av Camaron Sabalo, #406*, ☎ *669-913-9692*, is open Tuesday through Sunday, 5 pm-2 am. This is a lively Cuban bar with Cuban music and dancing, and Cuban foods. They also offer special events, for which you must purchase tickets.

Señor Frogs, *Av del Mar*, ☎ *669-982-1925*, is one of the most popular discos in town. The locals come here to mingle with party-addicted tourists. Drinks are fairly reasonable in price and the music is loud and modern. The most popular drink is the *coscorrones* (tequila shooter). There are rumors that some rowdy guests have danced on the tables late into the night. If you would like to eat while here, I recommend the ribs. Señor Frogs usually has good security and well functioning air conditioning.

A FROG OF MANY COLORS

Señor Frogs is one of those strange Mexican franchises that you find everywhere and in every form – it can be a clothing store, a disco or a restaurant.

Mundo Bananas, *Av Camaron Sabalo #131,* ☎ *669-986-4700*, is a catch-all with clothes, pool tables and a bar. That should just about cover all the needs of any customers.

Fiesta Mexicana, *Hotel Playa Mazatlan,* ☎ *669-913-5320,* has tradi-tional food along with a folkloric music and dance show. The meal is gour-met Mexican buffet, consisting of things like pineapple tamales, enchiladas with fresh cheese and smoked marlin tostadas. They serve unlimited domestic drinks. Shows run every Tuesday to Saturday from 7 pm to about 10:30 pm. The music comes from four states in Mexico and the dancing is exuberant, the costumes exquisite. They do things like the Fire and Machete dance, magic shows, a comedy act and the Mexican hat dance. The cost is $28 per person and $14 for children under 11. This is a professional show and a must to see at least once.

South to Puerto Vallarta

The coastal road between Mazatlan and PV is mostly undeveloped. The tiny villages along the way such as Concordia (page 191) and Rosario (page 193) are worth a visit just because they are so calm and Mexican. For the botanist or ornithologist, Teacapán is a must. If you have your own vehicle, the possible stops are innumerable. If traveling by bus, staying in Tepic and doing day/overnight trips is a good option.

Tepic

Tepic has all the conveniences of a big city coupled with the friendli-ness of small-town Mexico. I love the people, who always had time to tell me a story or show me something. The tourist office was so enthusias-tic about my visit they gave me a list of the special places in the area and got me to report back on them. The food was delicious, and the hotel I stayed in was exceptionally comfortable. The city is dotted with beautiful parks and squares and the main town square is always bustling with events. If you are in this region and not staying in the ocean town of San Blas (where 80 miles/120 km of unspoiled and undeveloped beaches draw many), then stay in Tepic.

■ Getting Here

By Plane

Amado Nervo Airport is about eight miles/12 km from the center of town and out past the bus station. It is named after the famous poet Amado Nervo, who was born in Tepic. I do not know of any other airport anywhere that is named after a poet. Serviced by Aero California, Mexicana and AeroMexico, it has flights from Mexico City, an hour away, and from Tijuana on the US border, about 2½ hours away. From here, you can fly to Puerto Vallarta and connect to other places from there.

AIRLINE CONTACT INFORMATION		
Aero California	www.aerocalifornia.de	☎ 800-237-6225 (Mx)
AeroMexico	www.aeromexico.com	☎ 800-237-6639 (US); 800-021-4010 (Mx)
Mexicana Airlines	www.mexicana.com	☎ 800-531-7921 (US); 800-509-8960 (Mx)

By Bus

It is a pleasant half-hour walk on Calle Insurgentes from the central plaza to the bus station. A cab will cost $2. The station is serviced by **Elite**, **Omnibus**, **Futura**, **Transportes del Pacifico**, **Norte de Sonora** and **TuriStar**. There are restaurants and a cafeteria at the bus station.

By Car

The main highway that goes through Tepic is Highway 15, which follows the coast all the way to the Guatemalan border to the south and the US border to the north. It is a four-lane toll road that is well marked with huge signs.

■ History

The first settlements in the area were at **Matanchen Bay** about 5,000 years ago. Around 350 to 650 AD, people started moving inland. Under Toltec influence they developed crops using terraces reinforced with fabric made from vegetable fibers. Between 700 and 1200 they began making ceramics, jewelry and stone and metal figurines. They also built the great ceremonial centers.

Central Pacific Mexico

Tepic has been a center for trade and commerce all through the 16th and 17th centuries and now is the center of government for the state of **Nayarit**. Although most of the area's historical events took place at San Blas, it was **Nuño Beltran de Guzman** in 1532 who started commerce in the area. At the same time the adventurous **Jesuits** went inland to spread the word. After they were expelled, the people of Tepic started planting tobacco and citrus fruits that grew well in the shadow of the two volcanoes, **Ceboruco** and **Sanganguey**. They soon realized that the volcanic soil, heavy rains and altitude of 8,500 feet/2,500 meters made the area good for grain, sugarcane, cotton and coffee, too.

The state of Nayarit was part of Guadalajara and the state of Jalisco, but turbulence led Nayarit to separate in 1884. It finally became a state in 1917, with Tepic as the capital.

> ♣ **LOCAL LINGO:** *The name* Tepic *comes from the Nahuatl Indian word meaning "solid rock" and the word was bastardized (I assume) to refer to the clay figurines found by archeologists near Tepic.Originally called Santiago de Compostela, the present name comes from the Nahuatl words tetl, meaning rock, and pic, meaning hard.*

TEPIC'S CITY SEAL

The final version of the seal was completed in 1993. It has seven human footprints that symbolize the seven Nahuatl tribes that formed the Aztec nation. The central part of the shield has the right side profile of an eagle devouring a snake. The eagle stands for strength of the sun and the snake for the value of the earth. The seal can be seen at the regional museum in the center of the city.

■ Services

 Post office, *Calle Durango #33 between Allende and Morelos, Monday to Friday, 8 am-6 pm, and until noon on Saturday.*

Hospital, *Paseo de la Loma, next to La Loma Park,* ☎ *311-213-7937.*

The **Police Station**, *Tecnologica #3200,* ☎ *311-211-5851,* is a long way from the center.

The **Tourist Office**, *on the corner of Puebla and Nuervo just past the Presidential Palace,* is one of the most helpful tourist offices in all of Mexico. Since most of them are exceptionally good, that says a lot.

■ Sightseeing

Amado Nervo Museum, *Zacatecas # 284 North,* ☎ *311-212-2916, hours unavailable,* is located in the house where this famous poet was born on August 27, 1870. He schooled in Tepic until he was 14 and then worked on the newspaper in Mazatlan. He then went to Paris, where he worked on *El Imparcial* newspaper and met Ana Cecilia Luisa Daillez, the love of his life. When he returned to Mexico he had become quite well known. Nervo died on May 24, 1919. Inside the house are numerous documents, many of the furnishings as they were when he lived here, photos of his wife and daughter and the big wooden desk where he wrote. The house became a museum in 1967. You can buy books of Nervo's poems here, but English translations are not available.

Quatro Pueblos Museum, *Hidalgo #60 West,* ☎ *311-212-1705, Monday to Friday, 9 am-7 pm (siesta 2-4 pm).* The property, an 18th-century colonial house, was made into a museum in 1992, with the five rooms dedicated to the local indigenous groups of the area. The first room has costumes and artwork of the Huicholes, including the intricate beadwork for which they are so well known. The second has artwork of the Coras, Tepehuanas and the Mexicaneras groups. This includes wall hangings and pictures. The third and fourth rooms have work from the Tepic, Ixtlan, Jomulco and Mexpan villages. All of these villages are located in the mountains, so the work is very different. The final room has work from the Pacific Ocean. Mostly this covers fishing implements and tools for building palapa huts.

Anthropological and Historical Museum, *Av Mexico #91 North,* ☎ *311-212-1900, 9 am-6 pm,* is inside a colonial building built in the mid-1800s by Felipe Liñan. In the last century, the German Consulate was housed here. It left in 1933 and the state school of Fernando Montaño operated in the building until 1948. It became a museum in 1949, originally displaying classical and neo-classical archeological items. In 1969 it expanded to include the bones of prehistoric animals found in the area. There is a permanent collection of ceramics (many of which feature tropical fruits) from the western cultures of the country. On the upper level is a huge crocodile from the San Blas area. It is more than 12 feet/four meters long. One room is dedicated to religious colonial art.

Museum of Juan Escutia, *Hidalgo #71 West,* ☎ *311-212-3390, Monday-Friday, 9 am-1 pm and 5-7 pm,* is in yet another 18th-century colonial house. Juan Escutia was one of the child heros of Chapultepec, the area in Mexico City where children held the Americans at bay for four days. It was in 1846 when Mexico declared war on the US and on September 11th of the same year, US General Scott attacked the Fort of Chapultepec in Mexico City that was defended by 632 soldiers from the Battalion of San Blas and 200 young cadets. As the battle raged, all the soldiers were killed. Eventually, the US Army entered the fort and, while still defending their land, five young cadets died. One was Juan Escutia. Juan's parents, José and Maria Martinez, lived here until 1869. Inside you will find the birth certificate of Juan, along with pictures of other Chapultepec heros. There are military uniforms and pictures of Juan as a cadet, along with the flag of San Blas and medals from that era. Juan Escutia was born in Tepic on February 22, 1827 and joined the military in 1847. When he was at battle in Chapultepec, he was the bearer of the flag.

Museum Aramara (Museum of Visual Arts), *Av Allende #329,* ☎ *311-216-4246, Monday-Friday, 9 am-1 pm and 5-7 pm,* has two rooms with permanent exhibits that feature paintings done by local artists. The six inside rooms have modern art, photographs and plastic arts. The late 18th-century colonial building was first a school and, later, the only sanatorium in the state.

Museum of Emilia Ortiz, *Av Ledro #192,* ☎ *311-212-2652, Monday-Friday, 9 am-1 pm and 5-7 pm,* has a permanent exhibition of this talented artist's work. She is not only an excellent painter, but also a poet and a journalist who received recognition from peers in those fields. Born in 1917, Ortiz has been an artist for over 70 years. The museum is well lit, with benches on which to sit and admire the works.

The Plaza has the Palacio de Gobierno, built in the 1800s, facing the 18th-century Cathedral of the Pure Conception of Mary and the 16th-

Tepic's plaza and cathedral.

century Temple of the Cross of Zacate. The temple originally was a Franciscan convent but today is home of the State Ministry of Tourism. The center of the plaza has a lovely fountain and there is always some type of event happening nearby.

A City Tour is offered for free by the town of Tepic. You must get your ticket an hour before the bus leaves from the kiosk on the plaza in front of the cathedral on Av Mexico and Amado Nervo. Even during off-season, this is a popular tour. It starts at 10 am and ends at 5 pm, and is conducted in Spanish only. The historical tour includes some of the parks and old buildings. The vehicle looks like a remodeled milk truck with rows of seats, but no doors. Being open air, visibility is good. This is an excellent opportunity to see Tepic.

■ Adventures on Foot

 Volcán Ceboruco is 8,000 feet/2,164 meters high. You can drive all the way to the crater during dry season. While on the highway, you will see remnants of the last eruption that took place in 1870, killing everyone in the surrounding villages. Previous eruptions occurred in 1567 and 1542. To get here, take a bus from Tepic to Jala, a colonial village at the foot of the mountain with less than 500 residents. Purchase all your drinking water and food here, as there is nothing available farther along.

> **FACT FILE:** This area is credited with growing the longest ears of corn in the world, some of which reach up to 19 inches/48 cm.

The Gothic-Romanesque-styled **Lateran Basilica** built in the 18th century is worth visiting while in the village. The old church (not the basilica on the plaza, but up from it) dates back to the 1500s. You can climb the bell tower for a look at the town. This old church, built in the typical Spanish style with white plaster and a bell tower to one side, once also served the convent next door. There is a **museum** in town, near the plaza, that has some maps, statues and ancient animal bones.

Stay at **Hospedaje Camberos**, *on Av Hidalgo, $,* if you want to spend the entire day on the mountain and are too late to get back to Tepic or if you just want to spend a day in this tiny Mexican village. The lady in the store next door will open the door for you with a key that looks like it should be for a prison rather than a home. There are two very clean bathrooms for the five tiny, basic rooms in the *hospedaje*. Each room has a bed with mattress and sheets. The two recommended restaurants in Jala are **Joya** and **Don Miguel**, both on Dom Conocido.

From Jala on the southern slope, walk along the cobblestone roadway that leads up the mountain toward the microwave towers. As you get near the top it becomes obvious that there are actually two craters, one beside the other. Near the rims of these are the microwave towers. From the towers you can follow a path toward the center and then to the top of the bigger cone. Steam still leaks up from underground, which means you should be careful where you plant your foot. One of the craters has a flat floor and numerous pine trees. This is a good picnic spot. There's also another picnic area that can be driven to. You will need hiking boots (runners won't do), water, warm jacket, food and sunblock to explore the volcano area. This is a magnificent hike. However, if you are the driving kind, you can get near the top with a vehicle.

■ Adventures on Water

Aguamilpa, a man-made lake, is 4.5 miles/seven km from Santa Maria del Oro. The 55,000-acre lake was created by damming Mexico's longest river, the Santiago, for the Aguamilpa Hydro Electric Power Plant. The 70-mile/100-km lake is surrounded by vegetated hills that pour scenic waterfalls into its waters. It is also a fishing lake where stocked bass is the draw. One lakeside lodge caters to anglers. **Aguamilpa Lodge**, *Bass Adventures*, ☎ *505-377-2372 (US), PO Box 995, Angel Fire, NM, 87710, $$$$$,* has 16 rooms and sits on a cliff overlooking the lake. An all-inclusive package available between November and April includes lodging, meals, drinks, boats and guides.

Mexcaltitlan is the Venice of Mexico because the streets of the town flood every rainy season. Located at the mouth of a river in a large lagoon, Mexcaltitlan is an island that is believed to be where the Aztecs first left to go inland and start the city of Tenochtitlan, now Mexico City. The small, round island is in a swamp/mangrove area and can be reached by hired boat, available at the dock (see directions below). The island's one village has one hotel and restaurants that specialize in making pre-Hispanic foods. There is a museum that holds the thousand-year-old stone carved with the eagle devouring a serpent. The museum also has artifacts from the indigenous people who lived here thousands of years ago. Buses from Tepic bus station go every two hours. You go first to Santiago, then on to Santispac. The road gets rough between Santispac and Mexcaltitlan. At the water, there is a dock where you can hire a boat to take you to the island. The cost is less than $5 round trip. If traveling in your own vehicle, leave it at the boat landing but lock it up and take all valuables.

■ Adventures in Nature

 Centro de Educacion Ambiental (Environmental Education Center), ☎ *311-212-9409,* is five miles/eight km from town, just 10 minutes by taxi. It is open 8 am-1 pm daily; admission is $1. This educational center promotes conservation, appreciation and investigation of the outdoors. Located on 26,000 hectares of forest, the center offers an extensive amount of flora and fauna for the public to enjoy. Swing bridges cross delicate canyon areas that feature every type of plant imaginable. With the lush jungle comes the numerous bird species that can be observed from special platforms. Because the jungle has gone back to its natural state, the temperature is always around 20°C/68°F and the humidity is high. An interpretive trail has 18 labeled points of interest and the main center has an audio visual show (in Spanish). Take with you insect repellent, a hat, binoculars (essential) and hiking boots or good runners. It will take about three hours to make the tour.

Laguna de Santa Maria del Oro is 30 miles/50 km southeast of Tepic and five miles/eight km from the town of Santa Maria del Oro. This crater lake measures one mile/two km wide and is surrounded by hills covered in pines and subtropical vegetation. Birding is the favorite activity, but people also come to swim or fish in the lake. Stocked with bass and tilapia, the lake yields fish weighing up to six lb/2.5 kg. Small restaurants around the lake serve the specialty called *chicharron de pescado* (fish sausage). Although motorboats have not been banned from the lake, Jet Skis have, a real plus for the eco side.

There are some lakeside cabins with private bathrooms, hot water and kitchenettes at the **Bungalows Koala,** ☎ *311-212-3772* (phone in Tepic because there are no phones at the lake). Tucked into bougainvilleas and snake plants, they are well kept and have potted plants decorating the brick buildings. There is also a restaurant. Those with RVs or tents can camp here. The bungalows are owned by Chris French and his wife, who first came to the area 20 years ago because they liked the name. They could have done better business moving to the coast, but they liked the climate of the lake and decided to stay. They are into preserving the environment and encourage the use of non-motorized transportation. This is truly a gem of a place.

The roads around the lake are barely rough tracks and hikers, bikers or horseback riders can spot the birds mentioned below and maybe find some new plant life not seen before in Mexico. It takes two hours to walk around the lake at a leisurely speed. You can purchase juice, water or a beer from one of the lakeshore restaurants.

BIRD WATCH: *Birds at the lake include grebes, pelicans, cormorants, herons, humming-birds, trogons, ducks, motmots, kingfishers, neotropical creepers, vultures, ospreys, hawks, flycatchers, chachalacas, sandpipers, swallows, kingbirds, cotingas, swallows, crows, jays, pigeons, doves, parrots, wrens, cuckoos, owls, thrushes, gnatcatchers, mockingbirds, woodpeckers and finches. The area has many resident birds, migratory birds and casual visitors.*

The church in Santa Maria del Oro village has a statue donated by Nuño Beltran (known to the people of the village as "Bloody" Guzman) in restitution for the murders he committed while trying to conquer the area.

The restaurants in town are **La Parroquia**, near the church, and **La Cocina Economica**, in front of the square. I have no information about these places.

■ Adventures in Culture

Los Toriles de Ixtlan del Rio is an archeological site about 60 miles/88 km from Tepic. Buses to Ixtlan leave every hour from Tepic and Guadalajara. At the village you can hire a taxi to take you to the ruins just one mile/two km west.

This is not a huge ruin, but it is unique because it has the only circular Maya temple found to date that is not an observatory. Occupied by the Tumbas de Tiro group around 300 BC-600 AD, the area covered approximately 200 acres. After the Tumbas de Tiro fell, the Aztatlan people occupied the town.

Ceramics found at the site were unique to the Chinesco, Ixtlan and San Sebastian areas. They featured predominantly red, orange, yellow and cream colors and the subjects were mainly women, war, work and music. The later ceramics made by the Aztatlan group were of smooth red clay. Found in the homes of the common people were earthenware pots and red tripod grinding mortars.

The later group of inhabitants perfected the use of metals and worked the metal into jewelry with intricate designs. They also used a lot of obsidian that was probably transported from Volcano Ceboruco, not far from Ixtlan. The obsidian was carved on both sides.

At the site, pit tombs were found. This method of burial is believed to have been practiced until 600 AD when the Aztatlan people took over. There is also evidence of stairways, drainage ditches, small residences, workshops, altars and palaces. Of course, the most impressive ruin at the site is the round temple called Ehecatl-quetzalcoatl. The two circular tiers have steps leading to the top where there are two pyramids. Adjoined to the circular tiers is the Palace of the Bas Relief and, in front of it, the main square with the Palace of the Columns flanking one side.

The site is open every day from 9 am until 5 pm. The information center has pamphlets from the National Institute of Anthropology and History. There are also bathrooms and a picnic area. Rumors have it that there will be a tourist lodge in the future.

There are numerous hotels in Ixtlan village and most are in the middle price range. The Plaza Hidalgo offers the most luxurious services, but it is not necessarily the best. Look around and compare to see what suits you best. The hotels mentioned below are recommended by the tourist office in Tepic. Most are along Av Hidalgo. **Hotel Colon**, *Hidalgo #359, 311-243-3919, $*, has 32 basic rooms. **Hotel Santa Rita**, *Hidalgo #125*, ☎ *311-243-2451, $*, is a tiny place with just a few basic rooms. It was originally called The Maya. **El Paraiso**, *Hidalgo #757*, ☎ *311-243-2000, $$*, has 20 rooms. **Plaza Hidalgo**, *Hidalgo and 5 de Mayo*, ☎ *311-243-2101, $$$*, is a four-star hotel with 42 rooms equipped with everything you need.

There are about 20 restaurants, including the **Three Gold Stars**, **Happy Chicken**, **Moby Dick** and **Fisherman**. Like everything else, most are on Av Hidalgo. If they look clean and serve what you want, give them a try.

■ Places to Stay

Hotels are spread around the city. There are numerous two- and one-star options beyond the plaza toward Av Victoria and then more west of the plaza but also toward Victoria.

Hotel Cibrian, *Amado Nervo #163, 311-212-8699, $*, has moderately large rooms with private bathrooms and tiled floors. The place is clean and the staff is friendly. It is the only decent and moderately priced hotel that is close to the square and it is my choice.

Motel del Sol, *Insurgentes & Prisceliano Sanchez, no phone, $*, is close to the bus station. If you are just passing through and need to sleep for the night, this is a clean and secure option that has a car park on the premises. However, if spending any time in Tepic, get into the center, where it is much safer.

HOTEL PRICE SCALE	
Price for a room given in US $.	
$	Up to $20
$$	$21-$50
$$$	$51-$100
$$$$	$101-$150
$$$$$	$151-$200
Anything over $200 is specified.	

Central Pacific Mexico

Villa Las Rosas, *Av Insurgentes # 100*, ☎ *311-213-1800, $$,* is across from the Hill Park and zoo. It has two floors with 30 rooms built around a courtyard. Each rather plain room has cable TV, air conditioning, tiled floors, private bathroom with hot water and ceiling fan. Parking is on site. The price of the room includes a continental breakfast in the Handrails Restaurant (7 am-10:30 pm). At night you can dance at the Faisan Disco, also on the premises, where the weekend begins on Thursday.

Sierra de Alica Hotel, *Av Mexico #180*, ☎ *311-212-0322, $$,* is half a block from the square and patronized mostly by Mexican businessmen. It offers laundry service, pharmacy, beauty salon, money exchange, safe deposit boxes, a travel agent and off-street parking. I did not find the hotel staff friendly, although those in the restaurant were. It is open at 7:30 am and serves excellent meals.

Hotel Las Palomas, *Av Insurgentes 2100*, ☎ *311-214-0238 or 800-713-8500, www.laspalomashotel.com.mx, $$$,* is fairly nice. It overlooks a busy street so rooms at the back are recommended. Each room has a private bathroom, cable TV, air conditioning, telephone and a sitting area. There are reading lights over the beds, the floors are tiled and there are large closets for your stuff. There is a restaurant, bar and parking.

Hotel La Loma, *Paseo de la Loma #301*, ☎ *311-213-2222, $$$,* is close to the park and zoo. This comfortable place has lush gardens surrounding a small pool. Rooms are clean and well furnished with cable TV, tiled bathrooms, ceramic floors, cupboards and night lights. Each room also has a sitting area with a small table. The staff is pleasant, the grounds well kept and the price is reasonable. There is a restaurant, bar and parking. La Loma is close to many good restaurants, although it is about a 10-minute walk to the plaza.

Hotel Melanie, *Blvd Tepic Xalisco #109*, ☎ *311-216-1888, $$$,* is a half-hour walk or a five-minute cab ride from the center of town. Its 43 rooms are set around a clean vegetated courtyard that has tile walkways. Unfortunately, the tile reverberates sound and makes it a bit noisy during times like carnival. There is air conditioning, cable TV, daily maid service, restaurant and laundry service.

Hotel Fray Junipero Serra, *Lerdo #23*, ☎ *311-212-2525, www.frayjunipero.com.mx, $$$,* is on the plaza. It has over 100 spacious rooms with air conditioning, carpets, private bathrooms, cable TV, telephones and safe deposit boxes. There is laundry service, pool and a restaurant that's popular with locals, This is a good deal.

Hotel Real de Don Juan, *Av Mexico and Juarez*, ☎ *311-212-1324, $$$,* is across from the Government Building, just off the plaza. The rooms are large, with queen-sized beds, private bathrooms, night tables and tables beside the windows where you can sit and watch the action on the street (if you are at the front). There is also a restaurant and bar.

Nekie (Fiesta Tepic) Hotel, *Av Insurgentes and Lago Victor,* ☎ *311-207-0768, $$$$,* has a 1940s atmosphere, but the place has been modernized to provide air conditioning, tiled floors, safe deposit boxes and cable TV. Its 240 big rooms have high ceilings. There is an outdoor pool, laundry service, parking, restaurant, beauty parlor, bar and gift shops. This is a five-star hotel with five-star service.

■ Places to Eat

There are a few dishes traditional to the province of Nayarit. *Pescado Sarandeado* is grilled fish cooked over mangrove wood. This dish may no longer be available since mangroves are now being preserved. *Pate de camaron* is a shrimp pâté and *taxtihuili* is a corn broth that has shrimp cooked into it. If you see any of these dishes offered, be certain to try them.

▶▶ **AUTHOR NOTE:** *Most of the better restaurants are away from the plaza and on or near Av Insurgentes.*

Sierra Hotel Restaurant, *Av Mexico #180,* ☎ *311-212-0322,* is a tiny place with a cozy atmosphere. The food is excellent and inexpensive. I had the chicken for $3.50 and the portion was big enough to fill me. What really impressed me here was the staff. They went out of their way to make me welcome and to give me everything I wanted. Then they turned around and let a beggar kid in to have something to eat.

Cheros, *Av Insurgentes #233, across from Alameda Park, no phone*, specializes in *banarilla*, an interesting dish of chopped barbeque pork or beef mixed with spices. A T-bone or New York steak costs $7.50. The meat I tasted had a smoked flavor and was tender. This is a popular place for those who want to enjoy a drink with their food. It's open 7 am-2 am daily.

La Mision de Trinos, *Hidalgo # 73,* ☎ *311-212-2180,* is a very clean place in the center of town that serves excellent food. Their *liquidos* are thick and their *huevos rancheros* (eggs with tomato and onion) are good. They serve international foods, so getting a sandwich or a good plate of chicken is easy. Prices are about $4 per meal.

AltaMirano, *Av Mexico # 105 South,* ☎ *311-212-1377,* is above the square beside the cathedral. You must enter the building and go to the back stairs and then up. The food is good, although not exceptional. The view is what you really pay for. They are open early, so breakfast is popular here. The coffee is good and the service reasonable.

Mariscos Lalo's, *Calle Allende and Ures,* ☎ *311-216-4421,* is popular for seafood. There is a take-out service and the lines are always long.

El Girasol, *Paseo de la Loma # 201*, ☎ *311-213-4293*, is close to La Loma Hotel and is a vegetarian restaurant. The food is excellent, considering this is a meat-eating nation. There are lots of salads.

Fu Seng, *Insurgentes #1199*, ☎ *311-214-5988*, is beyond Alameda Park and is a stark room with tin tables and plastic chairs. However, the stir-fried vegetables are excellent, and the prices are low.

■ Nightlife

Fundacion Nayarit, *Lerdo de Tejada #57*, ☎ *311-216-4064*, is the art center of the city. It opens at 10 am and, depending on the function, doesn't usually close until late. During the day you can have a cappuccino and a piece of cheesecake and enjoy the bohemian ambiance. There is art on the walls and a small bookstore that sells local poetry and self-published books. A calendar of events lets you know what is happening that month. Most events start at 8:30 pm and have a cover charge of about $1.50 per person. Offerings include things like "*Musica Romantica* by Los Sobrinos" and "Luis Lucachin Reading Ballads of Yesterday and Today." For me, this place was a real treat.

San Blas

The *Bells of San Blas* was written by Henry Wadsworth Longfellow. It was his last creation before he died on March 24, 1882.

> *What say the Bells of San Blas*
> *To the ships that southward pass*
> *From the harbor of Mazatlan*
> *To them it is nothing more*
> *Than the sound of surf on the shore,*
> *Nothing more to master or man.*
> *But to me, a dreamer of dreams*
> *To whom what is and what seems*
> *Are often one and the same,*
> *The Bells of San Bas to me*
> *Have a strange, wild melody,*
> *And are something more than a name*
> *For bells are the voice of the church*
> *They have tones that touch and search*
> *The hearts of young and old*
> *One sound to all yet each*
> *Lends a meaning to their speech*
> *And the meaning is manifold.*

This is the newest and, so far as I can tell, the most beautiful beach in all of Mexico. The 50 miles/80 km of sand and surf is dotted with a few estuaries and undisturbed by huge hotels. But that will change rapidly and my guess is that in 10 years my comments about the place and the hotels will be history. The town is a tiny fishing village of about 12,000 people and is surrounded by rainforests and mangrove swamps. At present those stretches of beach hold surfing waves, ruins from the early Spanish explorers, turtle sanctuaries and wildlife-riddled estuaries.

▶▶ **AUTHOR NOTE:** *The only drawback to visiting San Blas are the* **mosquitoes** *and the insects referred to as a* **sand fleas***, no-see-ums or jejenes (hay-HAY-nays). Avon's Skin so Soft is good for the jejenes and for your skin. Long shirt-sleeves and long pants are also a help. Insect repellent is a must. The reason there are so many insects is because there are mangrove swamps nearby. Don't let the insects stop you from coming; just come prepared.*

■ Getting Here

 Buses from Puerto Vallarta cost about $12 and take 2½ hours on a first-class bus. San Blas is two hours by bus from Tepic and four from Guadalajara.

The closest **airports** are in Puerto Vallarta, Tepic and Guadalajara.

■ History

San Blas, founded in 1768, became an important port for the Spanish. It was **Manuel Rivero y Cordero** who, under command of Carlos II, made San Blas the port for Spanish ships sailing along the California coast. The Customs House was the first one built in the New World and served as both a tax collection place for incoming goods and as a defense fort. It was also from here that **Fray Junipero Serra**, a Franciscan missionary, ruled the 15 missions along the coast. He arrived in San Blas on April 1, 1768 and, using two ships that had just been built in the harbor, started colonization of the area. Fray Junipero Serra died in San Carlos Barromeo de Carmelo on August 28, 1784.

COASTAL MISSIONS ESTABLISHED BY SERRA

1769 – San Fernando de Velicata and San Diego de Alcala

1770 – San Carlos Barromeo de Carmelo

1771 – San Gabriel Arcangel and San Antonio de Padua

1772 – San Luis Obispo de Tolsa

1776 – San Juan Capistrano

1776 – San Francisco de Asis

1777 – Santa Clara de Asis

1782 – San Buenaventura

■ Services

The **Tourist Office**, *Calle Mercado, Monday to Friday, 8:30 am-5 pm, Saturday until 1 pm*, has maps, a guidebook and pamphlets about the area. The staff speaks English and is quite helpful. They sell used paperbacks written in English.

Police, *Calle Sonola, across from the bus station*, ☎ 323-285-0028.

People at the **Health Center**, *Calle Campeche and Batallion*, ☎ 323-285-0232, speak only Spanish.

Post office, *Calle Sonora and Echeverria*, ☎ 323-285-0295, *Monday to Friday, 8 am-2 pm*.

■ Adventures on Foot

The **Mafia Hotel** is not a place you will want to stay, but it is interesting to walk around and have a look at what may have been had nature not intervened. The luxurious stone structure, located on the beach, has over 150 rooms overlooking the ocean. On the opening night, when even the president was there, an army of sand fleas (*jejenes*) attacked, sending the guests back to their homes in the city. Now the building is falling apart. Obviously, the owners had not heard of Skin so Soft by Avon – a sure-fire protection from the pesky biting bugs.

The Ruins, on Cerro de San Basilio at the northeast end of town above the cemetery, include the remains of La Nuestra Señora del Rosario Church and the Contadura, the counting house. The church was built in 1769 and was used until the late 1800s. The counting house was built with large stones and held together with little mortar. It had arched doorways. The old cannons around the building were used to keep British pi-

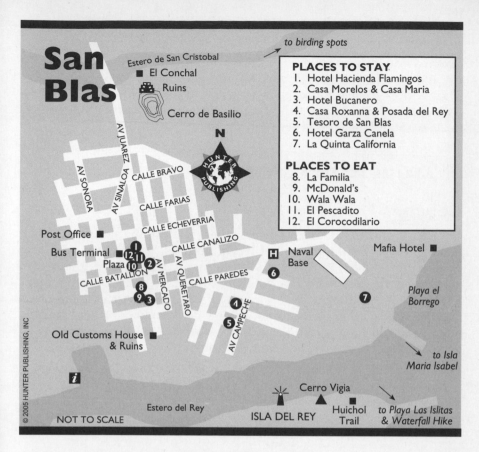

San
Blas

to birding spots

Estero de San Cristobal
■ El Conchal
Ruins
Cerro de Basilio

N

HUNTER PUBLISHING

AV JUAREZ
AV SINALOA
AV SONORA
CALLE BRAVO
CALLE FARIAS
CALLE ECHEVERRIA
CALLE CANALIZO
AV MERCADO
AV QUERETARO
CALLE PAREDES
AV CAMPECHE
CALLE BATALLION

Post Office ■
Bus Terminal ■
Plaza

Old Customs House ■
& Ruins

PLACES TO STAY
1. Hotel Hacienda Flamingos
2. Casa Morelos & Casa Maria
3. Hotel Bucanero
4. Casa Roxanna & Posada del Rey
5. Tesoro de San Blas
6. Hotel Garza Canela
7. La Quinta California

PLACES TO EAT
8. La Familia
9. McDonald's
10. Wala Wala
11. El Pescadito
12. El Corocodilario

H Naval
Base

Mafia Hotel ■

Playa el
Borrego

to Isla
Maria Isabel

Cerro Vigia

Estero del Rey

ISLA DEL REY

Huichol
Trail

to Playa Las Islitas
& Waterfall Hike

NOT TO SCALE

© 2005 HUNTER PUBLISHING, INC

rates away. During the 18th century, José Maria Mercado used this fortification to successfully keep invaders out.

FACT FILE: The first ship to arrive and be taxed here was the Chinese *Nao* coming from the East with silks and spices.

Although restoration was being done at the ruins, a recent hurricane took out a lot of the work. There is a $1 entry fee. There is a bathroom at the gate. Open daily from 10 am to 6 pm.

The old **Customs House** is located across the river from the docks. It is constructed of brick that is now crumbling. Next to the ruins is a new, rather nondescript Customs House but it, too, is not in use.

Isla del Rey is on the bay and is actually part of the peninsula, rather than an island. It is the sacred lands of the Huichol Indians and has a pilgrimage trail. The Indians came to this site every spring to worship the sea goddess, Aramara. Today they still come, dressed in traditional costume, to enjoy their spring celebrations. You must cross the estuary by boat to get here (50¢). The dock is across from Tesoro Bungalows.

Cerro Vigia, near ceremonial grounds of Isla del Rey, holds El Faro, the red-and-white striped lighthouse where you can get good views of San Blas. A trail from the dock passes scrub and the Huichol ceremonial ground before heading up the hill. You must cross the estuary by boat to get here (50¢). The dock is across from Tesoro Bungalows.

■ Adventures on Water

Beaches

 La Islitas Beach has the longest wave in the world, according to the Guinness Book of World Records. This wave is supposed to be about 20 feet long (six meters) and can carry the skilled surfer for a mile or more before petering out. The beach is five miles/eight km south of San Blas and buses pass by every half-hour. There are a number of beachside restaurants, some with hammocks where you can relax, read and enjoy a beer. You can be certain there will be many experienced surfers talking the talk and waiting for the "Big One".

Borrengo Beach is about half a mile down (south) on the beach and is where those who are into camping hang out. The bugs can be bad, so repellent is essential. Intermediate surfing is good along this beach, but you must bring your own equipment. Boogie boards are also fun here. Snorkeling is not good because of the murky water.

Waterfalls

El Cora Waterfalls are 30 feet/10 meters high. They are located just out of the town of El Cora on an old hacienda that was once owned by Germans. The revolution of 1910-1914 resulted in the land being confiscated by the new rulers. Petroglyphs dot the trail. The walk is not long and there is a cool pool to swim in at the bottom of the falls. The tiny stream that forms the waterfall empties into the river below. It can be crossed below the pool and a grunt up the side of the cliff will take you to another pool and falls. Take a bus (the white one) or drive from San Blas to El Cora town (10 miles/16 km) along the road to Santa Cruz/Tepic. Turn south at Tecuitata and go five miles/eight km to a loading platform where you can leave your vehicle. Follow the creek downstream. The final bit is steep, so hiking boots are recommended. Bring your bathing suit.

Tecuitata Waterfalls are near the village of the same name. Go the same way as to El Cora, only half a mile past the village of Santa Cruz get off the bus or turn downhill along a dirt road where the sign indicates Balneario Nuevo Chapultepec. At the bottom of the hill there is a waterslide, a restaurant and a small pool. Walk upstream through the jungle to the Arroyo Campsite and the waterfall. This waterfall is not as spectacular as El Cora, but certainly easier to reach.

■ Adventures in Nature

Birding

 According to the Audubon Society, San Blas is second only to Panama as having the largest number of bird species. There are many habitats – mangroves, mud flats, lagoons and offshore islands with thorn scrub and pine/oak woodlands – where you might spot rare and exotic birds.

> **BIRD WATCH:** *More common Mexican birds, like the blue bunting, the yellow-winged cacique and the mangrove cuckoo, will be easy to find. However, avid birders should keep a lookout for bare-throated tiger herons, lesser roadrunners, boat-billed herons, Colima pygmy-owls (these are so cute!), Rufous-necked wood-rails, rosy-thrush tanagers and military macaws.*

Most birders log over 200 species in a week. If you don't have a bird book with you, purchase the one at the tourist office, *Where to Find Birds in San Blas*. This book tells you of other places around town where birds can be seen. A spotting scope or binoculars is essential. Bring insect repellent.

 Where to Find Birds in San Blas, by Soalind Novick and Lan Sing Wu, is available by mail (178 Myrtle Court Arcata, CA 95521, US $4.50) or you can purchase it at one of the hotels/shops in town.

San Cristobal and **El Pozo Estuaries** are birder specialty places, but they are also rich with turtles, iguanas and crocodiles. The vegetation includes vines and giant ferns. Fresh springs run through the estuaries. The boat ride through this area goes for several miles, and San Cristobal estuary connects to the freshwater lake of La Tovara. The El Pazo inlet is where the annual fishing derby starts each year. Boats can be hired either at your hotel or at the dock. **Chencho, ☎ 323-285-0716**, takes morning trips to San Cristobal and the cost, depending on duration, is $50 for up to five people. He takes you up the river to the lake. You need not go all the way if you are interested in seeing the wildlife in the estuary. This must be negotiated with the boatman.

La Tovara Lagoon is reached by traveling through the jungle and mangrove swamp up the estuary where crocodiles are wild and protected. Because there are so many, seeing them will almost become ho-hum by the end of the trip. However it is the Northern potoos, a bird that likes to be out after dark, that is the big draw. Green kingfishers and great black hawks are also common. Along the way you'll see vines, bromeliads, mangroves and flowering plants. At the right time of year, large hordes of butterflies gather here. An interesting spot on your river journey is an old movie set with huts on stilts set along the water's edge. The trip goes to a spring where you can swim in cool waters and then have a drink or a snack at the restaurant near the dock. The pool is large and the water clear. The spring provides drinking water for San Blas residents. There are fish in the water. **Chencho** (see above), the famous river guide, has an evening trip to the pool that costs $40 for up to four people. He is at the dock midday taking reservations and may group you with other people to make a load of four. You leave around 4 pm and return after dark. It is a thrill to travel through the jungle after dark. The sounds are eerie. Birders Novick and Wu suggest you hire **Oscar Partida**, who speaks English and knows his birds very well. He can be contacted by phone, ☎ 323-285-0324, or at Las Brisas Hotel.

> ▶▶ **AUTHOR TIP:** *During peak seasons, when private boats are busy, the tourist office will put on a boat that is much cheaper than a private boat but also more crowded. See them at the office for details.*

Roca Elephante is a tiny island (a rock) just offshore to the northwest of the town that has both the blue- and brown-footed boobies as well as red-billed tropicbirds nesting. You will need to hire a boat at the dock to take you there. As you approach the island, swarms of frigate birds will cloud the skies. Peregrine falcons and pelicans also reside on Roca Elephante. You can't go onto the rock, but the boat will circle a number of times until you have had your visual fill.

Singayta Inlet is a jungle environment where El Manglar Environmental Center has built a traditional Nayarit village with a palapa hut that is used as an information center. Their objective is to protect the 260 species of birds in the surrounding forest. The organic nursery has prized orchids, some of which have taken four years to establish themselves. Near the huts are some Aztec petroglyphs. Boats are available to take people into the mangroves and lakes. To get here from San Blas, take the bus to Singayta (on the inlet and where El Manglar Environmental Center is located) from the plaza for a dollar each way. This is one of the most popular birding spots in all of western Mexico, even with the lush population of mosquitoes and sand fleas.

MEPG

The Mangrove Environmental Protection Group in San Blas was started in 1993 to protect the mangroves and surrounding land from mega-tourism and shrimp farms. Their main concern is education and enforcing the laws that have been passed. The president is Juan Garcia, a local businessman. Among other things, the group developed a bicycle path that leads from the entrance of town at Conchal Bridge, all the way to the bay and along the beach to Los Cocos. The most frequent users of this path are the oyster fishers.

Parque Nacional Isla Isabel is a bird and underwater sanctuary 52 miles/70 km from San Blas. It is a narrow volcanic island, one mile/1. 6 km long that has a deciduous forest starting to cover the lava base. The island was formed about 3.5 million years ago and has evidence of nine separate volcanoes. There are bare rocks, cliffs and sandy beaches surrounding the small coral reefs just offshore. In the center is a crater lake with water 18 times saltier than the ocean. The landscape is unmatched and the island is often called the Galapagos of Mexico. It is also a birder's paradise, with numerous seabirds; blue- and brown-footed boobies nest here.

 FACT FILE: The interesting thing about boobies is the sibling rivalry. The oldest bird will often kill its nest-mates if food is scarce.

There was at one time a huge colony of sooty terns on the island, but cats almost made them extinct. The cats were removed and the terns are recovering. Alongside the many endangered birds, Isla Isabel has a healthy community of amphibians, including the fake coral snake and the brown and green iguana. A research station operates for five months of every year, and visitors are welcome to camp as long as they bring all their supplies, including water. The researchers rely on local fishers and the navy to bring in water and supplies. **Ancla Tours** in Nuevo Vallarta, ☎ *322-297-1464*, takes people to the island. In San Blas, **Tony Aguayo**, ☎ *323-285-0364, at the end of Calle Juarez,* is a recommended guide. He charges about $200 per person (based on two people going) for a full-day island trip. His boat will hold about six people.

Cerro de San Juan Ecological Reserve, ☎ *311-213-1423,* is 6,200 feet/2,000 meters high and is another good hiking/birding area between San Blas and Tepic. It's about 15 miles/25 km from San Blas. The area has pine and oak forests.

BIRD WATCH: *Rare birds have been spotted in the San Juan reserve, including Mexican wood nymphs and Rufous-crowned motmots. Although not seen, the eared-poorwills have been heard. There are also yellow grossbeaks, woodcreepers, redstarts and buntings.*

There is a ranch-style lodge at the top of the mountain. To get to the reserve, you must take a bus from the center of town. On the way you can stop at El Mirador del Aguila and look for military macaws.

Crocs

Ejido de la Palma Crocodile Farm is three miles/five km south of Matanchen Village, near Las Islitas Beach. These crocs are in captivity. There is a freshwater lake on the site and the surrounding jungle houses butterflies, turtles and lizards. There is an entrance fee of $2 per person – the money goes toward the protection of the crocs.

■ Outfitters/Tour Operators

Bird Treks, *115 Peach Bottom Village, Peach Bottom, PA,* ☎ *717-548-3303 (US), 800-224-5399 (Mx), www.birdtreks.com,* offers a tour that starts in Puerto Vallarta. It takes half a day traveling to San Blas where you set up home base in one of the better hotels. The next seven nights are spent sleeping at the hotel, while the days are spent hunting birds with expert birders (who are also the tour leaders). The cost is $2,200 for an all-inclusive package from PV to San Blas and back. This does not include booze, personal supplies (such as mosquito repellent) or tips.

Wings Birding Tours, ☎ *888-293-6443, www.wingsbirds.com*, offers birding trips all over the world. I have worked with them in Bolivia and I know they are first class. Their website has a bird list that is far too long to put in here. The tour starts and ends in Puerto Vallarta, with most of the time spent in the San Blas area. This is a nine-day, eight-night tour that includes everything except the pen to tick off the birds seen. The cost is $2,450 per person for double occupancy. Wings allows only 12 people in a group, plus the leader.

■ Places to Stay

Casa Morelos, *Calle Heroico Batallion # 108,* ☎ *323-285-0820, $*, is between town and the beach and two blocks from the bus station. The guesthouse has clean rooms without private bathrooms and is owned by the same family who owns **Casa Maria**, just around the corner (same phone number). Both have communal cooking areas and gardens in which to sit. These are friendly Mexican establishments that are comfortable but simple.

HOTEL PRICE SCALE	
Price for a room given in US $.	
$	Up to $20
$$	$21-$50
$$$	$51-$100
$$$$	$101-$150
$$$$$	$151-$200
Anything over $200 is specified.	

La Quinta California, *halfway between town and the beach,* ☎ *323-285-0603, $,* has bungalows around a common courtyard that is thickly vegetated with every plant imaginable, including a strangler fig tree. The rooms are not big, but the kitchens are fully equipped with small stove and fridge. Each comfortable two-bedroom bungalow has enough beds to accommodate four people. Prices are reasonable. However, you can get weekly and monthly rates that are even more attractive. There is no daily maid service.

Rafael's Apartments, *Calle Campeche and Calle Hidalgo, $$,* has clean apartments that surround an enclosed garden that is second only to La Quinta's. The kitchens have full stoves (ovens included). The place is clean, safe and economical, but there is no phone or e-mail address so you have to take your chances. Hit town and head over here.

Casa Roxanna, *Callejon el Rey #1, www.sanblasmexico.com/casa-roxanna/, $$,* is a very neat and tidy little place that has a pool with an adjacent bar, and rooms with air conditioning, cupboards and cable TV. The kitchens are fully supplied with fridge and stove and have an apartment-sized working area. The décor is tasteful, the floors tile. The sitting area is large and there is laundry service and secured parking. The large bungalows sleep up to five people and the small up to three. This is a real gem and, as a birder, I could stay here for a month with no problem. The gardens are lush.

Bungalows Conny, *Calle Chiapis #26,* ☎ *323-285-0986, www.bungalowsconny.sanblasmexico.com/contact.html, $$,* is a Mexican hacienda-style hotel that is comfortable and clean. The rooms have air conditioning, television, two double beds, private bathrooms and hot water. Laundry service is offered. This place is a good find and just four blocks from the main plaza.

Hotel Bucanero, *Av Juarez #75,* ☎ *323-285-0101, $$,* is older and with a décor that is more interesting than most in town. In the garden is an anchor and a couple of stuffed crocs. The rooms have high ceilings and are cool, but dingy. There is a pool, but no restaurant. Note that the disco next door could keep you awake on weekends.

Posada del Rey, *Av Campeche #10,* ☎ *323-285-0123, $$/$$$, www.sanblasmexico.com/posadadelrey.* Some of the dozen rooms have air con-

Central Pacific Mexico

ditioning, but none of the private bathrooms has separate shower stalls. There is a small pool with a poolside bar, a beach-supply shop and a restaurant. The owners are friendly and will arrange tours for you. They speak English, French and Spanish.

Tesoro de San Blas, *Calle Campeche and Hidalgo,* ☎ *323-285-0537, www.geocities.com/dougcb68/tsb.htm, $$,* features rustic, three-room bungalows that have hot-water showers in the bathrooms, gas hot plates and refrigerators in the kitchens and a comfortable sitting space in the living rooms. The cabins are kept clean. There is a large maintained garden full of exotic plants like mango, banana and papaya. There is also off-street parking. One small room in the house is available for rent. The cabins are on the estuary so the view of the lighthouse adds to the sunsets. Birders like to use this as a home base because they can walk around the estuary when bird activity is high.

Hotel Hacienda Flamingos, *Calle Juarez # 105,* ☎ *323-285-0930 or 285-0485 (no English spoken), www.sanblas.com.mx, $$$,* is right in town close to the plaza. This is the restored German import house, first built in 1883 to receive goods from the orient. It was then called Casa Delius. The last officer to work at the Customs House was displaced in 1932 and had to find other work. His grandson purchased the building out of nostalgia in 1990 and started restoration that has been done to perfection. Photos of the family remain in the hallways that still have the original tiles. There is a pool, a fountain that works all the time and a lush garden. The eight rooms are as beautifully finished as the rest of the building and come with private bathrooms, air conditioning and coffee makers (coffee is supplied).

Hotel Garza Canela, *Calle Paredes # 106 South,* ☎ *323-285-0112, www.garzacanela.com/acommodations.htm, $$$,* has 45 large rooms with tiled floors, air conditioning and fans, satellite TV, safe deposit boxes and private bathrooms with all the amenities. Some larger rooms have a fully supplied kitchenette with fridge and stove. There is also a pool surrounded by a well-tended garden, private parking, laundry service, souvenir shop, travel agent and a babysitting service. Your breakfast and purified water is included in the price. The restaurant is open beam, with linen tablecloths, good service and homemade foods. This is a family-run establishment and their pride in excellence is obvious. The owners are friendly, helpful and knowledgeable about the area. They speak English and some German.

Miramar Paraiso Hotel, *Km 18 on the highway between San Blas and Puerto Vallarta,* ☎ *323-254-9030, www.sanblasyogaretreats.com, $$$,* is 20 minutes by bus from San Blas. This restored colonial mansion overlooks the ocean and has a path leading to the beach about 200 yards away. Two pools and palapa huts dots the lush grounds. There are six different styles of rooms, some with a balcony, some with extra-large windows and some that hold up to four people. All rooms have a private bathroom and shower. The Miramar is also a yoga retreat. Two yoga classes are offered daily: the morning class is more strenuous, while the evening class focuses on meditation and relaxation. They also offer a jungle survival course that would be of interest to anyone planning on hiking in the tropics in the future. Between classes you can do some exploring. The food is vegetarian and the lifestyle conducive to losing weight. They encourage daily hiking, Kombucha mushroom therapy and cleansing fasts. The lady who does the mushroom therapy also teaches dance, surfing and aerobics. Massage therapy is available. The owner does Huichol beadwork and will give lessons. Seven nights here, including meals and one excursion per day (minimum of four people) is about $1,200.

Camping

You can hang your hammock, pitch your tent or park your camper at **Mario's**, no phone, on Borrego Beach. It has restrooms, and food can be purchased. Although there are other places to camp, this is the most popular. You will need insect repellent.

■ Places to Eat

 El Delfin, *at Hotel Garza Canela,* ☎ *323-285-0610, 1-9 pm*, is extremely clean and the water is safe to drink. The cost for a dinner is about $10 per serving. This is a first-class restaurant and should be tried at least once – for that special night out. If you are tired of seafood, the steak here is excellent.

La Familia, *Calle Batallon #18,* ☎ *323-285-0258*, is best for dinner. Their seafood is famous – try their fried snapper. The décor is totally Mexican and the service is down-home friendly.

McDonald's, *Calle Juarez #35, 7 am-10 pm*, offers hamburgers that are nothing like the US chain version. These actually have tons of meat in them. Other meals are offered, too, but nothing that stands out. This is a popular place, which means the food is tasty and nobody gets sick from eating it.

Wala Wala, *Juarez #29, 8 am-10 pm daily except Sunday*. People come here for the fresh uncooked vegetables (they are safe to eat as they are washed in purified water). This, too, is a popular place, in part because of its simplicity and sparkling cleanliness. Meals cost under $10.

El Pescadito, *Calle Juarez and Canalizo,* is on the plaza. It comes highly recommended, although I didn't try it.

El Cocodrilario, *Calle Juarez and Canalizo, 8 am-10 pm*. The specialty here is spaghetti for $8 per serving. They have large servings and good service.

The Bakery, *Calle Cuauhtemoc,* around the corner from Posada del Rey, is the place to try great Mexican chocolate that has been baked into interesting cakes, cookies and tarts.

Jaltemba Bay

Jaltemba Bay is a wide palm-dotted bay that has four villages around it and one scenic island. The villages start at Punta Raza, a rocky point that serves as the southern tip of the bay. From south to north, they are **Los Ayala, Rincon de Guayabitos, La Peñita** and **La Colina**. The island, visible from all villages, is **Isla Peña**. The town of La Peñita is joined by a bridge to Rincon de Guayabitos two miles/three km away. La Piñita has one traffic light, so "laid back" is what you can expect here among the 8,000 residents. The most restful places are in Rincon de Guayabitos, although there are some splendid spots in busier La Peñita.

It is best to have your own transportation if you want to explore along the coast. If you haven't got a car, a guide with a vehicle can be hired. There is an informative web page sponsored by those from Casa Libertad. Key in www.members5.boardhost.com/CasaLibertad/msg/9216.html.

■ Getting Here

 From the center of Puerto Vallarta, you can take a local, second-class **bus** for the hour-long (a bit longer if traffic is thick) trip to Jaltemba Bay.

You can also take a **taxi** for about $50.

▶▶ **AUTHOR NOTE:** *Note that some of the hotels offer free transportation from the PV airport to their hotel.*

If flying to Puerto Vallarta, take a taxi from the airport to the first-class bus station just five minutes away and take a bus from there to La Peñita. The cost is about $5 one way; buses leave every half hour. Local buses run between the other spots along the bay.

Services

Tourist Office, *near the main highway on Av del Sol Nuevo,* ☎ *327-274-0693, Monday to Friday, 9 am-7 pm.*

Post office, downtown, *Monday to Friday, 9 am-1 pm, 3-6 pm.*

Clinica Renteria, *Calle Valle de Acapulco,* ☎ *327-274-0140.*

Caturera's Farmacia, *Av del Sol Nuevo and Tabachines,* not only dispenses medicines but also sells stamps, has a fax and gives tourist information not found on the web or at your hotel.

There are no **police** on Jaltemba Bay, which says a lot for the community.

Fiestas

The Virgin of Talpa is celebrated every May and the party lasts for about two weeks. The pedestrian walkway where most of the celebrations occur is decorated in palm fronds. There are fireworks, dances, elaborate costumes and special foods for sale along the walkway. Contact the Tourist Office for more information. Since this is low season, hotel reservations are not necessary.

Adventures on Foot

Golf

El Monteon Course, ☎ *327-303-2929,* is located in El Monteon village. It is a nine-hole, par-three (per hole) course that costs $30 to play, including transportation to and from your hotel in Jaltemba Bay or Guayabitos, your clubs, one set of balls and tees, lunch and a drink. What a deal! This information was given to me by Charlie and Mona Bryant of Casa de Ensueños.

Adventures on Water

Isla Islote is visible from anywhere around the bay. The island is a wildlife sanctuary. To get here, take one of the glass-bottomed boats found along the beach that cost $5 per person. The abundant sea life is spectacular and easy to see because the water is so clear and the waves so gentle. On the island are nesting birds such as terns, boobies and frigates. Snorkeling is good, too.

Catamaran *Fanta-sea*, Freddy's Tours, ☎ *327-274-9559 or 274-0248,* will take you on a tour/party for four unforgettable hours. On the boat, you can dance, drink and sing or just take photos to show others how much fun people can be. There are seats in the sun and in the shade, two bathrooms, a bar, safety equipment and lots of music. The cost is $60, including dinner.

Beaches

The south end of the beach starts at the rocky point and curves around to the little cove of Guayabitos, where there are palapa hut restaurants and fishing boats. Two miles farther north the beach becomes wider and offers good swimming and body surfing possibilities. People also windsurf along this stretch. Past La Peñita is more of the same, except the surf is a bit stronger so intermediate surfers can have some fun.

Take the road to the village of **Los Ayala** and, from the village, go down a dirt road to the beach. The water is calm and the swimming is excellent. There are places to eat and have a beer and, farther in, there are a few places to stay. If you walk south back toward La Peñita you will pass a cemetery that goes all the way to the water; the name of the beach is Playa los Muertos, or Beach of the Dead. Locals don't like cars along the beach so they have tried to block passage. However, you can walk around that. If you continue walking north, maneuvering around the coves, you will come to a turtle nesting area called **Playa Punta Raza**. Here, locals are trying to protect the creatures. If you are conservation minded and give them a hand, they may tell you when the turtles are due to hatch and let you come to watch. Seeing one of these giants of the sea ramble onto land, dig a hole and lay some eggs is a thrill, but even more thrilling is watching the little ones hatch and find their way into the water. The jungle behind the beach is lush and has numerous trails to get you up to the road (if you have a vehicle there). The beach is not good for swimming as there is a riptide here.

Playa Platanitos is north of Las Varas. It is a small cove with a white sand beach that stretches for 12 miles/18 km north and has a gentle slope. The beach is good for swimming as the surf is so gentle. Parts of the cove have vegetation coming right to the water. This is a fishing village with a few palapa-hut restaurants along the beach that serve fresh fish for less than $5 a meal. To get here, take the bus toward San Blas from Las Varas and get off at Platanitos. From there you can walk to the beach a little more than a half-mile away. This is a good destination for a day trip.

Along this beach is **Villa Exotica**, *www.vacation-rentals.org/p15949.htm, $$$$$*, which offers two-bedroom, two-bathroom villas. The villas have full kitchens, huge decks, air conditioning, satellite TV, hair dryers, microwaves, toasters and VCRs. There is a swimming pool, a Jacuzzi and a business office with Internet service. Kayaks and canoes are available, and there is even a telescope for those who want to stargaze. You can arrange for all meals to be included in the price.

■ Adventures in Nature

 Walking south toward Puerto Vallarta will always net you some birds that can be added to your list.

 BIRD WATCH: *Birds found in this area include rough-winged swallows, cowbirds, crows, grackles, anis, orioles, frigate birds, pelicans, vultures, boobies, hummingbirds, egrets, bitterns, coots, woodpeckers, gnatcatchers and kingfishers. Birders with a car should also visit* **Compostela**, **Santa Maria del Oro** *and* **Tepic** *(see page 215). The birds you can expect to see in those places are ant-tanagers, scrub euphonias, blackbirds, moorhens, gross beaks, buntings, cedar waxwings, peewees, flycatchers and great-horned owls.*

■ Adventures on Horseback

 Horse tours are possible at the stables next door to Cocos, **Retorno Las Palmas**, in Rincon de Guayabitos. Make reservations with Chorro at the stables (no phone). Rental is not expensive and the horses are gentle. On the other side of Cocos is a stall that rents Jet Skis.

■ Outfitters/Tour Operators

Bob Howell *at Mi Casa es Su Casa,* ☎ *327-274-0312,* offers wildlife-viewing trips that end at hidden waterfalls, old villages, coffee plantations or hot springs. He will also take you biking, fishing, snorkeling or hiking to an active volcano. Lunch, prepared by Vicky, Bob's business partner, is included. If you stay at their house for more than a week, pick-up and delivery at the PV airport is included. Trip costs vary depending on where you go and how long you are gone. A half-day hike with transportation to the trailhead should run $45.

Freddy Tours, ☎ *327-274-0453 or 274-0248,* offers two-hour whale-watching or sightseeing tours on the bay. They begin at 2 pm and last until 6 pm, just after dark. They also have snorkeling ($45 for half a day), waterskiing ($25 per hour) and nature tours ($10-$45, depending on

Central Pacific Mexico

what you do). Their boats are well equipped with safety equipment like vests, radios and shade. Fishing charters with a local fisher can also be arranged by Freddy's at a cost of $170 for two and $10 more for each additional person. All gear is supplied, but you must bring your own grub. There is a limit of two beers per person allowed on this excursion.

Aquatic Adventures, *Rincon de Guayabitos,* ☎ *327-294-1283*, has diving and fishing trips available for an hour or two or all day long.

■ Day Trips

Boca de Chila is 28 miles/45 miles north toward San Blas along Highway 200. Drive through Las Varas and, two miles/three km after that town, is a roadside *tienda*. This is the village of El Conchal – there is no other sign. The road going west (left) leads to the beach. You will need a four-wheel-drive vehicle or you must walk to get there. After about a mile or two, you will cross a cement bridge and then follow the stream for a bit before breaking out onto the sandy beach with an estuary at the one end. The beach is six miles/nine km from El Conchal and has nothing on it but a few anglers looking for a restful day rather than a catch. There is often someone around with a panga who can pole you up the estuary for $10 or so. The estuary will take four or five hours to travel and is similar to Tovara out of San Blas. The other thing that you can do is look for Spanish coins along the beach and near the estuary. Apparently, pirates used to hole out here while waiting for Spanish galleons to show themselves. There are crocs and iguanas in the estuary.

BIRD WATCH: *Birds are ubiquitous in the estuary area and include such species as the king bird, sandpiper, stilt, egret, cormorant, hummingbird, heron, flycatcher.*

Information about this trip to Boca de Chila was from Bob Howell's website, http://members5.boardhost.com/CasaLibertad/?poll.

Zacualpan, also north of Las Varas (six miles/nine km) and accessible by public bus, has an outdoor museum near the Pemex Station in the center of town, four blocks from the plaza. The museum has numerous petroglyphs, some similar to those at Alta Vista. These were found when the road was being built. Some have faces, others have symbols, some are round with flat surfaces and one is about two feet wide. A selection of the glyphs has been placed in the museums in Las Varas and Tepic. Those ones were found in two tombs six feet/two meters deep. After the stones were removed, the tombs were covered. Today, no one knows their location.

■ Shopping

The local **Thursday Market** starts at about 7 am and lasts until 2 pm. It is located next to the church in La Peñita. The market features indigenous art (huichol), local wares and produce, jewelry and an assortment of novelty items. This is an excellent place to purchase souvenirs.

■ Places to Stay

Andreas Bungalows, *Calle Retorno Gaviotas #2, $, www. geocities.com/andreasbungalows/mypage,* has five units, each with kitchenette, bedroom with one single and two double beds and a bathroom with a shower. The floors are tiled, the décor includes local hand-painted murals, and the furniture is chunky Spanish design. Rooms are set around a central courtyard and the building is barely five minutes from the beach. The bungalows are very clean and affordable. The owner, Irene Lopez Vences, is super-friendly, which makes this place better than home.

HOTEL PRICE SCALE	
Price for a room given in US $.	
$	Up to $20
$$	$21-$50
$$$	$51-$100
$$$$	$101-$150
$$$$$	$151-$200
Anything over $200 is specified.	

Bungalows Alexa, *Playa Los Ayala, no phone, www.guayabitos.com/ serv/hotels/alexa/index.html, $$,* has motel-style rooms with kitchenettes that are plain but clean. The kitchens have a stove and fridge, there is a sitting area and the floors are tiled. For the price and seclusion, this isn't too bad a deal.

Posada del Sol, *Calle Andando Huanacaxtle,* ☎ *327-274-0043, $$,* is spartan and spotless. Each unit has a full kitchen, private bathroom with shower, bedroom with ceiling fan, and some of the best pillows in Mexico. There is a nice patio. The *posada* is half a block from the main street.

Posada la Mision, *Retorno Tabachines #6, in Guayabitos,* ☎ *327-274-0357, $$,* is on the beach. The 20 clean rooms, located on two floors, are spaced around a pool in a central courtyard. They have tiled floors and archways that create a feel of old Spain, especially when the slow-moving ceiling fans are whirring. Units have a private bathroom, cable TV and hot water. There is a restaurant and private parking, but the big draw is the lush garden area with rubber trees and a huge old strangler fig.

Posada Real Hotel, *Av Sol Nuevo and Huanacaxtle, in Rincon de Guayabitos,* ☎ *327-274-0177, $$,* has rooms and bungalows. The bungalows are set around a verdant courtyard that has birds playing in the fruit trees. The rooms, at the front of the complex, have private bathrooms. There is a small pool, a children's pool with a water slide, a racquetball court and off-street parking.

Bungalows El Delfin, *Retorno Ceiba and Cocoteros,* ☎ *327-274-0385, $$,* has rooms with kitchenettes that include fridges, stoves, ceiling fans and purified water. They also have 15 bungalows that are much more comfortable than the rooms and suitable up to for four people. The pool is surrounded by greenery. Off-street parking is available. This is one of the more popular middle-of-the-range places available in Guayabitos.

Casa Libertad, *Calle Circuito Libertad #7, $$$, www.home.gci.net/ ~casalibertad/,* is a Spanish-styled bungalow that has white stucco and a red-tiled roof. There is bougainvillea around the new outside fence and the covered porch has red tile on the floor, arched wooden windows, rattan furniture and potted plants. There is also bright lighting and fans. The rooms have arched windows, open-beam ceilings, space galore and comfortable Mexican furniture. The walls have some art. A large upper terrace offers an expansive view of the bay. If the bougainvillea doesn't have enough color for you, the rose garden may. The gardens are under the care of the resident manager who lives in an apartment on the property. The rates change according to the number of days you are here. If you stay for six weeks, the rate drops to half ($42 per day). The owners are active in the community and work hard to make guests happy. The photos you see on the Internet don't begin to show the beauty and comfort of this place. The owners live in Alaska and you can contact them at 11000 Snowline Dr. Anchorage, AK 99507, ☎ 907-344-0986, e-mail casalibertad@ak.net. Their bulletin board is a great resource. If the web page listed above doesn't work for you, do a search for Casa Libertad and follow the links.

Mi Casa es Su Casa, *Flamingo 14 and Av. Sol Nuevo,* ☎ *327-274-0312, $$$,* is owned by Bob Howell and his business partner, Vicky, a character loved by everyone. Their two-story Mexican home is near the beach and across from a small rainforest. The two clean, comfortable bedrooms have balconies, night tables and tiled floors. The bathrooms (also clean) have lots of warm water. One room has an adjoining bathroom, while the other has a bathroom just outside the door. Breakfast is included, and the coffee is made from beans roasted and ground fresh every day. There is satellite TV in the common living room. There is a minimum two-night stay. Happy hour is held between 5 pm-6 pm and a margarita during this time is included in the price of the room.

They also have for rent a 400-sq-ft bungalow with a second-level patio of the same size. The bungalow has a living room, bedroom, bathroom and fully equipped kitchen. The floors in the kitchen and bathroom are all tiled. The bungalow comes totally furnished and includes microwave, electric stove, fridge, TV, dishes, toaster and blender, as well as air conditioning and satellite TV. Bicycles, beach gear and tennis courts are also available. Rental is $600 a month, including utilities. For those staying longer than a month in the bungalow or more than a week in the B & B, Bob includes an orientation visit to three villages.

Casa de Ensueños B&B, *Calle Golondrinas #19,* ☎ *327-274-1230, www.casadeensuenos.com, $$$,* has five spacious rooms overlooking the bay. They have king-sized beds, private bathrooms, bedside tables and ceiling fans. One room is wheelchair-accessible. The floors are tiled. The place is cleaned to a sparkle. Amenities include satellite TV, volleyball court, beach chairs and umbrellas, nooks around the property to hide in with a book, bikes (complimentary use) and a barbeque, making it as comfortable outside as it is inside. A complimentary sunset beverage is served each evening. The breakfast consists of fresh baked rolls, fruit and coffee and is served on the outside terrace overlooking the bay.

If arriving by car or walking from town, the following directions are from the entrance to the town at the highway. When you come to the T in the road at the tourist office, turn right. Follow Av Sol Nuevo and turn left on Pavo Real, right onto Flamingos and then left onto Golondrinas. The owners, Charlie and Mona Bryant, also have two large houses and two bungalows on the north end of the beach, next door to the trailer park. To see them go to www.oasisinmexico.com; if you are interested, you will have to e-mail the Bryants for information and rate details.

Decameron Los Cocos, *Retorno Las Palmas, Rincon de Guayabitos,* ☎ *327-274-0190, $$$,* is a great resort, but stay out of building #2 as it is dungeon-like. The 240 rooms have air conditioning, satellite TV, phones, a bathroom with shower and one king-sized or two double beds. There are four pools, three bars, three restaurants, a gift shop, a disco (usually not too swinging), laundry service, a massage parlor and tennis courts. This is a quiet place where nightlife is not the main draw, but you can rent bikes, kayaks, boogie boards and pedal boats to have fun all day.

Villa Corona del Mar, *Retorno Gaviotas #15,* ☎ *327-274-0015, www. villacoronadelmar.com, $$$/$$$$,* has eight rooms each with a private balcony overlooking the ocean. They have private bathrooms, rustic Mexican furniture, king-sized beds, night tables with bright lamps, purified water, fans and large closets. There are also two bungalows for rent that have living rooms, kitchenettes with dining areas and beds enough to sleep four. The bungalows that hold up to six people cost $129 per night. The property has a pool with a poolside bar, a Jacuzzi, and a tennis court. The outdoor kitchen is where your continental breakfast will be served each morning. There is also a restaurant.

La Casa de los Amigos, *Calle Mirador #3,* ☎ *327-274-0713 or 888-434-4673 in the US, $$$$, www.casadelosamigosmx.com,* is a Moorish-styled villa built in 1986 and designed by the famous architect Salvador Cache Perez. There are three guest rooms available, all with private bathroom and balcony overlooking the ocean. Breakfast is served on another balcony (not your private one) and includes fresh juice, fruits and buns. The house also offers a complimentary cocktail at about 5 pm. They have a Jacuzzi on the terrace, surrounded by a well-maintained garden, and there is purified water in your room. Should you wish, an in-room masseuse can be hired. *La Casa* offers airport pick-up in PV at no extra cost. The minimum stay is one week. The hospitality of this place is exceptional.

La Peñita de Jaltemba, *Calle Lazaro Cardenas #36,* ☎ *327-274-0776, www.casitadelapenita.ws/contact.asp, Rhope81333@aol.com, $$$$*, has seven suites located on two levels around a pool. They each have a living room, fully supplied kitchen with microwave and stove, private tiled bathroom and separate bedroom. The price includes pick-up from PV airport. The seven suites are all a different size and hold between two and six people. There is parking and a Jacuzzi. The gardens are well tended, with tiled patios and barbeque pits.

Villas Buena Vida, *Retorno Laureles #2,* ☎ *327-274-0756, www.villasbuenavida.com, $$$$*, has large, luxurious rooms furnished with traditional Mexican furniture. The suites have kitchens and some are wheelchair-accessible. There is also a pool. This is a large complex with white buildings that sparkle in the sun.

■ Places to Eat

Vendors at the western end of La Avenida have excellent food at excellent prices. If there is a crowd around the stall, you can rest assured that the food is delicious, safe and clean. Otherwise, walking along the beach and deciding on a place is often the best way to go. I can list only a few of the many possibilities.

Esmeralda's, *at Villas Buena Vida, Retorno Laureles #2,* ☎ *327,274-0756,* known as Victor's place by the locals, often has live entertainment such as jazz bands. The food has been recommended by a number of people and the specialty is a fish dish, known as *sarandeado*, that uses the freshest fish available. The entertainment, along with the food, makes this a very special place. Meals cost between $8 and $12.

Nina and Pedros Restaurant, *on the beach in Rincon de Guayabitos,* is excellent for lobster when it is in season. The cost is about $9 per serving with all the trimmings.

Rincon Mexicano, *Hotel San Carlos, Retorno Ceiba #2,* ☎ *327-274-0155,* offers authentic Mexican seafood at a cost of less than $10 per serving.

Piña Colada Bar and Grill, *Av Guayabitos #15,* ☎ *327-274-1211*, has the best fajitas in town. A full meal costs about $10. The roadside atmosphere is fun and very Mexican. They also cook up a mean steak if you are extra hungry.

Tukan Restaurant, *Carretera Federal # 200,* ☎ *327-274-0427,* serves local fresh shrimp, but is best known for its *milanesa,* a veal or pork steak pounded, breaded and fried (similar to Wienerschnitzel, served in Germany). For me, *milanesa* is like a fast-food meal, except it is really good. Each meal will cost $6 or $7.

Besa del Sol Restaurant, *on the beach in Guayabitos,* is considered the finest restaurant in the area. The tables are well spaced; you don't have to listen to your neighbor breathe. The place is clean, the kitchen newly renovated. A steak done to perfection costs $7.50. They also serve any exotic drink you could possibly want.

Jaqueline, *Retorno Cedro #4,* ☎ *327-274-0913,* has good Mexican food. It is on the beach in Guayabitos in the hotel of the same name. A meal seldom costs more than $8.

Hinde & Jaime's, *on the main street in Guayabitos*, should be called the Canadian Bar as there are more Canadians there than Mexicans. The atmosphere is saloon complete with a pool table. The food is also good – a supper of hamburger and fries runs about $6.

Restaurant Campañario, *Hotel Posada la Mision, Retorno Tabachines #6, in Guayabitos,* ☎ *327-274-0357,* has been a favorite for as long as there have been visitors to Guayabito. The Mexican-styled shrimp is good as are the burgers. A meal runs anywhere from $7.50 to $10 per person.

Cristobal, *on the beach in Guayabitos just down from Campañario,* is another favorite. Seafood is the specialty – if you want steak you will have to go to Besa del Sol.

■ Nightlife

Nightlife is not wild on this bay. The best I can muster up for you is the **Fanta-sea catamaran tour** offered by Freddy's. But new bars and discos open all the time, so ask other travelers.

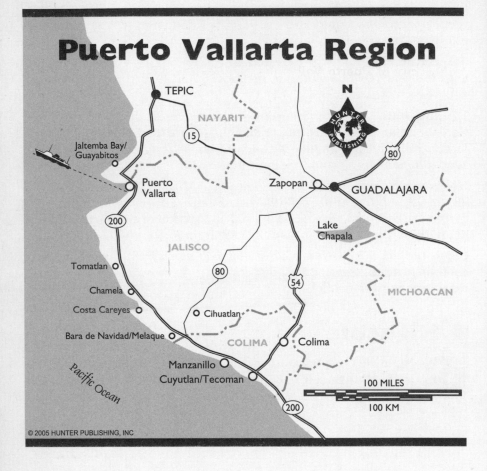

Puerto Vallarta Region

© 2005 HUNTER PUBLISHING, INC

Puerto Vallarta Region

Puerto Vallarta

The city of Puerto Vallarta is spread around the **Bahai de Banderas**, a sandy bay with a backdrop of the Sierra Madres. The town is divided by the **Cuale River**, and everything is referred to as being either north or south of the river.

The airport is about four miles/ seven km north of the Cuale River. Just south of the airport, large hotels, condominiums and resorts line the beach and main drag, along with restaurants, souvenir shops, dress shops, shoe shops, Internet cafés, night clubs, juice shops, tour agencies, massage parlors, car rentals and time-share hawkers.

East of the beach, residential homes climb the hills, dotting the lush vegetation with white-plastered walls and red-tiled roofs. This is where Elizabeth Taylor and Richard Burton first shared their love for each other. Ever since, millions of tourists have come to PV looking for the same type of romance.

WARNING

Puerto Vallarta has been a travel destination for a long time. The town has grown and changed. At one time, it wasn't safe to walk down the beach at night after you'd had a couple of drinks. However, the government has made the city safe for visitors by posting tourist police around town. As tourism increased, the occasional (and it takes only one in a thousand) visitor has behaved in a way that has been anything but commendable. They have been drunk, abusive, rude or insensitive to a Catholic culture. This has resulted in some locals losing their fondness for tourists. I was called a cheap Canadian because I wouldn't pay US $20 for a child's baseball cap. Bus drivers have taken tourists on goose chases – this happened to me and to others I spoke with. The timeshare salesmen are a big nuisance, though they are just trying to earn a living. If this type of treatment is going to bother you, do not go to PV; try someplace like Manzanillo or Mazatlan that hasn't been so inundated with visitors, or take an all-inclusive package and stay at your hotel.

■ Getting Here & Around

By Plane

Numerous airlines service Puerto Vallarta.

AIRLINE CONTACT INFORMATION		
Aero California	www.aerocalifornia.de	☎ 800-237-6225 (Mx)
AeroMexico	www.aeromexico.com	☎ 800-237-6639 (US); 800-021-4010 (Mx)
Alaska Airlines	www.alaskaair.com	☎ 800-252-7522 (US); 55-5282-2484 (Mx)
America West	www.americawest.com	☎ 800-363-2597 (US); 800-235-9292 (Mx)
American Airlines	www.aa.com	☎ 800-433-7300 (US); 800-904-6000 (Mx)
Continental	www.continental.com	☎ 800-231-0856 (US); 800-900-5000 (Mx)
Delta Airlines	www.delta-air.com	☎ 800-241-4141 (US); 800-123-4710 (Mx)
Mexicana Airlines	www.mexicana.com	☎ 800-531-7921 (US); 800-509-8960 (Mx)

If you are mobile (all your luggage in a big pack), you can hop on the city bus to town. To get one, walk out the front door of the airport and turn to your left where you can see a pedestrian bridge. Buses stop under the bridge. Choose one that says "centro" on it and away you go. The cost is four pesos. Otherwise, you must hire a taxi.

By Taxi

Taxis from the bus station or airport to the center of PV cost about $5. There is a taxi booth at the airport that sells tickets for your destination (thus preventing any haggling over prices). However, these ticket stands charge up to four times as much as the drivers on the street do. There are about a thousand taxis in town and they charge about $2 for trips around town. Always confirm the price before accepting the ride. Tips are not expected.

By Car

The big national chains are all here and, if you are going to leave the state, you should rent from one of these companies. That way, should you have a problem with the car, you can be serviced by one of their representatives wherever you are.

▶▶ **AUTHOR TIP:** *Always ask about taking a rental vehicle out of state, as some companies do not have insurance for their vehicles to leave the state.*

In order to rent a car you must have a major credit card, valid driver's license and recent photo ID. You must be at least 25 years old.

In low season, the average cost of a small car with air conditioning is between $23 and $35 a day. During high season, the cost goes to $40 or $50 a day for the same vehicle. This includes insurance and unlimited mileage.

Clover Car Rentals, *Villa Vallarta Shopping Center,* ☎ *322-224-0304 or 224-4910, cloverrentacar@prodigy.net.mx,* is a local company that charges $40 to $50 a day for a jeep, but you must stay within the state. The owner is honest and pleasant to deal with. His vehicles are in decent shape.

Thrifty, *Av Moctezuma # 3515,* ☎ *322-224-9280 or 224-0776, www.thrifty.com.mx*, is located at the airport. They will rent a VW beetle without air conditioning for $31 a day, including all mileage and insurance. In the event of an accident, Thrifty recommends that you call them for assistance before signing any papers.

Budget, *at the airport,* ☎ *322-224-2980,* offers a Chevy Pop for $175 a week, plus $12 a day for insurance and 15% tax. This works out to $286 a week. This is expensive for a small car. A Tsuru is $210, an Astra $245 and a jeep is $320, plus insurance and tax. A VW beetle is $140 plus.

By Bus

Long-distance buses depart for stations around the country from the Medina Bus Station north of the airport. Local buses go to the national station. For long-distance, first-class trips, budget between $4 and $5 per hour of travel.

The Estrella Blanca (Elite), ☎ *322-221-0850, 290-1001 or 290-1014.* Buses leave for Guadalajara at 5:30, 7, 8:30, 10:30 am, noon and 5 pm. The cost is $29.20 per person. They also go to Mexico City in the afternoon and evening at 5:15, 6:15, 7:15 and 9 pm daily. The cost is $66.10 and the journey takes 12 hours.

Primera Plus, ☎ *322-221-0095, www.flecha-amarilla.com,* charges $29.20 for a bus to Guadalajara. The price includes a sandwich and juice. The air-conditioned bus is a luxury liner and comes recommended for any trips in the area if their schedule is right for you. I traveled with them and was quite pleased. Buses to Mexico City leave in the afternoon/evening at 5:15, 6:15, 7:15 and 9 pm. The cost is $66.10 per person. They also have buses going to numerous destinations around the country.

ETN, ☎ *322-223-5665 or 223-5666,* has buses going to Guadalajara at 12:30 am, 1:00 am, 8:45 am, 10:15 am, 11:45 am, 1:00 pm, 2:00 pm, 3:30 pm, and 5:00 pm. They have one bus a day leaving at 7 pm for Mexico City and one at 10 pm going to Leon. This, too, is a luxury liner, but I found they were totally indifferent to trying to help me. They have a downtown ticket office at Calle 31 de Octubre #89 (next to hotel Rosita).

Transportes del Pacifico, ☎ *322-222-1015 or 222-5622,* has buses going to Guadalajara every hour starting at 6 am until 1:45 am daily. The cost is $26.50 per person. Buses for Tijuana leave at 12:15 pm daily and cost $82.30. This trip takes 34 hours. Buses to Mazatlan leave at 10:45 pm daily and cost $25.40. This trip takes seven hours. Buses to Tepic leave every 20 minutes starting at 4 am and take three hours. The cost is $11. Buses to Mexico City leave at 6 and 8 pm daily and take 12 hours. The cost is $66.10 per person.

TAP, ☎ *322-290-0119,* has buses going to 24 destinations around the country. I found the workers at the PV office helpful and honest. I would not hesitate to travel with TAP. They have buses going to Mazatlan at 8:10 am, 11:10 am, 1:10 pm, 3:10 pm and 5:10 pm. The trip takes seven hours and costs $25.70 per person. Buses for Mexico City leave at 5:10 and 7:10 pm daily. There is a one-/two-hour wait over in Tepic during this trip. The cost is $63.40. TAP also covers many destinations to the north, like Tijuana and Guaymas.

City buses cost four pesos per person, per ride. If you want to go from the center to the airport or bus station, take the bus labeled *Hotels* or *Aeropuerto*. If you want to go to the south end of town, take the bus labeled *Olas Altas*. This bus goes as far as Playa Muertos.

The buses from the center going to Mismaloya cost 45¢ and depart from Basilio Badillo. Those going to Nuevo Vallarta and Punta de Mita leave from the Medina Bus station or at the bus stop across from the Sheriton Hotel. They cost $1 each way.

Remember, no area code is needed when making a local call.

By Water

Water Taxis, ☎ *322-297-1637, 209-5004 or 209-5092,* go to Yelapa, Las Animas, Quimixto and Mahujuitas daily from Los Muertos Pier at the south end of town. They leave at 10:30, 11 am and 11:30 am. For those wanting to stay overnight, there is a boat leaving at 4 pm. The round-trip costs $18.

Dolphin sculptures on Puerto Vallarta's malecón.

■ History

The village of **Las Peñas** was founded in 1841. Before that, as far back as 600 years before Christ, the Xalisco and Nayarit kingdoms ruled the area. Nayarita was the god of battle and he fought bravely to conquer the most beautiful spot on the planet. After the gods lived here for a while, the Colhoa and the Toltecs came and planted their crops in the fertile ground. They also tramped through the jungles and over the hills to form a trail to what is now called Mexico City.

In 1524 **Francisco Cortes de San Buenaventura** and his men came upon the bay and decided to explore. He was met by locals who were prepared to fight to keep the land free of the white men. Among the men with Cortez was **Juan de Villadiego**, who carried a flag with the inscription, "In this I defeated and the one that carries me, it will defeat." On the other side was the image of Mary with the words "Mary, Mary, pray for us," below her. Just as the battle was about to start, a ray of light formed a halo on the Virgin. This was taken as a miracle. The battle was forgotten (the locals negotiated with Cortez) and Cortez named the spot **Valle de Banderaso**, or Bay of Flags.

Less than 20 years later in 1541, **Don Pedro de Alvarado** came to the bay and, after passing the rocks that guard the bay near Mismaloya Beach, he called the area Las Peñas (The Rocks). It was not until 1918 that the name was changed to Vallarta in honor of the Governor of Jalisco, Ignacio L. Vallarta.

But before it became Vallarta, the bay was used by those shipping gold and silver out of the country in boats that went around the tip of South America and across the Atlantic Ocean to Spain. The bay was also used as a refuge by pirates, like Sir Francis Drake, hiding from Spaniards.

The final note in history was the coming of **John Huston** with Richard Burton, Ava Gardner, Deborah Kerr and Elizabeth Taylor in tow. They were filming *Night of the Iguana*. Tourism began.

■ Services

i The **Tourist Office**, *Calle Juarez and Ascencio #1712*, ☎ *322-223-2500, Monday to Friday, 8 am-4:30 pm*.

Puerto Vallarta Convention and Visitors Bureau is useful if you need more detailed information. It is near El Cid.

Post office, *Mina #188, Monday to Friday, 8 am-6 pm, Saturday until 1 pm*.

The **IAMAT Clinic**, *Calle Lucerna #48*, ☎ *322-222-5119*, is coordinated by Dr. Alfonso Rodriguez. English is spoken. A second one is at *Rio Nilo 132, #8*, ☎ *322-293-0036*, and the third is at *KB3 Blvd Francisco Medina Ascencio, Plaza Neptuno D-1*, ☎ *322-221-0023*.

Gold's Gym, *Av Fco. Medina Ascencio, half a block from the Calypso*, is the largest in the world. If a work-out is what you need and you like an inside air-conditioned gym, then I recommend trying Gold's. Known worldwide, their equipment is always in good repair.

Spa Puesto del Sol, ☎ *322-221-0770*, is a European health spa across from El Faro at the Tennis Club. It has a gym with 40 machines and a full line of weights. They also hold aerobics classes and massage services.

Aztec Massage, *Venustiano Carranza #307 (upstairs)*, ☎ *322-222-4881*, offers therapeutic massages for pain relief and relaxation. They also do in-home service.

Publications

Vallarta Today is an English-language publication produced daily. It has the week's entertainment schedule featured on the second page. You'll find details about locally sponsored events, like the Vallarta Gourmet Festival that includes 23 participating restaurants, or the gourmet cooking classes offered by famous chefs and presented at the LANS Department store every Thursday.

The English-language magazine, *Vallarta Lifestyles*, has been around since 1990 and is sold at magazine stands for $2. This full-color, informative publication is directed at tourists. *Lifestyles* also puts out a free map and activity guide. *Vallarta Voice* is a free English-language publication that has news, events, reviews and profiles. It is published once a month from November to April.

The Times is an English-language newspaper that comes out on Friday. It offers local and national news (some US and Canadian news), as well as a crossword, horoscope and classified ads. This is a free publication.

Online, **www.virtualvallarta.com** has maps, photos and articles that offer the latest information about events in Puerto Vallarta.

■ Sightseeing

Vallarta Cigar Factory, *two locations, Libertad #100-3, next to the flea market, or Vallarta #252 at 5 de Febrero,* ☎ *322-222-0300 (for either place), Monday to Saturday, 10 am-9 pm, Sunday 10 am-6 pm*. The factory welcomes visitors to watch cigars being made from Cuban, Nicaraguan, Mexican and Dominican tobaccos. The workers make three grades of cigars. The lowest grade includes the Corona, Robusto and the Churchill. These cost between $3 and $5 each. The next grade includes the Café, Rothchild, Doble Corona and Torpedo, which sell for $5 to $9 each. Then there are the Corona Gorda and the Campaña that sell for $12 and $13 each. This is an interesting tour.

Museum of Anthropology, *Isla Rio Cuale, no phone, Tuesday-Sunday, 10 am-2 pm and 4-7 pm, $2*. The director presents a free lecture in English every Tuesday at 10 am on topics relating to Mexican anthropology. This small museum has a few artifacts from Mesoamerica, but mostly items found in pre-Hispanic tombs in Jalisco, Nayarit and Colima states.

Manuel Lepe Museum/Gallery, *Juarez 533,* ☎ *322-222-5515, Monday to Saturday, 10 am-5 pm*. The gallery/museum is world renowned for the contemporary art of Manuel Lepe. His work includes tiny ceramic angels, boats, airplanes, papier mâché, jewelry, posters and lithographs of original works. The museum/gallery has some items for sale. Lepe is well known throughout the United States, Europe and Mexico for his Naif style of painting (miniatures). One of his exhibitions at the Sciences and Industries Museum in LA drew over a million people.

Museo Ernesto Muñoz Acosta, *Francisco I Madero #272,* ☎ *322-222-1970, daily, 10 am-7 pm*. This museum has works from contemporary artists, including some by Sergio Bustamante and Manuel Lepe. They also carry some traditional work from the Huichol people. The museum likes to carry pieces from promising regional artists. This, like the Lepe Museum is also a gallery.

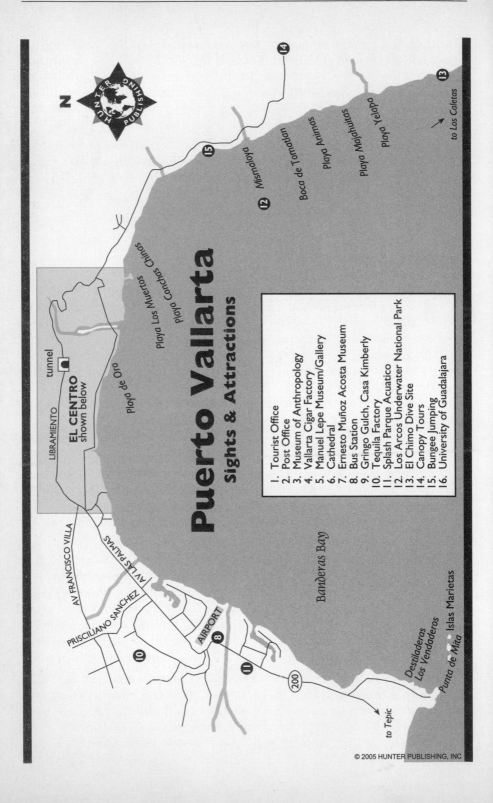

Puerto Vallarta
Sights & Attractions

1. Tourist Office
2. Post Office
3. Museum of Anthropology
4. Vallarta Cigar Factory
5. Manuel Lepe Museum/Gallery
6. Cathedral
7. Ernesto Muñoz Acosta Museum
8. Bus Station
9. Gringo Gulch, Casa Kimberly
10. Tequila Factory
11. Splash Parque Acuatico
12. Los Arcos Underwater National Park
13. El Chimo Dive Site
14. Canopy Tours
15. Bungee Jumping
16. University of Guadalajara

© 2005 HUNTER PUBLISHING, INC

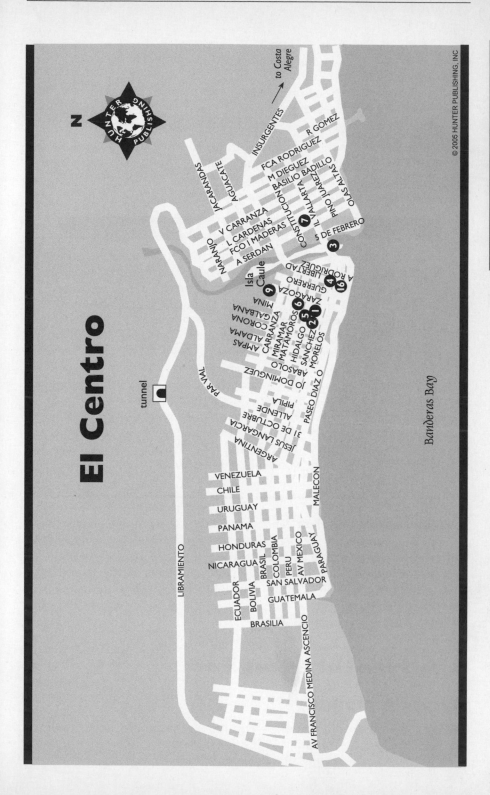

© 2005 HUNTER PUBLISHING, INC

El Centro

The **Virgin of Guadalupe Church** in the town center was built between 1929 and 1939. It was damaged during the last earthquake in the 1990s; restoration is in progress. Although the interior of the church is not exceptional, the outside tower is the city's crowning landmark. The tower has a wrought-iron crown with eight angels. The crown is a replica of the one worn by Carlota, the Empress of Mexico from 1864 to 1867.

Gringo Gulch is reached by climbing the stairs that go up toward the hills from the main plaza. Up the gulch you will find the former home of Richard Burton and Elizabeth Taylor called **Casa Kimberly**, *Calle Zaragoza # 445, open daily 9 am-6 pm, $6.*

THE GREAT LOVE STORY

Isolated beaches rimmed with palm trees lured John Huston to Puerto Vallarta in the 1960s to film *Night of the Iguana*. His cast included Elizabeth Taylor and Richard Burton. While working, the two fell in love. Richard bought Elizabeth a 24,000 square-foot house for her 32nd birthday. It was similar to his own that was perched on the hillside overlooking Bandera Bay. The houses were across the road from each other. The couple then built a pink and white walkway, called "the love bridge," between the two places so they could visit each other more discreetly. Elizabeth left Eddie Fisher, her husband at the time, and married Burton. Their story became one of the great love stories of our century. She owned the house for 26 years and, when she sold it in 1990, left nearly all of the possessions in the house. While on tour, you see posters, the original furniture, mementos and photos.

Tequila Factory, *Carretera Tepic, Km 12,* ☎ *322-221-2543, open noon-3 pm.* At the factory you will see how the tequila is made, learn some of the history of its making and, of course, taste a bit. Make reservations for your tour and then take a bus to Tepic or to the airport from the center of town (not far from the bus station) and get off at the factory or the airport (the factory is a five-minute walk north of the airport). After you taste, you can purchase. I did.

■ Adventures on Foot

Hiking & Walking

 The *malecón*, the walkway along the beach, was first constructed in the 1950s using tons of cement, stones and rocks. Most of the rock used was taken from the Cuale River. With the

Puerto Vallarta's malecón *makes a great place for a walk.*

rock not holding the earth back along the riverbed, there was tremendous soil loss during rains. The silt that was washed into the bay was filtered by sea cucumbers that hung out around the mouth of the river. For a time, the over-harvest of sea cucumbers created a problem with murky water being in the bay. However, present conservation practices now forbid the harvest so we again have clean water in the bay near the river and the cucumber population is increasing.

The *malecón* is formed by a series of retaining walls. During construction of the walls, roads were built to access the oceanfront area. The major construction road, beside the *malecón*, is now used as the main road.

The *malecón* is about three miles/five km long. Starting on the north side of the river, the bay stretches all the way around to Punta Mita. It is lined with restaurants, hotels, shops and people.

Golf

There are seven courses in PV, some designed by world-class golfers such as Jack Nicklaus, Tom Weiskopf and Robert von Hagge. To date, Hagge has designed 11 courses in Mexico.

FACT FILE: Because of the quality of its courses, PV was chosen as the place to host the EMC World Golf Cup in 2002, the Ford Collegiate Championships in 2001 and the USGA Junior Girls' Tournament the same year.

In addition to the world cup, Puerto Vallarta sponsors its own golf cup competition each year in mid-November. This is a high-profile event that lasts for three days and, so far, has included 120 amateur competitors from all over North America.

Flamingos Golf Club, *Tepic Highway #145, www.flamingosgolf.com.mx*, was designed by Percy J. Clifford and has 18 holes. It is a ways from town so they provide a shuttle bus from the Sheraton Hotel at 8 and 10 am; return trips are at 2 and 4 pm. You must reserve for pickup. This is a par 72, 6,452-yard course where the challenge lies in chipping, although the landing areas are about 40 yards wide on average. Low-season greens costs start at $115 per day.

LOCAL GOLF CHAMP

Lorena Ochoa, a young gal from Guadalajara, is often seen playing on the courses in PV. Lorena became a professional golfer in 2002 and has already earned close to $350,000 in prize money. Besides money, this champ has a list of awards that are longer than a child's Christmas wish list. Among them is the National Sports Award (presented by President Vincente Fox), Player of the Year Award and the Golfstat Cup. She has managed to achieve a seven-tournament winning streak. This record has been beat only by Byron Nelson, who had an 11-game winning streak. Also, in 2001 Lorena had the nation's lowest average score of 71.71.

Four Seasons *at Punta Mita on the Four Season's Resort property, www.fshr.com, no phone,* was designed by Jack Nicklaus. This 18 hole, par 72 course has one hole sitting on an island about 175 yards offshore. It is surrounded by the largest water hazard in the world and is the only natural-island green. If the water is too rough, or the tide too high for the little boat to take you to the island, an alternative green can be played. This is a semi-private course intended for hotel guests. The cost during mid-season is about $230 per person. Club rentals cost $35 and shoes $15. Caddies are not available on this course.

Marina Vallarta, *Paseo de la Marina, www.foremexico.com*, is within walking distance of most hotels. It was designed by Joe Finger and is a 6,700-yard, par 71 course. The obstacles are palms, tropical plants, wildlife and water fountains. There is a driving range, golf shop, chipping/ putting green and a full-service clubhouse. The property is owned and operated by the Club Corp International from Dallas. It is rumored that they have nearly $2 billion in assets and are considered the world's leader in operating country clubs and golf resorts. The cost to play is $120 a day and this covers the cart rental. Clubs can be rented for $20 a day. There is a discount for frequent players.

La Vista, *Circuito Universidad #653*, ☎ *322-221-0073, www.vista-vallarta-golf.com,* has two courses. One is a par 72 course that sits on 478 acres of palm grove dotted with tiny creeks. It is located on the higher grounds of the property. This course was designed by Jack Nicklaus. The second course, opened in 2001, was designed by Tom Weiskopf. The course runs through natural jungle, deep gorges and swift rivers. Both courses have 18 holes and are designed with challenges for both the amateur and the professional. The clubhouse includes practice facilities, restaurant, bar and golf shop. On-course beverage service is offered.

El Tigre, *Paradise Village, Av Paraiso, Km 800,* ☎ *322-297-0773, www.para-dise-mexico.com*, was designed by Robert von Vagge and Rick Baril. The course is an 18-hole, par 72, 7,239-yard run with 12 holes featuring water. The designers incorporated five or six tees per hole, extra-wide fairways, beach bunkers and lots of water. The clubhouse is huge and there is a 300-yard driving range and a putting green. Inside the club is a restaurant, bar, spa and golf apparel shop. The cost is $130 a game during high season and there is a special "twilight" price of $85 for those starting after 2 pm. Club rentals run $45 and shoes are $15.

Mayan Palace, *Av Paseo de las Moras, www.mayanpalace.com.mx,* is now open to the general public. If you think you can get past the time-share salesmen, you may like this course. It was designed by Jim Jimlipe and has 18 holes with water and sand hazards. The cost is about $130 for the 18 holes.

■ Adventures on Water

Beaches

 PV has 40 beaches open to the public. Those at the north end of the bay have soft white sand and shallow water, while those at the south tend to have coarser sand and deeper water. However, the south has many little coves hidden between the rocks where you can spend the entire day alone. To save confusion, the beaches have general names that were given to them years ago. As the city developed, smaller stretches of beach within the larger beaches have been named. This is to make directions more specific.

BEACH DANGER FLAG SYSTEM

There is a system of red, yellow and white flags that indicates possible dangers in the water.

- RED – The undercurrent is dangerous to swimmers and under no circumstances should you go into the area between the two red flags. Undertow is not to be ignored; it has caused many deaths.
- YELLOW – Jellyfish are in the area. To avoid being stung, do not go into the water between the two yellow flags.
- WHITE – The white flags mean there is some soft surf, but have fun.

Las Animas, Quimixto and **Yelapa beaches** can be reached only by boat. Las Animas, "Beach of the Souls," is strictly for snorkeling, sunning and eating. If it wasn't for its beauty, it would be almost boring. Food and drink are available along the beach at some of the palapa-hut establishments or from local ladies selling their homemade goods. Quimixto is a little village surrounded by reefs that divers can enjoy. Yelapa is another isolated village that has some rustic cabins, lots of birds and is quiet. To get here, take the water taxi in PV, hire a private boat at the docks, or use a tour company. Boats at Boca (see below) can also take you here.

Playas Conchas Chinas is a series of rocky coves south of Los Muertos. The name describes the spiraled shells found on this beach. To get here, take buses marked *Mismaloya* or *Boca* and get off where the sand looks good. **Mismaloya** is good for birding and it is also where you can see the movie set used in the filming of *Night of the Iguanas*. Once at the beach and hotel of the same name, walk south, past the hotel to where the Horcones River flows toward the ocean. Continue past the beachside restaurants to the set. The building behind is where stars lived while working. **Boca de Tomatlan** is the last beach going south that is accessible by bus/car. It is eight miles/13 km south of the town center. Boca is far more isolated than all the other beaches in the area and the swimming here is safe. *Pangas* (small boats) are available to take you to Yelapa, Las Animas or Quimixto beaches (see above). There are numerous little huts selling food and drink. The last bus returns to town at about 7:30 pm. These beaches are for surfing, sunning or fishing.

Los Muertos Beach starts south of the river and stretches for a mile or so. It is a favorite for swimming and wading as there is no undertow. Jet Skiing and parasailing are popular pastimes also. The banana boat ride here is fun and should be tried at least once. Equipment can be rented from any of the hotels along this section of the beach. **Los Muertos Pier** is also along this beach.

Playa de Oro is a long stretch of beach with a few rocky areas north of Los Muertos. The strip of beach includes Playa Camarones, Las Glorias and Los Tules. The sand is moderate to fine and the surf gets stronger the farther north one goes.

Punta de Mita is best for surfing. It is at the very north end of the bay. **Los Venaderos** is also to the north and offers good snorkeling and windsurfing. It is close to Las Marietas Island, a bird sanctuary and good snorkeling area. Boats can be rented from locals living around this beach. **Destiladeras** is, like Los Venaderos, close to Las Marietas Island and offers good windsurfing or snorkeling. To get here, take a bus going to Punta de Mita and, again, get off wherever the sand looks good. You will need to bring your own equipment.

Water Parks

Splash Parque Acuatico, *Km 156 on the Tepic Highway,* ☎ *322-297-0708, www.splashvallarta.com,* is a family-oriented water park that features 12 slides, all different speed levels, a river zone for the quieter splashers, and a children's pool. You can also swim with dolphins (advance reservations required). There are dolphin/sea lion shows, diving exhibitions and bird shows offered on an ongoing basis starting at 10:30 am; the last show starts at 5:30 pm. Check with the tourist office for times of specific shows. The cost to enter the park for the day is $10 per person.

Swim with Dolphins, ☎ *322-297-1252,* is a program offered by Vallarta Adventures. You can go to the pool and learn about dolphin physiology, anatomy, history, husbandry and training. Once in the water, you can feel a dolphin's skin and maybe even get towed by one. You can have a video made of your encounter. Life jackets are provided. Children must be five or older to swim with the animals. The cost is $130 to swim, $60 for an encounter and $240 for a full-day program.

Boating

A trip aboard *La Marigalante*, ☎ *322-223-0875, www.marigalante.com. mx,* costs $60 per person. This old-styled boat seen crossing the bay every day was built in Veracruz by the Asociacion Mar, Hombre y Paz (Association of Sea, Man and Peace) to commemorate the 500th anniversary of the discovery of America by Columbus.

A DEBT REPAID

When Columbus was sailing the *Niña*, *Pinta* and *Santa Maria*, he offered 10,000 gold pieces to the first man who spotted land. Rodrigo Detriana (whose real name was Juan Rodriguez Bermejo) saw the land and let Columbus know, but was never paid his reward.

The organizers of the Marigalante collected money from 33 American countries and took a 52,000 nautical-mile journey around the world, eventually landing in Seville, Spain. The ship carried the money owed to Rodriguez and had it placed in his name in the cathedral. During the journey, the crew collected enough memorabilia to stock four museums, one of which is on board the ship.

You can take a daytime cruise on the ship or an evening dinner cruise. The evening cruise starts with a mariachi band, has a rope-twirling demonstration and dinner, which includes shrimp brochettes, filet mignon and red or white wine. This is followed by a sound and light show that finishes with a firework display. The daytime cruise leaves in the early morning and includes a Mexican breakfast of eggs, refried beans, fresh fruit and juice. The show has a pirate theme that starts with the weighing of anchors and proceeds to a naval battle that uses water-filled balloons as artillery. The show ends with a pirate torture contest and a few sword fights that could involve a passenger or two. Lunch is barbequed chicken and ribs, rice, salad and corn. There is an open bar and part of the day is spent at one of the beaches along the bay.

To go on this ship you can book with any tour office (it is not possible to book direct). Or (I don't recommend this) you can go to a time-share event where you listen to the blurb about buying a chunk of paradise and, as a reward, you get the tour.

You can **learn to sail** with Vallarta Adventures (see page 265). They offer basic training and allow you to be as interactive as you choose. If you find that you don't like it, the crew on board will take over and you can relax instead. There is also a sunset cruise that includes wine and cheese, seafood hors d'oeuvres and an open bar. The boat is available every day.

Scuba Diving

Scuba diving is popular in PV mostly because of Los Arcos Underwater National Park that is just half an hour from the dock. There are two companies who can take you diving and the costs are comparable. They are **Ecotours Vallarta de Mexico**, *Ignacio Vallarta 243*, ☎ *322-222-6606 or 223-3130*; and **Chicos Dive Shop**, *Av. Diaz Ordaz # 772*, ☎ *322-222-1895, www.chicos-diveshop.com*. You must have your PADI certification with you or you will be required to take an in-pool session before the guides will take you down. Divers who have not been underwater during the last 12 months are required to take a refresher course.

Those not certified can take pool sessions taught by PADI certified instructors at the Sheraton, Canto del Sol, Velas, Crown Paradise, Vista Club, Mayan Palace, Melia, Nautilus, Westin, Las Palmas, Holiday Inn, Villa del Palmar or Embarcadero hotels. The lessons are offered daily from 10 am-5 pm. Courses include home study, classroom sessions, pool training and one ocean dive.

> **WARNING:** Be aware that not everyone who claims to have PADI certification does, in fact, have it. Just as the dive masters must see your PADI card, you should check theirs as well.

Los Arcos Underwater National Park, off Playa Mismaloya, has dives from 12 feet/eight meters down to 60 feet/20 meters. There are granite arches, caves and a wall that goes down about 1,800 feet/600 meters. The continental platform where the wall begins is located near the main arch. Numerous crags and crevices hide the black coral forest that is rejuvenating itself now that harvesting is illegal. Common wildlife includes rays, eels, morays, octopus and lobster. It takes half an hour by boat to reach the park. Night dives are done near the "Shallows of Christ" close to here, where lobster and octopus are said to be abundant. A number of small islands offer push-off points for snorkeling. Because underwater currents force plankton up near the surface, the number of fish feeding on them is enormous.

The **Marietas Islands**, often called the Galapagos of Mexico, are 21 miles/32 km or one hour by boat from the mainland. You can dive around caves, coral reefs and drop-offs, where there are mantas, turtles, dolphins and humpbacks (in season December to March). You can also combine diving with bird watching, as blue-footed boobies are known to hang out here. It is common to play with dolphins while in this area.

El Morro, just beyond the protected waters of the bay's north end, is four miles/six km past the Marietas and 1½ hours from PV by boat. This area is famous for its pinnacles that rise from the ocean floor and harbor sea life such as mantas, turtles, skipjacks and eels. This is a dive for experienced divers only.

El Sequial is also for experienced divers only. This impressive spot has sea sponges, groupers, snappers, mantas and sharks swimming around pinnacles and caves.

El Chimo is an hour from PV by boat at the south end of the bay. Here you will find eagle rays, damsels, sea fans and even some black coral. The ocean floor has a large plateau with a series of pinnacles, some of which form columns like those in a church. This, too, is a dive for the experienced only.

Corbeteña is two hours north of PV. It is often called "The Rock" and is considered one of the best dives in the entire country. In addition to the steep walls, caves and arches, wildlife attractions include giant mantas, sharks and (in season) whale sharks. Moderate currents and a dive depth of about 120 feet/40 meters make this a good spot for small groups of experienced divers.

Snorkeling

Majahuitas Beach is less than an hour from town on the south side of the bay. It is regarded as one of the most beautiful beaches in the PV area. Because of the wildlife sanctuaries along this coast that cause a spillover effect, the wildlife here is abundant. Large schools of tropical fish swim alongside turtles, dolphins and mantas.

Los Caletas has some drop-offs for diving, but it is better for snorkeling in the shallows where you may spot manta rays, turtles and a variety of fish. The beach area was first used by John Huston for his private beach. You can hike or kayak in the bay, read a book while swinging on a hammock or visit the spa and have a body massage or facial. However, everyone I spoke to who came here with a tour operator did not feel they got their money's worth. They said that the ride out takes an hour, the water for snorkeling is rough and the food is so-so. The scenery is beautiful, but you can get that at other places for much less money.

■ Adventures in Nature

Whale-Watching

 Whale-watching tours are offered by many companies in PV. Check to see which ones are most involved in the study and preservation of the whales before booking. At a minimum, choose so that some of your tour dollar ends up helping conservation. Whale season here is December to March.

WATCHING THE RULES

The government has set rules for observation of whales. Your boat must not be closer than 250 feet/80 meters to an animal and you must not be in the water (you must be in the boat) when approaching one. You must not obstruct a whale's passage in any way or touch one. Jet Skis, kayaks or boats with motors running are not permitted in the area while observing the animals. Your time in the area should not exceed 30 minutes and, if it is a pod that you spot, observation time is dropped to 10 minutes.

It is the responsibility of the paying tourist to see that these rules are implemented. Often, a tour company will want to please its clients by bending a rule or two just to be guaranteed the business and praise. Do not permit this.

For more information on the whales and how to help with their conservation, go to www.ine.gob.mx, or write to Direction General de Vida Silvestre, Av Revolucion #1425, Nivel 1, Col. Tlacopacm, San Angel, CP 01040 Mexico DF, ☎ 55-624-3655.

Humpback and gray whales can be spotted around Punta Mita at the north end of the bay and near the Marieta Islands. During the early part of the season, around mid-December, you may spot the whales doing their courting rituals where they swim side by side, bumping and rubbing each other, thus stimulating the hormones needed for reproduction. Later in the season you will see moms and kids floating around enjoying each other. Some tour companies carry an underwater microphone so you can hear whale sounds. The great gray whale spends its summers in the cool waters off the shores of Alaska in the Bering Strait. In September it starts its journey south to the warmer waters of Baja California and the mainland near PV. Once in the warm waters, the whales mate and the females give birth.

MEXICAN WHALE RESERVES

In 1948 Mexico signed an international agreement for the regulation of the hunting of whales in its waters. However, the agreement did little to actually stop whale hunting. It was not until 1972 that preserves were established. The first was **Laguna Ojo de Libre**. In 1979, **Laguna San Ignacio** was added to the preserve list and, in 1980, **Laguans Guerrero Negro** and **Manuela** were also declared preserves. These saltwater lagoons are all near the west coast.

Since most whales spend time around Baja California that is where most of the preserves were established. However, it was soon realized that many of the whale pods liked to hang around the PV area so that area also became a preserve. In 1993, the waters around PV were declared a UNESCO site.

Turtle-Watching

The Olive Ridley sea turtle arrives at Bandera Bay around the beginning of July each year to lay her eggs. This wonder continues until the end of November. Once the eggs are laid it takes six weeks for them to hatch. This means that you can possibly see turtles laying their eggs between

July and November and see the hatchlings between mid-September to mid-February. It is a thrill to sit on the sand and watch the little heads poke out of the shells. Then, no matter what obstacles stand in their path, they make their way to the ocean. Sometimes there are only a few turtles hatching, but if you are lucky you will be able to see hundreds.

For the best luck you should join a group that is involved in turtle preservation. These people know where the turtles are and when the hatchlings will start to break out of their shells. They also know what to do to keep them safe.

▶▶ **AUTHOR NOTE:** *Bounce, a static remover used in clothes dryers, tucked into your belt loop or buttonhole will prevent bees and mosquitoes from attacking.*

Birding

Birding is good along the rivers that run from the mountains down to the ocean. You can go as far as the village of El Nogalito or Tomatlan at the south end of the bay or walk along the bay and follow any path going inland. There has been 355 species of birds recorded in the area.

 BIRD WATCH: *Macaws, parakeets, trogons, magpies, jays, boobies, frigates, egrets and herons are common.*

For real birders, Ecotours (page 266) offers day trips, four-day trips and six-day trips to birding areas. They know exactly where the birds are.

■ Adventures on Horseback

 Rancho El Charro, ☎ *322-224-0114, www.ranchoelcharro. com,* offers rides ($60) through the jungle to a waterfall that is near a canyon.

Rancho Capomo, *Gorion #172,* ☎ *322-224-0450,* offers five-hour rides into the jungle that start at 9 am. There are bilingual guides and breakfast or lunch can be included. The ranch is in the mountains and the ride goes to a waterfall (there are many in the PV area) and back to the ranch. Rates are not advertised because they change regularly.

Rancho Ojo de Agua, *Cerra Cardenal # 227,* ☎ *322-224-8240,* also offers trips into the jungle and they do longer rides of up to four days. Stop by any tour office in town to book these trips or call them direct. See *Tour Operators*, below, for more details.

Horses are used for work as well as pleasure.

■ Adventures in the Air

Canopy Tours

There are two canopy tours in the PV area that offer the opportunity to swing from cables strung across the jungle at heights of up to 350 feet/110 meters.

The first tour is offered at Los Palmas in the Sierra Madre Mountains on private property owned by Vallarta Adventures. There are 14 observation platforms for wildlife observation. To get from station to station, you are harnessed into mountain climbing gear and sent across the cables. Some platforms are as far as 375 feet/120 meters from each other. This is not a tour for anyone afraid of heights. Macho men may want to try the optional extreme game where you swing to a platform, climb a net and then crawl across a rope ladder back to the starting platform. At the end of the tour, you must rappel down 55 feet/18 meters to the ground.

The price ($60 for the day) includes transportation to and from the site, plus all climbing gear. You should wear either shorts or pants and running shoes, although strap-on sandals are acceptable. You are allowed to bring a small pack with water in it, but cameras are not permitted for safety reasons.

You must be able to walk uphill for 15 minutes and have enough strength to climb a 15-foot/five-meter ladder. You must also be able to stand on a platform that is 3x3 feet/1x1 meter in size without hyperventilating, vomiting or fainting. Pregnant woman or anyone with heart trouble, seizures, no balance, or back, neck or shoulder disabilities should not join this tour. Children must be eight years or older to participate.

The second canopy tour goes through the treetops and across a river gorge 350 feet/110 meters below. It uses 1½ miles/two km of cable in a series of 10 zip lines that run between stations. Crossing the gorge is a real rush. The longest cable run is 1,000 feet/350 meters. After you have done this run, go down to the rock-lined river and swim in one of the natural pools or sit on a tiny sand beach.

The minimum age limit for either tour is eight years. To reach the second canopy site, catch a bus from La Jolla de Mismaloya at the south end of town. Buses depart at 8:30, 10 and 11:30 am, then 1 and 2:30 pm. Allow some extra time for travel, as occasionally they run late. See tour agents (page 265).

Pacific Bungee Jumping, ☎ *322-228-0670*, is south on the coastal highway toward Mismaloya, about a quarter-mile past the President Intercontinental Hotel at Km 9.2. Past the hotel, you'll see the bungee crane over the water. Jumping the 120 feet/40 meters toward the water can be fun and, since 1993 when the jump was established, there has not been a death. You have the choice of a full body or ankle harness. The jump is open 10 am-6 pm daily and reservations are not required. If you let them know ahead of time, they will supply you with an "I did it" certificate. This company also rents dune buggies to rod around in the sand. If taking a public bus from PV, go to the stop on the corner of Basilo Badillo and Insurgentes and take a bus marked *Boca* or *Mismaloya*. Ask the driver to stop at the bungee.

■ Adventures of the Brain

University of Guadalajara, *Libertad #105-1*, ☎ *322-223-2082, www.cepe.udg.mx,* has specialized courses for survival Spanish and for advanced levels. You can go for a few hours a day for one week, two weeks and four weeks. There are special children's classes from elementary to senior levels. There is also an immersion program where you can stay with a Mexican family. Intense, long-term courses are about $8 per hour, while the shorter-term, two hours a day for a week courses run $10 an hour.

■ Outfitters/Tour Operators

Rancho El Charro, ☎ *322-224-0114, www.ranchoelcharro. com*, offers rides through the jungle to a waterfall that is near a canyon. The guides are bilingual and the saddles cushioned. They take only small groups and welcome children. Trips can be anywhere from three hours to eight, although the five-hour trip is the most common. An all-day trip with guides and food costs about $100 per person. Otherwise, the cost is about $15 per hour, with guide. For real horse lovers, they also offer a full week of riding, camping out, staying in colonial haciendas and exploring mountains. This adventure runs just over $100 per day. El Charro has special pick-up points in PV and they will deliver you to your hotel at the end of the ride. You can book ahead via their website; they will respond with a confirmation. I found this company cooperative and quick to respond to anything I wanted.

Rancho Ojo de Agua, *Cerrada de Cardenal # 227*, ☎ *322-224-0607*, offers the same ride as above and they also do longer rides of up to four days. Prices for these rides should be negotiated. Tropical jungle rides depart 10 am or 3 pm and return at 1 pm or 6 pm. The shorter ride costs $47 and the longer ride costs $60, including lunch. They also have a sunset ride from 4:30-7:30 pm, dinner included, for $52. A long ride with an overnight costs $185, including meals. There is free transportation from town out to the ranch. Contact them to make arrangements.

Rancho Capomo, *Gorion #172, no phone*, has five-hour rides into the jungle that leave at 9 am from their ranch in the mountains. There are bilingual guides and breakfast or lunch can be included. The ride goes to a waterfall (there are many in the PV area) and back to the ranch. The cost is about $55.

Carnival Tours, ☎ *322-222-5174, www.carnival.com*, has a catamaran that goes to Los Arcos, Quimixto or Las Animas. The tour includes breakfast, open bar (for national drinks), snorkeling equipment, music and lunch (on the beach) that is either grilled fish, chicken in sauce, hamburgers or quesadillas. Their tours leave from the marina at 9 am and you should be there half an hour early to purchase your ticket. This company specializes in tours for the cruise ship crowd.

Vallarta Adventures, *Calle Mastil, Marina Vallarta and at Paseo Las Palmas #39-A, in Nuevo Vallarta*, ☎ *322-224-8354 or 226-3732, www. vallarta- adventures.com*, offers tours to some of the outlying villages, cultural tours to Huichol villages, whale-watching, scuba diving, snorkeling and a canopy adventure. They also have a variety of wildlife excursions where you can watch turtle hatching/egg laying (June-Sept., $60), watch for dolphins ($65, four hours), visit a crocodile rejuvenation program run by the University of Guadalajara ($32) or take a hike and look for birds in the jungle ($45, five hours). They also rent plastic, non-tip kayaks at a cost of $65 for six hours.

Mex Bike Adventures, *Calle Guerrero # 361,* ☎ *322-223-1834 or 322-223-1680 from Canada or the US,* run hiking and biking tours for all experience levels. Their 12-mile/20-km bike trip up the Cuale River takes three to four hours and costs $44 per person. This includes bike, helmet and refreshments. The bikes are 24-gear, front-suspension mountain bikes. Mex Bike will go with a minimum of three people.

Ecotours Vallarta de Mexico, *Ignacio Vallarta 243,* ☎ *322-222-6606 or 223-3130,* has been offering tours since 1991. Ecotours is owned by Astrid Frisch, a biologist, and Karel Beets, a specialist in sustainable development. Their excellent reputation in conservation has led them to work with the World Wildlife Fund, the American Museum of Natural History in New York, the St. Louis Zoo and the National Wildlife Federation. Ecotours offers diving, snorkeling, bird watching, hiking and kayaking, and is involved in the Humpback Whale Photo-identification project and in the Sea Turtle Conservation Program. Astrid is also involved in the inter-state protection of marine life. Ecotours is able to offer knowledgeable and up-to-date information to their customers about wildlife in the area. The people are downright friendly, treating everyone with respect even if their knowledge is limited. The cost of a two-tank dive is between $75 and $135, depending on the dive site and length of time it takes to get there. Snorkeling tours cost $70 per person and $42 for children under 12. The snorkeling tours include all equipment. Eight-hour whale-watching tours cost $80 for adults and $50 for children. This is the oldest company doing the whale-watching tours. The cost of the tour includes breakfast, lunch and all transportation.

Ocean Friendly Tours, *Paseo del Marlin #510,* ☎ *322-225-3774, www. oceanfriendly.com*, runs whale-watching tours during the winter and nature photography all year long. Whale trips run from 9 am-2 pm between mid-December and the end of March. This tour has an ocean specialist along as guide. They also have professional photos of ocean wildlife for sale.

Exotic Tours, *Av Diaz Ordaz #652, on the malecón next to the Hard Rock Café,* ☎ *322-222-8653, exotictours@hotmail.com,* has a showroom with videos, brochures, photos and a simulation of the ocean and jungle. Watch the TV monitors to see what can be done on each tour – beside a large papier mâché whale, a whale-watching video is playing, and among the jungle vegetation is another video about the canopy tour. A tremendous amount of work has gone into this showroom and seeing it will give you a good idea of what to expect. I highly recommend stopping in here. This company co-ordinates a lot of tours for other companies.

Open Air Expeditions, *Guerrero #339,* ☎ *322-222-3310, www.vallarta-whales.com*, offers numerous tours, including a whale-watching trip in

Banderas Bay ($75, four hours); turtle watching on the bay ($65, four hours); and spotting crocodiles at the University of Guadalajara Research Station ($32, four hours). You can also take a river trail hike ($55, five hours) or a kayak trip in a non-tip kayak ($65, six hours).

Canopy Tours, *Los Juntas de los Veranos*, ☎ *322-223-6060*, *www. canopytours-vallarta.com*, offers canopy tours that go over a canyon. A bus runs five times a day out to the site. Transportation, soda and insect repellent are included in the price, $60 for the day. They accept direct reservations only – that means either you book by telephone or online – up to one month in advance.

Chicos Dive Shop, *Av Diaz Ordaz # 772*, ☎ *322-222-1895*, *www.chicos-diveshop.com*, has been around since 1968 offering diving and snorkeling tours, diving courses and jungle tours. They know all the spots, and offer nitox tanks, night dives and custom trips. They also have a wide variety of rentals for those not carrying any gear. Pathfinders, a subsidiary company, offers dune-buggy trips twice a day (9 am-noon and 2-5 pm), every day except Sunday. The trip follows the Bay of Banderas and then goes along some jungle rivers and into the foothills. The cost for machine, helmet and water is $25 for the half-day.

Natura Expeditions, *Terminal Maritima*, ☎ *322-224-0410*, *www. naturaexpeditions.com*, runs hiking, biking and horseback riding trips into the mountains. Their hiking tour ($35, five hours) begins at a ranch in the mountains and you hike for three hours through the forest and jungle with an English-speaking guide who can point out different plants and their uses. Birders will find this a good walk. You will stop at a hot spring for a short dip midway during the hike. The trip includes transportation to trailhead, fruit, water, guide and shot of tequila at the end of the day. You should wear either hiking boots or good running shoes. Those not into walking can ride a sure-footed and well-trained horse ($45, five hours) along the Mascota River where the vegetation is lush and the bird life abundant. You will pass mango and banana plantations en route to the hot springs. Back at the ranch, you will be invited to feed the ostrich. This trip includes two hours travel time. The price includes transportation, horse, guide and water. Bikers travel off-road past plantations and small towns on a 21-gear, full-suspension bike. Along the way, wildlife will be spotted. The cost for this is $35, including your bike, water, equipment and guide. Add a dinner of barbequed ribs to any of the above trips for just 10 bucks. Natura also has a trimaran called *Simbad* that can carry 17 people. You can hire the boat fully equipped with a full bar and lunch or just the boat. The cost is $220 for an eight-hour day without the bar and lunch. This is a good deal.

B-B-Bobby's Bikes, *Miramar #399 at Iturbide*, ☎ *322-223-0008*, has bikes for rent to take either on your own or with a guide for the day or a week. They use the RACE brand of bike and supply helmets, gloves, shorts and water.

Rainbow Dancer Cruises, *Francia #487, ☎ 322-299-0936, www.rainbowdancer.com, or go to the Main Marina, off Av Escuela Naval Marina, across from San Javier Hospital.* The boat leaves the port every day except Sunday at 9:30 am. There is a $1 charge to enter the port and you can purchase tickets for the catamaran boat trip at the dock. The cost is $40 per person and half price for kids. This includes all meals and drinks on board ship. You start with breakfast on board as you travel to Los Arcos where you can snorkel. Lunch is in Quimixto at a local restaurant and the meal is included, although the drinks are not. Those wanting to ride a horse will pay an additional $13. The *Rainbow Dancer* caters to a gay/lesbian crowd.

Santa Maria Catamaran, *Los Muertos Pier,* leaves every day at 9:30 am and 10:15 am, and returns at 6 pm. Included in the price is a continental breakfast, fruits, lunch, open bar on board, snorkeling gear, kayaks, fishing gear, music to dance by and air conditioning in the bathrooms (how about that?). This boat visits Los Arcos, Las Animas and Quimixto. It is a wild time.

AnclaTur, *Cerrada de Playas #2, Nuevo Vallarta, ☎ 322-221-2244 or 322-278-2606 (cell),* has a 38-foot/12-meter catamaran called *Eleganz* that can hold 23 passengers.

FACT FILE: *Eleganz* was built in 2000 by Beneteau of France, one of the world's leading boat builders.

On board is radar, weather fax, water maker, GPS, echo sounder, auto pilot, auto life raft, VHF radio and satellite phone. For entertainment there is a CD stereo player, TV, VCR and video games for the kids (big and small). Watersports include a kayak, snorkeling equipment and fishing tackle. You can opt for the full meal plan which includes continental breakfast, snacks, lunch of tacos, quesadillas or enchiladas, and national alcoholic beverages for $30 a day, plus tax. The luxury plan, $48 per day, includes everything that is in the above plan, plus a beach lunch of shrimp or lobster (in season) or an entire fish and an imported bottle of wine. The boat, totally equipped with a full crew and experienced captain costs $5,000 a week.

■ Day Trips

Las Juntas village is 14 miles/22 km south of PV and can be visited as a day trip by using a local bus, your own vehicle or a taxi. Once there, you can do a horse trip up the river, swim for a while, hike up the river and/or eat and drink in the restaurant. There are two restaurants, one upstream from the other. **Chico's Paradise Restaurant**, ☎ *322-473-0413, www.chicosparadise.com.mx, open 10 am-6 pm*, is surrounded by jungle vegetation. Chico works with the local indigenous people so a lot of the profits go to them. The best dish is the beef brochette, served with rice, beans, French fries and salsa for $11. For dessert, try the caramel custard (flan). Chico's has the Santa Lucia waterfall at its side and is next to La Tuito stream that has swimming holes. I have no details on the second restaurant.

A run to Las Juntas should be done as a day trip from PV as there is no place to stay at Las Juntas. This is a popular destination.

■ Shopping

 Huichol Collection, *Paseo Diaz Ordaz #732*, ☎ *322-223-0661 and Morelos #490*, ☎ *322-223-2141*, are retail outlets carrying the best in Huichol art. The stores are run by locals who ensure that some of the profits return to the communities where the art originated. One of the newer styles of art is being represented by the solid beaded pieces that come in every size and shape imaginable.

Libros Libros Bookstore, *31 de Octubre (just south of Hidalgo Park)*, has both Spanish- and English-language books.

Indigera, *Juarez # 628*, ☎ *322-222-3007, five blocks north of the main plaza*, specializes in "Day of the Dead" art, but they also carry some exceptional crystal that has been decorated with 23kt gold leaf. They have some exquisite Huichol Indian art and unique masks. Because quality is good, prices are fairly high.

HUICHOL SYMBOLS

- The **Iguana** is the adviser of the future and the eyes of the spirit.
- The **bird** is the symbol of freedom and messenger of good.
- **Turtles** help the rain goddess and are considered good luck.
- **Corn** indicates health and prosperity.
- The **scorpion** is the protector of the peyote and the people.
- **Snakes** are intermediaries between humans and the spirit world.
- **Butterfly** is the symbol of good luck.

La Bohemia, *Constitución and Basilio Badillo,* ☎ *322-222-3164*, has a collection of unique resort-wear (clothes that look great in Mexico, but the pits once home). They also carry a line of jewelry and accessories that is quite exquisite. Prices are fairly high. La Bohemia sponsors a fashion show every Thursday at 1 pm at the Camino Real.

The **Flea Market** by the Rio Cuale Bridge holds numerous shops and *tiendas* selling everything from seashells to fine art. Prices have to be bartered here and you would be wise to look at other shops to have an idea of where to start (or end).

Habanos, *Calle Aldama #170,* carry the best Cuban cigars, including Cohibas, Montecristo, Cuaba, La Gloria, Cubana, Ramon Allones, Partagas, Upmann, Romeo y Julieta, Punch, Bolivar, Hoyo de Monterrey, Fonseca and La Flor de Cano.

CIGAR SAVVY

Some of the things to look for that guarantee Cuban quality are the red serial number of the Republic of Cuba on the cigar and under the box, and the factory code (several letters). It must have the brand of Cuba on it saying "Hecho a Mano."

■ Places to Stay

 There are 111 hotels registered with the tourist office in Puerto Vallarta. They vary in quality from zero to five stars, from the luxury timeshare places to cheap digs that are not even registered. It is beyond the scope of this book to list them all. Some are all-inclusive, which means, meals, entertainment and local booze is part of the package. The web page, www.puertovallarta.net, lists most of the hotels and gives a brief description. If you want specific things like golf courses, tennis courts or child-care that aren't included in this book, look on the net.

WARNING: When booking online, be aware that photos never show the cockroaches in the corner or the paint peeling from the ceilings. Never pay for your entire stay up front, just in case the real thing doesn't meet your expectations. If the place looks too good for the price, it may well be. Check www.tripadvisor.com for reviews about places you are considering. Some of the postings are obviously put there by staff, but others are legitimate and helpful when deciding on a hotel.

Timeshare hawkers will drive you bonkers in PV. If you are genuinely interested in purchasing, be careful. Timeshares are not always what they are made out to be. Give yourself at least 48 hours cooling-down time from when you are wined and dined by the salesman until you sign a contract. The Mayan Palace is about the largest timeshare in the area (and has the most hawkers).

HOTEL PRICE SCALE	
Price for a room given in US $.	
$.................	Up to $20
$$.................	$21-$50
$$$................	$51-$100
$$$$	$101-$150
$$$$$	$151-$200
Anything over $200 is specified.	

Remember, no area code is needed when making a local call.

LAP OF LUXURY HOTELS

The luxury places usually have a couple of pools, air conditioning, and a disco/bar and restaurant. They are big, sometimes with more than 500 rooms. Some are time-shares and all are above average as far as hotels go, especially when it comes to entertainment. Below are a few.

Camino Real, *Km 3.5 Barra de Navidad Hwy,* ☎ *322-221-5000*, $140-$550 per night, 337 rooms.

Four Seasons, *Punta Mita,* ☎ *322-291-6000,* $390-$790 per night, 140 rooms.

Hacienda Cora, *Calle Pelicanos #311,* ☎ *322-221-0800*, rates start at $177 per night, 67 rooms.

Hotelito Desconocido, *Carreterra A Mismaloya #479,* ☎ *322-298-5209*, $200-$280 per night, 27 rooms.

La Jolla de Mismaloya, *Km 11-5 Zona Hotelera Sur,* ☎ *322-226-0660*, standard rooms are $252-$282 a night, 303 rooms.

Marriott Casa Magna, *Av Paseo de la Marina #5,* ☎ *322-221-0004,* $90+ per night in low season, 433 rooms.

Melia Pto. Vallarta, *Paseo de la Marina Sur, #H7,* ☎ *322-226-3000,* has rooms as low as $110 per night, 357 rooms.

Premiere Buenaventura, *Calle San Salvador #117,* ☎ *322-226-7001*, $160-$290 per night, 83 rooms.

Sheraton Buganvilias, *Blvd Fr. Medina Ascencio 999,* ☎ *322-226-0404*, $80-$275 per night, 684 rooms.

Sunterra Vallarta Torre, *Paseo de las Garzas,* ☎ *322-224-0366*, no prices available, 66 rooms.

Puerto Vallarta

Places to Stay

1. Camino Real
2. Four Seasons
3. Hacienda Cora
4. Hotelito Desconocido
5. La Jolla de Mismaloya
6. Marriott Casa Magna
7. Melia Puerto Vallarto
8. Premiere Buenaventura
9. Sheraton Bugambilias
10. Sunterra Vallarta Torre
11. Hotel Belmar
12. Hotel Hortencia
13. Hotel Azteca
14. Posada Roger
15. Posada del Pedregal
16. Hotel Ana Liz
17. Hotel Castillo
18. Posada Real
19. Andale Hotel
20. Hotel Bernal
21. Hotel Club del Sol
22. Casa Kimberley B&B
23. Las Palmas
24. Hotel El Pescador
25. La Rosita
26. Playa Concha Chinas
27. Playa Los Arcos
28. Hacienda Buenaventura
29. Hotel Molino de Agua
30. Grand Club Marival
31. Plaza Pelicanos
32. Casa Turaki
33. Hotel Krystal
34. Presidente Intercontinental

EL CENTRO
shown below

LIBRAMIENTO

tunnel

Banderas Bay

AV FRANCISCO VILLA

AV LAS PALMAS

PRISCILIANO SANCHEZ

AIRPORT

Islas Marietas

to Tepic

© 2005 HUNTER PUBLISHING, INC

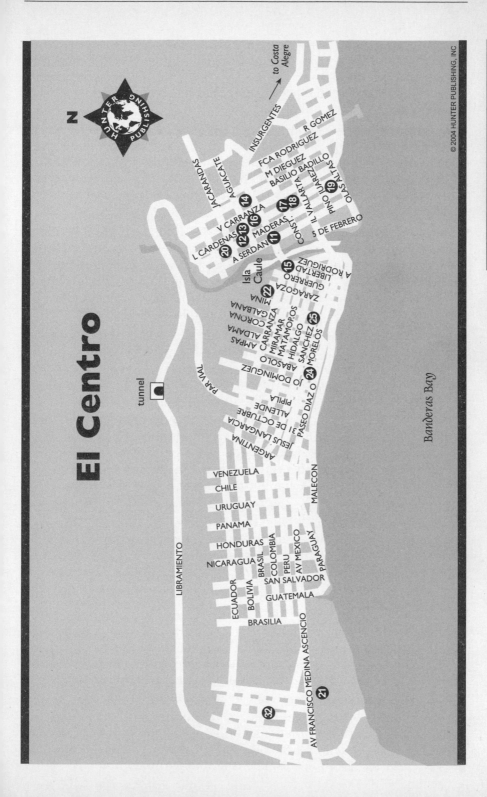

Puerto Vallarta Region

Hotel Belmar, *Insurgentes #161,* ☎ *322-222-0572 or 223-1872, $,* offers rooms at $13.50 per person without air conditioning. With air conditioning, the cost is a bit higher. This is a tiny hotel just 500 meters from the Playa de Los Muertos and three blocks from the *malecón*. Rooms are basic but okay.

Hotel Hortencia, *Calle Francisco Madero #336,* ☎ *322-223-3221, www. hotelhortencia.com, $,* has rooms with bathroom and fan. The hotel is in a colonial styled building and is clean. Part of the attractiveness of this hotel is its bright white walls. It also has rooms with air conditioning but the cost is $35 for a double and for that price you can get a lot better in one of the fancier hotels.

Hotel Azteca, *Calle Francisco Madero #473,* ☎ *322-222-2750, $,* has 40 rooms that are fairly bright considering the windows open onto a central courtyard rather than the street. There are two desks and nightstands in each room, plus fans. The place is hospital clean, the staff is friendly and it is quiet. Some rooms have kitchenettes. What more can one want for $18 a night?

Posada Roger, *Basilio Badillo #237,* ☎ *322-222-0836, profiled on www. puerto-vallarta.com, $$,* has 48 rooms decorated with heavy Mexican furniture. Each room has a private bathroom, cable TV, telephone, air conditioning and a fan. The hotel features a rooftop pool, surrounding gardens, currency exchange and safe-deposit boxes.

Posada del Pedregal, *Agustin Rodriguez #267,* ☎ *322-222-0604, www. mexonline.com / pedregal.htm, $$,* is a small hotel that has clean large rooms at reasonable prices. During low season, the owner will barter a little. The cost of a room with private bathroom and hot water is $30 for two people sharing a bed. You must pay for your room in advance.

Hotel Ana Liz, *Calle Francisco Madero # 429,* ☎ *322-222-1757, $$,* has small clean rooms with fans. Each room has its own bathroom. This place is a family run establishment and often has repeat customers. It is just a block from the beach, on the south side of the river.

Hotel Castillo, *Calle Francisco Madero # 273,* ☎ *322-223-1438, $$,* has 20 rooms with TV, fans and private bathrooms. Some rooms have cooking facilities. They offer discounts for longer stays.

Posada Real, *Calle Francisco Madero, no phone, $$,* is next door to the Castillo. This is a drab little place that has rooms with fridges, stoves and cable TV. Rooms for one person are $10 without a bathroom and $23 with. The same room costs $29 for two people. This place is overpriced.

Andale Hotel, *Olas Altas #425,* ☎ *322-223-2622, $$,* is above the Andale Restaurant in the center of town and has seven standard rooms and two, two-bedroom suites. The rooms have tiled floors, brick walls with iron-bared windows, closets, double beds, small reading lamps and tables. This is a very nice place to stay, not fancy but certainly fun.

FACT FILE: In 1980, José Peña and his burros helped build the Andale Hotel. The burros, treated like prized pets, were trained to carry the sand from the river up the stairs to the second level of the building.

Hotel Bernal, *Calle Francisco Madero #423,* ☎ *322-222-3605, $$$,* is an old place that has been kept clean and comfortable, although it is rather basic. The staff is more interested in the afternoon soap operas than in renting a room.

Hotel Club del Sol, *Blvd Francisco Medina Ascencio, Km 15,* ☎ *322-222-2188, www.hotelesclubdelsol.com.mx/vallarta, $$$,* is an average hotel with friendly staff. Their 103 rooms come with or without kitchenettes. All have air conditioning and fans, fridges, two beds, telephones and cable TV. There is a restaurant and sports bar on the property and a 180-foot/60-meter water slide. Prices are not bad at this middle-of-the-road place.

Casa Kimberley B&B, *Calle Zaragoza 445,* ☎ *322-222-1336, www.casakimberley.com, $$$,* is in the home previously owned by Richard Burton and Elizabeth Taylor. The nine bedrooms/suites in the Burton side of the house are named after some of the movies in which he starred. Just to be near the place where these two romantics lived is fun. There is a pool, bar and dining area, and you get to use the walkway over to the Elizabeth side where the museum is located. The rooms are luxurious, with tiled floors, private bathrooms, night tables, sitting areas and area rugs.

Las Palmas, *Paseo de la Marina # 161,* ☎ *322-224-0650, $$$,* has 221 rooms, each with private bathroom and balcony, cable TV, air conditioning and tiled floors. Some rooms have kitchenettes and the views are either of the ocean or their garden. This beachside hotel has two pools, a tennis court, a bar and four restaurants. There is laundry service available, beach and pool towels are provided and safe deposit boxes can be used.

Hotel El Pescador, *Paraguay # 1117,* ☎ *322-222-2169, $$$,* has 100 rooms in a large nondescript building on the beach. Most rooms have a balcony and they all have tiled floors, lamp, a nice closet area, air conditioning or fan and a private bathroom. There is a pool, lounge chairs (little shade) and a nice dining area. For a moderately priced hotel, this is a good choice. It is right down town and is the sister hotel to La Rosita.

La Rosita, *Paseo Diaz Ordaz #901,* ☎ *800-297-0144 from US (no local number), $$$,* has been around since long before my first visit to PV more than 20 years ago and has been consistent in the quality and service offered to its customers. It has over a hundred rooms, all clean and comfortable with rustic Mexican furniture, soft beds, tiled bathrooms, TVs (no cable) and fans. Some rooms overlook the ocean. There is a pool and restaurant and the price of the room includes breakfast. The central location is always a draw.

Playa Concha Chinas, *Carretera Barra de Navidad, Km 2.5,* ☎ *322-221-5763, $$$/$$$$,* is a tiny place with just 17 rooms, each a little different. They are done in tile and have small bathrooms, but some have a Jacuzzi on the balcony. There is air conditioning, safe deposit boxes and cable TV. Some of the edges are a bit worn, but not badly. By this I mean that there are chips in the paint, a few dustballs in the corners and maybe a spot or two on the window or shower door. The hotel is a little way from the center so it is quiet, yet it is easy to get into town if you need to. The beach is rocky and the jungle behind is close. The pool is not large and overlooks the ocean. There is a restaurant and laundry service.

▶▶ **AUTHOR NOTE:** *You can also purchase a 9,000-square-foot villa at the Real de Concha Chinas (different than the Playa Concha Chinas). The cost is just a million and a half (more or less). If interested, contact a real estate agent when in PV.*

Playa Los Arcos, *Olas Altas #380,* ☎ *322-222-1583, $$$/$$$$,* has 185 rooms mostly decorated in Mexican motif with tiled floors, skylights and balconies in some rooms. But some rooms are small and dingy. All bathrooms are minuscule and all the reports that I got said the beds were hard as cement. The staff is fine and the hotel is on the beach in the old section of town. Their breakfast, offered with some package deals, is good. Although they offer an all-inclusive package, I seldom recommend these because they limit your experience of the real Mexico.

Hacienda Buenaventura, *Francisco Madina Ascencio # 2699,* ☎ *322-224-6667, $$$/$$$$,* has 155 rooms that show a bit of wear. This is not a five-star, nor is it on the beach, but it is not a bad deal. The rooms are large with Mexican décor, balconies and telephones. There is air conditioning, an outdoor pool, cable TV, tour desk, money exchange, laundry service, bar and restaurant. Guests may use the facilities at their other hotel called, simply, The Buenaventura. It is in the hotel zone.

Hotel Molino de Agua, *Ignacio L. Vallarta # 130,* ☎ *322-222-1957, $$$/$$$$,* has guest cabins and rooms. The grounds have two pools, as well as parrot and monkey houses. The cages for the monkeys are not very big, and the animals don't look comfortable. There is also a problem with school kids using the pools and making the grounds noisy. However, the rooms are large and comfortable, though the beds are a bit hard. There are no TVs, which I sometimes regard as a plus. The hotel is in the very center of town, but because the grounds are large and walled, it is not noisy from street traffic. The staff is exceptionally accommodating.

Grand Club Marival, *Paseo Cocoteros, no phone, $$$/$$$$*, is in Nuevo Vallarta about half an hour (eight miles/12 km) from the center. Its 650 rooms, each with private bathroom, cable TV and air conditioning, run from $65 to $350 a night. There are six restaurants, seven bars, four pools, numerous tennis courts, a fitness center, an outdoor Jacuzzi, a games room, an arcade and a business center. Professional entertainers present each evening in one of the restaurants. Although the building was built in 1983, it has been renovated recently. This hotel is a long way from the center, but worth visiting at least for the show.

Plaza Pelicanos, *Calle Diego Rivera #120,* ☎ *322-224-4444, $$$$,* has over 400 recently renovated rooms with air conditioning, private bathroom, telephone and cable TV. Each is well decorated. There is a children's pool and an adult pool, a Jacuzzi, a games room and a babysitting service. This hotel offers many different packages with lures like free beach craft and night shows. However, I suggest you take only the room and maybe breakfast. It is far more fun to explore, unless you have just a few days and need an exotic place to crash.

Casa Tukari, *Calle Espana #316,* ☎ *322-224-7177, www.tukari.com, $$$/$$$$ (rates change according to the season),* is in a Mexican colonial-style house that has all the modern conveniences. All four rooms have a view of the garden, which has guava, lime and banana trees, plus a small pool. Each room has a telephone, ceiling fan and a fridge. There is also a Jacuzzi. A massage can be ordered from an on-site therapist who practices the Reiki technique, magnet therapy, light and sound therapy and aromatherapy. PV has been awarded the title of "the most friendly city in the world," and Casa Tukari certainly falls into the same friendly classification.

Hotel Krystal, *Av La Garzas Sur,* ☎ *322-224-0202, $$$$$,* has 405 rooms that cost between $170 and $500 each. The Moorish-style building is moderate in luxury and rooms have mini-bars, air conditioning, satellite TV and daily maid service. They have a pool, safe deposit boxes, bar, lounge, restaurants, tennis, racquetball, hot tub and fitness center. The breakfast buffet is good and lasts until 11 am. There is also an authentic show called "Fiesta" starting every evening at 7 pm.

Presidente Intercontinental, *Carretera Barra de Navidad, Km 8.5,* ☎ *322-228-0191 or 228-0191, $$$$$,* has 120 rooms with an ocean view and 97 rooms without. Fourteen suites have private Jacuzzis, five of them indoors. The three master suites have two bedrooms each, both with balconies and Jacuzzis on each balcony. The presidential suite has all this and a private pool. Services offered include a travel agency, a gift/magazine shop, a business center, a gymnasium, a tennis court and two restaurants. However, the hotel does not have a good reputation. It has a lack of security, a very small pool, and is often full of locals who really want to party on their vacation. The place is a bit tattered in places and needs a facelift. It is more than an hour's walk into town; taxis are generally used.

■ Places to Eat

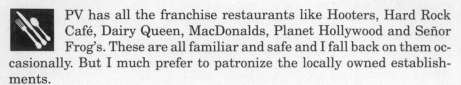 PV has all the franchise restaurants like Hooters, Hard Rock Café, Dairy Queen, MacDonalds, Planet Hollywood and Señor Frog's. These are all familiar and safe and I fall back on them occasionally. But I much prefer to patronize the locally owned establishments.

There are so many choices in PV that it is hard for me to make much more than a random selection and give my preferences. Explore on your own and find some of the gems I haven't yet been to.

GOURMET FEST

A 10-day gourmet festival held in mid-November is sponsored by 23 of the area's most prestigious restaurants. The fair starts with a reception cocktail party where you can schmooze with the chefs. It closes with a banquet that could only be called a food orgy. The festival also offers events like cooking classes and seminars directed at learning about foods, especially cheeses and wines. If you're in town during this time, check at the tourist office or at your hotel for times of events.

Este Café, *Libertad #336* ☎ *322-222-4261*, is a tiny place that has good fresh-baked bread, along with fruit, yogurt and granola, cakes, frappés, shakes or smoothies. The bagels are ordinary and the coffee is something like watered-down espresso. A coffee and pastry runs $4.50 – fairly expensive.

Al Taurino, *Paseo Diaz Ordaz #868,* ☎ *322-223-2817,* is an attractive, middle-of-the-road restaurant that has a good seafood stew ($8) cooked with lots of chilies. Portions are moderate.

La Piazzetta, *Olas Altas and Rodolfo Gomez #143,* ☎ *322-222-0650*, is open Monday to Saturday 1 pm-midnight. Pizza cooked over a wood fire is their specialty, but their veal scallopini is not to be overlooked.

Beanz American Café, *Olas Altas 490-7*, is open 8 am-midnight. Although they guarantee good coffee, they can't seem to guarantee good service. I waited by the counter for quite a while but couldn't get the attention of the waitress, even when I spoke to her. I went elsewhere.

Café Due Espresso Bar, *Commercial Center Villa Vallarta on Francisco Medina Ascencio,* ☎ *322-224-6567,* has excellent bread and good bagels. This is a good spot for a sandwich or breakfast with juice.

Pie in the Sky Coffee Shop, *I.L. Vallarta #150 at Aquiles Serdan,* ☎ *322-222-8411, www.puntamita.com/pieinthesky.htm*, serves good specialty coffees and pastries in its air-conditioned restaurant. They also sell cookies, Italian ice cream, carrot cake, cheesecake and bagels. The pastry is excellent. A piece of apple pie (made with real apples) and a coffee was $4. This was my favorite afternoon coffee spot.

Calypso Café, *Av Francisco Medina Ascencio #1939,* ☎ *322-225-4870*, is open every day and serves excellent coffee and pastries. The owner is a fellow from Pheonix who married a Mexican woman and decided to make PV his home. The place is air-conditioned, which is a draw during the hot muggy days. The computers are fast and cost around $2 per hour.

Ruben's Hamburgers, *Olas Altas #463,* ☎ *322-223-1445,* is the Mexican version of Burger King. The service is excellent, the meals large and the prices low. The deep-fried banana with ice cream is recommended, as is the baked potato. The hamburgers are served with lots of sliced onions – always a favorite with me – for just under $5. The restaurant is located on two floors. The bathrooms are spotless but, when I was there, they were missing toilet seats.

The RiverWay Restaurant, *Calle Morelos #101,* ☎ *322-222-6873*, has an excellent location near the beach, down by the flea market. Open for breakfast, lunch and dinner, this place has good food at low prices. Lunch is about $4 per meal. They often offer a second drink free if you have supper. Reservations are recommended during high season.

Mickey's No Name Café, *Morelos #460,* ☎ *322-223-2508, nonamecafe@ prodigy.net*, is a sports bar that specializes in barbeque ribs and chicken. The meat is good, but the portions are small and the prices are high. A two-for-the-price-of-one beer costs double what it would cost in some other restaurants. The service, however, is good and friendly.

Santa Barbara, *Olas Altas #351,* ☎ *322-222-4477*, offers Mexican and American food and their menu sports such dishes as a Reuben on rye, liver and onions, chicken mole and fajitas. They have a good selection of wines and, if you have room, homemade desserts are available. The prices are less than $20 a plate.

Planeta Vegetariano, *Iturbide # 270, just above Avenida Hidalgo,* ☎ *322-222-3073*, is open 8 am-10 pm. The breakfast buffet offers fresh fruit, oatmeal, tofu omelette, soy milk and hotcakes made without eggs or milk. There is also yogurt, fruit drinks and the best coffee in town. You get all you can eat for $3.50. Lunch or dinner starts at 11:30 and is served until 10 pm. For $5.50 you have the choice of five main dishes that include soup, salad bar, fruit drinks, tea, coffee and dessert. This is one of the best places in Vallarta. The restaurant holds about five or six tables, so go early, or just off regular meal times, so you can get a seat.

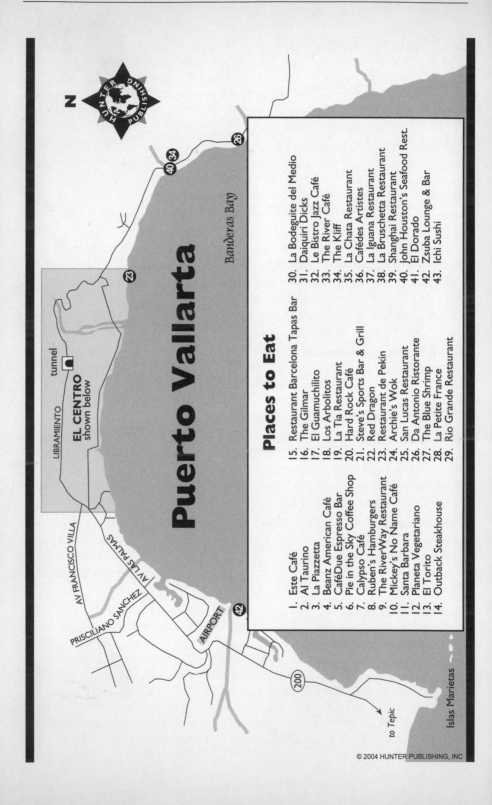

Puerto Vallarta

El Centro
shown below

Banderas Bay

Islas Marietas

to Tepic

Places to Eat

1. Este Café
2. Al Taurino
3. La Piazzetta
4. Beanz American Café
5. CaféDue Espresso Bar
6. Pie in the Sky Coffee Shop
7. Calypso Café
8. Ruben's Hamburgers
9. The RiverWay Restaurant
10. Mickey's No Name Café
11. Santa Barbara
12. Planeta Vegetariano
13. El Torito
14. Outback Steakhouse
15. Restaurant Barcelona Tapas Bar
16. The Gilmar
17. El Guamuchilito
18. Los Arbolitos
19. La Tia Restaurant
20. Hard Rock Café
21. Steve's Sports Bar & Grill
22. Red Dragon
23. Restaurant de Pekin
24. Archie's Wok
25. San Lucas Restaurant
26. Da Antonio Ristorante
27. The Blue Shrimp
28. La Petite France
29. Rio Grande Restaurant
30. La Bodeguite del Medio
31. Daiquiri Dicks
32. Le Bistro Jazz Café
33. The River Café
34. The Kliff
35. La Chata Restaurant
36. Cafédes Artistes
37. La Iguana Restaurant
38. La Bruschetta Restaurant
39. Shanghai Restaurant
40. John Houston's Seafood Rest.
41. El Dorado
42. Zsuba Lounge & Bar
43. Ichi Sushi

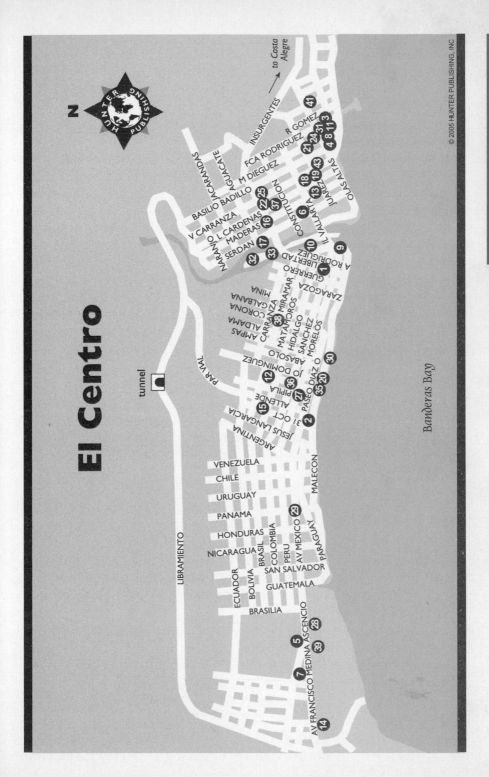

El Centro

© 2005 HUNTER PUBLISHING, INC

to Costa Alegre

tunnel

Banderas Bay

Av Francisco Medina Ascencio

Libramiento

Par Vial

Brasilia
Guatemala
San Salvador
Bolivia
Ecuador
Peru
Colombia
Brasil
Nicaragua
Honduras
Panama
Uruguay
Chile
Venezuela
Argentina
Jesus Langarica
31 Oct
Allende
Pipila
Paseo Diaz O
2 de Agosto
Malecon
Paraguay
Av Mexico

Insurgentes
FCA Rodriguez
R Gomez
M Dieguez
Basilio Badillo
Aguacate
Jacarandas
Basilio Badillo
V Carranza
Naranjo
O L Cardenas
Maderas
Serdan
Constitucion
I L Vallarta
Juarez
Olas Altas
Libertad
Guerrero
A Rodriguez
Zaragoza
Mina
Miramar
Corona
Galeana
Aldama
Matamoros
Carranza
Hidalgo
Sanchez
Morelos
Abasolo
Jo Dominguez
Ampas

El Torito, *Ignacio L. Vallarta #290,* ☎ *322-222-3784,* has world-famous barbequed ribs and chicken, plus a choice of over 100 liquors and wines. This is a large sports bar that has 25 television sets, all set at a different sport. El Torito has been in business since 1982, so they are doing something well.

Outback Steakhouse, *Francisco Medina Ascencio #4690,* ☎ *322-225-4906,* offers steaks done Australian style and served with a bonzer salad. For the seafood lover, they also have a catch of the day special that is superb. To finish your meal, try their "Chocolate Thunder from Down Under."

Restaurant Barcelona Tapas Bar, *Matamoros and 31 de Octubre,* ☎ *322-222-0510,* is open daily from 5 pm-midnight. If you like to sip fruit-flavored wine and munch on appetizers, then try this place. The food is good.

The Gilmar, *Francisco Madero #418,* ☎ *322-222-3923*, is between Aguacate and Jacarandas, across from the Bernal Hotel in the old part of town. A good spot for breakfast, it is open daily, 8 am-11 pm. The coffee is fairly strong.

El Guamuchilito, *Aquiles Serdan # 438,* ☎ *322-222-4360*, is open noon-11:30 pm daily. This is a steak and seafood restaurant that is fairly new. The food is so-so.

Los Arbolitos, *Lazaro Cardenas and Camino de la Ribera # 184,* ☎ *322-223-1050,* is open 11 am-11 pm daily. Try the onion soup for under $4 – it will fill you up. They also have flan (caramel custard) for $3.50, but the serving isn't big enough to satisfy me. See if you can talk them into a bigger piece.

La Tia Restaurant, *Pino Suarez #240 and Lazaro Cardenas,* ☎ *322-223-0667,* is open 8 am-10 pm. For breakfast, the French toast ($2) is great. They also make a fruit plate with yogurt and granola for $2.50. Suppers run between $7 and $21.

Hard Rock Café, *Av Presidente Diaz Ordaz #652,* ☎ *322-222-2230*. The restaurant is open 11 am-2 am, with the merchandise area open 10 am-1 am. An American chain famous around the world, the café is for those who need a touch of home.

Steve's Sports Bar & Grill, *Basilio Badillo #286,* ☎ *322-222-0256,* is a fish and chip joint that sells the cheapest beer in town. It is open daily 11 am-1 am and has both American and Canadian satellite TV.

Red Dragon, *Insurgentes # 323,* ☎ *322-222-0175*, makes the best Cantonese food in the city. They are open 1 pm-midnight and will even deliver to your hotel.

Restaurant de Pekin, *Olas Altas and Los Muertos Pier,* ☎ *322-222-8609*, is open noon-midnight every day of the week. The Pekin has been renovated so the atmosphere is exquisite. The menu has seven appetizers, five soups and two dozen main dishes. Their pineapple shrimp and Kung Pao chicken are spiced just right; anything with peanut sauce is good. The price is right, too.

Archie's Wok, *Francisca Rodriguez # 130*, ☎ *322-222-0411*, has been around since film director John Huston's day when Archie was Huston's personal chef. They specialize in Thai, Chinese and Filipino foods. This is a very good place to eat.

San Lucas Restaurant, *Cardenas and Insurgentes*, ☎ *322-222-3126*, is a pleasant eaterie that overlooks the street from its second-floor location. It is open noon-10 pm and specializes in seafood and steak.

Da Antonio Ristorante, *in the Presidente Intercontinental Hotel, Carretera Barra de Navidad, Km 8.5*, ☎ *322-228-0722*, is classy and romantic. The restaurant overlooks the bay and specializes in authentic Italian foods. You will pay El Presidente prices.

The Blue Shrimp, *Morelos #779*, ☎ *322-222-4246*, *www.theblueshrimp. com.mx*, is open noon-1 am daily. The décor includes relics of ancient ships and the walls are made to look like reefs. There are fish tanks interspersed around other sea-styled items and the room is lit with a blue light that adds to the underwater ambiance. Even the bathrooms are shaped like shells, the men's like a snail and the women's like a conch. The food is shrimp of every size prepared in almost any exotic style. I liked the coconut shrimp in a batter, covered in a coconut-milk sauce. There are so many varieties of shrimp, served in so many ways – the owners even managed to make a shrimp popcorn. Although there are other dishes, such as mahi mahi and tuna, shrimp is the real draw. This restaurant also has an excellent salad bar. They have the largest percentage of return customers in PV.

La Petite France, *Francisco Medina Ascencio Km 2.5*, ☎ *322-293-0900*, open 8 am-midnight daily. La Petite is a must for those who love French food, French wine, French décor and French service. The breakfast omelets, served in the garden, are a huge draw. I also liked the filet de poisson à la Petite France, a white fish with shallots, white wine and hollandaise sauce, all for $12.

Rio Grande Restaurant, *Av Mexico # 1175*, ☎ *322-222-0095*, open 8 am-11 pm, specializes in jumbo shrimp, red snapper and whatever the catch of the day may be. They have been in business since 1984, have air conditioning and offer the second drink free when you order one of the main dishes. For something special, try the crabmeat tacos.

La Bodeguita del Medio, *Malecón, Paseo Diaz Ordaz #858*, ☎ *322-223-1585*, will take you back to the 1940s in Havana with live Cuban music and delicious Cuban food cooked by a Cuban chef. The specialty is beans, rice and pork, spiced with hot chilies. Compliment this with a *mojito*, the drink of Hemingway, made with Cuban rum and lemon juice. Top all this off with a Cuban cigar, also available at La Bodeguita, and you'll go home to write your own version of *The Old Man and the Sea*.

Daiquiri Dick's, *Olas Altas #314*, ☎ *322-222-0566*, is open every day except Wednesday from 10:30 am-midnight. This is one of the restaurants that partakes in the Gourmet Festival each year (see above). It started as a small beachside hut and transformed over a period of 18 years into the gourmet establishment you see today. They serve dishes like filet of tuna in a sesame crust over ginger-braised spinach and sukiyaki sauce, or chunks of lobster sautéed with serrano chili pepper, tomato and asparagus. They have come a long way in 18 years. This is one of the best places to eat in PV.

Le Bistro Jazz Café, *on the island on Rio Cuale*, ☎ *322-222-0283*, is open every day except Sunday from 9 am-midnight. It offers some of the better wines available in PV. It is a romantic spot, especially when the jazz players are working. My favorite meal here is the coconut tempura shrimp royal served with a hot curry sauce. However, my husband had the filet mignon with mushrooms and baked potato and still says this was the best meal he ever had. (He says this a lot.)

The River Café, *Isla Rio Cuale #4*, ☎ *322-223-0788, www.rivercafe.com. mx,* is open noon to 11 pm daily and has live jazz music Thursday through Sunday evenings. The café hires the best chefs to cook your meals, which are served along the riverside walkway. This is a romantic spot and the food is very good. My waiter was eager to give me exactly what I wanted, yet he never hovered. The calamari is a specialty, but if you are tired of seafood, how about rack of lamb done with garlic and rosemary sauce? During high season, reservations are recommended.

Le Kliff, ☎ *322-228-0666 or 224-0976, www.lekliff.com,* is the classiest restaurant in town. Meals are served under the largest palapa roof in the world and the restaurant overlooks the ocean. It is most romantic to go before sunset and watch as the sun sinks into the ocean. The Kliff offers a huge variety of foods, all first class, for about $25 a dish. The house specialty is the fresh filet le Kliff, but I liked the tequila jumbo shrimps. The after-dinner coffees are an act in themselves. It takes two waiters to prepare one, as alcohol-laden liquid is poured from one decanter to another in a display of agility. It is good entertainment for the guests. Once mixed, the coffee is brought flaming to your table. This is a treat that should not be missed. They also have non-intrusive live entertainment.

La Chata Restaurant, *Paseo Diaz Ordaz #708*, ☎ *322-222-4790*, is a clean, tastefully decorated restaurant. The upstairs room overlooks the bay, which makes it a good place to take in the sunset while enjoying a meal. Prices are better than most along the *malecón* and the portions, although not large, are big enough for an average appetite. I had the ceviche, but it was not exceptional.

Café des Artistes, *G. Sanchez # 740,* ☎ *322-222-3228, www. cafedesartistes.com*, is open 6-11:30 pm daily. It is owned and operated by international prize-winning chef Thierry Blouet, whose creations are legendary. How about a prawn carpaccio with caviar sauce? Or honey-glazed roasted duck with a green lime sauce and pumpkin risotto? This is not for the diet-conscious. The restaurant has original art, an indoor stream and lush gardens. For all this you will pay about $20 a plate.

La Iguana Restaurant, *Lazaro Cardenas #311,* ☎ *322-222-0105,* is open daily (except Monday), 11:30 am-1 am. This moderately-priced Mexican restaurant offers all the standard Mexican dishes, but it is the seafood that is really good. Try the shrimp in a Mexican sauce served with rice. On weekends, they have a mariachi band and often host events such as a folklore show, cockfight exhibition (I'm not certain what this is, but I believe cockfights are now illegal) and fireworks. During the week there is no cover charge and there is live music for dancing.

La Bruschetta Restaurant, *Calle Corona #172,* ☎ *322-223-1177,* is a cozy little Italian restaurant that does not have a hawker at the door trying to lure you in. That was a big draw for me. I had the Caesar salad and some lasagna. The meal was delicious, but it barely qualified as an appetizer. I left hungry and unsatisfied. The cost for a salad and spaghetti was about $15.

Shanghai Restaurant, *Francisco Medina Ascencio, Km 2,* ☎ *322-224-1961,* is a first-class establishment that serves foods made closer to the Hong Kong style than the American "Chinese" style. Their shrimp in black bean sauce is delicious. A meal in this air-conditioned restaurant runs less than $10.

John Houston's Seafood Restaurant, *in the Jolla de Mismaloya Hotel, Hotel Zone South at Km 11.5,* ☎ *322-226-0660,* is a true seafood place that serves seafood appetizers, snacks, salads, soups and main dishes. Steak is on the menu, but the choices are limited. The octopus cocktails, done in a tomato sauce, were exceptional. Meals run about $15.

El Dorado, *Pulpito # 102,* ☎ *322-222-1511,* is open 9 am-9 pm and has been in business since 1961. Their specialties are seafood and Mexican dishes. Try the fried dorado. Meals are large and prices are just under $10 per serving.

Zsuba Lounge and Bar, *Paseo de la Marina #245 (near the faro),* ☎ *322-221-0669,* is open 1-11:30 pm. They serve traditional Japanese cuisine from sake and Sapporo beer to sushi, but you can also get a prime rib. This is a quiet place for a pleasant dinner. A meal costs between $10 and $15.

Ichi Sushi, *Juarez #797,* ☎ *322-222-6100*, offers Japanese meals that can be delivered to your hotel or eaten at the restaurant. They carry foods like makisushi, nigiri sushi, teppanyaki, temaki, teriyaki, yakitori, tempura, sweet-and-sour dishes and special combos. The meals run about $5 per serving.

■ Nightlife

The nightlife in PV is extensive and offers everything from quiet piano bars to rowdy discos. If candlelit dining is your thing, you have tons of options. You can get live entertainment, too; there are many folk shows. Walking the *malecón* is a favorite pastime, especially for locals. There is often a free show near the arches along the *malecón* and you can watch a light show on the old boat, *La Marigalante*.

For drinking, dancing and carousing, go to any of the bars near your hotel. Bars in areas near the hotels tend to be patronized by ex-pats and tourists, rather than locals.

Movie Theaters

▶▶ **AUTHOR NOTE:** *English-language movies always have Spanish subtitles in Mexico. Most films are North American productions.*

Cine Bahia, *Insurgentes # 63*, ☎ *322-222-1717*, has five screens featuring American- and Spanish-language films. They have three showings for each screen and the matinee is usually at 4:30 pm.

Cine Luz Maria, *Calle Mexico # 27*, ☎ *322-222-0705*, has two screens with three showings for each screen. They often have a low-cost matinee during the week.

Cine Versalles, *Av Francisco Villa # 799*, ☎ *322-225-8764*, has five screens with three showings for each screen.

Cine Colonial, *Calle Bolivia 141*, ☎ *322-222-1675*, has two screens with two showings every day except Sunday, when they have three and four showings, the first one starting at noon.

Music Scene

PV is developing an international music scene that is worth taking in. Go to the tourist office for updated information on who is in town and where they are performing. Violinist **Willie Royal** and guitarist **Wolfgang Lobo Fink** started playing here in 1990 and even though they now do world tours, they still come back once a year to perform. The Mayor of Margaritaville, **Richard Kaplan**, has performed with his two Macaws for 22 years in PV. The venue is the Playa de Oro Resort and he offers a blend of Jimmy Buffett, Willie Nelson and Kenny Loggins. **Antonio LeComte** is an award-winning pianist who plays new-age music. He was nominated by the Theatre Journalists Association for best original score in 1993. He is accompanied by **Bob Tansen**, and the two of them usually play at the Café des Artistes (see above). Other performers who come here include **Jethro Tull**, who plays the blues; **Alberto Perez**, who has been performing jazz for 15 years; and **Righoberto**, who plays classical guitar and is accompanied by singer, harpist and flautist **d'Rachel**. The best of the jazz artists are **Beverly and Willow**. **Ron Doering** directs the **Sweet Life** quartet and they often play at La Dolce Vita. Ron plays rhythm guitar and sings blues. There are more. Be sure to take in a few.

One of Puerto Vallarta's many bars.

Kalhua Bar, *on the* malecón *just north of the plaza, no phone*, is a popular place to put up your feet on the windowsill, have a tall drink and watch the sun fall into the ocean.

La Dolce Vita Restaurant, *Paseo Diaz Ordanz # 674*, ☎ *322-222-3852*, has live jazz every weekend starting at 9 pm and going till midnight. You can enjoy an excellent Italian dinner (about $12) here before the jazz starts.

Discoteca Valdez, *Guerrero #179, no phone*, is just off the main plaza and is a great hopping place for a dance or two.

Wild Coyotes Bar and Grill, *Venustiano Carranza #208*, ☎ *322-222-8324*, suggests that you should not only get drunk but get wild. This does not interest me, but the place is popular. It is located in the older part of town just two blocks from the beach.

Guadalajara

Guadalajara is the second-largest city in Mexico, with more than three million people. If the heat from the beaches is getting to you, a few days in Guadalajara and Laguna Chapala, just 30 miles/45 km from the center of the city, will give you a refreshing break. With the city sitting at about 5,000 feet/1,600 meters, the temperature averages at 22°C/72°F year-round. If this is still too hot, the lake always has a cooling breeze coming off the water.

Guadalajara is a sprawling city and the long-distance bus station is located a long way from the center, through the industrial area. In the center, plazas and parks are bordered by myriad historical buildings as well as restaurants and shops. Because of its lovely parks and gardens, the city is often called the City of Roses. It is also credited with being the birthplace of the mariachi bands and the Mexican Hat Dance.

Guadalajara is easy to get around. Public transportation is abundant and hotels are found in all areas of the city. The restaurants are a little harder to find, but they are excellent. If you're looking for a little bit of home, you can always stop at one of the franchises, like Dunkin Donuts, Pizza Hut and MacDonalds.

■ Getting Here & Around

By Plane

 The airport for Guadalajara is halfway between the city center and the lake. Buses and taxis commute between the center and the airport. The cost for a taxi is about $15.

By Bus

The long-distance bus station is new, large and well organized. Some of the better bus companies have private lounges in the terminal, reserved for their customers; you can't get into those areas until you have purchased a ticket.

To get into the city from the station, go out the door and behind the station to the main road where buses stop.

▶▶ **AUTHOR NOTE:** *Do not cross the parking lot to catch a bus that runs along the main road. Those buses make their way to the city only after they go in and out of numerous subdivisions.*

The best bus to take is TUR (blue in color and found at a separate stop from regular city buses). The city buses take longer and don't go directly to the plazas. However, to get on a TUR bus you must go to one of their specially designated stops. I often could not find one, so I just hopped onto a city bus.

A taxi to the center from the bus station runs about $10, well worth the fare if you have baggage.

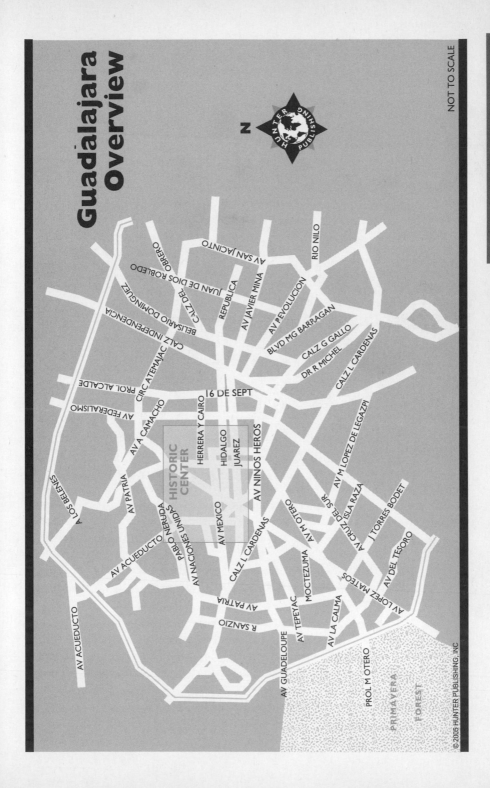

Guadalajara Overview

NOT TO SCALE

© 2005 HUNTER PUBLISHING, INC

First-class bus service goes to most places in Mexico almost every hour, although some may go to Mexico City before connecting with places like Oaxaca or Vera Cruz. Buses to Mazatlan go every hour from 5 am-9 pm daily; the trip takes seven hours. The cost is $31.50 one-way on a first-class, air-conditioned bus. Your ticket may include a sandwich and juice. Unfortunately, for confirmed readers like me, these buses also offer videos.

Carts for hire in downtown Guadalajara.

By Car

Driving in downtown Guadalajara is for those extremely skilled at stockcar racing, or for locals. There are large eight-lane highways around the city that are easy to drive.

The airport has all the international car rental companies like Hertz, Avis and Budget. To book in advance, do so online at www.rentalcar-momma.com/cities/guadalajara.htm. I have no phone numbers for the companies at the airport. The companies listed below are all off the airport compound.

Buelah Rent a Car, *Av Niños Heroes #968*, ☎ *333-614-1135*, has compact vehicles at competitive prices. This is a local company.

Alamo, *Av Niños Heroes #982*, is open 8 am-8 pm. A small Chevy standard will cost $270 a week, including insurance; a Venture Van, automatic, will cost $700, with unlimited mileage. Extra insurance is not included. To get coverage for collision you must pay an extra $15 per day.

Arrasa Rent a Car, *Av Lopez Mateos #62*, ☎ *333-615-0522*, has locations at Hotel Presidente and the airport. They have standard vehicles and suburbans ($750 a week). This is a local company.

By Subway

The subway, Tren Lingero, is an efficient and reliable way to get around. There are two lines; one going north and south and the other going east and west. Look for a subway sign (stairs going down) and, once downstairs, purchase your token from a machine beside the gates. The cost is $1 for a two-train trip. You will need correct change (a 10 peso coin). The trains don't operate after 10 pm.

The city has many attractive plazas.

■ Services

The **Tourist Office**, *Av Morelos just off the Plaza de Liberacion*, ☎ *333-614-0123*, *www.mexperience.com/guide/majorcity/ guadalajara.htm*, *setujal@jalysco.gob.mx*. Although they don't have a huge amount of pamphlets for visitors, they are cheerful and helpful. The best map of the city is put out by the Direcion General de Turismo y Promocion Economica and costs 50¢. It is available at the tourist office. In the event of an emergency, call their 24-hour hotline, ☎ 55-250-0123 or 800-903-9200.

The **post office**, *Independencia and V. Carranza, two blocks west of the central plaza*, is open Monday to Friday, 8 am-6 pm, Saturday, 9 am-2 pm.

Hospital Mexico Americano, *is on Colomos # 2110,* ☎ *333-641-3141.*

The **IAMAT Center**, *is at Francisco Zarco #2345,* ☎ *333-615-9542.*

Police. *For emergencies,* ☎ *060; for non-emergencies,* ☎ *333-617-6060.* You'll spot numerous police on bicycles around the tourist areas and they are always willing to help or give directions. Many speak a little bit of English.

Publications

The Colony Reporter, www.guadalajarareporter.com, is an English-language newspaper that has national and regional news, plus arts and entertainment, restaurant reviews, history, education and sports. They are available at any newsstand for 50¢. You can also subscribe from overseas from between $30 and $45 per year, depending on where you live.

■ History

 Guadalajara was first located where the villages of Nochistlan and then Zacatecas still stand. After repeated attacks by the Caxcan and Coca Indians, who were living in the area at the time, it was moved to its present site. The move is credited to Beatriz Hernandez, who, along with 60 other Spanish settlers, resettled in the Atemajac Valley. When there were other attacks in the Atemajac Valley, the settlers fought back and won. There is a commemorative monument of Beatriz on one side of the Degollado Theatre on the main plaza in the city.

■ Sightseeing

 Before doing anything in Guadalajara, get on a horse-drawn wagon and take a tour. The wagons are parked along the plazas downtown. Usually, the drivers speak some English and will give you a running commentary about the city for about $10 per hour.

The historical center has a collection of plazas between Hidalgo and Morelos streets. Plaza de los Fundadores is at the east end and Plaza Laureles is at the west end. The plazas form a Latin cross with the cathedral (built in 1616) at the center. The original 14 blocks of arched buildings around the plazas have increased to 30 since the city was first established.

Plaza Tapatia, the center of activity and tourism, can hold up to 15,000 spectators. The plaza is seven blocks long and crosses over Av Independencia at the east end. Degollado Theatre is on this plaza.

The Plaza de la Liberacion is between the cathedral and the Degollado Theatre. This plaza was originally called the Plaza de Las Dos Copas (Plaza of the Two Urns) because of the urn-like fountains in its center. That area also features a statue of Miguel Hidalgo, who helped liberate the Mexican people from slavery under the Spanish.

Plaza de Armas, across from Government House, has a bandstand that was brought from France when Mexico celebrated 100 years of independence. Band music is played there every Thursday and Sunday at dusk.

Plaza de Armas.

Plaza de los Laureles is what used to be the courtyard of the cathedral. Now, it has a fountain with the city's coat of arms. Opposite the museum on the north side of the cathedral is the Rotunda of Illustrious Jalisciences, a mausoleum that holds historical characters from Jalisco's past.

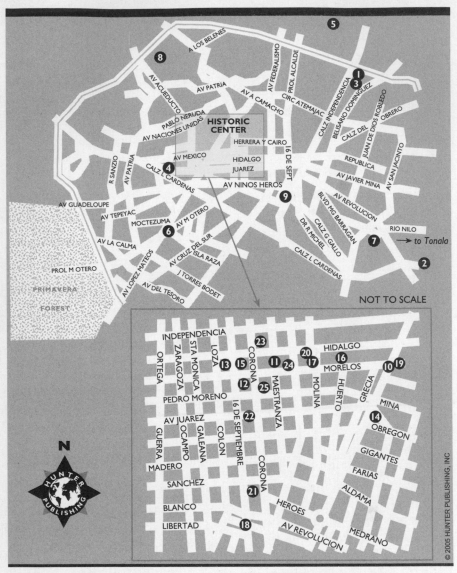

Guadalajara ~ Sights & Attractions

1. Zoo
2. Bus Station
3. Selva Magica
4. Museum of Art
5. La Barranca Oblatos
6. Los Arcos de Milenio
7. Telaquepaque
8. Zapopan
9. Agua Azul Park, Archeological Museum
10. Plaza Tapatia
11. Plaza de la Liberacion
12. Plaza de Armas
13. Plaza de los Laureles
14. Plaza de los Mariachis
15. Cathedral
16. Tourist Office
17. Theatre Degollado
18. Public Library
19. Cabañas Cultural Institute
20. St. Augustine Church
21. Plaza San Francisco
22. Exconvento del Carmen
23. Regional Museum
24. Museum de Cera, Ripley's Belive It or Not
25. Palacio Gobierno (Govt. House)

Plaza de los Mariachis starts at the San Juan de Dios Church and is one block long. It forms the top of the cross. Originally it was called the Plaza Pepe Guizar in honor of the composer who wrote the song *Guadalajara*. And, true to its name, you can often hear mariachi music being played here.

The Cathedral, in the center of the plazas, is not the original cathedral built in the city. The original did not have the two towers. In 1818 an earthquake devastated the first building and, when it was rebuilt, the towers were included. Built of gray stone, the church appears austere. However, the fine gothic ceiling, the elaborate arches and the stained-glass windows soften the austerity. The cathedral is dedicated to the Virgin of the Assumption. A painting inside by Bartoleme Esteban Murillo shows the Virgin going to heaven and is an example of colonial art. There is also a 200-year-old organ that is still being played. An image of Nuestra Señora de la Rosa, carved from a single piece of balsam, is also in the church. The carving was given to Mexico as a gift by Carlos V of Spain in 1548.

The Ministry of Tourism is housed in one of the mansions that originally belonged to Juan Saldivar, a settler with means during colonial times. Inside the courtyard are an attractive fountain and a well-preserved colonnade.

Theatre Degollado, a monumental structure with Greek columns and frieze over the portal, was built in 1856. In front of the theater is a fountain and to the side is the monument to the founding mother of Guadalajara, Beatriz Hernandez, holding up the flag of Mexico. Behind the theater is another frieze that is at ground level, which allows for better inspection. It depicts the day of February 14, 1542, when the Spanish won the battle for the Atemajac Valley. It is called El Friso de los Fundadores.

Today, the theater is home to the Jalisco Philharmonic Orchestra and the University of Guadalajara's Folk Ballet. If there is a concert performing while you are here, get a ticket from the tourist office, ☎ 333-614-0123.

Plaza de Armas features a fountain and the **Palacio de Gobierno** or government house, built in the 18th century. It now houses the state's legislature. The mural in the central stairway is by the famous painter José Clemente Orozco, who lived from 1883 to 1949. Orozco is considered one of the three great muralists of the last century. (The other two are Siqueiros, whose characters take on a similar appearance to Orozco's, and Diego Rivera, who did the intricate and sardonic murals that are in the Government House in Mexico City.) Orozco was influenced by Rivera and, in turn, influenced painters such as Jackson Pollock, Rupert Garcia and Leonard Baskin.

FACT FILE: Plaza de Armas is where Hidalgo made a speech in 1810 to abolish slavery.

Public Library, *Av 16 de Septiembre # 849,* ☎ *333-619-0480, Monday to Friday, 8 am-8 pm, and Saturday, 9 am-5 pm.* This library holds over 200,000 volumes from as far back as the 1500s. It is the oldest library in Western Mexico and is a pleasure to visit.

Cabañas Cultural Institute, *Hospicio #8, Plaza Tapatia,* ☎ *333-617-6734, Tuesday to Saturday, 10:15 am-8:30 pm, Sunday until 2:45 pm.* Constructed in the 18th century, the building has 23 interior patios and a domed chapel. Originally, this was an orphanage and named after the man who started it, Bishop Ruiz de Cabañas y Crespo. The dome of the chapel has a mural by Orozco called "The Man of Fire," which is considered one of the most important murals in the world.

SPIRITUAL ADVENTURES

Tarot Card Readings, *Casa de la Sra. Consuelo #248,* ☎ *333-658-6104,* is open for private consultations Monday to Saturday, 9 am-9 pm. The reader has 20 years' experience and will tell you about your love life, give you advice on your job, or confer with the dead. She can even help you with impotency. Such a deal!

San Agustin Church, *on the side of the Degollado Theatre,* was constructed in the late 16th century. It started as a convent, but now houses the music school of Guadalajara.

San Francisco Plaza, *Av Juarez and Av 16 de Septiembre, just a few blocks from the center*, features the San Francisco Church, which has three baroque-style sections. Walking around the outside of this church takes a long time if you want to see all the statues and carvings. Next to San Francisco is the Aranzazu Temple, built in the style of the mission churches with three distinct bells framed into one tower. Inside the church are religious artworks, including three baroque altar pieces, the only ones of their kind in the city.

Exconvento del Carmen (an ex-convent), *Av Juarez*, is a block up from San Francisco Plaza. No longer a convent, the building has been taken over by the arts community and now has plays, literary workshops, movies and visual art exhibitions. There is no entry fee. Stop by the tourist office for a schedule.

The Zoo, *Paseo del Zoologico #600,* ☎ *333-674-4488, Wednesday to Sunday, 10 am-6 pm, $3.* This place is so big (100 acres) that a tram is available to carry you from site to site. There are 360 species of animals here. The main attractions are the aviary, located in a double pyramid-styled building, the herpetarium that has 130 species of reptiles, spiders, scorpions, fish and amphibians. A night zoo houses nocturnal animals.

Selva Magica, *next to the zoo, open daily, 10 am-6 pm, and weekends until 8 pm, $1.* This theme park has about 35 different rides, including a wild roller coaster. Your entrance fee includes a dolphin show.

On the other side of the zoo is the **Planetarium**, ☎ *333-674-4106,* that has airplane exhibits along with space and astrological displays. See next page for details.

Museums

Regional Museum of Guadalajara, *Liceo # 60, on the main plaza,* ☎ *333-614-5257, Tuesday to Saturday, 9 am-5:45 pm, $3.* Originally the building was the San José Seminary, built in the late 1600s. It has been used as a seminary, a garrison, a men's college and, since 1918, a museum. The museum is divided into sections depicting different periods. The Paleontology Hall has fossils, including those of a huge mastodon complete with tusks. Another section features modern art.

Paleontological Museum of Federico Solozano, *Av DR Michel #520,* ☎ *333-619-7043, Tuesday to Saturday, 10 am-6 pm, Sunday, 11 am-6 pm. The cost is $1 to enter the museum and $2 for entry to the museum and Agua Azul Park next door.* The museum holds a collection of plant and animal fossils in seven different salons. All exhibition halls contain permanent collections, except for one. The main focus around the displays is the importance of preserving these items for the purpose of science. The exhibits are placed in cases on the floor in some rooms and you walk *above* them to have a good look. Guided tours are offered every day at 10 am, noon and 4 pm on weekdays, and at 11 am, 12:30 and 4:30 pm on weekends. A lot of money has been spent on this museum and it is well worth visiting. There is a café in the building and parking at the back.

Archeological Museum, *Av 16 de Septiembre #889,* ☎ *333-619-0104, Tuesday to Friday and Sunday, 10 am-2 pm and 5 pm-7 pm, 50¢.* This museum has objects from the Jalisco, Colima and Nayarit states. Some of the silver and gold items are exceptional in their craftsmanship.

Museum of Arts, *Av Juarez # 975, Tuesday to Saturday, 9 am-6 pm, Sunday, noon-6 pm, no entrance fee.* This building was the original University of Guadalajara. One of the contemporary showpieces is a mural by José Clemente Orozco. The artwork is well displayed and has good lighting.

Museum de Cera (Wax Museum) and **Ripley's Believe It or Not Museum**, *Av Morelos #215,* ☎ *333-614-8487, every day, 11 am-8 pm. Adults pay $5 for both museums, $3 for the wax museum only; children pay $2 for both museums and $1 for the wax.* The wax museum has historical figures, actors both national and international, and famous sports figures.

The Ripley museum has an eclectic collection of items from around the country. There is a souvenir shop inside.

Planetarium/Museum of Science and Technology, *Periferico North # 401,* ☎ *333-674-3978, Tuesday to Sunday, 9 am-7:30 pm, 50¢.* The Severo Diaz Galindo Planetarium is named after Jalisco's first astronomer. There are three areas to the museum; the planetarium, the astronomy hall and the scientific exhibitions. This is a hands-on museum where you can do things like make your hair stand on end.

▪ Adventures on Foot

Hiking

 La Barranca Oblatos canyon is in the Zapopan area of the city, along the Guadalajara/Saltillo Highway. To get here, follow the signs to Tonala-Matatlan and travel along Calle Belisario Dominguez. It ends at the canyon. The area opens at 6 am and closes at 7 pm daily. There is a parking lot (50¢ an hour) at the trailhead.

There are three viewpoints along the canyon. From Huentitan Lookout you can see where the Verde and Santiago rivers merge. Independence Lookout stands over the canyon and gives the best views of its depth. The canyon walls drop 1,900 feet/630 meters to the rivers below. The third viewpoint is the Dr. Atl Lookout, which overlooks Cola de Caballo Falls (Horsetail Falls) that drop about 300 feet/100 meters into the canyon. There are interpretive signs along the trails going around the area and a steep, bricked pathway leading into the canyon. Remember that if you go down, you have to come back up again. There are picnic sites along the rivers.

 FACT FILE: El Arcediano suspension bridge, which spans the rivers, was part of the original route into Guadalajara from Mexico City up until 1893.

La Barranca Oblatos was declared an ecological preserve in 1993 and covers an area of 2,842 acres. An estimated 5,000 visitors run down into the canyon and back each week for exercise. There is a hydroelectric plant at the site and a hotel in the canyon called Casa Colorada. However, I know nothing about the hotel.

Golf

Atlas Golf Club, *Km. 6.5 on the Chapala/El Salto Highway,* ☎ *333-689-2783,* is an 18-hole, par 72 course with 7,204 yards, designed by Joe Finger. Weekday fees are $25 for 18 holes, on weekends you pay $45. Caddies are required and cost $7. Carts are available. For an additional $10 you can use the sauna, steam bath, pool and showers. There is a restaurant on site.

Santa Anita Golf Club, *Km. 65 on the Guadalajara/Morelia Highway,* ☎ *333-686-0962,* is an 18-hole course designed by Larry Hughes. It costs $21 for nine holes during the week and $29 for 18 holes. On weekends and holidays 18 holes costs $45. Caddies are required and cost $7. The restaurant here is accessible to nonmembers, but you must be "recommended" by one of the five-star hotels in town before you are allowed to play.

Guadalajara Country Club, *Mar Caribe #2615,* ☎ *333-817-2858,* was designed by John Bredemus. There are 18 holes on this par 72, 6,821-yard classic-styled course. Green fees are $65 and caddies cost $10. The course, and its clubhouse, are open to visitors.

■ Adventures in the Suburbs

Los Arcos del Milenio (Millennium Arches), *Av Mariano Otero and Av Lazaro Cardenas,* is an impressive structure consisting of six arches designed by Julio Chavez Sanchez Sebastian, a famous Mexican sculptor. The arches cover 183,000 square feet/17,000 square meters, took 1,500 tons of metal to make and stand 150 feet/52 meters high.

FACT FILE: Sebastian also created the Door to Chihuahua in the city of Chihuahua and the Horse's Head in Mexico City.

Tlaquepaque

Tlaquepaque is the handicraft and art center of Mexico and has been a shopping/trading area since the Tonallan Kingdom ruled this part of the world. Today, the streets are lined with shops selling every art or craft ever made in Mexico. Some are of very high quality. But shopping isn't all you can do here. Visit **The Pottery Museum**, *Independencia #237,* ☎ *333-635-5404, Tuesday to Saturday, 10 am-4 pm, and Sunday until 1 pm, free.* Housed in a colonial mansion, the museum has been exhibiting art since 1954. Of special interest are the miniatures and elaborately designed pre-Hispanic pieces. The kitchen is also worth visiting. It has one wall decorated with traditional coffee cups.

PETATILLO

The Petatillo style of painting on ceramic pieces is a crosshatch design that looks like long strands of metal woven together. This design is difficult to achieve and has been used by artists for several generations.

The **Pantaleon Panduro Museum**, *Sanchez # 91,* ☎ *333-635-1089, Tuesday to Sunday, 10 am-6 pm, free*, displays the best pieces of pottery produced in the country for that year. There are contemporary and antique designs and some miniatures.

The central plaza will lead you to **El Parian**, a building with a food court where you can get just about anything to eat. From the plaza, continue on to the **Refugio**, *Donato Guerra # 160,* a cultural center that was once an asylum for women. It has been renovated and turned into a collection of chapels and singing rooms.

Walking between Tlaquepaque and Tonala you will pass some old mansions built before the 1900s.

To get to Tlaquepaque from either the bus station or the airport, take a taxi or city bus marked *Tlaquepaque*.

Tonala

Tonala, now an extension of Tlaquepaque, is the pottery center of the country. The word *Tonala* comes from the local Indian language and means the Place of the Sun. When the Spanish arrived, the village was governed by Atzahuapili, a queen who was known to keep numerous jewelers who designed elaborate pieces for her. Today, the area still has fine jewelry shops, but it has switched its focus mainly to ceramics.

There are about 400 shops in the area supporting artists who do both high- and low-temperature pottery. They also work with iron, stone, brass, copper, marble, papier mâché, textiles and glass. Some of the more interesting items are miniatures. Market days are Thursday and Sunday, when temporary stalls display food, herbal medicines and crafts, and magicians and street buskers offer entertainment.

▶▶ **AUTHOR NOTE:** *You may find shopping during non-market days easier, as there are fewer people.*

Visit the **Museum Nacional de Ceramica**, *Constitución #104,* ☎ *333-683-0494, Tuesday to Friday, 10 am-5 pm, and weekends, 10 am-2 pm.* There is no charge to enter but you must pay $8.50 for the use of a camera. The museum, housed in a colonial mansion, displays ceramics and pottery from around the state. There are hundreds of shops from which to purchase items made in Tlaquepaque and Tonala. For an overview, visit www.mexweb.com/tonala2.htm.

Zapopan

Zapopan is five miles/eight km northwest of the city center. To get here, follow Av Calzada Avila Camacho to Zapopan suburb, recognized by an ancient and decorative arch at its entrance. The walkway inside the arch, Paseo Teopiltzintli, is lined with bars, restaurants, gardens, fountains and shops. Continue along the *paseo* to Plaza de las Americas and the **Virgen de Zapopan Bascilica**, built in 1730 and now the largest pilgrimage site in Mexico. Every spring at the beginning of rainy season (March), the village becomes a hub for the pilgrims. At that time, the Virgin of Zapopan, a tiny image carved from corn-husk paste, is taken out of the Basilica to visit 130 parishes in the city. She is supposed to offer protection from rains and floods. On October 12th, when her tour is over, she is taken back to rest for the winter. About a million people welcome her back. After she is safely tucked away, the people enjoy a festival in the courtyard. The devotions to the virgin started when the original church collapsed in 1606, destroying everything but her. Besides her protection to the parishes, she also protects Guadalajara from lighting, plagues and storms.

Next to the Basicilica is the **Huichol Art Museum**, ☎ *333-636-4430, Monday to Saturday, 9:30 am-1:30 pm and 3:30-6 pm, Sunday, 10 am-2 pm.* A "must stop" if in the area. The art is done on shirts, knapsacks, pants, skirts, rings, necklaces and masks. Like petit point, the intricacy of the beadwork is amazing. Also nearby is the **Albarran Hunting Museum**, Paseo de los Parques #3540. It costs $2 to enter. The house looks like it was constructed in Africa and is stuffed with 270 animals that were killed by Benito Albarran, the original owner of the house. He traveled to five continents to get the animals.

Rodeos and Bullfights, *Plaza de Toros Nuevo Progresso, Av R. Michel # 577,* ☎ *619-0315,* has bullfights on Sundays between October and March. They start about 4:30 pm and cost $8-$15 to enter, depending on the seat (those in the sun are cheaper). They also have a two-hour rodeo show that starts every Sunday at noon. Across the street is the **Jalisco Stadium**, where football (soccer) games are played. See the tourist office in the center of town for game schedules.

■ Adventures in Nature

Parque Agua Azul, *Calz. Independencia Sur between Gonzalez Gallo and Las Palmas (you can also enter from Av. Dr Michel), $2 to enter the park and museum; $1 to enter the park only.* This is the most popular park in town. Located next to the Archaeological Museum in the southern section of the city, it has two areas connected by a bridge. A lush green section has a tree-lined walkway, called Avenue of the Musicians, with gardens on each side. Along here are benches and tables, as well as food vendors. But the most interesting things are on the other side of the bridge. They are the butterfly house, the orchid house, the solarium and the aviary. Guided tours are available hourly at the butterfly house. There is also the Concha Acustica, an outdoor stage where cultural shows are held. Ask at the tourist office on the main square in town about events.

Primavera Forest, *Km 20 on Highway 15*, is on the way to Tepic/Puerto Vallarta, before the tollbooth where the toll highway begins. The park has 154 square miles/400 square km of forest with picnic tables and walking/cycling paths. Birding is good here. There is a hot spring just over the hill from the park (you will see signs). The spring is on privately owned land and the owners charge to enter. To get here, pass the country clubs of Rancho Contento and Pinar de la Venta on Highway 15 (the road to Tepic/Puerto Vallarta). This is where the toll road begins. Watch for signs indicating the *Canon de las Flores* and *Ejido La Primavera*. This is where you turn and follow the signs to the site.

■ Adventures of the Brain

Español Para Todos, *Torres Quintero # 39*, ☎ *333-364-0897*, *www.espanolparatodos.com.mx*, offers all levels of language school with either a private tutor or group lessons. There are classes for beginners, business needs, advanced grammar or Latin American literature. The classes are for two hours a day, five days a week, and cost $150 per month. Private lessons cost $8 an hour. Studying literature, culture and the arts is $75 a month.

■ Outfitters/Tour Operators

During my visit, few tourist agencies could make arrangements for hiking, biking, rafting or birding excursions. Most seem to sell tickets to other places and book expensive hotels. You are mostly on your own to explore.

Andale Mexico, ☎ *442-212-2899*, *www.andalemexico.com/tour_tqexp. htm*, an Internet travel agency in Queretaro, offers a trip on the Tequila Express that runs to Tequila and Amatitan. It starts in Guadalajara and covers the tequila tour plus two nights in a hotel for $300.

Casas Tours, *Av Niños Heroes 22-C*, ☎ *333-657-8970*, *casatour@elturista.com*, can book tickets, hotels and tours around the country.

Convisa, *Av 16 de Septiembre #730-B,* ☎ *333-614-8228, convisa@prodigy.net.mx,* is downtown and can make all the usual plane or bus transportation arrangements.

■ Day Trips

The village of **Tequila**, at the foot of Tequila Volcano, can be reached by taking a bus from the old bus station or by taking a tour on the Tequila Express (see next page). The village of Tequila is classified as the "denomination of origin," meaning it is recognized internationally as the place that originally discovered tequila.

The volcanic soil deposited during eruptions makes the ground here (along with the ground in Amatitan, just down the road) perfect for growing the blue agave plant that is used in making tequila.

AGILE AGAVE

The mescal, or agave azul, is a cactus-like plant that is used to produce tequila, vinegar and sugar. Its leaves are also used for roofing and the stalks are used as construction beams. Threads pulled from the leaves are used for sewing and the spines can be used as nails. Once the plant has been cooked, it can be pressed into bricks.

If touring on your own, take a bus (or drive on the highway toward PV) from the old bus station and get off at **Arenal**, 45 km/30 mi from Guadalajara. Along the way you will see agave in the fields. In Arenal, go to the **Hacienda de la Providencia** (ask directions or follow the signs). The hacienda has been producing tequila for more than 100 years. Tours of the still and the colonial hacienda, decorated in period furniture, are available. From Arenal, take a local bus to **Amatitan** just six miles/nine km farther, where you will find the **Hacienda de San José del Refugio** that has been producing tequila since 1870. This is a mule-driven mill. After seeing the still, you will be taken into the cellars where the fermentation vats are sunk into the floor. This is the most unusual of the three distilleries along this route and really worth the stop. A factory in town, next to the Pemex station, produces handmade oak casks and barrels for the tequila industry. You can purchase a decorative cask that has side arms on it where tequila glasses can sit. After visiting Amatitan, catch another bus to Tequila, where you can again visit a tequila factory, (there are dozens from which to choose), have another taste of the sacred brew and hope that you can make it back to your hotel in Guadalajara. Tequila has the **Tequila Sauza Museum** on the town square. Inside is a mural that is reminiscent of Hogarth's Gin Mill. This one depicts the effects of tequila, rather than gin, on the general population. Just beyond the city you will see **Tequila Volcano** (9,500 feet/3,000 meters above sea level).

TEQUILA TWO-STEP

It takes eight to 10 years for the plant to grow to maturity. Once the heads, called cones, are ripe, they are picked and heated in ovens for 24 hours, then cooled for another 24 hours. The next step requires the cones to be ground, so the juice can be extracted. The juice is left in tanks for 72 to 96 hours. It is then distilled and left to age, which can take anywhere from a few months to several years.

To travel from one community to the next, take local third-class buses (they run every half-hour) from each village center about. If you find the tequila has gotten ahold of you, there is a private sanitarium in Tlaquepaque where you can get a very comfortable cure.

The **Tequila Express**, ☎ *333-880-9099, runs every Saturday (register by 10 am; the train leaves by 10:30 am), $55 for a return trip to Tequila.* It leaves from the Ferrocaril Mexicano Station, Camara National de Comercio for this full-day adventure. As you wait at the train station with your ticket in hand, a mariachi band will play for you. On the train, you can start your consumption of tequila or local beer. The train has reclining seats, tray tables and air conditioning. After a short time traveling, you will be served some vegetables and fruit. Once in the village of Tequila, you will be taken to the museum, located in a colonial house that once belonged to a tequila baron. It features harvesting implements, wooden carts and a collection of bottles. From there you go to the factory and actually see the production firsthand. The final stage of the tour includes a true Mexican fiesta, where you can eat traditional Mexican food served as a buffet. Back on the train (about 6 pm) the party continues with more mariachi and dancing in the aisles. By the time you're in Guadalajara, you will be ready for bed.

■ Shopping

Everyone comes to Guadalajara to shop for authentic high-quality art. The places to shop are mainly in the art centers of **Tlaquepaque** (see page 299) and **Tonala** (page 300). I have recommended a few other places in the city, but I also suggest you mainly walk the streets and see what appeals to you.

The enormous **Libertad Market** in the central square, is also called the San Juan de Dios Market. This spot has always been a market, even before the Spanish settled in the city. It sells mainly produce and items for

Guadalajara has some bustling market places.

use in the home, but tourists will also be able to find numerous handicrafts.

Omar Centeno, *Av Vallarta # 1075*, ☎ *333-827-1497*, sells high-quality fine art. Some of the bronze workings are magnificent (and expensive).

Handicraft House, *Calzada Gonzalez Gallo #20*, ☎ *333-619-1369, Monday to Friday, 10 am-4 pm, Saturday until 5 pm, Sunday until 3 pm*. Handicraft House features art from around the state, including over 2,000 ceramic pieces designed by Roberto Montenegro. There is also an exquisite collection of blown glass and metal handicrafts.

Artesanias Arzola, *Juarez #286*, ☎ *333-683-3761, or Fco. Madero #197*, ☎ *333-683-0134*, has unique articles such as frames, candlestick holders and birdcages (used to hold incense). They are made from gold, silver or copper.

Art V, *Av Tonala #273-A*, ☎ *333-683-5570*. If you are searching for hand-painted glass, this is one of the better shops. They bake their painted glass at 1500°F/800°C to ensure longevity. Numerous items sold here include party glasses, decorative glass chests and glass masks.

■ Places to Stay

Hotels are spread all over the city. There is one at the new bus station and many motels along the highway into town, but they are a long way from the center. If you have a car, they may be an option. Go to one that has off-street parking and use public transportation from there. The one hotel by the bus station is rather expensive, but if you are catching a bus early the following morning, it works out costing about the same as staying in town and catching a taxi both ways.

HOTEL PRICE SCALE
Price for a room given in US $.
$.................Up to $20
$$..................$21-$50
$$$...............$51-$100
$$$$ ....$101-$150
$$$$$ ....$151-$200
Anything over $200 is specified.

Hotels around the old bus station in town are numerous and cheap. The Royal is an example of what you will get.

Hotel Royal, *Los Angeles #115 at Reforma*, ☎ *333-619-8473, $,* is fairly clean. The rooms have color TVs, fans and hot water all day. If you take a room with two beds good for four people, the cost is just $20. This is a family-run establishment.

Guadalajara Hostel, *Maestranza #147*, ☎ *333-562-7520, www. hostelguadalajara.com, $,* is in the center just off the plaza and located in a building built in the 1800s. The hostel has 30 beds and is secure. There is hot water in the bathrooms, full kitchen facilities, lockers (bring your own lock), Internet access, a games room and laundry service. However, if sharing a room, it may be cheaper for you to stay at other hotels such as the Sevilla.

Hotel Seville, *Calle Prisciliano Sanchez #413*, ☎ *333-614-9172, $$,* is a three-star hotel that offers a double for just $22. Rooms are clean, although a few are not overly big. There are fans, TV, lots of hot water, fluffy towels and even a shower curtain in the tiled bathroom. The bedrooms are partially tiled and carpeted and each room has a closet and desk. The hotel personnel speak some English. There is parking available and a restaurant.

Hotel San Francisco Plaza, *Degollado #267*, ☎ *333-613-3256, $$,* is located in the center near the Degollado Theatre. This colonial house has 76 renovated rooms that are comfortable, but not plush. They are set around three inner courtyards. The biggest draw for this price range is the central location.

Posada San Rafael, *Lopez Cotilla # 619*, ☎ *333-614-9146, $$,* is a restored historical hacienda in the center of town. The 12 big rooms are comfortable and set around a central courtyard. The front door is always locked and kitchen facilities are available for those staying longer than a few days. There is air conditioning and the bathrooms are tiled and have hot water. I love this place. The staff is friendly and there is Internet access for a small fee.

Hotel Frances, *Maestranza # 35*, ☎ *333-613-1190, $$$*, is an elegant hotel with a historic past. The building, 375 years old, has always been a hotel. The entrance has a marble fountain and the inner courtyard is surrounded by arches held up by classical columns. The center of the courtyard has an enormous gilt chandelier and a wide stairway leading to the upper levels, where the rooms are located. When the building was remodeled in 1981, it was declared a national monument by the Governor of the state. Back in 1610 when the hotel was built it was called the Mezon de San José and provided short-term shelter for traders traveling from the northwest of Mexico to Mexico City. During renovations many of the early items were preserved. For example, what looks like garbage bins are actually troughs used to feed horses. In more recent years, the hotel was chosen as the site to film scenes for the movie *The Evil that Men Do*, starring Charles Bronson. The movie also has some of the owners in it. No two rooms in the hotel are alike, but the choice ones have a balcony facing the government building across the street. The on-site restaurant has a splendid lunch buffet for $5 per person.

Hotel Colon, *Av Revolucion #12*, ☎ *333-613-3390, $$$*, is a three-star hotel. The clean rooms have a TV, phone, tiled bathroom and carpet in the bedroom. There is a restaurant and front desk service 24 hours a day.

Hotel Nueva Galicia, *Av Corona #610*, ☎ *333-614-8780, $$$*, is a sister hotel to the Colon and is convenient for those wanting to be in the commercial area of the city. The rooms are clean and the English-speaking staff is friendly.

Hotel del Parque, *Av Juarez #845*, ☎ *333-825-2800, $$$*, is close to Plaza Revolucion. The rooms are simple and clean and the staff speaks some English. The big draw to this hotel is its jazz bar, one of the most popular in town.

Casa del Retoño B&B, *Matamoros #182*, ☎ *333-639-6510, $$$*, is in Tlaquepaque. This is an adobe-brick house built in traditional Mexican style. There are eight colorful rooms with private bathroom and tiled floors. The garden is decorated with potted plants and old trees where birds are often seen. Complimentary breakfast consists of juice, coffee, tea, milk, cereal, toast, yogurt and fruit. This is a lovely place.

Hotel Country Plaza, *Av Americas #1170*, ☎ *800-359-7234, $$$*, is close to the country club. It has 119 rooms, some wheelchair-accessible. The rooms are large, some with king-sized beds and sitting areas. They have carpeting, private bathroom, purified water and cable TV. There is a pool, tennis courts, a business center, laundry service, free parking and a casino.

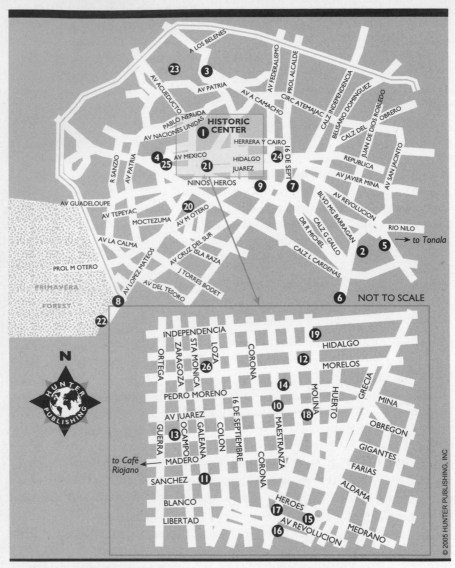

Guadalajara ~ Places to Stay & Eat

1. Hotel Royal
2. Casa del Rotoño
3. Hotel Country Plaza
4. Hotel Plaza los Arcos
5. Villa del Sueño
6. Hotel Casa Grande
7. Hotel Mision
8. Hotel Crown Plaza
9. Holiday Inn
10. Guadalajara Hostel
11. Hotel Sevilla
12. Hotel San Francisco Plaza
13. Posada San Rafael
14. Hotel Francis
15. Hotel Colon
16. Hotel Galecia
17. Hotel Aranzazu
18. Hotel Genova
19. Hotel Mendoza
20. Rincon del Sol Restaurant
21. Hare Krishna Restaurant
22. El Carnal Restaurant
23. Boni's Restaurant
24. Hacienda de Tequila Restaurant
25. La Charla Restaurant
26. Antigua Restaurant

Hotel Aranzazu, *Av Revolucion #110*, ☎ *333-613-3232, $$$*, is a Best Western Hotel. There are 468 rooms on 10 floors. Each has cable TV, a mini-bar, alarm clock, private bathroom, VCR and Internet connection. You have a choice of either two twin beds or one king-sized bed. The hotel has a restaurant, bar, parking, babysitting service, laundry, valet, a spa, pool and tennis courts. The buffet breakfast is expensive. Watch your bill in the restaurant.

Hotel Genova, *Av Juarez # 123*, ☎ *333-613-7500, $$$*, is another Best Western hotel, but much smaller than the Aranzazu. The 185 rooms on seven floors have either two doubles or one king-sized bed, mini-bar, cable TV, coffee maker and Internet connection. There is off-street parking, a restaurant, a beauty parlor, laundry service and a spa. Breakfast is included in the price, as is a welcoming tequila drink on arrival. They also provide a morning newspaper.

Hotel Plaza Los Arcos, *Av Vallarta #2477*, ☎ *333-615-1845, www. magnohotel.com.mx, $$$*, has large but spartan rooms, some with kitchenettes. Rooms are carpeted, and have a private bathroom with purified water, cable TV and a sitting area. Continental breakfast is included. There is private parking available. The hotel is close to the newest shopping mall in Guadalajara and to restaurants, bars, galleries and the Expo center. This hotel is associated with the Magno Hotel Chain.

Villa del Ensueño, *Florida #305*, ☎ *333-635-8792, $$$ / $$$$*, is located in Tlaquepaque. It is a first-class hotel/B&B with 18 large modern rooms/suites surrounding a central courtyard that has a heated pool, potted plants and deck furniture. There is a second pool indoors. The rooms are furnished with solid wood furniture and have open beam ceilings, fans, good lighting and tiled floors. The entire hotel is hospital clean. Internet service and off-street parking are available.

De Mendoza Hotel, *Av Carranza #16*, ☎ *333-614-2621, $$$$*, is a colonial building in the heart of the historical area. Each large room has a sitting area, air conditioning, cable TV, carpet, open beam ceiling, private bathroom, mini-bar and heavy wood furnishings. There is a pool, restaurant, bar, travel agent and off-street parking. The staff speaks English.

Hotel Casa Grande, *International Airport*, ☎ *333-678-9001 or 888-306-2487, www.casagrande.com.mx, $$$$*, has large carpeted rooms with private bathrooms, night tables with reading lights and sitting areas. There is a pool, a fitness center, a restaurant (7 am-1 am), a bar (5 pm-1 pm) and a business center.

Hotel Mision Carlton, *Av Niños #125*, ☎ *333--614-7272, $$$$*, has rooms with air conditioning, cable TV, private, tiled bathroom and a telephone. There is a restaurant, laundry service, a babysitting service, a pool, off-street parking, a bar, a barber shop and a business center.

Hotel Crown Plaza, *Av Lopez Mateos Sur #2500*, ☎ *333-634-1034, $$$$/$$$$$*, has almost 300 rooms on eight floors. All have private bathroom, air conditioning, comfortable beds and a sitting area. The well-tended grounds have a pool, a children's play area and two tennis courts. There is a gym, a beauty salon, massage service, a bar, a restaurant and babysitting service. The hotel also has free parking, an airport shuttle and even a kennel for Rover. The only drawback is the distance from the center of town. It is too far to walk. I sent my husband, John, out to pace the distance, but after two days of walking he gave up and returned to me by cab.

Holiday Inn, *Av Niños Heroes #3-89*, ☎ *333-622-2020 or 800-364-7700, www.selectgdl.com.mx, $$$$$*, is like any Holiday Inn found around the world. The rooms have a private bathroom, air conditioning (or heat, if need be), a table and a chair. There is a rooftop pool and a restaurant on site. There are special prices during off-season, but even these are international prices rather than Mexican ones. The service is good and the staff is helpful. Most speak some English.

■ Places to Eat

The people of Jalisco are especially proud of their food. If you see some of the items listed below on the menu be certain to try them.

JALSICO SPECIALTIES

- *Tortas ahogadas* is a meat-stuffed roll covered in a hot chili sauce.
- *Birria* is a spicy meat stew.
- *Menundo* is a dish made with tripe.
- *Pozole* is a corn-based soup.
- *Charales* are tiny fried fish.
- *Jejuino* is the traditional sour-sweet, non-alcoholic drink.

Antigua Restaurant, *Morelos #371*, ☎ *333-614-0648*, is open 8 am-10 pm daily, and on Friday and Saturday it stays open until midnight. This building was constructed in 1802 by a member of the Calzado family and is still owned by them. In 1802 the area that is now used as a restaurant was the Library of Santisima Trinidad (Holy Trinity). The family started a pastry shop in the rooms next to the library. It became popular and, eventually, expanded into a restaurant. Pastry is still their specialty. Antigua offers an excellent breakfast buffet for $5.80. The scrambled eggs have a unique spice added for flavor. Their evening specialty is *arrachera tapatia*, a spicy beef dish that is filling. Also good is the chicken Cordon Bleu (azul). The bar has live music on weekends.

Rincon del Sol, *Av 16 de Septiembre #61*, ☎ *333-683-1989*, specializes in Mexican food. The chilies in walnut sauce or mutton with seafood are the best dishes. A moderate-sized serving costs about $12. The food is always nicely presented.

Hare Krishna, *Pedro Moreno #1791*, ☎ *333-616-0775*, is a vegetarian restaurant that serves Indian cuisine. Their food is delicious, but I often have a hard time finding the restaurant open. Phone before you go.

Productos El Jardin, *Av La Paz # 1558*, ☎ *333-825-6885*, is a vegetarian restaurant that has an à-la-carte menu and a buffet. The cost for the buffet is $8. Drinks are extra.

El Carnal, *Av Lopez Mateos Sur # 6160, no phone*, is open every day from 10 am-7 pm. The restaurant specializes in seafood and their best meals are made with huge shrimp or lobster. The special Jalisco dish is *charales* (see above) and they also have the best ceviche in town. Unintrusive live music plays and there's an activity area for children. The off-street parking is a draw for those driving.

Boni's, *Av de las Rosas #543*, ☎ *333-647-2551*, in Zapopan, is a new-wave place that offers many vegetarian dishes. The cost is a tad expensive – around $9 for a large salad.

Hacienda de Tequila, *Av Hidalgo #1749*, ☎ *333-630-5090*, is a block from Av Las Americas. If you haven't had enough steak and tequila, then maybe you need to come here. They use Angus beef and their tequila is never watered down as it is in many bars in Mexico, especially the establishments that charge lower prices. The atmosphere is comfortable and quiet. A perfectly cooked steak costs $12.

Café Riojano, *Av 8 de Julio #164, between Cotilla and Madero*, ☎ *333-820-3323, bullyfo@yahoo.com.mx*, is a tiny place that offers delicious coffee and cake. This is a good midday hangout. An espresso is $1 and a latté is $1.50. If you want something sweet, try a chocolate soda.

Restaurant Chez Pierre, *Av España #2095*, ☎ *333-615-2212*, is open Monday to Saturday, from 1 pm-1 am. The restaurant, which has been in business for 32 years, offers first-class French cuisine cooked by famous chef Pierre Pelech. The best meal is the oysters and roast duck ($14). But no matter what you try, it will be good. The French like to take hours to enjoy a meal – plan to do the same when you come here. If in Guadalajara during Christmas, the meal served after midnight Mass is always exceptional. For this you must book in advance.

Unico Restaurant Folklorico, *Av Lopez Mateos Sur #4521*, ☎ *333-632-9222*, is open Tuesday to Saturday from 4 pm-1 am for meals and during holidays, until 3 am for music and dancing. This is a good spot for first-class Mexican food and entertainment. The Folklorica shows are at 4 and 9:30 pm, Tuesday to Saturday. There is valet parking until 1 am.

Genghis Khan, *Av Mariano Otero #1499,* ☎ *333-671-0130*, opens daily for supper at 5 pm. It is a large Mongolian-style restaurant with brass urns and shields that lend an exotic atmosphere (although they have given in to their conquerors and now serve Chinese food). Prices are somewhat high. A meal of sweet and sour meat costs $9 per serving.

Il Magazzino Café and Bar, *Av Manuel Acuña #2938,* ☎ *333-641-9775*, is an Italian restaurant that serves pastas, pizzas, fish and barbequed steaks. One of these dishes, with a bottle of imported wine, will run $25.

La Charla, *Av Vallarta # 1095,* ☎ *333-825-0393,* is open daily for breakfast. A full plate of *huevos rancheros* and toast costs less than $7. This is a very clean place set in a trendy part of town.

▪ Nightlife

 Don't stay out late in Guadalajara, as the city transforms itself from an interesting historical center in the day to a rowdy, brawling zone at night. Even in the quiet areas, beer bottles seem to fly out of windows and drunks take pleasure in sleeping along your walkway. If you want some entertainment, go to the bar in your hotel or plan on taking a taxi everywhere.

Alcatraz Prison Bar, *Marcos Castellanos # 114-Z,* ☎ *333-826-5886,* is a lively drinking joint/eatery that attracts locals wanting to drown their sorrows with lots of booze and loud music. However, I found it to be fun.

Peña Cuicacalli, *Av Niños Heroes #1988,* starts their live entertainment at 8 pm; a second show starts at 9 pm. They bring in artists from around the country for the shows. If you want to have a meal here, reservations are highly recommended.

Laguna Chapala

Chapala Lake, the largest natural lake in Mexico, is about 50 miles/75 km long and 13 miles/20 km wide. Although large in area, the lake is averages only 10 feet/three meters deep and is just 30 feet/10 meters at its deepest. The area is famous for its warm climate and has attracted over 6,000 Canadians and Americans as permanent residents, many of whom are artists. The lake is 30 miles/45 km from Guadalajara, about one hour by bus.

Currently, the lake's water level is low, making the dock and "lakeside" restaurants about a quarter-mile from the shore. The distance is so far

Boat/van takes passengers from the pier to the lakeshore.

that, if you hire a boat to take you around the lake, there is a bus to take you from the end of the pier to the shore of the lake.

Fluctuating water levels are not uncommon, although floods have been more common than droughts. The lake flooded for a few years in the 1940s and receded in the 1950s. It flooded again in the 1980s and is receding now. Since the building of the Maltarana Dyke in the 1950s, fluctuations have become more severe.

LEGISLATIVE LOOPHOLE

A mistake in legislation allowed foreigners to purchase land that was on the waterfront, so many North Americans living at the lake purchased the land they had previously leased. The law was in effect for only three months. Once the government realized what was happening, they changed the law so foreigners could no longer do this. They also cut off water supply to the lake, in the hope that the foreign landowners would sell the property back to Mexicans. A side effect of this move was that it caused the shoreline to recede a long way from business establishments.

LOCAL LINGO: *The word* Chapala *means "Place Soaked in Water," according to some, while others believe it means "Grasshoppers in Water."*

■ Getting Here & Around

 The **bus** to Chapala leaves from the old bus station in Guadalajara. You must pay 5¢ (50 centavos) to enter the bus station (once inside, toilets are free). Buses run once every half-hour between 5:30 am and 9:30 pm. The fare is $3.50 per person, each way.

Buses to other destinations around the lake can be boarded in Chapala, either at the station where the Guadalajara bus arrives, or a little farther up the street.

Lakeside Linea Profesional Rent-A-Car, ☎ *333-766-2555, Monday to Friday, 9 am-4 pm, and Saturday till 1 pm.* A Chevy with five-speed standard transmission costs $48 a day and includes insurance, tax and 155 miles/250 km of driving. For a week, the cost is $280, including unlimited mileage. The same model automatic costs $60 a day. A Nissan Sentra automatic with air conditioning costs $75 a day with 155 miles/250 km each day of free mileage, $450 a week with unlimited mileage. Insurance deductible is 10% of the value of the car in the event of theft and 5% in the event of collision. You are covered for two drivers at no extra charge, as long as each driver has a valid driver's license.

■ History

 Records show that the **Nahuatl Indians** lived in the area as early as the 12th century. Fishing in the lake was good and the climate comfortable. When **Franciscan Friar Antonio Tello** arrived in 1524, he found a large community. He started evangelizing and constructed religious buildings at Chapala and around the lake. Life remained rather isolated except for the religious activity until the 1900s, when elaborate homes started to spring up. Some of the hotels from that time are still operating today. Once the railroad was completed in the 1930s, more people came to settle. The railway made transportation to and from Guadalajara much more comfortable than the horse and buggy method used before. The trip was also nine hours shorter.

■ Services

The **Post office**, *Hidalgo #242B on the road to Ajijic, Monday to Friday, 8:30 am-3 pm, Saturday until 1 pm.*

Municipal Police, *Niños Heroes & Zaragoza*, ☎ *333-765-4444.*

Health Center, *F.R. de Velasco # 406,* ☎ *333-765-2623.*

Publications

El Ojo del Lago is a local newspaper publication in English, free for the visitor and packed with useful information from historical stories to cultural events. The *Lake Chapala Guide*, by Teresa Kendrick, has detailed information about the lake and its ecological history. It also has suggested tourist attractions, including details on how to reach them.

■ Festivals

October 4th is the **Festival of San Francisco de Asis**, Chapala's patron saint. Celebrations include a special church service followed by street dancing and parades.

■ Sightseeing

Historical Walking Tour

Chapala has some interesting historic houses. Prior to the 1900s, the only building around the lake taller than one story was the church. Then Luis Barragon, a Mexican architect, built his family home, an ostentatious mansion on Av Frederico Madero between Morelos and Niños Heros. It became the highest building in town. **Hotel Arzapalo** faces the lake at the end of Av Frederico Madero. It was built in 1898. **Hotel Nido**, along Calle Madero, is now the municipal office. It was built in the early 1900s and is located just north of Hotel Arzapalo and across from the Beer Garden, the longest-operating restaurant in Chapala. Inside the Nido are numerous photos of Chapala during the lake's high-water days. **Hotel Niza**, just a bit farther along Calle Madero, was built in 1908. **Villa Monte Carlo**, on Hidalgo just off Madero, was built in 1895 by Septimus Crow. He liked the area because he could treat his arthritis in the nearby hot springs.

During the late 1800s, a visit by the president made the area popular with the rich, and villas Ferrara, Niza and Josefina were built in a style similar to the Monte Carlo. These houses are the big mansions along the Madero. The church with the double steeples is the **Church of San**

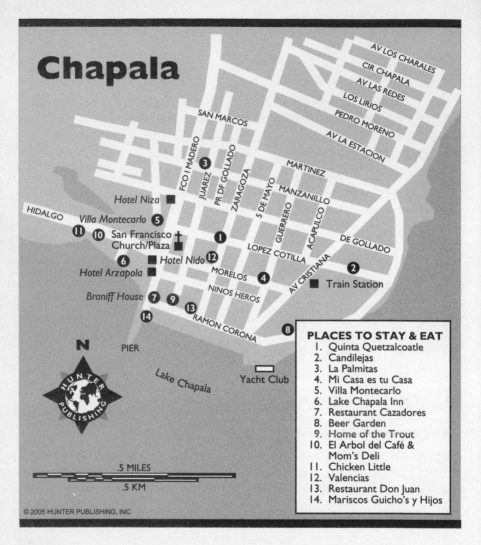

Chapala

AV LOS CHARALES
CIR CHAPALA
AV LAS REDES
LOS LIRIOS
PEDRO MORENO
AV LA ESTACION
SAN MARCOS
MARTINEZ
FCO I MADERO
JUAREZ
PR DF GOLLADO
ZARAGOZA
5 DE MAYO
MANZANILLO
GUERRERO
ACAPULCO
DE GOLLADO

Hotel Niza

HIDALGO
Villa Montecarlo ❺
⓫ ❿ San Francisco
Church/Plaza
LOPEZ COTILLA
❻ ■ Hotel Nido ⓬
Hotel Arzapola ■
MORELOS ❹
NINOS HEROS
AV CRISTIANA ■ Train Station
Braniff House ❼ ❾
⓭
⓮ RAMON CORONA
❽

N
PIER
Lake Chapala
□ Yacht Club

.5 MILES
.5 KM

© 2005 HUNTER PUBLISHING, INC

PLACES TO STAY & EAT
1. Quinta Quetzalcoatle
2. Candilejas
3. La Palmitas
4. Mi Casa es tu Casa
5. Villa Montecarlo
6. Lake Chapala Inn
7. Restaurant Cazadores
8. Beer Garden
9. Home of the Trout
10. El Arbol del Café &
    Mom's Deli
11. Chicken Little
12. Valencias
13. Restaurant Don Juan
14. Mariscos Guicho's y Hijos

Francisco, built in 1528 and reconstructed in 1580. The Queen Anne mansion that houses the Cazadores Restaurant, located on the street facing the lake, is called the **Braniff House**. It was built in 1906 by Luis Verdia and purchased by Alberto Braniff in 1906.

> **FACT FILE:** Although these Braniff's did not own the American Braniff Airlines, Alberto is credited with being the first to fly a plane in Latin America. He did this on January 8, 1910.

Farther along the street that follows the lake is the **Chapala Yacht Club**, constructed in 1910 by Chistian Shjetnan, a man instrumental in getting the rail line to the lake. Walking away from the lake toward the east end of town, you will find the old **train station**, built in 1930.

FACT FILE: DH Lawrence lived in the house at Zaragoza #307 and wrote *The Plumed Serpent* while here. He calls the lake "Sayula" in the book, but it is clearly Chapala.

Exploring Lake Villages

Touring the villages around the lake could take a few days, depending on your interests. This tour can be done by boat, car, bus or on foot. However, travel by bus or car gives you more time to explore.

▶▶ **AUTHOR NOTE:** *Boats cost far less when rented for the day, rather than by the hour. Negotiate with the operators located at the pier.*

I have listed the villages and their main attractions. Although Chapala is an interesting town, Ajijic has become a very popular destination and has all the tourist facilities you will need. Some make it a base camp for exploration to the rest of the area.

San Antonio Tlayacapan is an easy three-mile/five-km walk west of Chapala. The **Church of San Antonio de Padua** and the tower that is now part of the school are interesting. San Antonio is the patron saint of the village and his day is June 13th. The village celebrates for a week before with mass, fireworks, food and dancing. On the 13th, people from around the lake come to spread flowers around the streets and church and to help celebrate with an exceptional fireworks display. Overnight options in San Antonio Tlayacaoan are **Casa Tlayacapan**, *Colon # 100,* ☎ *333-767-0182*, or the **trailer park**, *Allen Lloyd # 149,* ☎ *333-766-0040,* which has a pool, clubhouse, satellite TV and flower gardens. There are numerous restaurants, including an Italian and a fried chicken place.

The traditional village of **Ajijic** is five miles/seven km from Chapala. It has cobblestone streets and adobe brick houses, and is now attracting tourists more frequently than Chapala. It is one of the oldest villages in Mexico, founded in 1531. The town has become popular for foreign artists to make their homes. If art is what you are looking for, this is a must stop. In the village is the **Rosario Chapel**, a beautiful stone building with a central bell tower. The plaza has been restored into an attraction. During the rainy season, you can walk to **Tepalo Waterfall**, reached by a trail that goes up the hill at the back of town. It's a fairly long walk that will take about two to three hours. Be aware that during dry season (November to March) there may be little or no water falling. There are numerous places to stay (over 20) and even more places to eat (over 50). Many of the B&Bs in this area are exceptional by world standards.

ARTSY AJIJIC

The annual **film festival** has been held in Ajijic every October/November since 1999. It has received international acclaim. Check at the tourist offices in Guadalajara, Chapala and Ajijc for details.

The **Ajijic Arts Society** has been instrumental in promoting local art. Among their members is Georg Rauch, an Austrian who developed his style in Mexico. **The Galeria Americas, Casa de la Cultura, Galeria Daniel Palma** and **Galeria de Paolo** are all first-class galleries that carry the works of Chapala artists.

The **Music Appreciation Society** promotes and supports concerts, dance performances and chamber music events. They are affiliated with the Degollado Theatre in Guadalajara.

San Juan Cosala is another mile/1.5 km past Ajijic. The big draw here are the hot springs that have temperatures of around 95°F/35°C. They are located at Km 13.5 along the Chapala/Joco Road at the Motel San Juan Cosala. The waters are said to help detoxify the body, although some believe the water is also good for arthritis. I think it is just good to soak in. The town has about 10 little places to stay; food is best around the Piedra Barrenada section of town.

Jocotepec (Place of the Citrus Fruits) is at the most western point of the lake. Although inhabited by locals for centuries, it didn't become a town until 1832. **Señor del Monte Church**, in the center, is worth stopping at. The festival honoring Señor del Monte (with pineapple?) is held on the third Sunday in January. Like the rest of the villages on the lake, Jocotepec has numerous places in which to stay and/or eat.

Poncitlan, 15 miles/25 km east of Chapala along the rail line (no trains running), is laid back and quiet. It has an old church made of stone with a triple bell arch on top. The old wooden door is rugged, thick and arched with stone. Just on the outskirts of the town are the ruins of the **San Jacinto Hacienda**. Also of interest is the **Convent of San Pedro and San Pablo**, built in 1553. On the altar of the convent's church is a sculpture of the Nuestra Señora del Rosario. It was given to the town by King Carlos V of Spain. There are a couple of hotels and B&Bs in town, as well as numerous restaurants. The most popular of these is El Patio on Emilio Carranza #45.

FACT FILE: It was in 1858 that the War of the Camichines occurred in Poncitlan. The altercations left numerous places destroyed. The local people defeated General Miramón and forced his army into the Santiago River. Miramón later became the youngest Mexican president to take office.

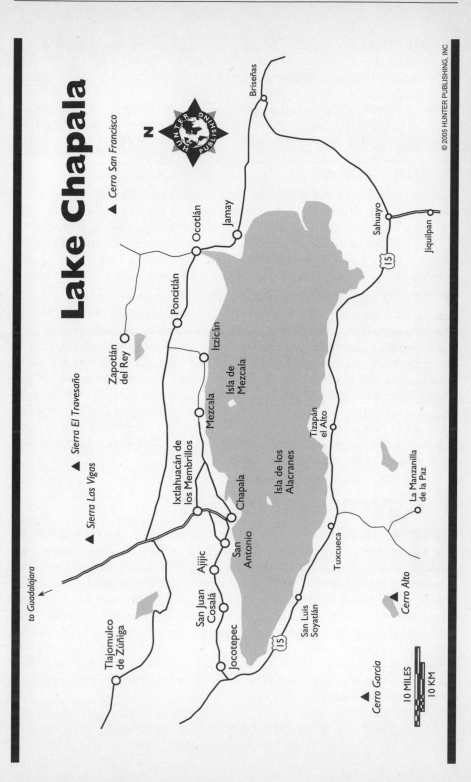

Lake Chapala

Ocotlan (Place of the Pines) is on the rail line at the eastern end of the lake and at the only natural outlet of the lake. The town was founded in 1530 and the imposing **Misericordia Church** was built in the 1800s. It features twin bell towers and outside niches that hold religious statues. Inside are records of the earthquake that destroyed the town. Another attraction is the **Anthropological Museum**, which contains rock paintings found in the nearby hills and along the northern lakeshore, along with ceramics created after the Spanish arrived. There are more than a dozen hotels in the village.

Jamay is at the eastern end of the lake and has been inhabited for centuries. The main attraction is the monument in the plaza honoring Pope Pius the IX. It stands about 100 ft/30 meters high and is carved from stone. Walking to the **Guadalupe Chapel** on the hill will give you an excellent view of the village and lake. There are three or four places to stay in town. Most people come here for the food; over a dozen good restaurants serve local lake dishes.

La Barca, founded in 1553, is not on the lake but rather on the Chapala Marsh where the Lerma River enters the lake. Birding is good here. It is **La Morena Hacienda**, now restored and made into a museum, that is the draw. The murals on the inside of the hacienda cover about 5,300 square feet/500 square meters of wall space. The paintings are of life around the lake in the 1800s and were done by Gerardo Suarez. He was inspired by the work of Casimiro Castro, whose lithographs published in 1855 were exceptional. You will notice from the mural that there were beggars in Mexico even then. There are about a half-dozen places to stay in town and twice as many restaurants.

■ Adventures on Foot

Stations of the Cross, just out of Ajijic, can be reached by walking. From the center of Ajijic, follow Galeana Street just east of the Ajijic Clinic. Go uphill. Within 15 minutes you will get your first view of the lake. During rainy season, the vegetation is lush and the flowers are numerous. In fact, the trail becomes hard to follow because the vegetation is so dense. However, in dry season the route is hot and dusty. Once past the crosses depicting the life of Christ during his last week on earth, you will come to a small chapel that overlooks the lake. Wear boots on this hike as the terrain is uneven and often has loose rocks. You will also need water, a hat and sun protection. It is about an hour up and half an hour down.

BIRD WATCH: *There are some birds in the Stations of the Cross area; eagles are common.*

■ Adventures on Water

 You can rent a boat at the pier to take you out to the islands. Boats cost far less when rented for the day, rather than by the hour. Negotiate with the operators located at the pier.

Isla de los Alacranes (Scorpion Island) is in the middle of the lake. Thankfully, the island is named for its shape, not for the insects. However, due to the appalling condition of the lake, the wildlife on this island has decreased.

DAMMED IF YOU DO

Eleven dams have been built up the Lerma River, a major contributor to the lake. Between the 1970s and 2002, the volume of the lake reduced by 83%. Because of the diversion of water, a waterfall that once plunged 150 feet/50 meters into the lake has also disappeared. The level of toxic chemicals is up so high that fish are mutating. Phosphorus is 80 times higher than permitted by international standards. This statistical information was taken from www.livinglakes.org/chapala/#biology. If you are interested in the health of this lake, go to the website or contact Sociedad Amogos de Chapala, www.amigos-delago.org, ☎ 376-765-5755 in Chapala.

Mezcala Island is interesting because it has the ruins of a prison. These include stone paths, crumbling walls and photogenic doors and windows. This was once a fort during the 1812-1816 Revolution, when locals took their stance against the Spanish. They fought heroically, trying to win independence for Mexico and finally succumbed to hunger and thirst rather than military defeat.

 An account of the fight has been published in the *Heroic Defense of Mezcala Island*, by Alberto Santoscoy, and is available as an e-book at www.epmassoc.com/catalog/175.php?sp=3. If this link is broken, type the book title in your search engine to find another link.

Bull's Cave on Mezcala has petroglyphs and rock paintings. You can take a boat to this island either from the village of Mezcala or from the pier in Chapala. The island is about 15 miles/25 km from Chapala.

■ Outfitters/Tour Operators

 Boats to go around the lake can be hired at Chapala ($33 for half an hour for up to eight people; $38 for an hour). Boats to Isla de los Alacrines cost $22 for half an hour and $27 for an hour. Rates go down when hired for longer periods of time.

Horses can also be hired at the pier in Chapala for trips around the dry lakebed. The cost is $10 an hour.

Charter Club Tours, *Plaza Montaña Center, Main Highway and Colon St,* ☎ *376-766-1777, charterclubtours@hotmail.com,* offers bus tours with bilingual guides. On Wednesday they have a tour around the lake; on Saturday they do a tour of Guadalajara city. Custom tours are available. Prices vary but, as an example, you can do a shopping trip to Guadalajara for just $7 (not counting your purchases). They also know when and where the monarch butterflies appear; ask them about it.

Viajes Vikingo, *Av Hidalgo # 225,* ☎ *376-765-3292,* can arrange your travels after you leave Chapala.

■ Shopping

 Artisans near the docks and lake sell souvenirs. However, if you want something special in the way of embroidery or ceramics, try **Galeria de Artesanos de Chapala**, *Av Madero #220,* ☎ *376-765-5487,* which carries a collection of work from local artists.

Isabel's Bazaar, *Hidalgo #76,* has exquisite paintings by Isabel. Also for sale are other items, like Mexican jewelry, but I think Isabel's paintings – many of which are less than $100 – are the best.

■ Places to Stay

 Each village around the lake has a bed and breakfast and a moderate hotel. The ones listed below are just a sampling. Be adventuresome and look for new ones – let me know when you find an exceptional establishment. The hotels in Chapala and Ajijic are numerous – and Ajijic has more places in the moderate price range.

Candilejas, *Lopez Cotilla # 363, Chapala,* ☎ *376-765-2279, $,* has 15 basic rooms with private bathroom and fans. This is a very well-kept place, run by an amiable man whose care of the gardens seems to attract guests. Just a block from the bus station, this is an excellent choice in this price range.

La Palmitas, *Juarez #531, Chapala,* ☎ *376-765-3070, $,* has 13 rooms that are without frills or private bathrooms.

Mi Casa es Tu Casa, *Guerrero # 190-A, Chapala,* ☎ *376-765- 5059, $$,* has large, clean rooms with private bathroom and cable TV. There is a laundry service and breakfast is included in the price. Vegetarian cooking is available upon request.

HOTEL PRICE SCALE	
Price for a room given in US $.	
$	Up to $20
$$	$21-$50
$$$	$51-$100
$$$$	$101-$150
$$$$$	$151-$200
Anything over $200 is specified.	

Los Dos B&B, *Calle Rico 191,* ☎ *376-763-0657, $$$,* in Jocotepec, has a pool, an artist's studio, extensive gardens and a shuttle bus just outside the house that will take you to and from town. The rooms are large and have private bathrooms. Breakfast, included in the price, is served on the patio.

Nueva Posada, *Donato Guerra #9, Ajijic,* ☎ *376-766-1344, $$$,* is a luxuriously restored hacienda. It has huge arched windows, high ceilings, ornate chandeliers and antique furniture. The stone staircase leading to some rooms is an amazing work of masonry. There are lush potted plants in every hall and a stone walkway leads to the pool that is hidden by flowering vegetation. The restaurant has a huge rubber tree in its center. The 17 rooms, located on three floors, are decorated with watercolors painted by local artists. This is an exceptional place.

Hotel Real de Chapala, *Paseo del Prado #20, Ajijic,* ☎ *376-766-0014, $$$,* has 79 rooms with air conditioning and private bathrooms. The hotel also has a restaurant, a bar, a pool, two tennis courts and a volleyball area. Everyone I spoke with recommended eating at the rooftop patio and restaurant because the food, service, prices and views can't be beaten. The rooms have air conditioning, night tables and a sitting area.

Quinta Quetzalcoatle B&B, *Zaragoza #307, Chapala,* ☎ *376-765-3653, $$$,* has nine rooms, some of which are wheelchair-accessible. Each room has a shower and bathtub, a sitting area and reading lights. They are also tastefully finished. There is a hot tub and pool on site.

FACT FILE: Quinta Quetzalcoatle B&B is where DH Lawrence wrote his famous novel, *The Plumed Serpent.* All you wannabe novelists may get some inspiration by staying here.

Villa Monte Carlo, *Hidalgo #296, Chapala,* ☎ *376-765-2024, $$$,* is the old house built by S. Crow (see *Walking Tour,* page 315) and has 48 renovated rooms with air conditioning and private bathrooms. If history is your thing, you may want to try this place.

Lake Chapala Inn, *Paseo Ramon Corona #23, Chapala,* ☎ *376-765-3070 or 800-501-9446, $$$,* has rooms with private bathrooms, king-sized beds, TVs, telephones, hair dryers and bedside reading lamps. There is a flowered terrace overlooking the lake and a tiny pool in the garden. There is also laundry service, a library and a music room.

■ Places to Eat

 Acapulquito Zone, *Ramon Corona,* ☎ *376-765-4595,* is located along the lakeshore, where numerous restaurants and bars are found. At Acapulquito's you will get delicious seafood for around $10 per meal. This is a favorite of ex-pats.

LAKE CHAPALA FISH DISHES

- *Carp roe* is whitefish.
- *Birria* is catfish.
- *Charales* – Charal is a small fish caught in the lake that has been used to make a traditional dish for hundreds of years.
- *Caldo michi* is fish soup.

Restaurant Cazadores, *Braniff House, Ramon Corona #18,* ☎ *376-765-2162,* is across from the lake. Save this elegant restaurant for a special lunch or dinner. The waiters are in black ties and vests, the food is good and the meal will take a few hours to consume.

The Beer Garden, *Ramon Corona,* ☎ *376-765-3817*, opened in 1929 and has been a popular restaurant ever since. There is a rooftop patio where you can enjoy the sunset while sipping a margarita or a glass of wine before the disco starts. It is located at the far end of the town, along what used to be the shore and across from the Nido Hotel.

Home of the Trout, *Paseo Corona # 22,* ☎ *376-765-4606,* is closed Monday. However, on Wednesday when they feature live music, reservations are necessary. The special on that day is chicken Cordon Bleu, which includes a margarita or white wine, nachos for an appetizer and dessert for a mere $10. Fridays they offer a steak and seafood combination for $12, including all the extras that you get on Wednesdays. They also serve things like stuffed squid or frog legs.

Mariscos Guicho's y Hijos, ☎ *376-765-3232, at the Chapala pier,* serves the best seafood in town. They also have some gourmet dishes like frog legs, caviar tacos and seafood soup.

El Arbol del Café (Coffee Tree), *Calle Hidalgo, no phone*, is the place to find a good cheesecake to go with your afternoon coffee. It is fun to hang out here.

La Casa del Waffle, *Chapala-Jocotepec #75, no phone*, is open 10 am-midnight every day except Tuesday. Come here for a late breakfast and, while sipping on a coffee, decide which of the 12 flavors of big Belgian waffles you would like. Options include things like mango and strawberry. The kids' favorite (and mine) is the Winnie the Pooh waffle, with honey. All meals are about $7.

Ajijic Grill, *Morelos #5,* ☎ *376-766-2458*, in Ajijic, offers a good Japanese dinner. They have a sushi bar – like a salad bar, only with sushi. They also have lunch specials that include dishes such as tempura, tonkatsu, yakitori and kushi age. Other non-Japanese dishes are quail and lobster.

Mom's Deli, *Hidalgo #79-I, Plaza Maskaras,* ☎ *376-765-5719,* has a different lunch special every day starting at 11:30 am. As an example, they have French dip sandwich or roast pork on Mondays and meatloaf on Wednesdays. The cost is $6 per serving and the meals are offered until the food is gone, so get here early.

Valencianas, *Morelos #209,* ☎ *376-765-4182,* has the best pizza in town. This is a rare find, as fish is the most common meal in the area.

Chicken Little, *Av Hidalgo # 101-B,* ☎ *376-765-4399*, is the most popular chicken-aria in town. There is a small seating area at the restaurant, but most patrons take the food with them and snack on the beach or at the docks.

Restaurant Don Juan, *Paseo Ramon Corona #3, no phone*, has fish and beef dishes, as well as *comida corridas* (daily meals) with three different choices each day. For an example, you can have either soup, pork chop, rice, beans and coffee, or fish soup, a filet of fish with rice and beans and coffee for $5.50. The food is good.

■ Nightlife

Because the lake has attracted many artists, the area is alive with workshops, theater performances, readings and art shows. Pick up local publications for information on these events.

The Costalegre
(Puerto Vallarta to Barra de Navidad)

The Costalegre stretches 80 miles/150 km south from the Bay of Banderas to Barra de Navidad. This section of coast was decreed by the president in the 1990s to be an ecological tourist corridor. He did not want it to be developed into another sprawl of luxury hotels. The corridor is bordered by Puerto Vallarta in the north, Colima in the east and Manzanillo in the south. Although there are a few huge estates and hotels along this stretch, most of the area remains remote, dotted only with isolated fishing villages. If you are totally self-sufficient, you can camp in some of these villages and beaches. However, I do not recommend this because the robberies in this part of the country have often been violent.

Besides sunning, surfing and wildlife viewing, windsurfing is good along this stretch of coastline. If you are independent and have your own car, you could spend a year exploring all the coves, bays and villages and never see them all.

WARNING: Because of the curves and narrowness of the road, do not drive along here at night. Large transport trucks use this highway and often drive in the middle of the road, squeezing any little guy onto the non-existent shoulder and down the bank.

To get here, take local buses from town to town (carry a map – the one I used was Mexico Pacific Coast by International Travel Maps, Vancouver), or drive.

Hotelito Desconocido, ☎ *322-223-0293 or 800-851-1143 from the US, http://hotelito.com,* is 60 miles/90 km south of Puerto Vallarta and three miles/4.5 km toward the coast from La Crus de Loreto along Highway 220. The hotel is one of Mexico's most ecologically friendly resorts. It offers an all-inclusive package that costs anywhere from $500 to $650 a day, depending on the season and/or a special sale. The packages include pick-up from Puerto Vallarta airport, four nights and five days for two people, breakfasts and dinners, tea and fruits all day, introductory use of the spa plus one massage and one body mud treatment, one mermaid bath and one facial, one horse trip, free use of kayaks and a trip to see the turtles. This is a luxury vacation geared toward the ecologically sensitive.

VIEW TURTLES HATCHING

Every August to February, Olive Ridley turtles lay their eggs on the beach here and, six weeks later, the eggs hatch. Because most sea turtles have three different egg-laying sessions two to six weeks apart, viewing these events is possible for almost six months. There is a biologist available at the hotel to answer questions and to help you find the turtles during their laying/hatching times.

The bungalows, called *palafitos*, are located over the estuary. They are constructed with natural products; the support beams are wooden poles, the walls are bamboo and the roof is thatch. Wood floors complement the thatched roof. The furniture is mostly rattan and the walls are decorated with antiques and local art. There is solar power for electrical use and candles are used for light at night. Each room has a ceiling fan, a mosquito net over the bed, a safe deposit box, a private bathroom and a bamboo shower stall. Bathrobes, soap, shampoo and body lotion is supplied. Breakfast and supper are served buffet style in the palapa hut overlooking the lagoon and lunch is served at the smaller beach club. Activities include wildlife-viewing, horseback riding, mountain biking, hiking, windsurfing, rowing, canoeing, volleyball and billiards. All of the equipment is supplied by the hotel.

 BIRD WATCH: *Birders can cross to the estuary where the bird life is rich. There is also a viewing platform for birders.*

The health spa has a steam bath, Jacuzzi, showers and massage chambers. They also offer specialized treatments such as aromatherapy, Swedish massage, Shiatsu massage, reflexology and a mud bath treatment that is said to stimulate metabolic functions and rejuvenate the skin. There is also the mermaid's bath or stone therapy (rocks are used to remove the stress from your body).

Tomatlan

This little village of 10,000 people is a good place to stop and shop if you are heading back to the beach roads. There are numerous places to eat and a few places to stay. If you are interested in wide-mouth bass fishing, then a trip to the dam is suggested.

■ Adventures on Water

 Cajon de Peñas Dam is the largest in the state and has a capacity to hold 186 billion gallons of water. This dam supplies water to Tomatlan and generates power for the area. Fishing for tilapia, bass, prawns and *bagre*, a catfish belonging to the *Doradidae* family (the species originated in Peru), is popular. Some people collect the tegolobo mollusk that lives here, which is known for its flavor. A family living near the dam and just off the road will rent you a boat for about $15 an hour. They will also prepare a meal for you. If you are self-sufficient, you can camp near the water. To get to the dam from Tomatlan, return to Highway 200 and go north (turn right at the highway) and follow it to the Km 130 sign. Turn onto an unpaved road toward Viejo Santiago and follow it for 11 miles/18 km to the dam. There are signs indicating both the dam and the village of Viejo Santiago.

Playa Chalacatepec is half an hour from Tomatlan by car and six miles/ nine km from the highway. Playa Chalacatepec encompasses three beaches in all. The north beach has gentle waves, making it good for swimming. It has a long expanse of sand protected by a rocky point at the center, where you can fish, watch for birds and find little coves in which to sit. The southern span of beach has strong surf. The entire beach is an exceptional stretch of land that is seething with birdlife. The remains of a pirate ship that sits on the sand here has become part of a legend that says there is gold at the bottom of the ocean, not far from the ship. From Tomatlan, return to Highway 200, turn south (left) and follow it for about 17 miles/28 km until you see a sign indicating Playa Chalacatepec. Turn toward the ocean.

■ Adventures in Culture

 The white **mission church** on the plaza was constructed between 1769 and 1774 and the bell in the tower is dated from 1730. Inside, two statues date back about 150 years and are considered exceptional pieces of art.

La Peñita Pintada (rock paintings) is along one of the small tributaries of the Tomatlan River. To get there, ask a taxi driver to take you to "La Pintada." The fare should be less than $5 for the one-way trip. He will take you to a spot on the Tomatlan River and you must walk from there. As you walk up the river, watch for a rocky outcrop and the painted wall that is filled with ancient hieroglyphics. The paintings are on the ceiling of the outcrop, 30-45 feet/10-15 meters above ground. The rock itself was hand-sculpted so that the paintings are protected from sun and rain. Some believe these paintings are very old, around 10,000 years, and like those found in Spain.

■ Places to Stay & Eat

 Hotel San Miguel, *Galeana #52*, ☎ *322-298-5522*, *$$*, has large, clean rooms with large windows, cable TV, air conditioning, tiled floors and sitting areas. The hotel has a pool, a restaurant, a bar and Internet connections.

Posada Carmelita, ☎ *322-298-5302*, and **Posada Lupita**, ☎ *322-298-5421*, *$$*, are in the center of town, but I have no information about them.

Quemaro

Quemaro is home to little more than Las Alamandas, a luxury hotel that has been featured in prestigious magazines like *Town & Country* and *Travel + Leisure*. The resort is a little way outside of the village.

■ Place to Stay

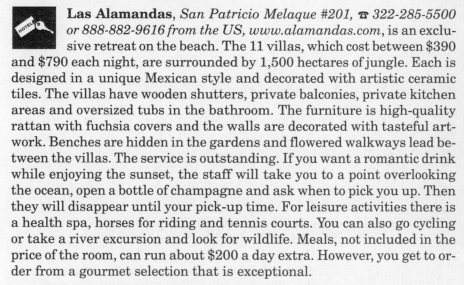 **Las Alamandas**, *San Patricio Melaque #201*, ☎ *322-285-5500 or 888-882-9616 from the US, www.alamandas.com*, is an exclusive retreat on the beach. The 11 villas, which cost between $390 and $790 each night, are surrounded by 1,500 hectares of jungle. Each is designed in a unique Mexican style and decorated with artistic ceramic tiles. The villas have wooden shutters, private balconies, private kitchen areas and oversized tubs in the bathroom. The furniture is high-quality rattan with fuchsia covers and the walls are decorated with tasteful artwork. Benches are hidden in the gardens and flowered walkways lead between the villas. The service is outstanding. If you want a romantic drink while enjoying the sunset, the staff will take you to a point overlooking the ocean, open a bottle of champagne and ask when to pick you up. Then they will disappear until your pick-up time. For leisure activities there is a health spa, horses for riding and tennis courts. You can also go cycling or take a river excursion and look for wildlife. Meals, not included in the price of the room, can run about $200 a day extra. However, you get to order from a gourmet selection that is exceptional.

Airport pick-up is included in the price. Those with their own plane can use the 3,300-ft landing strip. However, don't arrive at the gate without reservations, because the guards will not permit you to enter.

Puerto Vallarta Region

Chamela Bay

On the road to Barra de Navidad along Highway 200, at Km 72 El Super, is a road that leads to Chamela Bay and a delightful little fishing village (the turn off is signed Km 72/El Super). The bay holds four beaches referred to as Playas Perula, Fortuna, Chamela and Rosadas. The bay is dotted with small islands, some vegetated, some just large rocks with a name. There is little at the turnoff except a few stores, but the bay has some low-key places to stay, including a couple of RV parks. There are lots of places to eat.

▪ Adventures on Water

The best **snorkeling** is from Playa Perula, a wide expanse of gentle water and soft sand. Boats along the bay will take you around the islands to good snorkeling spots for $15 an hour. If you want to go for longer, a deal can be worked out. There are many palapa huts offering fish dinners for sale along this stretch.

Playa Fortuna is where the waves get a bit stronger, so body surfing and windsurfing can be good. There are also a few hotels and restaurants along this beach.

▪ Adventures in Nature

Cumbres de Cuixmala Reserve is a nature preserve bound on the north by the San Nicolas River, on the south by the Cuixmala River, and on the west by the ocean. The reserve goes about six miles/10 km inland. It has both deciduous and semi-deciduous forests that house a myriad of birds and animals. There are over 1,120 vascular plant species, some of which are considered threatened.

A LESSON IN BIOLOGY

A vascular plant is one that has xylem and phloem cells that conduct water, nutrients and photosynthetic products in all flowering plants, ferns and fern allies. Xylem cells transport the water and nutrients to the leaves of the plant and the phloem cells transport the photosynthetic products to the roots.

About 270 bird species use the reserve, 40% of which are migratory. Threatened bird residents include the yellow-headed parrot and the wood nymph. The reserve is also a healthy area for crocodiles.

> ### CROC ALERT
>
> One incident between a crocodile and human has occurred here. A fisherman was diving with a spear and he carried a sack of fish over his shoulder. He was bitten in the foot by a croc. It is believed that the croc was not after the man, but the fish.

Birding on the numerous small islands around the bay is good. **Isla Pajarera** is home to brown boobies and is also a good diving spot.

▶▶ **AUTHOR NOTE:** *The closest place offering dive gear rentals is Melaque, 45 miles/72 km south of Chamila.*

Isla Cocinas has a small birding beach. Watersports, especially windsurfing, are popular. **San Andres, Novilla, Esfinge, San Pedro, San Agustin** and **La Negrita** islands all provide wildlife-viewing opportunities. You can kayak around these islands (see *Immersion Adventures*, page 342, for information).

■ Places to Stay

 A one-lane village follows the shore of the ocean. Because finding places does not require directions, the hotels/motels don't offer addresses.

Don Pillos RV and Tenting, *$, no phone*, is at the south end of the bay at El Negrito. The $20 daily rate includes use of washrooms and showers. There are a few shaded areas to park an RV, but most are in the sun. The gate is locked at night.

Bungalows Mayar Chamela, ☎ 315-333-9711, *$,* in Chamela, has 18 rooms with kitchens, private bathrooms and fans. The site is clean and has a pool. This is a two-star property.

Chamela Motel, ☎ *315-333-9824, $,* is a three-story building with very plain rooms, all with private bathroom and hot water.

HOTEL PRICE SCALE		
Price for a room given in US $.		
$		Up to $20
$$		$21-$50
$$$		$51-$100
$$$$		$101-$150
$$$$$		$151-$200
Anything over $200 is specified.		

Hotel Vagabundo, *Independencia and Ballena,* ☎ *315-333-9736, www. hotelvagabundo.da.ru, $$,* in Perula, has simple rooms with private bathrooms, fans and tiled floors. A couple of bungalows also have kitchen areas for cooking. For added comfort, there is a swimming pool and numerous around the yard.

Playa Dorada, ☎ *315-333-9710, $$,* in Perula, has bungalows with two double beds, ceiling fans, bathrooms with hot water, full kitchens and small living rooms. The rooms in the main, three-story building have one double and one single bed, fans, private bathrooms and small sitting areas. There is a pool and the grounds are well shaded.

Centro Vacacional Chamela, ☎ *315-285-5224, $$,* is a clean place with 22 rooms right on the beach. They do not take reservations. There is a pool and well-maintained gardens. This is the best moderately priced place near Chamela (turn off at mile marker 66.5 on Highway 200).

Paraiso Costalegre Resort, ☎ *315-333-9778, $$$,* is at the old Villa Polynesia site. It has 11 cabins, two larger houses and 16 RV spots, as well as tenting. To guarantee shade, RVs park on a pad under a palapa roof ($12 per night). Shade trees dot the property. The rooms are inviting and have a private bathroom and comfortable beds. There is a large sign on Highway 200 pointing the way to the resort.

Villa Vista Hermosa, ☎ *877-845-5278 in the US, www.villavistahermosa. com, $$$$$,* sits on five acres on a hill overlooking the bay. The flowered grounds are well tended; potted plants surround the fountains and pool. If you prefer the beach to a pool, use the private cove just below the resort. Each villa is exquisite, featuring large beds in big rooms, tiled floors, brick walls, Mexican furnishings and air conditioning. There are numerous patios and hideaways where guests can sit. All meals are included in the price and you are even invited to sneak into the kitchen for a midnight snack. Wine is served with dinner. Gourmet meals are made using fresh fish, shrimp or chicken. Pick-up at the airport in Manzanillo or Puerto Vallarta can be arranged.

■ Places to Eat

Restaurant Tejeban, ☎ *315-333-9705,* is at El Super, on the south side of the Chamela River. **La Viuda Restaurant** is on the north side of the river at Km 64. On the other side of the bridge is **Don Lupe's Mariscos**. **Restaurant Tejeban** is a truck stop where chicken and hamburgers are the mainstay of the day, while Don Lupe's Mariscos sells seafood. I have no information about La Viuda except that it has been around for quite some time.

Beachfront palapa restaurants between Playa Fortuna in the north and Playa El Negrito in the south serve mostly seafood. You can expect to pay between $5 and $10 for large meals and much less for snacks. Beer runs $1.50-$2 for a large bottle.

Costa Careyes

This small bay has gentle waves and is good for swimming. At the village of Careyes, the shore becomes rocky with tiny stretches of white sand. Birding is good here.

■ Adventures in Nature

In 2002, the Mexican National Commission for Protected Areas set aside 17 marine turtle refuges as protected areas. One of these places is **Teopa Beach**, at the north end of the bay, where the workers have collected, protected and hatched over half a million eggs so far. The Mexican division of the World Wildlife Federation has joined forces with the National Commission to give these areas the highest form of wildlife protection in the Mexican system. For more information visit the World Wildlife Federation website, www.wwf.org.

■ Adventure on Horseback

Costa Careyes Polo Club, *no phone,* was established in 1989. It is three miles south of the Costa Careyes Resort. The greens are open mid-November to mid-April and the fees are $70 per game during the day, but $50 for early morning sessions. The club has two fields and games are played most weekends. Beginners and pros are both welcome to play and/or take lessons. There are about 40 horses available for rent to play the game.

Cuitzmala

Cuitzmala is 25 miles/44 km south of Careyes along Highway 200 and is the location of the **Goldsmith family mansion**. The Goldsmiths are descendants of the rich Bolivian A. Patiño, the first Indian since the days of the Inca to become rich. He made his money from mining. With things looking a bit shaky in Bolivia, Patiño moved his family to France and got into banking. Family fortunes grew. The mansion at Cuitzmala is just one of many owned by this family. The Alamandas Resort, just out of Puerto Vallarta, is also owned by them. Access to the beach near the Goldsmith mansion is restricted because part of the beach has been set aside as a turtle preserve.

■ Places to Stay

Casitas de La Flores, *Km 53.5 on the Barra de Navidad road,* ☎ *315-6510-240, www.mexicoboutiquehotels.com / thecareyes / index.html, $$$$$+*, has brightly colored Mexican pueblos that can be purchased or rented. They come with one, two or three bedrooms and fully equipped kitchens, air conditioning, cable TV and telephones. The tiled bathrooms are spacious, the balconies have views and there are plunge pools to soak in. The courtyards are decorated with exotic plants. This is a luxury five-star establishment, where the rent starts at $900 a day during low season. High-end pueblos with five bedrooms and seven bathrooms cost $2,000 a day.

El Careyes Beach Resort, *Km 53.5 on the Barra de Navidad road,* ☎ *315-351-0000 or 877-278-8018 from US and 866-818-8342 from Canada,* charges $225 to $550 per night for a pueblo-styled room that has air conditioning, cable TV, a private balcony and either a garden or an ocean view. Some rooms have private plunge pools, while others have an indoor Jacuzzi. On the property is a meandering pool, shaded in places by palm trees. There is also a full-service spa, a restaurant, a bar, tennis courts and a workout and weight room. Equipment is provided for watersports, including boogie boarding or kayaking. Horses and bicycles are also available for guests to use. You can even play a game of polo. El Careyes is another exotic place and the only one tucked into this little bay.

TURTLE TENDING

The beach near the Careyes resort is where the Carey turtles, now endangered, come to lay their eggs. The conservation practices around this event are strict and only respectful visitors are permitted entrance to the beach to watch the laying or hatching of the eggs. The Careyes Beach Resort will escort those interested in seeing the turtles (see previous page). However, any beach where a Carey hawksbill turtle decides to come ashore is now under strict protection according to the Mexican National Commission for Protected Areas and this beach is part of a preserve.

■ Places to Eat

 Playa Rosa is a waterfront restaurant that serves good quesadillas and lobster (in season). Meals cost between $6 and $12. No waterskiing, Jet Skiing or spear fishing is permitted in the area around the restaurant. Open noon until 10:30 pm.

Tecuan

This village is at Km 33 on Highway 200. There is a sign at the turnoff that leads to an abandoned hotel perched on a cliff. The hotel is six miles/10 km down the road toward the beach. This is where the movie *I Still Know What You Did Last Summer* was filmed. In the movie, the hotel was called Tower Bay after the lighthouse that still stands. The hotel was originally built by a Mexican general who wanted to give his president a gift, but the general died before it was completed. The general's son took over the project for a while, but lost interest. Sadly, the place has since been stripped of anything valuable. The beach here has strong waves due to the long expanse of unprotected beach and the westerly winds. The surf here is for the adventure surfer only. Swimmers should not venture into the water as the undertow is extremely strong. However, the wildlife viewing is good at the lagoon below the hotel, and you can see wildcats, crocodiles, snakes and turtles.

 BIRD WATCH: *The Tecuan area has herons, egrets, pelicans and grebes.*

Tenacatita

This village is five miles/eight km off the main highway toward the ocean. Turn toward the ocean at the Km 30 sign. Going in the opposite direction leads to Agua Caliente. The village of **Rebalcito** (with hotel) is two miles/three km before the beach. Some travelers stay here and walk down to the water.

Tenacatita is a tiny village that has a few palapa huts along the beach selling seafood and beer. The beach is two miles/three km long and is good for snorkeling and swimming. It is also popular for catching lobster, octopus, crabs and snails.

LOCAL LINGO: *The name* Tenacatita *means "colored rocks" in Nahuatl. The town was named after the reddish rocks seen at the south end of the bay. It is believed that locals used to cut pieces of stone from the rock to build into their homes.*

Because indigenous people have lived here for centuries, it is possible to find pieces of pottery and figurines in the hills near the bay, especially after a heavy rain when the water washes away the earth.

■ Adventures on Water

 At the mangrove swamp near the lagoon behind the isthmus and Playa la Boca, *pangas* can be hired to take you upriver in search of wildlife. See *Tour Operators*, below.

▶▶ **AUTHOR NOTE:** *Playa la Boca has knee-deep black sand and lots of sand fleas, especially at night.*

The bay is one of the best in the country for **snorkeling** because of the calm water. The sport is especially popular at a spot called **The Aquarium**, located to the right of the village and over the hill. This route will also get you to **Playa Mora**, which has a colony of black coral. Black coral is now protected and only a small amount is harvested each year. It is recommended that you not purchase black coral jewelry so that even less will be harvested. Damselfish are often seen in this area.

 FACT FILE: It takes black coral a hundred years to grow half an inch.

Playa de Oro is known for the American steamship (named *The Golden Gate*) that sank on July 27, 1862, killing 250 people and losing $1.5 million in gold. The vessel caught fire and sank just offshore. Only 80 people survived. Two years after the accident, a few cases of gold were recovered. In the 1960s, the ship was found and salvaged. It was just 50 yards from the shore. It is believed that a lot of the gold is still out there and, occasionally, someone finds a piece washed up on shore. Look for some. This is a popular spot for snorkeling and diving. Diving gear and guides can be hired in Malaque or in Manzanillo.

■ Adventures in Nature

A walk along this shore will bring you to a huge rock at the water's edge that looks a bit like a mini Macchu Piccu. There you will find a small cave inhabited by **bats**.

WARNING: Be careful when in the water near the cave, as the waves are very strong.

■ Outfitters/Tour Operators

The **Palapa la Sirenita restaurant** has boats for trips into the mangroves that cost $25. The excursion will take a few hours.

■ Places to Stay

Remember, no area code is needed when making a local call.

Hotel Paraiso de Tenacatita, *Av Tenacatita # 32*, ☎ *315-353-9623*, *$*, has 13 rather small and plain rooms that have either a fan or air conditioning. They are located around an inner courtyard.

Hotel Costa Alegre, *El Rebalsito*, ☎ *315-351-5121, $*, has simple rooms with air conditioning and fans. There is a restaurant on site.

HOTEL PRICE SCALE	
Price for a room given in US $.	
$	Up to $20
$$	$21-$50
$$$	$51-$100
$$$$	$101-$150
$$$$$	$151-$200
Anything over $200 is specified.	

Playa Tenacatita Trailer Park, *Av Tenacatita, across from Hotel Paraiso*, ☎ *333-115-5406 (cell)*, has 15 RV spaces with water, sewer and electricity. They cost $15 a night, with discounts for longer stays. The gate is kept locked at night.

Las Villitas Club Deportivo, *Av Tenacatita # 376*, ☎ *315-355-5354, $$$*, has large and small bungalows with kitchens. Each bungalow has a full stove, fridge, stools, TV, tiled floors, white walls and fans. The larger bungalows have sitting areas separated from the bedrooms by a curtained window. The place is funky and painted in every bright color imaginable. However, everything is very clean. Guests can rent mountain bikes.

Blue Bay Village, *Km 20.7 on Highway 200*, ☎ *315-351-5020 or 800-258-3229*, is a five-star all-inclusive resort. It has over 200 rooms and suites; rooms go for $110 during low season and suites run $490 during high season. There are two restaurants (one buffet, one à la carte), four bars, a disco, a snack bar, pool, sauna, tennis courts, a gym and an open-air theater that has nightly shows. The hotel also offers horseback riding, boats and watersports equipment for rent.

FACT FILE: Blue Bay Village is called *Los Angeles Locos* by the local population The original owners were so rich that, to the locals, they seemed to be wasting money coming to this isolated spot, hence the name.

Punta Serena, *Km 20 on Highway 200, beside Blue Bay Village,* ☎ *315-351-5100 or 800-551-2558, www.puntaserena.com, $$$$*, is an adults-only holistic spa resort with 26 rooms. According to *Spa Magazine*, Punta Serena offers "a heaven of tranquility and true personal pampering... where you can free your mind, spirit and soul with a (clothing optional) stroll along the beach." I agree that the hotel is first class. It offers treatment programs that include facials, body wraps, exfoliation treatments, massages, Mexican sweat lodges, manicures and pedicures. There are two hot tubs, a spa with sauna, a steam room, an indoor Jacuzzi and a fully equipped gym.

■ Places to Eat

There are numerous eateries along the beach, and more restaurants at Rebalcito. **Restaurant Yoly** is recommended for good Mexican food if you want to walk the two miles/three km up to the highway and on to the village of Rebalcito. There are no taxis available. I have no phone listing for this restaurant. However, prices are under $10 for a seafood dinner.

In Tenacatita, **Chito** and **Fiesta Mexicana** *(no phones)* are close to one another. Both offer Mexican food for reasonable prices.

Restaurant Palapa la Sirenita, ☎ *315-351-5208,* has dinner specials on Tuesday *(tomales)* and Friday *(birra de chivo,* or goat meat) for $8 a meal. The cozy place with just 10 tables has been in business for almost 20 years.

Cihuatlan

This town of 20,000 people is 22 miles/33 km from Barra de Navidad. Besides visiting the plaza, golfing at Tamarindo and walking the Marabasco River, there isn't much else to do here.

■ Adventures on Foot

Hiking

 At the side of the **Marabasco River** about four miles/six km from town is a painted rock with circular engravings on it. The rock sits in the middle of a field. Walk up the river (the same side as the town) to reach it. You can also ask a taxi to take you here, but the river is good for swimming, so I prefer to walk.

Golf

El Tamarindo resort has an 18-hole, par 72, 6,682-yard course that features some of the most dramatic golfing scenery in Mexico. After the ninth hole, players can stop for a drink at the snack bar before going down the shallow green to a stretch of rocky coastline. There, they play three holes along the shore and end at a par five on the last hole. Signs warn you not to go into the bush looking for golf balls as snakes and other dangerous creatures inhabit the brush. The cost to play is $150 for green fees and cart and $25 for the mandatory caddy. A tip is extra and expected.

■ Adventures in Nature

Playa Peña Blanca, at the north end of the beach that is south of the village, is under protection when turtle eggs hatch. You will need special permission to pass this way during that time. For more information about the protection, visit www.wwf.org. For permission to visit the area when turtles are active, speak with a tour operator in Manzanillo (page 367).

The white rock just off shore that is covered in bird-dung gives the place its name. The bird most commonly seen here is the blue-footed booby. This is also a popular dive site because of the canyons and the artificial reef that was created in 1996. To rent diving gear you must go to Manzanillo (page 367).

La Vaca Mountain is a scenic spot along the beach, but it is inundated with ATVs every day from 9 am to 3 pm. For a thrill in speed, you can join a tour that starts at Peña Blanca and goes for three hours along the beach, through a river, around the mountain and back again. The faster you go, the better. The machine (Honda TRX-250), a scarf, helmet and goggles are included in the cost of the tour.

‎ers/Tour Operators

‎d & Trails Adventures, *Rancho Peña Blanca,* ☎ *315-‎7,* offers a tour to La Vaca by high speed ATV. Prices are ‎ailable.

Playa Boca de Iguanas

Turn at Km 17 off Highway 200 and follow the road for one mile/two km down to the beach. There is no local bus service here, so you must either have your own car or, after taking a bus, hike in from the highway. Boca has a hotel, two trailer parks and a restaurant. Camping is popular along this five-mile/eight-km beach that stretches all the way to La Manzanilla. The beach has a very gentle slope and not much undertow, so boogie boarding is a popular sport.

Hotel Tenacatita was destroyed by an earthquake. Its remains are great to poke around in, and the marshy area behind the beach is good for birders. Just walk down the beach toward Manzanillo to reach the ruins.

■ Places to Stay & Eat

Hotel Boca de Iguanas, *no phone*, has very basic rooms and **Coconuts by the Sea**, ☎ *315-338-6315, info@coconuts-bythesea.com,* is a private house with a couple of rooms for rent. It is set on a hill above the hotel. There are a few restaurants along the beach.

Playa Manzanilla

This is not to be confused with the larger center of Manzanilla, a little farther south. To get here, turn at Km 13 off Highway 200 and follow the dirt road down a mile. Those without a car can walk from the highway. The village begins along the beach where Boca de Iguanas leaves off five miles away and stretches from Boca to here. The beach has gentle waves and palapa food places (there are also lots of restaurants in the village). There are numerous guesthouses for rent if you want to stay awhile, plus a few smaller, basic hotels for shorter stays. Internet access is available. This is turning into another desired destination.

Adventures on Foot

Take the **waterfall hike** starting at the footbridge on the road going to Campo. Turn left at the river and follow the trail past an odd tower with a thatch roof. Continue along the road/trail that runs beside the river to a goat farm with a gate across the road. Pass through, but be certain to close the gate. Once back on the river follow a small trail on the left or walk on the riverbed if there isn't too much water. The walking gets a bit rugged farther in, and eventually you will come to a pool with high rocks around it. The waterfall is at the far end. It is never dry, although in summer it is just a trickle.

Adventures on Water

For a tour of the bay see Pancho, Alex or Monty at **Restaurant Fiesta Mexicana** in Tenacatita, ☎ *315-338-6316*. They can take you out to view dolphins, turtles and whales (in season). The cost is $30 per hour for the boat and guide. The boat will take up to six people. Anglers should also contact the guides at the Fiesta.

Adventures in Nature

The **mangrove swamp** in this area is being studied by Earthwatch. The mangroves here play a role in preventing erosion and damage to the coral reefs. They provide housing for fish and crocodiles and migratory and residential birds. Especially important in this region is the boat-billed heron. The delicate environment of the mangrove is being threatened by tourism due to the demand for more luxurious hotels.

DOING GOOD

If you are interested in preserving the area, learning about it, or if you would like to join a study group coordinated and led by university professors, visit www.earthwatch.org. If you are observing on your own, be sensitive to the environment. This means don't litter, use muscle-powered vehicles and stay on the trails.

Adventures on Horseback

Horseback riding is possible along the beach for $10 an hour. Daniel Hallas, ☎ *315-351-5059*, is the owner of the horses and he can be e-mailed at dlh3648@yahoo.com. He also offers a ride to the waterfall (see previous page) for the same price.

■ Outfitter/Tour Operator

Immersion Adventures, *at La Manzanilla (third house on the right)*, ☎ *315-351-5341, or at the Campamento Ecologico on the beach walking toward Boca de Iguanas,* has tours for all skill levels. A very active itinerary includes four or more hours of paddling and an hour of snorkeling. Duration can be adjusted to suit your energy level. Birding is also offered. Trips cost about $115 per person, per day, and includes all kayaking gear. If you want to tour without a guide, you can rent kayaks by the hour. Organized trips run to Tenacatita Bay, where there is good snorkeling over the fringe coral reef. From the bay they enter La Vena mangrove estuary, where birding is big. This trip from La Manzanilla takes about 10 hours and costs $37. The **Careyes Bay** trip is good for strong paddlers who can hold their own for a few hours. Parts of the bay have high cliffs and rugged landscape. Good kayak control is required. They stop at a tiny beach called Esmeralda, where the group snorkels. This nine-hour trip costs $100 per person, per day.

■ Shopping

Manzanilla is developing into an artistic community with numerous ex-pats. I was surprised at the number of artists working here and I am certain that I have listed only a few below. If you want to take home something unique, a piece of original art may be just the thing. The talent here is amazing. There are numerous art shops in the village where you can browse.

ARTISTS TO LOOK FOR

Sylvain Voyer is a Canadian landscape artist who has been active in Canada for years. He has worked with the Canadian Artists Representation, Alberta Art Foundation and Medici Art Foundation. He also taught art at the University of Alberta. Sylvain went to Mexico to paint in 1988 and had a major exhibition in 1992 of his work that portrayed Maya ruins of the Yucatán as the subject. He later started painting the west coast of Mexico. His list of commissioned paintings is long.

German **Sara Henze** was influenced by her father, an abstract artist. She studied at the School for Visual Art and Design in Cologne. After a few distractions (school and kids) she returned to painting. She does a mix of abstract and realistic portraits in bold and muted colors. You can find her works in La Manzanilla.

I know little about **Stephanie Doucette**, but she does a lot of Mexican portraits, some of which incorporate mystical figures.

Ron Stock does faux-naif style paintings that have tremendous detail in simple scenes.

Carlos Kieling offers an assortment of designs featuring everything from Van Gogh to Shakespeare and abstract t-shirt designs. He also likes to paint wildlife.

Jack Rutherford, an American painter and writer, paints pieces that are influenced by Picasso's style. His work is varied and his exhibitions numerous.

▪ Places to Stay

One-star **Posada del Cazador**, *Maria Asuncion #183*, ☎ 315-351-5000, $, is at the north end of town. It has basic rooms with fan and private bathroom.

Hotel Puesta del Sol, *Calle Playa Blanca #94*, ☎ 315-351-5033, $$, has basic but clean rooms with private bathrooms and fans. The rooms are located around a central patio. There is a porch with a fridge, sink and gas stove for guests to use. There is also a pool. The hotel is just one block from the beach at the south end of town.

HOTEL PRICE SCALE
Price for a room given in US $.
$.................Up to $20
$$..................$21-$50
$$$................$51-$100
$$$$ ....$101-$150
$$$$$ ....$151-$200
Anything over $200 is specified.

Posada Triton la Manzanilla, *Calle Concha Molida #12 and Punta Roxana*, ☎ 315-351-5124, $, is at the north end of town. This is a very basic establishment.

Posada Tonala, *Av Maria Asuncion #75*, ☎ 315-351-5474, *www.posada-tonala.com*, $$, is a tiny hotel with rooms on two floors built around a common sitting area. Each room has a double bed, TV, fan or air conditioning, tiled floor, bed lamp, desk and private bathroom with hot water. Run by a German couple, the place is sparkling clean and right on the beach. There are also three spacious bungalows for rent that are just as clean and cozy as the rooms. They cost between $25 and $60, depending on the number of guests. Monthly rates are available.

Eileen's, ☎ 315-351-5383, *eizack1@yahoo.com*, $$, has two nicely decorated rooms with private bathrooms and double beds. The rooms open onto a garden patio furnished with deck chairs. Full kitchen facilities are available for guest use. The house is decorated with artistic tiles, the halls are dotted with potted plants and the building is spotless. This is a unique guesthouse with exceptionally low rates. Guests get the luxury of eating meals cooked at the owner's cooking school.

Calypso Hotel, *Calle Anden de la Calechosa #10*, ☎ *315-351-5124, $$*, is a neat and tidy little place with eight rooms and three bungalows. The rooms have private bathrooms, desks, fans and tiled floors. The décor is plain but clean.

Hotel Fiesta Mexicana, *Km 8.5 on highway to Melaque/Barra de Navidad*, ☎ *314-333-2181, $$$*, has 194 rooms in a Mediterranean-style hotel. Each room has air conditioning, private balcony, TV, private shower, iron and board, and telephone. There is a restaurant, a bar, a coffee shop, a gift shop, private parking and a money exchange. The food in the restaurant is acceptable.

Villa Montaña, *$$$*, is on the hill above town and is perfect for everything from a writer's retreat to a family adventure. There is no TV, telephone or Internet, but there is a guest kitchen. Both bedrooms have a private bathroom and mosquito nets over the beds. There is lots of patio space and gardens with hammocks around the property.

Casa Maguey, ☎ *315-351-5012, www.casamaguey.com, $$$*, has three bungalows fully equipped and ready to move into. Just bring food and drink. There is tile on the floors and rattan furniture throughout. Each bungalow has a private bathroom and a separate living room and is surrounded by gardens. There are no pets allowed.

La Casa Maria, *Calle Los Angeles Locos and Concha Molida*, ☎ *315-351-5044, www.lacasamaria.com, $$$$$*, has camping ($5 per person) and a number of little cozy cabins that can sleep up to six people. They have kitchens with small fridges, microwaves and all needed cooking utensils. The bedrooms are large. This funky place is just five minutes from the beach.

El Tamarindo Golf Course and Resort, *Km 7.5 on the road to Melaque/Barra de Navidad*, ☎ *800-397-0877, $$$$$*, has one of the nicest pools in the area. There are thatched-roof villas with wooden floors and private plunge pools on the decks. The rooms were remodeled in 2001 and each has a telephone, data port, air conditioning, wardrobe and bathrobes, as well as a covered terrace, dining area and private garden. Villa rates run between $235 and $670 for two people, per night. This includes the use of all non-motorized sports equipment, the fitness room and the tennis courts. The big draw is the golf course. You will be offered a welcoming drink when you arrive and breakfast is included in the price. Despite the luxury, you may find the service a bit lacking. The staff seems disinterested in the welfare of their guests when things go wrong.

■ Places to Eat

Eileen's, ☎ *315-351-5383*, serves a choice of two meals each day at 6:30 pm. Reservations are required. The eating area is on the rooftop of Eileen's house. The day I was here, she served pecan-covered dorado (fish) with pumpkin-seed green sauce and vegetables and rice. The other choice was chicken breasts with lentils and green beans. All meals come with a salad and homemade dressing. The cost for my meal was $12.50, and the cheesecake with mango sauce was an extra $3. The food was excellent.

Martin's, *center of town,* is open daily from 8 am-11 pm, but closed on Thursday. This large palapa-hut restaurant serves things like home-made soup for $2.50 and a Caesar salad big enough for two for $8. The enchiladas, also very good, cost between $5 and $6. The view of the ocean is as good as the food.

Martha's, *near the garden in the center of town,* has the best tacos in Mexico. They are like sandwiches, only you get to put a hundred times more flavors into them. This is a family-run establishment and the owners are friendly. The food is excellent.

Jolandas, *Playa Blanca #43,* ☎ *315-351-5449,* is open Thursday to Monday, 3-10 pm. The bar is open an extra hour at night. This is the funkiest place along the Costalegre (Happy Coast) and also the most popular for dinners with the young surfers.

El Quetzal, *one block from the beach*, is open 8 am-11 pm. Meals such as roast duck or rabbit are highly recommended. The good thing about this café is that it is open for breakfast – with coffee and *huevos rancheros* for about $3.

Palapa Joe's, *Calle Maria Asuncion on the beach*, is open 8 am-9 pm. It's a good place to eat. The food is mainly fish, but the fish is exceptional. Just sitting here and having a beer with the in crowd is fun too.

Barra de Navidad/Melaque

As is common in Mexico, these two towns are so close together, they are considered the same place. Barra is located on a sand spit that forms the southern end off the bay and separates the bay from the Laguna de Navidad. At the south end of the bay and across from the tip of the spit is the entrance to the lake. Just offshore are Isla de Navidad and San Patricio de Melaque, called simply Melaque. These two islands are good for birding. Isla de Navidad is also a destination for those who love golf and luxury and have lots of cash to fulfill their needs. The island has 1,235 acres of developed land that includes the golf course, two marinas, a tennis ranch, a spa, a night club and a number of private villas and condominiums. If you are interested in staying on the island, see *Places to Stay*, below, for reviews of the island's Grand Bay hotel, which even has a golf course.

■ History

 Cortez wrote to Charles V of Spain describing a port along the coast that was strategically well situated. Some believe the port he referred to was Navidad. However, historically, **Francisco de Hijar** is given credit with finding the bay in 1535. He named it Puerto Xalisco.

According to historian Tony Burton, in his book *Western Mexico – A Traveler's Treasury*, the bay was of interest to the Spanish long before Hijar arrived because they had heard rumors that Isla de Navidad was inhabited only by women who had a cache of pearls. Naturally, the Spanish sailors thought they could save the women from their man-less fate by coming to the rescue. When Hijar arrived, he and his men were sadly disappointed. All they found were rebellious locals, most of whom were men.

On December 25, 1540, **Viceroy Don Antonio de Mendoza** arrived to put down Indian uprisings. Because of his arrival date, he renamed the place Navidad, which means "Christmas" in Spanish.

The port became a good naval base for the Spanish. In 1564 they sent an expedition from here to the Philippines under the leadership of Miguel Lopez de Legazpi and Friar Andres de Urdaneta. The expedition was successful and led to the Spanish conquering the Philippine Islands.

Today, the Spanish/Mexicans are still trying to entice men to the area, although they are no longer using the lure of stranded women laden with pearls. They have developed a 27-hole golf course and a luxurious hotel.

■ Services

 Post office, *Calle Nueva Espana, Monday to Friday, 8:30 am-4:30 pm, and Saturday until 1 pm.*

▪ Adventures on Water

> **SURF TURF**
>
> Surfing in the area requires some social etiquette. Some locals are territorial about their place on the beach, so it has become customary to go first with either a tour operator or a local so that you can be introduced to the Mexican surfers. When they see that you are not a threat to their waves, you will be left to surf solo.

Beaches

 Playa Principal is the main beach in Barra. It is a bit steep and at the south end near the lagoon, surfers are able to catch a few strong waves. Body surfers and paddlers should be careful here as there is an undertow. Windsurfing is a good sport for this area. Surfboards can be rented in Melaque from the tour office next door to La Paloma Art Studio.

Playa Laguna is the beach beside the jetty. It is small with gentle waves and is good for kayak paddlers. The lake is not good for swimming because the water is stagnant.

> **BUGS BUG OFF!**
>
> Mosquito repellent is essential while you travel the Pacific coast. The mangrove swamps that border the beaches and separate them from the mountains are a great breeding place for insects. If you have not brought your own (I recommend Deep Woods Off that is 95% DEET, available in Canada and the US), then **Autan Classic**, manufactured by Bayer de Mexico, is good alternative. It can be purchased at most department stores. Mosquito coils, called **Raid-O-Litos** in Mexico, will also help when sitting at a palapa-hut restaurant or in your room at night. Malaria and dengue fever, spread by mosquitoes, are a problem usually after rainy season only. The incidence of these diseases in Mexico is low. For the *jejenes* (sand fleas), use an oil; **Skin-So-Soft** by Avon is a good one.

Playa Melaque is the beach near the town of the same name. The beach has a steep slope so the waves break close to shore. This area is not good for snorkeling except for a tiny spot at the west end of town that has some calm water.

■ Adventures of the Brain

Amiga's Spanish Lessons in Paradise, *Mazatlan between Sinaloa and Jalisco, www.easyspanish.net,* teaches conversational Spanish in private and semi-private classes. Field excursions are included. Their method of teaching has students speaking while doing practical tourist things like bargaining in the market or looking for a room. They also teach slang, a useful part of any language. Lessons are available from November to April and cost $15 an hour for private lessons, $12 an hour for semi-private and $7.50 an hour for group lessons with three to six students.

■ Outfitters/Tour Operators

Sea to Sierra Outdoor Adventures, *Ejidatarios #4, Barra de Navidad,* ☎ *315-355-7140, www.seatosierra.com,* offers bike tours to places like Tenacatita, El Tecuan, Boca de Iguanas, Las Joyas, Colimilla on Isla Navidad and Cihuatlan. Their bikes have front-end suspension and are in good shape and the beers served after a ride are cold. Sea to Sierra specializes in safe, off-road biking and tours from two to six hours a day. Most tours are vehicle-assisted (if you conk out, you can ride in a car). Helmets, water and bikes are included in the price of about $100 per day. Beer is a little extra. The company also runs horseback riding trips that cost between $20 and $25 per hour, depending on how many people ride. The minimum is two people for two hours.

South Swell Surf Shop, *16A Benito Juarez, Melaque,* ☎ *314-872-2457 (cell), is open 8 am-7 pm daily.* South Swell rents snorkeling and surfing equipment and also offers surfing lessons in English or Spanish. They run $10 per hour, plus the cost of the board. To rent the boards without lessons costs $12.50-$20 a day or $8-$10 for a half-day, depending on the type of board you use. Snorkeling sets rent for $9-$10 per day and boogie boards are the same price. They run guided trips to other beaches for $50 a day, plus the cost of gasoline. This shop keeps up to date on water and wave conditions for surfers.

Fishing guide **Alfredo Molinas**, ☎ *315-355-6049,* is good. Call him and make an appointment. He knows where the fish are located.

■ Places to Stay

There are hundreds of places between Barra and Melaque. Some are basic; others, like the one on the island, are beyond the financial reach of most of us.

In Barra

Hotel Caribe, *Calle Sonora,* ☎ *315-355-5952, $,* has very basic clean rooms and a nice sitting area on the porch as well as a rooftop patio.

Hotel Delfin, *Morelos #23,* ☎ *315-355-5068, $$,* is on the lakeside of the spit and across from the Sands Hotel. This is a fairly large place with arched open hallways overlooking the street. It is clean and the big rooms each have a private bathroom. The disco down the street that at one time was a bother has been closed due to popular demand.

HOTEL PRICE SCALE	
Price for a room given in US $.	
$.................Up to $20	
$$..................$21-$50	
$$$................$51-$100	
$$$$ ....$101-$150	
$$$$$ ....$151-$200	
Anything over $200 is specified.	

Posada Pacifico, *Mazatlan #136,* ☎ *315-355-5359, $$,* is a motel-style place with rooms on two floors located around a central courtyard. Each large room has a private bathroom and ceiling fan.

Casa de Don Ramon, *Del Galeon,* ☎ *315-355-6114, www.pathcom.com/ ~msclarke, $$,* is next to the harbor master's office and is recognized by its yellow and red wall surrounded by red bougainvilleas. If you like flowers, this is a good place. Each of the five rooms has a screened window, a fan and air conditioning, and a private bathroom. Guests have access to a communal patio and a kitchen equipped for light meals.

Casa de Marco, *Miguel Lopez de Legazpi #60,* ☎ *315-355-6091, www. casademarco.com, $$$,* has one- and two-bedroom apartments for rent by the week; one is wheelchair-accessible. Located close to the beach, the hotel also has a pool. The kitchens have a fridge, a microwave, a toaster, a blender, a coffee maker, an iron and pots, pans and dishes. There is also cable TV, a stereo CD player and an in-wall safe. There is a balcony for each suite. This clean spot is an excellent choice for those who want to stay in Barra for awhile.

Bungalows Mar Vida, *Mazatlan # 168,* ☎ *315-355-5911, $$$,* has five air-conditioned bungalows with kitchenettes, private bathrooms and hot water. There is a pool on site. The hotel is very clean and safe.

Casa Chips, *198 Miguel Lopes de la Gaspi,* ☎ *315-355-5555, www. casachips.com, $$$/$$$$,* is a beachfront hotel that has been operating for more than 10 years. It has seven rooms, each with ceiling fan, two queen-sized beds, small fridge, private bathroom and arched windows facing the street or the ocean. There is also a full apartment, a studio and a sunset suite for rent. Some suites have a balcony. The comfort level and tasteful décor of these places is commendable. The hotel's beachside café offers barbequed ribs for $8 per serving on Tuesday. It's open 9 am-9 pm.

The Sands, *Morelos #24*, ☎ *315-355-5018, $$*, has been a popular spot with travelers for years because of its nice pool and well-kept gardens that feature caged monkeys. The rooms all have private bathrooms, fans, tiled floors, wooden-framed windows and tasteful furnishings. Breakfast is included in the rate. The hotel has the lagoon on one side, the ocean on the other and a pool with a bar at one end. The disco, which at one time kept guests awake, has now closed.

Hotel Cabo Blanco, *Bahia de las Navidades #3*, ☎ *315-355-5170, $$$$*, has 83 rooms and is the most luxurious hotel in town (excluding the Grand Bay Isla Navidad hotel). It is set on the canal and is a bit of a walk from the beach. The rooms are small, but there is a pool with a bar, and a children's playground. This hotel, because of its location, likes to offer an all-inclusive package. Most people who have stayed here are happy with what they got.

In Melaque

Although most people stay in Barra, Melaque is just two miles up the road.

Hotel de la Costa, *Calle Ignacio Vallarta # 19*, ☎ *315-355-5126, $$*, has 20 rooms in a clean place without frills.

El Palmar Beach and Tennis Resort, *Calle Esmeralda and Zafiro, across from the Bungalows Pacifico in the Obregón section of town*, ☎ *315-355-6263, $$$*, has a nice pool and garden, plus tennis courts where you can meet and challenge other players. The rooms have two beds, purified water, very large bathrooms, tiled floors and apartment-size fridges. One- and two-bedroom apartments are available, too.

Attractive **Hotel Club Nautico**, *Gomez Farias # 315*, ☎ *315-355-5770, $$$*, has 56 rooms with air conditioning, fan, balcony, cable TV and telephone. There's a small pool and a restaurant, El Dorado. English is spoken.

Hotel Monterrey, *Calle Gomez Farias # 27*, ☎ *315-355-5004, $$$*, is near the bus station and a good choice if you have arrived by bus and don't want to search too far for a place to stay. It is an attractive hotel with an enclosed courtyard. The 22 rooms are moderate in size and have private bathrooms and fans. There is a restaurant, bar, off-street parking and a pool. Two bungalows with kitchenettes are available. The hotel is near the beach.

Isla de Navidad

The Grand Bay Isla Navidad Hotel, ☎ *315-331-0500, www.wyndham-vacations.com*, costs between $520 and $600 a night for a golf/room package. This includes your room, your game and breakfast for two people. You can also stay for a mere $380 a night without the golf game. There is no extra charge for up to two children under the age of 10. Visit their website to learn about other package vacations.

The hotel has 200 rooms with private balconies overlooking the bay or out to the mountains. They feature tasteful décor, air conditioning and ceiling fans, tiled floors and muted fabrics. The bathrooms are all marble and there are in-room safes. Bathrobes are supplied and hypo-allergenic bedding is available. Each room has cable TV, coffee maker, fridge, hair dryer and iron. A plate of fresh fruit and bottled water is delivered daily. The place is gargantuan and oozes sexuality.

There are three tennis courts, a workout room, putting green, private marina, three swimming pools, a bar, a restaurant and a private beach. The childcare facilities have skilled workers who are able to entertain the kids for hours. Travel around the island is complimentary, as are daily newspapers. You are welcomed by a doorman, and photo ID and a credit card are required upon check-in for any extras. The lobby bar has a view of the beach and lake, and live music most nights.

All your food needs will be fulfilled. The Grand Café is a casual restaurant that serves meals either inside or on the terrace. There is a swim-up bar in the main pool, a sandwich and beer restaurant beside the pool and Antonio's, a formal dining room featuring Continental cuisine and Mexican seafood dishes. Take your pick from over 200 brands of tequila. The décor includes original paintings by well-known artists.

If the hotel is not upscale enough for you, there are some villas available. The smallest, called the **Albatros**, undoubtedly named because of its size, just 8,600 square feet/800 square meters. There are three bedrooms, a kitchen, living room, a palapa-roofed hut beside the small pool and a two-car garage. The other villas go up to 13,450 square feet/1,250 square meters in size. Inquire for rates.

The Meson Doña Paz is a tri-level mansion where guests can stay in rooms if they don't want a villa or the expanse of the large hotel. It has a restaurant, two cocktail bars, a pool with bar, a whirlpool, an exercise room and a tennis court.

The **golf course** is a par 72, 27-hole course designed by Robert Von Hagge. It offers views of the ocean, the mountains and the lagoon and is tucked between the hill on the island called Cerro del Caracol and the marina. The huge clubhouse has a bar, a restaurant and a pro shop that offers instruction for a fee. It is built in colonial style, with terra cotta tiles to contrast the polished marble. The bathrooms are segregated and include showers, sauna and a Jacuzzi. Guests can have Turkish baths and massages, or work out in the gym. Non-guests pay $260 each to play a round. Rental clubs are $50, gloves are $20, and a caddy is mandatory.

If you are interested in staying on the island, contact Hotel Operator and Reservations, *Ruben Dario 1262, Colonia Providencia, 44630 Guadala-*

jara, Jalisco, Mexico, ☎ *333-641-5326 or 800-849-2373 in Mexico City,* for general information.

■ Places to Eat

In Barra

 Casa Chips, *Miguel # 198,* ☎ *315-355-5555,* is open 9 am-9 pm daily. This is a beachside café that has snacks and drinks all day. On Tuesdays it offers barbequed ribs for $8 per serving. This is a popular meal; if you want to be guaranteed a dish, make reservations.

Cenadura Esperanza, *Av Veracrus, no phone*, has Chinese food that is always such a treat after a steady diet of rice and beans or chicken. The stir-fried vegetables are highly recommended. The cost is under $5 per serving.

Mar y Tierra, *Av Lopez de Legazpi, no phone,* at the east end of town is where to go when you want a Mexican meal or a hamburger served with a special flare. Meals cost under $8.

Restaurant Ambar, *Av Veracruz # 101A,* is open 5 pm-midnight. The upstairs restaurant serves French cuisine and crêpes. Even if you don't want to do a whole delicious meal here, come for an after-dinner drink and a crêpe.

Popeye's Restaurant, *Av Miguel Lopez de Legazpi #44, no phone,* is on the beach at the point where the *malecón* starts. Their specialty is seafood, and they offer a fantastic avocado and shrimp salad. Shrimp wrapped in bacon and stuffed with cheese is another favorite. Prices are high, $10+ for a meal.

Panchoz Restaurant, *Av Miguel Lopez de Legazpi # 53,* ☎ *315-355-5176,* has some long-resident parrots to entertain you while you eat. Panchoz' specialty is ceviche, a pickled fish dish that is super as an appetizer or as a main meal. The fish is "cooked" in lime juice and the tartness is especially good if you are thirsty. The cost is $5-$10 for a dish.

Mr Crocodile Lucky, *Calle Morelos #26,* ☎ *315-355-8205*, open Tuesday to Sunday noon – midnight, is the place to go for Italian dishes. Pizza, spaghetti and lasagna are all recommended along with a cool beer. Meals cost less than $10.

Café and Jugos Manhattan, *Calle Lopez de Legazpi,* opens every day at 7:30 am and closes at 3 pm. It is inside the Alondra Hotel, which was still not open when I was there. However, some shops inside were doing business. Breakfast coffee is a specialty of the Manhattan, but the carrot cake for under $3 a slice is also worth your time.

In Melaque

It is often nice to walk to this village for a meal. You get a change of scenery and can share your presence (and dollars).

The Alcatraz, *Av. Lopez Mateos (upstairs) near the trailer park at the east end of the street, no phone.* Try their Chicken Alcatraz – onions, green peppers and chicken served in a hot-pot. This is one of the most popular restaurants in Melaque.

Highly recommended **Pedro's Fish and Chips**, *Alejandrina # 38,* has garlic and Cajun shrimp, both hot and delicious. They are open only for supper, 5-9 pm every day except Sunday. Meals cost about $8.

■ Nightlife

 Terraza Bar Capri, *Av Miguel Lopez de Legazpi # 119, Barre de Navidad*, is open 2pm-2 am. Their happy hour runs from 6-9 pm daily. There are pool tables, a nice dance floor and recorded music.

Club Felix, *Calle Jalisco #48, Barre de Navidad,* has tables inside and outside on the street. This is a popular meeting place where you can have a peaceful drink and talk. However, the benches don't have backs, so you may want to sit inside where there are chairs.

Manzanillo Region

Manzanillo

The mountains, covered in thick green vegetation, almost touch the ocean at Manzanillo. Between the mountains and the water are jagged rocks. Together, the three terrains give the bay a dramatic affect. The old town of Manzanillo is a port, but a very clean one. The only time that you may get an unpleasant impression of the city is if

you arrive by bus. If that happens, you will see the grottiest section of town before you see the splendor. However, to rectify this, the city is building a new station close to a green strip of mangrove that is rich in bird life.

Manzanillo center.

There are a few hotels in the old town; most are dingy, but the Colonial and the Bahai are worth considering (see page 369). There is not much in the way of beaches in town. To hit the sand, you must travel about four miles/seven km to the hotel area. The term "hotel area" is a bit of a misnomer because it looks more like a middle-class suburb with shopping malls, gas stations, dress shops and car dealerships than it does a resort area. The hotels, for the most part, aren't even visible from the main streets.

One of the big draws to Manzanillo is that, after sunning for a few days, you can take a one-hour bus ride into Colima and visit some historical sights or travel the mountains just another half an hour away. One of these mountains is Mexico's most active volcano, El Volcán de Fuego, a true thrill to visit.

■ Getting Here & Around

By Plane

 The airport, about 15 miles/25 km from Manzanillo, is serviced by America West, Alaska Airlines and Aeromar, which flies from San Antonio and Houston in the US and books through Vista World Travel.

AIRLINE CONTACT INFORMATION		
Aeromar	www.vistaworldtravel.com	☎ 800-880-8068 (US)
Alaska Airlines	www.alaskaair.com	☎ 800-252-7522 (US); 55-5282-2484 (Mx)
America West	www.americawest.com	☎ 800-363-2597 (US); 800-235-9292 (Mx)

By Taxi

The cost of a taxi into Manzanillo from the airport, about 45 minutes away, is $27. From the airport to Barra de Navidad, about 20 minutes away, is $22. You can also take a mini-van, located outside the terminal, into Manzanillo for $7. Taxis cost $2-$5 from town to the hotel areas.

▶▶ **AUTHOR NOTE:** *You'll see ticket stands at the bus station selling taxi tickets. The cost of getting a taxi this way is almost four times higher than hiring a taxi yourself once outside the door.*

By Bus

Buses come from Colima every hour and from Guadalajara three times daily. When arriving by bus, take a city bus or a taxi to the area you have chosen to stay. The hotel area is between four-12 miles/seven-20 km from the bus station.

A city bus costs 45¢ per person and can take you to either end of the peninsula or to the center of the old town. Walking from the bus station into the old town takes half an hour to 45 minutes.

By Car

Driving is good in the area because the road is well paved, the signs are clear and the traffic is light.

> ### DARING DRIVING
>
> It is legal to make a left turn from the right lane in Mexico and, if there is an accident, the car that was farthest ahead on impact is the one in the right. In the event of an accident, if you have broken a law by drinking and driving, your insurance is invalid.

Hummbug, *www.divemanzanillo.com/autorental/buggy.htm (reservations through website only)*, is a small car with open sides and back and a roof held up by poles. This little vehicle rents for $50 a day, has a standard transmission and holds up to five people. It goes a mere 40 mph/ 60 kmh and uses very little gas. It is popular for those running up and down the beach road during the day, but for safety reasons do not take it on the highway at night.

Auto Rentals de Mexico, *Crucero las Brisas #749*, ☎ *314-333-2580, www.gomanzanillo.com*, has everything from Volkswagen bugs ($50 a day) to a Suburban with air conditioning ($150 a day). This large company, found throughout Mexico, is very good to deal with.

ODIN Car Rental, *Blvd Miguel de la Madrid #11825-A*, ☎ *314-333-1112, odinmanzanillo@yahoo.com.mx*, has the same variety of cars that are available at any other company. The bonus is that they will pick up and deliver your vehicle anywhere in Manzanillo. The cost for a VW Serina is $31.50 a day.

National Car Rentals, *Miguel de la Madrid #1070*, ☎ *314-333-0611, interent@bay.net.mx*, is a bit more pricey than other companies. For example, a Chevy without air conditioning costs $46 a day or $276 a week (including unlimited mileage, insurance and the 15% tax). A car with air conditioning costs $53 a day.

▶▶ **AUTHOR NOTE:** *The thing I liked about National was that they were much more interested in telling me the truth about road conditions and driving in Mexico than they were in renting me a vehicle. I highly recommend you deal with Silvia.*

■ History

 Cortez saw Manzanillo in 1522 when he ordered Gonzalo de Sandoval to look for places in which to build ships, but it wasn't until 1527 that Alvaro Saavedra came to start ship construction. He named the bay **Santiago de la Buena**. However, after the business was established, pirates came and used secluded bays along the coast as a refuge, so the shipbuilders left. But the huge trees in the area were a great draw to shipbuilders, and in 1825 the port once again became a major shipbuilding area. In the early 1900s, the city was linked to the rest of the country by rail lines and, finally, by paved highways. When shipbuilding declined, the city became an important port. Today, Manzanillo has seen a growth spurt and the port is busier than ever, hosting ships from all of America and the Far East.

■ Services

 Tourist Police, ☎ *314-336-6600*
Federal Police, ☎ *314-336-5677*

Tourist Office, *Blvd Miguel de la Madrid #1294,* ☎ *314-333-3838, www. manzanillo.com.mx.*

Publications

Manzanillo and the State of Colima, Facts, Tips and Day Trips*, by Susan Dearing, is a local publication that has a plethora of facts and tidbits for the visitor. Look for it around town or purchase it directly from Susan Dearing for $30, AP 295, Santiago, Colima, Mexico 29961. You can also order online at www.gomanzanillo.com/guidebook/index.htm.

■ Sightseeing

 University Archeological Museum, *Glorieta San Pedrito,* ☎ *314-332-2256, Tuesday to Saturday, 10 am-2 pm and 5-8 pm, and Sunday, 10 am-1 pm, $1.* This museum opened in 1996 in a modern building. It has a collection of 20,000 pieces, although more than

Manzanillo

Sights & Attractions

1. Sailboat traffic circle
2. Archeological Museum
3. Old Town
4. San Gabriel Caves
5. El Salto Waterfalls
6. Las Hadas Golf & Marina
7. Zona de Tolerancia

N

Laguna de Cuyutlan

Laguna de Cuyutlan

to La Ventanas Beach

5
to

4
to Colima,
Tecoman & 4

2

7

3

Laguna
San Pedro

Laguna de Las Garzas

AV DE LAS GARZAS

BLVD MIGUEL DE LA MADRID HURTADO

1

Bahía de La Buena Esperanza

Bahías de Manzanillo

Playa Salagua

Playa Hadas

6

Playa Perla

LA PUNTA

to airport, La Boquita
& Miramar beaches

Playa Audencia

Bahía de Santiago

NOT TO SCALE

2,000 are seldom on show at any given time. The five rooms are Manzanillo, Regions of the State, Mesoamerica, Pre-Hispanic Jewelry and Temporary Exhibitions. Two sunken tombs from the Comala period that were built between 300 and 500 AD are always on display. The reconstruction is exceptionally well done. There are also some bone and shell fragments and painted textiles that were found at Del Tesoro beach not far from the city.

ZONE DE TOLERANCIA

Manzanillo has a **zona de tolerancia** (a tolerated zone), where some bars allow table dances, lap dances and more. In fact, everything legal is permitted and the live entertainment is checked by a doctor once a week. Motels de Paso is where you can hire a room by the hour to accommodate the entertainment. This area is near the docks in the old section of town.

Cockfights are common, but I do not advocate the sport. If you are interested, purchase Susan Dearing's book about travel in Manzanillo or visit her website, www.gomanzanillo.com, for event information.

■ Adventures on Foot

Hiking

 San Gabriel Caves are eight miles/12 km south of Ixtahuacan. To get here, take a bus to Ixtahuacan and then a second bus to San Gabriel, a tiny village at the top of a hill. From there it is a five-minute walk to the entrance of the cave. Inside, you will walk along a 50-foot/15-meter shaft before you come to the main chamber. Its walls are filled with stalagmites and stalactites of every color and formation you can imagine. This was once a ceremonial cave and has a tiny man-made pyramid that was built up on one side to accommodate the slope of the cave. To enter you must have a guide approved by the Department of Tourism. Guides can be hired in Ixtahuacan; ask at the restaurant on the plaza. Alternately, work with a tour company in Manzanillo.

Golf

El Tamarindo Country Club, *Km 7.5 on the Melaque to Puerto Vallarta Highway,* ☎ *800-397-0877.* This course was designed by Robert Trent Jones II and David Fleming. It is a par 72, 18-hole, 6,682-yard course. The first hole (a par four) offers a nice warmup of 371 yards and requires a bit of skill to avoid the jungle. By the third hole you are near the beach. According to *Golf Odyssey Magazine,* holes six, seven, eight and nine may be the best string of four holes in the world. Holes six and seven have a dogleg and a double dogleg to work around and the eighth has a trap-protected green that is bordered by the ocean. The ninth hole overlooks the rocky shore of the bay. A snack bar located at the ninth offers views of the ocean. At the holes near the ocean, it is claimed that more shots are taken with cameras than with clubs.

> **WARNING:** On the last nine holes, don't look for lost balls in the jungle, as the snake population there is high.

La Manta Raya Golf Club at Las Hadas, *Av Vista Hermosa*, ☎ *314-331-0101*, is a par 71, 18-hole course with the 15th and 18th holes crossing water. The 18th is called the million-dollar-island green. The longest hole on the course is 538 yards. There are 46 sand traps, 15 water hazards and 25 side bunkers. The course opens at 7 am daily and the last tee time is 5 pm. The cost is $96 for 18 holes and $56 for nine. A cart is $45, caddy $15 and shoe rental is $25 for 18 holes. There is an amateur tournament here each November. Check at the club for more information.

LAWS OF GOLF

- The practice green is always twice as fast or twice as slow as the other greens.
- Your bag always has either two or 200 tees.
- If your ball falls on the driving range it is probably because you did not aim it there.
- A visible ball in the rough is not yours.
- You must always face the wind for 16 holes.

Santiago Golf Club, *Av Camaron #1-A*, ☎ *314-335-0410*, is a nine-hole, par-36 course with 3,284 yards from the back tees. The course was designed by Larry Hughes and goes through the foothills and around a salt-water lagoon. It is open 7 am to 6 pm; reservations are required. Lessons are available and there is a pro shop.

Tennis

There are courts at **Club Santiago**, **Las Hadas** and **Maeva**, but hotel guests get first refusal. If the courts are not booked, then you can go in for a game ($15 an hour).

Gym

Siluett Gym, *Blvd Costero Miguel de la Madrid and Las Hadas*, ☎ *314-333-2260,* has all the gym equipment needed to get rid of last night's dinner and drinks. They also offer classes in aerobics, kickboxing and technical indoor cycling.

■ Adventures on Water

 El Salto Waterfalls at Peña Colorada is a double-tiered fall that drops about 60 feet/20 meters into a pool that is used for swimming. From a cliff at the side of the pool, divers plunge into the cool water. The jungle around the river is dense and vegetated with plants found in rainforest environments. Strangler figs are common, as are ferns and air plants. This waterfall is fed by the Minatitlan River. To get here, drive past the water slides at Peña Colorada to the bottom of the hill. Cross the iron bridge and park. Follow the path from the parking area to the steps leading down to the river. Don't be afraid to float through the narrow passage between the rocks to a second waterfall and another swimming area. It is quite safe. There is a 50¢ charge to enter the area.

Scuba Diving

Although Manzanillo is not known internationally as a diving destination, that is slowly changing. There are two artificial reefs in the area, one south of Manzanillo, called Tepalcates, and the other at Elephant Rock. In 1998, new sea mounds were discovered just a few minutes from the shore. These mountains lie just 30 feet/10 meters below the surface and are swarming with wildlife. Some of the common species are globefish, sea urchins and manta rays. Most of the following information about dive sites is taken from Susan Dearing's *Underworld Scuba.*

> **WARNING:** There is a phenomenon known as **rebalses** here, whereby strong wave action causes problems for divers. Always check with the local dive shop for weather/water conditions before going out.

Los Frailes has visibility down to about 75 feet/25 meters, where there are stony corals and sponges. Often, a six-foot/three-meter moray is spotted here, along with groupers, hogfish and triggerfish. This spot is off the very tip of the Juluapan Peninsula at the north end of the bay.

Elephant Rock is at the north end of the bay just off the Peninsula de Juluapan. The area has underwater tunnels that run about 150 feet/50 meters through the mountain. There are canyons, crevices and underwater arches, as well as coral reefs and a surging blowhole. Puffers, turtles and whale sharks are often found here. This dive goes from 20 to 60 feet/ six to 20 meters down and can have a strong current; this is for more experienced divers only.

Los Carrizales is in a narrow inlet in the bay north of Audiencia Beach and is where the Grand Canyon, a quagmire of cracks and crevices that house octopus and lobster, is located. It is also the location where a ship with $1.5 million worth of gold burned and sank. You may get lucky and pay for your dive with what you find. See Playa de Oro, page 336, for more details. This dive goes from 25 to 100 feet/10 to 30 meters deep.

Drowned Rock has a visibility of about 75 feet/25 meters and features walls and canyons. This is a good place for spotting large schools of tropical fish. It is in Manzanillo Bay.

Peña Blanca is a white rock out on the bay where whales and manta rays like to play. The volcanic fissures, crevices and caves make this a challenging dive. It runs 45-100 feet/15-30 meters and is for experienced divers only.

Las Ventanas Lagoon is a seahorse sanctuary where you can see these well-camouflaged creatures. Although some grow up to a foot in length, they are hard to see. Those with a bulge in the tummy are pregnant males. Now this is woman's lib at its best.

Snorkeling

La Boquia Beach at the north end of the bay is good for snorkeling. There is a coral reef and a sunken ship.

Playa Audiencia, in front of Hotel Sierra along the hotel strip, is the most popular spot for snorkeling. Visibility is about 40 feet/12 meters and the bottom is white sand, so the fish are easy to see. Damselfish, yellowtails, eels and stingrays swim among the soft corals, while angelfish, trumpet fish and balloon fish hang around the area. You need not go more than a few feet from shore to see the fish and usually the wave action is gentle. However, you should swim at least a few feet from the rocks in case one of the few large waves pushes you against them.

Elephant Rock is at the north end of the bay just off the Peninsula de Juluapan and is excellent for snorkeling. There is a secluded little beach here where you can rest between swims. You may be able to hook up with a diving boat going to the rock and do some snorkeling.

Sportfishing

Manzanillo is known as the Sailfish Capital of the World because of the number of trophy fish that have been taken from these waters. Over 70 game fish can be caught in the area. Of the most popular, sailfish and dorado are here year-round, while marlin and tuna are usually caught from November to March. There is a limit of one fish per tourist. See page 367 about boats for hire.

The International Dorsey Tournament, *contact Club Deportivo de Pesca,* ☎ *314-336-7265,* has been held every November and February since 1954 and attracts anglers from around the world. The fish caught must be between eight and 12 feet/2.5 and four meters in length to qualify. The International Tournament is held the first week of November and costs $500 per pole to enter. There is over $80,000 in prizes. The National Tournament is the first week of February and admission is $200 per pole. Prizes are up to $50,000. The Torneo Fiestas de Mayo take place during the first week in May and cost $200 per pole to enter. Prizes are about $50,000 in all. Boats entering the tournaments must go at least 10 miles/16 km from shore, have radios, life vests and heads (bathrooms). These are catch-and-release tournaments.

Watersports

Explorer Manzanillo Catamaran Sunset Cruise, *Las Hatas Marina,* ☎ *314-331-0101,* leaves on Monday, Thursday and Saturday at 4:15 pm for a three-hour tour of the bay. This is a double-decker boat where you can sit either in the sun or below in the shade. It can hold up to 300 passengers. You will pass Elephant, Three Wise Men and Rhinoceros Rocks. Along the shore, luxurious residential homes dot the hillsides. Between December and February, you may be lucky enough to see whales. Dolphins on the other hand, are around all year so the chance of seeing one of them is good. The cost for the cruise is $33 per person and includes water, sodas and national alcoholic beverages.

Banana Boat Tours are available from some hotels along the bay. A banana boat ride is a wild event where you get a number of people on a yellow inflatable that resembles a banana. Once in the middle of the bay, you bounce around trying to get everyone else but yourself thrown into the water. It's like a bucking bronco ride on water and, the more people on the vessel, the rougher the ride. Life vests are provided.

Beaches

There is some great surfing around Manzanillo at places like Olas Altas beach.

▶▶ *Anyone interested in the real big stuff should contact* **Alan Delgado**, ☎ *314-333-1565, www. gomanzanillo.com/surfing/index.htm, who runs a surf club.*

Cathedral in Guadalajara

Above: View of Acapulco's bay

Below: Surfer, Puerto Escondido

Above: Haze over Monte Alban

Below: Church, Patzcuaro

Monte Alban

Above: Monarch butterflies

Below: Street with church, Concordia

Above: Guadalajara cathedral at nighttime

Below: View of Ixtapa shorline

Cabañas Cultural Institute, Guadalajara

Cathedral of Oaxaca

Santiago Bay, like many bays along the Mexican Pacific, has a series of beaches. Some are good for snorkeling, some for surfing and some for swimming. Santiago stretches from the Juluapan Peninsula on the west to Santiago Peninsula on the east which, in turn, forms the northern shore of the Manzanillo Bay.

La Boquia is at the north end of Santiago Bay, where the lagoon empties into the ocean. This beach has gentle surf and is popular with locals. Windsurfing, swimming, diving and snorkeling are good. There are umbrellas for rent along the shore for $3 per day. The palapa restaurants are a sure hit for a snack or a full meal.

Miramar, in front of Club Maeva, starts where the pedestrian walkway goes over the highway. This is a good boogie boarding and surfing area. There are a number of stalls renting boards, inner tubes and horses. The beach has a gentle slope, fine white sand and an easy surf.

Playa Santiago, at the south end of the bay, is the oldest beach in the area. It has many inexpensive hotels along the shore. The water is calm and clear, the slope of the beach gentle. Behind Santiago is a hill dotted with eye-catching villas; they are sparkling white with red-tiled roofs that give the area an exotic flavor.

Audiencia Beach is at the south end of the bay on the rocky Santiago Peninsula. Audiencia is where Bo Derek and Dudley Moore filmed *10*. Hotel Sierra is located on the best part of this beach. The two ends of the beach are rocky and good for snorkeling and diving. Jet Skis, boogie boards, inner tubes and banana boats can be rented from stalls along the beach. You can climb to El Faro Lighthouse or La Reina Lookout for a good view of the Manzanillo area.

Playa Perla is a tiny beach near the yacht club. It has good snorkeling and diving; many people come for night dives to see parrotfish that gather in the shallows on the north side.

Playa Hadas is a secluded cove where Las Hadas Golf Resort and Marina are located. It is difficult to get onto the hotel beach even though, in Mexico, it is against the law to block off beach access. I don't know what would happen if you walked through the lobby and onto the "private" beach.

Playa Salagua is next to Karmina Palace, where the Salagua River enters the ocean. The river is often used by locals for swimming, but the beach itself has high waves and a strong undertow, so it is no good for swimming. It is, however, a good place for experienced surfers. You can rent umbrellas and buy refreshments from the palapa hut establishments just to the side of the Palace.

Manzanillo Region

FACT FILE: Playa Salagua was host to pirates and buccaneers 150 years ago. During high trading times with the East, the Manila Galleon often stopped here, bringing items from China and Japan. These items were paid for with Mexican silver.

Manzanillo Bay is the largest bay in the area and stretches from Karmina Palace all the way to the harbor in the old town. Waves are unpredictable and can be as high as 10 feet/three meters or as gentle as a ripple. Some people, during the calm times, like to snorkel in the bay. The area nearest the harbor, called Playa Las Brisas, is often deserted. This is a good spot to sit at a restaurant and watch the ocean liners come and go.

La Ventanas is west of Laguna de Cuyutlan. The beach has a blowhole, called the *bufadora* in Spanish. It throws a column of spray into the air every few minutes and is a popular tourist destination.

■ Adventures in Nature

 Where to Watch Birds in Mexico, by Steve Howell, covers 100 sites and about 1,000 species.

 Guide to the Birds of Mexico and Northern Central America, also by Steve Howell, describes 1,070 species and covers Mexico and Central America down to northern Nicaragua. The guide features 71 color plates, plus maps.

Laguna San Pedro is off the highway that joins the beach strip to the center. Take repellent, binoculars and follow any of the trails that lead from the road toward the water.

BIRD WATCH: *This mangrove area is good for birding; lilac-crowned parrots, white-throated magpies, San Blas jays, orange-breasted buntings, flamulated flycatchers (rare) and rosy thrush-tanagers are just a few species you may see at San Pedro.*

Cuyutlan Lagoon at the south end of the bay is the largest saltwater lake in the state. The vegetation along the lagoon is mostly white mangrove. These trees are very salt-tolerant and have a unique root system that grows above high-water levels. Seedpods develop on the ends of these non-immersed roots and, after they ripen, fall onto the ground and grow. The roots above the water also facilitate the exchange of gases.

Some mangroves are able to filter saltwater through their roots, while others release the salt through leaf pores. Mangroves are home to birds, reptiles and land animals. You can take a boat tour through this lagoon. See *Tour Operators*, below.

 BIRD WATCH: *Cuyutlan is a good place to spot herons, pelicans, gulls and ducks.*

Laguna de Juluapan is at the north end of the bay near La Boquita Beach. Because Manzanillo hasn't been overrun with tourists (although there are a lot of hotels), rarer birds are still easy to spot and there are a large number of different species.

 BIRD WATCH: *Laguna de Juluapan is home to yellow-crowned night herons, social flycatchers, ruddy ground doves, star-throats and broad-billed hummingbirds. There are also orioles, cowbirds, seedeaters and woodpeckers.*

■ Outfitters/Tour Operators

Underworld Scuba, *Plaza Pacifico, Av Audiencia, B-29,* ☎ *314-333-0642, www.divemanzanillo.com or www.goman-zanillo.com/scubamex/index.htm,* has been working in the area for close to 15 years and has been used by high-powered media companies like The Discovery Channel and *Travel + Leisure* magazine. Underworld Scuba is a PADI Dive Center and an accredited CMAS Dive Center. All four instructors are members of the PADI Professional Association of Diving Instructors. They take both divers and snorkelers, a maximum of six divers per boat so you are assured of personalized attention. All gear is included in your dive/snorkel package. They also offer special dives and night dives for the more experienced. Two-tank dives to two locations, including all transportation, cost less than $70 per person. Discounts are offered to people who book more than one day of diving with them. Dive lessons are available. Snorkeling is done Thursday to Sunday, with a minimum of four people, for just under $30 per person. Considering the professional help you are getting from these people, this is a deal.

This company will also take you on a city tour or a plantation tour where you will learn tidbits about the area (like what Jimmy Buffett's favorite drink is or where the most popular bar in the 1940s was located). They run cultural tours and wildlife observation tours, special archeological tours and they take people hiking to the volcanoes of Colima. The prices are about the best in town, their English is perfect and the safety level is high.

Manzanillo Region

Most of the information about diving was taken from Susan Dearing's website. Susan can be found at Underworld Scuba. She has been diving in the area for a long time and comes highly recommended. Her publication, *Manzanillo and the State of Colima, Facts, Tips and Day Trips*, is a local publication that has a plethora of facts and tidbits for the visitor. It is sold around town. Or you can purchase it for $30 directly from Susan Dearing, AP 295, Santiago, Colima, Mexico 29961 or at www.gomanzanillo.com/guidebook/index.htm.

> **WARNING:** There are hundreds of hungry Mexicans who claim to be scuba diving instructors, but are not. Always check certification cards and remember that even these can be fake. The best advice I can give is to dive with a reputable tour operator. It may cost a few dollars more, but at least you will be reasonably safe. Seems cheap by my standards.

Pacific Water Sports, *Hotels, Club Maeva, Sierra, Las Hadas and Playa de Oro,* ☎ *314-331-0101,* are open 9 am-5 pm daily. They have water sports equipment like kayaks, banana boats and boogie boards for rent. They also offer tours on a catamaran for wildlife viewing or for a sunset cruise. Prices are competitive and the equipment is in good shape.

Club Deportivo de Pesca de Manzanillo, *Manzana G Lote 3, Parque Industrial Fondeport,* ☎ *314-336-7265,* is located at the inner port in the old town. Come here to hire skilled fishermen to take you out. All have radio-equipped boats, are licensed and have a set rate of $250 a day.

The Cooperativa de Servicios Turisticos de Manzanillo, ☎ *314-331-0101,* operates from Las Hadas docks and is the same as the Club Deportivo de Pesca. These people are environmentally sensitive and follow safety rules. An average boat goes out for about five hours and can carry up to eight people. The cost is around $250 for the day.

Manzanillo Ecotours, *Blvd Costero Miguel de la Madrid, Km 15,* ☎ *314-333-1707,* offers photography tours into the jungle or caving trips. Ecotours also can take you kayaking or snorkeling. No prices are available at this time.

Auto Tours del Mar, *(no address available),* ☎ *314-357-3503*. Federico, the owner and tour guide, speaks English and is willing to drive you on any custom tour in an air-conditioned GMC Suburban. The cost is $100 per day for everything but your food and drink.

Neptune Diving and Sport Center, *Km 14.5, Miguel de la Madrid,* ☎ *314-334-3001,* has diving and snorkeling trips around Manzanillo. They will also take children snorkeling. The cost for a two-tank dive is $75; $70 if you have your own gear. They also offer certification lessons;

three days costs $280. Snorkeling is $35 for adults, half-price for kids between eight and 10 years, and free for kids under eight.

■ Shopping

The Flea Market is opposite Club Maeva on the Santiago Peninsula. It has handicrafts, especially those made with seashells. What is exceptional in artwork are the handmade candles. Walk through the market and have a look.

Santiago Outdoor Market is on the main strip along the peninsula and is open only on Saturday mornings. Go and taste the tacos, fruit-flavored drinks and fried *churros* – a donut-like pastry, cooked in thin strips and filled with a caramel or vanilla cream. They are excellent!

■ Places to Stay

In the Old Town

Hotel Emperador, *B. Davalos #69*, ☎ *314-332-2374*, *$*, has small rooms that are popular with backpackers. They have just a bed, a small table, a bathroom (slippery floors when wet) and ceiling fans. There is a nice balcony above the street that is shared by all the guests.

Hotel Miramar, *Av Juarez #122*, ☎ *314-332-1008*, *$*, is comparable to the Emperador with rooms that are just as dim, although they are larger. The bathrooms are also large, but dark. There is a communal balcony. The hotel is at the opposite end of the *jardin* in the center of town. The owner was pleasant, but some of the clients looked a bit rough.

HOTEL PRICE SCALE		
Price for a room given in US $.		
$		Up to $20
$$		$21-$50
$$$		$51-$100
$$$$		$101-$150
$$$$$		$151-$200
Anything over $200 is specified.		

Hotel Colonial, *Fco. Bocanegra # 26 and AV. Mexico*, ☎ *314-332-1080*, *$$*, is an old establishment that has two floors of rooms around a central courtyard that is presently used mainly as a restaurant. The rooms are white plaster with red-tile floors and heavy wood furniture, and have access to a balcony that surrounds each floor. The place is clean to a glitter and is the most comfortable place in the center of the city. There is also air conditioning, private bathrooms and daily maid service.

Hotel Bahia, *Hidalgo #134*, ☎ *314-332-6487*, *www.hotelbahia-manzanillo.com.mx*, *$$*, is a good hotel that has 74 clean rooms with tile floors and white walls. Each rooms has a TV, telephone, desk, chairs and night tables. This is a good place to stay if you want to be in the heart of the city. However, there is no negotiating on the rate.

On the Bay

The bay area is divided from the center by the landmark called the "white sailboat" and buses go either north or south of this landmark. The area that goes north from white sailboat looks more like a residential area along a beach, while the land going in the other direction looks like a tourist hotel zone. Along the north are numerous small hotels, some exceptional, most quiet, and all on the beach. These are interspersed with restaurants, garages, condominiums, tire repair shops, souvenir shops and hardware stores. It is obvious that Manzanillo is not totally dependent on tourism for its survival, and the fact that so many people work keeps the hawkers down to a minimum.

The southern strip has both large and small establishments, shopping malls, tourist office, car rentals, restaurants and shops. The residential homes are not along the beach, but rather on the hill behind it.

Hotel del Mar, *Fco. Villa #51*, ☎ *314-333-1150, $$, hoteldelmarmanzanillo@yahoo.com.mx,* is two blocks from the beach. There are a number of rooms from which to choose and some are a good deal if you are on a budget. The large rooms have a small sitting area and cable TV. There is air conditioning in some rooms, fans in others. The bathrooms are large and have separate showers. The place is clean, but a bit dingy. Rates are $22 for two, $27 for three and $33 for four people. There is also a cabin for rent that will sleep up to eight people for $70 a day. This includes a kitchen with stove and fridge.

Hotel Maria Isabel, *Blvd Costerno Miguel de la Madrid, Km 14,* ☎ *314-333-0298, $$,* is next to Juancito and is okay, but not the greatest. The rooms have fans, TV and hot water.

Hotel Hawaii, *Blvd Miguel de la Madrid, Km 13.5,* ☎ *314-334-3014, $$,* is a bit more expensive than some of the others close by, but it is very well kept. The rooms are medium-sized and tastefully decorated. They have TVs, fans and private bathrooms. The owners are helpful, speak a little English and the beach is just 300 feet/100 meters from the hotel.

Hotel Star, *Av Lazaro Cardenas #1313,* ☎ *314-333-1980 or 333-2560, $$,* is a small, family-run hotel that has friendly staff. The rooms are of average size and have tiled floors and white painted walls that give them a bright and clean appearance. They also have a TV. There is off-street parking and the hotel backs onto the beach.

Hotel Las Brisas, *Av Lazaro Cardenas #1243,* ☎ *314-333-2716, $$,* is a lovely little place right on the beach, close to the sailboat turnaround. The clean rooms are large enough to hold a sitting area complete with couch. All rooms have air conditioning and fans, as well as a private bathroom. Also available are suites with kitchenettes, some big enough to hold six people. The large courtyard contains a small swimming pool. This is a good deal.

Hotel Playa de Santiago, *Playa de Santiago,* ☎ *314-333-0055, $$,* has rooms with ceiling fans, TV and private bathroom. There is a pool and tennis courts on site.

Hotel Brisas del Mar, *Av Lazaro Cardenas #1301,* ☎ *314-334-1197 or 334-1153, $$/$$$,* is a bright white and blue building on the beach. The rooms are large and have sitting areas and come with air conditioning or fan. All rooms are clean and have cable TV. The small pool in the courtyard is often full of kids. You can also rent a villa with a full kitchen for $45.50 per day for one person; $60.50 for two and $85 for three or four. Rent it for an entire month for just $600. This is a good deal.

Hotel Santa Cecilia, *Blvd Miguel de la Madrid #893,* ☎ *314-334-2244 or 800-696-7979, www.hotelsantacecilia.net, $$$,* is a lovely little place overlooking the ocean. The large rooms have air conditioning, private balconies, fans, cable TV and a fridge/bar. There is a pool, off-street parking, a restaurant and a bar, a play area for children and an Internet service. Ask about discounted rates for longer stays. The staff is friendly and helpful.

Hotel Marina Puerto Dorado, *Av Lazaro Cardenas # 101,* ☎ *314-334-1480, $$$,* is located at Playa Las Brizas. It has rooms and suites, all with air conditioning and private bathrooms. The suites have kitchenettes and some hold up to six people. There is a restaurant and pool.

Hotel La Posada, *Av Lazaro Cardenas #201,* ☎ *314-333-1899, $$$,* is on the beach. This pink California stucco building with brick archways at the entry has all the charm of Spain. There is a central patio shaded by flowering trees and shrubs. The 24 rooms are well decorated with antique chests and Mexican rugs. All have private bathrooms, air conditioning and balconies that offer an ocean view. There is complimentary coffee available all day and breakfast is included in the price. Drinks from the bar work on a self-serve honor system. There is also a pool and off-street parking. However, there are no TVs, Internet, telephones, clocks or radios. For me, that's a real plus.

Hotel Marbella, *Blvd De la Madrid, Km 9.5,* ☎ *314-333-1102, $$$,* is on the beach, close to good restaurants. The hotel has 100 rooms, each with air conditioning, cable TV, private bathroom and balcony. The floors are tiled, the closets big, and the reading lights over the beds are bright. There is a pool, tennis courts and off-street parking available. This is a well-kept and decent place.

Hotel La Pergola, *Blvd Costera Miguel de la Madrid, Km 11.5,* ☎ *314-333-2265,* is a cozy place with 18 large tiled rooms that have private bathrooms, fans, air conditioning, sitting areas, cable TV (50 channels), two double beds, night lights and large closets. The small pool is located in a courtyard that is filled with vegetation. There is also a bar and restaurant, a business center and off-street parking. The restaurant is very popular.

Hotel Plaza Manzanillo, *Blvd Costero Miguel de la Madrid # 1164*, ☎ *314-334-0681 or 800-640-6161, $$$*, has 44 rooms on three floors that are around a central courtyard and swimming pool. The rooms on the main floor have patio doors opening onto the pool and the ones on the upper levels have balconies. The rooms are clean and have private bathrooms, telephones, air conditioning, fans and cable TV. There is off-street parking and a restaurant on site.

Hotel Palma Real, *Peninsula de Tuluapan*, ☎ *314-335-0000, $$$*, is at the north end of the bay near L'Recif. The spacious rooms come with cable TV, air conditioning, marble bathroom and a mini-fridge. The courtyard has an attractive deck and sitting area that surrounds two pools. The pools are joined by a stream that has a current in it. There is also mini golf, volleyball and a games room.

Hotel Tucanes, *Av Del Tesoro*, ☎ *314-334-1098, $$$*, is a five-star hotel that keeps the balconies of each room private by growing borders of lush vegetation. The 103 rooms have air conditioning, cable TV, mini-bars, telephones and marble bathrooms, some with Roman tubs. The kitchenettes, also part of every room, have fridges, microwaves and coffee makers. There is a games room, off-street parking and a restaurant and lounge. The hotel is across from the Hadas golf course (see page 361). The pool is divided in two by a bridge and there is a poolside restaurant. An airport shuttle is provided free of charge.

Dolphin Cove Inn, ☎ *888-497-4138, www.dolphincoveinn.com, $$$ / $$$$*, is a small hotel perched on the hillside overlooking Manzanillo Bay. A walkway leading down to the beach has lounge chairs and tables along the way. There is a small pool on site and a restaurant open for breakfast, lunch and dinner. The 35 large rooms each have a bathroom, kitchenette and either a terrace or balcony. There are numerous styles from which to choose, but all are clean, comfortable and decorated with Mexican tiles. The two-bedroom suite costs $190 during low season and $210 during high season.

Villas Los Angeles, Calle La Cima, ☎ *314-333-1702, www.villaslosangeles.com, $$$$ / $$$$$*, sits on the hill above Santiago Peninsula. The villa has suites with one, two or three bedrooms (some with Jacuzzi), fully equipped kitchens, marble bathrooms, telephones, cable TV and balconies. The suites are decorated Mexican style with hand-painted tiles, natural woods and rattan furniture. There is a well-maintained garden and a pool in the courtyard. Rates range from $110 for a one-bedroom unit to $200 for a two-bedroom suite with a Jacuzzi in the bedroom.

Manzanillo

Places to Stay, Eat & Party

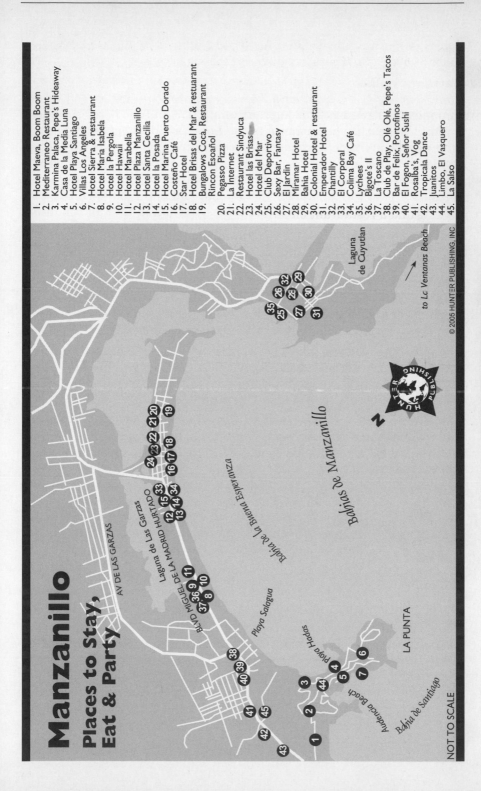

1. Hotel Maeva, Boom Boom
2. Mediterraneo Restaurant
3. Karmina Palaca, Pepe's Hideaway
4. Casa de la Media Luna
5. Hotel Playa Santiago
6. Villas Los Angeles
7. Hotel Sierra & restaurant
8. Hotel Maria Isabela
9. Hotel la Pergola
10. Hotel Hawaii
11. Hotel Marabella
12. Hotel Plaza Manzanillo
13. Hotel Santa Cecilia
14. Hotel la Posada
15. Hotel Marina Puerto Dorado
16. Costeño Café
17. Star Hotel
18. Hotel Brisas del Mar & restuarant
19. Bungalows Coca, Restaurant
   Rincon Esoañol
20. Pegasso Pizza
21. La Internet
22. Restaurant Sindyuca
23. Hotel las Brisas
24. Hotel del Mar
25. Club Deportivo
26. Sexy Bar, Fantasy
27. El Jardin
28. Miramar Hotel
29. Bahia Hotel
30. Colonial Hotel & restaurant
31. Emperador Hotel
32. Chantilly
33. El Corporal
34. Colima Bay Café
35. Lychees
36. Bigote's II
37. La Toscano
38. Club de Play, Olé Olé, Pepe's Tacos
39. Bar de Felix, Portofinos
40. El Fogon, Señor Sushi
41. Rosalba's, Vog
42. Tropicala Dance
43. Juanitos
44. Limbo, El Vasquero
45. La Salso

Bahías de Manzanillo

Laguna de Cuyutlan

to La Ventanas Beach

© 2005 HUNTER PUBLISHING, INC

Laguna de Las Garzas

AV DE LAS GARZAS

BLVD MIGUEL DE LA MADRID HURTADO

Bahía de la Buena Esperanza

Playa Salagua

Playa Hadas

Alameda Beach

Bahía de Santiago

LA PUNTA

NOT TO SCALE

Rooms on the second level that have two double beds and a kitchen area go for $95 a night. There is a discount for longer stays.

Karmina Palace, *Av Vista Hermosa #13,* ☎ *314-334-1313 or 877-527-6462 from the US, $$$$$, www.karminapalace.com*, has its golf course running about two blocks along the main street and the hotel is set back toward the beach. The entrance to the hotel is a huge archway and the flower gardens inside have eight interconnecting pools, all with waiters ready to bring you food or drink. The smaller suites are just under 900 square feet and have balconies, two double beds, stocked mini-bars, sitting areas with couches and coffee tables, and bathrooms with marble showers, tubs and double sinks. All rooms and suites have air conditioning and ceiling fans, two cable TVs, private safes and telephones. Special prices are available that run just under $200 a night, but the larger two-bedroom suites can cost $1,000 a night in peak season. The hotel offers all-inclusive packages.

This is part of the Reef Regency Vacation Club, which specializes in luxury treatments for their guests. For example, the spa offers massages, body treatments, facials, salt scrubs, manicures and pedicures.

From the hotel you can take a boat cruise at sunset, go deep-sea fishing, ride a horse, snorkel or scuba dive, rent a car or an ATV, or head to the spa for a massage. The on-site tourist office will arrange tours of Colima, Manzanillo, Barra de Navidad or Cuyutulan.

Las Hadas Golf and Marina, *Av Vista Hermosa,* ☎ *314-331-0101 or 888-559-4329, www.brisas.com.mx, $$$$$,* is the hotel you can see from many beach locations that has a white lighthouse with an exterior spiral staircase.

FACT FILE: The name *hadas* means "fairies" and comes from the time when ships would see nymphs dancing on the water in the bay. Science has proven that the "nymphs" are a phosphorescent image that is caused by plankton, but the name and myth lives on with the hotel.

The famous Bolivian silver-mining family, the Pateños, built the hotel in 1975. The architect was José Luis Ezquerra de la Colina of Spain. The combination of Mediterranean, Moorish and Mexican styles makes the place a unique landmark. There are 234 spacious rooms and suites with satellite TV, mini-bars, safes, balconies, hair dryers, bathrobes, huge closets with interior lights, ceiling fans and air conditioning, and marble bathrooms with oversized tubs. Some suites have private pools in the rooms. One of the rooms can accommodate a wheelchair.

The 18-hole golf course is rated as one of the top 100 in the world and it sits on 15 acres. The marina can hold 70 boats. Equipment is available for water skiing, kayaking, paddleboating, scuba diving and snorkeling. There is a meandering swimming pool and a quarter-mile of private beach. Massages, reflexology, personal trainers, facials, manicures and pedicures are available. There is also a weights room with a tennis court close by. There are five bars/restaurants/lounges that serve food from 6:30 am until 11 pm daily. If you visit their website and watch for promotional deals, you can get a room, including complimentary welcome drink and breakfast, for as low as $160 a night.

Los Sueños del Mar, ☎ *314-335-0482 or 800-376-8854 (reservations only from US and Canada), www.LosSuenosDelMar.com, on the Peninsula de Juluipan just north of Manzanillo, $$$$/$$$$$*, is a secluded B&B just 20 minutes from the airport by car or taxi. Breakfast is served on the sundeck among papaya, frangipani, limes, bougainvillea, palms and avocado trees. Stone fountains in the garden offer birds fresh water in which to splash and a dipping pool allows the guests to do the same. Two guest rooms are on the lowest level of the three-story house, and each room has its own terrace, full bathroom and a stocked fridge. Two guesthouses, located at the bottom of the hill below the garden, are private, but their lower level doesn't compromise the views of the ocean where, in season, whales can be seen with their young. These houses have fully equipped kitchens that include toaster ovens, microwaves, blenders, bean grinders, coffee makers and kitchen utensils. They also have four-piece bathrooms, air conditioning and fans, feather beds, satellite TV and Internet connections. Gourmet meals are available, or you can hire a chef to cook in your house. These are luxury accommodations. I suggest you visit the website. It will help make your mind up quickly.

Pepe's Hideaway, at Las Hadas, ☎ *314-333-0616, www.pepeshideaway. com, $$$$$*, is a private place on the beach and on the property of Las Hadas Hotel. A little cove with golden sand is below Pepe's and is protected by rocky cliffs. Six palapa-roof bungalows, painted in bright Mexican colors, have king-sized canopy beds, private bathrooms, ceiling fans and balconies. There is a pool or you can swim in the cove. Rates run between $100 and $150 per person, per night, including a full breakfast, snacks like guacamole and ceviche all day long, the main meal of the day, and all your drinks. The meals are gourmet and delicious to eat. Service is top notch.

Hotel Sierra, *Av La Audiencia*, ☎ *314-333-2000 or 800-333-3333 from the US or Canada, $$$$$*, is a long-time favorite. This high-rise, located on a volcanic-sand beach in a sheltered bay, has 332 rooms with tiled floors, air conditioning, cable TV, telephones, mini-bars, marble bathrooms and lounge chairs on the balconies. There is a pool, a sauna, a massage parlor, tennis courts, a golf course close by, laundry service, a car rental agency, a gift shop and a babysitting service. There are three restaurants and a nightclub. Their all-inclusive packages must be booked through an agent. However, recent reports say that the Sierra has been taken over by new owners who do not take care of the place, so some rooms are dirty and musty and the plumbing leaves a lot to be desired. The staff, too, is overworked and, as a result, a bit grumpy. Maybe it is time for this hotel to have a rest from demanding tourists.

Hotel Maeva, *Santiago Peninsula, Km 12.5,* ☎ *314-335-0595, $$$$$*, offers rooms with everything included for $210 a day, per person. The grounds cover 90 acres of well-maintained gardens and the hotel has about 500 rooms and suites with air conditioning, phones and cable TV. There are four pools, a gym, a mini-golf course, a water slide park and 12 tennis courts. The all-inclusive packages offer horseback riding, field sports, snorkeling and watersports. There are four restaurants, two bars and a disco.

Casa de la Media Luna, ☎ *877-391-1329, www.casamedialuna.com*, is on the hill at Las Hadas, overlooking the ocean, in one of the most exclusive neighborhoods in Manzanillo. For one or two persons during high season from December to May, the cost is $300 a day, $1,050 if there are seven or eight people staying. The cost drops to $250 a day during low season for the same arrangement. This hotel offers privacy and luxury. The rooms have living rooms with wet bars, foyers with powder rooms, dining rooms with stereo systems and kitchens with breakfast nooks. The living rooms contain card tables, books, games and satellite TV. Ceiling fans are throughout the apartment. The walls are white, the ceilings beamed and the floors tiled. Upstairs are four bedrooms with central air conditioning, two large bathrooms and balconies leading from all the bedrooms. One of the gigantic marble bathrooms has a view of the ocean. There is a pool and Jacuzzi on the property. There is a cook, a team of chambermaids and a house manager to look after things. The cook allows you to choose the menu. If you want to live like a king, even for just a week, rent this villa. There is a minimum stay of three days.

■ Places to Eat

In the Old Town

 Roca del Mar, *21 de Marzo #204,* ☎ *314-332-0302,* in Casa del Marina beside the *jardin*, has pleasant staff. However, the "cowfish" that was passed off as snapper should be avoided. Their chicken fared no better; it was greasy and overcooked. Cow-fish, for those wondering, is a piece of cheap beef pounded and cut into the shape of a fish and fried. The dish cost twice as much as a piece of beef.

Café Costeño, *Av Mexico and Calle Juarez,* ☎ *314-333-9460,* has the best *latte* in town. However, their pastry is a bit heavy for the hot climate and I found the cheesecake stale. This may be due to the fact that I was there during low season and things didn't sell as fast as they should.

Colonial Hotel Restaurant, *Fco. Gonzalez Bocanegra # 28,* ☎ *314-333-0168,* is expensive, but the food is excellent and the portions large. I had a T-bone steak that was done exactly the way I had requested. This is not common in Mexico. The Colonial offers a good lunch of the day for $5.

Restaurant Chantilly, *Av Juarez and Madera,* ☎ *314-332-0194,* is popular at all times of the day. It is open 7:30 am-10:30 pm. The breakfast I had was nondescript and they didn't have the first thing I ordered. They did, however, make boiled eggs – a difficult thing to get in Mexico. For an ordinary but good Mexican meal, I would suggest coming here. They have live music on Saturday nights.

On the Bay

Café Costeño, *Av Lazaro Cardenas,* ☎ *314-334-9460,* has the same owners as the one in town. The large thatch-roofed building can be seen from the sailboat circle. The restaurant is open for breakfast and stays open until after the last dinner patron leaves. Their specialty is coffee – you get the bottomless cup at breakfast. Most meals cost less than $10.

Restaurant Sinayuca, *Av Lazaro Cardenas #1500,* ☎ *314-333-1594,* has great lemonade, served cold (50¢ for a large glass). They also have a delicious meal of the day for reasonable prices. It is nice to sit in the shade of this place and rest.

L'Recif, *Cerro del Cenicero,* ☎ *314-335-0900,* is open November to May from 6 to 11 pm. Reservations are recommended. This classy restaurant is located on the top of Cerro Cinecerro, or Ashtray Hill. Legend has it that ancient humans living here burned people and animals before offering the ashes to the gods of the sea. The restaurant doesn't do this. You will need to take a taxi to get here and then plan on spending a few hours enjoying both the view and the meal. The candlelit tables, covered in fine linen, offer a romantic setting for drinking a bottle of wine. L'Recif serves international dishes and they charge international prices. However, the reviews of this place have been mixed. I was satisfied, but others I spoke with were not. They claimed the food was not worth the price.

El Caporal, *Blvd M. de la Madrid, on an alley that runs between Sol Deposito and the SIX Convenience Store, no phone,* is open noon until 7 pm. The live music shows seem to draw Mexican families. The raffles are another draw – sounds odd, but it is Mexican gambling at its cheapest. The food is all Mexican and inexpensive ($5 per meal).

Colima Bay Café, *Blvd M de la Madrid,* ☎ *314-333-0168,* has a Señor Frog's atmosphere. The action doesn't start until after 10 pm and there is no cover charge if you eat dinner ($3 if you don't). The best meal is the

Manzanillo Region

jumbo shrimp, for about $12. Drinks are expensive. The café is on the beach and has tables outside.

Mediterraneo Restaurant, *Blvd Miguel de la Madrid, located at the Salagua stoplight near the tourist office,* ☎ *314-333-0323*, has some delicious meals, like Greek salad with shrimp that is large in flavor and portion size. They also offer vegetarian food. The lasagna comes highly recommended. If you fish, you can bring your catch here and they will cook it for a price. Thursday, Mexican night, brings an all-you-can-eat buffet for $9.

Portofinos Pizza, *Blvd M de la Madrid,* ☎ *314-334-1333*, has good pizza but the ravioli and lasagna are excellent. The pizza is done in a wood-fired oven, which adds great flavor. The place is quiet and has a restful atmosphere. The Mexican decorations are not obtrusive and the cost is less than $15 per meal.

Bigote's II, *Blvd Miguel de la Madrid #3157,* ☎ *314-334-0341*, serves seafood. This has been a popular place for a long time. The shrimp cooked in a white sauce and served over rice is excellent for $10 a serving.

La Toscana, *Blvd Miguel de la Madrid #3177,* ☎ *314-333-2515,* serves Italian cuisine and, from what I hear, the lamb is the best in town. However, the Caesar salad is not as good. The food is made fresh; enjoy a drink and the ambiance while waiting. They are open seven days a week. These chefs also own Willy's, a French cuisine restaurant that was, and perhaps still is, the most popular place in town. They are competing with themselves.

Pepe's Tacos, *Blvd Miguel de la Madrid, Km 7.5,* ☎ *314-333-1859,* has excellent food for less than $10 a meal. The barbequed pork with melted cheese is a specialty of the house, as is the *frijoles charros* (bean soup).

La Salso, *Blvd Costero Miguel de la Madrid at the Soriana Shopping Center,* ☎ *314-334-1489*. Although they carry other seafood specialties, like fish with tamarind or mango sauce, I personally liked the shrimp ceviche for less than $10 a meal.

Ly Chees, *397 Calzada Niños Heroes,* ☎ *314-332-1103*, is on the dock and overlooks the water. The atmosphere is excellent, as is the food. They serve Cantonese-style meals in huge portions cooked with very fresh vegetables. The cost is less than $10 per serving. There are rumors that this place may have to be relocated. If you hear it has moved, please drop me a note to comments@hunterpublishing.com.

El Fogon, *Blvd de la Madrid, Km 10,* ☎ *314-333-3094, opens at 6 pm*. It has atmosphere, cold beer, complimentary appetizers and spicy soups. The most interesting meal is the grilled ostrich (*avestrus*). This restaurant is in a rustic wooden cabin next to Señor Sushi.

Señor Sushi, *Blvd de la Madrid, Km 10,* ☎ *314-333-0982*, is great if you want a change from Mexican food. The sushi is excellent and nicely chilled. Meals cost under $10.

Limbo, *Av Audiencia, Plaza Pacifico,* ☎ *314-334-1562,* opens after 6 pm. Its great hot wings ($4), when combined with a beer from the tap, can't be beaten. This is the only place in town that you can get draft beer.

El Vaquero, *Av Audiencia,* ☎ *314-334-0129,* up from Plaza Pacifico, offers free chips and salsa as an appetizer. This is a first-class steak house where you pay by the kilo. They serve the meat on a hibachi or a hot plate at your table. Closed Monday.

TASTY DISHES

Coimote is marinated swordfish cooked with cociñero chiles and served on a fried tortilla. Enjoy this with *tuba*, a liquor made from the coconut palm, or *tequino*, a fermented corn drink served cold with lemon and ice. For dessert, have some *cicadas*, toasted and candied coconut (sweet!).

Hotel Sierra, *Av La Audiencia,* ☎ *314-333-2000*, is the place to go for a Sunday brunch buffet ($10 for all you can eat). The buffet has everything, from fresh fruit to eggs to toast.

Rosalba's, *Blvd Miguel de la Madrid, Km 13.5,* ☎ *314-333-0488*, is north of the Premex station on Santiago Peninsula. This Mexican restaurant offers a daily special for just four bucks. It includes soup, meat, rice, beans and dessert. The meal changes every day. The place is clean and comfortable, the service good and the beer very cold.

Juanitos, *Blvd Costera, Km. 14.3,* ☎ *314-333-1388*, is open 8 am-11 pm. It is one of the most popular restaurants in town with North Americans and has been since the 1970s. Their coffee is excellent, their banana milkshakes are thick, their barbequed ribs spicy and their prices low. A meal with a non-alcoholic drink is about $8. Additionally, you can buy American newspapers, there is Internet available and you can have a photocopy done. This is called diversity in business. Owner John Corey knows everything about the area. If I have failed to give details about something specific, see John.

■ Nightlife

Bar de Felix, *Blvd Miguel de la Madrid, Km 9.5,* ☎ *314-333-1875*, is one of the most popular bars in town and it is owned by the same people who own the Vog (below), another hot spot.

Manzanillo Region

Vog, *Blvd Miguel de la Madrid, Km 9.5,* ☎ *314-333-1875,* is open 10 pm until 3 am. The $5 cover charge includes a light and sound show at midnight. This is the most popular disco in town and it may be the loudest, too. There is a dress code; no shorts or t-shirts. If the music and dancing gets to be too much for you, then go next door and play a game of pool.

Boom Boom, *Av Miguel de la Madrid, Km 12.5, in Hotel Maeva,* ☎ *314-331-0800,* closes at dawn and is one of the liveliest sports bars in town. If the name is any clue, maybe you need to bring those earplugs I suggested in the *What to Pack* section.

Olé Olé, *Blvd Miguel de la Madrid, Km 7.5,* ☎ *314-333-1622,* is a comedy club. Acts change every month, but to enjoy them you must understand Spanish. There is billiards in the front of the bar and a lounge in the back. Watch your bill and your change.

Sexy Bar and **Fantasy** are in the Zona Tolerancia (ask a taxi driver to take you here) and next door to each other. They feature striptease and table and lap dancing. There is more offered here than the strip show and dancing, but the more you do, the more it costs. Tips go into the g-strings of the girls and you must put the money in place without touching her skin. Women can go to these bars, but they must be escorted by men. As a general precaution, men should not take more money with them than they are prepared to lose.

Tropicala Dance Hall, *Blvd Miguel de la Madrid, Km 14,* ☎ *314-333-2474,* has live music and the cover charge ($5) includes a buffet snack bar. Open Thursday to Saturday from 10 pm-3 am. The place is air-conditioned.

Club de Play, *Blvd Miguel de la Madrid, Km 7.5, no phone,* is a restaurant, video bar and dance hall. I did not visit this place, but it was recommended.

Colima

One of the world's most active volcanos is just half an hour by car from Colima. The city itself is the capital of the state sporting the same name and is not, except for its gardens and plazas, an attractive city.

The downtown area has two magnificent parks and the outer part of the city is modernizing itself to include things like air-conditioned malls. An earthquake hit the city on January 21, 2003 with a magnitude of 7.6 on the Richter scale. Twenty-five people were killed and almost 300 injured. Major buildings were damaged, but reconstruction is well under way.

■ Getting Here & Away

 ETN, ☎ *312-312-5899*, **Elite**, ☎ *312-312-8448*, **Primera Plus**, ☎ *312-314-8027*, and **Omnibus de Mexico**, ☎ *312-314-7190*, all have buses that run about once every other hour to either Manzanillo or Mexico City, where you can catch a bus to other regions.

■ History

 Artifacts found in this area indicate that people started farming in the Colima area around 1600 BC and that by 600 AD they had become quite sophisticated in their music, arts, agriculture and occupations. The items that have revealed the most about this civilization have been found in tombs. As agriculture developed and expanded, the city became a trading center.

After the Spanish arrived, Franciscan monks followed so they could evangelize. The monks established their first chapel around Ajuchitlan, a few miles from Colima, below Vulcan de Fuego.

Today, artists seem to like the exceptional climate here and they, too, have set down roots.

■ Services

 Tourist Office, *Hidalgo #96*, ☎ *312-312-4360*, *www. visitcolima.com.mx*, *Monday to Friday, 8:30 am-3 pm and 6-9 pm, Saturday until 1 pm.*

Post office, *Av Madero # 203, Monday to Friday, 9 am-3 pm and 5-8 pm.*

Police, *Av 20 de Noviembre*, ☎ *312-313-1434 or dial 06.*

Medical Center, *Maclovio Herrera #140*, ☎ *312-312-4044*, is in the center of town. There is a little English spoken here.

■ Sightseeing

 The Plaza in the center of town features the colonial-styled government house on one side and the cathedral next to it. The plaza itself is filled with tropical plants and flowers that are interspersed with ornamental swans. There are three colonnades through the park, all lighted by decorative lampposts. The central bandstand was brought from Belgium in 1891 and hosts the State Musical Band every Thursday and Sunday for the entertainment of the locals.

The Cathedral, designed by Lucio de Uribe and constructed in 1894, has a neoclassical façade. The city continues to preserve the cathedral's unique appearance, which is threatened with each of the frequent earthquakes. The quake of 1941 damaged the building so badly that it was left unusable for several years. The cathedral is consecrated to the Virgin of Guadalupe, the patron saint of Mexico. Every December, pilgrims come to worship in honor of the saint.

Government House was also designed by Lucio de Uribe in the French neo-classical style. Uribe began the work in 1877, but didn't finish it until 1904. Like the cathedral, the government house has seen numerous earthquakes, some that were quite damaging, but the construction has been repaired to an admirable quality. Above the main balcony is an antique clock brought from Germany in 1891. Beside it is a replica of Mexico City's Dolores Bell. Inside, the hall walls are decorated with murals painted by Jorge Chavez Carrillo in 1953 to honor Miguel Hidalgo on the bicentennial of his birth.

Regional Historical Museum, *Morelos #1 and Reforma,* ☎ *312-312-9228, Tuesday to Saturday, 9 am-6 pm, Sunday, 5 pm-8 pm, $3*. This mansion was built in 1848 by Juan de Dios Brizuela as his residence; after he died, it became the Hotel Casino. In 1988 it was converted into the Historical Museum. The main floor holds permanent exhibitions of archeological items and folk art from sites around the state. The museum's main attraction is the reproduction of a tomb that shows how items were placed around the deceased in order to help him/her enter into the next life. Tunnels led to a large domed crypt where the bodies were laid to rest.

POTTERY

The interesting thing about the pottery of this area is that pieces depict domestic life, rather than gods, as is common. These sculptures are of women, men, dogs, parrots, snakes and working tools used in the fields.

The upper level of the museum was expanded to include items from the time when the people of Mexico first came in contact with the Spanish until the early part of the last century when the revolution occurred. There are things like horse-drawn buggies and items of clothing.

Iguana Museum, *Medellin # 66, daily, 10 am-5 pm, $2*. This is a unique museum featuring the leathery-skinned ancestors of the dinosaurs. You can visit by guided tour offered in Spanish only. The museum also runs tours to other areas of the region; ask the staff.

Casa de Hidalgo, *Degollado and Independencia,* is another Lucio Uribe project that was started in 1871 but took over 20 years to complete. Many cultural events take place here and it is the home of the University of

Colima

SIGHTS & ATTRACTIONS
1. Plaza, Cathedral, Govt House & Gregorio Quintero Garden
2. Regional Historical Museum
3. Casa de Hidalgo
4. University Museum of Folk Art
5. Alfonso Michel University Art Gallery
6. Museum of Western Cultures
7. Federal Palace
8. Iguana Museum
9. San Felipe de Jesus Church
10. Nuñez Garden
11. Piedra Lisa Park
12. Parque Regional Metropolitano
13. El Chanal Archeological Site
14. La Campana Archeological Site

PLACES TO STAY
15. Hotel La Merced
16. Hotel Maria Isabel
17. Hotel Maria Victoria
18. Hotel Villa del Rey
19. Hotel America
20. Hotel Los Candiles
21. Hotel Ceballos

PLACES TO EAT
22. Trebol, Los Portales
23. El Charco de la Higuera
24. Fonda San Miguel
25. Los Naranjos

NOT TO SCALE

Manzanillo Region

© 2005 HUNTER PUBLISHING, INC

Colima Folk Ballet. If the doors are open, go in and see the rich décor. If there is an event on while you are in town, be certain to purchase a ticket and go. Information about the events is available at the tourist office.

University Museum of Folk Art, *Gabino Barreda and Manuel Gallardot*, ☎ *312-312-6869, Tuesday to Saturday, 10 am-2 pm and 5 pm-8 pm, Sunday, 10 am-1 pm, $1*. This museum is dedicated to folk art and has the most complete collection in all of Mexico. Just inside the doors are *mojigangos*, or puppets, that stand about 15 feet/five meters high. They are used during the February Fiesta of Charrotaurinas held in honor of San Felipe de Jesus. Farther inside are masks, costumes, ceramics, toys and weapons. This museum is very well laid out.

Alfonso Michel University Art Gallery, *Vicente Guerreo #35*, ☎ *312-312-2228, Tuesday to Saturday, 10 am-2 pm and 5-8 pm, Sunday, 10 am-1 pm, $1*. This museum is housed in two mansions that have been adapted to hold the museum yet keep the charm of colonial homes. There are both temporary exhibits and a permanent collection of Alfonso Michel. Paintings, graphics, sculptures and photographs from national artists are on display. The town library is located in this building.

Museum of Western Cultures, *Av Calzada Galvan*, ☎ *312-313-0608, Tuesday to Sunday, 9 am-6:30 pm, $1.50*. Take a taxi to this museum as it is over two miles/three km from the center. It has a large collection of pottery and stone artifacts from pre-Hispanic Mexico. The first museum was founded in the late 1950s with a donation from Maria Ahumada de Gomez, a self-taught archeological researcher from Villa de Alvarez who collected works of the country's indigenous people. Her collections went to many "homes" before this structure was built in 1980 to hold her treasures. The main floor has artifacts and the second floor has more flora and fauna, clothing, weapons, musical instruments and art pieces.

Federal Palace, *Av Madero # 203, Monday to Friday, 9 am-3 pm, and 5-8 pm*. Lopez de Lara built the palace in 1906 and it changed hands many times before being purchased by the city's famous writer, Blas de Ruiz. It wasn't until the early 1900s that it became a government building. This is where the post office is now located. The national shield was placed on the outside over the main doors in 1936. The murals inside on the second floor are by artists Madame de la Merced Zamora and Antonio Cedeño.

Gateway to Camino Real, *Junction of the Manzanillo Libramiento and the Camino Real Blvd*, is a contemporary sculpture of a palm tree with 10 golden leaves, each symbolizing the municipalities in the state. The gateway was designed for the millennium by the Mexican sculptor Sebastian, who also designed the sailfish in Manzanillo. The gateway is made of enameled iron, stands 650 feet/210 meters tall and is 60 feet/18 meters wide. It weighs 70 tons.

San Felipe de Jesus Church, *Constitución #70*, is often referred to as the *Beaterio* or Church of the Sagrario, because so many precious items have been moved into it from the cathedral. (The cathedral suffers so often from earthquake damage that the city decided to house precious items in San Felipe, where earthquake damage has never occurred.) Inside are documents signed by important heads of state. The carved wooden columns you see are made of cedar. Next to the church is a little park with lots of flowers.

■ Adventures on Foot

Gregorio Quintero Garden, behind the cathedral, is a well-kept flower garden with a lovely stone fountain in the middle. Beside the fountain is a monument dedicated to Gregorio Torres Quintero, a Colima educator who taught a unique and easy way of learning to read and write. On weekends, you can enjoy an outdoor craft market here.

Piedra Lisa Park, *Calzada Galvan*, is another park decorated with numerous flowering plants and tall trees. The gardens are dotted with park benches and ornamental lights. There is also the slippery stone for which the park was named. Legend says that if you slip on this stone you will come to live in Colima. Children have a lot of fun "slipping." At the entrance to the park and on the corner of Av 20 de Noviembre is a monument standing eight feet/three meters high in honor of King Coliman, for whom the city was named. Coliman was said to have defended the area against Spanish attacks. He died in 1523 in battle against Gonzalo de Sandovla. The bas-relief on the monument depicts the battle. There are also two inscriptions; one says "Stronger than history, your legend is both destiny and privilege," and the other says "Colima here exalts the virtues of your ancestry as a definition of patriotism."

Parque Regional Metropolitano, *Calle Degollado, southwest of the plaza and on the Colima River, daily, 8 am-7 pm (water slides open Wednesday to Sunday, 10 am-4:30 pm)*. The 25 acres of land is divided into two sections. One consists of a wave pool with water slides and a forested area that has a small zoo and the other has a lake where you can rent a rowboat. There are eateries at the park and picnic areas where you can barbeque.

Nuñez Garden, *Calle Juarez and Revolucion*, was called the *Alameda*, or the New Plaza, when it was first created in 1858. It was built under the orders of General José Silverio Nuñez, who was in the legislature from 1857 to 1860. After he was charged with war crimes and put to death, the park was named something else. When he was later exonerated, the city decided to rename the park in his honor. This happened in 1915. The park is the home of the Lira Colimense, an orchestra founded and di-

Manzanillo Region

rected by José Levy. These gardens, in my opinion, are the nicest in this city of flowers.

■ Adventures on Water

 La Maria Laguna is 15 miles/25 km north of Colima and is good for birding. The lake sits in the shadow of the volcanoes and has cedar, giant fig, ash and sapodilla trees in the forests surrounding the lake. This is a crater lake that formed in the cone of a now extinct volcano. There are picnic tables and barbeque pits around the lake. Some of the trails lead to good views of Fuego that can be seen puffing away up the valley. In the evenings, you can see a reflection of the volcano in the lake's still waters. A hiking trail here runs for three miles/four km to Yerbabuena, where you can get an even better look at the volcano. To get to the lake, take a bus from Colima to San Antonio and then a taxi from there to La Maria. The driver will let you off at the Ejido la Maria, where there is a gate. Pay the $1 entrance fee and walk through the gate and along a paved path to the lake. There are cabins for rent at El Ejido, ☎ 312--320-8891. They sit on a hill above the lake and feature kitchens and bathrooms with hot water; they rent for $25 a night. If you opt to stay here, you must bring everything with you, including water-purifying tablets or bottled water.

Laguna Carrizalillos is another lake in the San Antonio area. To get here, take a bus to San Antonio and then a taxi or a second bus to the lake. Campsites at this lake cost $5 a night to pitch a tent or park an RV. A tourist facility rents boats and plastic kayaks ($10 an hour) for paddling around the lake. They also offer horse tours (about $25 an hour).

■ Adventures in Nature

Volcano Tours

There are two volcanoes standing side by side. **El Volcán de Fuego** is active and is the younger and smaller of the two, standing at 13,000 feet/4,000 meters. It is located eight miles/12 km south of the other, **El Nevado de Colima**, which stands at 14,300 feet/4,500 meters. Nevado de Colima is about 53 million years old and has not erupted in modern times. It is the sixth-highest mountain in Mexico and, although its steep sides are slightly eroded, it maintains a classic cone shape. Fuego, on the other hand, has been spewing fire for millions of years. It is estimated that there have been about 30 eruptions since the Spanish arrived in the early 1500s, making the volcano one of the most active in the world. It is believed that about 4,000 years ago Fuego had an enormous spill that caused cataclysmic results. Since then, although it has never repeated that performance, it has had many smaller eruptions. It seems that earthquakes, so common in the area, cause activity to increase on the mountain. The 1985 quake resulted in many new cracks opening on the hill and the mountain spewed ash and molten rock for weeks. In 1869 a small cone developed just east of the main crater. It was named El Volcáncito (Little Volcano).

FACT FILE: The temperature of the molten rock inside the volcano is close to 1,500°F/ 815°C.

Being in the vicinity of a volcano when it is rumbling or throwing rocks is an amazing thrill. The earth trembles, the sound becomes deafening and rocks the size of cars fall like rain. Fuego can be observed from the summit of Colima or from the western slopes at la Yerbabuena. If you are totally independent, you can go to Yerbabuena on your own and hike up to get good views of the volcano. However, I highly recommend hiring a guide; a good guide can show you a lot more than you would find on your own and provide some degree of safety, since they know the area. See Tierra Verde Expeditions or Aztec Tours, below, for information.

■ Adventures in Culture

El Chanal Archeological Site, ☎ *313-4946, Tuesday to Sunday, 9 am-5 pm, $2.50*. This site is four miles/six km past Av De Los Maestros on Calle Carranza. First explored by archeologist Vladimiro Rosado Ojeda in 1945, El Chanal was the first to be explored in the state. It covers 124 acres on either side of the Rio Verde that contain an important ceremonial pyramid and a ballpark. So far, only four acres have been excavated. Colima state has few carvings of the gods that were worshipped by pre-Hispanic people, but at El Chanal, there are reproductions of Tlaloc, Ehecatl and Xipe-Totec. There is also part of a stairway along the pyramid that is in good shape and a bas-relief with a carved calendar motif.

La Campaña Archeological Site, *Av Tecnologico, Villa de Alvarez,* ☎ *313-4946, Tuesday to Sunday, 9 am-5 pm, $2.50*. La Campaña (The Lookout) covers about 120 acres of land between the Pereyra and the Colima rivers. The main monument, the Adoritorio Central, is a square-based platform made from river stones. The platform may have had wooden and thatch temples at one time. A second platform beside the main one is not quite as large. This site has been recognized as an archeological zone since 1917, but work didn't start on it until 1994 and is presently ongoing. Archeologists have found over 50 buildings and15 plazas, making this one of the biggest sites in Western Mexico. Also here are underground tombs, drainage canals and roadways. It is believed that there were people living here as early as 1500 BC, but most of the construction visible today was from about 900 AD.

■ Outfitters/Tour Operators

Azteca Tours, *Av San Fernando #533 (room #10)*, ☎ *312-314-6437*. Gilles Arfeuille of Azteca Tours is a volcano specialist who offers an excellent trip. You have a choice of either observing the volcano after a short hike or rapelling down into the inactive volcano and hiking to one of the lakes. Azteca Tours will also take you to Nevado de Colima National Park and to the east side of the volcanoes. This hike goes to 13,000 feet/4,000 meters, where you will be able to look across to the active volcano. Strong and curious hikers can go to the summit of the inactive volcano in the park, but a permit is required and the tour must be booked at least two days in advance. Azteca also offers a trip to Yerbabuena to view Fuego. This is a bit easier than going to the east side of the volcanoes. A full day (about eight hours) on the mountains costs $85 per person, with all equipment supplied (unless you camp overnight, in which case you will need your own sleeping bag and warm clothes). The guides speak Spanish, English and French.

Tierra Verde Expeditions, *Priscillano Perez Amora #727*, ☎ *312-308-1007*, *tierra_verde2001@yahoo.com*, offers extreme sports around Colima. Their experience and lust for fun are commendable. Paragliding or hang-gliding with experienced guides costs $77 a day. This includes transportation, equipment, pilot and some refreshments. Generally, the company needs three days' notice and they will take no more than three people at a time for gliding. If you are a large group, contact them to make special arrangements. Hikers can head out to visit the snow-topped volcano on an eight-mile/12-km route to the top for $65. There's an alternate, less expensive hike for those who want to see the fire and smoke spewing into the air without reaching the summit. This trip includes everything: transportation, entry fees, drinks and a restaurant meal. It includes a stop at Carrizalillo Lake and the Alejandro Rangel Hidalgo Museum in Norgueras. For scientists, guided trips to the volcano can be adjusted to fit your needs. Talk with the company. There is a minimum of two people per hiking trip and a maximum of 20. Participants must be in good physical condition. The guides all speak English and can be hired by the day. The cost is $50-$80 a day, depending on the activity.

■ Day Trips

Head to the village of **Los Ortices** and the **ruins of Tampumacchay**, a privately owned park/museum/hotel about 12 miles/18 km south of Colima on Highway 110. Watch for the sign indicating Los Ortices, the name of the hotel. The grounds are littered with petroglyphs, mortars and pestles and there is a ceremonial mound. The museum displays jewelry, copper money, clay idols and incense burners, as well as mammoth teeth found in a gorge near the property. The items are believed to be from 1,500 to 2,000 years old. You can visit the shaft tombs here ($2), but only with a hotel guide. **Los Ortices Hotel** (you'll see it) has small basic rooms without air conditioning, a pool, restaurant and bar.

The village of **Comala** is located on the road to Nogueras (see below) and is known as the Ciudad Blanco (White City) of Colima. It was first made famous by Juan Rulfo in his novel *Pedro Paramo*. The town is white, all the homes are whitewashed and most have a red-tiled roof. The plaza has a string of street-side restaurants where you can sit and enjoy a beer or a pomegranate or tamarind punch. The church on the plaza was built in the late 1700s. An active arts community here makes unique wooden furniture, as well as some things that can be taken home, such as picture frames, lamps and small tables. These items are made mainly of mahogany or parota wood and finished with wrought iron trim or painted with images of birds, flowers or coffee plants. There are numerous shops on the square. To get here, take a bus from Colima that stops along Calle Degallado. The sign in the bus window should say "Comala." Buses run every half-hour.

To reach the village of **Nogueras**, six miles/10 km north of Colima, take a taxi ($5) or a bus going toward Comala. The bus stops along Calle Degallado in town. Be sure to visit **La Hacienda de Nogueras Museum**, *no phone, Tuesday to Friday, 10 am-2 pm and 5:30-7:30 pm, weekends, 10 am-6 pm, $1*. The museum has been under the management of the University of Colima since 2000. Built by Captain Juan Vicente of Nogueras, the hacienda housed the family who made their living by growing sugarcane and manufacturing sugar. As you approach the hacienda, you will see the remains of a chimney from the sugar plant. In 1873, the hacienda went bankrupt and was purchased by the Rangel family who ran the mill until the 1917-1927 revolution. After that time, the property was reduced to a few acres and, in order to survive, the crop was changed from sugarcane to lemons. Alejandro Rangel was the last of the family to own the hacienda and he relied more on selling art than on running the lemon orchard. He remodeled the mansion, put in display cases to hold the artifacts and built a *horno*, or oven room. Instead of making bread, he filled the rooms with ceramics and artifacts found on the property. One display case has figures that show different congenital defects that were reproduced in clay by the pre-Hispanic artists. They include such physical problems as cleft palates and clubbed feet. Another room has a collection of Christmas cards, some of which are historical pieces that illustrate the lives of people like Philipe II of Spain. Four rooms in the house hold the works of Alejandro Rangel Hidalgo. In addition to these art and anthropological areas, there is the Margarita Septien Fun House, made for children but enjoyed by adults.

This is one of the better museums in the region and a definite must as a trip from Colima or from Manzanillo. There is a restaurant and gift shop on site.

In the yard, next to the house is a **chapel**. You can also enter an underground tomb where some of the pottery pieces that are now in the museum were found. Entire families were sometimes buried in these tombs, along with their servants and pets. Other precious items like jewelry and pottery were also found in the tombs.

ARTIST HIDALGO

Alejandro Rangel Hidalgo was a painter, collector, designer, illustrator and set designer. Born in 1923 in Guadalajara, Alejandro traveled in 1947 to Europe where he spent two years touring museums and major art centers. Upon his return to Mexico, he started working as an illustrator for writers. He then made some money at designing Christmas cards. These brought him awards such as the prestigious UNICEF award and the Colima Arts and Humanities Award. He moved on to working with metal, wood and glass. He also created set designs for the Colima Folk Ballet. He died at age 77 in Mexico.

■ Shopping

 Artesanias Colima DIF Estatal is on the pedestrian walkway that starts next to the cathedral. The DIF is a state-run co-op that carries arts and crafts made by artists living throughout the state. The street called **Andador Constitución** is a good place to go from shop to shop looking for artistic items of good quality.

Plaza San Fernando, *Av De Los Maestros and Carranza,* is a modern shopping mall that has everything from ice cream to Internet access to clothes shops. But there are no souvenir shops.

Alvaro Obregón Market, *Guerro and Ignacio Sandoval,* is open daily from 7 am to 4 pm. This local market sells fresh fruits and vegetables, as well as pottery and ironworks from Comala and Villa de Alvarez. There are also food stalls where you can try some local foods not usually found in the tourist restaurants. Markets are always so interesting to explore.

■ Places to Stay

Hotel La Merced, *Plaza Nuñez, Calle Hidalgo #188*, ☎ *314-312-6969 or 314-2734, $,* has been a popular hotel for years. The thing that attracted me most was the well-tended garden. The rooms are clean, although not fancy, and have private bathrooms. The owners are friendly. There is good security and a large car park.

HOTEL PRICE SCALE
Price for a room given in US $.
$ . . . . .Up to $20
$$ . . . . $21-$50
$$$ . . . . $51-$100
$$$$ . . . . $101-$150
$$$$$ . . . . $151-$200
Anything over $200 is specified.

Hotel Maria Isabela, *Blvd Camino Real and Av Felipe Sevilla del Rio,* ☎ *314-312-6262 or 800-221-8478, $$$,* is about a mile from the center and is a good deal. The 150 rooms are generally clean, the two restaurants are excellent and the hotel has live entertainment in the lounge. There is also a pool.

Hotel Maria Victoria, *Blvd Camino Real 999,* ☎ *314-312-3138 or 800-713-5283 or 888-815-7995 (US, Canada), mariavictoria@colima.podernet.-com.mx, $$$/$$$$,* has large rooms with a sitting areas, air conditioning, private bathrooms, cable TV, mini-bars and balconies. There is also a pool and restaurant. This is probably the best hotel in the city.

Hotel Villa del Rey, *Blvd Camino Real,* ☎ *314-312-2917, $$$/$$$$,* has 100 clean rooms near the university and is often near full. This is always a good sign. The rooms have private bathrooms, fans and sitting areas. There is a coffee shop on site.

Hotel America, *Morelos #162,* ☎ *314-312-0366, $$$$,* is in the center of town and its colonial décor is attractive. The rooms are large, with air conditioning, cable TV, telephones and private bathrooms. There is a popular restaurant and the staff is helpful. The place is hospital clean.

Hotel Los Candiles, *Blvd Camino Real #399,* ☎ *314-312-3212, $$$$,* is just down from the University of Colima. Each of the 75 large rooms has air conditioning or fan, cable TV, tiled floors and a private bathroom. They surround a pool. However, look at the room before you pay, as a few are a bit battered. The grounds are fairly well kept. There is a car park, safe deposit boxes and taxis available all the time. The hotel is away from the center, but bus service into town is frequent.

Hotel Ceballos, *Portal Medellin #12,* ☎ *314-312-4444, www.hotel-ceballos.com, $$$$,* is a colonial building on the plaza overlooking the Jardin de Libertad. The rooms are large and well kept, with private bathrooms, air conditioning and cable TV. The restaurant has tables on the street. This place is popular with Mexican businessmen.

Manzanillo Region

■ Places to Eat

 Trebol, *Degollado # 52*, ☎ *314-312-2900*, has a good meal of the day at noon that usually comes with tortillas, instead of the more common rice or potatoes. The service is excellent. Trebol is very popular, so arriving right at noon is not a good idea.

Mariscos Silva, *Insurgentes #556*, ☎ *314-314-9782*, is a ways from the center but is a destination that people go out of their way to reach. You can eat in their comfortable restaurant or take a package of goodies home. One of their specialties is shrimp ceviche.

Los Portales, *Morelos 25*, ☎ *314-312-8620,* on the plaza just up from Trebol, is another popular lunch spot. If you can't get into Trebol, try these people. They have tables on the street. The meal of the day comes recommended. If you're here for dinner, try the chicken cooked in a tomato sauce.

El Charco de la Higuera, *Calle Madero*, ☎ *314-313-1092*, is open 8 am to midnight and is six blocks west of the central plaza. Barbequed meat and most typical Mexican dishes cost less than $10 a meal. It has a nice atmosphere.

Fonda San Miguel, *Av 27 de Septiembre #129*, ☎ *314-314-4840*, has regional food and is popular with locals. The meals are all under $10.

Los Naranjos, *Gabino Barreda #34*, ☎ *314-312-7316*, is open from breakfast until after-dinner dessert time and serves everything from toast and eggs with coffee to a hamburger and fries or a full steak dinner. The atmosphere is pleasant, the place clean and the prices under $10 for dinner and $5 for breakfast. The food is fairly good. Los Naranjos is in the older part of town.

■ Nightlife

 The **University of Colima Folk Dance**, *Hidalgo Theatre*, ☎ *314-312-5140,* is performed every Saturday at 7 pm from December to March. This is one of the best dance groups in the country and you should try to take in a show. The group is directed by Rafael Zamarripa who, in the last 20 years, has taken it to perform in Canada, the US, Guatemala, Panama, Puerto Rico, Spain, Belgium, France, Holland, England and Switzerland. To find out more, visit www. ucol.mx/arte/grupos/index.php and click on any group you wish to know about. This is a Spanish-language site.

Manzanillo to Playa Azul

Cuyutlan

This little village can be visited as a day trip from Manzanillo or as an overnight. It is much quieter than Manzanillo.

■ Getting Here & Away

Cuyutlan is about 40 miles/65 km from Manzanillo. **Buses** leave every half-hour or so from the bus station in the center of Manzanillo's old town, by the docks. You can also hire a **taxi** for about $20. Cuyutlan is small; you can walk around town or take a taxi.

■ Sightseeing

Cuyutlan Salt Museum is a half-hour walk north from the village. From Cuyutlan, walk two very long blocks north of the *jardin* (plaza) and you will find the salt museum on the left side. It is housed in a barn made of hand-hewn boards. The barn and the storage buildings are about 100 years old. There are whalebones, photos of when the *Adventures of Robinson Crusoe* were filmed here in 1951 and tools from the salt mines from about the mid-1800s. Most impressive is to see how salt is mined.

ALL THINGS SALTY

Sea salt is used for other things besides consumption. For example, magnesium and boron is taken from sea salt and used in chemical fertilizers. The remaining minerals are given additives to make them whiter and to prevent water absorption. The product is sold as table salt. The additives preventing absorption also prevent absorption by the body. Some scientists believe that refined salt causes a myriad of ailments, including arthritis and decreased sexual capabilities. So, one of the answers is to use non-refined sea salt with all its natural elements. This is available at the salt museum.

■ Adventures on Water

 The beach at **Cuyutlan** is famous for the Green Wave, a huge swell that produces towering waves of up to 45 feet/15 meters in April and May. (The green color comes from the phosphorescence caused by marine plankton.) This beach is a haven for surfers who come by the hundreds and wait, play, wait and, when they see it, get the thrill of riding this wave. This is not a good swimming beach, but it is really a treat to come and watch the experienced surfers here. There are numerous places where you can rent boogie boards and umbrellas.

El Paraiso Beach is seven miles/10 km south of Cuyutlan and is lined with numerous palapa huts where you can eat reasonably priced food. The beach itself has dark sand and gentle surf, so it is better than Cuyutlan for swimming and body surfing at certain times of the year.

■ Adventures in Nature

El Tortugario Ecological Center, ☎ *313-312-4455, Tuesday to Sunday, 10 am-6 pm, $2,* is three miles/five km south along the beach from Cuyutlan. Since there is no government funding for this organization, a donation beyond the cost of entry is greatly appreciated. Considering the work they are doing, it is easy to contribute. This is a marine conservation center that houses turtles, crocodiles and iguanas. Turtles of all sizes are raised and studied for a short while before being released into the ocean. The center receives many of its eggs from poachers, who dig them up the morning after the mother has laid them on the beach. The center re-buries the eggs in a protected area. After the hatchlings emerge, they are put into saltwater pools where they are fed. When they are big enough and their survival possibilities increase, they are released into the ocean. If you are there at the right time you can volunteer to collect eggs or help with the feeding and tagging of hatchlings. From the sanctuary, you can continue along a trail to Palo Verde Estuary.

The trails that run between **Palo Verde Estuary** and El Tortugario Ecological Center go through jungle where numerous birds and amphibians can be seen. If you are a real birder, hire a boat at the dock (down from the plaza in the center of town) to take you into the estuary, a mangrove heaven for wildlife. If you want to hire a boat, David Renteria comes recommended. He has a knowledge of English and knows the estuary well.

▪ Shopping

Cuyutlan is famous for its **coconut palms** and the artistically carved coconuts are different here than anywhere else. You will get character faces depicting locals or a combination of local faces to make one face. This is so much more attractive than the usual monkey. Barter for price – $10 is not unreasonable considering the hours of thought and work that go into the carvings.

▪ Places to Stay

El Paraiso Hotel, *El Paraiso Beach*, ☎ *313-317-1825, $,,* has plain, clean rooms with fans that rent for about $20 a double. There is also a restaurant and pool with a nice deck.

HOTEL PRICE SCALE		
Price for a room given in US $.		
$		Up to $20
$$		$21-$50
$$$		$51-$100
$$$$		$101-$150
$$$$$		$151-$200
Anything over $200 is specified.		

Hotel Morelos, *Hidalgo 185*, ☎ *313-326-4013, $*, has 40 rooms in an old colonial building; all recently redecorated with bold colors and refurnished with carved wooden furniture. Each room has private bathroom with hot water. There is a new patio with a pool that is shaded and cool. The restaurant here is one of the better places to eat in the town.

Hotel Bucanero, *Paseo de los Estados*, ☎ *313-326-4005 or 800-024-3136, $$*, has 49 rooms with private bathrooms and fans. The pool is in the center of a courtyard and everything around the hotel sparkles white. There is also a restaurant and bar on the premises.

Hotel San Rafael, *Av Veracruz*, ☎ *313-326-4015, $$*, has 30 rooms in all, some overlooking the ocean. Each has a fan and private bathroom with hot water. The furniture is carved wood and the rooms are clean. Some have private balconies. There is an inviting pool that is both large and clean and an open-air restaurant.

Hotel Fenix, *Hidalgo 201*, ☎ *313-326-4082, $$*, has 28 rooms in a two-story building that has an open-air walkway running past the rooms. These rooms have been refinished, but retain their traditional Mexican atmosphere. Most overlook the street. The hotel is owned by a Mexican/American couple, so those who don't speak Spanish (but do speak English) will have no problems getting information. There is a restaurant.

Hotel Maria Victoria, *Veracruz #10*, ☎ *313-326-4004, $$$*, has 80 rooms, some with balconies that overlook the ocean. The rooms are on three levels and set around a central courtyard. Each clean room has a

Manzanillo Region

private bathroom with hot water, fans and bedside tables with lamps. The pool is small and the beach is close. There is a restaurant.

■ Places to Eat

There are numerous places along the beach where everyone goes to eat. Most serve fresh seafood at low prices (less than $5 a plate). Stop anywhere that appeals to you. You can't go wrong.

El Bucanero, *Paseo de los Estados,* ☎ *313-326-4005,* is one of the better places in which to eat. Try the shrimp del diablo (devil's shrimp). The spices are not excessively hot and the meal is good. The cost is $9 per serving.

Tecoman

This little colonial town is good to use as a base if you want to visit some secluded beaches and still have the comfort of a hotel. The most common occupation is farming and the area is known as the lime capital of the world.

> ### DID THE EARTH MOVE FOR YOU?
>
> Tecoman sits in an earthquake zone (as does a lot of Mexico). Three tectonic plates – the North American, the Rivera and the Cocos – come together near here. The Rivera and the Cocos are being consumed beneath the North American plate. The Rivera moves about three-quarters of an inch/2½ cm per year, the Cocos about 11 inches/27½ cm. The strongest quake in recent times registered 8.4 on the Richter scale. The one that hit in September, 1985 was not as strong, but it was the most devastating, killing 9,500 people and injuring 30,000.

■ History

First visited by Spaniards in 1523, it wasn't until 1581 that Luis de Velasco granted the area town status and people started settling. For the next hundred years, the town prospered. The early 1800s saw battles between the Spanish and local inhabitants. In 1847, an earthquake destroyed the town but, like the phoenix, it rose again to prosper and grow. In 1952 it was given city status. This brought pride to the people, a civic pride that is obvious even today. The town has about 10 gardens and parks that are well cared for.

■ Adventures on Water

Beaches

To visit the following beaches, either drive your own vehicle along Highway 200 taking the secondary roads down to the beaches, or take a bus to each hamlet from the center of Tecoman and then walk to the beach.

Playa El Real is six miles/10 km south of town. There is nothing sheltering this bay, so surfing is good. The sand is fine and the tides are gentle. There are numerous palapa huts along the beach that sell refreshments.

Playa Boca de Pascuales is another mile/1.6 km south and is good only for experienced surfers because of the strong waves that break both right and left with enormous power. The table talk in the evenings is about the thick lips and high faces (of the waves, not the people). Surfers say that some waves are so deep that you don't see daylight when riding one. On the road going to the beach the Enramandas restaurant is reported to be good. However, there are lots of palapas along the beach where refreshments can also be obtained.

Fishing here is a mainstay. At the lagoon, the ocean water rushes into the lake and crossing the mouth is always rough. Away from the mouth, anglers catch *cocineros* or *toros*, bait fish that are used to attract porgy fish that can easily weigh in at 40 lbs/17 kg. *Cocineros* are also kept for eating.

Playa de Tecuanillo is a narrow beach with fine sand and a gentle slope. The waves are gentle and swimming is a favorite pastime for locals. Palapas along the beach sell refreshments.

Boca de Apiza is 20 miles/32 km south from Tecoman and is a peaceful little place where the Coahuayana River flows into the ocean. It also forms the Michoacan/Colima border. The beach spreads to the south from the village here, which has one basic hotel, though most people come here to camp. The beach is good for self-sufficient campers, and beachcombing seems to be a favorite pastime. To get here, take a bus going south to Apiza and get off at the Boca de Apiza turnoff. It is a three-mile/five-km walk down the road to the beach.

Laguna de Amela, 12 miles/20 km east of Tecoman, is a deep lagoon surrounded by hills cloaked in thick tropical vegetation. There is good birding and fishing here, and there's a small fish cooperative. The most common catches are tilapia and catfish.

Laguna de Alcuzahue is five miles/eight km from Tecoman and has a crocodile reserve. Banana, lemon, tamarind and coconut plantations surround the lake, which has tilapia, robalo and cuatete fish. Small boats are available for rent.

MORELET'S CROCODILE

This freshwater amphibian is an immigrant to the area and was imported from eastern Mexico (the states of Quintana Roo, Chiapas and the Yucatán) for environmental experiments. The purpose was to see if the habitat would be compatible and the population would increase. It did.

First identified in 1924 by Dr. Schmidt as a separate species, the Morelet is found only in the New World. The females lay between 20 and 40 eggs in a clutch and they have been known to protect their hatchlings from predators.

FACT FILE: Crocodiles and caiman almost became extinct after the skin hunts of the 1940s and 1950s, when sales of products made from croc skin amounted to about $500 million US per year.

■ Outfitters/Tour Operators

Vazquez Montes, *Abasolo #171*, ☎ *313-324-3333*, can organize boat rentals and guide services. The other company in town is **Avitesa**, *Av Lopez Mateos #220A*, ☎ *313-324-2359*. I know nothing about these two companies except that they exist.

■ Places to Stay

Remember, no area code is needed when making a local call.

Gina Hotel, *Javier Mina #460*, ☎ *313-324-3045*, *$$*, has 51 simple rooms with private bathrooms and hot water.

Gran Fenix, *Javier Mina #429*, ☎ *313-324-0791*, *$$*, is across the street from Gina and has 42 rooms that are similar to those at the Gina.

Hotel Bugambilias, *Hidalgo #39*, ☎ *313-324-1055*, *$$*, has rooms with private bathrooms and fans.

Hotel Real, *Av Insurgentes*, ☎ *313-324-0100*, *$$$*, has 81 rooms with air conditioning, private bathrooms and cable TV. There is a pool. This is the best (and most expensive) hotel in town.

Hotel Tecoman, *Av Insurgentes # 502*, ☎ *313-324-2768*, *$$$*, is not too far from the Real and is also a good hotel. The rooms have air conditioning, private bathroom and cable TV.

Playa Azul/
Caleta de Campos

■ ■he road between Playa Azul and Tecoman to the north is long and sparsely populated. Driving along this road at night is not recommended, and even during the day it can be hazardous. There have been shootings and armed robberies, some resulting in death. The police patrol the highway, but they can cover only so many miles at one time. Always travel in a convoy of at least two vehicles. Although camping on a secluded beach sounds romantic, it is also dangerous in this area. Those wanting to surf and stay at the surf camps on some of the wilder beaches should go where there are a lot of other people.

Gas stations along this stretch are also sparse; there is one between Tecoman and Playa Azul. Staying in the industrial sprawl of Lazaro Cardenas a little farther down the coast is not advisable as there is nothing there for visitors. Plan on going farther along.

■ Adventures on Water

 The undertow at **Playa Azul** isn't always dangerous, but most of the time it is very strong and getting pulled out is possible. Only experienced surfers should use this beach.

■ Adventures in Nature

Villa Dorada Turtle Camp is active from July to the end of November, when the adults come ashore and lay their eggs. Then, six weeks later, the eggs hatch and the little ones make their way to the ocean. This is always a thrill to watch. In one season, an estimated 14,000 turtles are born. The survival rate, when no protection is given to the hatchlings, is often less than 10%.

■ Places to Stay

Playa Azul Hotel, *Venustiano Carranza*, ☎ *753-536-0090, $$$*, has 71 moderately-sized rooms with air conditioning or fans, cable TV and private bathrooms. There are two pools, one with a water slide, the other that is excellent for swimming. There is a ping-pong table, a restaurant and bar, laundry service and off-street parking. The patio is like the jungle with its lush vegetation. The hotel is also close

HOTEL PRICE SCALE	
Price for a room given in US $.	
$.	Up to $20
$$.	$21-$50
$$$.	$51-$100
$$$$	$101-$150
$$$$$	$151-$200
Anything over $200 is specified.	

to the beach. A trailer park at the back of the hotel has electrical hook-ups, toilets and showers. This park is always full, even though the spots are tiny.

Hotel Villa Dorada, *4.5 miles / 7.5 km from Playa Azul just out of Playa Calabazas,* ☎ *753-314-8102 or 800-719-8587, $$$,* has 26 bungalows, each with one or two bedrooms, living room with TV, dining room, kitchen with stove and fridge, and bathroom with hot water. Breakfast is included in the rate. There is a pool and restaurant on site, as well as tennis courts, volleyball courts, a basketball court and table games. You can also rent ATVs to rod around on if things seem a bit too quiet. Summer months are often booked with time-share users.

Hotel Maria Teresa Jerico, *Av Indepencia #626,* ☎ *753-536-0005, $$$,* is a three-star hotel with 42 large rooms that each have private bathroom, air conditioning and cable TV. There is a pool, a restaurant, a bar and a nice garden. The hotel is just three blocks from the beach.

Hotel Maria Isabel, *Av Fcd. Madero,* ☎ *753-536-0016, $$,* has 20 rooms set around a patio that is decorated with potted plants. The clean rooms have fans, private bathroom and cable TV. There is also a small pool.

Rio Nexpa Rooms, *north of Caleta de Campos on the Nexpa River, no phone, $$,* is set among palms and close to some great surf. The rooms are in a building that has a palapa roof with open pole ceiling, bamboo walls and frond facing. The four rooms have ceramic tiles for decoration, woven straw mats and driftwood towel racks. They open onto a central dining area. Guests share two bathrooms on the same floor as the rooms. The cost is minimal for a room and extra people can sleep in the loft for $3 extra. For surfers, this is an exceptional deal. There is room for a total of 10 guests at the hotel. The place is comfortable, the waves perfect and the owners helpful.

Patzcuaro to Ixtapa/Zihuatanejo

Patzcuaro Lake & Village

Patzcuaro Lake is about 200 miles/300 km from the coast, but the archeological sites near the lake are what attracted me to it. Getting here for a day trip from the coast is not possible as the drive in a private vehicle is seven hours; public transportation takes longer. An overnight stay should be planned. There are a few places in the village of Patzcuaro and a small hotel on the island of Janitzio.

■ History

The lake was inhabited by people for thousands of years and the kingdom who ruled this area just before the Spanish arrived, the Parapecha, were so strong they were never subjects of the Aztecs. When the first Spaniards arrived in 1521, they brought disease that was devastating. Tens of thousands of people died due to smallpox. Weakened by disease, the Parapecha were unable to defend their city. The Spanish robbed the ancient temples of their gold and jewels.

The land around the lake is dotted with the remains of this once proud nation plus tiny colonial villages containing churches and missions dating back 400 years. **Vasco de Quiroga**, in 1533 was the first priest to start a settlement. He built a mission with a hospital and a college where local people could learn to read and to study medicine. Quiroga died in 1565 at the age of 95 and is still held in honor by the local people today.

■ Getting Here & Around

Buses that go around the lake leave from the central bus station about a mile/1.6 km south of the town. City buses go from the bus station to the town center every five minutes. Buses also run from the center of town to the dock on the lake; taxis cost $5 to the lake.

■ Sightseeing

Patzcuaro Village

 The village has two plazas. One is dedicated to Quiroga, the first bishop of the area and the man responsible for the building of most missions around the lake. The second plaza, **Plaza Chica**, is dedicated to Gertrudis Bocanegra, who helped the local people during the war for independence from Spanish rule. Bocanegra was shot near the main plaza for her activities. Plaza Chica has a library containing a mural painted by Juan O'Gorman that is considered exceptional.

Market day in the village is every Friday and it's when people from around the lake come to sell and trade their wares. The **Casa de Once Patios**, an ancient nunnery, is the place to look for local arts and crafts on non-market days. There are only five of the 11 original patios left on that building.

Make a point to see the hexagonal tiled bath at the **Madrigal de las Altas Torres**, two blocks from Plaza Queroga. It is worthwhile seeing. The museum of **Popular Art**, *Calle Quiroga and Lerin, Tuesday to Saturday, 9 am-7 pm*, is located in the old **College of St. Nicholas**. It contains pottery and copper works, traditional masks, religious objects, lacquered objects and cornhusk items. Some of the interesting floor tiles in this building contain cattle vertebrae. In the backyard is a wooden cabin and the base remains a Parapecha ceremonial site.

Going uphill along Av La Paz from the main plaza is the **Basilica of Nuestra Señora de la Salud**, built in 1543. Quiroga banned holy images dressed in cloth so the Indians wouldn't put their own idols into Spanish-styled garments and call them Catholic. The people had always made images of their gods, so they complied to the rules and made a corn- and cane-paste Virgin. She sits on the altar of the Basilica and is said to perform miracles. Quiroga's remains are in the **masoleum** at the entrance to the Basilica. The old customs house, the **Real Aduana**, is on Calle Ponce de Leon, off the main plaza.

Lake Villages

Local buses travel from village to village around the lake.

At the eastern end of the lake, 11 miles/18 km from Patzcuaro, is **Tzintzuntzan**, famous for its pre-Hispanic key-shaped pyramids known as *yacatas*, one of which was dedicated to the hummingbird. (The name of the town is supposed to sound like the wings of the bird.) The *yacatas* are near the lake and less than a half-mile from the center of the village. Although this was once a huge city of about 100,000 people, the excavated area covers less than a square mile. The oval mounds at the site don't look like much from a distance, but once you walk around the compound and see how they were constructed, they become impressive. The Great Platform has five *yacatas* on top of it, plus a few buildings, one of which was the palace. The five *yacatas*, before the arrival of the Spanish, held up the temple of Curicaueri, a god-king of the Parapecha. The side of the great platform that faces Patzcuaro has been built up and reconstructed. Scientists believe that the lake once came up to the walls of the platform and the two ramps seen below were boat docks. The area is open 10 am-5 pm and the entry fee is $2.50. This includes a visit to the tiny museum.

Back in the village of Tzintzuntzan is a **Franciscan mission**. The monastery (part of the mission), built with red and black volcanic rocks, still stands, as does the **Convent of Santa Ana** that was once the hospital chapel. The windows and archways of the mission are decorated with carved angels and seashells. There is an open chapel at the monastery from where the friars used to preach to Indians. The olive trees in front were supposed to have been planted in 1530 by Vasco de Quiroga, the bishop who founded the mission at Patzcuaro.

Tzintzuntzan is known for the glazed black and white pottery originally designed by Miguel Morales in the 1920s. Many locals have duplicated this art and have it for sale.

The village of **San Pedro Pareo** has a church with early stone carvings that include the sun, moon and animals. Prior to the arrival of Catholicism, this spot was dedicated to the Tarascan Indian's moon goddess Xaratanga. The mission of San Pedro has these ancient carvings beside figures of Peter and Paul. Inside the church is the black Christ of Jaracuaro, a pathetic figure obviously suffering pain and malnutrition.

The village of **Uricho** has a church with a Moorish ceiling and a gilded altar. **Erongaricuaro** is known for its plaza and shops selling cotton fabrics. The Franciscan monastery in the village has a carved relief similar to the one in Tzintzuntzan. If you're looking for a guide, contact **Francisco Castilleja**, ☎ 434-344-0167, who speaks Spanish, English and French.

The village of **Quiroga** sells crafts such as stone carvings that are replicas of the mission reliefs, but there is little else of interest. Just up from there is **Puacaro**, which has a freestanding bell tower and a priest's home.

Zacapu was the home for the highest of Tarascan dieties, Curicaueri. During colonial times, a Franciscan monastery was built here and it has another shell/animal-adorned façade. There is also a statue of Jacobo Daciano wearing his pilgrim's hat. Religious murals can be seen inside the nunnery beside the church, and the hospital chapel across the street that now houses nuns still has a richly gilded altarpiece.

Naranja de Tapia is just up the road from Zacapu and has a church
built in 1733. The ceiling is said to contain some of the best paintings in
Mexico.

■ Adventures on Foot

 For a view of the lake and the surrounding area, climb **Volcán
del Estribo Grande**. It is about 2.5 miles/four km from the
center. To get here, walk from the plaza to the west along Ponce
de Leon. It will turn to Teran, Calle Paseo and, finally, Cerro del Estribo.
Keep climbing to the top.

■ Adventures on Water

 Janitzio is the island in the lake that can be seen from town. To
get here from Patzcuaro, hire a boat at the town docks. A
collectivo goes to the docks from the central plaza, or you can
hire a taxi. Boats cost $2 to Janitzio and they leave when full. The first
departs at 8 am and the last boat comes back about 5 pm. It takes less
than half an hour to get there. Boats also go out to the islands of Yuñuen,
Pacanda and Tecuen farther offshore for about $5. There are places to
stay on Janitzio if you get stuck here.

A photo of the lake taken from the boat could have a fisherman throwing
a butterfly net like those often depicted in advertising posters of
Michoacan. The nets, when in the air, look like the wings of a butterfly.
Apparently, the nets are used only for tourists.

The island takes about an hour to visit. The walk up to the 120-foot/40-
meter **José Marie Morelos** statue in the center of the island is difficult.
The entry fee to the site is $2 and you must have the correct change. Nu-
merous restaurants on the island offer Mexican foods, including the delicious *caldo michi*, a tomato-based fish chowder.

■ Adventures in Culture

 The ancient village of **Ihuatzio** is where the people lived before
the Spanish arrived. Its pyramids are believed to have been
handmade, stone by stone. As you walk toward the archeological zone, you will see the two pyramids, partially reconstructed. To the
north of them is the King's Causeway, along which priests walked while
taking part in religious processions. In the opposite direction from the
causeway are the three yacatas mounds, barely noticeable because of
their deteriorated state. Beyond the mounds is a collection of stones
placed in a circle that form what scientists believe to be an observatory.

There is evidence that these ruins belonged to at least two separate civilizations, but both were created in the second millennium.

To get here, take a bus marked "Ihuatzio" from Plaza Chica (Plaza Bocanegra). It will take 20 minutes to reach the ruins. Tell the driver to let you off at the *ruinas*. Admission is free on Sundays and $2 at all other times.

■ Places to Stay

 In addition to the places listed here, there are less-expensive options, such as the three-star Meson del Gallo and Posada San Rafael.

The **Fiesta Plaza Hotel**, *Plaza Chica (Bocanegra)*, ☎ *434-342-2516*, *$$$*, has 60 rooms with cable TV and private bathrooms. There is a restaurant.

Hotel Mansion Iturbe, *Portal Morelos #59*, ☎ *434-342-0368*. *$$$/$$$$*, is a 17th-century colonial home that once belonged to Francisco de Iturbe. He gave it to his daughter as part of her dowry. The coffee shop, Café Doña Paca, opens at 8:30 am and it serves coffee with special star-shaped sugar cookies that are delicious. The hotel rents bicycles for about $25 a day.

Hacienda Mariposas Resort and Spa, *two miles/three km from town on the highway to Santa Clara*, ☎ *434-342-4728*, *www.hacienda-mariposas.com*, *$$$$$*, is a first-class place with a pool.

■ Places to Eat

Primo Pizo, *Plaza Quiroga*, offers a chicken dish smothered in a walnut sauce that is excellent. **El Viejo Guacho**, *Iturbe*, has empanadas and pizza. They also have a good salad tossed with a homemade dressing. For the classic French meal that starts with escargots and ends with dessert and cheese, head to **La Cocina de los Angeles**, *on Lazaro Cardenas #158*.

Ixtapa/Zihuatanejo

Zihuatanejo and Ixtapa are like the old and new towns of Puerto Vallarta. But Ixtapa, three miles/five km from Zihuatanejo, is the Mexican government's idea of a resort with high-rise hotels and expensive restaurants, rather than the early unplanned development found in PV.

Manzanillo Region

The town of Ixtapa was started in the 1970s on a coconut plantation and mangrove estuary.

Ixtapa (White Place) is administered by FONATUR, a federal agency that is interested in land sales and development. The section that goes away from the beach where the hotels, condos and time-shares are located, is a peaceful area with modest (and luxury) homes surrounded by lush tropical vegetation.

Zihuatanejo (Place of Women) is the seat of government for the municipality, but was first a fishing town. To this day, it remains quaint, with narrow streets and friendly people. Fishing is still a major occupation for the 50,000 inhabitants living in the two towns.

■ Getting Here & Around

By Plane

 Airlines flying into Ixtapa are Frontier Air, Continental Airlines, Mexicana Airlines, AeroMexico, Alaska Airlines and America West Airlines. They fly regular scheduled flights from cities in Mexico, the US and Canada. Some also offer charter specials; contact your travel agent for information.

AIRLINE CONTACT INFORMATION		
AeroMexico	www.aeromexico.com	☎ 800-237-6639 (US); 800-021-4010 (Mx)
Alaska Airlines	www.alaskaair.com	☎ 800-252-7522 (US); 555-282-2484 (Mx)
America West	www.americawest.com	☎ 800-363-2597 (US); 800-235-9292 (Mx)
Continental	www.continental.com	☎ 800-231-0856 (US); 800-900-5000 (Mx)
Frontier Air	www.frontierairlines.com	☎ 800-432-1359 (US)
Mexicana Airlines	www.mexicana.com	☎ 800-531-7921 (US); 800-509-8960 (Mx)

By Taxi

Taxis to and from the airport are $20 from Zihua and $22 from Ixtapa for up to four persons. Taxis in town are $1.50 minimum and between the two towns run about $5 one way. To reserve or hire a taxi for the day, ☎ 755-554-3680, 554-4583 or 554-3311. Small vans also do the airport runs and cost $6.50 to Zihua and $7.50 to Ixtapa.

By Bus

The bus station is 1.5 miles/two km from Zihuatanejo center. **Estrella de Oro** and **Estrella Blanco** offer first-class trips throughout the state of Guerrero. Taxis outside the station cost $2 for the trip into town. The **Monacas Express**, Calle Rube #6, ☎ 800-685-7575, has direct service to Uruapan and Morelia.

Local buses are great for getting around and cost far less than taxis. They are also far more interesting. Around town or to the beaches just north or south of town, the cost is 50¢.

By Car

Remember, if someone in the left turn lane is signaling to the right, it probably means that they want you to pass them on the right. This is common practice in Mexico.

> **WARNING:** Be aware that the isolated highways in this area are dangerous due to highway bandits. Also, farm animals, pedestrians, cyclists and potholes are common on secondary roads and cannot be seen once darkness falls. Stay off the highways at night. If you get into any car difficulty, contact **Los Angeles Verdes** (The Green Angels), ☎ 800-903-9200. Their service is free, but they do appreciate a tip.

Hertz, ☎ *755-554-2590, at the airport, or at Nicolas Bravo #13,* ☎ *755-554-2255, in town.*

National Car Rental, ☎ *755-554-8429, at the airport or at Hotel Fontan,* ☎ *755-554-2255, in town.*

Dollar Car Rental, ☎ *755-553-0397, at the airport or Av N. Bravo #13,* ☎ *755-554-5366, in town.*

Budget, *Centro Commercial Los Patios #19,* ☎ *755-553-0206,* in town have cars for $80-$100 per day, including insurance.

■ History

Prior to the coming of the Spanish, a Tarascan leader settled in the area and built a barrier on the beach so women and children could safely swim here in the sheltered waters. The barrier, built on Los Gatas, still provides a calm swimming area. The Indian people called the area Cihuatlan. This was soon changed to Ciguatanejo, almost the same name we use today. The 1800s brought pirates and privateers who used the calm bays for shelter and the open waters for treachery. In the early 1900s, entrepreneurs came to export some of the fine hardwoods available in the surrounding hills. In the mid-1970s, Douglas S Cramer (who produced *Love American Style*) began filming the television comedy show *The Love Boat*, which took place on a modern cruise ship, one of Princess Cruises' boats. The show was on the air for a total of 25 years and reruns are still playing. In 1987, and after joining Aaron Spelling in the production, *The Love Boat* was rated as one of the best prime-time shows. It has been translated into 29 languages and shown in 93 countries. Through this series, Zihua was discovered and Ixtapa was developed to attract tourists.

■ Services

 Tourist Office, *2nd floor in the bus station*, ☎ *755-554-2355, or at La Puerta Shopping Center, Ixtapa*, ☎ *755-553-1968, 8 am-9 pm weekdays*. Like the rest of the Mexican tourist services, these offices are helpful and cooperative.

Post office, ☎ *755-554-2192, Monday to Friday, 9 am-3 pm, Saturday until 1 pm*. The PO is five blocks straight up from the beach and three blocks east.

Police, *Calle Limon*, ☎ *755-554-2040, or in Ixtapa, across from the Hotel Presidente*, ☎ *755-553-2008*.

IAMAT Center, *Nicolas Bravo #71-A*, ☎ *755-553-1711, or Col. Centro, fax only, 755-554-5041*. The center's English-speaking coordinator, Rogelio B. Grayeb, can be reached by cell at ☎ 755-1335.

Clinica Maciel, *Calle Palmas #12*, ☎ *755-554-2380*, is open 24 hours a day and offers both dental and medical services.

US Consular Agency, *Hotel Fontan, Ixtapa*, ☎ *755-553-2100, 553-2772 (fax), or 044-755-557-1106 (cell) while in Mexico. From the US, dial 011-52-755-553-2100, 52-755-553-2772 (fax), or 52-755-557-1106 (cell)*.

Yoga with Sylvia, ☎ *755-557-8418, Hotel El Paraiso Real, La Ropa Beach, Tuesday to Friday, 9-10:15 am, Saturday, 11 am-12:15 pm*. Sylvia offers private lessons upon request. These are English classes and cost $10 for a one-hour session.

Publications

Another Day in Paradise is Zihua's only English-language magazine. It comes out once a month and can also be accessed online at www.zihua-ixtapa.com/~anotherday/. It is an excellent publication with informative, clearly written articles. Be certain to pick up a copy.

▸▸ **AUTHOR NOTE:** *If you must use the long-distance telephone to reach home, make the call and have the person call back. It is much cheaper to call to Mexico than it is to call from Mexico. Private companies, such as Primus or Pioneer, advertise good connections to the US, but the cost can be up to $10 per minute. Visit www.saveonphone.com for the service that will best serve you.*

■ Festival

The **International Guitar Festival**, www.zihua-ixtapa.com/zihua/guitarfest/participants.php, is held every April in Zihua. The venues vary around town and a visit to the tourist office will give you the schedule. The festival draws musicians such as Emiliano Juarez, based in Madrid, Spain, and Ed Ivey, who writes and produces blues music. JL Stiles, a ragtime and blues guitarist, has played his 12-string guitar at the festival numerous times, and Jenny Kerr, an American and regular at the festival, has entertained audiences up to 120,000 people in Europe. Each year the list of high-powered entertainers gets longer. If you are in town during this event, it is a must to take in. Visit the website for dates and a line up of the entertainment.

■ Sightseeing

Archeological Museum of the Grand Coast, *on Olaf Palme along the Paseo del Pescador,* ☎ *755-554-7552, Tuesday to Sunday, 10 am-6 pm.* The story of the "Place of Women" is slightly varied at this museum. They say that the women goddesses rose in the afternoon to lead the sun into Mictlan, the world of the dead, so it could give faint light to the deceased. The women then bathed in the gentle waters protected by the rocks.

There are six rooms here that display artifacts from about 50 archeological sites covering the influences of Olmec, Teotihuacan, Tarascan and Mexican societies. The first room has objects from settlements along the coasts of Jalisco, Nayarit, Colima and Guerrero. Rooms two and three carry objects that have been found at Tierras Prietas and at Cerro de la Madera in Zihuatanejo. The fourth room has cultural artifacts from village life in the area between 200 and 750 AD. The last two rooms cover the more recent history of the area. Some of the items are exceptional, like the pottery from Tierras Prietas that suggests the people practiced deforming the head of infants much like the Maya did. Other pieces indi-

Manzanillo Region

cate the importance women played in the life of the people. Artifacts are well displayed and the lighting is good.

■ Adventures on Foot

Hiking

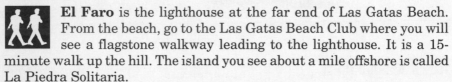 **El Faro** is the lighthouse at the far end of Las Gatas Beach. From the beach, go to the Las Gatas Beach Club where you will see a flagstone walkway leading to the lighthouse. It is a 15-minute walk up the hill. The island you see about a mile offshore is called La Piedra Solitaria.

Golf

El Club de Golf Palma Real has golf, four tennis courts and two paddle courts. The 18-hole, par 72, 6,898 yard course was designed by Robert Trent Jones. It is located on Ixtapa Blvd near Hotel Barcelo, ☎ *755-553-1163 or 553-1062*. Although reservations are unnecessary, I suggest you book in advance to play during high season. Green fees are $75 ($45 after 3:45 pm for nine holes), cart fees $35, caddie fee $20 (you must use either a cart or a caddie) and club rentals $22. Tennis and paddle courts are $45 or $16 after 7 pm. Golf lessons are available. There is a pool, restaurant and bar at the club, plus a mobile bar on the green. The course is open seven days a week all year.

Marina Ixtapa Club de Golf, ☎ *755-553-1424 or 553-1410, marina-ixtapa@prodigy.net.mx*, is an 18-hole, par 72, 6,793-yard course designed by Robert Von Hagge. There are water hazards on 14 of the holes. Their pro is Oscar Fernanedez Cole. The green fees are $94 ($80 after 2 pm) in high season and $59 ($50 after 2 pm) in low season. Groups of 10 or more get a reduced rate of $85 in high season and $50 in low season. Carts are included in the fee and caddies cost $20, clubs $30. Golf lessons are available. There are two tennis courts on site, a bar and restaurant, and a mobile bar on the course. The course is open every day, year-round.

Tennis

There are courts at almost all the hotels in Ixtapa, but only the Hotel Villa del Sol in Zihuatanejo makes its court available to the public. There are also public courts at both golf courses.

■ Adventures on Water

Fishing

 The big fish in the bay include marlin, sailfish, yellowfin tuna, dorado and wahoo. Of the smaller fish, roosterfish, snappers, groupers, mackerel and yellowtail jacks are the most common. Catch-and-release fishing is commonly practiced. In early 2004, over 500 sailfish arrived in the waters here, and more than 200 were actually landed (one weighed 165 lbs/75 kg). Anglers use bonito as bait and catching three or four sailfish in a day is common; the lucky few will catch up to eight or nine. Fly-fishing is also becoming popular. One group landed 25 bonitos and a 47-inch dorado, while another group got a 20-lb/eight-kg yellowtail jack. Most fishing is done within 10 miles/six km of the shore. The fishing here is so good that articles have appeared in *Saltwater Sportsman, Field and Stream, Marlin Magazine* and the *South Coast Sportsman* espousing the possibilities.

FISHING CHART FOR IXTAPA/ZEHUATENEJO

Pacific sailfish are here all year, except March and April.

Pacific blue marlin and **black marlin** are available February to May.

Yellowfin tuna are caught here from December to May.

Dorado is a possible catch in January, February, June to September, November and December.

Wahoo swims these waters from September to February.

Roosterfish are here from June to February.

Sharks, **groupers** and **barracuda** are in the waters here year-round.

Snook is available from June to December.

The November **Tag and Release Fish Tournament** includes using both fly and conventional tackle. Proceeds from this tournament go to the Children's Wish Foundation. For scoring, sailfish receive 100 points; marlin, 250; swordfish, 300; and spearfish, 300 points. Dorado and tuna are measured by weight and the person who gets the biggest catch is awarded the trophy. Anyone who lands and tags a fish gets an extra 25 points and anything caught on a fly rod earns double points. If that fish is tagged, an additional 50 points is added to the score. Dead fish are disqualified. All catches and tags must be verified by the on-board observer. The International Game and Fish Association rules apply, except that the captain, mate or other fisher may set the hook and then must immediately pass the rod to the angler. No one is permitted to touch the rod, reel, or line except to guide the line on the reel. Visit www. ixtapasportfishing.com/tournament, for information and registration forms. Fishing licenses are provided by the captains of the boat. There is also an inshore division that is only for fly-fishers. This is a catch-and-release event. Registration fees are $650 for a team of two, $850 for three and $1,050 for a team of four. In shore, teams of one or two cost $650. Daily prizes run between $100 and $200.

The **Dolphinarium**, *at the Magic World Aquatic Park, Paseo de Los Garzas (next to the Ixtapa Palace Hotel),* ☎ *755-533-1359, 10 am-noon and 4-7:15 pm daily (high season), noon-4:30 pm (low season), $6.50.* Groups of up to 18 people enter the water and swim with dolphins. There are 15 minutes of instruction before the 45-minute swim. For children there is also a Muppets Theater that teaches them about the evolution of dolphins. The dolphin swim costs $60.

Beaches

Playa Principal is the beach in Zihuatanejo where the pier is located. This is not a swimming beach, but from here you can catch a water taxi to other beaches or charter a fishing boat. There are restaurants along El Andador de los Pescadores, the walkway that borders the beach.

Playa Manzanillo is between Principal and Playa Larga, but still on the bay. The two islands just offshore are Isla Ixtapa and Los Morros de Potosi, once a favorite hiding place of pirates. The government wants the islands developed, but ecologists want them preserved. If you are interested in fighting development, write to the Secretary of Ecology and Natural Resources (SEMARNAT), www.semarnat.gob.mx/wps/portal, and make your opinion known.

Playa Madera is part of the main bay, east of Playa Principal. It is considered safe for children and has fine sand and gentle surf. The beach runs for about 600 feet/200 meters and has many restaurants and hotels.

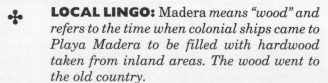

❖ **LOCAL LINGO:** Madera *means "wood" and refers to the time when colonial ships came to Playa Madera to be filled with hardwood taken from inland areas. The wood went to the old country.*

Playa la Ropa has the best swimming in town. The beach has a gentle slope and little current or surf. You can parasail or take a banana boat ride. There are restaurants, hotels and equipment rental stalls along this stretch. Often, Latin music is played for the entertainment of the entire beach.

Manzanillo Region

BIRD WATCH: *Birders at Playa la Ropa should watch for the magnificent frigate birds with their eight-foot wingspan that allows them to soar all day long with barely a wing movement. Also here is the pelican, with its nine-foot wingspan. This bird comes in two colors, white and brown, and the latter can dive up to 60 feet / 20 meters for its supper. These birds can also hold up to three gallons of water in their beaks. The brown booby, also seen here, has a 4.5-foot / 1.5-meter wingspan and is recognizable by its bluish feet and bill.*

The beach got its name when a boat from the Orient, full of silks, sunk just offshore. The silks were eventually washed into shore and the name of the beach (*ropa*=clothes) was born.

The estuary behind this beach is a crocodile preserve that can be visited. A donation toward the upkeep of the crocs is always appreciated.

CROC FACTS

Crocodiles are carnivorous predators that eat fish, crabs, birds, turtles and small mammals. Some even eat smaller crocs. They catch their food by surprise attack and most prey is drowned before being eaten. Usually, crocs are not interested in tasteless humans. If they are warning you to get away, they will grunt. The females lay between 20 and 60 eggs in each nesting that occurs during dry season. The young hatch within 90 days, which is usually at the beginning of rainy season.

Playa las Gatas is a small beach with a little offshore reef that is easy to snorkel out to. There is quite a bit of underwater wildlife here, but nothing much bigger than an angelfish. On the south side of the beach dramatic south-swell waves arrive about 10 days a year. They form dramatic tubes and move slowly enough for the surfer to position him/herself inside before they start to break over the rocks. Some locals are possessive of this wave and the best advice for surfers is to wait outside the group until the locals miss one. These waves run all day long and are not affected by the onshore winds. Among locals, a scrape on the coral or sharp rocks is called "the hand of the tiger." If your face gets it, they say you've been "kissed by the tiger." Regardless of how you get it, the wave will be worth it.

This stretch of beach has restaurants and banana boats for rent.

Playa Larga is a three-mile/five-km walk from Playa Principal and is ideal for beachcombing, horseback riding and sitting at the beach-side restaurants. The ocean surf and currents are strong here, so swimming is not recommended.

El Palmar, in Ixtapa, is two miles/three km long and offers all watersports and safe swimming. Shacks along the beach offer numerous equipment for rent – boogie boards, banana boats, windsurfing boards, Jet Skis, waterskis and boats – and also offer para-glide rides. If you want to windsurf or kayak, move a bit north and use Quieta Beach.

▶▶ **AUTHOR NOTE:** *Many of the beaches between Quieta and Linda are private with no public access (even though this is illegal in Mexico).*

Playa Linda, just beyond the private zones, is a long beach that is good for beginner surfers. The spot near the mouth of the river has big waves when there is a north or west swell. For swimmers, this is also a nice beach. The river offers clean water during dry season, but during wet season it is murky. Birders often come here.

Ixtapa Island is a 10-minute boat ride from Playa Quieta. Boats are located in front of Club Med. The cost is $3 for the round-trip. The first boat usually leaves around 10 am, the last one returns about 5 pm. There are four beaches on the island and the only beach without restaurants is Carey Beach, which is used only for sunbathing. There are shallow dive/snorkel spots among the rocks that form canals containing many fish. Snorkel gear can be rented at the huts around the beaches. A mask and flippers runs about $10. Waves in the area run from none to moderate; most are low. Sea life and coral are the attractions.

Beaches North of Ixtapa

Playa Atracadero has little except palms, sand, surf and sun. There are some tide pools that are often fun to explore. Otherwise, the beach is deserted. To get here, take a bus north to Joluta, 40 miles/60 km from Zihua, and walk two miles/three km down the gravel road to the beach. Bring all your beer, food, suntan lotion. If you have become addicted to the music, bring that, too.

Playa Llanos is a small village about 10 minutes north of the Troncones Beach turnoff. The actual beach is three miles/five km from the village near the highway. It is undeveloped except for a few palapa hut restaurants. The surf is not strong because rocks in the bay break the strength of the current. There are numerous tide pools to explore and, for some reason, this beach usually has a lot of shells after the tides retreat. Oyster fishers come here at midday to unload their catch onto waiting transport trucks.

Playa Majagua is 20 miles/30 km north of Zihua and is accessed by taking the road to Troncones and then continuing from Troncones down to the ocean. Majagua is a tiny fishing village with a few houses and a few palapa restaurants that specialize in oysters and lobster. It is also the location of Cueva del Tigre (see *Adventures in Nature*, below). La Boca, at the north end of the bay, is where the river enters the ocean. Surfers congregate at La Boca when the surf is strong.

Majagua has one place to stay, the Kandahar Beach Resort (see *Places to Stay*, below).

Playa Troncones is a small beach community with a population of less than 1,000. It is 22 miles/37 km north of Ixtapa. For a quiet vacation with little to do but watch wildlife, peer into tidal pools or comb the beach, this may be your spot. Bird watching is considered good and the surfing is for beginners. Tour companies can take you diving, snorkeling or fishing. This is a good spot if you want a quiet base from which to explore other areas such as Zihuatenejo or Colima. There are well over 20 places to stay and about half as many restaurants, plus numerous palapa-hut eateries. Of the hotels, there are economical surfer's camps and basic rooms, bungalows and villas. See *Places to Stay*, below.

Beaches South of Ixtapa

Barra de Potosi is a little village at the south end of the 10-mile/15-km beach. A lagoon here opens to the ocean and is surrounded by mangroves. You may spot a caiman or two hanging around the shore. There are numerous restaurants along the beach where seafood is the meal of the day. This beach is popular with locals because the surf is mild and the sand slopes into the water gently, so it is good for children. Barra has several hotels.

 BIRD WATCH: *Birding is good by the lagoon and in the mangroves. Some common sightings are pink flamingos, roseate spoonbills, white pelicans and blue herons.*

Diving

There are a total of 35 good sites in the area, and there's even a shipwreck in the main bay. Water temperatures and visibility vary with weather and other conditions. The most common sea life are octopus, lobster, turtles, whales, manta rays, sea horses, dolphins, sharks, starfish, sea urchins, conch, coral, cucumbers, puffers, flounder, moray eels and stonefish (highly venomous).

Islas Blancas is in front of the Ixtapa hotel zone and boats are available at Playa Linda or Zihuatanejo Bay. These dives require good guides, so hire only people from a reputable company with certification cards. Islas Blancas has eight locations where one can see underwater life, caves, coral and large fish. Dives go as deep as 100 feet/30 meters. You can also do night dives here. The waves are usually moderate to high. Except for Zacatoso where snorkelers can swim, the area is for experienced divers only.

Sacramento is a chain of pyramid-shaped rock formations 20 minutes by boat northeast of the bay. Six spots here have schools of fish to admire. The dive goes to 100 feet/30 meters and the waves are moderate to high. There are spots for the advanced and the basic diver and there is snorkeling at Morro de Tierra, nearby.

Punta Ixtapa, at the far end of the bay, has a few shallow sites with almost no current or wave action. Small sea life is the attraction and the visibility goes to about 50 feet/15 meters. This area just off the pier at Playa Linda is mostly for snorkeling.

La Majahua Bay has five shallow sites for the less experienced diver. Visibility goes to about 70 feet/20 meters and starfish, sea cucumbers, crabs and lobster are the most common things to see.

Caleta de Chon, also on the bay, has a visibility of 45 feet/15 meters and almost no current, so it is good for beginners, night dives, photography and snorkeling.

Piedra Solitaria is out from the lighthouse and, because of the different depths, it attracts the largest variety of sea life. The walls are high and the visibility goes to 150 feet/50meters. However, the area does have high and moderate currents that require experience on the part of the diver. This is one of the best places to come for underwater photography.

Morros de Potosi is about an hour southwest from Zihua Bay and is one of the most popular spots for experienced divers. It has caves, vertical walls, cliffs and tunnels. The corals are old, forming good crannies for sea life. There are strong currents here, although there are protected areas where snorkeling can be enjoyed. Bajo de Afuera, with a depth of 130 feet/40 meters, is especially interesting because of its arches. However, the currents are strong.

■ Adventures in Nature

 The tiny village of **Majagua**, 20 miles/30 km north of Zihua, is the location of the **Cueva del Tigre**. To visit the cave, you must go with a guide (see *Tour Operators*, page 418). You access the cave by rappelling into it. Inside are bats (I do not know what kind).

Near the village of **Angangueo** is where you can see one of the most remarkable events in nature. In November, monarch butterflies come to hang out for the winter, mate, and then rise in huge clouds to form their cocoons. Tens of thousands of butterflies cover tree trunks and shrubs. When they light, they are called cloud bombs.

 FACT FILE: When the 250 million monarchs arrive in Mexico each fall, each acre of land contains about four million pairs of orange and black wings.

Scientists Cathy and Ken Brugger discovered, in 1975, that the butterflies winter in Mexico each year. Up until that time no one knew what happened to them each autumn. Because they arrive in Mexico around Dia de los Muertos (Day of the Dead), some Mexican people believe that these are spirits of dead children or lost warriors. When the monarchs return north in the spring, it is the sign for people to plant their crops. This occurs in March, when the monarchs are crawling on the ground (in the form of caterpillars) looking for milkweed to sustain them until they develop into butterflies again. It takes three or four generations for these creatures to reach southern Canada. There are numerous monarch sanctuaries in the area; El Rosario Sanctuary and Sierra Chincua Reserve are two that allow tourists to visit. Because the forests in the area are endangered due to logging, it is imperative that locals earn money from tourism revolving around the monarch and its preservation.

▸▸ **AUTHOR NOTE:** *Because of its flashy behavior, the monarch has been dubbed the Elvis of the insect world.*

Angangueo has many guides offering tours to either El Rosario or Sierra Chincua Reserve. Guides cost about $10 each and a horse costs an additional $4. Entry fee to the sanctuary is $3 per person. The guides' eyes are trained to see the butterflies and a good guide will point out where they are resting. There are many monarch sanctuaries in the area. Over 35,000 tourist visit El Rosario and Sierra Chincua Reserve each year.

▸▸ **AUTHOR NOTE:** *Because the town and sanctuary are at a higher altitude than the beach, you should carry a sweater to stave off the cold. The walking is on an uneven surface, so wear good hiking shoes. Once in the sanctuary, be careful not to step on butterflies that may be on the ground. Also, do not touch the trees where they are clustered.*

Manzanillo Region

To get here, catch a bus from Ixtapa/Zihuatanejo to Mexico City and transfer to a bus going to Ciudad Hidalgo. From there, jump on another bus headed to Angangueo.

 If you can, pick up a copy of the book written by Dr. Robert Michael Pyle (aka Butterfly Bob) called *Chasing Monarchs: Migrating with the Butterflies of Passage*. It's published by Houghton-Mifflin.

■ Adventure on Wheels

 The Azatlan Ecological Park has a bicycle/jogger/in-line skate path that starts at the marina in Ixtapa, follows the golf course and continues. From town and along the golf course is about three miles/five km. The second section continues to Playa Linda, another three miles/five km away. This part follows Herionda Mountain and is known as the Azatlan Park. The vegetation is thick, and the area is patrolled by security to ensure safety. The next section continues along Paseo de los Viveros and Paseo del Palmar. The area is shaded in parts because of the huge trees bordering the path. The path's total length is 10 miles/15 km.

■ Adventures in the Air

 Take an **ultralight plane** to get an eagle's view of the area. There are three levels of flying, with the first being an introduction to the sport. There is nothing more eerie than to be gliding over the land with almost no sound but the wind in your ears. It must be what an eagle feels when he soars. The ultra-lights used here are made in France. For those who don't know, the motor is used only to get into the air. Once you're up, it's all about nature, wind and gravity.

■ Outfitters/Tour Operators

 Ixtapa Sport Fishing Charters, *Stroudsburg, PA,* ☎ *570-688-9466, www.ixtapasportfishing.com*, has been fishing in these waters since 1989 and they know where and when to get the big ones. They also organize the Tag and Release Tournament every November (see page 411). Their website has all the latest fishing information pertaining to this area. Their boats include eight 28-42-foot cruisers that cost $295-$445 a day. They also have nine 25-foot open fishing boats powered by 75 hp motors. These cost $210 a day. All boats come equipped with VHF radios, Penn International tackle (spinning and conventional reels from 12Ts to 80 TWs), dead bait and lures. Some have GPS systems.

The price also includes ice, dispatch fees and taxes. This company has been featured in *Field and Stream* and *Down Mexico Way* magazines. You must contact them in the US or e-mail them in order to book a boat.

> **WARNING:** Don't sign up to dive with Mr. Cheapo on the beach who has a can of paint and a brush with which he paints a sign claiming that he has PADI and NAUI qualifications. Always check credentials and dive only with a reputable company.

Hector Olea's Snorkeling Tours, *Manzanillo Beach,* ☎ *755-554-4311*, runs snorkeling tours on a 22-ft boat. As a local, he knows of many secret spots with excellent viewing. Lunch is nourishing and delicious.

Ixtapa Aqua Paradise, *Centro Comercial Los Patios #137,* ☎ *755-553-1510, Ixtapa or Puerto Mio #1, Paseo del Morro, Zihua,* ☎ *755 554-0460, www.ixtapaaquaparadise.com/trips.html*, are PADI certified. They offer great diving trips and diving lessons. A two-tank dive is $70 and a one-tank dive is $55 for certified divers. A trip to Morros del Potosi dive site is $90 for a two-tank dive; night dives are $65. Prices include tanks, weights and drinks on board the boat. If you need to rent all of the diving equipment, it will cost another $10 per person.

Ixtapa Zihuatanejo Sport Fishing & Tours (IXZI-Travel), *Hotel Qualton Club,* ☎ *755-552-0083, 755-101-3755 (cell) or 570-688-9466, 044-755-556-5093 (cell) in the US, www.zihuatanejosportfishing.net, or www. ixtapa- sportfishing.com*, has a variety of boats and tours. They can take you to the best fly-fishing areas around the bay (the most popular fish are the roosterfish, sailfish, tuna, dorado and marlin). Catch and release is the practice, and the captain's tag records are available for scrutiny. Their 38-foot custom cruiser with twin diesel engines, Penn International rods that have 30 TW, 50 TW, and 80 TW reels, navigational and fish-locating electronics, ice and life jackets, costs $400 for seven hours with a maximum of six people. If you want a smaller boat, they have a 26-foot *panga* with a 115 hp outboard motor. This one is equipped with everything the other boat has. The cost for seven hours with a maximum of four anglers is $190.

IXZI also offers an evening shopping trip with an English-speaking guide and an all-day regional tour starting at the museum in town and heading to the colonial town of Petatlan to see the famous church. You can visit fruit plantations and a tile factory. Their city tour is combined with a visit to the countryside and some horseback riding. Some tours are all day and some are just a few hours. Custom tours are available. Depending on what you do, prices run between $28 and $65 per person. The English-speaking guides share a lot of cultural information with their clients. This is a very good company.

Nautilus Divers, *Calle Juan Alvarez #33,* ☎ *755-554-9191, www.nautilus-divers.com*, specializes in diving tours. They charge $55 for a one-tank dive, $80 for a two-tank dive and extra passengers can tag along for $10 each if there is room. Night dives are $65 and a trip to Morros de Potosi is $90 with a minimum of four persons. Boats leave daily at 9 am and noon. They offer special prices if you do more than one day of diving and a discount if you bring all your equipment. Reservations should be made at least one day in advance.

Jaguar Tours, ☎ *755-553-2862, www.jaguartours.net,* is located in Troncones and operated by Bill Cooksey. He offers jungle hikes, cave tours, canopy-zip tours and hang-gliding excursions. Canopy zip-tours ($65) take place in Troncones, so there is no travel time. They are worth every penny. The fun starts with a guided nature hike up a mountain to a cavern. After an hour of exploring, learning about the plants and animals, you get zipped into a harness and swung down the mountain on a cable, stopping at strategic spots to see more wildlife. In the near future, there will be two courses from which to choose, one twice as long as the other. Nervous participants can take a half-swing, where you go only part way ($35). Jaguar also takes people hang-gliding ($75) from a special winch on the beach. The glide is guaranteed to reach 1,000 feet/300 meters of elevation. Bill also runs boat tours to observe sea turtles. The cost is $130 for the boat that holds up to six people.

■ Shopping

 Mercado Turistico de Artesanias, *Av Cinco de Mayo (near the park in Zihua) and on the Blvd Ixtapa in Ixtapa*. These markets have more than 250 *tiendas* with a plethora of crafts that come in a variety of qualities. Most items are handmade by local people and the quality is usually good. Prices in Zihua seem lower than those in Ixtapa. The hand-carved wooden fish are indigenous to the state, as are the *huaraches*, which are handmade leather sandals.

> **FACT FILE:** The markets were created by the municipal government in 1990 after the state passed a law that prohibited salespersons from hawking their wares on the beach or streets.

Silver that is sold in the better stores, or *platerias*, use silver that comes from the mines around Taxco, a colonial town in the state. Always be aware that if the price of the object seems too low, it probably is not genuine.

▶▶ **AUTHOR NOTE:** *All prices for precious metals should have the 15% IVA (value added tax) included in the price. This is the law.*

Petatlan village is known for its church on the main square and for its open-air **gold market** held in front of the church. Most of the stalls are open every day. The tour agent will be able to inform you if the stalls are closed due to a festival or other event. There are also archeological ruins near the town. To get here, take the bus marked *Petatlan* on Benito Juarez Street in Ixtapa. Tell the driver where you want to go and he will let you off near a stairway that leads to the street passing in front of the church. Walk three blocks to the plaza.

■ Places to Stay

Ixtapa and Zihuatanejo have numerous five-star hotels with hundreds of rooms. They offer few surprises. Below is a sample. Remember, no area code is needed when making a local call.

THE FIVE-STARS

All have a private bathroom, cable TV, air conditioning and purified water. Most run between $100 and $200 a night for a double.

Continental Plaza, *Blvd Ixtapa,* ☎ *755-553-1175*, has 152 rooms, two restaurants, babysitting service and Internet access.

Dorado Pacifico, *Blvd Ixtapa,* ☎ *755-553-2025,* has 285 rooms, five restaurants, four bars and two tennis courts.

Hotel Krystal, *Blvd Ixtapa,* ☎ *755-553-0333*, has 255 rooms, four restaurants, a gym, a pool, a disco and tennis courts.

Las Brisas, *Playa Vista Hermosa,* ☎ *755-553-2121,* has 423 rooms with private terraces, four pools, a gym, tennis courts, six restaurants and a huge garden.

Melia Azul, *Blvd Ixtapa,* ☎ *755-555-0000,* has 250 rooms, five restaurants, a pool, a Jacuzzi, a gym, tennis courts and nightly entertainment.

Posada Real, *Blvd Ixtapa,* ☎ *755-553-1925,* has 110 rooms, two pools, a restaurant, a bar and a Jacuzzi.

Presidente Inter-Continental, *Blvd Ixtapa,* ☎ *755-553-0018,* is an 11-story tower with 408 rooms, four restaurants, numerous bars, tennis courts, two pools and convention rooms.

Manzanillo Region

Qualton Club, *Camino Escenico,* ☎ *755-552-0083,* has 150 rooms with balconies or terraces, a pool, a restaurant and a bar. They offer all-inclusive packages.

Radisson Resort, *Blvd Ixtapa,* ☎ *755-553-0003,* has 275 rooms overlooking the water, a pool, two restaurants, a gym, tennis courts and a babysitting service.

Riviera Beach Resort, *Blvd Ixtapa,* ☎ *800-710-9346 or 888-809-6133 from Canada or the States,* has 173 rooms, a pool, a Jacuzzi, three restaurants, a bar, a gym, a spa with sauna and steam bath, two tennis courts and conference rooms.

Villa Paraiso, *Paseo del Rincon, Lote 1,* has 89 rooms with kitchenettes and balconies or patios, a pool, a gym, a tennis court, a restaurant and a bar.

HOTEL PRICE SCALE	
Price for a room given in US $.	
$	Up to $20
$$	$21-$50
$$$	$51-$100
$$$$	$101-$150
$$$$$	$151-$200
Anything over $200 is specified.	

Casa Elvira, *Paseo del Pescador #32,* ☎ *755-554-2061, www.zihuatanejo. com.mx/elvira, $,* has been around for a long time. The eight rooms are plain and clean, with fans and a shared bathroom. The garden shows the proprietor's pride of ownership and is where guests often congregate to visit. There is a restaurant and it, too, is popular.

Posada Citlali, *Vincente Guerrero #3,* ☎ *755-554-2043, $$,* has 19 rooms located on three stories that surround a courtyard filled with greenery. The no-trim rooms are small, basic and clean. They come with private bathroom and ceiling fans. This is a popular place.

Hotel Irma, *Adelita at Playa Madera, no phone, $$,* has 75 rooms with large balconies, red-tile floors, air conditioning and private bathrooms. There is a pool and the gardens are well kept. The charm of this place overrides any of its tatters. It is a ways from town.

Señora Leonor Ramirez, *Calle Adelita, no phone, $$$,* is near Playa la Madera. This comfortable place has spotless rooms. There is a courtyard and small pool that is surrounded with coconut palms, avocado trees, breadfruit trees and mango trees.

Hotel Villa Vera, *Av Morelos #165,* ☎ *755-554-2920, $$$,* has 45 basic rooms with private bathrooms and hot water. The floors are tiled and the walls are a glittering white, giving them a clean look. Some rooms have air conditioning, others have fans, and all have a TV. The rooms are on four floors, overlooking the pool. There is a bar beside the pool, a tobacco shop and private parking for guests. The owners live at the hotel and personal service is their main concern.

Casa Avila, *Juan Alvarez #8, no phone $$$,* has 27 rooms with double beds, air conditioning, ceiling fans, TV and private bathrooms. This hotel is on the beach and in the center of Zihua. Tata's Bar, a popular spot, is located on the premises.

Villas El Morro, *Adelita #59,* ☎ *755-554-2704, www.zihuatanejo-villaselmorro.com/habitaci.htm, $$$,* is set on a hill overlooking the bay. All rooms have air conditioning, fully equipped kitchens, sitting areas, king-size beds and TVs. You can even opt for a room with a private Jacuzzi and/or a balcony. Some rooms have a single bed for a child, who can stay for no extra charge if under the age of four. The well-maintained yard overlooking the bay has a pool. There is a restaurant, open every day but Sunday, from 8 am to 8 pm. This is a good deal.

The **Kandahar Beach Resort**, ☎ *617-669-1324 (US cell), $$$$/$$$,* is on the bay at Majagua and has eight one- and two-bedroom bungalows. They have fans, private bathrooms, kitchens, sitting areas and thatched roofs. There is a pool, restaurant and bar in a well-kept garden. They have a pool table, books, kayaks for rent and a masseuse ready to pound your flesh. From this resort you can fish, horseback ride or look for wildlife at the estuary that is just a 20-minute walk up the beach.

Casa Que Canta (Center of Well Being), *Camino Escenico,* ☎ *755-555-7000 or 555-7026, $$$$$, ($220-$500 per night for two), www.lacasequecanta.com,* is a spa resort with 18 air-conditioned rooms and suites. They feature hand-crafted furniture, ceiling fans, in-room safes, marble bathrooms with bidets, walk-in closets and complimentary mini-bars. Each has its own garden and gourmet breakfasts are served on your private patio that overlooks the bay.

Some of the unique treatments available at the spa include facials done with an electric wand or an electro-magnetic wave machine that stimulates your nerve endings. They also have eye-firming treatments. Massages last about 90 minutes and use techniques that combine reflexology and holistic medicine. You can also try one of the wraps that are supposed to get rid of toxicity and cellulite. These treatments are for men and women.

The water in the pool is constantly flowing. It starts at the Jacuzzi, goes to the two-tiered pool that cascades, at one end, over a waterfall and flows to the ocean. The only drawback is that there is no private beach in front of the hotel and the prices for meals and drinks are higher than they should be.

Villa del Sol, *Playa la Ropa,* ☎ *755-555-5500, www.hotelvilladelsol.net, $$$$$, ($250-$500),* is an award-winning resort designed by German engineer Helmut Leins. Located on the beach, the hotel has five pools, a gym, two restaurants, three bars and numerous activities to enjoy. The 35 rooms and 35 suites range in luxury from a standard room to the presidential suite. Rooms have air conditioning and fans, large towels, bathrobes, a hair dryer, satellite TV, electronic safes and DVD players. The simplest of accommodations is a split-level room that has a king-sized canopy bed, a night table, reading lamps, sheer curtains that match the canopy, a sitting area with a coffee table and tiled floors. The marble bathrooms are large and the balconies are furnished. All rooms are located in an adobe-like villa surrounded by tropical gardens and private terraces. The film library has a wide selection. The hotel specializes in honeymoon packages and weddings. This is luxury at its finest.

Playa Troncones

The choices available allow for the needs of almost every traveler.

The Casa de la Sirena, *www.casadelasirena.net, no phone, $$$$,* on the beach has rooms with air conditioning, private bathrooms and large showers, king-sized beds and tiled floors. There is a pool on site. You can rent the entire house, a room or a bungalow. There is a small pool here. The bungalows are more expensive and the price should be negotiated.

Another good place to stay is the **Abadia B&B**, *no phone, $$,* which has five huge rooms that are tastefully decorated. They feature sitting areas, ceiling fans, fridges and ocean views. There is a pool on site.

Casa Ki, ☎ *755-553-2815, $$, www.casa-ki.com,* is another tropical paradise with bungalows and rooms. Each has a king-sized bed, a refrigerator, a porch with a hammock, and a private bathroom with hot water.

Barra de Potosi

Places to stay in Barra include the three-star **Hotel Albergue**, ☎ *755-556-0026, $$;* and **Cabañas Margarita**, ☎ *755-556-0149, $$;* **Casa de El Paso de la Monarca**; and **Casa de Huespedes Juarez**. The last two are in the center of Angangueo, have no phone numbers, no stars and cost less than $20 per night. There is also **Hotel Villa Monarca**, ☎ *755-556-5346, $$$* along the highway toward Morelia.

■ Places to Eat

Café Casa, *Calle Adelita, no phone,* is a tiny place where your food is served in an outside courtyard. They have freshly brewed coffee at all times of the day, starting around 8 am. This is a breakfast must.

MEXICAN BEERS

Mexican beers are Tecate Light, Tecate, Indio, Pacifico, Victoria, Modelo Negro, Modelo Especial, Corona, Bohemia, Dos Equis and Sol. My opinion is that all Mexican beers taste similar. Certainly, all brands have the same alcohol content (3%).

Restaurant El Mirador, *Adelita #59,* ☎ *755-554-9013, at the Villas El Morro,* is open for breakfast and has pancakes for less than $3 a serving. For supper, try the marinated fish strips with onions and chili peppers for a mere $3.50 per serving. It is delicious.

Soleiado, *Plaza Ambiente,* ☎ *755-553-2101,* is open 7 am to midnight. This sidewalk café serves the best eggs benedict for $6, including toast and potatoes. The coffee is also delicious.

Casa Elvira, *Paseo del Pescador # 32,* ☎ *755-554-2061,* is open until 11 pm. It has been around for a long time and is popular. Fish and seafood are the draw. Try Elvira's skewer, a combination of seafood grilled over charcoal that gives the food a special smoky taste. This meal will cost about $9. Add a bottle of wine and you couldn't want more.

Villa de la Selva, *Paseo de la Roca,* ☎ *755-553-0362,* has been serving lovers (and hungry people) romantic dinners since 1982. The tiered terraces where the tables are located provide a private and secluded atmosphere. The international style food is excellent and the prices are high; $20 or more for a meal.

Restaurant Bandido's, *5 de Mayo and Pedro Ascencio,* ☎ *755-553-8072,* is open 11 am to 2 am every day except Sunday. This is a sports bar that offers live music every day during winter months. The music is often Cuban salsa, a treat for the mariachi-weary. The srimp tacos are good, as are the fish dinners. Prices are around $10 a meal.

Ristorante Beccofino, *Ixtapa Marina,* ☎ *755-553-1770,* is a first-class Italian restaurant with a top-notch wine cellar featuring wines from France, Italy, Chile, Spain and Mexico. The restaurant is part of the Ixtapa Gourmet Group, a prestigious group of chefs dedicated to creating the best recipes for their customers.

El Mango, *Calle Nicolas Bravo # 9,* ☎ *755-554-2421,* offers good hearty food in large portions at cheap prices. The place isn't fancy, but you can watch satellite TV while dining.

Ricomar *(no phone)* is in an alley across from Mango's and just off Calle Nocolas Bravo. They serve the best *pozole* in town (Thursday is *pozole* night in Zehua). *Pozole* is a meat stew made with either chicken or pork; green is chicken, red is pork.

Manzanillo Region

Casa Bahia, *Yacht Club in Zihu*, ☎ *755-554-8666*, is near Puerto Mio above the marina gas station. Famous for its selection of tequilas, Casa Bahia also serves some Hawaiian dishes that are not over-spiced. Costs run about $15 for an evening meal.

Casa Morelos, *Centro Comercial la Puerta, # 9, 10 and 18,* ☎ *755-553-0578,* open 7: 30 am to 11:30 pm daily, has a spicy fish soup for $5 that is large enough to be a lunch. The place is clean, but not fancy; the work goes into the food. This restaurant is also part of the Ixtapa Gourmet Group (see above, under Ristorante Beccofino).

El Pueblito, *Av Morelos # 249*, ☎ *755-554-8414*, is a garden restaurant that uses a wood-clay oven to cook some of the meals. On *pozole* night (Thursday), they have both white and green *pozole* (a chicken dish). During the rest of the week, try meals like the veal cutlets in peanut sauce or the lamb in green sauce. Other good dishes include beef tongue, sweet breads, crocodile steak and quail. The meals are all done Guerrero style. Guerrero is an area of Mexico that specializes in using wood in clay ovens for cooking. Meals are moderately priced (under $20).

Emilios, *Paseo de las Garzas, across from Ixtapa Palace*, ☎ *755-553-1585,* offers the best Mexican pizza in town, gourmet pizza that is. This can be complemented with a fresh salad. They also have exceptional barbequed ribs. A middle-sized pizza costs less than $10.

La Sirena Gorda, *Paseo del Pescador #90*, ☎ *755-554-2987*, is open 9 am to 11 pm every day except Wednesday. It serves the best fish tacos in town. The meal is so good that it has been recommended by *Bon Appetit Magazine*. Located on the waterfront, the restaurant also has a great atmosphere. The ceviche is recommended by me and so is the smoked fish. And no dessert can beat their coconut ice cream pie made with Kahlua.

Playa Troncones

La Cocina del Sol, *no phone*, has a trained chef who uses a wood-burning oven to cook some exceptional dishes. The restaurant has fresh bread for sale every day (also cooked in the wood-burning oven). A spring roll with watercress, carrots, bell pepper, cilantro and soy dipping sauce costs $4. A spinach salad with yogurt dressing costs the same. All sauces are homemade. La Cocina also has rooms available.

■ Nightlife

 Bay Club, *road to La Ropa*, ☎ *755-554-4844*, has live jazz music on the weekend. This is a treat. You should take a taxi home after an evening of entertainment here.

Señor Frog's, *Blvd Ixtapa,* is one of the wilder spots for after-dinner entertainment. This restaurant seems to be the big party draw in all Mexican beach towns.

Rick's Bar, *Av Cuauhtemoc # 5,* ☎ *755-554-2535,* is open Monday to Saturday, 5-11 pm. Besides drinks, the bar offers laundry service, hot showers, Internet access, tide tables and maintenance services for your yacht. Saturdays is Mexican Fiesta night and some of the performances are worth seeing. Students working their way through university perform here to make some extra cash, and their shows are often hilarious. On Friday nights, musicians have a jam session and visiting musicians can join in. Besides all this, the grill offers a good steak for $15. There is a $5 cover charge.

■ Heading to Acapulco

There are a few places of interest en route to Acapulco. San Valentin beach is not one of them

> **WARNING: San Valentin Beach** is a centuries-old turtle nesting ground and a popular haunt of thugs who drive away police so they can capture turtles and their eggs. It is difficult to access the 12-mile/18-km beach because of the armed guards who, besides killing turtles and mouthy tourists, are believed to traffic drugs. At the time of writing, this area was being protected by about 10 heavily armed bandits.
>
> My advice is to stay away and leave the problem to the local authorities. The best way to help stop this type of activity is to not purchase products made from turtles or their eggs.

This information was taken from an Associated Press article written by Natalia Para on January 20, 2004.

Papanoa village and beach are about 45 miles/75 km south of Ixtapa. The rugged cliffs along this stretch of road are more attractive than the beaches. The village is a bus stop for buses heading along Highway 200. Papanoa has one hotel, **Club Papanoa,** *Hwy 200, Km 160.5,* ☎ *755-648-3689 or 755-650-1571, www.hotelpapanoa.com, $$$,* on the highway overlooking the bay. The hillside where the hotel sits is dotted with palm trees and red-tiled walkways that lead to a nice pool. The 30 rooms have TV, air conditioning, private bathroom and a sitting area. There is a restaurant.

Puerto Vincente Guerrero is a long stretch of pristine beach that offers the only marina between Ixtapa and Acapulco. Although fishing is the big sport here, you can also watch turtles nesting or their eggs hatching during season. Beachcombing, snorkeling and diving are good activities here. To get to the beach, take a bus or car to the village of Papanoa and then catch a truck going to Puerto Vincente. Continue past Puerto Vincente about a half-mile to the Bahia la Tortuga Lodge. The only gringo you are likely to see in this area is John Lorenz, the owner of the lodge. **Bahia la Tortuga Fishing Lodge**, ☎ *956-592-6130 (in US), www. escapeixtapa.com/packages.html*, has a rustic house on a secluded cove. The rooms have air conditioning, private bathrooms, windows opening to the ocean and private entrances. It can hold 10 people comfortably, 12 people intimately. There is a beach house with a kitchen for guests to use and an area with hammocks for relaxing. Because of the isolation, the lodge offers all-inclusive packages. Three nights and four days, all inclusive (bed, meals, drinks, airport transfers and fishing in a boat), costs $545 per person. Six nights and seven days, all inclusive, costs $995. The cost for two days fishing (or whale-watching/snorkeling) is $495. This includes a room for two people, airport transfers and one meal a day. Other packages include all meals and drinks. Lobster cooked with garlic butter is one of the most common meals served. Lunch is often cooked on the beach and includes snapper or your catch of the day. This is a family run operation with experienced fishing guides (family members) to help you find a marlin, dorado, sailfish or even some of the smaller ones like roosterfish and snook. During the humpback whale migration (December-April), whales pass right in front of the beach hut. Over the years, the mammals have changed their route to avoid places like Acapulco and Puerto Vallarta, where there are so many boats. Vans at the lodge are available to take you to Ixtapa or to one of the lagoons where you can kayak or look for wildlife. There is snorkel gear available and the owners often take visitors to a waterfall in the jungle. This company prefers that you contact them personally before arriving at the lodge.

Piedra de Tlacoyunque Beach is reached by turning at the Carabelas Restaurant along Highway 200 and following the road about a mile down to the beach. This is an ecologically protected beach with heavy surf in places. Swimming isn't so good most of the time, but beachcombing is. There are no services except for one palapa hut that sells fried fish in high season.

TURTLE ALERT

This beach is a nesting ground for leatherback and Olive Ridley turtles. When it is time to nest, hundreds of these turtles head for the beach and lay their eggs. The turtles reach a length of seven feet/2.5 meters and can weigh 1,200 lbs/540 kg, so the beach gets a bit crowded. They lay 60 to 100 eggs per nesting; avoid walking where they have nested. A government camp here houses workers who try to protect the turtles.

Laguna Nuxco and Laguna el Plan are off the main highway and between the towns of San Luis de la Loma and Tecpan de Galeana. Neither lakes have any services, but birders may want to visit the area in search of birds that have, as yet, eluded them. However, with turtle-poaching going on along this stretch of coast, I would advise traveling here only with a large group and a tour guide.

Manzanillo Region

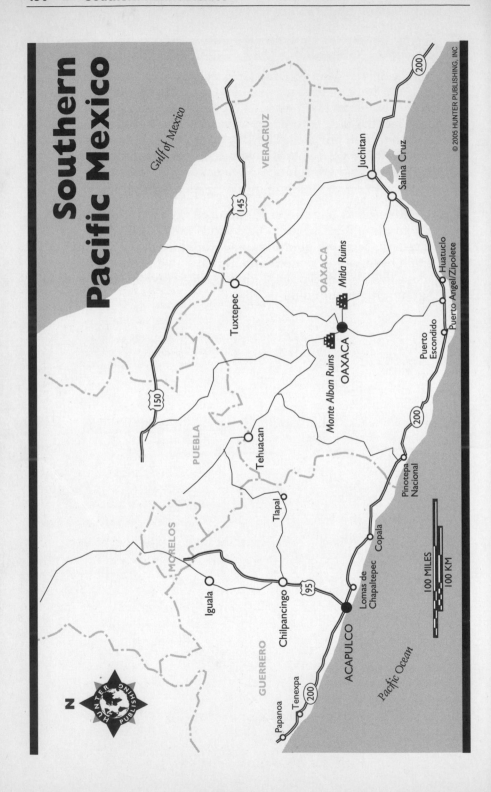

Acapulco & Southern Pacific Mexico

Acapulco

Once the desired destination of everyone going to Mexico, Acapulco suffered a depressed period due to over-development and pollution. That was in the early 1980s, but a massive clean-up operation in the '90s included water treatments and hotel renovations. Hurricane Pauline hit in 1997, washing thousands of homes down the hill and flooding the lowlands. Although it was a disaster and took many lives, the clean up was beneficial to all.

The town is set on a huge, gently sloping bay. The hotel area is like that of all resort towns along the coast. It has first-class businesses supplying every foreigner's desire. The older section of town at the south end of the bay is mostly for locals. It is where fishing boats come in at the end of the day and where mom-and-pop hotels offer simple rooms at moderate rates.

La Quebrada cliff-divers of Acapulco are world-renowned and should be seen at least once. The bars and nightclubs where some of the most expensive entertainment in Mexico can be found are around Icacos Beach and cater to the rich and wild. But there are also quiet piano bars and intimate restaurants, peaceful walkways and colorful parks. Acapulco has it all.

▸▸ **AUTHOR NOTE:** *The Golden and Diamond zones are like suburbs in Acapulco. Most other towns have one Hotel Zone. Because Acapulco was the first tourist destination along the Pacific Coast, it has had the chance to grow and grow. As a result, there are two zones, Golden and Diamond. There is also the center of town where the less expensive hotels are found.*

Southern Pacific Mexico

WORDS OF LEGEND

Acapulco comes from the Nahuatl words *acame* (reeds), *pul* (thick) and *co* (location), to mean Place of the Reeds. The legend about its name tells of Prince Acatle falling in love with the beautiful rain princess but, because he couldn't marry her, he started to cry and dissolved himself into a puddle of mud. (He sounds a bit soppy to me.) Where he dissolved, a reed bed started to grow. Meanwhile, the princess floated above as a cloud and, when she saw her prince had turned into mud, she also cried, adding more water to the puddle. When the reeds flattened, she died and dropped into the mud with her prince.

■ Getting Here & Around

By Plane

The international airport is 14 miles/23 km from the center. America West flies from Phoenix and Sacramento. Continental Airlines flies from Houston. Mexicana flies from Los Angeles, San José, Dallas, Denver, Chicago and Miami, with connections in Mexico City. American Airlines flies from Dallas. AeroMexico connects to all flights that pass through Mexico City. Delta Airlines flies into Mexico City and connects with AeroMexico.

AIRLINE CONTACT INFORMATION		
AeroMexico	www.aeromexico.com	☎ 800-237-6639 (US); 800-021-4010 (Mx)
America West	www.americawest.com	☎ 800-363-2597 (US); 800-235-9292 (Mx)
American Airlines	www.aa.com	☎ 800-433-7300 (US); 800-904-6000 (Mx)
Continental	www.continental.com	☎ 800-231-0856 (US); 800-900-5000 (Mx)
Delta Airlines	www.delta-air.com	☎ 800-241-4141 (US); 800-123-4710 (Mx)
Mexicana Airlines	www.mexicana.com	☎ 800-531-7921 (US); 800-509-8960 (Mx)

The trip from the airport into town can be done by public bus, caught outside the terminal, or by taxi. Buses take an hour; taxis should take about 20 minutes, depending on the traffic.

By Bus

There are numerous first-class bus companies that travel between Acapulco and Mexico City or Oaxaca, where you can transfer to anywhere else in the country. Second-class buses travel up and down the coast and inland to mountain villages. To get into town by taxi, leave the terminal and go to the opposite side of the street. Taking a taxi from here is much cheaper than taking one from the terminal.

In-town buses are of two types. **La Costera** buses are air conditioned and cost a bit more than the regular **local buses**. Destinations are marked on the windows.

By Car

Bigger cars cost more; Volkswagens cost less. Always barter and confirm the price. Remember, no area code is needed when making a local call.

There are numerous international companies at the airport and their prices run between $80 and $100 a day for a compact car. The companies are: **Alamo**, ☎ 744-466-9444; **Avis**, ☎ 744-466-9174; **Budget**, ☎ 744-466-9003; **Dollar**, ☎ 744-466-9493; **Europcar**, ☎ 744-466-0246; **Hertz**, ☎ 744-466-9172; **Saad**, ☎ 744-466-9179; and **Thrifty**, ☎ 744-466-9115.

> **WARNING:** Avoid driving the highway between Ixtapa and Acapulco, especially at night. This is where most incidences of highway robbery occur and they are often violent. There is also a poaching operation going on at the beaches between the two centers, so that area should be avoided by everyone.

By Boat

Acapulco Marina, ☎ 744-483-7498, can hold up to 30 boats. Facilities include 110/220 power, potable water, pump-out, satellite-dish connection, toilets, showers, ice and repair facilities. Visiting sailors have access to the marina pool, restaurant and hotel. There is an Immigration office in the city. When arriving by boat you should go to the Customs office on the *costera* (walkway beside the water) at the dock near the *zocalo*, close to Sanborn's Restaurant. It is open Monday to Friday, 8 am-3 pm; ☎ 744-466-9005. Immigration is also on the *costera*, across from the Comercial Mexicana, ☎ 744-484-9022. They are open Monday to Friday, 9 am-2 pm.

Southern Pacific Mexico

■ History

 The **Tlahuicas Indians** settled on the bay about the time of Christ and lived here until they were conquered by the Tlataoni, Ahuizotl, and, finally, the Aztecs.

Cortez arrived in 1530 and established another shipbuilding center along the coast and a commercial trading center for those traveling between the Philippines and Spain via Mexico.

After initial explorations around the area were completed, the bay became a favorite departure point for ships heading to the Orient. In 1532, **Francisco de Mendoza** headed down to the South Pacific and in 1539 **Francisco de Ulloa** went looking for the legendary cities of Cibola and Quivira. In 1540, **Domingo del Castillo** charted the first map of the west coast and in 1565 **Friar Andres de Urdaneta** arrived from the Philippines. He had charted a safe route to the Orient that would be used for the next 200 years.

Shortly after Urdaneta arrived, the bay became a heaven for rich merchant ships. Pirates followed and began filling their own coffers with goodies from the commercial boats. **Adrian Boot** built the present Fort San Diego in 1776 to counter pirate attacks. By 1592, **Viceroy de Velasco** had established a coach road from Mexico City to Acapulco and the town had become a city. The fort remained a Spanish stronghold during the war of independence and wasn't surrendered until October, 1821.

There were numerous skirmishes around the bay for the next hundred years, always fought for control of the fort and the commerce attached to the bay. Finally, a good road was built and it took only a week for intrepid travelers to get between Mexico City and the bay. The first hotel was built in 1934 to accommodate these travelers. This was followed by the construction of an airport in the 1950s and, shortly after, the city became a world destination for tourists.

■ Services

i **Post office**, *Palacio Federal, across from the steamer dock, Monday to Saturday, 8 am-8 pm,* ☎ *744-482-2040.*

Police, *Av Camino Sonora,* ☎ *744-485-0490,* or see one of the tourist police dressed in pith helmets.

IAMAT Clinic, *Hotel Fairmont Acapulco Princess,* ☎ *744-469-1000, ext. 1309, or Marques Hotels, Playa Revolcadero,* ☎ *744-484-2108.*

Tourist Office, *at the Convention Center,* ☎ *744-484-4416, daily, 9 am-9 pm.* Of all the offices in Mexico, this is the one from which I received the least cooperation.

Consulates

If your consulate is not represented in the *Appendix*, page 491, and you have a serious problem, visit the **Acapulco Convention and Visitors' Bureau**, *Av Costera M. Aleman #3111, Suites 204-205*, ☎ *744-484-7621*.

■ Sightseeing

 I always suggest visitors take a **city tour** just to gain the tidbits of information that always make a visit more interesting. City tours usually include the San Diego Fort (where the History Museum is located), the *Zocalo* and the cathedral, and La Quebrada cliff divers. Some tours also take in a bit of shopping. While being escorted around, you will learn how and where Hollywood stars played in the area, gossip about the cliff divers or how the pirates lived. Most tours cost $20 per person and take about four hours. See *Tour Operators*, page 445. Of course, most of these things can be done on your own.

The world-famous **La Quebrada cliff divers** jump off the side of a cliff, 130 feet/45 meters into the Pacific Ocean. The divers climb the cliff (no small feat in itself), pray to the shrine on top and then jump. The less-experienced divers usually jump from a spot partway up the cliff, while the old hands jump from the top. The secret and danger of the jump is that divers must hit the water when the ocean swell is at its highest. If they misjudge, it could cost them their lives. At one time, people jumped for money. Today, they collect money after the show. If you wander down to the cliff during the day, you may see younger divers learning from the old heroes. The night show has divers holding lit torches as they plunge into the waters below. A popular viewpoint is the patio of Hotel El Mirador, the first luxury hotel built in the city. Hotel Mirador charges $5 to sit on their terrace, but the excellent view makes it worthwhile. Plus, you can enjoy a drink as you watch. Divers perform at 1, 7:30, 8:30, 9:30 and 10:30 pm every day.

San Diego Fort, *La Costera #123 (across from Hotel Costa Club), Tuesday to Saturday, 10 am-2 pm and 5-10 pm, free*. Constructed in 1631 to protect the bay from marauding pirates, the fort is built in the shape of a pentagon to offer the best defense from all directions. When in operation, the fort was surrounded by a moat and capable of holding 2,000 men, their food, gear and ammunition. An earthquake destroyed the original fort in 1776 and it was rebuilt by 1783 with stronger walls, deeper moats and better vantage points. A historical museum is now located inside the fort. It features models of historical ships like those that were hidden at Puerto Marques by Sir Francis Drake. The museum also has items that Drake and his men searched for, such as embroidered silk tapestries,

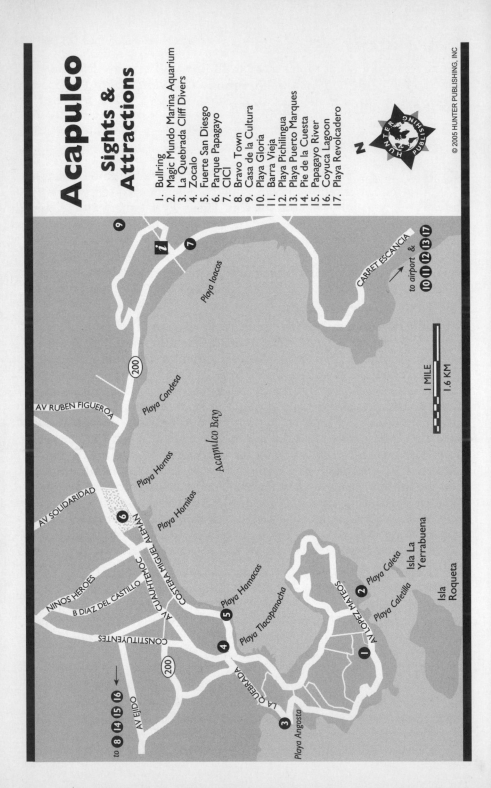

Acapulco

Sights & Attractions

1. Bullring
2. Magic Mundo Marina Aquarium
3. La Quebrada Cliff Divers
4. Zocalo
5. Fuerte San Diego
6. Parque Papagayo
7. CICI
8. Bravo Town
9. Casa de la Cultura
10. Playa Gloria
11. Barra Vieja
12. Playa Pichilingua
13. Playa Puerto Marques
14. Pie de la Cuesta
15. Papagayo River
16. Coyuca Lagoon
17. Playa Revolcadero

1 MILE

1.6 KM

kimonos, porcelain vases, jade Buddhas, inlaid chests and ivory carvings. This museum is worth a visit.

Nuestra Señora de la Soledad is the church on the *zocalo*. It is unusual with its Moorish-styled spires done in blue and yellow tiles. Inside, the church is ornate.

Casa de la Cultura, *Costera Miguel Aleman #4834*, ☎ *744-484-4004, weekdays, 9 am-2 pm and 5-8 pm, Saturday, 9 am-2 pm, free.* There is a small collection of archeological items, a Mexican art exhibition and an Ixcateopan gallery.

Corridas (bullfights), *Av Circunvalacion*, ☎ *744-482-1181*, across from Playa Caleta, are held every Sunday at 5:30 pm from January to March. Tickets for seats in the shade cost $20; seats in the sun cost a little less. Tickets can be purchased at the ring. You can purchase advance tickets from some tourist agents in the Hotel Zone. This is a cultural event and fun to watch.

Parque Papagayo, *Av Costera Miguel Aleman*, ☎ *744-485-9623, 9 am-9 pm, daily,* is an amusement park sitting on 52 acres across from Playa Hornos. There is a roller-skating rink, a race-car track, a space shuttle Columbia ride, roller-blading, skateboarding, billiards, video games, paddleboats and bumper boats in a little lake. The best part of this park is the aviary. There is no entry fee, but the rides cost money.

Bravo Town, *Carr. Federal, Rio Papagayo*, ☎ *744-471-3130, 8 am-9 pm daily,* is an eco-park where you can raft, climb, hike, observe wildlife or just enjoy the quiet. It is located on the Papagayo River. Rafting on the river includes a five-mile/eight-km run through Class II and III rapids and past high cliff walls. The pool is big enough to do laps and the climbing wall is made of natural stone. There is a restaurant and ample parking. This is a great place to spend a couple of days of organized and safe adventure. Rafting costs $50 for adults for half a day and $42 for kids between three and 12. However, if you have your own transportation to Bravo Town and don't have to be picked up, the price is $42 for adults and $22 for children between three and 12. To get here, follow the Federal Highway 200 going north toward Ixtapa for three miles/five km. Once past the second gas station, turn right (east) and follow the road to the river. Cross the river, turn left and follow the signs.

▪ Adventures on Foot

Golf

Club de Golf Pierre Marques, *Av Costera Miguel Aleman*, ☎ *744-484-0781*, is an 18-hole, par 72, 6,557/5,197 yard course originally designed by Percy Clifford and remodeled by Robert

Trent Jones for the 1982 World Cup Championships. This is a difficult course with lots of mature trees, 65 sand bunkers and 13 water hazards, as well as a wind factor to be considered. The course is presently undergoing a facelift and, as of January 2004, only nine holes were open. The new face, costing somewhere around $3 million, is being designed by Robert Trent Jones, Jr. Hotel guests pay $110; non-guests pay $125. Rental clubs are $35 and shoes are $10. Rates include carts on a shared basis; extra carts are $42 each. You can also play tennis here.

Club de Golf Acapulco, *Av Costera Miguel Aleman*, ☎ *744-484-0781*, has nine holes that, played twice, measure 6,898/5,801 yards and are par 72. The course was built in 1957 and designed by Percy Clifford. The cost to play is $40 for nine holes and $60 for 18. Clubs cost $16 and carts for nine holes run $16. A driving range is open 7 am-11 pm. Fees are $5 for 50 balls and $10 for a rental club for an hour. Classes are available for $20 an hour.

Fairmont Acapulco Princess Golf Course, *Acapulco Diamante*, ☎ *744-469-1000, www.fairmont.com*, is an 18-hole, par 72, 6,355/5,400 yard course designed by Ted Robinson. It has narrow fairways lined with coconut palms. The course is mostly flat with lots of trees, water hazards on 12 holes and numerous sand bunkers. The 18th hole is a dogleg par 4 around a large lake. Golf carts are mandatory. This course is considered tough. Call for rates and other information.

Vidafel Mayan Palace Golf and Tennis, *Av Costera de las Palmas*, ☎ *744-469-0221*, is an 18-hole, par 72, Robert Von Hagge design. I have no other information about this course.

Tres Vidas Golf Course, *Carr. Barra Vieja*, ☎ *744-462-1001, www. tresvidas.com.mx*, is an 18-hole Robert Von Hagge course. It is being upgraded and the architect has the golfer reaching the ocean on five different greens. The 25 mph winds that can gust up to 40 are one of the hazards. There are a total of nine interconnecting lakes to play around. The cost is $140 to play the 18 holes.

Tennis

Alfredo's Tennis Club, *Av Prado #29*, ☎ *744-484-0004*, has two night-lit courts. Rates ($15 during the day and $22 at night) include towel, refreshments and use of the swimming pool. Lessons are available.

Villa Vera Racquet Club, *Lomas del Mar #35*, ☎ *744-484-0333*, has tennis courts open day and night. They also have racquetball courts.

Club de Tenis, Panoramic, *Costera Vieja*, ☎ *744-484-3318*, has two courts on the hill overlooking the bay.

Park Hotel and Tennis Center, *Av Costera Miguel Aleman #127*, ☎ *744-485-5992*, has three courts. Hotel guests are given priority.

■ Adventures on Water

Beaches

 Playas Hornos and **Hornitos** each have rocky outcrops that are good for casting or watching the local fishermen. The safe-swimming area is enclosed by buoys, which also keep out motorized traffic.

Playa Condesa is in the middle of the bay and is a gay singles haunt where thong suits are the norm. There are numerous restaurants and palapa huts from where you can sit, drink, soak up the sun and enjoy the skin that happens to be walking by.

Acapulco is famous for its shoreline.

Playas Caleta and **Caletilla** share a cove on the south end of Peninsula de las Playas. Because the waters are protected, this is a good swimming area. Family-run hotels here are frequented by middle-class Mexicans.

Playa Tlacopanocha is a calm stretch of sand just south of the *zocalo* that is popular with families. Because of the water traffic, this is not a swimming beach, but rather a place to catch up on local gossip or buy some fresh fish. You can see locals repairing their nets. Photographers will find lots to capture on film.

Southern Pacific Mexico

Playa Angosta is the sunset beach. Located on the west side of the peninsula, it is the only beach that offers an unobstructed view of the sunset. It is also the most scenic beach on the bay. It is just down from La Quebrada, where divers leap into the water.

Playa Hamacas, in the center of the old town, is what's left of the fishing village of half a century ago. Come here to purchase fresh fish (if you have a place in which to cook it).

Entrance to **Playa Icacos** is at the CICI amusement park where the huge balloon is located. Some of the more expensive hotels may try to keep you from using this part of the bay, but that is illegal. This strip has some of the most expensive nightclubs in Mexico and the entertainment is first class. For watersports and balloon rides, this beach has many outlets that rent the equipment.

Playas Revolcadero/Diamante/Gloria are in the Diamond section, the wealthiest part of the city. Rough waves pound the white sand, making surfing and boogie boarding a good pastime. Windsurfing is popular here, too. The beaches are not recommended for swimming. Ultralight planes and horses are available for rent at the south end.

Barra Vieja, 15 miles/25 km south past the airport and along a stretch of palm-fringed beach, is where Tres Palos Lagoon enters the ocean. Herons nest in the foliage around the lake. There are boat-owners who will take you fishing or on a tour of the lake for about $10 an hour. There are also *caballeros* (cowboys) willing to rent you their *caballos* (horses) for about $15 an hour.

Playa Guitarron is near the Radisson Hotel. Large rocks on both sides of the beach are used as secluded tanning spots. There are also some boogie boards for rent here.

Pichilingue Beach is part of Puerto Marques Bay, where Drake used to hang out in the old days. Yachts still harbor here. This is also part of the Diamante area; rico-rico!

Playa Puerto Marques is part of a large bay and is lined with restaurants, bars and hawkers with boogie boards, balloon rides, banana boats, Jet Skis and even paddleboats. This is a very busy beach, especially during weekends in high season.

Pie de la Cuesta, a strip of beach about six miles/10 km north of Acapulco, runs a mile back from the Laguna de Coyuca de la Cuesta. The 28 square miles of lagoon are good for birding, although waterskiing is permitted. (This, in my opinion, gets rid of any birds pretty quick.) Over 250 species of birds have been reported around the lagoon. Because the surf on the ocean can be dangerous, the lagoon is often used for swimming. It also has mullet, catfish and snook for anglers. You can eat at any of the palapa restaurants along the beach

Cruises

Bay cruises are offered by a number of different boat companies. The **Fiesta Cabaret and Bonanza**, *Av Costera Miguel Aleman, Fiesta Pier,* ☎ *744-483-1803,* offer day- and night-time trips. *The Bonanza*, the daytime boat, has a swimming pool on board, as well as a platform that lowers to the water when the boat stops. *The Fiesta* cruise ($35) starts at 10:30 pm on weekends and holidays and has an open bar. **The *Aca Tiki*,** *Av Costera Miguel Aleman, Muelle Central,* ☎ *744-484-6140,* is a floating supper club that offers a three-hour cruise ($20) starting at 3 pm daily. It claims to be the world's largest catamaran. There is lots of alcohol and the entertainment is non-stop. ***Palao****, Costera #100,* ☎ *744-482-4313,* is a glass-bottom boat that leaves from the Ski Club pier downtown at 11 am and 1:30 pm for a four-hour tour ($35). A buffet lunch is offered while you circumnavigate Roqueta Island. **Yacht *Dinka*,** *Av Costera Miguel Aleman,* ☎ *744-482-6209,* operates from 10 am to 6 pm daily. *Dinka* is the largest glass-bottom boat in the bay. On their tours ($20), a guide enters the water to feed and attract fish so you get a better view. There is also a fairly long stop at Roqueta Island.

Roqueta Island has gentle currents around it. Glass-bottom boats leave for the island from Playa Caleta or the marina. The 45-minute ride costs $3 and passes the spot where a bronze statue of the Virgin of Guadalupe once lay at the bottom of the ocean (she was removed because she was corroding). There are two beaches on the island and swimming or snorkeling is recommended. A trail on the island leads to a lighthouse. A small zoo (closed Tuesday) has birds and a few animals.

OCEAN CLEAN-UP

Some outfitters have formed a non-profit organization, **Proteccion Ecologica Subaquatica**, PO Box 65C, Acapulco, ☎ 744-486-1803, www.geocities.com/rainforest/1834/ecampo.html. They offer ecological diving weekends; you go down to clean the ocean floor, help with reef recovery programs or work on other underwater ecological chores that need to be done. Subaquatica also has a turtle protection program. On their website is an excellent description of the life cycle of turtles.

Diving/Snorkeling

The bay offers many good places to ctach a glimpse of life under water.

Piedra del Elefante, at the south end of the bay, is a favorite spot for intermediate divers.

Rio de la Plata, also at the bay's southern end, is an underwater ship dive.

Roqueta Caves, near Le Quebrada, go down to 40 feet/12 meters. This has to be a morning dive because the cliff-divers use the spot at other times of the day.

Piedra de la Hierba Buena is an underwater shrine that was once the home of a bronze virgin. It is just off Roqueta Island. There is a small reef housing tropical fish. Currents are gentle, but the danger of motorized boat traffic around the island is great. There have been deaths (not necessarily here) when boats have come in contact with swimmers/divers.

> **WARNING:** Be careful where you swim/snorkel. The motorized water traffic is heavy on the bay during high season and accidents happen. Being chewed by the motor of a boat is not a good way to end your vacation.

Rafting

The **Papagayo River** has Class I to Class V rapids. The usual five-mile/eight-km run at Bravo Town (see page 445) takes in Class II and III rapids. Orchids, cacti, armadillos, deer and tropical birds hide in the bushes near the river. A life jacket and helmet must be worn and are supplied by the company.

Watersports & Water Parks

Shotover Jet, *Av Costera Miguel Aleman #121, Hotel Continental Plaza, #30*, ☎ *744-484-1154*, takes visitors on a thrill run in a heavy aluminum jet boat that travels 40 mph, spraying water and fumes all the way. The promise of wildlife is a bit stretched. You speed through the canals of the Puerto Marques Lagoon where the first *Tarzan* films were shot. For a thrill, the boat will sometimes make 360 degrees turns. Trips depart from the Revolcadero Beach every 15 minutes daily, as long as weather permits (I believe they stop in the event of hurricanes). Life jackets are provided. Boats carry 12 passengers in a tiered seating arrangement so everyone gets the same view and spray.

For less manic activities, this company does rafting, trekking, rappelling, climbing and canyoning from Bravo Park on the Papagayo River. Hikes are usually two-day expeditions. Rates run from $50 per person for rafting to $250 for a two-day guided hiking tour.

Magico Mundo Marino Aquarium, *between the Caleta and Caletilla beaches*, ☎ *744-483-1215, 9 am-6 pm daily, entry fee is $3; additional fees for Jet Skis, river kayaks, etc.* This is an aquarium with indoor and outdoor exhibits, water slides and scuba lessons. You can also rent Jet Skis, inner tubes and kayaks.

CICI, *east end of the Costera by Playa Icacos*, ☎ *744-481-0294, 10 am-6 pm daily, $6*. This huge watersports park has artificial waves, water slides (one that is 180 feet/80 meters long), an aquarium and a dolphin and seal show. You can swim with the dolphins; the cost for an hour of this fun is close to a hundred bucks.

■ Adventures in Nature

Coyuca Lagoon/Pie de la Cuesta, 6.5 miles/10 km north of Acapulco, is the most important natural attraction in the area. (Pie de la Cuesta is the spit of sand separating the lagoon from the ocean.) To get here, take a local bus north toward Ixtapa and get off at the fork where the police station and the first-class bus station are located. More adventuresome travelers can take a bus to Embarcadero, a fishing village on the lagoon. It has a restaurant and boats for hire to visit nearby islands. Boat tours take a few hours and cost about $8 per person.

About 10 miles/16 km long and five miles/eight km wide, the lagoon is surrounded by palms, water hyacinths, vines and bromeliads. The water is only 23 feet/seven meters deep, but it holds 14 species of edible fish, including robalo, lisa, pargo and carp. There are also freshwater shrimp and crabs.

The Barra de Coyuca is opened three times a year to allow some water in or out of the lagoon so that it keeps a consistent level. This is especially important during rainy season.

BIRD WATCH: *Islas Presidio, Montosa and los Parjaros are bird sanctuaries that hold black and white herons, pelicans, ducks, marabou storks, avocetas, gulls and other migrating species.*

Scenes from *The African Queen, Tarzan* and *Rambo II* were filmed here. **Isla Montosa** has a dock and restaurant on the shore. **Isla Presidio** was once a prison but has been converted into a paradise for birds. It was used by the Spanish to keep dangerous prisoners (who, they believed, would not be able to escape). During that time there were sharks and crocodiles in the lake. Now there are no sharks, but there are still a few crocs. One resident croc, called Candelario, is housed in a tank on **Montosa Island**.

If you're out here and need a bite to eat, head to **Café Lagoona**, *Pie de la Cuesta*, ☎ *744-460-4687, open noon-8 pm daily*. It offers things like *empanadas* with melted gouda cheese, fresh shrimp and fresh avocado salad with tomato, basil and manchego cheese served with homemade dressing. You can have your meal in the privacy of a palapa hut holding only one table, or you can eat inside in the open-beamed room with white linen tablecloths. A full meal costs $10 or less.

Cacahuamilpa Caves are just out of Pilcaya and 32 miles/52 km from Taxco on Highway 166 (Taxco is four hours by car from Acapulco). Guided tours at the caves leave on the hour starting at 10 am; the last tour goes at 5 pm. Each tour lasts two hours and costs $3. The caves are in Cerro de la Corono, a limestone mountain ridge that has many karst features. Electric lights illuminate the interior. This cave system was discovered in 1834 by Manuel Saenz de la Peña and was decreed a national park in 1937. Part of it was mapped in the 1920s, but only 10 of the 45 miles/70 km have been explored. A level one-mile/1.6-km walk takes you into chambers as high as 250 feet/80 meters, but the average height is 120 foot/40 meters. Many of the stalagmites and stalactites reach from floor to ceiling and look like a fountain, a throne, a goat, a bell tower and a gargoyle. This is a spectacular trip.

The best way to visit the caves is by car. Alternately, catch a bus to Taxco from just outside the bus station in Acapulco. Buses leave every hour starting at 8:30 am – look for the sign *Grutas* painted on the window.

■ Adventure in the Air

Paradise Bungee Jumping, *Costera Marina, Aleman #107,* ☎ *744-484-7529, www.bungee-experience.com/list.htm,* is near Condesa Beach. This jump is into a pool 165 feet/50 meters below. The cost is $60 for the first jump and half-price for any others. After you jump, you receive a t-shirt. A photo of yourself costs $10 and a video costs $20 extra. This has to be the ultimate adrenalin rush.

FRENCH FIRSTS

The A J Hackett Company – first in the world to do bungee jumping – runs this operation. They started by doing an unauthorized jump off the Eiffel Tower in 1987. They follow the New Zealand standards of safety and have launched more than a million jumps. They also have companies in France, Germany, US, Australia and New Zealand.

Sky Flight, *Playa Revolcadero,* ☎ *744-484-8575,* flies ultra-lights that can soar at 60 mph/90 kmh with a headwind. This company guarantees a height of at least 1,000 feet/300 meters. Call for rates.

■ Adventures on Horseback

Guided horseback rides are available at **Playa Revolcadero**, ☎ 744-443-1906, for about $10 an hour. Call ahead, or just head down to the beach and ask around. You can also inquire at your hotel about other horse rentals.

■ Adventures of the Brain

If you find someone to teach you **survival Spanish** in Acapulco, expect to pay $15 an hour. Visit the tourist office for information on private tutors. Most Spanish schools in the region are in Cuernavaca.

Idiomas & Aventuras, *www.study-spanish.com*, has an integration program where you live with a family, go on cultural trips and study Spanish in-between. They offer four lessons a day with a maximum of four students in each group, and students are tested before being placed in appropriate groups. Minimum stay is two weeks and new courses start every Monday. A two-week all-inclusive course costs $990. Three weeks costs $1,434. They also offer private lessons; two weeks cost $1,310. This is a Swiss-based company.

■ Outfitters/Tour Operators

Fun Fishing Factory, *Costera Aleman #100 (near the* zocalo*)*, ☎ 744-482-1398, offers excellent snorkeling and diving trips. The cost for your first dive is $65, a second one on the same day is $35. Snorkeling, with equipment provided, is $25 per person. This company can also supply private American yachts and/or take you fishing. Prices depend on where you go and what you use. Owner Christina Spivis has been taking people on tours for over 30 years and knows the hot spots. Everyone I spoke with who used this company was totally satisfied.

Bravo River Rafting, *Carr. Federal, Rio Papagayo*, ☎ 744-471-3130 or *Costera Miguel Aeman #121, Hotel Continental Plaza #30*, ☎ 744-484-1155, *www.bravotown.com*, offers a thrilling adventure down the Papagayo jungle river. Their riverside base camp in Papagayo has a swimming pool, a natural rock rappel-training wall, a climbing wall, a restaurant and bar, souvenir shops and a photo shop. The company also offers hiking tours.

Divers De Mexico, *Av Costera Miguel Aleman #100-Club de Esquies*, ☎ 744-482-1398 or 483-6020, are close to the *zocalo*. This company has been in business for 40 years and they know the waters around Acapulco very well. They are affiliated with Fun Fishing, above. They are PADI approved and have good boats. Their focus is on fishing. The boats are comfortable, well equipped and have passed the American Coast Guard Standards for safety. The staff is friendly, willing to help and are most knowledgeable about the area. They especially know how to find the big fish. Fishing rates depend on which boat you take and for how long. Diving rates are $65 for a half-day, one-tank dive.

Acuario Tours, *Av Costera Miguel Aleman #186-3*, ☎ *744-485-6100*, *www.acuariotours.com*, can arrange local tours, transportation or make hotel reservations.

Turismo Caleta, *Andrea Doria #2*, ☎ *744-484-6570*, runs city tours, lagoon trips and yacht excursions.

ViisaTor, *Anton de Alaminos #208*, ☎ *744-484-1605*, *www.viisatravel. com.mx*, offers numerous excursions, including a 3½-hour city tour ($30) and an all-day lagoon tour ($60). An English-speaking guide and hotel pick-up and drop-off in an air-conditioned vehicle are included.

Acapulco Scuba Center, *Paseo del Opescador*, ☎ *744-482-9474*, *www. acapulco.com/en/tours/scubacenter*, has many years of experience fishing and diving. They are PADI certified and offer lessons. They charge $65 for a two-tank dive for certified divers and $65 for a one-tank dive for novices. The cost for snorkeling is $35 for four hours. They include refreshments on their trips.

Hermanos Arnold, *Av Costera Miguel Aleman #302*, ☎ *744-482-1877*, *9 am-6 pm*, organizes scuba diving and snorkeling trips. This company has equipment rentals, offers lessons and has a small restaurant where you can enjoy a drink after your excursion.

■ Shopping

 In Acapulco, vendors and local hawkers are everywhere. Some have shops and some are on the beach selling crafts and silver (although this practice has been made illegal). Goods come in every price range and quality.

You buy anything you can get in the US and a few things extra at the huge **Gran Plaza** that dominates the *costera*, the walkway beside the water.

Mercado de Artesanias, *Av Costera Miguel Aleman, 9 am-9 pm daily*, is a traditional marketplace four blocks from the downtown Sanborn's. Hand-embroidered dresses, hammocks, ceramics and onyx chessboards abound between t-shirts, baseball caps and seashell crafts, rolls of toilet paper and piles of face soap or shampoo.

■ Places to Stay

It seems to me that the aim of the hotels is to provide the most luxurious environment imaginable where every sensual craving of the body can be satisfied. Mexico, in general, and Acapulco, in particular, is able to fulfill these desires. Acapulco has over 400 hotels with a total of 3,000 rooms, most of them comfortable. Rates run from $50 to $1,000 a night (some even go for $10).

Hotel Maria Acela, *La Paz #19*, ☎ *744-482-0661*, *$*, has 20 rooms that are basic and clean. This is more a guesthouse than a hotel.

Etel Suites, *Pinzona #92*, ☎ *744-482-2240*, *$*, has rooms in two buildings perched on a hill overlooking the city. The rooms come with air conditioning and fans, hot water and kitchenettes that are fully furnished. Discounts are offered on longer stays. This is a clean and comfortable option. The rooms are constantly being repaired, the staff is friendly and there is a pool.

HOTEL PRICE SCALE
Price for a room given in US $.
$..................Up to $20
$$..................$21-$50
$$$...............$51-$100
$$$$ ....$101-$150
$$$$$ ....$151-$200
Anything over $200 is specified.

Torre Eifel Hotel, *Inalambrica #110*, ☎ *744-482-1683*, *$*, has 25 rooms set on a hill overlooking La Quebrada. They are basic and clean, with fans and hot water. There is off-street parking. This is a good deal for the budget-minded. However, the walk from town to home is uphill.

Asterias Hotel, *Quebrada #45*, ☎ *744-483-6548*, *$*, is a tiny place with just 10 rooms around a pool and patio decorated with plants. The rooms have private bathrooms and fans.

Maria Antioneta Hotel, *Teniente Azueta #17*, *$$*, has 34 basic but clean rooms with fans and hot water in private bathrooms. The rooms are secluded from the street and the place is comfortable.

Hotel Villa Nirvana, *Av del la Fuerza Aerea #302, Pie de la Cuesta*, ☎ *744-460-1631, www.lavillanirvana.com*, *$$*, has bungalows and rooms that have private bathrooms and hot water. Some have a kitchenette and a private terrace with a hammock. The hotel is enclosed and has private pool and beach access. A restaurant serves great food. This is an affordable, non-luxury place that is just great. Discounts are available for longer stays. Public buses into town leave from just outside the gates.

Puesta del Sol, *Pie de la Cuesta*, ☎ *744-460-0412*, *$$*, has basic, clean rooms with fans and private bathrooms. The grounds are well kept and have lots of palm trees, a lawn, vines and bougainvilleas. This place is a favorite with budget travelers.

Southern Pacific Mexico

Hacienda Vayma, *Pie de la Cuesta,* ☎ *744-460-2882, $$,* is a funky, artsy place with basic rooms set in little buildings named after artists. Rooms have fans and private bathrooms. The restaurant here serves the best food in Pie de la Cuesta. A rooftop terrace and volleyball courts are available. The hotel is located on the beach.

Maris Hotel, *Av Costera Miguel Aleman and Magallanes,* ☎ *744-485-8440, $$,* has 84 standard rooms each with private balcony, air conditioning, bathroom and cable TV. There is a restaurant, bar, beach club and pool.

Hotel Majestic, *Pozo del Rey #73,* ☎ *744-483-2885, $$,* has 210 rooms on the beach, each with air conditioning, private bathroom with hot water and cable TV. There is a beach club, tennis courts and a gym. Watersports equipment can be rented from the hotel.

Sands Hotel, *Calle Juan de Cosa #178,* ☎ *744-484-2260, $$,* has rooms and cabins with air conditioning, cable TV and private bathrooms with hot water. There is a pool, restaurant, private parking, squash courts and Jeep rentals on site.

The villa-style **Hotel Ukae Kim**, *Av Pie de la Cuesta #356, $$$,* has 20 rooms with hot water and air conditioning. The little villas are painted in bright colors and each has a private terrace and tropical garden. The buildings surround a pool.

> ▸▸ **AUTHOR NOTE:** *Hotel Ukae Kim adds a 20% surcharge for use of a credit card. This is an illegal practice. If it bothers you, report the hotel to the credit card company.*

Suites Alba de Acapulco, *Gran Via Tropical #35,* ☎ *744-483-0073, $$$,* requires a minimum stay of three nights. The hotel, with 292 rooms, is on a hill on the peninsula overlooking the bay. There are gardens, water slides, three pools, a Jacuzzi, a mini market, restaurant, bar, parking lot, tennis courts and games room. Each room has air conditioning, a kitchenette, a balcony or patio, a dining area, a fridge, ceiling fans and cable TV. This place sounds good, but is overpriced. Also, it is a long way from town, with no public transportation close by.

Romano Hotel (Days Inn), *Av Costera Miguel Aleman,* ☎ *744-484-5332 or 800-325-2525, $$$,* has 279 rooms with air conditioning, cable TV, good views and everything else you can expect from this chain. There is also a huge pool and deck. Not a bad deal.

Hotel Romano Palace, *Av Costera Miguel Aleman #130,* ☎ *744-484-7730, $$$,* is on Condesa Beach. It has a pool, two restaurants, two bars, tennis courts, parking and a currency exchange service. All rooms have air conditioning, safes, satellite TV and free movies, fridges, balconies, ceiling fans, writing desks and kitchenettes. The bathrooms have fluffy towels, hot water and hair dryers.

Acapulco Park Hotel, *Av Costera Miguel Aleman #127*, ☎ *744-485-5992*, *$$$/$$$$*, is a motel-like structure that has 88 rooms across from the Plaza Bahia. The hotel has been renovated to look like a colonial building. The rooms come with double beds, tiled floors, air conditioning, cable TV, fridges, kitchenettes and large bathrooms with hot water. Some rooms have balconies and all rooms are clean. On the premises are three tennis courts, a bar and a swimming pool in the garden and ample parking. Many people have said that the staff is exceptionally helpful.

Romance Inn, *St. Vista de Brisamar #6 (behind the navy base)*, ☎ *744-481-2176*, *$$$*, has rooms on three floors. Each room is small and cozy with double beds, cable TV, kitchenette, fridge and balcony. There is a pool overlooking the bay and a restaurant. Breakfast is included in the price. It is a long way from the center of town.

Hotel Copacabana, *Tabachines #2*, ☎ *744-484-3260*, *$$$/$$$$*, is in the Golden Zone. The hotel has a restaurant, a poolside bar, an oceanfront bar and a lobby bar that often has live entertainment. There are two Jacuzzis, an outdoor pool, beauty salon, souvenir shops, laundry service and beachfront lounge chairs. Each room has air conditioning, private balcony, sitting area with a table, a mini-bar, cable TV and a large bathroom with hair dryer.

Park Hotel & Tennis Center, *Av Costera Miguel Aleman #127*, ☎ *744-485-5489*, *$$$/$$$$*, has been renovated into a colonial-style hotel and each of the 88 rooms has air conditioning, Spanish TV, a private bathroom with hot water and a fridge. Some rooms have balconies. The spotless rooms are located around a garden and pool. There are three tennis courts and a bar. The hotel is on the beach. Many people have said that the staff are exceptionally helpful.

Avalon Excalibur Acapulco, *Av Costera Miguel Aleman #163*, *$$$/$$$$*, caters to the tourist by offering boogie boards, banana boats and kayaks to its guests. Its 425 rooms have air conditioning, private balcony, either an ocean or mountain view, a coffee maker, complimentary coffee, a hair dryer, an in-room safe, an iron and board, a large bathroom and a modem/data port. There is a restaurant and outdoor pool on the beach, a gift shop, a kids' pool, a bar, babysitting service and a fitness room. The staff speaks English and the service is excellent.

Hotel Calinda Beach, *Av Costera Miguel Aleman #1260*, ☎ *744-484-0410*, *$$$/$$$$*, is in a classy-looking tower away from the beach. There are two pools overlooking the beach, two restaurants, babysitting service, laundry service and off-street parking. The 360 rooms feature average décor and each has air conditioning, coffee maker, hair dryer, in-room safe, mini-bar, iron and board, and cable TV.

Fiesta Inn Acapulco, *Av Costera Miguel Aleman*, ☎ *744-484-2828*, *$$$/$$$$*, has 500 large rooms, each with private balcony, air conditioning, coffee maker with complimentary coffee, electronic door, hair dryer, iron and ironing board, cable TV and large marble bathroom. Some rooms are wheelchair-accessible. There is a small pool, a restaurant, parking facilities, a fitness center and a gift shop on site. This hotel is accommodating in its service and the rooms are kept spotless. You can often get discounted rates that make staying here a good deal.

La Palapa Hotel, *Av Fragata Yucatán #210, $$$$,* is a luxury hotel in the Golden Zone. It is the second-tallest building in the city and is constructed so that every suite has an ocean view. There are sleeping areas in each suite, plus a living area with a kitchenette completely furnished and ready to use. Each apartment has air conditioning, a hair dryer, an in room safe, an iron and board, a modem/data port connection, a fridge and a color cable TV. The odd-shaped pool in the courtyard features a bridge over the narrowest section and a swim-up bar. Complimentary lounge chairs are available on the beach. If you don't want to go downtown for dinner, there are three restaurants and three bars in the building. There is also a money exchange, a laundry service and a beauty salon. Watersports equipment can be rented and scuba diving and snorkeling excursions can be arranged at the front desk.

Las Palmas, *155 Av Las Conchas,* ☎ *744-487-0843 or 52-744-487-1282 from the US, $$$$,* caters to the gay community. Located in the Golden Zone, it has a clothing-optional rooftop terrace that features a Jacuzzi overlooking the bay. Some rooms have private sundecks, Jacuzzi tubs and safes. All are bright, furnished with traditional Mexican furniture, and have air conditioning, ceiling fans, cable TV and tiled floors. Bottled water is available, breakfast is included and a complimentary drink is offered each evening. The restaurant serves vegetarian food.

Quinta Real Acapulco, *Paseo de la Quinta #6, no phone, $$$$$ (prices from $210-$330 a double),* is on the ocean in the Diamond section of town. The hotel itself is top notch, with elegant rooms decorated in high quality furniture and original Mexican artwork. They have king-sized beds, soft lighting and a few luxurious extras. There are the usual amenities such as air conditioning, high-speed Internet access, in-room safes, hair dryers, bathrobes, mini-bars, cable TV and huge marble bathrooms. Outside are two pools, a Jacuzzi, a beach club and a beachside restaurant. The pools are on different levels above a lawn that overlooks the beach. One pool is long enough to do laps. Behind the hotel is a hill covered in jungle vegetation.

Acapulco Princess, *Playa Revolcadero,* ☎ *744-469-1000 or 800-223-1818 or 800-441-1414, www.fairmont.com, $$$$$,* has a total of 1,017 rooms ranging in price from $120 to $1,000 a night. This includes the use of the golf course. There are also four pools, a saltwater lagoon with waterfalls, 11 tennis courts, five restaurants and bars, a health club and spa with 17 treatment rooms. Some rooms are wheelchair-accessible.

Acapulco

Places to Stay & Eat

PLACES TO STAY
1. Fairmont Pierre Marques
2. Las Brisas Acapulco
3. Hyatt Regency
4. Acapulco Princess
5. Fiesta Inn Acapulco
6. Hotel Copacabana
7. Maria Acela
8. Torre Eifel Hotel
9. Asterias
10. Villa Nervana, Hotel Ukae Kim
11. Acapulco Park
12. Romano Palace
13. Avalon Excaliber
14. Calinda Beach Hotel
15. Alba de Acapulco
16. La Palapa
17. Quinta Real Acapulco
18. Las Palmas
19. Romance Inn

PLACES TO EAT
20. Puetsa del Sol
21. Hacienda Vayma
22. La Gran Torta
23. Licha Tamales
24. Loncheria Chatita
25. Café Esteban
26. Fat Farm
27. Bahia Restaurant
28. Casa Nova
29. Beto's
30. El Campanario
31. El Olvido
32. La Cabana
33. 100% Natural
34. Palladium
35. Andromedas
36. Copacabana
37. Baby O
38. Señor Frogs

AV RUBEN FIGUEROA
200
AV SOLIDARIDAD
NINOS HEROES
B DIAZ DEL CASTILLO
AV CUAUHTEMOC
COSTERA MIGUEL ALEMAN
CONSTITUYENTES
200
AV EIDO
to 10
LA QUEBRADA
AV LOPEZ MATEOS
CARRET ESCANCIA

Playa Icacos
Playa Condesa
Playa Homos
Playa Hornitos
Acapulco Bay
Playa Hamacas
Playa Tlacopanocha
Playa Angosta
Playa Caleta
Playa Caletilla
Isla La Yerrabuena
Isla Roqueta

1 MILE
1.6 KM

N

HUNTER PUBLISHING

© 2004 HUNTER PUBLISHING, INC

Southern Pacific Mexico

Hyatt Regency Acapulco, *Av Costera Miguel Aleman #1,* ☎ *744-469-1234, $$$$$,* has 640 rooms. Some are luxurious suites, others standard rooms, but all are large and clean. Many have private balconies overlooking the bay and all have large closets, air conditioning, cable TV, electronic key cards and marble bathroom. There are two outdoor pools, a landscaped garden, spa, Jacuzzi, steam bath, sauna and massage room. Services include a tour desk, travel agency, photo service, babysitting, beauty salon, currency exchange and laundry. Often, the Hyatt will put its rooms on sale for a considerable discount; check online. Taxis (beetles) from the hotel to the center of town cost $3-$5 one way.

Willow Springs Spa, *Playa Revolcadero,* ☎ *744-466-1000 or 800-441-1414, www.fairmont.com, $$$$$,* has 320 rooms located on the beach. There are two pools, two golf courses, a putting green, tennis courts, 14,000 square feet of spa, two restaurants and a bar. There are treatment rooms for facials, massages, wet treatments, Swiss showers and more. The rooms have all the luxury of what Fairmont calls a "six-star" hotel.

Las Brisas Acapulco, *Car. Escenica Clement #5255,* ☎ *744-469-6900, www.brisas.com.mx, $$$$$ ($176-$416 double).* Las Brisas, eight-10 miles/13-16 km from town, is only for those who want to get away from everything. The pink and white stucco resort is set on 40 acres of tended hibiscus gardens set on a hill overlooking the bay. Each of the 300 rooms is a private *casita* that has a private or semi-private pool and its own terrace. The luxurious rooms have air conditioning, mini-bars and marble bathrooms. Hotel amenities include a sauna, a fitness center, two pools and a tennis court. Since each *casita* is positioned for privacy, jeep service is provided to take you anywhere on the property. Just call. Some reports say that this hotel is losing its elegance through lack of maintenance, but others say the service makes up for the chipped paint. Pay for just one night and, if it doesn't meet your needs, move on. If privacy and rest are your needs, then I think you'll stay.

Fairmont Pierre Marques, *Playa Revolcadero,* ☎ *744-466-1000, www. fairmont.com, $$$$$,* is a large luxury hotel with 334 rooms. It is closer to the airport than to downtown. The hotel has five restaurants and three pools, and sits on 480 acres of tropical gardens dotted with fountains and statues. Guests can use the amenities of the Fairmont Acapulco Princess next door, which include a tennis court, spa and numerous restaurants. Each room has air conditioning, cable TV, purified water, a writing desk and Internet access.

FACT FILE: The Fairmont Pierre Marques was once the private haunt of John Paul Getty.

Casa Condesa, ☎ *744-484-1616, www.casacondesa.com, $$$/$$$$$*, caters to the gay community. This is a small and intimate B&B. Rates include airport pickup, full breakfast and an open bar for local spirits and soft drinks. They also offer special package deals. The pool has a furnished deck and the bedrooms are funky and decorated with modern art. They feature TV, night tables and soft lights. There is a guest area in the house where you can sit to read a book. Casa Condesa comes with a few house rules. Minors (under 18) are not allowed (it is against the law to have a relationship with a minor in Mexico; please respect that law while here). No drugs except aspirin, please. Check out time is 2 pm, and you must make arrangements if you need to stay longer. Rowdy characters will be sent to their rooms. Nude bathing is permitted on the roof or by the pool. Pets are not welcome. The final rule is no peeing in the pool.

■ Places to Eat

 Acapulco has all the franchises you will find at home like McDonald's, Pizza Hut, Hooters, Hard Rock Café, Denny's, Sanborn's, Burger King, Taco Bell, Wendy's, and so on. However, I urge you to try some Mexican places.

Puesta del Sol, *Pie de la Cuesta,* ☎ *744-460-0412,* is open 7 am-10 pm. It has the best breakfasts around. Try the *huevos puesta del sol,* which are cooked with hot sauce and crushed tortillas, topped with cheese and served with refried beans. Yum. Their sea bass and lake white fish are excellent supper dishes and cost between $4 and $5.

Hacienda Vayma, *Pie de la Cuesta,* ☎ *744-460-2882,* has the best home-made pasta in the area and their pizzas are cooked over wood fire. Meals cost between $5 and $8. But the ceviche is the big draw and costs less than $4 for a good-sized helping.

La Gran Torta, *Av La Paz #6,* is open 8 am until midnight. Tortas are Mexican fast food. They are beef, chicken and pork and cost less than $5.

Licha Tamales, *Av Costera Miguel Aleman #322,* ☎ *744-482-2021,* is open 6 pm-midnight and specializes in tamales (corn paste wrapped around spicy meat, rolled into a banana leaf and steamed). Tamales are delicious, and in Mexican homes they are made during fiestas. The cost is $2 for a good sized snack.

Loncheria Chatita, *Av Azueta and Hidalgo,* is a Mexican place that specializes in *pozole,* a spicy chicken or pork stew that's delicious. They also make potato pancakes that are good for breakfast. For $5 you will be full for most of the day.

Café Esteban, *Av Costera Miguel Aleman,* ☎ *744-484-3084*, has fresh breads, cakes, pies, cookies, baguettes, coffees, lattes and cappuccinos – all are far too good to miss. While enjoying the air conditioning and a cappuccino, read a newspaper and tuck into a slice of cheesecake.

Fat Farm, *Av Juarez #10 and Felipe Valle,* ☎ *744-483-5339*, is open 8 am to 10 pm daily. I love the name. Their specialty is breakfast, starting with strong coffee. I recommend the banana pancakes with chocolate sauce. An entire breakfast will cost $4.

Bahia Restaurant, *Av Costera Miguel Aleman, located in the Sheraton Hotel,* is open 6 pm-midnight. It is a surf 'n turf place. The portions are not large, the service is quiet and the price is much higher than that of a meal served at a palapa hut along the beach. However, the wine selection is really good.

Casa Nova, *Escenica la Brisas #5256*, is open 7 pm-midnight. This is a good Italian restaurant that has great pastas for less than $10.

100% Natural, *Av Costera Miguel Aleman #3111,* ☎ *744-484-8440*, specializes in health foods such as yogurt shakes, fruit salads and soy burgers. I suggest the fruit salad with yogurt, granola and honey as a satisfying way to start the day.

Beto's, *in the Las Brisas area at Playa Condesa,* ☎ *744-484-0473*, has both class and atmosphere. Try the Thai shrimp with sesame oil, ginger, Thai chile and hoisin sauce. This is spicier than anything you'll find in Mexican cuisine. Because of the popularity of this restaurant, reservations are essential, especially during high tourist season. Meals run $15-$20.

El Campañerio, *Calle Paraiso,* ☎ *744-484-8830*, sits on a hill overlooking the city. The restaurant is in an old monastery and the atmosphere is elegant, with lit torches on the walls and candles on the tables (and sexy waiters). Try the filet mignon, served with a good bottle of French red wine. The meal will be costly, but worth it.

El Olvido, *Av Costera Miguel Aleman,* ☎ *744-481-0203*, is open 7 pm-midnight daily. It is a moderately expensive restaurant that offers gourmet food in a fairly elegant setting. Octopus salad with mango dressing is something I would go back to Acapulco for and the guanabana sherbet with *zapote* is a good follow-up to dinner. Expect to pay $20-$25.

La Cabaña, *east end of Playa Caleta, Old Acapulco,* ☎ *744-482-5007,* has been in business for over 50 years. It started out as a palapa hut along the beach that served good seafood. This was a favorite restaurant of *Tarzan* during his vine-swinging days in Mexico.

TARZAN

Johnny Weissmuller was the original Tarzan the Ape Man, and he made 12 movies between 1932 and 1948. *The Mermaids* was filmed in Acapulco and was budgeted for $1 million, not a paltry sum in those early post-war years. Weissmuller starred with Brenda Joyce (the second Jane, after Maureen O'Sullivan stopped playing the part). Tarzan and Jane lost popularity in the 1950s because of their excessively exposed skin.

■ Nightlife

Palladium, *Car. Escenica*, ☎ 744-465-5490, *10 pm-5 am, $3*, is the largest club in town with capacity to hold about 1,000 people. The pink neon glow from the dance floor can be seen from anywhere on the entire bay. The design is that of ancient Egypt and it seems to encourage seductive behavior from the modern Cleopatras. This is a popular place for celebrities to party.

Andromedas, *Av Costera Miguel Aleman*, ☎ 744-484-5602, *10 pm-5 am, $3,* has a medieval atmosphere. The entrance requires that you cross a stone ramp, pass through torch-lit doors and get beamed upon by people shining lights from the tower just inside. Inside, a mermaid swims in a tank next to the dance floor. This bar is for the young and wild.

Club Copacabana, *Av Costera Miguel Aleman #58*, ☎ 744-484-4358, *8 pm-4 am, $2,* is known for its huge cocktails and Latin music. Open to the beach, it can add a romantic flavor for those not wanting to stay inside. This is for the night owls.

Baby'O, *Av Costera Miguel Aleman #22*, ☎ 744-484-7474, *www.babyo. com.mx, 10 pm-5 am, $3,* is a disco that attracts celebrities (so I am told). This is for the younger, deafer Mexico City crowd who are looking to bump and grind until sunrise.

Señor Frogs, *Escenica #28, Rosarito Beach*, ☎ 744-446-5734, *www. frogs-charlies.com.mx, 11:30 am-3 am, no cover,* has taken over the spring-break partiers. There is often dancing on the tables (and more) by the time the restaurant/bar closes at 3 am. If you need some help getting onto the table, order the Mother of all Margaritas, guaranteed to get you going.

■ Heading to Puerto Escondido

If you are on your way south from Acapulco on Highway 200, a couple of places are worth a stop.

Southern Pacific Mexico

Playa Ventura is a little community with few services except for some palapa-hut restaurants that cook things like fresh fish or *huevos* and a rustic little hotel that offers a peaceful stay. Although the name of the town is actually Juan Alvarez, it is called Playa Ventura because the Ventura family owns most of the beachfront. The best pastime here is watching for wildlife. There are a couple of places that will let you pitch a tent or park your RV under their palapa huts. Take things slowly, ask around and, after an invitation, make yourself at home. The surf can be strong, so swim where the rocks break the water a little.

While here, visit **Lake Chautengo**, 20 miles/35 km north of Playa Ventura. There are mangrove swamps and the lake empties into the ocean. The bird life is good because of the isolation. Boats for lake exploration can be hired from locals either in Ventura or Chautengo for $10-$15 an hour. The trip to the lake by bus from Ventura is a full day's adventure and fun to do. Go first to Copala and then hook up with another small truck that is going to Cruz Grande. A third truck will take you to the lake. The locals here will look after you – just put your hands out and say, "la-GOON-a choo-tengo." They'll head you in the right direction. To my knowledge, there are no places to stay near the lake, but there are a few restaurants along the beach.

La Caracola, *Playa Ventura,* ☎ *741-852-8062,* is owned by Aura Elena Rodriguez. It has some thatched-roof rooms with or without kitchenette that are totally rustic, with bamboo walls and wood floors. The rooms have fans and foam mattresses on plywood beds. This is not your five-star, everything-American place. There is a tiny pool and the yard is loaded with palm trees. The property is on the beach and birds are numerous. You can rent a horse or burro and go fishing or surfing. Boats can be rented from locals or the hotel owners. Riding a horse or donkey is fun and fishing in a boat with a butterfly net is a skill that is fun to learn. Locals will take time to teach you.

To get to Playa Ventura by car, follow Highway 200 south from Acapulco for 90 miles/155 km to Copala and take the road leading to the coast. By bus, take a bus to Copala and then get on a local truck to the village. Trucks have a canopy for shade and seats along the sides. A taxi from Copala to Playa Ventura will cost about $30 for the half-hour ride.

Pinotepa Nacional, on Highway 200 as you head south, is a village of about 25,000 people. The culture here has been influenced little by globalization; locals still wear traditional clothes, conduct business in the markets and eat traditional foods.

> ✤ **LOCAL LINGO:** *The town name comes from the Aztec words,* pinolli *(crumbling) and* tepetle *(mountain). To the Mixec people, the most prominent indigenous group in the area, the place was called* Nu-Yu-uku, *meaning "Place of Salt."*

Market days (Wednesday and Sunday) draw people living in the surrounding hills, who come to trade, gossip, eat and maybe even drink a bit. The market is the main reason for you to stop here, and many people come to buy handwoven cotton garments that feature embroidery. They are worth taking home and keeping.

Hotel Carmona, *Av Porfirio Diaz #127,* ☎ *741-543-2222, $,* at the west end of Pinotepa, is a three-story hotel with clean rooms featuring private bathrooms, air conditioning and kitchenettes. There is also a pool and garden on site. This is the best place to stay. If the Carmona is full, try **Las Gaviotas Centro**, *Calle Poniente #3, just up from the plaza,* ☎ *741-543-2626, $,* which offers some fairly large rooms with air conditioning. Other rooms have fans and all have private bathrooms. There is a restaurant at the hotel. There are a couple of smaller, more basic places to stay, too. If you have a tent, camp at **Rio Arena** (follow the dirt road on the east side of the bridge). You'll see the waterfall at Rio Arena from the road. La Roca restaurant is located at the site.

Puerto Escondido

This funky little village sits, in part, on a mountain overlooking the bay, and has been a special destination for surfers for over 25 years. They found it in the 1970s and would like to keep the place to themselves. It is the "pipeline" wave that brought the first surfers. A pipeline is a tube of water that sucks the surfer through a tunnel of water to the other end, often a long way down the beach from where they started.

■ Getting Here & Around

There are no direct flights from the US to here, so the area lends itself to more adventuresome travelers.

By Plane

AeroMexico and Mexicana Airlines have daily flights from Mexico City and Oaxaca to Puerto Escondido. However, due to high winds in the area, the airstrip is often closed and planes can't land.

AIRLINE CONTACT INFORMATION		
AeroMexico	www.aeromexico.com	☎ 800-237-6639 (US); 800-021-4010 (Mx)
Mexicana Airlines	www.mexicana.com	☎ 800-531-7921 (US); 800-509-8960 (Mx)

Taxis from the airport cost $40-$50 if booked inside the terminal. If you go out of the airport and away from the terminal, the cost drops considerably. The fare will depend on your bartering skills; start at about half the fare offered by cabs at the terminal. I recommend taking the hourly suburban van on weekdays that costs $3.50 per person. Tickets for this can be purchased in the terminal near the baggage claim area.

Taxis in town to and from anywhere in the center cost $1.50 during the day and $2 at night.

By Bus

First-class buses come from Oaxaca (7½ hours), from Mexico City (12 hours) and from Acapulco (four hours). It is a long run, and the night buses have often been robbed. It's best to take day trips along the stretch of highway between Puerto Escondido and Acapulco.

■ History

 Called the hidden cove, Puerto Escondido has been occupied by people for almost 4,000 years. After the Spanish arrived and built the fort at Ixtapa/Zihuatanejo, they came south to conscript local labor to work in the fields. During the 1800s, the Indians were given parcels of land of their own to work, but because of their communal sense of belonging, they were soon relieved of their land by foreign entrepreneurs and again left to work as laborers. As progress chugged on, roads and railways were built, stores were opened, trade increased and, finally, the surfers arrived.

HISTORIC REVIVAL ALIVE IN THE ARTS

There is a unique little twist to the history here. The south side of town is called the **Felicita Zona**. Felicita was the last princess of the Pasqual Indians and daughter of Pontho, the last chief, who lived here. Felicita fell in love with an American soldier who was injured in the Battle of San Pasqual on December 6, 1846. She never got to marry him. The story was written in play form by Dr. Benjamin Sherman and performed annually from 1927 to 1932 in Felicita Park which, according to more legend, is where the Indians accused of various crimes were punished. The pageant was revived again between 1970 and 1972 and then again in the mid-1980s. Today, the Rotary Club of Puerto Escondido sponsors it. If you are around in May when performances are held, be certain to see the show.

▪ Services

Post office, *Av 7 Norte and Oaxaca*, ☎ *954-582-0959*.

Police, *on Highway 200*, ☎ *954-582-0498*.

Hospital Santa Fe, *Calle 3 Poniente*, ☎ *954-582-0541, Monday to Friday, 9 am-8 pm, weekends, 9 am-2 pm,* offers outpatient services.

Publications

El Sol de la Costa is a free English-language newspaper produced in town. It is full of information about local events and has music and restaurant reviews.

▪ Adventures on Foot

The **Cliffside Path** is a walking trail that partly follows the shoreline. It runs along a cement and stone walkway built into the side of the cliff, mostly at sea level. Some spots overlook tide pools and stone benches provide resting places where you can watch for wildlife. To get to the trailhead, go from the main beach to the jetty and find the path at the outcropping of rocks west of the fishermen's lockers. The entire route is less than 2.5 miles/four km and takes about an hour to complete.

▪ Adventures on Water

Aguas Termales Atotonilco are 15 miles/25 km west of Puerto Escondido near the village of San José Manialtepec. The springs are just over a mile from town up Manialtepec Canyon. They have been used by the 16 different groups of indigenous peoples for centuries. The water is supposed to have medicinal properties. The legend attached to the springs states that, after soaking here, you will appear much younger than you are. To get here, take a local bus to the village of Manialtepec and walk up the river. You can also join a tour; many companies offer transportation to the town and then a horseback ride to the springs (see page 462).

Beaches

Playa Carizzalillo is the most westerly beach along this strip. If coming by roadway (bus or taxi) you will be let off at the campground above the beach. Walk carefully down the steep hill. The waves are gentle and the water is safe for children swimming. Beyond the rocks is Punta Colorada, not a good surfing place for beginners. This is where the International Boogie Boarding Competitions were held in 2003.

BIRTH OF THE BODY BOARD

Body boarding was first tried on July 7, 1971 by Tom Morey, a surfer with a math and engineering background. On that day in Hawaii, Morey carved a piece of polyethylene foam into a small board and covered it with newspaper. He found the board worked well and in 1973 patented the board and named it the Morey Boogie. It sold for $10. Morey placed an advertisement in *Surfing Magazine* and less than five years later he was selling about 80,000 a year. (Info taken from El Sol de la Costa.)

Puerto Angelito is actually two beaches separated by a rock outcropping. It has lots of palapa restaurants serving good fish and cold beer. The swimming is excellent because it is a sheltered cove, and snorkeling is also safe.

Playa Principal is where fishermen launch their boats and you'll also find water taxis and pleasure boats for rent.

Playa Marinero is the best spot for swimming. It is located just before the rock outcroppings that separate this beach from Playa Zicatela. Europeans often come to sunbathe topless.

Playa Zicatela is the most popular surfing beach in the area, with waves big enough to satisfy even the most experienced surfers. Some call it the best surfing beach in North America. The famous "pipeline" wave is found at this beach and is what put Escondido on the surfing map. Be aware that the great surf causes a strong undertow that can be unsafe for the casual swimmer.

WARNING: Playa Zicatela is not a place to camp or walk alone. There have been some horrid incidences here that have resulted in some very bad press. To counteract the violence, the government has installed lights and three armed policemen patrol the beach during the day.

■ Adventures in Nature

Parque National Lagunas de Chacahua is 50 miles/70 km north of Puerto Escondido off Highway 200. The park includes a series of lagoons – Manialtepec, Chacahua, Lagartero and Chacahija – linked by mangrove swamps and surrounded by rolling hills. The park was created in 1937 and now falls under the care of the National Institute of Ecology. It covers 30,000 acres.

The main attraction here is the black orchid. This is one of the few places in the world where the orchid still grows wild. According to some specialists, there are 11 different vegetation zones in this park, mostly deciduous. Tree species include the dragon tree, which grows in the hills, and the mesquite tree, which grows on coastal dunes. There is also savanna with palms and wetter areas with willow. The large variety of vegetation attracts numerous birds and amphibians. There have been 275 species of birds spotted in the area, and visitors usually see 40-60 species on each birding trip.

 BIRD WATCH: *Expect to see roseate spoonbills, white-fronted parrots, boat-billed herons and bare-throated tiger herons.*

You might be lucky enough to spot a river otter, jaguarundi or opossum, and you're likely to see many crocs. The park is also a turtle sanctuary and the center for the Turtle Assistance Ecological Camp. Local boats can take you in search of birds, turtles and crocs. Laguna Manialtepec has the most migratory birds. Most people visit only Lake Chacahua or Lake Manialtepec.

The best way to see the park and spot wildlife is to have a tour guide. Talk to tour agents if you are interested in specific wildlife. Some agents can take you on custom tours deeper into the jungles. See page 462.

The waves where the Chacahua Lake enters the ocean are huge. There is also a very small coral reef offshore and tiger sharks have been spotted here.

■ Adventures of the Brain

 Instituto de Lenguajes Puerto Escondidio, *Carretera Costera and Col. Marinero (in front of the Cruz Azul Cement Company),* ☎ *954-582-2055, www.puertoschool.com*, is a small teachers' cooperative established in 1999. Their ultimate aim, besides teaching Spanish, is to have foreigners volunteer their time in the areas of their own expertise to benefit the community and the visitor. The school is located at Playa Zicatela, just a few feet from the beach. You can take the home-stay option and live with a local family or you can attend hourly lessons (as many hours as you want in a day) in a small group or solo. There is no minimum or maximum length of study. However, the minimum recommended time is two two-hour lessons a week. At least one workshop is recommended so that you can use the language.

The cost for private lessons is $10 an hour. If there are two in a group the price drops to $8; three people, the price drops to $6; four or more people pay only $5 an hour. Home-stay programs cost $150 a week. There is a one-time admin fee of $20 and a deposit is required to confirm your place. Home stays include room and board close to the school. There is also a pseudo home-stay option, where you stay in a small family-run hotel and have a private room, but still join the family in the main area of the hotel for meals and to practice conversation.

The school also offers salsa lessons, Oaxacan cooking classes, surfing and local art. Rates run $10 an hour and drop as the group size increases. For example, a surfing lesson is $15 an hour for one, but if two people particpate, each person pays just $10.

■ Outfitters/Tour Operators

Hidden Voyages EcoTours, *Dimar Travel Agency, Av Perez Gasga #905,* ☎ *954-582-0734, www.wincom.net/~pelewing/ hvecotur.html, 7: 30 am-10 pm.* This companies works with a professional ornithologist who acts as a guide on birding trips to Lagunas de Chacahua Park. The guides are also knowledgeable about plant life in the park. On each trip they take between four and 10 people. The five-hour trip (including 3½ hours on a boat) costs $40 per person. Binoculars are provided.

Hidden Valley also offers a sunset cruise with English-speaking guides/naturalists that take you to a lagoon where white water lilies and Lily Walker jacana birds are found. After the birds tuck in for the night, you get to sip a glass of complimentary wine and watch the night arrive. The four-hour trip costs $40 per person. Also on offer is a three-four-hour walking bird tour ($15) that goes into the foothills behind the bay.

Ana's EcoTours, *Hotel Rincon del Pacifico,* ☎ *954-582-1958*. Ana is a local guide licensed by the Secretary of Tourism. Born in the area, she is knowledgeable about wildlife and sensitive to its needs. Ana takes horse tours to a waterfall in the mountains. She also does some birding tours.

Margarito Bustamante is a local guide who lives in Las Negras, about 10 miles/16 km from town, but hangs out at El Cafecito in Zicatela Beach. He has his own canoe and knows where to spot wildlife in the park. He charges about $10 an hour and will take up to four people. If he isn't in his "office," ask in Las Negras.

■ Places to Stay

 Posada Real, *Playa Bacocho,* ☎ *954-568-8496, www.posada-real.com.mx, $$$$,* is a Best Western hotel with 100 rooms set on a hill overlooking 1,500 feet of private beachfront. The hotel is surrounded by flower gardens. The rooms are large and well decorated with stone walls and tile floors. They each have private bathroom, sitting area, hot water, air

HOTEL PRICE SCALE	
Price for a room given in US $.	
$	Up to $20
$$	$21-$50
$$$	$51-$100
$$$$	$101-$150
$$$$$	$151-$200
Anything over $200 is specified.	

conditioning and satellite TV (with English channels). There is laundry service and an open-air restaurant that overlooks the beach. The staff is helpful and many speak English. The only negative is that the hotel is on Bacocho Beach, between the airport and downtown. Since it is not recommended to walk around after dark, you should take a cab into the center.

Hotel Arco Iris, *Calle del Morro, Playa Zicatela,* ☎ *954-582-1494, $$,* has 20 large rooms that have private patios and ocean views. You can rent hammocks for use on the balcony. The place is clean and comfortable and the gardens out back are exceptional. There is a pool and restaurant that is reported to have good food. This is one of the most popular places in Puerto Escondido.

Hacienda Revolucion, *Av Revolucion #21,* ☎ *954-582-1818, $$,* has a number of rooms and little *casitas* for rent that are painted white to emphasize their cleanliness. They have private bathrooms, fans and a terrace with hammocks. The bathrooms are tiled and well lit. Laundry service and a safe deposit box are available. The entrance to the hotel has the façade of an old mission bell tower. Inside, the patio features rich vegetation and has a number of benches. This is a really good deal.

Hotel Rincon del Pacifico, *Av Perez Gasga #900,* ☎ *954-582-0193, $$ with fan and $$$ with air conditioning.* This lovely little place has rooms around a central courtyard decorated with potted plants. Each room has wide windows overlooking the courtyard, air conditioning, a fridge and cable TV. Economical rooms are available with fans, rather than air conditioning.

Castillo de Carrizalillo, *Calle del Castillo,* ☎ *954-582-1771, http://my. tbaytel.net/castillo, $$,* is a castle-like B&B operated by a Canadian man. It has round turrets at the corners of the building, each topped with a red-tiled roof. Rooms have a private bathroom, a tiled floor and a large window. This is a tiny place with only five exquisitely decorated rooms. Breakfast is included. The owners speak English, French and Spanish. This is a great place, if you can get in. I suggest booking ahead.

Hotel Nayar, *Av Perez Gasga #407, up hill from Adoquin,* ☎ *954-582-0113, $$,* has some rooms with air conditioning, others with fans. The rooms are not huge, but they are comfortable and have writing desks, private bathrooms, double beds, night lights and tiled floors. There is a pool and small walled garden. For the price, you can't go wrong.

Hotel Mayflower, *off the Adoquin,* ☎ *954-582-0422, $$,* has a number of choices, including a dorm. This is considered the youth hostel of the town. Some rooms have balconies and ocean views. Most have a private bathroom and ceiling fans (the dorms do). There is hot water and purified drinking water available and a communal guest kitchen. There is a rooftop bar. The owners speak English, Spanish, French and German.

Hotel Jardin Real, *Bacocho Beach,* ☎ *954-582-2963, $$/$$$,* has 29 rooms with private bathrooms, tiled floors, large windows and TVs. There is a pool and fairly well-kept grounds surrounding the motel-style building. The swim-up bar has a waterfall and is close to the restaurant. For the party crowd, this is a good spot. You drink, swim and sleep in places that are all within a few feet from each other.

Hotel Barlovento, *Camino al Faro, Calle 6a, Sur #3,* ☎ *954-582-0220, $$$,* is a California stucco-designed place with rooms on different levels. Each simple room has a large window, a high ceiling, air conditioning, a cable TV, a fridge, a private bathroom and tiled floors. There is a pool, restaurant and bar, as well as ample parking on site. The hotel is a short walk from the beach.

Acuario Bungalows, *Calle del Morro, Playa Zicatela,* ☎ *954-582-0357, $$$,* is a rustic place patronized by the surfers. The rooms are small, though some do have kitchens. There is no air conditioning. However, there is a gym, a surf shop, an Internet café and a vegetarian restaurant.

Hotel Flor de Maria, *Playa Marinero,* ☎ *954-582-0536, $$$,* was built by an Italian couple. It is located on a side street just up from the main part of the beach. The hotel is exceptionally clean and the restaurant has good food. There is a rooftop pool and bar. I heard rumblings about the staff being fearful of the boss.

Hotel Paraiso Escondido, *Calle Union #10,* ☎ *954-582-0444, $$$$,* is an upscale Mexican hotel that uses red tile, ornamental iron and clay bricks for decoration. The 18 rooms have big windows, hand-painted tiles, wall paintings and all the comforts of a first-class hotel. The building is perched on the hill overlooking the bay and catches the breeze. The yard is nicely groomed and there is a large pool in the center of the lawn.

Hotel Santa Fe, *Calle del Morro, Playa Zicatela,* ☎ *954-582-0170, $$$$,* has spacious rooms with TV (three channels), air conditioning and fans.

There is a hot tub in some bathrooms, but the water is often cool. The restaurant serves vegetarian and vegan cuisine. There are two pools in the garden and the hotel is close to the beach.

■ Places to Eat

Cafecito, *next to Bungalows Acuario at Zicatela Beach,* ☎ *954-582-0516,* has been a favorite breakfast hangout for years. Cafecito has two restaurants side by side. One is El Cafecito, the other is Restaurant Cafecito. Both restaurants are run by the same people. Because of popular demand, they expanded their business. Their coffee is the best in town.

La Gota de Vida, *Av Gasga, no phone,* has vegetarian dishes, soups and great *liquados* (shakes). Try the *banana con leche*. Prices are moderate.

Mario's Pizza, *Av Gasga,* ☎ *582-0570,* is at the east end of the pedestrian zone. Pizza is for sale whole or by the slice at reasonable prices.

Taqueria la Playita, *Av Oaxaca and 2nd across from the newsstand, no phone*, offers the best tacos in town. A roll of meat on a spit continuously cooks. Add some onion, tomato and spice and you are set. The cost is less than $5.

Sakura, *calle del Morro, Zicatela Beach, no phone,* is a Japanese place that is very popular. A full meal costs $7 per person.

Junto al Mar, *west end of the Adoquin, no phone.* This is an upscale restaurant that serves seafood. It comes highly recommended by many who have eaten here.

Mariposa, *Av Juarez #208, no phone,* is the best place to fill up on delicious red meat. Their steak is second to none in town and costs under $10.

Hotel Santa Fe Restaurant, *Calle del Morro, Playa Marinero,* ☎ *954-582-0170,* in the hotel of the same name, is *the* first-class dining place in town. Dress is casual, service is good and the food is excellent. They have traditional Mexican dishes, seafood and vegetarian cuisine. Prices are high; a meal will run $15.

Bananas, *Av Gasga,* ☎ *954-582-0005,* is open 7:30 am-1 am daily. They have everything from fruit crêpes to *huevos rancheros*. During happy hour (5-9 pm), they offer gourmet specials. Prices are moderate.

Papaya Surf Restaurant, *Zicatela Beach at the south end, no phone.* The pasta here is homemade and the fettuccine with meat is excellent.

■ Nightlife

 The Split Coconut, *no phone*, has been moved to the Hotel Jardin Real in Bacocho. Besides the food that they claim is better than ever, they have US Direct TV that you can watch while lazing at the pool. Happy hour is 2-4 pm daily and ladies get free drinks during that time on Tuesdays. Swimming is free on Thursdays during happy hour.

Tequila Sunrise, *just off Av Adoquin, no phone*, is one of the most popular bars in town.

Puerto Angel/Zipolete

This has been a busy port since the 1840s when it was first built for the coffee barons who were shipping their produce to Europe. Now it is an almost busy tourist town. The tourists are the budget-minded ones who want to hang out under a palapa and drink tequila. The beaches stretch for miles in each direction and the well-protected bay is split in two by a river. Two miles/three km west of the main bay is Zipolete, or Playa Amor, one of the few nude beaches in Mexico.

■ Getting Here & Around

 Puerto Angel is 25 miles/40 km north of Huatulco and 40 miles/ 60 km south of Puerto Escondido. Vehicles must endure the steep decline from the Sierra Madres on Highway 200 for six miles/nine km to the coast in order to reach the town and beaches. There is no air traffic.

A **bus** from Mexico City or Oaxaca takes eight-12 hours to get here. Local buses go up and down Highway 200 and take about two hours from/to Huatulco.

■ History

 Zipoltee means "Beach of the Souls" or "Beach of the Dead" in Zapotecan language. The Indians used the area as a religious site and there is an archeological camp.

It was fairly quiet here until the hippies of the 1960s started to arrive, hang out, smoke a bit of *ganga* and sell beads to live. Then it became a nude beach, barely tolerated by locals. Today, grass huts along the shore can be rented for reasonable prices and many palapa-hut restaurants are ready to cook you a meal or serve you a beer.

▪ Adventures on Water

Beaches

Playa Principal is in the main part of the bay where fishermen bring in their catch shortly after noon each day. Small restaurants line the beach, ready to cook some of the fresh fish.

Playa Panteon is connected to Principal by a walkway that passes around the cliffs. More restaurants line the beach.

Zipolete is two miles/three north of Panteon and can be reached on foot. A series of restaurants, cafes and services (such as telephones and Internet cafés) line the route. Zipolete has three beaches. **Playa Amor** is the nude beach. **Playa Agustinillo** is the next one going north and is good for snorkeling and swimming. **Mazunte** is an open beach good for watching nesting sea turtles. There are numerous coves and tiny bays and stretches where you can spend hours without seeing anyone else. This is definitely a place for the young; seldom did I see anyone over 40. The currents are strong along this stretch of beach as there is no breakwater. The undertow is especially dangerous and the beach has seen many deaths – remember the original name of the place.

▪ Places to Stay & Eat

Shambhala, *at the west end of the beach just past the rocks,* ☎ 954-584-3153, *$,* has five cell-like rooms and 10 cabins without private bathrooms. The floors are cement, the roofs are thatch and the lighting is provided by candles. Each bed has a mosquito net over it. You can also hang a hammock here for a small fee. Showers and flush toilets are in a separate building. Shambhala is for

HOTEL PRICE SCALE		
Price for a room given in US $.		
$	Up to $20	
$$	$21-$50	
$$$	$51-$100	
$$$$	$101-$150	
$$$$$	$151-$200	
Anything over $200 is specified.		

those who are into health food and drug-free bodies (alcohol is considered a drug here). It is a rustic and peaceful place and the most popular choice of backpack travelers. The restaurant serves vegetarian dishes.

Lo Cosmico, *across the road from Shambhala, $,* has cabins with cement floors and no electricity (candles are used). The showers and toilets are in a separate cabin. Rooms farther up the hill have private bathrooms; lower ones do not. The restaurant, owned and operated by the same people, offers crêpe specialties.

Las Casitas, *between Lo Cosmico and Shambhala, $$,* has tiny bungalows with kitchenettes and private bathrooms. Electricity comes from solar panels. There is a restaurant at the hotel that serves excellent food.

Lyoban, *in the center of the village,* ☎ *954-584-3177, $,* has hammocks for rent and rooms with private bathrooms. A laid-back, funky place, Lyoban is great if you want to be in town.

L'Achemista, *near Shambhala*, is open for dinner only. The food is international and excellent. A meal costs less than $6 per person.

Huatulco

Huatulco is a resort area at the foot of the Sierra Madres that has a series of nine bays with 30 beaches, some accessible only by boat. Almost all the hotels are on Tangolunda Bay, which has the most impressive beaches.

 LOCAL LINGO: *The name* Huatulco *means "Place where Wood is Adored" in Mixteca language.*

The area offers golf, watersports, shopping and dining, and the government has set aside some ecological preserves to attract eco tourists.

The government is trying to keep Huatulco from becoming an urban sprawl like a few other resort towns along the coast. If they pull it off, this will remain a beautiful spot. If you decide to come here, pay for only a few nights at your hotel and look around until you find exactly what you want.

■ Getting Here & Around

By Plane

 The airport, on Highway 200, is about seven miles/12 km west of town. It has domestic and international flights and is serviced by AeroMexico, Mexicana, Contintental Airlines, American Airlines and Air Canada. The cheapest airfares coming here are charter flights. Some small, local airlines fly to Oaxaca and Mexico City from here; check the airline desks at the airport.

AIRLINE CONTACT INFORMATION		
Air Canada	www.aircanada.com	☎ 888-247-2262 (US, Canada)
AeroMexico	www.aeromexico.com	☎ 800-237-6639 (US); 800-021-4010 (Mx)
American Airlines	www.aa.com	☎ 800-433-7300 (US); 800-904-6000 (Mx)
Continental	www.continental.com	☎ 800-231-0856 (US); 800-900-5000 (Mx)
Mexicana Airlines	www.mexicana.com	☎ 800-531-7921 (US); 800-509-8960 (Mx)

Taxis will cost about $50 if hired at the airport terminal to go into town. Taxis hired on the road away from the terminal cost 65% less. Those staying at the resorts will have pickup arranged by the resort. If you're going to Puerto Escondido, hire **Viajes Diamar**, ☎ 954-582-0734, to take you there for $8 per person. The van must be full for Diamar to make the trip.

By Car

Budget, ☎ *954-581-0036,* has a booth at the airport.

> **WARNING:** Advantage Rent-a-Car, *Hotel Castillo Huatulco, Blvd Santa Cruz #309,* ☎ *954-517- 0051,* is a company that you should avoid. It has been reported that they do not respect their contracts, nor do they fill reservations on time.

Driving to Acapulco takes 4½ hours, Oaxaca 10½ hours, and Mexico City 10 hours.

Driving along the highways is not recommended after dark.

By Bus

The first-class buses from Mexico City, Oaxaca and Acapulco usually go to La Crucecita first; from there you must catch a local bus to Huatulco. First-class buses are offered by **Cristobal Colon** and **Estrella Blanca**. The terminal is on Calle Gardenia. The bus to Barra de Navidad stops at Av Lopez de Legazpi. The overnight bus to Mexico city takes 12 hours and costs $40. Oaxaca buses leave during the day (at least once an hour) and at night. The eight-hour journey costs $20.

▪ History

In the mid-1800s, Acapulco was difficult to access and Tehuantepec was disintegrating, so Huatulco became one of the best ports along the southern coast. In 1831, the Colombo arrived with General Vincente Guerrero, then Mexico's President, who, at the time was a prisoner of the Spanish. They landed at the main beach and transferred Guerrero to Oaxaca where he was tried, convicted and condemned to death. He was executed on February 14th of the same year. No messing around with appeals in those days.

▪ Adventures on Foot

Canyoning

Canyoning on the Copalita River requires that you wear a helmet, life jacket, harness and ropes (provided by the tour company). This trip starts with a float down the river (feet first) to the first 45-foot/15-meter waterfall. The guides make certain you don't go over before being harnessed and lowered down. The next drop (60 feet/20 meters) is just a few feet along and drops down into a narrow canal. This drop takes quite a bit of time and help from your guide.

Rock Climbing

Piedra del Pacifico is a set of cliffs at the mouth of the Copalito River, where it enters the ocean. Climbers often come to play at this rock. Another great spot is the **Piedra de Moros**, near the community of the same name. It is a gigantic mound of rock that was originally formed from underwater eruptions. Now it is a play bubble where tourists hang on to ropes and rappel down.

Golf

Bahia Tangolunda Golf Course, *on Tangolunda Bay,* ☎ *958-581-0001,* was designed by Mario Schjetnan Dantan in 1991. It is a par 72, 18-hole, 6,870-yard course next to the beach. Sand traps and natural lakes challenge the golfer. The most beautiful green is right on the beach. There is a restaurant and clubhouse. Beware of the resident croc that likes the water sections of the course. Fees are $63 per day with a shared cart. The reduced fees are a real bonus because this is an excellent course as judged by serious players.

Bring your own equipment as the rentals are not in very good shape. The pro shop sells only balls and tees and those are overpriced. Also, bring insect repellent; the mozzies are huge and hungry.

■ Adventure on Water

Beaches

 Maguey has palapa restaurants where you can have a cold beer or a seafood meal or both. This is the biggest hustle and bustle beach in the town.

Cacaluta has sand dunes that are always good for sunset photographs. You may also see the odd all-terrain vehicle churning up the landscape. It's part of the machismo scene.

Conejos is a swimming and snorkeling beach that has light surf and a gentle drop off. Locals offer horses for hire along this beach ($10 an hour).

Tangolunda is the area's most developed beach and you can rent all manner of watersports equipment here. The waves are strong and the beach, except for a small section at one end, is fairly steep.

Chahue is the largest of the beaches and home to several new luxury hotels. A marina is being built on this bay. It is a pretty spot with steep sand dunes along the edge.

Santa Cruz, was originally the harbor and shipyard built by the Spaniards. Cruise ships now come in here. It has La Bufadora, a blowhole where water comes shooting up through the rocks like a geyser. You can hire a boat to take a cruise of the bay at Santa Cruz. Hector, at the Barcelo Resort, has a desk in the main lobby and he takes daily tours of the seven bays. The tours include a swim and snorkel at San Agustin Beach and a meal on Maguey Beach. (See *Tour Operators*, below.)

Organo is a swimming and snorkeling beach.

Chachacual has mangroves coming down to the ocean. Birds hang out here waiting for birders to find them. This is, as I have said earlier, considered the prettiest section of the entire area.

San Agustin is popular with divers who come to visit a little island and some reefs just offshore. Snorkeling is also good in this bay.

Copalita River can be explored in a boat or while on a raft/kayak trip. The lower, first section of the river runs through a bird sanctuary and jungle terrain. This section takes half a day. The full river trip, from source to sea, takes three days. It covers Class III and Class V rapids and features some serious drops. The middle section of the river has Class III and IV sections with some turbulent water accented by standing waves. For the experienced kayaker, this is often a destination river. The Alemania section, the upper part, has Class IV and V sections that requires skill and technical knowledge of river running. It passes through steep slopes and canyons with narrow channels that force the water to churn through. There are pullout/put-in places for all three sections.

Diving

Scuba diving in the area offers some coral reefs, cliffs and crags and tiny underwater islands. There are 15 different dive spots on the bay where you will see rays, globefish and schools of tropical fish. The corals include moose horn and beds of black coral. There are octopus, jellyfish, moray eels, sharks, yellow jacks, snappers and, on occasion, whales and dolphins. Corals are found at Cacaluta, La India, Chachacual, Riscalillo and San Agustin sites. Confer with a tour operator as to which dives would suit you the best.

■ Adventures in Nature

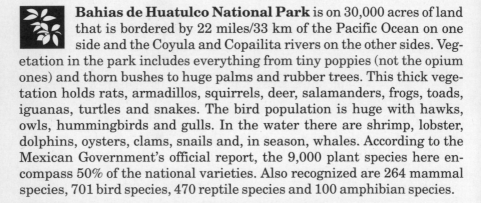

Bahias de Huatulco National Park is on 30,000 acres of land that is bordered by 22 miles/33 km of the Pacific Ocean on one side and the Coyula and Copailita rivers on the other sides. Vegetation in the park includes everything from tiny poppies (not the opium ones) and thorn bushes to huge palms and rubber trees. This thick vegetation holds rats, armadillos, squirrels, deer, salamanders, frogs, toads, iguanas, turtles and snakes. The bird population is huge with hawks, owls, hummingbirds and gulls. In the water there are shrimp, lobster, dolphins, oysters, clams, snails and, in season, whales. According to the Mexican Government's official report, the 9,000 plant species here encompass 50% of the national varieties. Also recognized are 264 mammal species, 701 bird species, 470 reptile species and 100 amphibian species.

■ Outfitters/Tour Operators

I found it very difficult to get exact prices from these companies, but the average cost to hire a guide and boat runs $10-$15 an hour. A half-day tour is usually between $25 and $40. Full-day tours are around $100 a day.

Ecoaventuras Huatulco, *Guamuchil # 208*, ☎ *958-587-0244*, is just a block east of the *zocalo*. They specialize in wildlife tours, especially on the lower Copalita River. They also organize cycle, rafting and kayaking trips.

Piraguas Adventures, *Plaza Ozxaca, #19, La Crucecita*, ☎ *958-587-1333,* organizes fishing excursions on the bay. Rates are $250 a day on a good boat with a lower deck. This price includes fishing gear.

Turismo Conejo, *Av Guamuchil #208*, ☎ *958-587-1529,* has birding tours and jungle exploration trips to some rock hieroglyphics.

Zona de Aventura Extrema, *Av Rio Coatzacoalcos, #12,* ☎ *958-587-1264,* caters to younger people who want more challenging excursions. Talk to them if you want to paddle the upper Copalita River or do some rappelling and climbing.

Hector has a desk in the lobby of the Barcelo Resort (no phone). He does a seven-bay tour that includes a swim or snorkel at San Agustin Beach and lunch on the beach at El Maguey. Food and snorkel gear cost extra. Hector also runs a coffee plantation tour where you will see the complete process of making coffee, from bean to drink. This excursion includes a trip includes a trip to a waterfall.

Camino Real Zaashila Huatulco service center, *Blvd Benito Juarez #5,* ☎ *958-581-0460,* will arrange a horseback riding trip to Rancho Caballo de Mar for $45. Trips start at 10 am and 2 pm and last 3½ hours. For the afternoon trip, bring a swimsuit, as a swimming/eating/drinking break is included. Long pants and shoes suitable for riding are recommended. Food and drink is included in the price.

Leaward Divers, *Plaza Oaxaca, 1st floor, #18, Zocalo in La Crucecita* ☎ *958-587-2166, scubahector@huatulco.net.mx, 9 am-2 pm and 5-9:30 pm; or at Tangolunda Beach next to Alamo Rent a Car,* ☎ *958-581-0051.* This company has been in business since 1989 and they know the best dive and snorkel places around. Of these, there are about 13 sites from which to choose with depths between 20 and 50 feet. For bay dives, they charge $55 for a one-tank dive that will last about two hours, $75 for four-hour, two-tank dive and $65 for a two-hour night dive. A two-tank dive at San Agustin Island, including a one-hour boat ride each way, costs $100 and lasts about seven hours. Snorkeling costs $20 for two hours. This company also offers discounts for students, multiple dives and groups, as well as to those who have their own gear.

▪ Places to Stay

 Like all the resort towns along the coast, Huatulco has many places to stay, although it hasn't quite reached the level of Acapulco or Puerto Vallarta. Many of the hotels offer tremendous luxury. I can't begin to write about all of them. My reviews below cover just a sample of what is here.

▸▸ **AUTHOR NOTE:** *Never book and pay for your entire vacation ahead of time. If things are not up to expectations, move on.*

There are numerous places in **Crucecita**. I have included just one to let you have a destination should you arrive late and have to stay there before finding a place on the beach.

Posada Michelle, *Gardenia #8, in Crucecita,* ☎ *958-587-0535, $$,* has small, clean rooms with large beds, cable TV and air conditioning.

Hotel Las Palmas, *Av Guamuchil #206,* ☎ *958-587-0060, www.tomzap. com, $$,* has 25 basic rooms a block from the plaza. They have tiled showers, cable TV and air conditioning. Free parking.

HOTEL PRICE SCALE	
Price for a room given in US $.	
$	Up to $20
$$	$21-$50
$$$	$51-$100
$$$$	$101-$150
$$$$$	$151-$200
Anything over $200 is specified.	

Hotel Binneguenda, *Av Benite Juarez #5,* ☎ *958-587-0077, $$$,* is a hacienda-style hotel built around a central courtyard with pool. Ceramic tiles and pottery decorate the hacienda. Each room has colonial furnishings, a small balcony, satellite TV, air conditioning, safe deposit box and tiled floors. The bathrooms are large.

Hotel Castillo Huatulco, *Av Benito Juarez at Santa Cruz Beach,* ☎ *958-587-0135, $$$,* has small, comfortable rooms with cable TV and air conditioning. There is also a pool and off-street parking.

Posada Chahue, *Calle Mixie and Mixteco, at Chahue Beach,* ☎ *958-587-0945, $$$,* has large modern rooms that are clean and comfortable. They feature air conditioning, tiled floors, private bathrooms and big windows. This is a Best Western Hotel.

Agua Azul la Villa B & B, *on the hill above Conejos Beach,* ☎ *958-581-0265, $$$/$$$$,* is a Canadian-run (must be good!), place that has eight little *casitas* tucked into the hill. The place is spotless, attractive and affordable. Food served in the on-site restaurant is delicious. Coming from cold Canada, the owners know how important a good breakfast is and they provide it. The garden in back features a two-tiered pool.

Gala Resort Huatulco, *Blvd Benito Juarez #4,* ☎ *958-581-0000, $$$$$,* has 300 air-conditioned rooms, three restaurants, three bars, lighted tennis courts and two outside pools, a kiddy pool and a supervised children's program. Watersports equipment is available for rent.

Quinta Real Huatulco, *Blvd Benito Juarez #2,* ☎ *958-581-0428, $$$$$,* is a relatively tiny palace with only 27 air-conditioned rooms that have TVs, in-room safes and marble bathrooms. Some rooms have whirlpools. The architecture features domed roofs, balconies, brickwork and white plaster that reminds me of a Tunisian mosque. The hotel has all the luxury of a *cazbah*. Views from the balconies are excellent and the green and black iguanas that skitter around during afternoon feeding time are not to be missed. Birders will love the grounds for finding new species to add to their lists. I can't say enough about the elegance of this place.

Camino Real Zaashila Huatulco, *Blvd Benito Juarez #5,* ☎ *581-0460, $$$$$,* is a Mediterranean-style hotel with high arches and white plaster walls. Most of the 130 air-conditioned suites have private pools. There are two restaurants and two bars, an outdoor 500-foot/175-meter, free-form pool, a Jacuzzi and lighted tennis courts. Watersports equipment, such as boogie boards and kayaks, can be rented. Rooms cost as much as $1,000 a night.

Crown Pacific Huatulco, *previously called the Magni Hotel, Benito Juarez #8, $$$$$, (office is in Cancun)* ☎ *998-881-7206*. This all-inclusive resort sits on the hill overlooking the bay, just 300 yards from the beach. The 135 suites each have a wet bar, fridge, safe, hair dryer, TV, large terrace overlooking the bay and a sitting area. The food, served buffet style, includes domestic drinks from the bar and wine with lunch and dinner. You can dine inside or in the garden. The food is gourmet, the table setup formal, with linen tablecloths, china dishes and silverware, water and wine glasses. Snorkel gear, boogie boards and scuba equipment are supplied. You can do water aerobics, play water polo and water basketball, use the fitness equipment and steam room, or play volleyball or tennis.

Sheraton Barcelo Huatulco, *Benito Juarez,* ☎ *958-581-0055, $$$$$,* is a contemporary Mexican building that was selected for the 1998 Condé Nast Gold List for everything from its beaches and hotel décor to the array of activities it offers. The 347 rooms have air conditioning and other amenities common to this type of hotel. There are three restaurants, two pools and four tennis courts. However, the food has been reported as mediocre, bordering on bad. I have been told it has no variety, no presentation and no flavor.

Las Brisas, *Tangolunda Beach, no phone, $$$$$,* is set on 50 acres of manicured lawn and colorful vegetation that slopes down to three private beaches. There are five restaurants, a business center, car rental, massage room, off-street parking, five outdoor pools, a health club and tennis courts. There's even an archery range. This is probably the most distinctive hotel on the bay. The rooms are exquisite.

■ Places to Eat

Most of the five-star hotels have restaurants that serve good food in an elegant setting. Head to La Crucecita if you want to get away from the beach scene. Buses go all the time, carrying the workers from the luxury hotels to their homes in La Crucecita.

Café Dublin, *Carrizol # 504, La Crucecita,* ☎ *958-589-2633,* is an Irish pub (who could have guessed?) and restaurant. They serve strong coffee and cold beer, neither of which you can find in Ireland. There is also a book exchange. The atmosphere is what draws people to this place.

Jarro Café, *across from the Sheraton on Benito Juarez, no phone,* has good breakfasts that include banana pancakes, one of my favorite dishes.

La Pirata Pizza and Chicken, *at the Hotel La Marina at Santa Cruz Beach, no phone*, is known for good chicken and reasonable prices ($6).

The Oasis, *La Crucecita, on the plaza*, ☎ *958-587-0219*, is a sushi bar that also has good, large salads (Mexican restaurants often serve minuscule salads). A second Oasis restaurant just a block away has a bit more atmosphere. The dining area there is in a central courtyard with a nice fountain.

Sabor de Oaxaca, *Av Guamuchil #206 in La Crucecita, half a block from the plaza*, ☎ *958-587-0060*, is considered the best in Huatulco. It is open 7 am-midnight daily. I recommend the combo, a selection of 10 traditional Oaxacan dishes that include *quesillo*, *cecina* (chili pork/beef), *tasajo* (filet), *chorizo* (sausage) and *chiles rellenos* (stuffed chilies). The combo meal costs $18 for two. They also make excellent *mole*, a chocolate-based sauce that is served over chicken.

Oaxaca

The city of Oaxaca has been a bohemian hangout for over 25 years. It can accommodate any class of tourist. The main reason to come to Oaxaca is to sit around the square at one of the street-side cafés, to visit Monte Alban and to purchase some black pottery.

■ Getting Here & Away

By Plane

 There are frequent flights between Mexico City and Oaxaca and a few flights that are direct to cities in the US. AeroMexico, Mexicana Airlines and Aviacsa fly into Oaxaca.

AIRLINE CONTACT INFORMATION		
Aviacsa	www.aviacsa.com.mx	☎ 888-528-4227 (US); 800-711-6733 (Mx)
AeroMexico	www.aeromexico.com	☎ 800-237-6639 (US); 800-021-4010 (Mx)
Mexicana Airlines	www.mexicana.com	☎ 800-531-7921 (US); 800-509-8960 (Mx)

The airport is about four miles/six km from the center of town, a $10 cab ride. However, a small van caught outside the terminal will cost only $3 per person. There are no public buses going from the airport into town.

By Bus

The main connecting city to Oaxaca is Mexico City. **Cristobal Colon** and **Autobus del Oriente** are the best first-class buses that travel between these two places. It is a six-hour journey and there are 17 buses going daily. However, numerous companies offer service in all directions from Oaxaca, so going all the way to Mexico City is not always necessary. Check at the bus station, *Heroes de Chapaltepec #1036, 11 blocks north of town*, for your desired destination. The bus station is a 30-45-minute walk from the center. Public buses run from the terminal into town for 50¢ (catch one across the street from the entrance). A taxi will cost $3 for the same trip.

By Car

Driving to the Oaxaca Valley offers the advantage of being able to visit most of the ruins with little difficulty. **Budget**, ☎ *958-515-0330*, **Hertz**, ☎ *958-516-2434*, **Avis**, ☎ *958-516-0009*, and **Alamo**, ☎ *958-514-8534*, all have outlets in town and at the airport.

∎ History

People have lived in the Oaxaca Valley for over 8,000 years. **Mitla** has cave paintings that tell of life during early times. After the cave dwellers, the **Olmecs** were the next civilization who left evidence of living here. They arrived around 5,000 years ago and left gigantic stone carvings of their gods. Around 2,500 years ago Monte Alban was built and the residents enjoyed a prosperous life trading with other kingdoms living as far away as Mexico City and the Pacific coast. They developed the skill of working with obsidian and produced exquisite ceramic pieces. Monte Alban declined about 1000 AD.

 LOCAL LINGO: *The name* Oaxaca *in the Zapotec language means "People of the Clouds."*

The Spanish colonized the area in the mid-1500s. At the same time, Jesuit missionaries introduced Catholic gods. The Indians gave up their Aztec gods and started worshiping at Spanish churches.

∎ Services

Tourist Office, *Independencia #607*, ☎ *958-516-4828, 9 am-8 pm daily, except Sunday.* This is one of the few tourist offices in Mexico that was not cooperative with me.

Southern Pacific Mexico

Police, *Calle Aldama #108*, ☎ *958-516-2726.*

Post office, *Plaza Alameda de Leon,* ☎ *958-516-2661, 8 am-7 pm week-days, until 1 pm on Saturdays.*

Hospital, *Diaz #400,* ☎ *958-515-1300,* is at the north end of town. There is little or no English spoken here.

■ Adventure in Culture

Monte Alban

 This site was populated for thousands of years. Archeologists have divided the major periods into five subdivisions. These periods pertain to the entire valley, rather than just the one ceremonial site.

TIME GOES BY

Period I is when civilization first came to the valley. People had gods, temples, priests and held religious ceremonies. They constructed buildings with near-vertical walls that featured stepladder-type access to get from one level to the next. Near the end of Period I, the people learned to make stucco and use it on their floors. They inscribed stones with hieroglyphs and numbers. The use of numbers suggests the understanding of a calendar. Both houses and tombs are of two designs, one superior to the other, indicating a social class system.

Jade and shell objects are associated with the later part of this period. The Dancers Building in the lower level of the north platform at Monte Alban is from this period.

Period II begins about 100 BC and is recognized by the huge stones that were used in house construction. The use of door lintels, also made with huge stones, was introduced during this period. Building J at Monte Alban and Caballito Blanco on the hill near Yagul are good examples of this construction. The people also started carving tablets – one can be seen in Building H at Monte Alban. Stelae also started appearing during this period. The ceramics had painted designs and the jade jewelry pieces were beautifully carved. The most famous of these is the head of a bat, which is now on display in the Anthropological Museum in Mexico City.

Period III had changes that were influenced by the people of Teotihuacan, now called Mexico City. The Zapotec culture flourished during this time. The people reconstructed Monte Alban and it is mostly their work that we see in the ruins today. The most predominant changes were the construction of the temple platforms and the sloping walls on the buildings. The stones used here are small and cut so they appear to look like bricks. Stairways were incorporated into the buildings and were no longer like ladders. The buildings were also covered in stucco and painted red. Patios, built in the homes of the aristocracy, had small openings that led to other patios and formed a complex design of interconnecting homes.

During this period, ball courts formed a double "T" shape and a stone in the center indicated the starting point of the game. Tombs also became ornate and the inside walls had fresco paintings depicting humans. Tomb 28 at Yagul, one of the finest found, was made during this period. By the end of Period III, tombs were ornate and contained cornices and tablets. In Tomb 104 at Monte Alban, an urn was found in a niche by the entrance. Other tombs contained carvings of human heads inside.

Pottery developed and was painted in numerous colors (polychrome) and showed intricate designs. During the latter part of this period, the quality of pottery declined, but the pieces featured more gods. By 750 AD, when this period ended, the great plaza of Monte Alban was completed.

Period IV continued until the 1200s. Not much changed during this period, except that the culture seemed to be in decline. The most significant work was at the Lambityeco site, where some buildings were decorated with splendid friezes and sculptures.

Period V reflects the influence of the Mixtec culture in the Oaxaca Valley. It arrived about 1200 and ended with the coming of the Spaniards. The cities developed many palaces, or large mansions, while the importance of the temple platforms decreased. The houses were extensively decorated with murals made of mosaic stones that required no cement to hold them onto the walls. The finest of these is found at Mitla. Other sites, such as Yagul and Matatlan, also showed this type of mosaic work. Some gold pieces housed in the Anthropological Museum in Mexico City come from this period. The most notable is the "skinned god" made out of gold by the lost-wax casting process. The piece was found in Tomb 7 at Monte Alban. Also in that tomb was a gold necklace with six hanging images held together with rings, a gold, multi-strand necklace, pearls, turquoise and intricately carved jaguar bones.

Southern Pacific Mexico

Monte Alban.

Monte Alban is on Jaguar Hill, eight miles/12 km from the center of Oaxaca. It is open 10 am-5 pm daily. There is a charge of $3 to enter. The ruins are accessible by car or bus. Buses (25¢) leave from the second-class bus station on Calle Trujano in town about once every hour. You can also book onto the tour bus that leaves from Hotel Señorial or Hotel Rivera de Angel, both in the town center. This is the easiest way to go and it costs less than $10 per person for transportation both ways.

At the entrance to the ruins there is a restaurant, a museum and a gift shop with many books about the area written in English.

The main plaza measures 900x600 feet/300x200 meters and forms a perfect rectangle. The hill had to be dug out to hold the plaza. At one time, the platform held temples, but because wooden beams were used, the temples have not remained. Near the ball court is a metal stele honoring Dr. Alfonso Caso, principal excavator of the site. The ball court itself has a round center stone that may have been used to begin the game. Each corner of the court has a niche – its purpose is unknown. The upper level of the court has the walls of four temples.

From the plaza, walk south to Building II, the top of which has a small temple with five pillars at the front and another five at the back. This temple never had walls. The next building, built during Period II, has little of interest. The palace between the two buildings had 13 rooms and a wide staircase. Continue past the south platform. Behind it is the Deer Building. Beside the south platform is a well-preserved building called the Dancer. The stone carvings along the stairs leading to the top of the platform depict humans in odd positions. There has been a lot of speculation as to what the humans represent, but the general belief is that they are prisoners awaiting execution.

On the way back to the parking lot you will pass Mound X that is from Period II. It is well preserved because it was built over by subsequent civilizations and it wasn't until excavations took place that the entire building became uncov-

Stone carving.

ered. Just beyond this building is Tomb 104, with walls painted with religious scenes that are still in perfect condition. Inside this tomb was a niche that held an urn with the figure of a noble man dressed in a headdress that featured the image of Cocijo, the Zapotec rain god.

Other Villages

There are numerous other villages in the valley and anyone really interested in Mexican archeology should either rent a car to get around or join a tour. All ruins can be visited by joining a tour or by taking local buses to the villages and then walking to the sites. If driving to Cuilapan and Zaachila, take the road to Monte Alban, southwest out of town, and turn left at the huge sign just beyond the bridge that crosses the Atoyac River. Follow that road to Cuilapan and then to Zaachila. If going to Mitla, Yagul, Dainzu or Lambityeco, take the main road out of town to Highway 190. Turn left at the highway and proceed in a southerly direction until you come to the sign stating where to turn for the village you wish to visit.

Cuilapan has a monastery and church that were built in the 16th century. This is where a clay sculpture of a young man was found with inscriptions, believed to be a calendar, on his chest and head.

Zaachila was the last Zapotec capital where we know the names of the leaders. There are some large stones inscribed with hieroglyphs in the

Southern Pacific Mexico

town. One of the tombs has a bas-relief that represents a priest with a turtle carapace used as a shield.

Dainzu has a ball court, plus a pyramid with buildings, apartments and patios. Some of the stairways are still in good shape and a stele with a human figure is in exceptionally good condition.

The buildings at **Lambityeco**, just off the highway, were first constructed around 700 AD, just as Monte Alban was declining. One of the friezes from this ruin had a bearded man as the main subject.

Mitla is just beyond Lambityeco and is the second most famous ruin in the valley. The buildings are located on two sides of the ravine formed by the Mitla River, and some were still occupied when the Spanish arrived. One of the palaces, called the Palace of the Columns, has numerous rows of carved mosaics decorating one wall. The doorway of this palace is divided into three openings. One archeologist calculated that this building required 100,000 cut stones. There are two tombs at the palace. The second tomb has a stone support column called the Column of Life. Legend says that if you put your arms around the pillar, it will tell you how long you have to live. It never told me anything even though I listened for a long time. There were also cave paintings found here.

Yagul had an acropolis with temples and palaces on it, plus a fortress on the hill beyond the main city. One of the tombs is decorated with carved human heads. There is also a ball court and a nice area called the Six Patios.

■ Places to Stay

If you want to see many of the ruins in the valley, you will need to stay a few days. There are numerous of places to stay in Oaxaca, but I review just a few to give you a base.

Hotel Las Golondrinas, *Tinoco and Palacios #411*, ☎ *951-514-3298, $$*, is a popular hotel because it is clean, comfortable and attractive. The 30 rooms are located around a central courtyard that is decorated with potted plants, most of them flowering. Large rooms have matching décor, comfortable wood furniture and private bathrooms with hot water. However, the beds are like cement. The guest sitting room has books to read. Laundry service is available. Call ahead to book a room, as this hotel is popular.

Hotel Antequera, *Av Hidalgo # 807, no phone, $$*, is a block from the plaza. This little place has 19 rooms that are clean and well decorated. They have sitting areas, bathrooms with hot water, tiled floors and night lights. The service is excellent and the atmosphere quiet. I recommend this place over the Señorial that is on the plaza.

Hotel Fortin Plaza, *Av Venus #118*, ☎ *951-515-7777*, *$$$$*, is on the hill just below the highway. This six-story building is a good landmark and visible from almost anywhere in town. However, it is a bit away from the center. The rooms are large with balconies and sitting areas. There is a restaurant. This is a Best Western Hotel.

Misión de los Angeles, *Calzada Portirio Diaz # 102*, ☎ *951-502-0100*, *$$$$$*, *www.misiondelosangeles.com*, is the upscale place in town. Each of the 150 rooms has large windows, balcony, cable TV, sitting area and private bathroom. There is a pool, a well-tended garden, off-street parking and a restaurant on the property. Like the Fortin Plaza, this hotel is a ways from the center.

■ Places to Eat

The best advice I can give is to play bohemian and sit at any of the sidewalk cafés along the plaza. I could (and often do) spend hours here watching the action and enjoying a coffee or beer. The climate of Oaxaca is conducive to such a lifestyle. However, there are many good restaurants around town that are worth trying.

For breakfast, everyone goes to **Primavera**, *Av Hidalgo, on the plaza*, ☎ *951-516-2595*. The coffee is the best and they have good omelets, too. Their pancakes should also be tried.

Alfredo da Roma, *M. Alcala #400*, ☎ *951-516-5058*, is in the center of town and serves Italian dishes. The pizza is delicious, but the lasagna is also excellent. Meals cost under $10.

Tito's Coffee Shop, *Garcia Vigil # 116*, ☎ *951-516-7379*, is the place to stop for afternoon coffee and cheesecake. Prices are reasonable, the cake is fresh and the coffee is strong.

Head to **La Brew**, *Garcia Vigil #409*, ☎ *951-516-9673*, for strong coffee and waffles (the big Belgian kind) served with lots of fruit. A breakfast or lunch of this kind is about $6.

La Casa de la Abuela, *Hidalgo #616*, ☎ *951-516-3544*. The name, when translated, means Grandma's House. And good food she serves in her house. The cuisine is traditional Oaxacan. Try the chicken covered in *mole* sauce and served on a plate of hot rice ($7 for a large plate).

■ Nightlife

Evenings should be spent on the plaza, one of the most beautiful in all of Mexico, enjoying the climate and the people. If you want to party, go back to the beach.

Appendix

Recommended Reading

■ Nature

📚 ***Where to Find Birds in San Blas***, by Soalind Novick and Lan Sing Wu, is available by mail (178 Myrtle Court Arcata, CA 95521, US $4.50).

📚 ***Where to Watch Birds in Mexico***, Steve Howell, A&C Black Publishers, 1999. Covers 100 sites and about 1,000 species.

📚 ***Guide to the Birds of Mexico and Northern Central America***, Steve Howell, Oxford Press, 1995. Describes 1,070 species and covers Mexico and Central America down to northern Nicaragua. The guide features 71 color plates, plus maps.

📚 ***Chasing Monarchs: Migrating with the Butterflies of Passage***, Dr. Robert Michael Pyle, Houghton-Mifflin, 2001.

■ History

📚 ***Heroic Defense of Mezcala Island***, by Alberto Santoscoy is available as an e-book at www.epmassoc. com/catalog/175.php?sp=3. If this link is broken, type in the book title in your search engine to find another link. The book is an account of the fight between the people living on Mezcala Island and the Spanish.

■ About the Chihuahua al Pacifico Railroad

 Unknown Mexico by Carl Lumholtz, Sunracer Publications, PO Box 86492, Tucson, AZ 85754, sells for $20 + $2 shipping and handling.

 Silver Magnet by Grant Shepherd, Sunracer Publications, PO Box 86492, Tucson, AZ 85754, sells for $20 + $2 shipping and handling.

Glossary

■ THE CALENDAR

dia	day
semana	week
mes	month
año	year
domingo	Sunday
lunes	Monday
martes	Tuesday
miercoles	Wednesday
jueves	Thursday
viernes	Friday
sabado	Saturday
enero	January
febrero	February
marzo	March
abril	April
mayo	May
junio	June
julio	July
agosto	August
septiembre	September
octubre	October
noviembre	November
diciembre	December

■ NUMBERS

uno	one
dos	two
tres	three
cuatro	four

cinco . . . . five
seis. . . . . six
siete . . . . seven
ocho . . . . eight
nueve . . . . nine
diez . . . . ten
once . . . . eleven
doce . . . . twelve
trece . . . . thirteen
catorce . . . . fourteen
quince . . . . fifteen
dieciséis . . . . sixteen
diecisiete . . . . seventeen
dieciocho . . . . eighteen
diecinueve . . . . nineteen
veinte . . . . twenty
veintiuno . . . . twenty-one
veintidós . . . . twenty-two
treinta . . . . thirty
cuarenta. . . . . forty
cincuenta. . . . . fifty
sesenta. . . . . sixty
setenta. . . . . seventy
ochenta . . . . eighty
noventa . . . . ninety
cien. . . . . hundred
ciento uno . . . . one hundred one
doscientos . . . . two hundred
quinientos . . . . five hundred
mil . . . . one thousand
mil uno . . . . one thousand one
dos mil . . . . two thousand
millón. . . . . one million
primero . . . . first
segundo. . . . . second
tercero . . . . third
último. . . . . last

■ CONVERSATION

¿Como esta?. . . . . How are you?
¿Bien, gracias, y usted? . . . . Well, thanks, and you?
¿Que pasa?. . . . . What's happening?
Buenas dias. . . . . Good morning.
Buenas tardes. . . . . Good afternoon.
Buenas noches. . . . . Good evening/night.
Nos vemos. . . . . See you again.

¡Buena suerte! . . . . Good luck!

Adios. . . . . Goodbye.

Que la vaya bien . . . . .Goodbye (used for someone special)

Mucho gusto. . . . . .Glad to meet you.

Felicidades. . . . . Congratulations.

Feliz compleaños. . . . . Happy birthday.

Feliz Navidad. . . . . Merry Christmas.

Feliz Año Nuevo. . . . . .Happy New Year.

Gracias. . . . . .Thank you.

Por favor. . . . . Please.

De nada/con mucho gusto. . . . . You're welcome.

Perdoneme. . . . . Pardon me (when bumping into someone).

Permitame . . . . . . Pardon me (when passing in front of someone).

Desculpe. . . . . .Excuse me (when interrupting conversation).

¿Como se dice esto? .What do you call this?

Lo siento. . . . . I'm sorry.

Quiero... . . . . .I want/I like...

Adelante. . . . . Come in.

Permitame presentarle.... . . . . .May I introduce...

¿Como se nombre? . . . . .What is your name?

Me nombre es... . . . . .My name is...

No se. . . . . .I don't know.

Tengo sed. . . . . .I am thirsty.

Tengo hambre. . . . . .I am hungry.

Soy gringa/gringo. . . . . .I am an American (female/male).

¿Donde hay...? . . . . .Where is there/are there...?

Hay... . . . . There is/are

No hay . . . . .There is none

¿Que es esto? . . . . .What is this?

¿Habla ingles?. .Do you speak English?

¿Hablan ingles?. . . . . . Is there anyone here who speaks English?

Hablo/entiendo un poco . . . . .I speak/understand a little Spanish.
  Español

Le entiendo. . . . . .I understand you.

No entiendo. . . . . .I don't understand.

Hable mas despacio por favor. . . . . . . .Please speak more slowly.

Repita por favor. . . . . Please repeat.

¿Tiene...? . . . . .Do you have...?

Tengo... . . . . I have...

Hecho... . . . . I make/made

¿Puedo? . . . . .Can I?

¿Permite me? . . . . May I?

La cuenta por favor .The bill, please.

bolsa. . . . . bag

muchila. . . . . backpack

■ TIME

¿Que hora es?.............................What time is it?
Son las...It is...
... cinco.. five o'clock.
... ocho y diez. .... ten past eight.
... seis y cuarto. .... quarter past six.
... cinco y media. .... half past five.
... siete y menos cinco. .... five of seven.
antes de ayer. ....the day before yesterday.
anoche. ....yesterday evening.
esta mañana................................this morning.
a mediodia......................................at noon.
en la noche. ....in the evening.
de noche. ....at night.
mañana en la mañana/mañana mañana. ....tomorrow morning.
mañana en la noche. ....tomorrow evening.

■ DIRECTIONS

Llevame alla ... por favor. ....Take me there please.
¿Cual es el mejor camino para...? ....Which is the best road to...?
Derecha.. Right.
Izquierda....................................... Left.
Derecho/directo...........................Straight ahead.
¿A que distancia estamos de...? ....How far is it to...?
¿Es este el camino a...?...................Is this the road to...?
¿Es cerca? ....Is it near?
¿Es largo?..................................Is it a long way?
¿Donde hay...? ....Where is... ?
... el telefono..............................the telephone.
... el baño. ....the bathroom.
... el correos. ....the post office.
... el banco. ....the bank.
...casa de cambio .... the money exchange office.
... estacion del policia. ....the police station.

■ ACCOMMODATIONS

¿Que quiere?............................What do you want?
Quiero un hotel... ....I want a hotel that's...
... buena. .... good.
... barato. .... cheap.
... limpio. .... clean.
¿Dónde hay un hotel buena? ....Where is a good hotel?
¿Hay habitaciones libres?.........Do you have available rooms?
¿Dónde están los baños/servicios?.....Where are the bathrooms?
Quiero un habitacion ....I would like a room.
habitacion sencillo............................. single room.
habitacion con baño privado. ....room with a private bath.

habitacion doble. . . . . .double room.
baño comun . . . . without a private bath/with a shared bath
ducha . . . . shower
¿Esta incluido? . . . . .Is that included?
¿Puedo verlo? . . . . .May I see it?
cama. . . . . bed
cama matrimonial . . . . double bed
¿Algo mas?. . . . . .Anything more?
¿Cuanto cuesta? . . . . How much?
¡Es muy caro!. . . . . .It's too expensive!

■ FOOD

comer. . . . . .to eat
pan . . . . bread
carne . . . . meat
papas . . . . potatoes
leche . . . . milk
frutas . . . . fruit
jugo. . . . . .juice
huevos. . . . . eggs
mantequilla. . . . . butter
queso . . . . cheese
agua mineral . . . . mineral water
cerveza . . . . beer
pescado . . . . fish
helado. . . . . ice cream
arroz. . . . . rice
ensalada . . . . salad
jamon . . . . ham
pollo. . . . . chicken
toronja. . . . . grapefruit
naranja . . . . .orange (the fruit)
mariscos. . . . . seafood
sopa . . . . soup
vino tinto . . . . red wine
vino blanco. . . . . white wine

Consulates

■ American

Acapulco, Hotel Continental Plaza, ☎ 744-484-0300 or 485-7207. Call only for specific emergencies.

Hermosillo, Edificio Sonora, Planta Baja, ☎ 662-217-2375, Monday to Friday, 9 am-5 pm.

Mazatlan, Playa Gaviotas #202, across from Hotel Playa Mazatlan, ☎ 669-916-5889, Monday to Friday, 8 am-4 pm.

Nogales, Calle Campillo, Edificio del Estado, 2nd Piso, ☎ 631-913-4820, Monday to Friday, 8 am-4:30 pm.

Puerto Vallarta, Zaragoza #160, Vallarta Plaza, ☎ 322-222-0069, Monday to Friday, 10 am-2 pm.

■ Austrian

Acapulco, Calle de Juan R. Escudero #1, 1st floor, ☎ 744-482-5551, Monday to Friday, 9 am-noon.

■ Australian

Mexico City, Ruben Dario #55, Col. Polanco, ☎ 555-101-2200, Monday-Thursday, 8:30 am to 5:15 pm; Friday, 8:30 am-2:15 pm.

■ British

Acapulco, Costera Miguel Aleman, ☎ 744-484-1735. This is an honorary consulate, so calling to make an appointment is necessary.
Mexico City, Lerma 71, Col. Cuauhtemoc, ☎ 555-242-8500, Monday-Thursday, 8 am-4 pm; Friday, 8 am-1:30 pm.

■ Canadian

Acapulco, Centro Comercial Marbella, ☎ 744-484-1306, Monday to Friday, 9 am-5 pm.

Mazatlan, Playa Gaviotas, # 202, ☎ 669-913-7320, Monday to Friday, 9 am-1 pm.

Puerto Vallarta, Zaragoza #160, Vallarta Plaza, ☎ 322-222-5398, Monday to Friday, 1-4 pm.

■ Finnish

Mexico City, Monte Pelvoux 111, 4th floor, Lomas de Chapultepec, ☎ 555-540-6036. Call for hours of operation.

French

Mexico City, Lafontaine 32, Col. Polanco, ☎ 555-171-9840, Monday to Friday, 9 am-noon and 3:30-6:30 pm.

German

Mexico City, Lord Byron #737, Col. Polanco, ☎ 555-283-2200, Monday to Thursday, 7:30 am-3:30 pm; Friday, 7:30 am-3 pm.

■ Italian

Acapulco, Gran Via Tropical #615-B, ☎ 744-481-2533. Call for hours.

Mexico City, Paseo de las Palmas, ☎ 555-596-3655. Call for hours.

■ Japanese

Mexico City, Paseo de la Reforma #295, 3rd floor, Col. Cuauhtemoc, ☎ 555-202-7900. Call for hours.

New Zealand

Mexico City, José Luis Lagrange #103, 10th floor, Col. Los Morales, ☎ 555-283-9460, Monday to Thursday, 8 am-4 pm; Friday, 8 am-1:30 pm.

Swiss

Mexico City, Torre Optima, Av. De las Palamas #405, Col. Lomas de Chapultepec, ☎ 555-853-5520, Monday to Friday, 9 am-noon.

Index

Index

TRAVEL NOTES

TRAVEL NOTES

TRAVEL NOTES

TRAVEL NOTES